Who is this King of Glory?

Alvin Boyd Kuhn

Must Have Books
503 Deerfield Place
Victoria, BC
V9B 6G5
Canada

ISBN: 9781773238173

Copyright 2021 – Must Have Books

All rights reserved in accordance with international law. No part of this book may be reproduced or transmitted in any form or by any means, electronic or mechanical, including photocopying, recording, or by any information storage or retrieval system, except in the case of excerpts by a reviewer who may quote brief passages in an article or review, without written permission from the publisher.

Who is this King of Glory? –

A Critical Study of the Christos-Messiah Tradition

"What profit hath not that fable of Christ brought us!" (Pope Leo X)
INTRODUCTION

The pick that struck the Rosetta Stone in the loamy soil of the Nile delta in 1796 also struck a mighty blow at historical Christianity. For it released the voice of a long-voiceless past to refute nearly every one of Christianity's historical claims with a withering negative. The cryptic literature of old Egypt, sealed in silence when Christianity took its rise, but haunting it like a taunting specter after the third century, now stalks forth like a living ghost out of the tomb to point its long finger of accusation at a faith that has too long thriven on falsity. For that literature now rises out of oblivion to proclaim the true source of every doctrine of Christianity as Egyptian, the product and heritage of a remote past. The translation of the Egyptian Book of the Dead, the Pyramid Texts, and the Book of Thoth lays on the table the irrefutable data which show that, far from being the first gleam of true light in a world previously benighted in heathenism, Christianity was but a poor and crippled orphan, appearing – after the third century – without evidence of its true parentage and sadly belying in its outward form the semblance of its real ancestral lineage. The books of old Egypt now unroll the sagas of wisdom which announce the inexorable truth that not a single doctrine, rite, tenet or usage in Christianity was a new contribution to world religion, but that every article and practice of that faith was a disfigured copy of ancient Egyptian systematism. Christianity, it proclaims, not only did not register a single advance in any line of wisdom or truth, but deplorably vitiated and disfigured the beautiful structure of religion which it ignorantly adopted and so wretchedly purveyed as its own alleged new creation. The shadow that pursued the faith with the semblance of outward similarity for sixteen centuries, now resolves into the substance of veridical proof of original identity. The entire body of Christian doctrinism is now seen to be nothing but revamped and terribly mutilated Egyptianism. Through the chance stroke of a trench-digger's pick Christianity is brought to book to face its Nemesis. The heathen parentage that it strove so desperately to deny and the marks of which it so sedulously endeavored to obliterate in the early centuries now rises from the dead past to charge its ungenerous offspring with faithlessness and deceit. And Christianity, as Edward Carpenter so frankly asserts, must now acknowledge its parentage in a pagan past or, failing to do so, must perish.

The entire Christian Bible, creation legend, descent into and exodus from "Egypt," ark and flood allegory, Israelite "history," Hebrew prophecy and poetry, Gospels, Epistles and Revelation imagery, all are now proven to have been the transmission of ancient Egypt's scrolls and papyri into the hands of later generations which knew neither their true origin nor their fathomless meaning. Long after Egypt's voice, expressed through the inscribed hieroglyphics, was hushed in silence, the perpetuated relics of Hamitic wisdom, with their cryptic message utterly lost, were brought forth and presented to the world by parties of ignorant zealots as a new body of truth. The only new thing about it was the pitiable exegesis that inspired and accompanied the reissuance. But the sheer fact that even amid the murks of ignorance and superstition the mere ghost, shell, husk and shadow of Egypt's wisdom inspired religious piety to extremes of faith and zealotry is singular attestation of its original power and majesty. Only by acknowledging and regaining its parenthood in that sublime pagan source will Christianity rise at last to its true nobility and splendor.

There can be no question of this necessity on its part. Almost alone one significant item enforces it. From the scrolls of papyri five thousand to ten thousand years old there comes stalking forth to view the whole story of an Egyptian Jesus raising from the dead an Egyptian Lazarus at an Egyptian Bethany, with two Egyptian Maries present, the non-historical prototype of the incident related (only) in John's Gospel. From the walls of the temple of Luxor, carved there at a date at least 1700 years B.C., there faces Christianity a group of four scenes that spell the non-historicity of four episodes purveyed as history in the Gospel's recital of the Christ nativity: the angel's pronouncement to the shepherds tending their flocks by night in the fields; the annunciation of the angel to the virgin; the adoration of the infant by three Magi; and the nativity scene itself. Egypt had used the symbol of a star rising in the east as the portent of coming deity for millennia anterior to the Christian era. Egypt had knelt at the shrine of the Madonna and child, Isis and Horus, for long centuries before a historical Mary lifted a historical Jesus in her arms. Egypt had from remote times adored a Christ who had raised the dead and healed the lame, halt, blind, paralytic, leprous and all afflicted, who had restored speech to the dumb, exorcized demons from the possessed, dispersed his enemies with a word or look, wrestled with his Satan adversary, overcome all temptation and performed the works of his heavenly Father to the victorious end. Egypt had long known a Jesus, Iusa, who had been born amid celestial portents of an immaculate parenthood, circumcised, baptized, tempted, glorified on the mount, persecuted, arrested, tried, condemned, crucified, buried, resurrected and elevated to heaven. Egypt had listened to the Sermon on the Mount and the Sayings of Iusa for ages. Egypt had known a Jesus who long antedated the Gospel Messiah and who presents to the student some one hundred and eighty items of identity, similarity and correspondence in word, deed and function with his later copy.

But Egypt's Christ was not a living person. It would have been equally fatal to Christianity if he had been. But the fact of his non-historicity rises now out of the past that Christianity thought it had sealed in oblivion forever, to strike the death-knell of a false and spurious religion. The Gospels' "life" of Jesus turns out to be nothing but the garbled and fragmentary copy of an Egyptian prototype who never lived, but was a purely typal dramatic figure, portraying the divinity in man. With this one revelation of lost truth the structure of historical Christianity topples to the ground. It must be replaced by a purely spiritual Christianity. In the splendid light of ancient Egypt Occidental religion can now find its way from Medieval darkness to sunlit truth. The Dark Ages can be brought to their dismal end at last.

The ineptitude of scholarly acumen in the face of the mountainous evidence supplied by the study of comparative religion, especially since the recovery of Chaldean and Egyptian antiquities, surpasses all belief and flouts all conscience. It has been exhibited on so colossal a scale, with consequences of the direst nature, that the question whether ignorance or deliberate chicanery engineered the total suppression of truth that has glared its overwhelming obviousness in the face of studentship, inevitably rises to the foreground of thought. It must be assumed that both ignorance and disingenuousness combined to produce the catastrophic result. A thousand big and little items of comparative religion, many of them sufficient in their single weight to clinch decisive determinations fatal to Christian claims, conspire to erect a positively impregnable fortress of proof of Christian errancy. This mass of data has been blithely ignored, brazenly flouted, or damned with slighting notice, by the ecclesiastical regime which would lose its easy hold on the masses by honest recognition of the truth.

The lesson of European Renaissance history has not been assimilated in its full import. Christian Europe, groping in early Medieval darkness for centuries following the violent extinction of Platonic Academies and schools of esoteric philosophy and religion, regained a portion of the lost light in the fourteenth century when re-established contact with Greek literature brought to light the long-buried works of classic Hellenic wisdom. This recouping of cultural status went far to illuminate the night of Christian gloom. But it can be seen now that it did not go far or deep enough to effect a complete restoration of the full glory of ancient intellectual brilliance. Greece had much to offer to a Europe blinded by theological obscurantism. But its gift was a secondary and derived product, not the original and genuine treasure. That had been lost in the silence of Egypt's desert expanses. Now, in the fullness of time, the Occident is destined to enjoy its final Renaissance to the full heritage of ancient culture. Once again Christian Europe will experience a "Revival of Learning," as the lingering smudge of Medieval obfuscation is wafted away by the pure breath of a recovered Eastern civilization. This time it is Egypt, whose hidden wisdom is released by the finding of the Rosetta Stone, that will enlighten the last areas of Medieval nescience.

The primary truth of human culture which is presented by all sage religions of antiquity is the fact that there resides deeply embedded in the core of man's constitution a nucleus of what, for want of a better designation, must be called a divine spark or sun. The glow of Christliness – a thing at once both chemically radio-active and intellectual – in us is indeed the hope of our glory. Modern science, through the work of Dr. George W. Crile, late head of the Cleveland Medical laboratories, has rediscovered what the ancient sages were familiar with – the radiant SUN in man. "Every man," proclaimed the ancients and the Medieval "Fire Philosophers," "has a little SUN within his own breast." This sun is the Christ in man, a nucleus of fiery divine spirit-energy. All the Christs in antiquity were denominated "Sun-Gods." The names of nearly all of them are the immediate words for the sun, or epithets appropriate to the solar orb. "All things are the products of one primordial Fire," assert the Chaldean Oracles. Life nucleates glowing centers of this fire throughout the universe in the radiant cells of its physical body, which are the suns. Every creature that his life shares a portion of this pervasive fire, which is the rock of its hope for evolution to its greater glory. St. Paul avers that Christ – in man – is the Rock. And so ancient drama represented the Christ figure himself as saying to Peter, whose name means "Rock" in Greek, "Thou art Peter and on this Rock will I build my church." There is no other enduring Rock in man's life on which the assembly of deified mortals – the church – could be founded. And obviously the community of Christified beings could not be established on any spiritual Rock external to man's own immanent subjectivity.

The rock of human culture thus being established as a fiery power within man's own breast, Christianity becomes chargeable with the most opprobrious of all possible accusations. It can be indicted for the crime of being the only religion that in large measure destroyed the force of man's inspiration and incentive to cultivate this divine solar light within his own bosom. It did this by diverting the direction of its followers' effort from the inner self-culture of a purely subjective consciousness to the worship of the Christ as embodied in one man in history. Granted that there is a powerful and effective psychology in the adoration of an ideal model of perfection, the main issue here involved can never be dodged. No matter how emotionally, how fanatically the worshipper pours out adoration to a person in objective life, the work of his own evolution is not accomplished until he effectuates the ultimate divinization of the nuclear potentiality of deific fire within his own self-controlled area of consciousness.

The balanced forces of human uplift would be thrown into immediate chaos if it were in the end possible for a man to achieve his apotheosization vicariously, or in any other way than through his own effort. By virtue of the fact that man was provided from the start with the presence of a unit of divine fire within the heart of his conscious being, he was adequately equipped to fight his own way to the goal of glory. The only treason of which religious devotion could become capable was the setting up of a fetish outside the life of consciousness, which would divert a single iota of resolute will from the culture of the resident deity. Christianity is the only religion in the civilized world that has perpetuated this treason. The point is inexorably established by logical thought as well as demonstrated by the historical sequel. The matter is beyond debate. By so much as the exaltation of a personal Jesus has beguiled human devotion away from the inner direction in the individual's task of perfecting his own innate divinity, by precisely that much has the outer presentation weakened the strength of mortal struggle to the light. It is psychological, but it is mathematically measurable. The amount measured is the item that ends all argument. If the worship of a Judean carpenter has taken any time and absorbed any psychic effort that could have been expended in the culture of divine graciousness within the heart of humanity, it has by so much held back the evolution of the race.

Christianity has taught its adherents, so to say, to play around the fringes of the cultural problem instead of bearing with all their psychic force directly upon its heart. It has hypnotized their devotional mentality under the spell of a promise of vicariousness which is itself subtly conducive to the weakening of the native nobility of man's true selfhood. It has made of its millions – what Nietzsche so thoroughly detested – groveling beggars, reveling in the turpitude of sin-confession and praying for God to have mercy on their unworthiness. It has made them wretches pleading piteously to be saved. How it has ever been assumed that a God of good sense would enjoy seeing his creatures, whom he has himself divinely endowed with a portion of his own Mind, writhing in worm-of-the-dust sycophancy at his feet, is beyond rational understanding. It is naturally to be presumed that he would take far greater delight in seeing them standing up in the might of their incipient divinity and making a fight of it. The morbid cast of mentation generated in millions of Christians over sixteen centuries by the doctrinal falsification of the esoteric meaning of "sin" is perhaps the most lamentable spectacle presented to the world in all time. That a religion could so far lose touch with sober sanity as to expect that it could exalt and edify man's spirit by grinding it down into the dust is evidence at once of its complete divagation from basic sound truth.

It is a grave question whether the ecclesiastical system and movement known as Christianity has any right to its name. So far from being the cult that brought in a true Christ-worship for the first time in "heathen" darkness, it was indeed – after the third century – the one system that destroyed such a true worship. Ancient cults bent all effort upon the cultivation of the god within man. This is the nucleus of the only true Christianity. In its genuine sense there has been no Christianity in the Occident since that fatal third century. Historical Christianity has substituted a personal fetish for the real Christos, the inner Fire of Love. No matter how appealing the figure substituted, it never can do the work of actual soul culture. And history has sealed this verdict. It is almost certainly true that in no quarter of human life has history so obviously and glaringly demonstrated the want of mankind's reliance upon the god instinct in the heart of the nations as has been evidenced by the horrifying spectacle of inhumanity and animal savagery put on display by the so-called Christianized nations. Christianity has never led the fight for culture. On the contrary, it has hung like a drag-wheel on the car of real cultural and scientific advance for many centuries. It has struck at every pioneer in the progress of true culture. Its highest practical aim has rather been to maintain an average level of decency in traditional forms of social life. Much incidental good of course has emerged from an effort to which millions of good people, in more or less ignorance of historic truth, have consecrated their life's devotion. But never has it been the single aim and objective of the Christian ecclesiastical system to ground the aspirational life of its devotees upon the one-pointed quickening of the Christ within all hearts.

A fairly considerable number of books have been written to defend the thesis of the non-historicity of Jesus, George Brandes' *Jesus a Myth* being a typical example. All of them have advanced data of weight and validity. But none of them has presented the real argument in the case. This springs from the material now available from ancient Egypt's fount of sage sapiency. From a hoary civilization comes the literature that ends all debate by offering the incontrovertible evidence that the Gospels are not and never were histories. They are now proven to have been cryptic dramas of the spiritual evolution of humanity and of the history of the human soul in its earthly tabernacle of flesh. The thesis, universally held by Christian theologians, that these Gospel books were "written" after Jesus lived and from the eye-witness record of his objective "life," must yield place to the knowledge that they first appeared in the second century, having long been held in the secret background of esoteric religionism. The allegation that the publication of the Gospels can not be explained or accounted for unless a great Teacher had lived whose life inspired their writing, must give way before the understanding that their appearance was due to the breakdown of esotericism, or the violent popular incursion into the secrecy of esoteric polity, and the dragging forth of the arcane books and the dramas of the occult spiritual life from the Mystery holy of holies.

A noted present-day clergyman in New York City, the eminent Dr. John Haynes Holmes, has declared in a printed sermon – Christianity's Debt to Judaism; Why Not Acknowledge It? – that Christianity drew its Founder from the Jewish people, along with five-sixths of its Bible, the Hebrew Old Testament, as well as everything that the character Jesus has spoken in the New Testament. Practically every word uttered by the Christ figure in the Gospels is to be found in the Mishna, the Gemara, the Talmud and the Hagadoth of the Jews, he asserted. But what now must be the astonishment of the eminent minister to be confronted with the mountainous evidence that all the material of both Christian and Hebrew systems has emanated from ancient Egypt's crypts of secret wisdom! Truly the Rosetta Stone is to be the Nemesis of a falsity that has shrouded religion in gloom and obscurity and shot it through with insincerity and dishonesty for some twenty-four centuries.

It is a sign of the aberration in religious thinking now prevailing that the presentation of the case for the non-historic Christ will run afoul of many persons of general probity who, even when measurably convinced that the Jesus story is a fable, as Pope Leo X so glibly asserted, will still adhere to the persuasion that it is better to suppress the bald and revolutionary truth and prolong the "beautiful illusion" of the Christ's personal existence. The original perpetration and now the perpetuation of blank falsehood concerning the fact of Jesus' existence is argued to be morally justifiable, even highly good, on the ground that it has wrought a prodigious psychological and moral beneficence. But this is, at bottom, to argue that Christianity can be better promoted by a lie than by the truth. We are adjured by the holy scriptures of that same faith that our only freedom comes from knowing the truth. While the world is hoping and planning to establish the better course of its life upon four fundamental freedoms, it might be well to remind ourselves that in a democracy there is a fifth freedom upon which the salutary influences of the four and all other freedoms are dependent and contingent, and that is the freedom of all to be put in possession of the truth, to the farthest limit of its availability. In minor situations it often appears both judicious and beneficent to withhold the truth. But the justification is always secondary to larger objectives and temporary. Every situation must ultimately be resolved by a facing of the truth. Final issues ever demand that life be met on its own terms. The extensive concealment of historical truth at once argues something unlovely and sinister. A great world faith, soliciting the loyalty of millions, could offer no surer evidence of its integrity than an unbroken record of instant eagerness to examine and accept every sincere presentment of the truth. This work is given forth with no other motive than to present the available evidence beating upon an issue of transcendent importance. In the hurly-burly of human affairs truth is not always welcome or pleasant. That is understandable. But far more vital is the understanding that it must be faced. Our attitude toward truth-seeking is one of the supreme tests of our worthiness to take on the responsibilities and enjoy the liberties of a democracy.

Lest it be assumed that the author's implied charges of dishonesty in Christian leadership spring from a personal animosity against Christianity, he takes the liberty to insert here a few sentences taken from a brief article in The New York Times of present date (Nov. 29, 1943) reported from a sermon of the Rev. Bernard Iddings Bell, eminent Episcopalian clergyman, preached in St. Paul's Chapel of Columbia University on Nov. 28. By inference Dr. Bell charges the Church with dishonesty, and nobody believes that he does it from "spleen." He said that present-day civilization "needs above all things a restored humility and a renewed honesty in two high places – the universities and the churches." "From kindergarten to the Ph.D. degree," he added, "our educators help their students to run away from ultimate decisions. . . . The universities have become resorts for the pursuit of instrumental tricks rather than of fundamental and immutable truth. And then our educators, having abdicated from their ancient and honorable post as keepers of the sanctities of truth, cry out in their pride their all-sufficient greatness."

"The churches, too . . . make of themselves pious clubs, daring not to rebuke the brazen multitudes for fear of loss of membership and money; and having sunk to the low estate of men pleasers, insist they hold the future of mankind in their proud hands."

The sun of man can not be too long beclouded with the fogs of hypocrisy and bigotry. Its mighty power will dispel them in due season. A new day of its shining arises with the accidental stroke of a soldier's pick on a slab of stone.

Chapter I

FAITH WEDS FOLLY

To the conscientious student who will give to the matter sufficient time and reflection it becomes a conviction that the most devastating cultural calamity that has befallen the human race in all its history was the degradation of the esoteric spiritual purport of ancient scripture into a debased literal and historical sense, entailing centuries of mental benightedness and spiritual thwarting, that took place at about the third century of the Christian era. And in this catastrophic conversion of cosmography, evolutionary pictography and racial history over into alleged factual occurrence, the single feature most signally fruitful of age-long fatuity was the transformation of the dramatic figure of the Christos, or divine essence of man's nature, over into a historical person. It is not too much to say that the withering wind of this distorted doctrine spread its blight upon all sane comprehension of the sublime message of ancient sacred literature over all the sixteen centuries since that fatal epoch. Indeed the truth of the situation warrants the statement that the injection of a living man into the spiritual drama in the place of the personified divine Ego in man has held the rational mind of the Western world in the grip of the most arrant superstition to be found in the history of civilized humanity. This work will amass the data to support the sharp asseveration that this was the central item in the entire debacle of theological systematism which then ensued and which must be rated as the most tragic catastrophe in world history. The causes that led to the fatal transference of character from the dramatic personification of an element in human consciousness into an alleged man of historical entification will be the central theme of this essay. To what inadequate degree the iniquitous consequences of the blunder can be seen and delineated, these will be dealt with in the unfoldment. But the task involves little less than the penetrating analysis of all ancient sacred writ, and the amassing of a vast array of factual data and basic argument in support of the momentous conclusions adduced in the sequel. The power of tradition, and more especially religious tradition indoctrinated in the childhood of many generations, is so overwhelming that the effort of this work to clarify the status of the great doctrine of divine Messiahship in ancient scripture will almost certainly be received with the cry of blasphemy from the shocked partisans of orthodoxy. All the obloquy that has been concentrated in the word "Anti-Christ" will be flung upon the undertaking. For this reason it is desirable to state at the outset that, on the contrary, the task is motivated by the highest possible reverence for the Christ ideal as the core of all religious culture. So far from being an attempt to devastate the benignant efficacy of the role of the Christ in religious practique, it is expressly the aim of the study to establish that efficacy upon its true psychological bases. This purpose entails the revelation of the true in place of the false grounds of the claim of the Christ ideal upon our reverence. Instead of being a vicious attack upon the sanctified name and function of Christhood, it is directly an effort to redeem that name and function from centuries of impious desecration that should have been seen all along as the real grounds for horrified indignation. When rightly viewed in relation to all the facts in the case, it must be conceded that the justification for resentment at a real sacrilege against the Sonship of God weighs heavily on the side of the book, and is not on the side of the inevitable hue and cry of violent condemnation that will greet it. In the face of this anticipated raucous chorus of vilification of the book's aim and intent there is hurled the forthright declaration that this is an utterly sincere and consecrated attempt to rescue the sacred name of the Christ from an ignominy already heaped upon it over long centuries. There is abundant warrant for asserting the righteous character of the motive on the ground of its aim to redeem the conception of Christhood from the incredible error and falsification that have befouled it for ages. As Socrates and Plato so thoroughly demonstrated by a masterly dialectic, the only source of evil in connection with anything is the failure to grasp its true status and function in a perfect balance between excess and deficiency. Nothing is good, say these two profound thinkers, unless its basic raison d'être is clearly apprehended and its use fulfilled in exactly balanced proportion. The record of historical frightfulness that has emerged into actuality over many centuries because of the unbelievable miscarriage of the first true conception of the character and office of the Messiah is overwhelming justification of a sincere effort to remold the mistaken view to its original truth and beauty. In final curt statement the high intent of this work is to end the sway of an entirely false and stultifying idea of the nature of the Christ and inaugurate the dominance of the only conception that truly honors it. The thesis, then, is to demonstrate that the Christ was a grade of distinctly divine consciousness that is coming gradually into rulership in humanity, and being this, it was nothing else. It was not a man.

Just as the conception of the Biblical Adam as man, generic, is a true envisagement of the meaning of the term and yields intelligible significance in exegesis of ancient scripts, but becomes both ridiculous and unintelligible when taken to mean "a man," so with the Christos. The conception of the Christ as man in his divine genius, or the God in man, opens at once the whole of scripture to lucid and consistent intelligibility. It is indeed the "key" to any true grasp of the whole sense of that revered body of primeval literature. But the instant the concept is shifted from man divine to a divine man in an historical personage, dire confusion, entanglement in contradiction, ridiculous inconsistency and the eeriest "historical" nonsense are thrust into the structure. The concept of the Christos as the godly higher Self in man meets the tangled riddle of the exegesis of the Bibles with complete satisfaction of every intellectual demand, and no other concept does so. The concept of Christ as a man immediately afflicts the entire exegetical situation with hopeless sabotage. Used as the "key," it jams the lock and opens nothing to the reasoning intelligence. But it does open something to the unreasoning psychic and emotional aptitudes of less intelligent folk: the hypnotic gullibility of religious piety and a pitiable slavery to religious superstition. And the quantity of the tragedy wrought in the world by the prevalence of these two psychological forces makes perhaps the most lugubrious chapter in human history.

The concept of the Christ as "a man," who ate, drank, slept, walked and spoke as any mortal, is beyond any possibility of refutation the most fatuous ideation that ever found a place in the effort to rationalize human religious experience. No less has it been at the same time the most baneful influence in blocking the cultural enterprise of grasping the central power and fullest unction of that experience. Here again the truth of the situation runs in a direction exactly counter to that commonly believed. Pious orthodox opinion is wholly aligned to the idea that the historical Jesus is the most positive assurance of the individual Christian's salvation and the active agent of its realization. This work ventures, doubtless for the first time in religious discussion, to fly directly in the face of that presumption with the claim that it is this very idea of the Christ as a historical person that has stood as the most concrete obstacle in the way of that salvation! The whole essay must be taken as the evidence advanced in support of that amazing reversal of all accepted belief. The basis of this strong contention will be the undeniable fact that the thesis of the historical Jesus has taken the mind and aspiration of all devotees outside themselves to an alleged man of Galilee, when the whole effort at spiritual growth and cultivation of our divinity must be focused within the depths of our own consciousness. It is no rank untruth to say that the cult of the historical Jesus has stood squarely between men and their immanent God and tended to keep them apart from each other. It has thwarted the culture of their own divinity. It would seem as if St. Paul wrote with this cogent realization in mind when he fairly shrieks at us: "Know ye not your own selves, how that Jesus Christ is within you?" He is not a man outside yourselves; he is the God whom you keep buried so deeply in your own hearts and minds that you do not know he is there. It is a notable thing that august ancient spiritual science rightly regarded it as a sinful aberrancy for one to worship a power outside one's self, or a deity lodged elsewhere than in the inner shrine of one's selfhood. Medieval and modern blindness has reversed this direction of aspiration, and with calamitous consequences. Some sixteen centuries of spiritual benightedness have produced for historical record the pitiful and demoralizing spectacle of millions of misguided votaries turning outside themselves for salvation and pleading with an alleged personal figure on the stage of remote history to enter their lives and transform them into loveliness, all the while neglecting the voice of the only real Christos that ever existed, their own instinct for goodness, truth and love. It was a turn that almost alone proved sufficient to effect the total abortion of the Western world's religious endeavor for a millennium and a half. It alone holds the legitimate answer to the insistent question, propounded in every epoch when gross barbarism rises to crush the nobility of spiritual culture: – why has religion failed to avert humanitarian catas- trophe? Failure in religion's practical effort is certain to follow as long as a meaningless worship is paid out to the divinity alleged to be embodied in one single historical savior, while the principle of divine mind within the self is left totally uncultivated. Granting some psychological virtue to the adoration of a historical paragon, it is still admitted in all religious discussion that men can be saved in the end only by their own righteousness. No world savior was ever sent into the world to save men from the task of saving themselves. Ever memorable and oft quoted are the lines of Angelus Silesius, Medieval mystic:

Though Christ a thousand times in Bethlehem be born,
But not within thyself, thy soul shall be forlorn;
The cross on Golgotha thou lookest to in vain
Unless within thyself it be set up again.

If any actual vicarious atonement or salvation were possible, the whole purpose for which souls from the celestial empyrean migrate to earth to further their evolution would be thwarted. Each soul must become the dynamo and citadel of its own strength, or there would be inequity and chaos in the counsels of evolution. Life grants nothing to any unit of being that it has not earned. To do so would be to introduce favoritism and particularity into the universal economy. The importance of this argument merits a fuller consideration, and additional treatment of it will enter the study later on.

The enormous fatuity of the concept of humanity's Savior as a man must be examined in the light of a more candid scrutiny than any to which it has heretofore been subjected. Indeed one of the bases of quarrel with it is the very fact of its having been accepted without either psychological or historical critique of a thoroughgoing kind. The closer and more keenly one brings reason and data to bear upon the matter the more clearly it is seen that the very vogue and sway of the idea has been made possible only through the almost total default of the rational faculty and its displacement by sheer unction of faith. It is perhaps the most notable example and instance of the power of the psychological elements of mystical pietism to override and paralyze the rational elements in religion. For at any time in many centuries it needed only a half minute's cool and steady facing of the realities of the situation to bring to view in the sharpest of outlines the utter irrationality of the presupposition that the power able to redeem human weakness to godlike status could be embodied and expressed, wielded and effectuated to its grand purpose, in the person of a man. The sheer thought that the savior of mankind from evolutionary undevelopment to perfection could be a man, or a power, no matter how divine, lodged in the body of a man in history, is such an anomaly, so out of line with all known natural process, that merely to pose the idea to the mind and hold it steadfastly there in the light of all its ancillary implications, is to see it for what it is – an utterly baseless creation of distorted religious fantasy. Merely to face the thought that the whole evolutionary advance of mankind across the gulf of undeveloped capacities from animal through human to divine nature was alleged to be effectuated and instrumentalized by the forces embodied in a single man at a given date in history, is to see the notion in all the glaring baldness of its inherent absurdity. The human mind can readily enough envisage as a modus consonant with reality the elevation of humanity from brute to philosopher, from savagery to Christhood, through the injection from without or the regeneration from within of a light and power to change base selfishness to divine charity, and thus redeem the race. But it can contemplate this process as operative only through the sweep of an influence which pervades the mass of mankind, animating all hearts and enlightening all minds, after the natural analogy of a little leaven raising the whole lump. That is a methodology which the human mind can grasp and accredit as harmonious with veritude. But that this vast regeneration of the race should be implemented by and dependent upon the birth and existence of a single historic individual, even through the inspiration of his resplendent example, is a concept that grows more weird, crass and chimerical the longer it is held in the focus of thought. It has in fact held its grip upon millions of minds solely by virtue of the total dearth of intellectual candor and the mental paralysis induced by rabid elements of emotional religiosity. It can not for a moment bear the light of reason. It can live only in the dim twilight of intellectual stultification wherein the clear outlines of the rational problem can not be distinctly discerned.

There is indeed a natural revolt in the character of all normal men and women against the thought of their accepting salvation purchased for them by another, the more so if the price of the ransom is for the vicar pain and suffering. What person of wholesome instincts wants to be saved by the sacrifice and oblation of another free being? Who that has the slightest iota of moral integrity would wish to live under the obligation of indebtedness for his evolutionary redemption to the sacrifice of another? Mankind cherishes a natural sense of the moral turpitude of taking what one has not won. It introduces whim into the normal order wherein man looks confidently for the reign of law. It is repugnant to man's inherent sense of right. Vicarious salvation was one of the items of theology that led Nietzsche to cry out his bitter denunciation of Christianity as "slave morality." Not merely the superman, but any man worthy of the name wants to face life and nature on their own terms and with his own resources, and will hold in contempt the man or faith that accepts the boon of salvation in the spirit of a craven. The purchase of man's redemption by the "shed blood of Christ," in the literal sense in which it stands as a doctrine of Christianity, is indeed one of the heaviest marks of Christianity's doctrinal degradation. (Happily it can be made rationally acceptable, as can all other doctrines, through a restoration of the true esoteric significance.) The learned Celsus in the third century tells us that Christianity appealed to and welcomed only the slaves of Roman tyranny, men and women of the most abject position. It was held in the lowest contempt by Pliny, Seneca, Tacitus, Suetonius and the more intelligent groups generally. It was rejected by all who were genuine enough to despise the self-confessed ignominy of letting a historical scapegoat bear the burden of achieving their karmic immunity. The gross teaching of an ersatz salvation of man, the race's restoration to its lost Paradise by way of the nailing of a quivering body of human flesh on a wooden cross on a given day, has been an insuperable obstacle to the swallowing of the Christian epos by thinking people down the ages. Vicariousness on any grounds is an unnatural and bizarre methodology; but the vicarious salvation of the human race through the sacrifice of a person in history transcends in fatuity the crassest fetishism of any wild children of forest and sea isle. Nature nowhere authenticates such a procedure to rational comprehension. It has stood as the weirdest anomaly in rational effort, defying all plausible explanation or fitness, thwarting all sincere search for true light, and taxing even the blindest of pious faiths to accept it as an inscrutable mystery. All this irrational thesis was held for centuries in spite of the total dearth of any logical answer to the difficulties involved in the practical problem as to how the divinity historically embodied in one person could become and remain effectual for the evolutionary divinization of all the other children of humanity. Jesus might be in himself a mighty reservoir of divine essence, a veritable dynamo of godly unction. But how it was to be made available for all other men, how transferred from him to a distribution amongst all others, by what transmission wires or channels it was to pass from him into the lives of those "believing on him," on what conditions it was to be received by some and denied to others, or what pleas, prayers, sacrifices or cajolery were necessary to draw it forth from him, – all these elements of the practical or factual operation of Jesus' saving grace to deify all men have never had an answer. And they can never have a rational answer. The groundplan and framework of Christian theology has ever had an artificiality that has rendered it a weird and fantastic thing in all conscientious effort at rationale. The spectacle of an omnipotent creator of all the worlds setting a trap to catch his own creatures by tempting them to sin, then condemning them to eternal misery in consequence of their inevitable "fall," and afterwards negotiating with them to appease his wrath on condition that his own Son, only begotten, consent to die in their stead, has stood for sixteen centuries as the rock foundation of that religion which shouts down all others with its vociferous claims to all-highest excellence among the faiths of earth. Through the force of the wholly unaccountable magnanimity of the man Christ in sacrificing himself to save a reprobate humanity, the minds of the countless millions of Christian devotees over the centuries since his "death" may have been, as the hymn sings, Lost in wonder, love and praise.

But it is even more certain that they have been hopelessly lost in total incomprehension. Forced to swallow it by the overwhelming combination of ecclesiastical authority and unreasoning faith, they have yet been nearly choked by its unpalatability.

It is probably the opinion of millions of votaries of the atoning blood of Christ the man, that his saving grace has been made accessible to them, distributed to them, by his still-living active presence and his personal attention to their lives individually. Granting the continued existence of his individual personality after these two thousand years on some "spiritual" plane of being assumedly in touch with earthly affairs, there must be faced the infinitely complex problem of explaining how the consciousness of one man is able to give attention to the multitudinous details in the lives of millions of mortals at every moment of every day without cessation; how he is able to read the conscious content of innumerable minds and hearts with particularity and accuracy and adopt appropriate measures of spiritual strategy to answer the spoken and unbroken prayers of all these; how, in short, he is able to be a very present help in trouble in millions of complex situations all the time, and act in relation to all of them with impeccable accuracy and unfailing justice. Blind zealotry blots out this problem from the uncritical minds of the masses and priestcraft is warily content to let the dangerous dog lie asleep. It is not made the subject of debate. But if occasionally a hint of the dilemma is ventured, such a minor obstacle to piety is swept lightly aside with the ever-handy reminder to such intellectual temerity that with God all things are possible, and with the only-begotten Son of God no less. Surely the almighty hand of Supreme Deity could manage a trifling difficulty of the sort, and at any rate

God moves in a mysterious way
His wonders to perform.

To minds submerged in the aura of miracle and overborne by pious authority and sacerdotal glamor, all things in a mysterious theology were made palatable. Jesus' pronouncement that "thy faith hath made thee whole" and his assurance that by faith we can move mountains into the sea had paved the way for the triumphant march of religious gullibility and the obscuration of reason. It is granted that we must have faith where we do not yet have knowledge. What else can a dependent mortal creature do but have faith in the beneficence of the universe? But a universal Power that is itself an all-embracing intelligence would not ask its creatures, who are destined to embody all degrees of that same intelligence, to hold to any specific formulations of faith the substance of which contravenes our reason and the regular courses of natural law. Our faith must rest upon and be supported by the inviolability of law and not take its stand upon any fantastic scheme that flouts what we do know and sets at odds all our reason- ing faculties. With either flaming zealotry or stolid indifference holding the critical faculty of the masses in abeyance, and occasional outbreak of rational inquiry smitten down with vengeful violence, the problem of how the man Jesus, dead ages ago, could still be the divine guest in billions of human hearts all at once and all the time, was held in leash.

Again, it is undoubtedly the thought of hosts of minds adjusted to miraculous possibilities of many sorts that Jesus' still-potent spirit was detached from the limitations of his personality or even his earthly mind and, continuing to float about in some form of a ubiquitous presence like a permeating atmosphere, functions with a sort of automatism like air rushing in, wherever there is a spiritual vacuum or spiritual pressure. It is conceived that somehow that mind which St. Paul adjures us to let "be in" us as it was also in Christ Jesus pervades the world like a stratosphere and is there for us to register and lay hold of after the fashion of tuning in spiritually with the proper wave-length. But how the efficacy of such a vibrational force could be linked with and still dependent upon the personal Jesus of history, is in no way apparent or explainable. There is no necessary or factual connection. Divine consciousness or grades or rates of it may indeed conceivably be about us, bathing us in the universal aura of their supernal vibrations. But that any of them should have derived their origin and their present presence and operation from a man in history is again a matter that asks for our acceptance of a wholly irrational theological dictum.

This general notion receives some support from Jesus' own assurance that when he left earth he would send the Paraclete, the Comforter, who would guide us into all truth and be the ever-solicitous monitor at our elbow. But all that this does is simply to rename the ubiquitous influence. It transfers the generative power from the personal Jesus to an impersonal principle. The new divine comforter must distribute his consciousness over as much ground as the personal mind of the risen Jesus would have to cover. Strangely enough one of the very phrases which the Greek theologians of the ancient philosophical religion used to picture the pervasive scope and functioning of a divine element in humanity was that "the gods distribute divinity." But this was in reference to the distribution of a seed fragment of God's infinite and universal mind to every creature according to its rank in evolution. The presence of potential divinity distributively in all levels of life is not a crotchety but a quite reasonable and natural procedure. It is indeed one of the great features in the early philosophies that gave form to basic Christianity. It is readily conceivable that a type or degree of supernal mind or consciousness does pervade the universe, an ethereal essence, so to say, of which evolving entities such as man can partake through the development of a receptive capacity in their own brain and nerve mechanism. To make God's infinite largesse available to man some such method of impartation on the one hand and appropriation on the other must be conceived as provided by the Oversoul of the world. But this is not the problem that is crucial to the tenability of the idea of a historical Jesus carrying out the part assigned to him in theology. He is there alleged to fulfill the function of saving millions of souls through his individual agency both during his life and for thousands of years after his death. If to substantiate the still operative power of Jesus Christ when he is no longer living, recourse must be had to the hypostatization of his personal mind as a universally pervasive cosmic atmosphere, the entire force of the method of explanation goes to weaken still further the claim for his historic personal existence and to strengthen that for his purely spiritual nature.

It is not conceivable that the mind of one personal human being could reach and save billions of mortals. Therefore, to postulate a conceivable method by which such a mind could administer salvation to myriads in all ages, that mind must be released from any attachment to personality and characterized anew as a cosmic mental emanation or diffusion of mental substance. This deduction from the premises at once erases the personal Jesus from the picture of theology, if not in his life, then certainly from the moment of his death. If to render his mind operable for salvation its connection with his personality must be severed, then its connection with any personality is seen to be a clearly unnecessary, indeed impossible requirement. And this brings us face to face with the final outcome of this argument, which is that that mind which was in Christ

Jesus would have existed, has existed and does exist, entirely independently of the fact or the question of any man's historical presence on earth. For no more did Jesus originate that mind than does the radio mechanism originate the sonata that it renders in your room. Any man can catch it, as does the radio, from an omnipresent univer- sal vibration, register it and give it expression on this plane of being. The vibration-wave of the sonata is in your room whether there is a radio present to reproduce it on the plane of your senses or not. The Christ consciousness was present as a cosmic outflow of divine thought energization, whether or not any man of requisite organic sensitivity lived to become its tubes and amplifier. The best that can be done for Jesus' uniqueness in this purview is to assume that perhaps he was the first man in history (if he lived) who was equal to making that register and that expression. But such a claim is bizarre from the first instant. It would have to rest on pure conjecture and assumption. And against it would be arrayed a host of vital considerations, such as that research now discloses that all the highest and truest sermons he allegedly preached to found a saving religion had been uttered by sage men centuries before him. If his message was the first release of the wisdom of supernal divine mind to humanity, it should have towered in grandeur and beauty to immeasurable height above anything taught antecedently. Organized ecclesiasticism has been bold enough for centuries to flaunt this legend before its following.

But the discovery of the Rosetta Stone and the Behistun Rock has put an entirely new complexion on the study of comparative religion, opening up whole vast areas of ancient literature from which it is seen that Christianity itself drew the body of its material. The disconcerting result of all this for the Christian position is that it definitely refutes the claims as to Jesus' founding the first true religion and, far to the contrary, thrusts upon the apologists for these claims the difficult task of defending this sole emissary of deity to earth against the charge of wholesale literary plagiarism! If when he came to uplift humanity with a shining spirituality never before dreamed of, the best he could do was to repeat the sagas of early Greek, Chaldean, Persian, Hindu, Chinese and especially Egyptian wisdom, on what does the claim for his supreme uniqueness and matchless exaltation rest?

Then, of course, there is that other predicament arising from the egregious claims of the Christian party, which, had it ever been frankly faced by ecclesiasticism, would have left the Occidental world in better situation. It is the matter of God's leaving the world prior to the year thirty-three or thereabouts without any chance to be saved by appropriating the mind of Christ. That the mere opportunity for the operation in humanity's evolution of the saving principle of God's grace should have been held off until the birth of a babe in Bethlehem at a given year in history, and not have been freely accessible to righteous men antecedently, needs nothing more than its clear statement to advertise its preposterousnss. It would be to say that the normal course of human evolution was held in abeyance, estopped, until the man Jesus arrived. One of our Christmas hymns sings

Late in time behold him come,
Offspring of the Virgin's womb.

It is of course an absurd idea that the road to human elevation was not opened until the man-Christ, Jesus, landed on the planet at a late epoch in the race's career. This is one of many twists and quirks which Christian dogma has asked its votaries to accept, to the dislocation of their rational mentality.

Chapter II

MYTH TRUER THAN HISTORY

It would seem to remove the discussion from the province of rational dialectic and throw it into the field of abnormal and precarious psychic phenomenalism to introduce an argument that has been frequently advanced by a number of people that is by no means inconsiderable. It must, however, be given a place in the debate if only for the reason that it arises from a special type of experience that appears to be actual among a surprising number of people who are at any rate sincere in their report and interpretation of it. It falls in a domain of psychology that has for the most part been shunned by academic investigation, its phenomena being commonly rated as abnormal, eccentric and unauthentic, categorized in fact as mostly self-delusion or hallucination. It has lately received some open countenance from scholastic authority and has been admitted to the field of legitimate study under the name of parapsychology. It may be better recognized under the designation of psychic phenomena. At any rate the phenomenon in question has been presented by many persons in modern religious groups of spiritistic character as a real experience of themselves or others testifying to them, and such is the veridical and empirical nature of the occurrence that for them it settles the entire debate categorically and summarily. The arguments based on it sway the attitude of thousands on the theme of this work and it therefore merits presentation and critique.

The point is advanced by mediums, psychics, clairvoyants and sensitives, to the effect that they can testify directly to the fact of Jesus' historical existence because, forsooth, they have seen him and talked with him, in inner vision! His personality is not a matter of doubt or speculation, because he has appeared to them in his shining form! They have seen him as St. Paul saw him on the road to Damascus. Their need of faith is lost in the certitude of sight. To these persons the debate is closed with their declaration that others may argue – they have seen. This phenomenal experience, commoner than is generally supposed, must, however, be subjected to a critical scrutiny that it apparently has not hitherto received. This is the more desirable because these reports of the appearance of a radiant personage to the inner sight of many people are both too voluminous and seem too sincerely founded to be thrust aside with the cry of hallucination. As evidently veridical psychic phenomena they prove an interesting theme in themselves. It seems to be necessary to concede that visions of the sort are actually seen. The shining apparition seems to these seers to be present in reality. Whatever it may truly be and however to be explained, it is evidently actually seen. The point at issue for our discussion is not the veritude of the experience or the veracity of the psychics; but what the thing proves. The critique is not directed at the fact, but at its interpretation. The position taken is that such apparitions present no necessary or valid evidence for the existence of the Gospel Jesus in Judea nineteen hundred years ago.

The identity of the personage of light in the radiant vision can not be other than a matter of presumption. Upon asking any of those who have "seen Jesus" in their subjective world how they have identified their spiritual visitant with the man of Galilee long dead, the answer is invariably: "Why, of course it was Jesus; I know it was he." On top of this one will be informed that he looked just like the pictures of him, or that the visionary recognized him by his whole appearance, as being just what he or she expected. Or the startling assertion will be made that he talked and declared his identity as Jesus, or even displayed to view the nail marks in his hands and feet. These rejoinders may seem at first glance to be pretty formidable testimony, but they are evidence not so much for the existence of the Galilean long ago as they are of the total failure of the clairvoyants to think out the implications of their assumption. They offer glaring evidence also as to the extraordinary capacity of persons endowed with these unusual gifts for psychic impressionability and intellectual credulity, if not gullibility.

Looking first at the latter, the "varieties of religious experience" include a wide range of phenomenalistic susceptibility. Old men have dreamed dreams and young men have seen visions. Saints have had rapturous exaltations, seers have beheld apocalypses and mystics have been wafted aloft in ecstasies. These experiences have abounded in great multiplicity, variety and profusion – unless the record is one long train of fiction and falsity, delirium and delusion. There is Joan d'Arc, there is Swedenborg, there is Madame Guyon and a legion of others. Modern students of this side of psychology assert that a thought is in reality a shaped figure in the mental ether; and assert that if thousands of people hold the same picture of such a person as the Christ in mind with great intensity and devotion for a continued period, the thought-form will become reified, hypostatized or substantialized to the extent that it will drift into the mental purview of psychic sensitives and be seen and mistaken for a veridical appearance. Modern psychology might catalogue it as an entification of the unconscious or subconscious object of much devotion. There are strange and uncanny possibilities in nature's bag of tricks. There are denizens in more worlds than the solid physical. It seems evident that many people have seen a personage of luminous tenuousness in their subjective world. But all proof is wanting that their testimony as to the identity of the apparition has any validity.

There is no field in which people generally are more gullible than in that of religion. Nowhere else are the bars of the critical judgment so quickly and completely let down for the entry of superstition, the supernatural, miracle, magic and marvel. Indeed no Christly claimant would be accredited unless he could do "mighty works" to awe the multitudes. If he can not heal the sick and raise the dead he is no Christ. But the impotence to which these tendencies reduce the reasoning faculty in devotees is perhaps nowhere better seen than in the situation here portrayed. These psychics testify unhesitatingly and with total conviction that the figure of light they have seen is the still-living Jesus of Nazareth, without a moment's pause to reflect that no one can identify a figure seen now with another person never seen at all! Identification can function only on the basis of previous knowledge or acquaintance. No one can identify the figure seen in a vision with the historical Jesus. The assumption that they can do so is ridiculous. Logic rules it out. Their claim that the figure is that of Jesus is based on pious assumption and can be nothing but sheer guess. The eyes can not identify the appearance of a person unless the eyes have seen him before, or his photograph or likeness. The figure seen matches the popularly conceived appearance of Jesus, and Jesus is the only historical person they can think to call it. The claim that the apparition resembles the pictures of Jesus in books and prints is the weakest item in the "identification." In fact it reduces the entire claim to blank folly. In spite of gratuitous assertions of the existence of portraits of the Galilean, assuredly there has never been an authentic picture of the man, even if he lived.

How can the apparitional Jesus look like his portraits when there were no portraits? If even in hallucination the visionary Jesus does resemble the conventional portrayals, we may have before us here an interesting psychological phenomenon. For the fact would seem to lend some support to the "occult" theory that the general communal thought-picture of Jesus, based on the customary portraits seen for centuries, has actually entified a spiritual thought-formation of the man in the image of his published likenesses. The allegation of pictorial resemblance is final proof of the purely subjective character of the visions and their inadmissibility as testimony in the case. What they give evidence of is some extraordinary capacities of the human psyche, not remote past history. The proof of connection between present subjective event in these cases and past objective event is totally wanting. The phenomena manifest in this realm are far too uncertain, undependable, even dangerous, for the practical uses of life. As a final observation on the point, one is permitted to express a robust doubt whether, if the living spiritual counterpart of some other ancient personage, unknown and unpictured through the centuries, should present itself before the inner gaze of these psychics, they would have any ability or means of identifying the specter. Could they identify, say, Apollonius of Tyana?

There is, however, another consideration that falls within the realm of psychology which has far more direct pertinence to the great question. The inquiry faces the task of evaluating the psychological influence and spiritual or cultural serviceableness of the idea of the personal Jesus as against the conception that makes "him" to be a high type of universal consciousness or principle. The defense of the historical point of view invariably lays vast store upon the claim that any vital religion, at any rate Christianity, could never have generated effective psychological dynamism among millions of followers if based only upon the characterization of the Christos as sheer principle. It required the living Jesus to generate in the Christian movement the driving power that it has become. Jesus must have lived, is the argu- ment, if only because such a life in actuality was necessary to give the religion based on it just that vital psychological reinforcement that it has manifested. He must have lived because it can be shown that it was most eminently desirable, from a psychological point of view, that he should have lived. The conception of Christ as principle could never have developed enough dynamic force or fervor to have enabled Christianity, so to say, to effectuate itself.

It must be stated that the outcome of this phase of the argument can have no direct evidential bearing upon the question of the historicity of the Christ. To prove that his existence was highly desirable does not prove that it was a fact. But the point is given a quite extraordinary importance in the debate, and this not without reason. It strikes close to the central nerve of the whole Christian system. That system bases its unique efficacy upon the claim that it alone of religions offers to believers a living God. The only time God ever came to earth in person, he outlined for humanity its true religion, the Christian. By many people this point of the psychological power of the historical Christ is maneuvered into the place of central importance in the whole discussion. They urge the claim that the Christ was sent into personal embodiment for the express purpose of providing mankind with one historical example of divine perfection, and assert that the whole argument stands or falls with the question of the psychological value of his example. Such an example was necessary to effectuate the religious salvation of the world. Jesus must have lived because such an ensampler was a psychological necessity. God had to send his Son in answer to this inherent need. It would be unthinkable that such a need would not have been providentially met. Therefore Jesus did live. The broad prevalence and strength of this position calls for an exhaustive critique.

It can be conceded at the outset that in the effort of a divine hierarchy of overlords to humanize and eventually divinize an animal-born race, the advantage of the employment of a living example would be evident. God or his hierarchical agents, archangels, demi-gods, heroes, divine men, could not but be fully aware of the powerful force and virtue of a concrete example of perfection set before the eyes of mankind. It would both quicken and stabilize the general human inclination to strive after the ideal. It would give solid and constructive form to that aspiration by focusing its drive upon a spe- cific set of ideal characteristics embodied and manifested in the exemplar. It would thus prevent the waste of infinite quantities of devotional force spent in direction toward ill-defined goals. The great divine man would stand before the world and lure all men unto him by the attractive power of his shining beauty. No other impartation of inspiration from God to man could make its salutary influence so effectively fruitful of constant good stimulus. A divine model of perfection would uplift the world through the magnetically moving force of his example. The gods must know that humanity is psychologically set and disposed to ape a paragon. The dynamic moral power of an embodied ideal is ever great. This psychological disposition well prepared the stage for the presentation to the world of its ideal hero, the Christos.

The gods did know that man would ape the divine paragon, and they did present the hero, the great sunlit figure of Christos, in every religion of antiquity.

With the keenest incisiveness it must be contended, as perhaps the prime spiritual motive of this study, that the argument based on the psychological beneficence of a divine ensampler for the human race falls out in favor of the non-historicity, and not, as almost unanimously believed, of the historicity. This astounding assertion must be vindicated against the general mass of contrary opinion.

If all other things were equal, naturally the impressive force of an ideal of perfection embodied in a living man would be conceded to be more effective for character in the lives of devotees than would the same paragon depicted only in the figure of a drama. A life lived on the same terms as our own would emotionally impress all mortals more powerfully than would any fictional representation. But all other things are not equal in the case of the Christ. There are elements in the theological situation environing the figure of the Gospel Jesus that make the difference between the two quite abysmal.

The first great divergence is in the fact that theology has made of the historical divine man the only possible such figure in the human record. Jesus is in the religion that exploited him the only-begotten Son of God. He is the only embodiment of the Father's glory and cosmic presence ever manifested in human form. He is totally unique and lonely. No man can match his perfection.

This fact of his solitary uniqueness at once destroys whatever psy- chological value his incarnation in a man of flesh might otherwise have. It defeats the very purpose for which an ensampler is designed – the effective working of the lure of his perfection under the force of the assurance that by striving the aspirant may achieve identity or equality with the ideal one. If it is published beforehand that the worshipped Personage is the unattainable and forever unapproachable Ideal, the springs of devotion and zeal are dried up at their very source. Why strive, why aspire, why copy, if it is to be all in vain? The glistening paragon becomes only a romantic ideal, the more radiant and bright-hued because of its eternal remoteness and inaccessibility. It is placed there only for mortals to gaze and gape at in awe and marvel. But it is rendered useless for the very thing claimed as the strength of the argument from psychology, the inspirational power of the life lived to be a moving example for us. The manipulators of the psychological factors in the ecclesiastical enterprise, in straining to assure the Christly figure of perennial reverence and worship of the romantic sort by placing him on an inimitable level of perfection and uniqueness, unwittingly sacrificed the very element in the psychological situation that it was most ardently hoped to gain by the procedure. To keep him secure in his lofty place of adoration they weakened the force of his ability to stimulate emulation. He is the stainless One, incapable of sin; men are doomed sinners, who must in craven fashion plead with him for salvation from innate degeneracy.

Thus the luminous picture of the mighty paragon has not worked out, and can not work out, as a triumphant force designed to elevate character by the cogency of its living reality. It has in fact operated directly to defeat that effect. It has left men facing a hopeless effort and turning from resolute zeal for attainment to sunken morbidity expressed in the conventional theological ideas of sin and its dog, remorse. Before the Ideal the eyes of sinning man have been lowered to the ground with sense of unworthiness and self-depreciation; they have not been lifted up to face the revealed divinity as the possibility of man's own accomplishment. Before the figure of the man-Christ man has made himself abject, groveling in unmanly beggarliness before the unbearable glory of the One who stands clothed in unattainable majesty.

The psychological influence of this only-begotten manifestation is further decisively emasculated by the accompanying theological doc- trine that this one epiphany of God's nature was not a man of our own earthly evolution, but came directly from the hand of supreme Deity, a product of divine fiat from another world. Though frequently emphasis is laid upon his community of nature with us, still he is exotic, a transplantation from the empyrean. He did not need to go through the long evolutionary gateway of our humanity, but was already a citizen of the cosmos, a dweller with God before the worlds were, existent before Abraham was. Though so high, he yet condescended, abased himself, to become for a generation one among us, sharing our immature nature without yielding to its seductions. He had not come up the long road of development from unicell or moneron to man, but came down from the skies full-panoplied in cosmic resplendence, to lay for the time being his glory mildly by, as the Christmas hymn has it. His coming was not an act of common brotherhood of a creature kindred with us, but a condescension and a gratuity, arbitrary in cosmic counsels and unrelated to natural contingency. He was a pure gift from the Gods. The Father's whim and his own munificent spirit of self-sacrifice brought him here. The merit was his; ours the unmerited benefit. So again the alleged great psychological efficacy of his exemplary life is annulled by the strangeness and vast remoteness of his nature from our own. He is no brother but a distant ambassador who deigns to visit us for a season and labor with us, but can not abide with us forever. He must in a moment return to the celestial palace, sending a substitute to remind us of his one charming sojourn with us.

But the crux of the debate on the psychological efficacy of a paragon is not reached until the matter is approached from the side of the great question of the relative potency of two forces, one operative from without the subject, the other from within. This crucial point of discussion must be given thorough treatment. Though it is not critical or decisive for the question of Christ historicity, it looms as perhaps the most portentous phase of the entire survey. It is not too sweeping an assertion to aver that the whole psychological beneficence of religion stands or falls with the outcome of the discussion of the historicity of the Messiah. It stands if the world savior be proven an element, a divine leaven, within the soul and conscience of all humanity. It falls if he be reduced to the futile stature of a man in history. For it is the contention of this study that the moral effect upon general humanity of being taught to look for salvation to a savior in the person of a historical man is inherently and inevitably degrading to the immanent divinity of man. Beyond doubt this strong asseveration will be violently disputed. It will be contended that it runs counter to every obvious envisagement in the situation. Nevertheless it is urged here that these alleged obvious implications seem obvious only in consequence of many centuries of inculcation of a false view which has overridden and subjugated open minds, and that they would lose their obviousness if they could be considered in the light of pure reason and apart from ingrained habitudes of pious assumption. Had the opposite view been sanctified by such age-long approbation it, rather than the first, would carry the weight of obvious rectitude with it. For, of the two possibilities, surely the method of human salvation that would instinctively at first sight commend itself as the obviously more natural one would be that which places the agency of universal salvation from evolutionary dereliction in a power lodged within all men, as against an extraneous and uncertain influence somehow, but in no understandable way, shed upon us under certain peculiar conditions by one person in history. Obviousness is obviously with the method of a general distribution of a divine spirit among all men to act as a leaven of righteousness and self-transformation, and it is certainly less clearly with a method that makes all men dependent upon the unaccountable self-immolation of one only-begotten Son of God. The one is in consonance with man's every normal instinct of natural procedure; the other strains at blind faith to swallow its artificially bizarre and fantastic features. The latter view, be it averred, has only won its place in the acceptance of millions of purblind devotees through the stultification of their reason by the ceaseless exploitation of the forces of religious faith. The irrational flaunting of the Biblical text "for with God all things are possible" has further tended to keep the door open to the influx into less critical minds of every conceivable absurdity in the theological field. The introduction of boundless irrationality in doctrinism was initially made when in the third and fourth centuries the esoteric interpretation of scripture yielded to the frightful debasement of exoteric literalism. The whale's swallowing of Jonah was no more difficult for piety than the ecclesiastical swallowing of the Jonah allegory and all its brother myths in their literal form. The tragedy of its successful accomplish- ment – as far as it has been successful – has lain in the necessary preliminary derationalization and paralysis of millions of simple minds before the natural gagging and choking could be overcome. Blind faith and the peculiar weakness of the human mind in face of the alleged supernatural were the instruments of the tragic intellectual dupery. The noble scriptures were intended to gain and hold the perennial reverence of all intelligent minds; they were never designed to enslave minds with the fatal fascination of a fetish.

Once the historical status was assigned to the Christ principle the words, "look to Jesus, the author and finisher of our faith," have exercised a damaging sway over countless minds. To those who knew that Jesus, esoterically comprehended, was the dramatic type-figure of the divinity within us, the words carried not fatality but uplift and inspiration. The difference in the two cases clearly limns the difference in the psychological character of the two influences. This work advances the proposition that it is psychologically hazardous at any time for people to place their divinity in a person or locale outside themselves. To do so involves the inevitable repercussion on average minds that their salvation is to be vicariously won. The disastrous consequence of this reaction must in the end be the enervation and atrophy of spiritual effort and initiative on the part of the individual to win his own redemption.

The effect of the doctrine of salvation through the intercession of the Son of God – a salvation which the doctrine implies we had in no wise ourselves earned – could not be, as claimed, an intensification of the personal effort at righteousness. The very words of scripture were to the effect that man's righteousness in the sight of God is as filthy rags. Every presupposition of the doctrine as presented emphasized the uselessness of effort and the casting of our burden upon Jesus' shoulders. "What a friend we have in Jesus!" has been sung in full-throated unctuousness. His own invitation to the weary and heavy-laden to come unto him and find rest has had an all-too-ready response in the literal sense. Taken wrongly these words have gone far to impair the natural sturdiness of spiritual character in millions. By a psychology that was hardly subtle, but simple and direct, they militated to turn the conscientious resolution of the individual away from the actual cultus of his own immanent deity in thought, word and deed, while he pursued the chimera of vicarious salvation through pleading with his personal Redeemer. He was told that the more abjectly he confessed his own folly and failure, the more effective would be his plea in the ears of the compassionate Savior of men. In looking to Jesus in a man of flesh the devotee neglected the indwelling Jesus, and would inevitably do so in the exact ratio of his ignorance and his gullibility.

This is a simple proposition and is quite self-evident. It is the law of nature that an organism or a function not used atrophies. Man has in a lifetime only a given quantity of psychic energy. If he expends it in one direction, the possibility of expending it in another is diminished by so much. The only Christos that is available for him is that hidden divine love within him. If he wastes his soul-force in straining to induce an exterior personage to intervene in his evolutionary effort on his behalf, he loses by so much the fleeting opportunity to cultivate his indwelling guest. It is necessary to put this with categorical cogency, because it will be brushed aside as inconsequential. It is close to being the crux of the entire problem under discussion. A man can not at one and the same time serve two masters, the one within and the other without. Neither can he reap the fruit of an ardent cultivation of his potential divinity while pouring out all his psychic ardor upon the person of a Galilean peasant.

Not only will it be said that this can be done, but it will be claimed in addition that the adoration of the Judaean carpenter is itself the prime stimulus and incentive to the end of one's inner spiritual culture. This brings us back to the question of the relative psychological power of a living or of a mythical and dramatic Christ. The great cry of the proponents of the historicity is that the psychological power of a living historical example must surely be greater and more beneficent than that of a purely dramatic figure. History, it is urged, is real, whereas a myth is fictional. This debate is of critical importance, because if the Christos of the Bible was not a person of flesh, he becomes, as would be said, nothing but a character of pure fiction. He is a myth. And many books have been written to prove that he is only a myth. How, it will be asked in vigorous spirit, can a mythical figure be presumed to exert as strong a psychological force upon the world as a Jesus in real life? As hinted briefly before, the unique strength of the position of Christianity is claimed to lie in this one item of the reality of Jesus' living demonstration or epiphany of God in humanity. It holds up to its following the assurance of ultimate victory based on the one divine fait accompli in history. Jesus was a living example, and not a mere theological promise unaccompanied by accomplishment. Jesus' life is the one solid rock of veritude upon which mortal man can build his hopes. What is a myth compared with this?

This is the argumentative situation as viewed from the point of naïve exoteric simplicity. It is not, however, the view revealed to deeper esoteric reflection. Esotericism understands something about the myth that is quite unknown to the uninitiated general mind. The ancient sages knew something concerning the myth that the modern mind has never grasped. It can now be said with certitude that the whole genius of religious and philosophical culture escaped the grasp of Occidental civilization as a result of the third-century loss of this certain understanding of the nature and utility of the myth. It is time, after centuries of stupid nescience, that modern ignorance of a vital matter be enlightened. Enlightenment on this detail may yet save religion and humanitarian culture, menaced dangerously by our blind failure to concentrate upon the one cultus of a higher selfhood in man that alone can redeem the world from immersion in the lower levels of consciousness and motivation.

What was known of old, and must now be proclaimed anew with clarion blast, is that the myth, as employed by ancient illuminati in Biblical scripture, is not fiction, but the truest of all history! So far from being fiction in the sense of a story that never happened and is therefore false to fact, it is the only story that is completely and wholly true! The myth is the only true narrative of the reality of human experience. It is the only ultimately true history ever written. It is a picture and portrayal of the only veridical history ever lived. All other so-called history, the record of people's acts and movements, buildings and destructions, marchings and settlings, is less truly history than the myth! The latter is the realest of history, as it is the account of the actual experience of life in evolution. Real as history is, it is finally less true than the myth. The myth is always and forever true; actual history is never more than an imperfect approximation to the truth of life. Even as a perfectly faithful record of what actually happened, book history is far from being true. This is an admission so commonplace that every courtroom is on guard against the testimony of witnesses because of the incapacity of the human senses in making an impeccable record of event. No history book ever contained a precisely true account of occurrence. No two historians ever wrote identical narratives of a war or a nation's life. The writing of actual history has never been other than the more or less careful exercise of the chronicler's constructive imagination.

On the other hand the myth is, as nearly as the highest human-divine genius can construct it, a clear picture of the more real import of life itself. It is possible for conscious beings such as men to live through actual events of history and yet largely, at times completely, miss the reality, in a profounder philosophical sense, of the very experience they undergo. What history thus misses the myth expresses. History is never more than a partial slap-stick comic or heavy tragic flirtation with the deep realities; the myth is a clear delineation of them. The myth is no more a fiction than a good photograph is a fiction. It is a true picture. In the hands of semi-divine mythicists of old it was a splendid photograph of something that is of far greater utility to men whose divine destiny entails a struggle for spiritual culture than any uncertain chronicle of man's tawdry fights and scrambles could ever be. It was made to be a glowing pictograph of those basic archai, those eternal principles of truth, those immutable laws of growth and structure which are the everlasting essence of all being. So the myth is ever truer than history. It is a portrayal of the meaning and structure of all history. It pictures and preserves forever for the grasp of unfolding divine consciousness in man that golden light of true realization which alone elevates his historical experience above animal sensuousness and vegetative existence.

With this revised comprehension of the myth it is now possible to approach with better qualification for a successful resolution of difficulties the matter of the historicity and the psychological potency of the central figure in the early Christian and all antecedent systems. That central figure was in the myths and in the religious dramas of most ancient nations for thousands of years B.C. It stood there drawn and limned by the astutest dramatic genius the race has ever produced, to be the perennial reminder to all men of all religions of their own divine endowment, and to serve as dynamic instruction in the methods of attaining its progressive evolution in and through history.

In the counsels of the Sages, who were men of our own humanity graduated in earlier cycles to the place of mastership and perfected knowledge of the whole earthly evolution – St. Paul's "just men made perfect" – the problem facing them in their task of giving to early humanity compendia of truth and wisdom that should guide the race through the course of self-controlled unfoldment was one that called for a determination of the best practical method of both holding before man the ideal of all his striving and stimulating his steady zeal to pursue it. It is not known now as it was in ancient days that a grade and council of perfected men, risen through humanity to divinity, stood in the relation of tutors and teachers to infant humanity, and prescribed codes of morals, religion, philosophy, law, mythology, literature and art, as well as mathematics, science and physics, not to forget agriculture, for the beginnings in civilization and culture. These are the authors of the great sacred books of antiquity, the instructors in pyramid building, the founders of human progress. Their graduate status at once explains the otherwise inexplicable phenomenon that has bewildered and confounded the savants of modern knowledge, – how it was that races that were still in the semi-barbaric stage already held in their possession tomes of the most exalted wisdom and philosophical insight, as well as moral purity, which their own undeveloped mentality could not have produced.

These men, both by evolutionary selection and by humanitarian choice on their own part, performed the function of formulating the cultural heritage of the human race, particularly in the domain of religion and philosophy. One of the greatest of the problems confronting them in their sublime work was the choice of method by which mankind could be most deeply impressed with the sublimity of the divine goal toward which the race was struggling and most intelligently spurred on to attain it. The plan adopted by the counsels of the most august wisdom was based on the decision to place before the world systems of religion, in which the outline of the drama of life, the place of the world in the cosmos, the place of man in the hierarchy of being, the moral conflict leading to evolution, and the eventual deification of humanity at the "end of the age" or cycle, should be clearly set forth for the behoof of all generations. In order that there should be no possibility of man's missing the mark, or failing to understand exactly the goal of perfection to which his whole incarnational series was destined to lift him, the Sages resorted to the measure of placing at the very heart of every religious system an ideal personage who should typify and personify man himself, in his dual nature as human and divine, struggling forward to the consummation of his high glory. This central character embodied the divine element that was to deify mankind, and the drama depicted the final victory of the god within over the lower forces in the human compound.

The figure was of course that of the Christos, who in his last triumph is clothed in robes of solar light, to indicate that the deity within man is of kindred essence with the sun and that as man progresses toward his final exaltation in glory his garments shall be white as the light and his righteousness shall cause him to shine like the sun in the kingdom of his Father. In this glorious character men could see pictured their history, their destiny and their eventual conversion into angels of light. This was the model, the archetype, the paragon of excellence decided upon by the council of perfected men to be made central in every religion given to the early nations, as their chosen means of most cogently impressing humanity's millions through the ages to strive after the shining ideal of divinity. In order that historical man could never forget that ideal or drift away from it, the Sages incorporated in every religion this very copy and replica of the man become God, so that it needed only for men to look at the model to see the image of their own life and their apotheosization. If mankind needed to be stimulated to the good life by the force of a divine ensampler, the Sages saw to it that the great spiritual allurement was provided. The radiant figure of the Sun-God, man himself divinized, stood at the heart of every old religion. High wisdom comprehended that mortal men needed to have a picture of their own glorious goal set before their eyes. The picture was given. The psychological power of a paragon to lure impressionable mankind was recognized and the paragon supplied. The whole history of man was diagrammed and with consummate genius depicted in a great drama, with the Sun-God always the central and significant character. It is known that the features and play of the drama were of such impressiveness and moving power that no device of human conception could have transcended the purificatory, or as the Greeks called it, the cathartic moral efficacy of this representation. It was a veritable baptism of the spectator and candidate in transfiguring elevation of consciousness.

It will presumably still be urged that if these exalted personages possessed the wisdom attributed to them they must have known that the example of one living Christ on earth would be more effective for salutary influence than any number of dramatic figures. At least two considerations weighed against their holding any such opinion or acting upon it. They realized for one thing that merely to present to the world one living example of perfect humanity would defeat the very psychology they aimed at. It would have been pointless and superfluous in a world that was to be taught that the rough road of evolution would bring every man to Christhood. Again they knew that it would be both confusing and disconcerting to intelligent people everywhere to proclaim the advent of one perfected soul in unique isolation, when it was already the general knowledge of instructed men in early days that more than one of humanity's chain had reached the mark of the high calling of God in the Christos, that a number would attain it in every age, and that all men would eventually do so. The proclamation and the production of one only example of accomplished divinization would have been meaningless and lacking in significant virtue in a world that was intended to be rightly instructed on fundamental verities. If there were but one living paragon, only one generation would see him, and if he was an obscure person like the Galilean, only a few hundred persons would know of him through personal contact. The sheer difficulty of having his name, fame and life and teaching advertised to the rest of humanity would have to be managed against real obstacles. If he himself proclaimed his unique divinity, how could he make ignorant, blind humanity accept him? His heralding by angels and portents might readily fall afoul of the general ancient vogue of such things, and pass unheeded.

It was not perhaps even considered for a moment that a purely typical ideal figure would serve to inspire men less than a living example, because every man, it was known, became a living example in the proportion in which he embodied the ideal in his life and person. Nothing was thus to be gained by a historical example that could not be better won by the ideal type impersonation. There was no point in producing one living paragon to prove to the world that man could become divine, when it was already known that all men would in due time become divine. All mortals, as they became intelligent, knew that they had the struggle of evolution before them and that perseverance would land them at the gates of godlikeness. What they needed was the vivid dramatization of the quality and character of that perfection toward which they were to aspire. These were clearly and impressively outlined in the dramatic type figure. The essential ingredients for compounding the most efficacious virtue in an ensampler were all present in this situation. Nothing was lacking that a living man-Christ could have supplied. The prime element was the knowledge that every man must be his own savior. This item of philosophical truth being known, the dramatic model possessed more sanely compelling force than a living personation. The knowledge of universal salvation robbed the latter of any advantage over the other. An embodied Christ would have been an impressive spectacle, but not overwhelmingly or inordinately so, for the knowledge that men were advancing into the highest stages of purity and illumination everywhere at all times deprived the fact of its uniqueness. One perfected man would not have been one alone, but one among many.

It is sharply to be recognized that the mere presumption of superior psychological advantage in a living type figure became possible only with the decay of knowledge that man's upward progress is the work of the individual himself in conjunction with nature, and the consequent entry of the vicarious concept through the corruption of ancient divine philosophy. In the end the orthodox presupposition that human salvation demanded the driving force of a personal God in the flesh, so far from proving its natural correctness, demonstrates only that the world's keenness of philosophical insight had been blunted to the degree that a totally insupportable thesis could be imposed upon the millions without a chance for successful repudiation.

The momentous task of providing nations and peoples with a divine model and exemplar was accomplished by the sagacious tutors of the race through the institution of a ritual drama designed and formulated to produce the most beneficent effect. It was adopted as the method that most readily met the terms of natural expediency and practicability. It would minister in full to the psychological needs of a race endowed and constituted as mankind was. With transcendent genius the Sages formulated the systems of myths, allegories, fables, parables, numerological structures and astrological pictographs such as the zodiac and the planispheres or uranographs to supplement the central ceremonial drama. The whole structure was, however, fabricated with such esoteric subtlety that, the keys once lost, the system has defied the best of medieval and modern acumen to recapture its cryptic import. The divinity in man being a portion of the ineffable glory of the sun, and necessarily therefore typified by it, the great scenic portrayal was built upon the solar allegory, and the successive phases of man's divinization were enacted around the solar year in accordance with the significance of the orb's monthly and seasonal positions. Ancient religion was for this reason called solar religion or "sun-worship." Temples were built to the sun and hymns to the sun written to extol its splendor as typical of man's inner splendor. The meaning of the drama thus interwoven at every turn with the movements of the great natural analogue and type of our divinity, every detail of the ritual would receive an enormous enhancement of impressiveness and meaning for celebrants, who would be subjected in this way to the greatly magnified psychic power that was generated by the co-ordination of their highest spiritual conceptions with the redoubtable truth of nature. Ancient sapiency linked spiritual law and natural law together in a kinship and correspondence that endowed the former with all the impregnable certitude of the latter. This link between the two aspects of truth was broken about the third century, and religion has ever since been crippled by want of a reinforcement so naturally strong. The modern religious consciousness has to make shift as best it can in almost total privation of the vital sources of assurance and stability which flowed into the mind from the correlation of its spiritual tenets with natural truth. Every theological presentment must necessarily fall upon mental comprehension with a manifold strength if it is immediately seen to be corroborated by the open facts of nature.

Mystical experience will be vastly certified to intelligence if it can be illuminated by the glow of meaning emanating from natural symbols. A graphic representation of hidden meaning is always far more effective to stamp the mind with living images than language of itself can accomplish. Hence the resort to drama in the first place, and next to a drama that was based on and interwoven with the most obvious of all natural phenomena – the rise and setting of the sun in the daily round and the larger counterpart of the same routine in the seasonal cycle. These two daily and annual operations, the alternate victory and defeat of the sun, typify of course the very gist of the whole human drama, the soul's descent into its "death" in mortal body and its recurrent resurrection therefrom. This is the core of the central theme in all religious scripture. The daily sinking of the sun at eve in earth or ocean, and its rising again in the east at dawn, or its yearly descent to the south in the autumn and its succeeding return northward in the spring, all prefigure the descent of the soul, a unit of God's own conscious mind, into incarnation in its 'night" or "winter" of "death" and its subsequent resurrection from the tomb of the body. The fact that ancient insight allied tomb and body in one meaning is astonishingly indicated by the identity of the Greek words, soma, body and sema, tomb.

In this ceremonial drama the central figure was the sun-god, or Son of God, the Christos, Messiah. He was likewise the Avatar, the Bodhisattva, the World-Savior. A generic term for him was The Coming One, or "The Comer" in Egypt. And never until the decadent epoch that fell like a pall upon early Christianity in the third century was the Messianic Messenger ever thought of as "coming" in the sense of being born as a person in the world. This is a fact of momentous significance. The many world saviors antecedent to Jesus were types and not persons born in history. They were typical characters portraying that spirit of divine charity which should transform and transfigure human life from the rapacity of the beast to the graciousness of unselfish love. Its "coming" would be its gradual growth and its mounting sweep in the hearts and minds of humanity as a whole. It would not be "born" until it came to overt expression in the active lives of mortals. Its taking root and gradually expanding in world consciousness was likened unto the planting and flourishing of the tiny mustard seed in the Gospel parable. No Christos can possibly "come" into the world except it arrive on the waves of charitable impulse that well up in individual and mass motivation. No Christ can bring godliness in his single person. No Messiah can impart it to men in the mass by any other method than the transforming of all hearts through the throb of Christly compassion and the exaltation of all minds into the likeness of the Christly intelligence.

Treated cursorily already, the argument that for full inspirational suggestiveness humans must have their faith fortified by the assurance that one man at least actually did attain to Christhood and manifest the ideal of perfection, must receive somewhat fuller scrutiny. Its force was already weakened by the consideration that the one character in history alleged to have furnished mortals this assurance was not a man of our own evolution, and had not attained his divinity over the same pathway that we must tread, but was an immaculate emissary from inaccessible heavens, a guest from remote empyreans. It must be accentuated that this situation introduces into the picture the negative depressing influence of man's realization of his own hopeless inferiority, the impossibility of his stepping up beside the Christ. In striking contrast to this the method adopted by the Sages obviated any such disastrous negativism. It carried with it the invincible certainty of attainment for every man. There was never a question of achievement, but only of effort, method and perseverance. The very manner of the presentation of the ideal figure carried the presupposition of final victory to the aspirant. The type was exhibited on no other grounds than that it was the picture of what could be achieved by all. Obviously there could be no sense or reason in holding before all men in all religions the type of what they could not attain. Attainment was an inevitable implication of the representation from the outset. One man's superb attainment could only add evidence to what was already known. But the proclamation that only one man had ever reached the goal would have thrown dismay into minds long assured of the high destiny of all. Heraclitus' discerning observation that "man's genius is a deity" had placed a god in potentiality deep within the heart of every life, and the envisaged prospect of divinization was simply a long growth of latent into active powers and faculties, a process that could be in no wise affected by the birth of any exceptional personage. That the eventual deification of all humanity should be considered to depend upon such a birth would have been received in ancient times with bewilderment and total incomprehension. When the true nature and terms of the problem of human spiritual advancement were succinctly understood, there was no way in which the Bethlehem event on the historical plane could be given a place of crucial importance in the universal task.

It will be seen that the entire argument for the historicity on the grounds of its superior psychological influence collapses finally under the force of the admission, which must be made by all parties, that even if Jesus of Nazareth lived and is the Vicar of God on earth, every man must work out his own salvation on exactly the same terms as though he had not existed! Since Jesus can not come to any man and take his evolutionary problem off his shoulders and effect his salvation for him, the only psychological value left to the fact of the historicity is reduced to the mere force of a sort of hero-worship. The Jesus life and character, his sufferings and virtues, can stimulate devotion and desire to emulate. His lofty moral preachment sets a norm for ideal human attainment. The very contemplation of his pure life and radiant divinity inspires an answering nobility in millions of lives.

The power of a noble example, the more especially one enhanced in beauty by centuries of pious glorification, is not questioned. But the same beauty and indeed the same lofty spiritual preachment was afforded imitative devotion in the case of the sun-god figure. In the end the sublime figure of the type character was there purely for inspirational incentive, standing free from any suggestion of vicarious salvation for the adorer. It moved to noble effort, but in not the least hint did it delude the worshipper with the fatuous notion that any power save his own consecrated struggle could win his salvation for him. The greater the claimed psychological power of the historical Jesus over the devotee, the greater the tragedy of delusion thus wrought upon millions, since this stimulating influence has never been detached from the concomitant imputations of vicariousness inseparably linked with it in Christian theology. Thus the greater part of the alleged beneficent force of the living example in the end evaporates into pure delusion not unattended with disastrous consequences.

A few sentences in the preceding chapter alluded to a situation brought to light by the study of Comparative Religion and Mythology which adds further vast weight to the probability that the whole enormous body of psychological prestige exerted by the belief in the historical Jesus is grounded on a chimera and not on a fact. The events in the alleged life of Jesus are pushed closer and closer to the point of myth by the astounding fact that, as the ever-clearer implications of these studies show, they are seen to match with nearly perfect fidelity the similar cycles of purely allegorical "events" in the dramatic and mythic representations of some sixteen or more – indeed probably fifty or more – earlier type figures recorded in ancient sacred Bibles of the nations. It is certainly to be regarded as more than passing strange that when the only-begotten Son of God did descend to earth to implant the genius of the one true religion to save mankind, his life only copied or matched in great detail the dramatized typal characters or sun-gods of antecedent religions. And the earlier figures whose careers he repeated were definitely non-historical or at best legendarily semi- historical, such as Zoroaster, Orpheus and Hermes. The Christians of the third and fourth centuries were plagued to distraction by the recurrent appearance of evidence that revealed the disconcerting identity of the Gospel narrative in many places with incidents in the "lives" of Horus, Izdubar, Mithra, Sabazius, Adonis, Witoba, Hercules, Marduk, Krishna, Buddha and other divine messengers to early nations. They answered the challenge of this situation with the desperate allegation that the similarity was the work of the devil! The findings of comparative religion and mythology constitute at this epoch a far more deadly challenge than they did in the third century, for there is the massive body of the Egyptian religious literature to increase the mountain of identities between Christian and antecedent pagan gospels and there is less of Christian hypnotism to overcome now than at the earlier date. In more formidable form than ever before the Christian proponents must face the open implications of the query that springs to mind out of these comparative religion discoveries, why, if the model life had already been proclaimed by numerous Avatars before Jesus and he therefore had nothing new to add, the need or occasion for his passionate sacrifice at all? The model he displayed had already been on view in nearly every ancient nation for centuries! So far from being the climax and grand consummation of a series of ever fuller revelations, his advent was rather an anti-climax. The enlightened and emancipated study of comparative religion, vitally reinforced by the discovery of the Rosetta Stone, bids fair to become a veritable Nemesis to the exorbitant claims of Christianity. It was these momentous disclosures of identity in the material of Christian and pagan literature that gave impetus to the present undertaking, provided the data for proof and lent overwhelming warrant to all the major conclusions to be reached. And it is this body of evidence that sweeps in with crushing force to devastate every one of the arguments from psychology that have been considered. In its totality it constitutes a bulwark of strength on the side of the non-historicity that must be rated virtually inexpugnable.

It can now be stated with little chance of refutation that the Gospel "life" of Jesus had been written, in substance, for five thousand years before he came. The record is in Egypt. An Egyptian Jesus – Horus – had raised an Egyptian Lazarus from the dead at an Egyptian Bethany, with an Egyptian Mary and Martha present, in the scripts of that an- cient land that were extant at least five thousand years B.C. And a carving in relief, depicting scenes of angels announcing from the skies to shepherds in the fields a deific advent, of an angel, Gabriel, foretelling to a virgin that she should be the mother of the Christos, of the nativity in the cave, and of three sages kneeling in adoration before the infant deity, had been on the walls of the temple of Luxor at least seventeen hundred years B.C. The Virgin Mother had held the divine child in her arms in zodiacs on temple ceilings for millennia before the Galilean babe saw the light. What indeed becomes of the grandiose message he brought and the shining light of deific perfection that he flashed on the world, if both were already here long before he came?

There remains another spectacular aspect of the psychological problem to be dealt with, not now of the influence of the divine personal advent, but this time having to do with the psychological phases connected with the sheer fact of how the world could recognize the Christ in Jesus or any other embodiment. How could he be known and identified on the historical arena? The amount of mental ineptitude displayed by votaries with minds drugged into doltishness by the overweening power of "faith" and literalism is everywhere great in religion. But hardly everywhere does it show itself in such glaring inanity as in this item. In the process of converting myth over into "history" the transformers swallowed many a camel of factual ridiculousness or impossibility without choking. But surely it must occur to even palsied minds that the matter of knowing or recognizing as the one divine Avatar in all history a man who is declared to have been in all respects like other men save without sin, is a thing that lies beyond the realm of all human practicability. The whole matter of his recognition and identification as uniquely divine has been so aureoled with romantic suggestiveness, so exotically perfumed with semi-celestial fragrance, that it is quite impossible for votaries to bring their minds to take a realistic view of the practical possibilities in the case. It seems impossible to bring them out of the shimmering roseate light of adoration and mental sycophancy and have them face the blunt realities of such a situation. Not a man or women of them but would say that if Jesus appeared to them tomorrow as he appeared in his daily mien in Judea, they would immediately recognize him and be so overwhelmed that they would instantly prostrate themselves in adoration at his feet. This is questionable; but what is not questionable is that if another cosmic figure equally divine appeared tomorrow in the guise of ordinary humanity these folks would not recognize him. By what credentials would any man of "regular" human appearance, even with the saintliest of faces, enable us to distinguish him from the commonalty of the race and accept him as the one cosmic divine being, God's only Son, come to earth? How could any spectator determine from looking at him that he was the one person in all ages set apart from the generality of mankind and really a god from the skies? Such a rating and such a distinctive uniqueness could not be determined from looking at any man in mortal flesh. Every age, indeed every community, has seen men of not only saintly appearance and bearing and wisdom, but of saintly life. Thousands of such people have lived lives essentially as blameless, innocent and charitable as his. How could any man in person exhibit unmistakably the marks of the supra-human distinctions claimed for Jesus in his life by Christian ecclesiasticism? These claims included first his uniqueness in all history as the only-begotten Son of God; then the totally novel and only single instance of a life utterly sinless and pure; then his cosmic election as the Logos of God, according to John's first chapter description; then his role as the second person of the cosmic Trinity; then his commission as the agent of man's evolutionary salvation; and finally as the embodied fulfillment of all ancient Messianic hope and realization. How could such qualities and functions be seen by merely looking at a man of ordinary human constitution? What stupefaction of mind is necessary to nurse the belief that the people of his day could identity him as the impersonation of all the exceptional and wholly unnatural characterization ascribed by religious fetishism to him must be left to the students of abnormal psychology to determine. It will be howled at this analysis that it is an attempt to treat a sacred thing in ribald fashion. On the contrary it is an attempt to take the situation exactly as Christian apologists represent it. If caricature is introduced it emanates from the side of ebullient faith and not from honest realism. The travesty of all natural possibility in the case is created by that naïveté of mind which even the learned theologians of every age down to the present have displayed in this matter. They have based many an argument or exegesis on the bald assumption that any person coming in sight of the man Jesus would have been at once overpowered with awe and would have known that he was looking at the only cosmic deity ever seen on earth. The sheer sight of his person would elucidate at once all the theological implications of his celestial errand. Forsooth he carried unmistakable credentials of his cosmic character with him in look, speech, majesty. Cosmic character shone all about him, glowed in his face, bearing, speech. The universal ascription to him of such egregious persuasion raises the next question as to how, if these were so, the humble people he was alleged to have contacted came to be instructed in the difficult art of recognizing cosmic characteristics. There is no evidence that the public of today has knowledge of any way to identify cosmic character.

Part of the rejoinder to this would be that he told the multitudes that he was the Son of God, the Messiah they were eagerly waiting for, the true vine, the celestial shepherd, the door and the way. They did not have to surmise; he gave them explicit information. In answer to this argument it need only be suggested that if people and popular attitudes of that day were in any way like what they are today, there is nothing that could have advanced the evidence of his cosmic mission that would so unfailingly have discredited his professions as his own statement that he was the one and only Son of God. It is the one sure token that the present age would accept as certain evidence of his not being what he claimed. Words that could appropriately and impressively flow from the mouth of the personified solar deity in a great ritual drama would create a riot in an actual street scene. One has but to use constructive imagination realistically for a moment to be assured of the vast improbability of the personal Christ's being recognized for what he is claimed to have been in theology. If this is not convincing enough, let some claimant to divine status try it today! Were he the man with the saintliest mien, with the spiritual mystic's benignant physiognomy and uttering the holiest of precepts, the moment he went about proclaiming his unique cosmic status a police call would in an hour be necessary to rescue him from the clownish roughness of the crowd. And the thing that would arouse both pity and subtle resentment in the crowd would be the evidence of general witlessness and lack of good sense thus flaunted in their faces. It is of course easy to ridicule or cheapen an essentially holy thing or a sincere action. Raillery is no true answer to real sincerity. Still pious religionism has asked us to accept without smiling a host of situations in the context of theological and Biblical interpretation that are wholly outlandish or screamingly ridiculous (such as the picture of Jesus riding into Jerusalem on the first Palm Sunday sitting astride the backs of two asses at once!). It is after all no service to any man so to reduce his powers of judgment under the sway of religious infatuations that he is unable any longer to apply his faculties to envisage events realistically. The many events of Gospel narrative would take on quite a different aspect in the minds of gullible believers if they could be viewed in the broad light of factual realism instead of through the glamor of uncritical acceptance.

The assumption that a mob of people could "spot" an Avatar – much less the only cosmic one in world history – in any ordinary pious man of saintly appearance merely by looking at his physical person, is one of those implications of Christian doctrinism that has been painted upon the tractable imagination of millions until all power to view the circumstance through the eyes of actual occurrence has been lulled into stupor. Even in India, where holy men openly do parade their pretensions to sanctity, the self-advanced claims of one Yogi to the unique cosmic distinctions predicated of Jesus would be looked at askance. Various disquisitions on the Gospels and the life of Jesus often seriously picture the multitude as suddenly realizing in the Galilean peasant the physical fulfillment of all epic religious prophecy. And Joseph Warschauer, in his The Historical Life of Christ, dissertates on the theme of Jesus' own awakening, at about the stage of his baptism in the Jordan, to the "humble" realization that he was to be in his single person the one living embodiment of divine messengership from God to humanity, and that through the brain, nerves and blood of his one little body were to flow the currents of a power that should redeem the human race. Even in spite of the fact that the whole ancient world looked for the coming of Messiah, and the exoterically taught masses expected it in the form of a living person, how the idea could have taken form in the mind of any intelligent man that his own body would be the vehicle or incorporation of that cosmic power is a glaring feature of the situation not explained by Warschauer or any other apologetic writer. It is left to the omnivorous camel-swallowing maw of that great monster of the genus of stupid religious gullibility, that ever-faithful animal that has carried on its back the priestcraft of the world, to ingest it without choking. The paralysis of the mass mind by the narcotic power of pious indoctrination affords one of the sorriest spectacles in all history. The cry for sanity in religion through the play of keen critical faculty will be met with violent reprobation by offended traditionalists. "There is no wild beast like an angry theologian" was the comment of the philosophic Julian, the Roman Emperor following Constantine. It has lost little of its truth in the intervening time.

This matter of the impossibility of the recognition of God's only Son in mortal flesh has been treated with sufficient cogency, yet it is of such importance that it needs all the elaboration it can receive. It is difficult to present it with adequate impressiveness. It will be next to impossible to bring minds habituated to wholesale acceptance of the romanticism that has been built like a halo around the person of the Jesus figure to any fully detached and emotionally unprejudiced view of the matter. Psychology knows full well the hypnotizing force of religious inculcations implanted on the sensitive plate of the mind in childhood. They produce what the psychologists have called a conditioned reflex. This is hard to supplant or overcome by any merely mental presentation. It often persists even when the reason negates it. Said W. J. Bryan, "I would accept every statement in the Bible literally, no matter how it contravened my reason." This well illustrates the massive emotional predisposition that is being dealt with here. "A man convinced against his will is of the same opinion still." Reason has an almost insuperable weight of psychological skullduggery to overcome and push aside before it can gain a hearing at all. In the religious domain the reign of reason has been challenged and its sovereignty abrogated by the usurpation of irrational elements that spring from mysticism, and that carry an alleged higher authority than "mere" intellectuality.

The mind itself is supposed to be transcended and overridden by something called spiritual intuition or direct vision of God. The failure of the effort to harmonize the rational and irrational elements in religion has been the crux of the great debacle of human sanity in this most important area of culture. It is a question demanding a volume for adequate handling; but as touching the subject under discussion it may be summed up with the statement that even if there are aspects of cognition and realization that transcend reason, their deposit in consciousness can not be presumed to have authority or credence in flat despite of reason. Evolution developed reason as an instrument for the guidance and safe progress of the human monad in the earthly life. It would be working at odds with its own purposes if it at the same time deployed another faculty that proved reason unsafe. Anything that is salutary to the welfare of the organism must in the end prove to be in consonance with reason; otherwise there would be, so to say, a self-contradiction within the constitution of being itself.

Yet it is believed that in spite of arrant psychologization and mental obsessions of the deepest tenure a movement's vivid imagination used in the reconstruction of the "life" of Jesus in its every-day aspects will carry home to any sane mind the full and indisputable truth of the assertion that the world could not possibly recognize a Person of the Cosmic Trinity if such a Person could be supposed to come to earth in human body. Ages do somewhat differ in set and temper, but it could hardly be contended that there ever was an age in which the appearance of a self-proclaimed cosmic Avatar would not be greeted with the utmost skepticism and derision by all classes of people. There are not rationally conceivable any credentials such a claimant could present that would allay incredulity, overcome suspicion, implant credence and carry certitude. The impregnable truth of the matter is that such a claimant could not be accepted in seriousness, could not be identified in the character and role claimed, could not be recognized and known as outside the category of a human being of ordinary stature. In Eastern lands where yoga phenomena of healing and other extraordinary occurrences were common and understood without marvel, not even his performance of miracles and the incidence of portents would prove to be cosmic credentials. The argument is long, but it can be condensed and concluded with the bald assertion, supported by every common sense consideration, that the presupposition posited by nearly all writers on "the life of Christ" as to Jesus' being recognized by the populace or the age as the only-begotten Son of God ever to appear on the planet merely by seeing his person, is from bottom to top the most outlandish chimera of nonsense ever to creep into the deluded minds of pious people.

So drugged indeed is the traditionally indoctrinated mind of religious susceptibility that it has no intelligent comprehension whatever of the great body of peculiar doctrine that it has, like a boa-constrictor, attempted to swallow. It is in no sense realistically aware that in upholding the historical Jesus it is accepting not only the personalization of a divine principle, cosmic love, but also of the cosmic Aeon of the Gnostics, the Demiurgus or Cosmocrator of the Greeks, the Ra of Egypt and finally the Logos of John and the second person of the creative Trinity. The unthinkable crassness of this acceptance has never once occurred to people in whom "faith" operates in place of thought. When the sarcolatrae or worshipers of a Christ in the flesh, transformed the Christly principle into a mortal man, they did not know or consider what went naturally with it, what mighty powers and functions the slender body of the man Jesus would have to carry. They did not reckon with the many ancillary implications of the transfer. It did not occur to them that the character claimed for Jesus had to cover also the power and range of the Lord of the Cosmos, and that his body would then have to contain the unimaginable creative energy assigned to this person in the hierarchy. For what is the Logos? God the Father is the supreme generator, planner, designer and creator of the universe. God the Son, the Logos, is that universe in its manifested creation. The Logos is God's boundless power and wisdom deployed in the active work of creation. The Logos is the infinite force that upholds the galaxies of countless solar systems and carries on their evolution. It needs only a moment of sober reflection to reveal the degree of stupefaction necessary to induce any mind to believe that the cosmic power great enough to create the infinite hosts of the suns and their planets could have been contained in the tiny body of a Judean peasant on one of the smallest of planets! If the tiniest billionth of such a mighty force were infused somehow into the mortal body of a man on this earth it would burn it to a crisp in a second. This idea that Jesus the man could be the second Person of the Trinity is as dire a hallucination as any that has ever been perpetrated even in the name of religion. Allegiance to a doctrine that has to be secured by an ecclesiastical system at the price of so frightful an obfuscation of the thinking genius of man is itself a tragic affliction. The whole situation which has made such an abnormality possible is an enormity of ghastly proportions and of ominous portent. The Logos, forsooth, embodied in the person of a carpenter! We hold the Greeks in derision for – as we allege – believing that Jupiter, the God of heaven, was a man who ran off with Io and other beautiful maidens and could be jealous or vindictive. It is now known that the Greeks were only toying with a marvelous imagery. But modern moronism is not saved by allegory. In sober earnest we have claimed that the unimaginable cosmic might of the Logos that swings the galaxies through their orbits came to earth and was a man of flesh! Jesus, the second Person of the Trinity! That millions have for centuries been made to "believe" such folly is a sickening realization. This was one item in the catastrophe that was precipitated on half a world for sixteen centuries as a result of turning myth and drama into alleged "history." A heavy price to pay for bad scholarship! The pious faith of the ignorant Church Fathers did not save them from precipitating the Western world into the Dark Ages, the blame for which has been laid at the door of an innocuous "paganism" of the northern lands of Europe, whose systems of a profounder esotericism were ruthlessly destroyed by advancing "Christianity" of the literalized variety.

Perhaps it is now possible to round out the argument as to the comparative psychological influence of a historical Christ and a dramatized typical Christ figure. Since the indwelling activity of Christos is the basic indispensable factor in salvation, anything that weakens it must be held detrimental to critically vital values. The great struggle in the human breast between the impulses of the natural man and the implanted seed of divine growth is ever so critical, the forces of "evil" resident in the carnal man so persistently powerful, and the issue of the conflict at all stages so delicately balanced, that any influence which in the least degree lessens the developing strength of the inner god, or which detracts from the personal effort to exercise its powers, dangerously imperils the outcome and the individual's evolutionary destiny. As the worship of the historical Jesus does, by the very measure of its sincerity, divert attention from the culture of the inner spirit, it becomes perilous to that degree. In the end there is no dodging this issue in the moral field of our life. It is incontestable that the exact amount of psychic energy that we expend in actualizing our reliance upon a historical savior is so much less available for our task of developing the inner deity.

While the outer savior is receiving our devotion, the inner Christ is permitted to lie unawakened. Mankind is so constituted psychologically that by so much as it can lean upon extraneous help it will not exert itself in its own behalf. The purpose of life in the flesh is to force souls who have come here from the empyrean to exert themselves against pressure, stress and strain in order to develop their greater potential divinity. It needs to be said in clarion tones for the benefit of overweening piety and uncritical faith, that any influence which in the least degree diminishes the individual's conviction of the necessity of reliance upon his own hidden divinity must inexorably be calamitous for his progress. The image of Jesus the man and the theological teaching of his power to save us intrude to break the force of the knowledge that our only savior is within. And never will the mortal man be able to bring the full resultant of his living experience in the world to bear upon the problem of his evolutionary growth until he divests himself of all artificial props and stands squarely on his own feet, making his fight alone. Only when he meets the exigencies of his life here by calling upon the resources of his potential savior within him will he be fulfilling the conditions requisite to cultivate that savior's dynamic possibilities. If in the stress of experience he habitually looks to a hypothetical power outside himself, he lets the real powers of his own divinity lie fallow.

Much so-called "spiritual science" of current development has worked on the assumption that a technique adequate for attainment of consummate results in this field involves only subjective effort. In the wake of the popularization of Hindu mysticism in the West practice has taken the direction of an inward retirement. Values in consciousness are sought by way of detachment from sensual experience and contemplation of purely spiritual things. But this movement stands sorely in need of the reminder that the seed power or sheer potentiality of Godhood in man requires for its development something more than mere meditation upon divine things. The spirit might dwell eternally in the world of abstraction if it could follow its own inclination, as a man might choose to lie comfortably in bed instead of getting up and exerting himself for desirable ends. But if it did so it would never achieve its evolution. It would never grow. God could have no children if his spirit did not go forth into an intercourse with matter, the eternal Mother, and implant the seed of a new birth in her universal womb. For the birthing of his progeny, the gods, archangels, angels, heroes and men, there is needed the conjunction of spiritual potentiality with the active energies of what the Greeks called physis, or nature. Clear down the diapason from God to atom every power of mind or soul has to be linked with its sakti, or physical energy, if it is to implement its ideal structure for creative purposes. Spirit can not evolve when not in relation to matter. It lies static, inactive; it is sheer ideal abstraction. To actualize its thought structures, to bring its creative designs to pass, it must be wedded with matter. It must use the energies loaded in the atom of matter to realize its entelechy (Aristotle), or final purpose. The whole flow of evolution, therefore, depends upon the stimuli provided by the contingencies arising in and from the soul's experiences in material body. Without matter spirit can have no experience. Not the transcendent but the immanent deity grows. Says Emerson, "The true doctrine of the Omnipresence is that God exists in all his parts in every moss and cobweb."

The conditions of experience bring latent spiritual capacity to active expression under the impact of the strong forces at play in the world of nature. Spirit awakes and exerts itself by virtue of the necessity of responding to the incidence of blows from the side of matter. Even the dangers threatening the existence or welfare of its own body, its instrument, on the good state of which its own unfoldment depends, elicits its unexercised powers.

The concept of world salvation by a personal redeemer not one's own inner deity is thus inexpressibly wide of the mark for the basic meaning of religion. If the one and only begotten Son of God performed the racial redemption, the god within each man would be deprived of the opportunity for growth which is created only with the dawn of full consciousness of its own entire responsibility for the consequences of acts. Any influence that depletes the utter reliance of the outer personality upon the inner deity is an interference with the planned economics of moral and spiritual evolution. It should have been noted in the study of homiletics that manifestations of divine help, as if coming from an outside savior assumed to be Jesus – in olden times the tribal god – generally occur when one has exhausted all known or available helps and is forced by dire anguish to call upon some spiritual or cosmic agency in last despair. From this it might be assumed that a degree of inner agony is just the stress needed to arouse sleeping divinity to active exertion. Thus the exigencies of the outer man in mortal experience prove to be the agencies of the divinization of the inner man. And the Christ of the age-old ritual dramas was the type of the divine Self in humanity undergoing the strain, stress and strife requisite to bring to light the grand epiphany of his solar glory.

What can be said for the psychological influence of the historical Christ is that the concept has engendered in Western civilization for sixteen centuries a massive emotionalism and sentimentalism arising from thought of his personal life and sufferings, which, if it can be shown that the Gospels are not histories but spiritual dramas, that their contents were in existence thousands of years before his alleged date, must be seen at last as the most prodigious waste of psychic force, the most devastating hallucination and the most stinging humiliation of pride in human history.

It may be appropriate to close this preliminary survey of the more obvious features of the discussion with consideration of another item that is closely related to the psychological utility of the Christ conception. In fact it is the nub and core of the final judicial determination of the relative merit of the two opposing theories. If it can be determined finally that, of the two, one is entirely necessary for the beneficent working of its effects on humanity, and the other not indispensable, but only an adventitious accompaniment of the first, the verdict for superior utility must go to the necessary one. As between the Christ in the heart of all children of God and the Christ in one man, the first is the one both primarily and ultimately necessary for the redemption of the individual. It is a condition sine qua non; the other is merely superfluous and accessory at best. Had there been one personal Christ or a thousand, it is still the leaven of Christliness in the soul of a man that must save him. It is the agency that must be present and operative even if the other be extant. The other could be dispensed with and salvation still be effected. This could not be put vice versa. If the immanent Christos be not a reality in consciousness, the historic Jesus can avail nothing for the suppliant. Salvation could be won without his existence – as it must have been done before he lived! For all his life and death it could never be won without the saving grace of the impersonal Immanuel. The historical Christ is therefore only a superadded and supernumerary theological luxury. He is a negligible element in the system of redemption, in no wise indispensable. So far from being true that the scheme of human salvation rests critically and centrally upon him, the truth is that it does not even vitally need him. It could do without him. He is surely not the keystone of the arch or the cornerstone of the temple. The structure rests solidly on the presence in all men of the deific leaven, and if he enters the picture it is as mere adornment. He is not basic but extraneous and decorative. His addition to the theological equipment makes the house of religion more attractive to people of emotional susceptibilities. His humanity, especially his infancy, babyhood, childhood and the imagined pains his frail body suffered in Passion Week, make a strong appeal to emotional sympathies and thus help perpetuate the institution of religion.

The story is a long one, but to it this work is dedicated, with the motive of restoring Christianity to its original exalted purity and of redeeming it from the degradation of having crucified anew the spiritual Christ in the heart on the cross of a material concept in human thought as "wooden" as the alleged "tree of Calvary."

The Logos was made flesh, yes, but not only one hundred and eighty pounds of it.

Chapter III

TRUTH WEARS A MASK

The logical point of departure for the investigation is the study of ancient methodology in the writing of sacred literature. It has been quite largely due to modern ignorance of a special methodology employed in such writing, one bearing no relation or kinship to any known technique in our period, that misinterpretation of arcane books has come about. In spite of voluminous authentic testimony to the fact of such an extraordinary literary method, scholars down to the present day have failed to take note of the evidence for it, and have with unmitigated obduracy flouted the claims for the fact and its overwhelming implications for our understanding the whole of ancient lore. The consequences have been disastrous over the whole range of religious interest. It is therefore necessary to begin with a scrutiny of the peculiar style of representation which was indigenous to the ancient mind and its approach to the grasp and expression of religious truth.

If it can be shown that the ancient sages wrote their great books of wisdom in a form that was purely typological or representative, and in no sense objectively historical, a presumptive argument of nearly clinching force will be established in favor of the non-existence of Jesus, as far as the New Testament is concerned. If practically the only documents in which his "life" is recorded are proven to be non-historical literature, the presupposition is well grounded from the start that he was not a living man but a typical personification of the god in man. The entrenched interests of ecclesiastical orthodoxy have persistently withstood the claims and the evidence for the correctness of this thesis, but it can be said in the face of such resistance that the case for it is established beyond the point of speculation or further controversy. If this is still controverted, it is designed to present in the work at hand a volume of data that will render the case virtually impregnable at last.

The purpose of this chapter is to adduce plentiful witness that the sages of antiquity wrote their Bibles in a method of designed cryptology and as much to hide their real meaning as to reveal it. Contrary to all modern reasoning and expectation, they did not write for the obvious purpose of informing, instructing or enlightening the largest number of people. Rather it is evident that they wrote primarily to preserve from popular desecration a treasure of recondite spiritual wisdom and cosmological truth, that was designed to be transmitted as nearly intact as possible from early antiquity to all later ages. Ancient literary interest centered about the safety and purity of a great jewel of knowledge, and not, as in modern days, about the most rapid general purveying of every item of discovery to the largest number of people possible. The golden motive in writing the sacred books was not how quickest to get truth to the populace, but how most surely to keep the great secrets of divine teaching untarnished by the populace, for the benefit of those of every age who would use them aright. To preserve the heritage of truth intact, and not to disseminate it among the illiterate and unappreciative masses, was the primary aim of the writers of the arcane books.

This aim and purpose dictated a peculiar type of writing, obviously one not directly open and simple in meaning, but one of indirection and disguise. Books were therefore composed in what is known as the esoteric method. An inner profounder and always more spiritual meaning than the one ostensibly carried by the outward sense of the words was intended to be embodied, and the expectation was that it would be divined by the more intelligent segment of society and missed by the unworthy and uncultured. For the attainment of this end the great cosmic, evolutionary, philosophical and religious truths, along with the vital data for understanding, were expressed, "not in dialogues, but in a wide variety of typical representations, the main forms of which were drama, myth, allegory, nomenology (or name structure), number formulations (as chiefly in the Pythagorean system), and astrographs, or pictorial designs drawn on the open face of the sky about the star clusters. The aim was to dramatize or pictorialize truth and evolutionary process, and to this end there was invented, through the exercise of the most profoundly astute insight ever exhibited by the illumined human brain, an entire language of symbolism, composed of an alphabet of symbolic characters drawn from living nature, ranging from atom to earth-worm or beetle to stars and gods. The great archaic texts of wisdom were therefore not only collections of myths, allegories and dramas, but they were couched in a language of the most extreme subtlety, ability to read which conditioned upon the profoundest knowledge of the science of natural analogy. The symbolic characters in this cryptic alphabet were by no means mere algebraic x's in the fashion of a cipher code or system. They were actual biographs of the idea to be expressed, living and objective types of the thing connoted. This very fact alone presupposes as the foundation for adeptship in the handling of such a language a knowledge of life and of nature that would be the acquirement of only the most perspicacious philosophical genius. It would require a volume in itself to reconstruct the science of correspondences or analogy resting on the kinship or parallelism known to subsist between the two worlds of objective and subjective reality, or as Emerson puts it, "betwixt the inner spirit and the outer matter," by virtue of which the discerning mind of man can interpret the outer phenomena as the counterparts or reflection of the inner consciousness. Nature is the analogue of the spirit; the world is the antitype of the soul. The universe is the physical construct of the Creator's thought, and therefore he who can handle the alphabet of the hieroglyphs of divine ideation in the objective presentment of nature can read God's mind after him. Natural forms thus become a living language of the most nearly divine comprehension man is capable of, and afford him the most voluble vehicles or symbols of the clearest expression he can frame. As the most penetrating insight into the profounder aspects of both consciousness and nature were prime essentials for such usage, obviously the mastery of a science so recondite would be confined to a minority of the most developed individuals. These were of course the philosophers, the illuminati, the hierophants of the temples and the initiates in the Mysteries. They were the members of the group to which was entrusted the custodianship and transmission of the Arcane Philosophy.

A cryptic typology and a symbolic alphabet or language were then the essential structural features of the ancient esoteric literary methodology. The logos of esotericism is a theme of the utmost profundity, which taxes the human mind to grasp its rational essence. It again would take a volume to expound, since its analysis would run deep and broad into the nature of life and consciousness alike. There is no room in this work for any full attempt at elucidation of the abstruse subject, though much of the work bears pretty closely upon the central answer. It may be in the end the gist of all effort at comprehension of the secrecy of initial world wisdom to understand simply that as the full inner meaning of life is as deep as the deepest mind of man, the attempt to render that full meaning for the grasp of lesser minds must be couched in terms and forms that will lay the heaviest toll of intelligence and sagacity upon the faculties of the student or aspirant. The answer is in part also inwoven with human psychology, by the conditions of which nothing but these living symbols can in the ultimate awaken in sluggish men the quickened flare of genius for the apprehension of the most real sense and values. It is recognized in all education that the drama carries far greater psychic impressiveness than the best of spoken language. We can learn a mighty lesson from the Greeks who in their dramatic rituals effectuated a mighty moral purgation in the consciousness and character of the auditors which was spoken of under the designation of "catharsis." It was known to them that the drama could be used to work a purification of the innermost springs of thought and conduct in the individual, as the beholder was made to live over vicariously in the persons of the actors the crises and heroic or tragic episodes of the human moral conflict depicted on the stage. The whole intent of the drama and the Mystery ceremonials was to bring the force of the most impressive living realization home to the inner consciousness of the audience personnel, and to stamp in the most vivid manner upon the susceptibilities of the participants the deepest sense of the incarnational drama in which all mortals are adventuring. It needs no elaborate dialectic to make clear the perception that drama carries a far more effective power for impressing moral issues upon the mind than any language can achieve. It is a copy of living reality; it is life itself in the particular and in miniature; and it is all drawn up in such a form as to present to the mind the structural nature of both action and meaning. In pain and its happiness. It gathers up a tangled or loose thread of unrelated occurrence and displays the fateful pattern of weal or woe into which it is being woven by the shuttle of life – or, as most ancients saw it, of many lives. As to the symbolism in language, it was of the same order of rationale as the drama, but cast in smaller scale. Both the drama and symbolism draw their dynamic psychological effectiveness from the fact that they bear to truth in the large the relation of truth in miniature. It was the knowledge of the early teachers of mankind that all smaller process was a diminutive copy of all larger process, or of life process in any measure. The law of life was universal. Therefore all forms of its expression, large or small, exemplified the same one law. The microcosm, they said, was a tiny reflection of the macrocosm. The fragment bore the image of the whole. Man was made in the image of God. The atom and the world are alike descriptive of the universe. Each revealed the pattern, and there is but one pattern, though it has endless modifications in minor detail. Man is looking at the whole of truth when he looks at any living part of creation. It is more than a poet's fancy that all of God is present everywhere, and that every common bush is aflame with deity.

Hence all nature is an alphabetic language, and every form is a symbol. Autumn is the eternal symbol of death and spring of resurrection. The leaf is the alphabetic character that reads repeated incarnation for the life of the tree. The seed is the greatest of all hieroglyphs, for it is the end product of one cycle and at the same time the beginning stage of the next, thus furnishing the key to the whole ongoing process of life. The career of a dragon-fly is the whole epic of human life lived in the four worlds of sense, emotion, thought and spirit, typed in the old language by earth, water, air and fire. The symbol is therefore a powerfully moving photograph of life and reality, a thumb-nail portraiture of the whole vast meaning of the cosmos. Language is itself nothing but a designed set of symbols. But symbols taken directly from nature have the additional cogency of being parts of life itself in immediate view. In dealing with symbols man constantly bathes his mind in reality. They are his safeguards against folly and error. They are his perennial instructors. They unfold before his eyes the forms and designs of the pattern of life. Says Emerson: "A good symbol is a missionary to convince thousands."

In its power over the human mind language comes close to deserving the term magical. Symbols, therefore, have been employed in the sphere of philosophy and religion to wield upon general consciousness a kind of potent charm akin to spiritual "magic." This is indeed the true magic. For thought is the great Magician of the cosmos, transforming one thing into another and calling the worlds into being by the wand of its vibrational power. The simple and natural meaning of the word "magic" is this power of mind to throw matter into the form outlined by thought. Thought makes or mars lives; it is the eternal prestidigitator. Its legerdemain brings the invisible to visible appearance.

All this is implicit in the nature and use of the symbol. The picture of truth presented by it imprints its image upon the open tablet of the mind. Through the rapport which the part feels with the whole, the unit of consciousness with the entirety of consciousness, and the instinctive urge of the fragment to re-become one with the All, the impact of a symbol upon mind anywhere is inevitably to awaken in it a stir of latent cognitive delight, the impulsive thrill of its recognition of its harmony with all being. This recognition and delight become life's truest guide to rectitude. Symbols keep the mind aligned with truth. They hold it in line with verity. They save it from vagary and fantasy. Such is the magic might of the symbol.

This magic is finally the ground of esotericism. It is admissible without cavil that mystic susceptibility to the wizardry of symbols would be developed and become operative in even step with the individual's growth in culture. It would be a manifestation of strength of genius and a high degree of intellectuality. Obvious it is then that a literature conceived on the basis of a science so profound, expressed in its recondite symbology and dependent finally upon the possession in its recipients of the astute faculty requisite for its due appreciation, would have to be cast in a language of esotericism. Inevitably failing of comprehension amongst the populace, it would appeal to the more sagacious and the more illuminated. The norms of culture were set by the more intelligent minority, as they must ever be. The wardship of culture is in the hands of a small group, whose deeper criteria of value at once set store by things which are beyond the mob, and thus esotericism is inexorably introduced into the cultural or religious situation.

It has been necessary to elucidate the nature and bases of esotericism because the stubborn recalcitrancy of savants in the time since the closing of the Platonic Academies in the fifth century has imposed on a truth-seeking scholar the task of vindicating it against the in- orthodox refutation of its legitimacy. It remains next to array in considerable volume a mass of data that will establish beyond further evasion or quibbling the fact of its ancient prevalence and its place in the methodology of scripture writing.

It is to be understood at the outset of this enterprise that, considerable as is the evidence amassed here, it is only a tiny portion of what might be assembled if all books could be consulted. Indeed that presented here is merely additional to what has been collected in an earlier work, The Lost Light. It is by no means the main body of such authentication. The quantity given here could easily be trebled or quadrupled. In the face of such an amount of testimony the question will arise in many minds why the scholars of our day and previous periods should have so obdurately held out against the indisputable regnancy of esotericism in the ancient literary field. Substantiation of the position taken will call for much quotation of documents and authorities.

A modern theologian agrees with the fundamental rationale of the esoteric method. Benjamin W. Bacon, of Yale Divinity School, in his valuable work, Jesus and Paul, (p. 207) says that just as in modern times we are conscious that truth may be imparted often more effectively by fiction than by plain statement, so it was with the ancient world, but in much higher degree. To this another modern, the Harvard Santayana (Dialogues in Limbo, p. 185) adds his confession that "allegory has its charms when we know the facts it symbolizes, but as a guide to unknown facts it is perplexing; and I am another lost in your beautiful imagery." Strange that the philosopher should admit his incapacity to follow natural imagery when he himself employs it in many beautiful analogies, and the general requirement of intelligence is no greater than necessary to see the fine allegorism in such a quotation as this from the same work of his (p. 56): "The soul, too, has her virginity and must bleed a little before bearing fruit." Are we to assume that natural parallelism is permissible when used by modern poets, but to be distrusted when employed by the philosophic sages with more systematic handling?

How truly the same thinker came to stating the full truth with regard to a greater chapter of history shown in his statement (Winds of Doctrine, p. 50) that "it seems to many of us that Christianity is indeed a fable, yet full of meaning if you take it as such." This is forthright corroboration of the basic thesis of this study, which claims that the scriptures yield their true meaning only when taken as allegory and fable, and yield nonsense when taken as history. It is worth completing his statement: "for what scraps of historical truth there may be in the Bible or of metaphysical truth in theology are of little importance; whilst the true greatness and beauty of this, as of all religions, is to be found in its moral idealisms, I mean, in the expression it gives, under cover of legends, prophecies, or mysteries, of the efforts, tragedy and the consolations of human life. Such a moral fable is what Christianity is in fact; . . ." Here is great sanity of discernment, and it largely tells the whole story of religion. Yet the same mind shows confusion again when he writes (Winds of Doctrine, p. 33): "Even the pagan poets, when they devised a myth, half believed in it for a fact." There is no tangible evidence anywhere to vindicate this stricture. To be sure, they "believed" in their myths when comprehended esoterically; but surely none but the grossest of ignorant folk ever "believed" in them as factual occurrence. That enormity of childish folly was reserved for the modern academicians.

Bishop Laurence in the preface to his work on the Book of Enoch (p. xlvi) says that the singular and fascinating "system of allegorical subtleties" predominant in the philosophies of the East is as inseparable from Oriental modes of thought and expression "as the shadow is from the substance."

Bulfinch (Age of Fable, p. 12), in writing of the creation of the world, says that "the ancient pagans, not having the information on the subject which we derive from the pages of Scripture, had their own way of telling the story." As to which it may be observed that it is possible to say now that the ancient pagans had these same and many more scriptures long before we had them, and knew infinitely better what they meant than we do. But it is noteworthy that he admits they had their own peculiar method of writing the account.

One of the most direct revelations of the basic interrelation of symbols with consciousness is given in a sentence from Proclus, the fourth century expounder of Platonism who was nearly equal in esoteric wisdom to the master himself, in which he says that "the paternal nature disseminated symbols in souls," and through the world. This statement pierces closer to the heart of the rationale of the science of symbolism than anything ever likely to be said in the elucidation of that abstruse science. The divine creative or paternal mind, or Logos, has scattered symbols through the world and placed in souls a power capable of being excited by their impingement on the outer sense. This is an item of Greek philosophy that could profitably be brooded over by thinkers today. It would tend to dispose us to a more friendly and harmonious relationship with outer nature, and would reveal to us anew the indispensable truth known to the Egyptians that, as Gerald Massey puts it, "the symbolical can only be interpreted by the natural." This must be so for the very sound reason that generally the symbolical is the natural. For nature is herself the greatest lexicon of symbols extant. Massey enlarges upon this theme when he says (Book of Beginnings, II, p. 37) that "typology consists of various things set forth by means of one original type. Symbolism was a mode necessitated, not a system designed, because the one principal type had to serve many purposes of expression." This, it has been seen, was true because there is but one universal law, and this one law, seen in every phenomenon, has to serve as the one norm of interpretation.

This discernment of Massey is corroborated by the observations of C. O. Müller, who is quoted by Lundy (Monumental Christianity, p. 18):

"Ancient Greece possessed only two means of representing and communicating ideas of the Deity – Mythus and Symbol. The mythus relates an action, by which the Divine Being reveals himself in his power and individuality; the symbol renders it visible to the sense by means of an object placed in connection therewith. . . . The symbol is an external visible sign with which a spiritual emotion, feeling or idea is connected. The mythic representation can never rest upon arbitrary choice of expression; so, too, the connection of an idea with a sign in Symbolism, was natural and necessary to the ancient world; it occurred involuntarily; and the essence of the symbol consists in this supposed connection of the sign with the thing signified. Symbols in this sense are evidently coeval with the human race; they result from the union of the soul with the body of man: nature has implanted the feeling for them in the human heart. The human face expresses spiritual peculiarities; and so all nature wore to the ancients a physiognomical aspect."

With the art or science of the interpretation of nature's physiognomy the ancient sages were profoundly conversant. It is one of the greatest of all "lost arts." Lundy adds to Müller's perspicacious analysis the observation that "if the mythos has no spiritual meaning, then all religion becomes mere idolatry, or the worship of material things," i.e., the symbols in their literal reference. "But we have seen symbols of Oriental Pagan religions which indicate a supreme Power and Intelligence above matter; and also how early Christianity abhorred idolatry."

Proclus in his great work on the theology of Plato speaks of "all the fables, therefore, of Plato, guarding the truth in concealment." And he adds that

"if certain persons introduce to us physical hypotheses of Platonic fables . . . we must say that they entirely wander from the intention of the philosopher, and that those hypotheses alone are interpreters of the truth contained in these fables which have for their scope a divine, immaterial and separate hypostasis and which, looking to this, make the compositions and analyses of fables adapted to our inherent anticipations of divine concerns."

Which is to say in plainer terms that those who take a physical or historical meaning out of the allegories, mistake the intent of the great dramatist and blindly miss the sense; while the true import is to be found in a mystagogical perception of truth deeply veiled.

The same great philosopher, speaking of the "mystic ceremonies" of the Mysteries, says that "every part is full of symbolical representation, as in a drama." Thomas Taylor, editing Proclus' work, says

"the reader may perceive how adultery and rapes, as represented in the machinery of the Mysteries, are to be understood when applied to the gods; and that they mean nothing more than communication of divine energies, either between a superior and subordinate, or subordinate and superior divinity."

He adds that the "apparent indecency" of these symbolic depictions had nothing to do with their "mystic meaning," but that they were indeed "designed as a remedy for the passions of the soul; and hence mystic ceremonies were very properly called akea, medicines, by the obscure and noble Heraclitus." Drama and symbol used as moral medicines!

Taylor in his Introduction to the philosophy and writings of Plato, quotes Proclus as saying that those who treat of divine concerns either speak symbolically and fabulously, or through images. Some, he asserts, speak according to science, but others according to inspiration from the gods. He states that those who attempt to set forth the nature of the gods through symbols are Orphic, whilst those who use "images" are Pythagoric.

"For the mathematical disciplines were invented by the Pythagoreans in order to a reminiscence of divine concerns, to which, through these as images, they endeavor to ascend. For they refer both numbers and figures to the gods."

It is notable that the Platonic philosophers rated the mathematical discipline and the contemplation of the numerological structure of the universe as the very highest and most direct path by which the human mind could approach a rapport with the divine. (In the light of which statement it may perhaps be true that Albert Einstein, the famed physicist of our day, when, in response to his challenge to the clergy to put an end to their preachment of an anthropomorphic God, he was bluntly told by them to stay in his own mathematical field and not presume to invade one in which he was not intelligent, might be considered to stand closer to an apprehension of divinity than his clerical detractors.)

Proclus then elucidates the reasons "when the ancients were induced to devise fables," and this remarkable passage is worth quoting if only for the sake of reminding a science-ridden age that it is utterly wrong in continuing to hold in contempt one of the greatest of all sciences, analogy.

"In answer, then, it is necessary to know that the ancients employed fables, looking to two things, viz., nature and our soul. They employed them by looking to nature and the fabrication of things as follows: Things inapparent are believed from things apparent and incorporeal natures from bodies. For seeing the orderly arrangement of bodies, we understand that a certain incorporeal power presides over them; as with respect to the celestial bodies, they have a certain presiding motive power. As we, therefore, see that our body is moved, but is no longer so after death, we perceive that it was a certain incorporeal power which moved it. Hence, perceiving that we believe things inapparent from things apparent and corporeal, fables came to be adopted that we might come from things apparent to certain inapparent natures; as, for instance, that on hearing the adulteries, bonds and lacerations of the gods, castrations of heaven and the like, we might not rest satisfied with the apparent meaning of such like particulars, but may proceed to the inapparent, and investigate the true signification. After this manner, therefore, looking to the nature of things, were fables employed."

There are passages in the books of the ancient philosophers that fairly shout – to the discerning student – their regal wisdom in our ears, and this is one of them. Had the potential enlightenment in these words been caught and held by the scholars of the earlier centuries and incorporated in western philosophy, the entire history of Christian Europe and America would have run a happier course. The fogs of religious insanity would surely have been dissipated by the intelligence that would have arisen from contemplation of God's natural handiwork, seen as the analogue of the verities of the unseen spiritual world. The irrational and fanatical mysticism inspired by the preachment of sheer faith would have been replaced by a mysticism of rational foundation, springing from the reading of the eternal mind in the open book of natural revelation. And Paul's adjuration to add knowledge to faith would have averted the endless sickening horrors of pious bigotry and persecution. The great science of analogy has been contemned even in spite of St. Paul's complete endorsement of Greek insight in his amazingly clear and simple statement that "that which may be known of God is manifest," and that "the invisible things of Him" may be clearly seen, by looking at the visible world around us. The long and gruesome train of ills that have been engendered by the medieval and modern contempt for ancient "paganism," the mawkish and revolting scorn heaped upon the alleged "primitive" child-mindedness of past civilizations spiritually more enlightened than our own, would have given way to a cultural sensitivity that must surely have kept the pages of the historical record free from the black stains they now bear. The spectacle of the supercilious contempt shown toward an ancient culture by a civilization that has not even evolved the intelligence to comprehend its subtleties has darkened the human outlook on life and defeated the power of the light to break through the darkness and shed its benignant rays of intelligence and sanity upon the world. It was so much easier for a mentality that could not comprehend the Greek myths to cast the stigma of its own incapacity upon the framers of the myths than to admit its proper applicability to itself. It is time that it be proclaimed in ringing tones that the alleged incomprehensibility of the myths is due to modern doltishness and not to ancient ignorance. Wisdom was so deeply grasped that the symbols which alone could awaken its cognition have left us gaping and mocking, incredulous and uncomprehending.

Had not the illustrious Platonic literature been pushed aside for a spurious and emasculated version of it, we could have been better instructed by such a sentence as this, which Proclus adds to the foregoing: "It may always be said that a fable is nothing else than a false discourse shadowing forth the truth, for a fable is the image of truth." Had we the discerning sense to lay hold of the great fact expressed in his next sentence – "But the soul is the image of the natures prior to herself" – for a grasp of which the study of the whole of the great Orphic-Platonic system is requisite – we would be in better position to accept his conclusion that "hence the soul very properly rejoices in fables, as an image of an image." And we could then follow his last sentence in the paragraph: "As we are therefore from our childhood nourished in fables, it is necessary that they should be introduced."

Staggering rebuke to the stolidity of this age is implied in his further exposition:

"The poetic fable abounds in this, that we must not rest satisfied with the apparent meaning, but pass on to the occult truth. . . . But it is defective in this, that it deceives those of a juvenile age. Plato therefore neglects fables of this kind and banished Homer from his Republic, because youth, on hearing such fables, will not be able to distinguish what is allegorical from what is not."

As it was unthinkable for us of the modern world in 1914 to believe that in a few years the whole fabric of human liberty that had been built up by centuries of struggle against tyranny would be toppling to ruin, so it must have seemed unthinkable to Plato and, seven hundred years later, to Proclus that the long-enduring structure of esoteric philosophy could be torn down and its ruins submerged under the debris of literal and historical nonsense. A juvenile age indeed!

What could be clearer than Proclus' statement that "the Orphic method aimed at revealing divine things by means of symbols, a method common to all writers of divine lore (theomythias)?" (The word means "God-myth.") And he quotes Plutarch (De Pyth. Orac., xviii): "Formerly the wisdom-lovers exposed their doctrines and teachings in poetical fiction, as for example Orpheus and Hesiod and Parmenides and Julian, the so-called Apostate. . . . Many of the philosophers and theologians were myth-makers. . . . Concerning the myths of the Mysteries which Orpheus handed down to us, in the very things which in these myths are most incongruous, he drew nearest to the truth. For just in proportion as the enigma is more paradoxical and wonderful, so does he warn us to distrust the appearance and seek for the hidden meaning. Philostratus asserts that in the Iliad the poet was philosophizing in the Orphic manner."

Plutarch (De Daedal., Frag. lx, 1, 754) writes that

"the most ancient philosophers covered up their teachings in a lattice work of fables and symbols, especially instancing the Orphic writings and the Phrygian myths."

"That ancient natural science both among the Greeks and foreigners was for the most part hidden in myths of an occult and mysterious theology containing an enigmatical and hidden meaning, is clear from the Orphic poems and the Egyptian and Phrygian treatises."

G. R. S. Mead, in Orpheus (p. 51) quotes Pico della Mirandolo, Italian occultist of the Renaissance, as writing:

"He who does not know perfectly how to intellectualize sensible properties by the method of occult analogy, will never arrive at the real meaning of the Hymns of Orpheus."

Mead further endorses Thomas Taylor, the enlightened interpreter of Plato:

"Taylor says that the Grecian theology was first 'mystically and symbolically' promulgated by Orpheus. . . . To understand that theology, therefore, we must treat it from the point of view of mysticism and symbolism, for no other method is capable of extracting its meaning."

And Mead adds Proclus' assertion that

"the whole theology of the Greeks is the child of Orphic mystagogy, Pythagoras being first taught the 'orgies' of the gods ('orgies' signifying 'burstings forth,' or 'emanations,' from a insert greek) by Aglaophemus, and next Plato receiving the perfect science concerning such things from the Pythagorean and Orphic writings."

In his book New Platonism and Alchemy (p. 6), Alexander Wilder makes the unequivocal statement: "There was in every ancient country having claims to civilization an esoteric doctrine, a system that was designated WISDOM, and those who were devoted to its prosecution were first denominated Sages or wise men. . . . Pythagoras termed the system he gnosis ton onton, the Gnosis or knowledge of things that are. Under the noble designation of WISDOM the ancient teachers, the sages of India, the magians of Persia and Babylon, the seers and prophets of Israel, the hierophants of Egypt and Arabia and the philosophers of Greece and the West included all knowledge which they considered as essentially divine; classifying a part as esoteric and the remainder as exoteric. The Rabbis called the exterior and secular series the Mercavah, as being the body or vehicle which contained the higher knowledge."

Clement of Alexandria, Christian philosopher of the third century tersely said that "it is requisite to hide in a mystery the wisdom spoken." This is the echo of St. Paul's "wisdom hidden in a mystery." No statement could be more explicit than Clement's:

"All, then, in a word, who have spoken of divine things, both barbarians and Greeks, have veiled the first principles of things and delivered the truth in enigmas and symbols and allegories and metaphors and such like tropes."

In speaking of the exoteric version of the fables and allegories Origen, Clement's learned pupil and one of the prime formulators of early Christian theology, asks: "What better could you have for the instruction of the masses?" Paracelsus (Vol. I, p. 17) centuries later wrote that it was "the property of the common herd to take false views of things." It is certainly true that almost every conception harbored in the minds of the 'average man" today, as in the past, concerning the true meaning of the deeper things of theology, is atrociously in error.

In Orpheus (1, p. 60) Mead declares: 'These myths are not only set forth in verse and prose, but were also represented pictorially and in sculpture in the Adyta of the temples."

"Myriads on myriads of enigmatical utterances by both poets and philosophers are to be found; and there are also whole books which present the mind of the writer veiled as that of Heraclitus' 'On Nature,' which on this very account is called 'the Obscure.' Similar to this book is the Theology of Pherecydes of Samos. And so also the work of Euphorion, the Causae of Callimachus, and the Alexandra of Lycophion." Mead follows these statements with the observation that while the veiling of high truth under gross outer symbols could in a pure state of society be done without moral damage, nevertheless a degenerate age would run the risk of stopping at the outer symbol, forgetting the inner reference and thus would plunge religion into grave dangers of fatal misconceptions.

Also in Orpheus (p. 24) Mead, describing the discipline enforced in the Mysteries, says:

"Another and most important part of the discipline was the training in the interpretation of myths, symbols and allegory, the letters of the mystical language in which the secrets of nature and the soul were written so plainly for the initiated, so obscurely for the generality. Without this instruction the mythical recitals and legends were unintelligible."

Sixteen centuries of unintelligibility that still enshrouds the great myths of antiquity surely add unimpeachable corroboration to Mead's assertion. Mead says the allegories may be interpreted either microcosmically or macrocosmically, but in either case yield the meaning of the evolution of mind.

In his magnificent Encyclopedia of ancient symbolic literature Manly P. Hall declares that nearly every religion of the world shows traces of astrological influences, and that the Old Testament of the Jews, its writings breathing the aura of earlier Egyptian culture, is a mass of astrological and astronomical allegories.

In a long passage in his great work on the theology of Plato Proclus points out how the master philosopher holds back the use of fables among those who through incapacity and shallowness would conceive only a perverted meaning from reading them, yet assents to their employment among those who are able to penetrate into the hidden mystic truth veiled by them. So, he says, Plato rejects the "apparatus of the fables" in the Republic and in certain dialogues, but admits them in the Cratylus, where "these things Socrates indicates in the Cratylus, jesting and at the same time being serious in what he says." Proclus says that in the Fourth Book of The Laws Plato celebrates the life under Saturn, obscurely signifying the hidden meaning "through fabulous fictions." The Cratylus is a splendid example of the easy victimization of the alleged towering modern intelligence by ancient astuteness in concealment. Present academic opinion still contends that in the Cratylus Socrates spent an afternoon in punning. He points out such "puns" as that the Greeks called the body soma and the tomb sema, and the pundits of today still can see no suggestive connection between the two words, in spite of the fact that hundreds of times the Greek philosophers have told us that in Orphic theology the soul while in incarnation in the body was as though dead in its tomb. "The body is the sepulcher of the soul" is almost an axiom of Greek philosophy. Behind every one of Socrates' "puns" hides some great and luminous item of the piercing Platonic insight into deep mysteries.

A vivid forecast of all later imbecility of the masses in religious superstition is made by Proclus for Plato when he says that while Plato "allows the poets that are inspired by Phoebus to signify things of this kind obscurely and mystically, he excludes the multitudes from hearing these things because they believe without examination in the fabulous veils of truth." Proclus speaks of the proper intelligence "unfolding the concealed theory which they contain."

Socrates hints at the deep psychological springs of the symbolic methodology when he writes in the Phaedrus "that an alliance to the demoniacal genus, prepared the soul for the reception of divine light, excites the phantasy to symbolic narration."

Proclus states that Orpheus "greatly availed himself of the license of fables." And once more he avers that Socrates (Plato?) "narrating the types and laws of divine fables, which afford this apparent meaning, and the inward concealed scope, which regards as its end the beautiful and natural in the fictions about the gods," dodges the mental stolidity of the crass to reach the subtler intelligence of the initiated.

The second-century esotericist, Plutarch, says that "so cautious and reserved was the Egyptian wisdom in those things which pertained to religion"; "and like them Pythagoras conveyed his doctrines to the world in a kind of riddle." In reference to Plato's last book, The Laws, written "when he was now grown old," Plutarch says that Plato threw off the esoteric mask, spoke not "in riddles and emblems, but in plain and proper terms" of the more recondite aspects of truth. In De Iside et Osiride (IX) Plutarch states that if the choice of king fell upon a soldier, "he was immediately initiated into the order of the priests and by them instructed in their abstruse and hidden philosophy, a philosophy for the most part involved in fable and allegories and exhibiting only dark hints to us in many instances, particularly by the sphinxes, which they seem to have placed designedly before their temples as types of the enigmatical nature of their theology."

In the same work (XI) Plutarch elucidates one of the animal representations of a god in such a fashion as to enable the dullest brain to catch a concealed meaning behind a symbol and to get an inkling as to how they operated the symbolic language.

"When you hear, therefore, the mythological tales which the Egyptians tell of their gods, their wanderings, their mutilations and many other disasters which befell them, remember what has just been said, and be assured that nothing of what is thus told you is really true or ever happened in fact. For can it be imagined that it is the 'dog' itself which is reverenced by them under the name of Hermes? It is the question of this animal, his constant vigilance and his acumen in distinguishing his friends from his foes, which have ever rendered him, as Plato says, a meet emblem of that god who is the chief patron of intelligence."

And in another passage Plutarch tells his age that if one will hear and entertain the story of these gods from those who know how to explain it consistently with religion and philosophy, and will steadily persist in the observance of all those holy rites which the law requires, and moreover will be disposed to the conviction that to form true notions of divine natures is more acceptable to them than any sacrifice or mere external act of worship can be, one will by this means be entirely exempt from any danger of falling into superstition, an evil no less to be avoided than atheism itself.

Gerald Massey, the profoundest and most discerning of Egyptologists, in his fine work, The Natural Genesis (Vol. II, p. 378 ff.) writes:

"The lost language of celestial allegory can now be restored, chiefly through the resurrection of ancient Egypt; the scriptures can be read as they were originally written, according to the secret wisdom, and we now know how the history was first written as mythology."

He adds that the Revelation assigned to John the Divine is the Christian form of the Mithraic Revelation, that in the Parsee sacred books the original scriptures are always referred to as the "Revelation," and that the Bahman Yasht contains the same drama of mystery that is drawn out and magnified in the Bible Revelation. He asserts that the personages, scenes, circumstances and transactions are identical in both. Each revelation relates to the Kronian allegory and in both the prophecy is solely astronomical. He explains that Egypt is the mother of the world's primeval religion and that the myths of Egypt were the origin of the Mysteries of the world. The main theme of most of his voluminous work is that the Hebrew "miracles" are nothing but the original myths of Egypt, misread as history. In his Reply to Prof A. H. Sayce he says:

"I have amply demonstrated the fact that the myths were no mere products of ancient ignorance, but are the deposited results of a primitive knowledge; that they were founded upon natural phenomena and remain the register of the earliest scientific observation."

He hammers endlessly on the point that the whole grand structure of luminous ancient doctrine crashed to ruin on the rocks of the early Christian stupidity which converted into literal history a vast body of drama and allegory that "was never anything but frankly mythological." And he has written thousands of pages to support his contention that what purports to be "history" in Christian systematism was actually pre-extant as Egyptian mythology. He cites as proof of his main thesis the fact that the Biblical material is found to be nonsensical and chimerical, in fact impossible, as history, but becomes lucidly intelligible and possible as myth. The massed material of his great volumes goes far to substantiate this claim.

He calls attention to the fact that the Jesus character both in the Gospels and in the Gnostic Christian work, the Pistis Sophia, announces to the inner circle of his initiated disciples that he will speak with them freely "from the beginning of the truth unto the completion thereof . . . face to face without parable." Parable was the declared method of his speaking to "them that are without" the circle of the initiated. In the full release of light and knowledge to the trained disciples parable and myth could be discarded for direct revelation.

We need the directness of Massey's phrasing of the following passage, the truth of which is of ominous import for civilization: "The human mind has long suffered an eclipse and been darkened and dwarfed in the shadow of ideas the real meaning of which has been lost to the moderns. Myths and allegories whose significance was once unfolded to initiates in the Mysteries, have been adopted in ignorance and reissued as real truths directly and divinely vouchsafed to mankind for the first and only time! The early religions had their myths interpreted. We have ours misinterpreted. And a great deal of what has been imposed on us as God's own true and sole revelation to man is a mass of inverted myths. . . . Much of our folk-lore and most of our popular beliefs are fossilized symbolism."

His great contention – with Max Müller – was that the Märchen and folk tales are not reflections, but refractions, or distorted popularizations of the original mythos, and that, contrary to Müller's assertions, it was the mythos that passed into the folk tale and not the folk tale into the mythos. The myths were first and the Märchen were their product, through the inevitable deterioration which all esoteric truth sooner or later undergoes when floated among the unlettered masses. "Typology and mythology are twins from their birth and one in their fundamental rootage." (Nat. Gen. I, 313.)

In the same volume, preceding page, Massey has a long and enlightening dissertation on the nature of the gods as just the "elementary powers of nature," and he reads the logical conclusions from the fact that they were represented symbolically by the animal types. Much other material is assembled to depict the wide variety of figures under which the gods and goddesses were exhibited. The hundreds of religious insignia, emblems, types and figures which Sir James Frazer presents but is powerless to interpret in his famous The Golden Bough, Massey clarifies with astute penetration into cryptic meanings. "Mythology" he says, "is one as a system of representation, one as a mold of thought, one as a mode of expression, and all its great primordial types are practically universal."

Testimony of another life-long research student in the field of archaic philosophy confirms Massey's conclusions. Godfrey Higgins, in his monumental work, The Anacalypsis, (p. 441) says that

"one thing is clear – the mythos of the Hindus, the mythos of the Jews and the mythos of the Greeks are all at bottom the same; and what are called their early histories are not histories of man, but are contrivances under the appearance of histories to perpetuate doctrines . . . in a manner understood by those only who had a key to the enigma. Of this we shall see many additional proofs hereafter."

The Anacalypsis is some 830 pages of additional proofs. Page 446 of this work gives his final summation of his life of investigation:

"When all the curious circumstances have been considered, an unprejudiced person will, I think, be obliged to admit that the ancient epic poems are oriental allegories, all allusive to the same mythos, and that many of these works which we have been accustomed to call histories are but allegorical representations of mythologies, of the secret doctrines of which I am in pursuit and which have been . . . concealed and perpetuated . . . for the initiated, under the veil of history."

He makes the unequivocal statement that "two clear and distinct meanings of the words will be found; one for the initiated and one for the people. This is of the first importance to be remembered." He quotes Niebuhr as showing that what we call early Roman history was "mere mythos," and explains that this will account for what on any other thesis is incredible, the "degree of superstition" evidenced by the Romans. He cites an Englishman, Lumsden, as saying that events purporting to be Roman history are drawn from the heroical legends of Greece and therefore must have been copied from them; that they were not copies of one another, but all drawn from a common source; and were in fact the remnants of a mythos almost lost but constantly renewed, discoverable everywhere in the East and West – "new Argonauts, new Trojan Wars," and the like. The works of early writers without exception were "deeply tainted with allegory," he declares elsewhere. "The mythos, not history, is the object of the writer."

It is to be presumed that Higgins erred in saying that the ancient sages Plato, Pythagoras and others disguised the doctrines of wisdom because they were too sublime for the mass of mankind; but he agrees that they did disguise them, alleging that this concealment laid the foundation for the priesthoods "whose interest it became to take care, by keeping the people in ignorance, that the doctrines should always remain too sublime for them." Higgins seems not quite to have arrived at the point of seeing that mystic truth is by its own nature esoteric, and disguise is not entirely artificial, but rather natural to it. He contends that there have been writers against "the modern or exoteric Christianity," "but never have we had a Hobbes, a Herbert or a Bolingbroke to endeavor to discover their secret." He earlier states that the Oriental sects were in the habit of using figurative language to disguise their metaphysical doctrines from the vulgar, but he says this gave their enemies the opportunity, by construing them literally, to represent them as absurd and outlandish. He connects the myths closely with astrology. He states that the book of Genesis was considered by most if not all of the ancient Jewish philosophers and Christian Fathers as an allegory.

What testimony could be more explicit than that of the Psalmist (Psalm 78) who says: "I will open my mouth in a parable; I will utter dark sayings of old which we have heard and known and our fathers have told us"? And how could he have anticipated that these "dark sayings" would lead to sixteen centuries of a nearly total obfuscation of sense and sanity in the religion of half the world? In the wake of this quotation Massey observes:

"It was the same with the Hebrew teachings brought out of Egypt as with the Egyptian writings, of which Origen observes, 'the priests have a secret philosophy concerning their religion contained in their national scriptures, while the common people only hear fables which they do not understand. If these fables were heard from a private man without the gloss of the priest, they would appear exceedingly absurd.'"

Moses, avers Massey, received two laws on the mountain, the written and the oral. This oral law was the primitive tradition that contained the Apocrypha, the secret doctrines of the dark sayings and parables, the clue and key to all their hidden wisdom. That which was written was intended only for the ignorant outsiders; the interpretation was for the initiated. With the written version of the Jewish sacred books alone in our possession, we have been locked outside and left there without the key.

Origen's teacher, Clement, speaks of the necessity of hiding in a mystery the wisdom which the Son of God had taught; of the hindrances which there were in his day to his writing about this wisdom, lest he should cast pearls before swine; of the reason why the Christian Mysteries were celebrated at night, like the Pagan ones, because then the soul, released from the dominion of the senses, turns in upon itself and has a truer intelligence of the mystery of God "hid for ages under allegory and prophecy," but now revealed by Jesus Christ, and only spoken of by St. Paul "among such as were perfect" (perfected in the Mystery initiations), giving milk to the babes and meat to men of understanding; and of those mysteries as entered upon through the tradition of the Lord, or the great oral transmission from those divinely illuminated. Massey insists we can not understand the thought of primitive man without first learning the language of symbols in which it was expressed, and says that "the wisdom, or Gnosis, so carefully hidden and zealously guarded in the past" can not be regained by mere pious lucubration. To recover it we must resort to the aid of the same nature-logic that the sages used to give it expression.

Origen makes a categorical declaration of the esoteric sense when he says (Contra Celsum):

"The learned may penetrate into the significance of all oriental mysteries, but the vulgar can only see the exterior symbol. It is allowed by all who have any knowledge of the scriptures that everything is conveyed enigmatically."

We turn to Philo and Josephus, both living about the time of the "historical" Jesus. There is a tradition that Philo was converted to Christianity by Peter. If it is credible it would put him in close touch with the very earliest Christian sentiment. His testimony should carry considerable weight in the argument. He writes (D.V.C.):

"Now the interpretation of the sacred scriptures is based upon the understanding in the allegorical narratives; for these men look upon the whole of their law-codes being like to a living thing, having for the body the spoken commands, and for the soul the unseen thought stored up in the words . . . unwrapping and unrobing of the symbols . . . and bringing to light the naked inner meanings, for those who are able with a little suggestion to arrive at the intuition of the hidden sense from the apparent meaning."

Massey says that Philo "Platonizes the myths," reading new ethical meanings into them. But Philo's forthright declaration on the esoteric method is found in his terse assertion, when speaking of the rib of Adam: "The literal statement is a fabulous one; and it is in the mythical that we shall find the true." For those who in spite of a mass of such testimony from eminent and godly men of the past continue to assert that there never was any genuine and sincere esoteric knowledge, it is desirable to quote another statement from Philo:

"Now I bid ye, initiated men, who are purified as to your ears, to receive these things as mysteries which are really sacred, in your inmost souls, and reveal them not to any one who is of the number of uninitiated, but guard them as a sacred treasure."

"In the Mosaic writings," says Josephus (Preface to Antiq.) "everything is adapted to the nature of the whole, whilst the lawgiver most adroitly suggests some things as in a riddle and represents some things with solemnity as in an allegory; those, however, who desire to dive into the cause of each of these things, will have to use much and deep philosophical speculation."

He again (Ibid.) says that all the sacred writings have a reference to the nature of the universe; whilst the legislator, Moses, speaks some things wisely but enigmatically and others under a fitting allegory.

What authority from antiquity can be cited with more weight than the first historian, Herodotus? In dealing with the Mystery celebrations of the Egyptians held on a lake within the sacred precincts of the temple as Sais, dramatizing the birth, life, death and regeneration of Osiris, he says that he considers it impious to divulge the name of the god.

"On these matters," he goes on, "though accurately acquainted with the particulars of them, I must observe a discreet silence. So, too, with regard to the Mysteries of Demeter (celebrated at Eleusis in Greece), which the Greeks term 'The Thesmophoria,' I know them, but I shall not mention them, except so far as may be done without impiety."

One must ask why such direct testimony from credible men of the ancient world should be flouted by modern savants. The effort to discredit the existence of a real esoteric system in the ancient day makes liars of nearly all the outstanding philosophers of the early world.

H. Y. Evans-Wentz, in his work The Tibetan Book of the Dead, states that archaeological research has now proven that the Mysteries consisted of symbolical dramatic performances open only to the initiates and neophytes fit for initiation, illustrating the universally diffused esoteric teachings concerning death and resurrection; and that the doctrine of the transmigration of the soul into animal bodies was not intended to be taken, as it has been by the uninitiated, literally, but symbolically, as in Plato's Republic. Herodotus (ii, 122) is cited as documentary support for the statement.

Alexander Wilder, previously quoted, in reference to the Bacchic Mysteries says that every act, rite and person engaged in them was symbolical; and the individual revealing them was put to death without mercy. So also, he adds, was any uninitiated person who happened to have heard them. Here is strong evidence that the ancients surely believed they had a secret supremely worth safeguarding from desecration.

The noted modern Egyptologist A. E. W. Budge, says that every act of the ceremonial dramas was symbolical in character and represented some ancient belief or tradition.

"And there was not the smallest action on the part of any member of the band who acted the Miracle Play of Osiris, and not a sentence in the Liturgy which did not possess importance or vital significance to the followers of Osiris."

Again he says that it is this "emblemism," spoken of by moderns as fetishism and idolatry, that has had a false construction put upon it, mainly by missionaries and travelers, although the Christian religion, he asserts, has been evolved from the same identical germ and on somewhat similar lines. Emblemism he explains as a merely external formula of an inner cult worship.

Though the charge would have far more fitness if made against the Christians after the third century, it was made even in the days of Grecian philosophy by Diodorus Siculus, who tells us that the Egyptians treated the Greeks as impostors because they reissued the Egyptian mythology as their own history. If the Greeks were guilty of converting myth into history, it merely indicates that that process of esoteric degeneration which inevitably set in in every occult religion had begun early and has continued ever since. Celsus, the learned Jew in debate with Origen, chuckles over the (literal) account of the Christian deluge with its ridiculous ark and impossible physical details, finding it a part of his own mythology literalized and amplified. Tom Paine, Voltaire and Ingersol chuckled in the same fashion later.

The Roman poet Sallust even classifies the fables as theology of the physical and animistic sort. He enlarges on the characteristics of each. He says the theological belongs to philosophers, the physical and spiritual to poets, but an intermediate mixture of both belongs to the initiatory rites (Greek: teletais), "since the intention of all mystic ceremonies is to conjoin us with the world of the gods."

The Jewish Maimonides comes up with the declaration that Genesis, taken according to the letter, is absurd and extravagant. Whoever should find the true sense of it ought to take care not to divulge it. This, he says, is a maxim which all the sages repeat to us, respecting the exact meaning of the work of the six days. If anyone should discover the true meaning, he should be silent, or speak of it only obscurely and in an enigmatical manner.

An important statement is found in that venerated work on the first three centuries of Christian history, Baron Von Mosheim's "History."

"It is not, therefore, Origen who ought to be termed the parent of allegories amongst the Christians, but Philo . . . many of the Jews, and in particular the Pharisees and Essenes, had indulged much in allegories before the time of Philo, but of this there can be no doubt, that the praefects of the Alexandrian school caught the idea of interpreting Scripture upon philosophical principles, or of eliciting philosophical maxims from the sacred writers by means of allegory, and that by them it was gradually propagated amongst the Christians at large. It is also equally certain that by the writings and example of Philo the fondness for allegories was vastly augmented and confirmed throughout the whole Christian world; and it moreover appears that it was he who first inspired the Christians with that degree of temerity which led them not infrequently to violate the faith of history and wilfully to close their eyes against the obvious and proper sense of terms and words . . . particular instances of it . . . may be shown from Origen and others, who took him for their guide, and who, manifestly, considered a great part both of the Old and New Testaments as not exhibiting a representation of things that really occurred, but merely the images of moral actions."

One can express with a sigh the wish that the discerning practice of Origen and Philo had persisted down the centuries!

The Schaff-Herzog dictionary of religious terms gives four meanings for such a name as "Jerusalem," following the gradient of classification laid down by Philo. Literally the name means the city in Palestine; morally, the believing soul; allegorically, the Church; and anagogically the city of heavenly peace, located only of course in consciousness. While this scheme of interpretation permits it to mean the geo- graphical town, it by no means confines it to that rendering, which the historical view does.

In the Anti-Nicene Library (Vol. XXIV, p. 127) in the section of Selections from the Prophetic Scriptures we read:

"We must therefore search the Scriptures accurately, since they are admitted to be expressed in parables, and from the names hunt out the thoughts which the Holy Spirit . . . teaches by imprinting his mind, so to speak, on the expressions . . . that the names . . . may be explained and that which is hidden under many integuments may, being handled and learned, come to light and gleam forth."

Jowett, Plato's academically accredited interpreter (Thomas Taylor's most discerning work being frowned upon) writes: "I am not one of those who believe Plato to have been a mystic or to have had hidden meanings," – this in the face of evidence that is mountainous in height and weight.

It is now far over a century since C. F. Dupuis published his once-famous and still valuable work, L'Origine de Tous Les Cultes, in which he asserted that John the Baptist was a purely mythical personage, and identified his name with that of the Babylonian Fish-God, Ioannes, of the

Berosan account.

We should not omit reference to a statement by Isaac Myer, the learned Kabalist scholar, in his work The Oldest Books in the World (VII):

"There was undoubtedly an extremely subtle and sublimated thought in existence among the learned of the ancient Egyptians which modern thinkers have not yet fully grasped and which busied itself mostly with endeavors to arrive at the bond uniting the unknown and the known or materially existing; this was more especially limited to a religious philosophy and in that mostly to the spiritual nature in man. The mural paintings on the walls in ancient Egyptian tombs are not for decoration; they are symbolical and mystic and the figures thereon are intended for a religious purpose."

In the Gemara of the Jews, it is said that he who has learned the scripture and not the Mishna "is a blockhead." The Bible, they say, is like water, the Mishna like wine, the Gemara liked spiced wine. The law is as salt, the Mishna as pepper, the Gemara as balmy spice. To study the Bible can scarcely be considered a virtue; to study the Mishna is a virtue that will be rewarded, but the study of the Gemara is a virtue never to be surpassed. Some of the Talmudists assert that to study the Bible is nothing but a waste of time. The Gemara embodied the anagogical or esoteric interpretation.

Rabbi Simeon Ben-Jochai, compiler of the Zohar, taught only the esoteric signification of doctrines, orally and to a limited few, holding that without the final instruction in the Mercavah the study of the Kabalah would be incomplete. The Kabalah itself says (iii-folio 1526, quoted in Myer's Qabbalah, p. 102):

"Each word of the Torah contains an elevated meaning and a sublime mystery."

"The recitals of the Torah are the vestments of the Torah. Woe to him who takes this garment for the Torah itself. The simple take notice only of the garments or recitals of the Torah, they know no other thing, they see not that which is concealed under the vestment. The more instructed men do not pay attention to the vestment but to the body which it envelops."

Godbey, in his searching work, The Lost Tribes a Myth (p. 697), asserts that the Jews lost the origin and meaning of the term "Israel" more than two thousand years ago.

"There is no agreement in their ancient literature upon that point. All record and tradition of the old Peniel sanctuary where Jacob became 'an Israel' has been lost."

But one of the most revealing intimations that the Christian movement early departed from the genius and spirit of the well-known esoteric methodology is found in a sensational passage quoted in Mead's Orpheus from Origen in his work Contra Celsum:

"The story of Dionysus and the Titans is a dramatic history of the wanderings of the 'Pilgrim-Soul.' And curiously enough we find the story of the resurrection of Dionysus . . . compared by the most learned of the Christian Fathers with the resurrection of Christ. Thus Origen (Contra Celsum IV, 171, Spenc.), after making the comparison, remarks apologetically and somewhat bitterly: 'Or, forsooth, are the Greeks to be allowed to use such words with regard to the soul, and speak in allegorical fashion (tropolegein), and we forbidden to do so?' . . . thus clearly declaring that the resurrection was an allegory of the soul and not historical." (Orpheus, pp. 185-6). It will be well to place alongside of Origen's lament over the deterioration of splendid allegory into crass literalism the unguarded utterance of Synesius, a Bishop of Alexandria after Origen's time: "In my capacity as Bishop of the Church I shall continue to disseminate the fables of our religion, but in my private capacity I shall remain a philosopher to the end." By the "fables" he meant the mass of literalized legend which the Fathers purveyed to the ignorant laity, of which Celsus says that they were so outlandish that even a stupid child's-nurse would be ashamed to tell them to children. And what he meant by remaining a "philosopher" would shock the churchmen who have for centuries decried the great Platonic and Neo-Platonic systems which, in spite of their protestations, have contributed so much to the foundations of Christianity. The unedifying spectacle of a Bishop fooling the populace with fables he knew were fictions, whilst he fed his own mind upon the deeper meanings of philosophy from pagan schools, goes far to support the claims made in this work and elsewhere as to the nature and causes of the terrible calamity that befell Christianity in the third century, ending in the conversion of allegory into a literalized Gospel and the befuddlement of the world.

From current reading we take a remark made by G. R. G. Mure, in his small work on Aristotle (p. 230), relative to the force of figurative or symbolic language:

"The eye for an effective metaphor is, in fact, a mark of genius and unteachable. And in devoting more space to illustrating that form of metaphor which depends upon analogy, – as when old age is described as 'Life's sunset,' – Aristotle means, perhaps, to mark the manifestation within the poet's imaginative world of that hierarchic order of analogous stages which pervades the whole Aristotelian universe. The last and least important element in tragedy is spectacle."

From Esdras (XIV, 6, 26 and 45) we take the following passages:

"These words shalt thou declare, and these shalt thou hide. And when thou hast done, some things shalt thou publish and some things shalt thou show secretly to the Wise."

". . . . and Highest spake, saying, The first that thou hast written publish openly, that the worthy and the unworthy may read it: but keep the seventy last, that thou mayest deliver them only to such as be wise among the people. For in them is the spring of understanding, the fountain of wisdom." It is Mosheim who in his famous history of the early Church (Vol. II, 167) discloses how the matter of esoteric writing and cryptic meaning became a nub of controversy between Origen and his opponents. It is well to quote Mosheim's statements in full for the sake of their explicitness. He is referring to Origen when he says:

"Certainly he would have had no enemies if he had merely affirmed, what no one then called in question, that in addition to the sense which the words of Scripture convey, another sense latent in the things described is to be diligently sought for. This will be manifest if we consider who were the men that inveighed so bitterly against Origen's allegories after he was dead. I refer to Eustatius, Epiphanius, Jerome, Augustine and many others. All these were themselves allegorists, if I may use that term; and would undoubtedly have commended any man, as a great errorist, who would have dared to impugn the arcane sense of Scripture. . . . There must, therefore, have been something new and unusual in Origen's exigetics, which appeared to them pernicious and very dangerous.

"The first and chief was, that he pronounced a great part of the sacred books to be void of meaning if taken literally, and that only the things indicated by the words were the signs and emblems of higher objects. The Christians who had previously followed after mystic interpretation let the truth of the sacred narratives and the proper sense of the divine laws and precepts remain in full force; but he turned much of the sacred history into moral fables, and no small part of the divine precepts into mere allegories.

"Nearly allied to this first fault was another; namely, that he lauded immoderately the recondite and mystical sense of Scripture, and unreasonably depreciated the grammatical or historical sense. The latter he compared to earth, mud, the body and other things of little value; but the former he compared to the soul, heaven, gold and the most precious objects. By such representations he induced the expositors of Scripture to think little about the literal sense of passages and to run enthusiastically after the sublimer interpretations."

All this is so directly valuable a contribution to the inner story of the great catastrophe that overtook early Christianity that the long quotations can be forgiven. Here we see the most learned of the Christian Fathers, Origen, clinging tenaciously to what he knew was the true method of esoteric interpretation, but already beset by the subversive and crippling insistence on the literal and historical rendering which spelled devastation for the true meaning of scripture. This was the beginning of the tragedy that has engulfed all spiritual exegesis of holy writ ever since. Origen was the last champion of a true Christianity going down to defeat under the swelling tide of Philistine crudity of mind.

A good part of the reason why the literalists feared Origen's method escapes in a naïve paragraph from Mosheim, who says that it appears strange that a man of so much discernment as Origen was should not have seen that his use of allegories and denial of the historicity of scripture would place directly into the hands of the Gnostics and others whom he sought to persuade to Christianity "the very means of overthrowing the entire history of the life and death of Christ." Unquestionably this strikes close to the heart of the whole matter. Once having committed itself to the personal and historical resolution of the Christos figure, the ecclesiastical power could not give countenance to the allegorical interpretation. The validation of the latter would present an immediate and constant menace to the whole historical structure of Christianity. Ever since early times it has had to battle with the implications of comparative religion study to avoid the general acceptance of conclusions massively obvious on the side of allegorism. With Egypt's evidence now available, the day of reckoning can no longer be held off.

Mosheim sets forth Origen's stated view that, as "the philosophical grounds of Christian doctrine are wrapt up in figures, images and facts in the sacred volume," if "we adhere to the literal meaning, that harmony between religion and philosophy can not be found." Mosheim admits that "in the objections of the enemies of Christianity, there are not a few things which can in no way be fully cleared up and confuted, unless we abandon the grammatical and historical sense and resort to allegories." This goes far forward strengthening Origen's (and this work's) general position, and is recommended to the close attention of all modern literalists and fundamentalists.

So extended an array of data has been necessary to establish the existence and influence of the esoteric method in the whole of ancient literature. It must be kept in mind that, lengthened as it is to the point of prolixity, it is only a tiny segment of what could be adduced. The significant fact in reference to it is that in spite of the mass of authentic evidence the effort has persisted in academic circles to maintain a denial of both the employment of such a distinctive method and its obvious and momentous involvements. It is by no means an unwarranted assertion to hint that the hostile attitude toward esotericism has been an item in the policy of a great conspiracy, operative ever since the third century, to diminish the influence of the pagan teachings. Evidence to support such a forthright statement is not wanting, although, as Sir Gilbert Murray has noted, most of the evidence supporting the pagan side has been destroyed by the Christians. Whatever the motive actuating a resort to the method of violence to negate an important fact in religious history, it must be held in any case a hazardous enterprise to flout the truth. It argues something less than full intellectual integrity, something sinister and disquieting. The world is still waiting for a good and adequate explanation of the harsh measure that prompted the closing of schools that purveyed such lofty wisdom and sage philosophy as the Platonic Academies of sapient Greece in the fifth century. According to von Mosheim, Origen "introduced the whole of the Academy into Christian theology." Bishop Synesius preferred "philosophy" to lying legend. Neo-Platonism brought to the modern Dean Inge his highest illumination in religion. It will call for a good case indeed to defend the suppression of truth and light of this sort.

In our longer view it becomes ever more patent that in the ignorant policy by the Church the world witnessed the triumph of irrational piety and fanatical zealotry over rational religion. The mystical and the rational sides of the religious motive, expressed in general by two quite diverse types of human beings – the one the feeling, the other the thinking – have always been at variance and often in conflict in the movement, and the resurgent sweep of one or the other has marked the epic of religious history. Hardly any event in the annals of mankind has wrought more serious consequences than that sudden and overwhelming change of character in early Christianity from a philosophical religion to one of devotion and feeling, so fateful for later times. The Christian world is still enthralled by the iniquitous influences to which this portentous event gave birth. It is with the design of breaking the deadening spell of much of this irrational enchantment still operative today that the great massing of data in this work is undertaken.

Chapter IV

WISDOM HAUNTS THE COUNTRYSIDE

It might be presumed that the authentic status of myth and religious allegory had been sufficiently demonstrated. But it should further greatly strengthen the whole case and prove of vital worth on its own account to assemble additional data that will reveal an even closer tie between the myths and the basic genius of all religion. This research will enable us to establish a connection between myths and another ancient mode of religious expression, a link which is little known or suspected by modern students. Indeed it will answer in large part the great question as to the origin of the myths. The conclusion reached by the investigation will again almost certainly be warmly disputed. A shorter chapter will suffice to present what must surely be considered an important body of evidence.

The collated data point to an origin of the myths in a place which itself vastly enhances their innate and fundamental kinship with religion. Lacking more accurate knowledge about them, we have been disposed to think that the myths were an independent and whimsical creation of the free fancy and childish imagination of peoples whom we have insisted on dubbing "primitive." That they were not thus an arbitrary product, unrelated to the profoundest philosophical wisdom and the highest spiritual insight of the ancient world, is evidenced by the material here collected. The evidence almost indisputably indicates their origin from an older religious institution or expression – the ritual drama. The myths find their basic character and their unity at last in the features of a great universal dramatic rite, the importance of which has been too stubbornly belittled and neglected through the force of Christian prejudice, even where its very existence has been granted.

First spokesman is no less an authority than Sir James Frazer, author of The Golden Bough. From his lectures (p. 374) we take his item: 'We shall probably not err in assuming that many myths, which we now know only as myths, had once their counterpart in magic; in other words, that they used to be acted as a means of producing in fact the events which they described in figurative language. Ceremonies often die out while myths survive, and thus we are left to infer the dead ceremony from the living myth."

Corroboration is added by H. J. Rose (Folk-Lore, p. 104): "The legend has pretty certainly grown out of the rite, as usually happens." Says Miss J. E. Harrison in her Themis (p. 328): "A mythos of the Greeks was primarily just a thing spoken, uttered by the mouth. Its antithesis or rather correlative is the thing done, enacted."

Significant is the sentence from Prof. A. B. Cook (quoted in Lord Raglan's work, The Hero): "Behind the myth (of the Minotaur), as is so often the case, we may detect a ritual performance." J. A. K. Thomson, in Studies in the Odyssey (p. 54) states that not only is the myth the explanation of the rite; it is at the same time the explanation of the god, – the central character in the rite. Forthright is the testimony of A. M. Hocart in The Progress of Man (p. 223):

"If we turn to the living myth, that is, the myth that is believed in, we find that it has no existence apart from the ritual. The ritual is always derived from some one and its validity must be established from its derivation. . . . Knowledge of the myth is essential to the ritual, because it has to be recited at the ritual."

Prof. Malmouski (Notes and Queries in Anthropology) writes:

"Psychologists like Wundt, sociologists like Durkheim, Herbert and Mause, anthropologists like Crawley, classical scholars like Miss Jane Harrison, have all understood the ultimate association between myth and ritual, between sacred tradition and the norms of social structure. . . . Myth as it exists in a savage community, that is, in its living primitive form, is not merely a story told but a reality lived. It is not of the nature of fiction such as we read today in a novel, but it is a living reality, believed to have once happened in primeval times and continuing ever since to influence the world and human destinies."

It must be pointed out that lack of keen discernment is shown in claiming that an intelligent view of the myths ever accepted them as having actually occurred, or that they were not known to be pure fiction in their outward form. Error and confusion at once enter the moment we attribute to them any other than typical reality. The whole miscarriage of ancient meaning sprang from the incorrigible tendency to assert that the ancient intelligent people believed their myths. There is the great chasm of difference between saying they believed them and saying they believed in them, and the chasm is that between truth and error. Never did intelligent people believe them; they believed what they represented, typified, adumbrated. The whole issue of right and wrong appraisal and judgment of them and the ancient hangs on this distinction. This work for the first time insists that this distinction is the critical point in the evaluation of all ancient literature. The first blows in the wreckage of archaic spiritual systems fell when the shadow of this misconception crept in upon the mind of the early Christian following.

Correcting the apparently slight, but really formidable misconception, it is necessary next to repudiate utterly this same writer's views on the myths, as thus expressed:

"We can certainly discard all explanatory as well as all symbolical ex-interpretations of these myths of origins. The personages and beings which we find are what they appear to be on the surface, and not symbols of hidden realities. As to any explanatory function of these myths, there is no problem which they cover, no curiosity which they satisfy, no theory which they contain."

This opinion needs refutation because it will be seconded by many readers who are instant in opposition to anything that extols the religion of "paganism." How any scholar acquainted with the facts of the ancient ritualism, and possessed of ordinary reasoning power, could asseverate that the ceremonies were entirely meaningless, is beyond comprehension. This is to accuse Plato, Euripides, Sophocles, Aeschylus and a long list of antiquity's most celebrated men of perpetrating a performance, presented annually before thousands of people, that was in the end nothing but gibberish. The actions and speeches in the drama reenacted the experience of mankind in its evolutionary cycle; yet this critic asserts that there was no problem or construction bearing relation to reality in the mythic representation. Criticism of this sort is farcical, and represents a total failure to grasp meanings which, however faintly apprehended by the unschooled, can still be discerned by any intelligent mind. So gross a misjudgment of a great form of an- cient culture is inexcusable. From a stupendous amount of such biased incompetence in assessing the value of early formulations in religion and philosophy the world has suffered incredibly.

While putting forth the questionable conjecture that the myth had nothing to do with speculation or exegesis, any more than with historical data, the next witness, Lord Raglan, English author of a most valuable work, The Hero: A Study in Tradition, Myth and Drama, contributes to the discussion a body of data, comment and cited material that goes far to make the case impregnable. His work stands as one of the first open-minded approaches to the investigation of the world's hero-legends, folk lore and Märchen, and adduces evidence which negates the historical view of the hero stories. He is perhaps the first modern to clarify the distinction between legend and real history.

He classifies the myth roughly as little else than the form of words which accompanies the performance of a rite. Citing the incongruity of the content and form of the myth with the ordinary products of the folk (to whom all previous consensus had assigned their origin), he states the highly important conclusion that the literature of the folk is not their own production, but comes down to them from a source above them. The author here brings out in clear and irrefutable fashion the discernment that it has been a great error to attribute the creation of folk lore to the folk themselves. The myths were made for the folk, but not by the folk. They were constructed with a view to catch the popular fancy and be retained easily in the folk memory. To claim that they were originated by the folk is to argue that the products of the highest cleverness and genius came from the ranks of the untutored and ignorant. The tales and ballads lived amongst the folk, but they were not their creation.

But to the modern student Raglan's statement that, since they were not an indigenous folk production, they must have come down to them from above, is mystifying. This is due to the failure of modern thought to envisage properly the ancient prevalence of esoteric spirit and methodology. There should be no more skepticism about the realities of esoteric truth and teaching than about the situation in any college, where faculty, representing the acquired wisdom and maturity of an older generation, presides over and instructs the members of a younger generation, its pupils. The from above in Raglan's pronounce- ment hints at nothing more weird and exceptional than the fact that more enlightened sages from time to time since remote days have contrived to issue for the benefit of the general mass of uninstructed humanity bodies of truth encased in the amber of popular legend, ballad, castle-tale and household fable. From above here signifies no super-intelligence achieved by the spiritually illumined aspirants, whether in ancient days or since.

The myths came down through the ages from a distant source in a mountain-spring of attained wisdom. Raglan presents this view and strengthens his conviction regarding it by a citation from Budge, the Egyptologist, who says (From Fetish to God in Ancient Egypt, p. 156):

"It would be wrong to say that the Egyptians borrowed from the Sumerians, or the Sumerians from the Egyptians, but it may be submitted that the literati of both peoples borrowed their theological systems from some common but exceedingly ancient source."

Budge here spoke more truly than he has done at other times. His words are indeed the truth on this matter, so largely missed otherwise. Raglan declares that a dozen learned writers show that the religious systems of many countries possessed many fundamental characteristics in common. They were obviously systems designed for the good of the community by the proper performance of the given ritual. This possession of a common religious denominator by many nations looms as vitally important, since it becomes the backbone of the argument that all the myths had one common origin in a primal construction wherein all the ingredients were at hand from the beginning.

Raglan's outline of the pervasive features of the ritual is a valuable summary. He says in effect that the basic pattern consisted of a dramatic ritual in which the death and resurrection of the king, who was also the god, performed by priests and members of the royal family, were the central events. There was also a sacred combat, in which the victory of the god over his enemies was won, and a triumphal procession, participated in by the neighboring gods, also an enthronement, with a ceremony by which the destinies of the state for the year ahead were determined, and finally a sacred marriage. Somewhere in the drama was interjected the recitation of the story whose outlines were enacted in the ritual. This was the myth, and its repetition engendered a strong psychic potency equal to that of the ritual itself. From the start the words and the actions were inseparably united, although in the course of time they became separated and each gave rise to its own literary, artistic and religious forms.

He states a little farther on (p. 154) that while the separation of Greek myth from its accompanying ritual may be due in part to the ancient philosophers, who composed allegories which seemed to tear the myth apart from the ritual, the divorcement of the two is chiefly due to modern classical scholars who have failed to recognize the close connection between Greek poetry and Greek religion and who have likewise missed the fact that the Greek descriptive writers such as Herodotus and Pausanius never cite a myth apart from a reference to some rite or to some sacred locality.

If at any time the sages composed myths that had no connection with the ritual, it could only have been that there was no structural or organic linkage with it. It is hardly possible to conceive how they could have composed myths unrelated to the ritual, for all the myths were picturizations of the same elements of meaning which the ritual portrayed. Perhaps not distinctly related in form, but related in meaning, to the ritual they must have been.

Raglan says that Miss Jennie Weston (From Ritual to Romance, p. 176), after dealing with a large group of Grail stories, concludes that these stories "repose eventually not upon a poet's imagination, but upon the ruins of an august and ancient ritual, a ritual which once claimed to be the accredited guardian of the deepest secrets of life." But so strong is the inveterate tendency to assume that history must somehow be interwoven in ancient constructions that Miss Weston supposes that certain historical outlines have crept into these narratives. Nothing but later ignorance and exoteric degeneracy ever compromised with the pure myth to the extent of insinuating historical reference into it.

A penetrating judgment is pronounced by Raglan (p. 225) when he definitely asserts that the myth took its rise from the dramatic features of the ritual, and that all traditional narratives show, by both form and content, that they derive neither from historical fact nor from imaginative fiction, but from acted ritual. There can be little doubt, he states, that all drama is the product of ritual drama. The dramatis personae, even when they are given historical names, are not individuals but types.

The Homeric poems, he says, have the form of dramas. The drama, he insists, was originally a religious ceremony, and the whole community shared in it. (The Hero, p. 240.)

Mr. MacCulloch, in alluding to the Algonquin stories, says: "All form part of a mythological cycle dealing with the life of the hero-divinity, Manabush." Raglan subjoins that the Homeric poems are all mythological cycles dealing with the lives of hero-divinities; but, he ventures, nothing so arouses the fury of scholars as the suggestion that these cycles are based on ritual, or sprang from it. He says they take the Tale of Troy as sober record of historical fact, woven together from scraps of romantic fiction. As there is nothing in the Bible that can not be found in antecedent literature, so, Raglan contends, there is nothing in "Homer" that can not be found elsewhere. Who was Homer? – he asks. And he answers with the pronouncement of Prof. J. A. K. Thomson, that "Homer" was the title given to the victor in the minstrelsy contest held at the festival of Apollo at Delos. He was the eponymous-hero of the hymn-singers and sacred dancers, and was a personification of the Delian Apollo.

"The hymn," says Prof. Thomson, "has given birth to the heroic-epos. For these 'men and women' are the old local Daimones, – Achilles, Helen and the rest. Their legends have combined to form one great legend recited at the Delian festival in honor of Apollo, the father-god of all the Ionians. . . . The hymn gradually added to itself more and more of the inherited or borrowed legends of the Ionian race until it grew into the proportions of all 'Homer.' And as Homer was the traditional author of the original hymn, so he remained the traditional author of all the rest."

Mr. W. F. J. Wright is cited as saying that the name of Troy is widely associated with mazes and labyrinths, and that various instances in the Iliad correspond with known features of a once widespread maze ritual. And Prof. Hocart is drawn on as authority for the datum that there are twenty-six common features which characterize the installation of kings in all parts of the world; and the inference is that these common features stem from a common source, the ancient spiritual drama.

Raglan says the conclusion is inevitable that such characters as the ogre, giant, devil, dragon, troll, cannibal and sorcerer are nothing but titles for a personage acting in a liturgy, representing the terrifying demon of the initiations. There is much indeed to support the expressed view of Raglan (p. 220) that the character known as the Horned Man was taken from the ritual and became invested with real life, gaining a status in popular belief far more real than that of any historical character. Perhaps Jesus is more real as mythical hero than as a once-living person. Anent this Raglan expresses his astonishment that Sir James Ridgeway should have been misled into taking the stock figures of myth for actual people.

The principal characters in the ritual are two, a hero and a buffoon who meet with various adventures together and live on terms of the greatest familiarity – naturally, since they represent the god and the animal nature of man, who live together in the same body! And this accounts for the special privilege accorded the fool to jest at the expense of the castle baron, and for the horse-play and buffoonery permitted at the Saturnalia and the autumn equinoctial festivals (surviving in the rough mischief of our Hallowe'en), when higher and lower, god and irresponsible joker in man, were placed on the same level of existence. Fools were considered sacred on the seventh day, symbolizing the raising of the animal man to his human-divine dignity on the Sabbath, the seventh and last "day" of the cycle.

The incarnation of the divine soul in man's animal body is the basis of all the legends of the sorcerers' turning the hero or his men into animals, or their disguising themselves as animals. The Hallowe'en animal mask is the survival and replica of the same thing, for the masks were originally the hides of animals! The prominence given this phase of the drama's meaning is attested by what Raglan writes (p. 261). He says that a prominent feature of every type of traditional narrative is the man in animal form, or the animal that can speak. Persons disguised as animals are so universal a feature of ritual and drama as not to need demonstration, he avers. And the answer to the query why ancient Egyptian ritual was performed largely by people in animal masks, and why Greek gods and goddesses were so often represented as animals or birds, holds in its symbolic purport one of the central items of the drama of human life. For the religion of these early peoples throbbed with an innate sense of kinship with nature and religious ideas were sympathetically adumbrated and reflected by nature's phe- nomena. Participants in the Mithraic Mysteries wore animal masks. Obviously the masks typified the outer personality of man, for the Latin word for "mask" is persona, and man's personality is an animal body!

It is quite worth a moment's digression from data to exegesis to say that the world's failure over many centuries to read the simple explication of this animal typism, as dramatically depicting the incarnation of the soul in the human-animal, and not the beast-animal, body, has buried the trap to catch untold millions of religiously simple-minded people in its disguised subtlety. Had the esoteric implications of the drama been kept in ken, all that mass of lucubrated assertion by numberless writers that the ancients endorsed the belief in transmigration of the once-human soul into the bodies of animals at death, would not have disgraced the pages of literature. Scholars, historians and sociologists can now be told that they have been shooting, not at an authentic poacher in the garden, but at a scarecrow.

Raglan cites that the Council of Trent believed that people can take the form of animals! The ancients, as we have seen, are accused of "believing" their myths. It was only the later Christians that believed them, with both humorous and tragic results.

Greek drama, like Egyptian, is predominantly tragic, because what moderns term "happiness" was not the one supreme motif of the human experience, as envisaged by Greek philosophy. By etymology "tragedy" means "goat-song." The goat was of course the zodiacal Capricorn, coming at the winter solstice, when the sun, typifying the soul in the dead "winter" of its incarnation, was in the throes of "death" as the scapegoat to carry the onus of man's redemption. For obviously man's only possible redeemer – from benightedness, nescience, animal carnality – is his own soul. If it can not make the grade into charity, love and compassion, what else can uplift him? Let the Church which has gulled its childish millions by substituting a historical for an immanent scapegoat, answer.

This concludes the limited assemblage of data to demonstrate that the myth came from the pristine ritual drama. If it is not enough to prove the point, there is doubtless much more material of perhaps greater strength that could be found and presented. The fact, if considered sufficiently demonstrated, might seem to be remote from any bearing on the question of the Jesus historicity. It is indeed not remote. If it can be shown that the Christ of the Gospels was a myth- ical character, we could then confidently look for agreement of all aspects of this mythical figure with the central character-personage in the ancient religious ritual, out of which the myths grew. Comparative religion study has already demonstrated this close relationship of the two figures, the Christ of the mythos and the Sun-God of the ritual. Some material in the present work may further strengthen that identity. If the ritual and the myth are shown to be in point of fact practically identical, and the features to match closely the characterizations of the Gospel Jesus, a strong presumptive case has already been established in support of the conclusion that the Gospel hero was but another of the many mythical type-figures, and not a Galilean peasant.

Chapter V

FANCY'S FABRIC TURNS INTO HISTORY

The story turns next to a chapter in revelation that must strike all but a few readers as incredible beyond all possibility of its being the simple truth. Even if the weight of the evidence submitted seems indubitably to support the position, it will still fail acceptance by many. It will leave even those convinced by the presentation shocked, bewildered, incredulous. That so gross a blunder, both gigantic and stupid, could have been perpetrated, and that it could have been foisted upon the world's intelligence for sixteen centuries without detection by the united acumen of all scholars over that period, will appear impossible. It will be the giraffe whose existence the farmer denied while looking it up and down. It will come close to upsetting Lincoln's witty apothegm, and almost prove that all the people can be fooled all the time, or for sixteen centuries. It brings the disconcerting realization that after all fifty million Frenchmen can be wrong. The upset of cherished maxims of human polity is distressing. The foundations of homiletics will be shaken. So vast a miscarriage of wisdom, embroiling the mental life of millions for centuries in the darkest superstitions, setting spiritual culture back for ages, will seem too enormous a price to pay for a mere misreading of myths. A consequence of such enormity would seem out of all proportion to the apparently trivial nature of the cause.

But the misreading of myths and allegories, fables and dramas, brought the historical Christ into hypostatization, euhemerized the central spiritual conception in all religion, and thus emasculated what was to have been the most potent dynamic of the whole religious life. It left the world chasing a chimera instead of focusing effort on the culture of spirituality. It threw a possible great civilization under the pall and handicap of the most fantastic conception that ever misdirected the moral genius of man into eccentric and bizarre and eventually cataclysmic channels. It killed the psychological efficacy of the whole religious enterprise, diverting zeal from the one pivot point where zeal alone counts, – the life of the inner consciousness and seat of character, the soul.

The revelation thus heralded and now to be substantiated by accumulated documentation, is the colossal blunder, perpetrated from the third century on, of mistaking myth, drama, ritual, allegory and other forms of typical representation for objective history, and following this by turning the body of myths into alleged occurrence. This chapter and indeed the entire work is the answer to the raucous chorus of protestation that will arise on all sides against the possibility of such a thing, declaring it absurd and demanding the evidence to prove it. In many quarters the declaration will be laughed out of court and given no chance to present its credentials. It can be said in patient appeal for examination of the supporting data that the closer one looks into the matter, the more completely does the apparent absurdity fade away and probability increase to certainty. When scrutiny has been carried on penetratingly enough, the absurdity of its being true turns quite around and gives place to the absurdity of any other view. Not only can the mistake be established on factual evidence, but the perception that a mistake has been made supplies the only hypothesis that yields a full and consistent explanation of all the data extant in the case. It alone provides a formula which solves all the difficulties and tangles involved in the problem. If this is so, it must be accepted and accredited as substantial proof. For if research elicits a formula which enables all the data to be explained rationally and consistently by its key, the formula is considered as satisfactorily established. The key that fits all locks must be the master key. A thousand questions, complications, inconsistencies, contradictions, illogicalities in current interpretation both of scriptural text and historical implication are resolved into entirely consistent intelligibility when the true key is applied. If this resultant can not be accepted as ultimate proof of the correctness of the thesis, it at least gives it the field over every other proposal that does not so resolve the difficulties with half the consonance and reasonableness.

The ancient illuminati depicted the soul's experience in this life by means of myth, drama, allegory and pictorial ideograph; and in the third century the increasingly ignorant Christian laity and the decreasingly intelligent Christian priesthood conspired at last to convert the whole into supposed history. That is the whole story in a thimble. But we can not go far with it in the thimble. Its full detailing demands a great elaboration. It is frankly the gigantic task to support the claim against determined and crafty opposition, for the very obvious reason that esotericism did not openly proclaim or defend itself, and therefore its defense is not in evidence in rebuttal of opposing claims. The opposition also has possessed the enormous advantage of being able to destroy all the evidence of the other side, a point which has been strikingly mentioned by Sir Gilbert Murray in his studies. It seems clear that a case which must be upheld by the destruction of opposing evidence stands already prejudiced as a weak one.

But there are times when history itself enacts an amazing drama of poetic justice in the operation of moral forces. So long as the voice of ancient Egypt's wisdom was hushed in silence, so long as the Egyptian papyri and stelae could not be read, the pious imposture could go on. Nearly two millennia passed, with Egypt's testimony unavailable. But in the fullness of time Napoleon's Colonel, Broussard, dug up the Rosetta Stone and Napoleon wisely saw its possible value. It is questionable whether, for direct cultural value to all races, any event, battle or reformation in human history surpasses this simple discovery of an entablatured rock. It is fast proving the ghost of retribution, the instrument of justice, the Nemesis of a Christianity fostered by ignorance and superstition. It opens up the vast treasure-house of ancient Egyptian literature, where, once exposed to view, there lies before our eyes the full and incontestable evidence of Christianity's false claims. That literature supplies the direct missing links in the body of comparative religion study, a study which proves beyond cavil that Christianity was not the first pure divine release of the one "true religion," but only at best a badly mangled copy of earlier Egyptian religion. So far was it from being an advance or improvement over pagan cultures that it is possible to say it was not even a good reprint of them, was in fact a vitiation and sheer caricature of more perfect ancient systems. However much this sounds like the vilest heresy and contumacy in flouting the traditional poses of orthodoxy, the truth should not be suppressed merely because it shocks those who prefer to hold to the set grooves of acceptance and who for a hundred reasons are unwilling to face a humiliating readjustment. Conservatism ever finds an error, when coupled with security, a more comfortable companion than truth admitted to the house with disturbing consequences. Only after new truth has slowly crept into the general body and settled itself commodiously amongst the former elements, will the conservative group adopt it, with the lying manifesto that they had been standing for the innovation all the time. Particularly has this been true of religious conservatism. The last to yield old ground to new positions, it is yet the loudest to extol the new form when finally it has established itself firmly. History supports this analysis.

The Rosetta Stone and Champollion's marvelous work in deciphering its cryptic hieroglyphics will force Christianity to face its pagan origins and admit at last its long-denied parentage in the ancient Egyptian wisdom. It has spurned its true ancestry, and having in the meantime heaped obloquy and contempt upon it, now finds it humiliating, when the true descent is established, to accept the connection. But it must do so or – perish. It can no longer support its claims in the face of contradictory evidence, which, with the release of Egypt's hidden wisdom, the rediscovery of the "lost language of symbolism" in which all ancient scriptures were written and the recovery of the buried esoteric meaning of all ancient religion, has been raised in height and volume from hillock to mountain size. With candid truth-seeking as its guiding star, there needs to be instituted a sincere scholastic research of all available documents to trace the causes, motives and circumstances of that devastating surge of forces which swept over the masses in the Roman Empire about the third century and with fell violence stamped out the cult of esoteric wisdom and closed up its schools and academies. With dispiriting unanimity the religious historians and Christian writers hail the suppression of the Mystery Brotherhoods and the philosophical schools as the happy ending of a degenerate paganism and the beginning of a Christianity of spiritual purity. By what distortions or chicanery of logic or sophistry the extinction of the great Plato's still unexampled wisdom, Socrates' magnificent dialectic of truth and Aristotle's consummate perspicacity can be twisted into a triumph of truth over error and the bright dawn of a new day for humanity, is surely not easily discerned. The logical inconsistency of the position is brought vividly to light in the historical phenomenon that transpired a thousand years later, when the strength of the whole Christian system was by the Medieval schoolmen built up on the foundations of the books of the same Plato and Aristotle, the obliteration of whose philosophies from the early Christian doctrinism was hailed as the end of world benightedness and the beginning of world enlightenment. During some earlier centuries of the Medieval period Plato's Timaeus was the principal authority for Christian exposition; and for nearly a thousand years later Aristotle was the venerated master for all the Schoolmen, with Aquinas in the lead, of the regnant Church. Forsooth, then, it was a benison to humanity to have earlier closed their great colleges under the sycamores of Greece! This is the crooked logic of factual history and in the light of it the world can see at last that Christian claims and Christian acts do not lie straight in the same bed. Had it not been for the Arabians and Moors the Schoolmen would probably never have had a Plato or Aristotle manuscript to found Medieval Christianity upon. The Christian propaganda office has vociferated a thousand times that the closing of the Platonic academies in the fifth century ended the Dark Ages of paganism and heralded the era of true religion. The Catholic Church vociferates with equal vigor that the revival of Aristotelian philosophy and its use as the bulwark of a rationalized Christianity was again the end of the Dark Ages of later Europe. It is a little confusing to be told that the world was saved by the suppression of Grecian esoteric wisdom and saved again by its renaissance. A fuller survey of some aspects of this muddled situation will be undertaken in a later chapter.

The marshaling of data to corroborate the positions taken will again require much quotation of authorities. The pointed force of documentary statements is in large measure lost when reported indirectly. The apology for so much direct quotation is that a work of this kind, combating universally accepted theses and putting forth conclusions which will be everywhere challenged, has no recourse but to summon a powerful array of authoritative statement to its side. The importance of the issues involved will amply justify the extensive citation.

We can put confidence in the sincere utterance of a fair-minded scholar like Mr. G. R. S. Mead, when he makes the following impressive statement (Did Jesus Live 100 Years B.C.?, p. 12):

"Canonical Christianity gradually evolved the mind-bewildering dogma that Jesus was in deed and in truth very God of very God, unique and miraculous in every possible respect; and the Church for some seventeen or eighteen centuries has boldly thrown down this challenge to the intellect and experience of humanity. . . . It is because of this stupendous claim, which has perhaps astonished none more than Himself, that the Church has brought upon herself a scrutiny into the history of her origins that it is totally unable to bear."

We can do no better than continue with some exceedingly valuable declarations from the pen of Gerald Massey, which, however heterodoxical they may appear to the orthodox, cut to the heart of the truth with startling incisiveness. This clear-eyed scholar, with the open pages of Egypt's symbolical and analogical wisdom under his gaze, showing the complete case for the derivation of Christian material from that august source, stood at a vantage point where few others have stood. Facing this perspective, his decisive advantage was his possession of both penetrating insight into things Egyptian and an unprejudiced open mind. It is to be hoped that our return to sanity and our more piercing discernment into ancient religion may bring us at last to see what he saw ahead of us, and may dispose us to do belated justice to the name of this truth-seeking student whom our blindness cheated of his legitimate honor and reward in his lifetime.

Massey says that the Mosaic account of the creation is allowed by the most learned of Jewish Rabbis, by Philo, Paul and certain of the Patristics to be a myth or symbolical representation; yet the whole structure of the Christian theology is founded on the ignorant assumption that it was not mythical but a veritable human occurrence in the domain of fact. As history, he avers, the Pentateuch has neither head, tail nor vertebrae. It is an indistinguishable mush of myth and mystery. He notes a logical consideration that has been missed by blind zeal to countenance the impossible in a religion of fanatical faith, but that must be granted much validity as an argument. This is the fact that had the Pentateuch been a real history, Palestine and Judea ought to have been found overstrewn with implements of war and work, both of Hebrew manufacture and that of the conquered races, whereas, outside of the Book, no evidence of the numberless combats and the devastation of Jehovah's enemies in great battles is to be found. Also the country of a people so rich that King David in his poverty could collect one thousand millions of pounds sterling toward building a temple is found without art, sculptures, mosaics, bronzes, pottery or precious stones to lend credence to the Bible story. Proofs of Bible "history" will not be found, avers Massey, not though Palestine be dug up in the search. And how fatuous after all to think of digging in the earth to find the proofs of spiritual myths and allegories! No amount of archaeology can prove a myth.

But there was bound to come a time when the ancient world would begin to write history of the factual sort, or when, as recondite learning and deeper esoteric comprehension waned, the process of weaving actual history into the texture of the myths would make headway. In nearly every land the custodians of the myths sooner or later intermixed some national history with the spiritual dramas. As is so clearly evidenced in Virgil's Aeneid, the temptation was almost unconquerable at times for the hierophants of religion to interweave the brighter deeds or virtues of a regnant king in the ritual drama, the more particularly since the king in all ancient countries did become the national type and personation of the Sun-God of the temple ceremonies. Kings were almost invariably named after the spiritual Sun-King of the drama. The titles of the Emperor of Ethiopia and Oriental monarchs still testify to this old custom. As nearly as can be determined, the time when this transition from myth to history occurred in Jewish history was in the days of Hezekiah. From then on the allegories of the descent of the gods to earth are made to run into and blend with a line of historical personages. This process, as Massey saw it, so confused the impossible situations found in myth and allegory with the ostensibly possible facts of history that to accredit the narrative as history the mind had to entertain many bizarre and fabulous incidents under the rating of miracle. The blending of history with myth opened the door to the entry of that derationalizing scourge born of religious ineptitude, the belief in miracle, Massey contends. It created the susceptibility to take stock in prodigy, the supernatural, the ominous, which nearly all minds engender from a literal reading of the scriptures. Massey feels that religion has unsettled men's minds by its glorification of the miraculous and the supernatural, when the whole basis of its true strength and salutary influence for humanity lies in its inculcating the majesty and divinity of the ever-present miracle of the natural. He attests that the sane ancient religion was founded upon the natural, the highest spiritual verities being everywhere presented in the light of their analogy with some natural phenomenon. Massey would have endorsed Emerson's wise discernment that "the true mark of genius is to see the miraculous in the common." The Hebrew writings were preserved, Massey continues, on account of the sacred mystery that lay underneath the veil of symbol, the veil that Isis boasted no man had lifted from her person. The writings were held in sanctity because of what they veiled; but to the Christians their sanctity goes no deeper than the veil, and is bred and kept alive only by ignorance, "absolute, unquestioning, unsuspecting ignorance of the meaning of symbolism." With them the veil itself is the treasure, and they know not the real treasure beneath it. And since they have centered all the sanctity in the veil, when that is torn off, all the sanctity is lost for them. They have disciplined no faculty which would enable them to see the real treasure when it is exposed to view. They howl that their treasure has been stolen away from them, when only the ornamentally carved lid of the treasure chest has been removed. And this indeed has been the tragedy of the situation. Voltaire, Paine, Ingersol, the Encyclopedists, the Deists, the atheists and the Freethinkers and religious skeptics generally have effectively torn away and trampled under foot the outer garments of Bible myths, all unaware that these clothed the body of truth. The revelation of the absurdity of Bible allegory, taken as supposed history, broadcast by these efforts, set on fire in millions of minds a burning resentment against the whole institution of religion, and the Bible, theology and priestcraft as its criminal accessories. They see nothing in religion worth saving. This upsweep of rationalism, as reaction against centuries of omnicredulous faith, threatens to abolish religion from the earth. This is the price the world is paying for the loss of symbolic genius in the third century. Nothing will save the cult of genuine religion from this menacing hand but the quick restoration of the knowledge that there is no absurdity and nonsense, but only grandeur of truth, when the scriptures are read as sublime spiritual allegories instead of histories. Nothing will stay the besom of devastation but the quick recovery of the lost language of symbolism. For nothing else will bring to light the treasure beneath the veil.

Massey maintains (Book of the Beginnings, Vol. II, p. 180) that when the Hebrew scriptures were translated into Greek in the third century B.C. by some Alexandrian Jews, the process of elimination of the esoteric is very visible. Dates were altered to conceal the true sense. And after the allegories had been transformed into histories, the true or symbolic reading according to the principles of the secret tradition was forbidden to be taught in schools. The Pharisees were so fearful of the popular despoliation of the Apocryphal wisdom by the unworthy that they sought to prevent the teaching of writing to the masses.

Testimony that Massey is correct in saying that myth and history inevitably tend to merge into one is found in the book of a writer whose aim is to disprove the mythical interpretation of the scriptures. T. J. Thorburn, in his The Mythical Interpretation of the Gospels (p. 120), writes:

"The myth proper is an explanation of some occurrence in nature – not in history – which deals chiefly with legend in its early stages. The personifications which take place in myths, however, help to link nature with history and to parallel events and persons in history with the phenomena of nature. Thus the legendary and even historical stories often become paralleled, and even confused with mythical ones. . . . In this way it is possible that John (and in a certain sense . . . Jesus also) became analogues of personified natural phenomena."

Very instructive for us today is Thorburn's next sentence:

"To the modern and European mind this process obscures and weakens the historical character of the human counterpart; to the ancient and Oriental mind it merely added vividness and reality to his picture."

It seems likely that the writer of this sentence did not catch the profounder significance of his own words, which hint at a superficial meaning when really great truth is being uttered. He did not realize that "the human counterpart" of the mythical analogue was man collectively, and not only some characters in Gospel narrative. And what dialectic or logical justification there is in his using the word "merely" in his last sentence it is difficult to see. It seems to be there as evidence of the insatiate impulsion in orthodox minds to cast a slight upon pagan systems at every turn. One of the high purposes of the mythicizing tendency of ancient scripture was directly to "add vividness and reality" to the productions. The writer's insertion of the word "merely" commits him to saying in effect that the adding of vividness and reality to sacred narrative was something trivial and inconsequential. If the method succeeded in adding vividness and reality, it at least accomplished something that has been lamentably lacking in later presentation of religious material. But Thorburn, in the very effort to discredit the utility of ancient mythicism, has splendidly stated its entire validity. His charge that the admixture of myth in scripture has obscured and weakened the full force of its educative power has a semblance of truth in it only because the interwoven myth has been uncomprehended. The presence of myth in the record has been a stumbling block only because all power to interpret it had been lost. It still remains true that the understanding use of myths by the ancients did vastly enhance the vividness and reality of the truths thus poetically embellished. But it turns out that a statement meant to deprecate the influence of the myth really concedes the claim for its high utility. Thorburn's unpremeditated admission states with great precision the signal distinction between the ancient sagacious use of the myth and the modern ignorant miscomprehension of its function.

Massey divides humanity into two classes, the knowing and the simple, and says that the knowing ones kept back the esoteric explanation of the myths to let the belief of the untutored masses in the real history take root. "The simple ones, like Bunyan, 'fell suddenly into an allegory about the journey on the way to glory,' which allegory, they were led to believe, was purely matter of fact."

The great truth of history remains to be faced, Massey insists, that the Gospel of "Equinoctial Christolatry" was written before, with a totally different rendering, and that the sayings, dogmas, doctrines, types and symbols, including both the cross and the Christ, did not originate where we may have just made acquaintance with them. This cryptology was written before in the books of secret wisdom, now interpretable according to the recovered Gnosis. It was pre-extant in the types which now have been traced from the lowest root to highest branch. It was inscribed before in the records of the past drawn on the starry skies. The truth is that the real origines of the cult of true Christolatry (not Christianity) have never yet been reached; hardly indeed have they even been suspected, because of the supposed "New Beginning" in human history which was taken for granted by those who knew no further. The evidence for all this, however, could not have been adduced before the mythology, typology and Christology of Egypt were discovered in the keeping of the mummies and disinterred from the vaults of the dead. Now, fortunately, the lost language of celestial allegory is being restored, chiefly through the resurrection of ancient Egypt, and scriptures can be read in the sense in which they were originally written.

In The Book of the Beginnings (Vol. II, p. 226) Massey says that one of two things is sure: "either the Book of Enoch contains the Hebrew history in allegory, or the celestial allegory is the Hebrew history. The parallel is perfect." Nor is there any escape by sticking one's head in the sand and foolishly fancying that the writer of the Book of Enoch amused himself by transforming a Hebrew history into celestial allegory and concealing its significance by leaving out all the personal names. "On the contrary it is the allegory which has been turned into the later history." Sacred history may and does begin with mythology; but mythology does not commence with history.

Massey's claim here has been disputed as a farcical fancy; but it can not be waved aside with a mere snort of ridicule when the evidence has to be faced. The Book of Enoch certainly contains the same characters as the sacred and secret history of the Jews, and as these belong to the astronomical allegory in the one book, that is good evidence of their being mythical in the other. There is no doubt that the Book of Enoch is what it claimed to be, the book of the revolutions of the heavenly bodies, with no relation whatever to human history. It should be subjoined to Massey's last statement that he does not mean that the celestial allegory, while it has no reference to human history objectively, is not all the while the allegorical portrayal of the meaning of all human history. The same is true of the book of Revelation.

Tersely he says that the Hebrew miracles are Egyptian myths, and as such, and only as such, can they be explained in harmony with the nature and reasoning principles of the mind. Held as miracles they are amenable neither to natural fact nor to rational rating. "The sacred writings of the world are not concerned with geography, chronology or human history. The historic spirit is not there. This is so in writing as late as the Talmud." What started out to be the type of history came to be taken as the matter of history, as ignorance submerged the keener diagnosis. The hidden significance fades out from less competent mentality and slips away, letting in more and more the "historical" assumptions. How slow the modern mind has been to see this process at work! Massey promises to restore the lost key hidden in Egypt by the data of comparative religion, which will be remorselessly applied.

Godfrey Higgins is found standing beside Massey in these general conclusions. In The Anacalypsis (p. 366) he writes his rebuke to ecclesiastical insincerity in forceful terms:

"How can any one consider the infinite correlations found in comparative study and not see the mythologic nature of nearly all epic poetry and early 'history'?"

"Mr. Faber, Mr. Bryant and Nimrod have proved this past doubt. . . . Our priests have taken the emblems for the reality. . . . Our priests will be very angry and deny all this. In all nations, in all times, there has been a secret religion; in all nations, in all time the fact has been denied."

Another passage declares vigorously that it all raises a very unpleasant doubt in his mind, after long consideration, as to whether "we really have one history uncontaminated with judicial astrology." He adds that Sir William Drummond has shown that the names of most of the places in Joshua are astrological, and Gen. Vallency has shown that Jacob's prophecy is astrological also, with a direct reference to the constellations. To this probably Jacob referred when he bade his children read in the book of the heavens the fate of themselves and their descendants.

Higgins quotes Bryant as saying that it is evident that most of the deified personages never existed, but were mere titles of the Deity, or of the Sun, Deity's universal symbol, and for our solar system, Deity's embodiment, as was earlier shown by Macrobius. Nor was there ever any such folly perpetrated in ancient history as the supposition that the gods of the Gentile world had been natives of the countries where they were worshipped. Bryant well observes that it was a chief study of the learned to register the legendary stories concerning the gods, to conciliate the absurdities and to arrange the whole into a chronological series – a fruitless and drudging labor. "For there are in these fables such inconsistencies and contradictions as no act nor industry can remedy. . . . This misled Bishop Cumberland, Waker, Pearson, Petavius, Scaliger, with numberless other learned men, and among the foremost the great Newton." As to the last name, it is not so certain that the great Newton was so completely misled. He states in his Principia that he was led to his great discoveries by many implications of the esoteric study, especially in the books of Jacob Böhme, the shoemaker esotericist. Bryant then goes on to demonstrate that the whole of such material, if literally understood, was a mass of falsity and rubbish.

Higgins makes the direct charge that sublime philosophical truths or virtues have been clothed with bodies and converted into living creatures. Starting with the plausible attempt to screen them from "the vulgar eye," the purpose of concealment worked with such thoroughness that the generality of men came at last to treat them in a literal sense. He attributes the change which resulted in the loss of the esoteric sense to the inevitable fluctuations that come in the run of evolutionary progress.

But the chief fault he places where Massey and others lay it – at the door of a designing priesthood:

"That the rabble were the victims of a degrading superstition I have no doubt. This was produced by the knavery of the ancient priests, and it is in order to reproduce this effect that the modern priests have misrepresented the doctrines of their predecessors. By vilifying and running down the religion of the ancients they have thought they could persuade their votaries that their new religion was necessary for the good of mankind; a religion which in consequence of their corruptions has been found to be in practice much worse and more injurious to the interests of society than the older."

This is frank talk, but nearly every scholar who has covered the ground of the ancient situation with a mind not set in advance against the pagan religions, has felt that this is essentially the truth. One such expression may be given. It is from the pen of the modern Harry Elmer Barnes (The Twilight of Christianity, p. 415):

"What might have happened to western society if the teachings of Jesus had been literally applied, we can not well know with any precision. There seems little doubt, however, that the total results of Christianity to date have been a decisive liability to the human race. There is no doubt whatever that Christianity has actually produced more suffering, misery, bloodshed, intolerance and bigotry than it has ever assuaged or suppressed."

Massey (Luniolatry, p. 2) says there is nothing insane or irrational in mythical representation when the allegorical connotation is thoroughly understood.

"The insanity lies in mistaking it for human history or Divine Revelation. Mythology is the repository of man's most ancient science, and what concerns us chiefly is this – when truly interpreted once more, it is destined to be the death of those false theologies to which it has unwittingly given birth."

Allegories misinterpreted as supposed history have created a veritable cult of the unreal which is blindly believed.

Commenting on the cry that he would take the living Jesus away from believers, he retorts that we can be none the poorer for losing that which never was a real possession, but only a psychological wraith which deluded us with its seeming substance. To find the true we must first let go the false. In Goethe's words, until the half-gods go, the whole gods can not come.

Massey says pointedly that there is no greater fraud than that which grew out of the historical interpretation of early legend. This factitious "history" is forever at war, he affirms, with all that is prehistorically true. It not only misinterprets the legend, which would have its own value if rightly scanned, but misrepresents the actual history of early days.

Massey stands firmly on the blunt assertion that the doctrines and dogmas of Christian theology are derived from Egypt and its arcana, and holds that this must be admitted when better acquaintance with that mine of recondite wisdom is made. The door to its adyta is only now opening. The pre-Christian religion was founded on a knowledge of natural and verifiable facts, but the Christian cult was founded on egregious faith which swallowed all that was impossible in fact and unnatural in phenomena. Current orthodoxy is based upon a deluding idealism, derived from literalized legend and misconstrued mythology. The ancients handed over to later generations the science of the human soul, and the Christians have lost it. They substituted the phantom of faith for the knowledge of truth. They propagated a religion that could live only on blind belief, and persecuted all those who would not blindly believe. They shut out the light of nature from their sealed domicile and compelled all others to live in the same dark prison.

The ancient legends and myths do not tell us lies, Massey insists. The men who created them did not deal falsely with us or with nature. "All the falsity lies in their having been falsified through ignorantly mistaking mythology for divine revelation and allegory for historic truth."

Lord Raglan cites Prof. W. Gronbeck (Vol. I, p. 249) in a passage that shows true discernment of the situation which has bred no end of confusion in all philosophical effort:

"In the history of the sacrificial hall the individual warrior is sunk in the god, or, which is the same thing, in the ideal personification of the clan, the hero. This form of history causes endless confusion among later historians when they try their best to arrange the mythical traditions into chronological happenings and the deeds of the clan into annals and lists of kings, and the confusion grows to absurdity when rationalistic logicians strive by the light of sound sense to extricate the kernel of history from the husks of superstition."

This is an accurate, though partial, analysis of the general course which esoteric degeneration has taken, supporting Massey's robust contention that the Märchen are the distorted wrack and debris of the myths. Until this basic perception of the truth of the relation between general folk lore and religious origins is gained, the efforts of modern studentship to evaluate the place and significance of this important aspect of human interest will be so much groping in the dark and continually missing the truth.

A part of the process of degeneration of esoteric mythology appertaining closely to Christianity is well delineated by G. R. S. Mead in his fine work on Gnostic Christianity, Fragments of a Faith Forgotten (p. 118). He writes that in its popular origins the Christian movement had deeply entangled itself with the popular Jewish traditions, which were innocent of all philosophical or kabalistic mysticism, that is, esotericism. But as time went on, either men of greater education joined the ranks or the leaders were forced to study more widely to meet the arguments of educated opponents, and consequently more liberal views obtained a hold among a number of Christians. In time also other great religious traditions and philosophies contributed elements to the popular stream. All such more latitudinarian views, however, were still looked upon with suspicion by the "orthodox." And before long even the moderate esoteric proclivities of Clement and Origen were regarded as a grave danger; so that with the triumph of narrow orthodoxy and the resultant hostility to learning, Origen himself was at last anathematized. It may not be conclusive proof of the evil transformation of good myth into bad history to cite this broad change in Christian polity in those early centuries; but the fact that such a change of posture took place lends to the contention that trends in the direction of literalism and historization of scripture were strongly in current at the time.

Express confirmation of one of the stages described by Mead is at hand in the statement of an eminent modern theologian, Benjamin W. Bacon, of Yale Divinity School, in his work, Jesus and Paul (p. 23). He declares that by creditable estimate Christianity lost one half of its following to Marcion and other Gnostic "heretics" bent on tearing it away from its Jewish associations and making it over in the true likeness of a Greek Mystery cult of individual spiritual realization. This was the movement which Mead has spoken of, due to the influx of Platonic and esoteric philosophies from Alexandria and Hellenic centers. It was an effort on the part of the more knowing ones to save Christianity from the debacle toward which it was fast heading through the corruption of the sound esoteric teaching. Almost every apologist for Christianity has hailed the defeat of the Hellenic philosophy's incursion into the early theology of the Church as the triumph of the faith and the salvation of Christianity. A fuller treatment of this chapter of Christian history is reserved for other connections in the study. It must suffice for the moment to say here that if by the repulse of Greek philosophy the Church gained the ignorant masses of the people, it not only failed to help their unintelligence, but further it lost its own power to bring spiritual light and rational nourishment to the more illumined of mankind.

It may be that there is an exoteric rendering of spiritual allegory that would purvey true meaning to the lower brackets in the intellectual scale. The supposition prevails that the truths of life can be made simple, for the simple. It has rarely worked out that way. In all historic cases where the esoteric rendition has been lost and the exoteric substituted, the popular conceptions of the profounder purport have become, not truth simplified, but truth distorted into untruth. There perhaps could and should be the milk for babes as well as the meat for stronger digestion. But, as it has worked out in actuality in the course of history, the exoteric milk, once it is dispensed among the populace, always tends to become churned into a little-nourishing cheese. Instead of instructing the simpler minds in simpler aspects of the truth, it ends by plunging them into myriad forms of outright error. In the historical sequel, it is sadly to be said, it has been proven that esotericism has carried the true meaning and exotericism only a false caricature. The exoteric doctrine has ever mistaught the popular mind. So Massey says: "An exoteric rendering has taken place of the esoteric representation, which contained the only true interpretation." And he gives the reason: wisdom designed for the enlightenment of the inner spiritual consciousness of evolved men "was converted into history" for the secular mind and "all turned topsy-turvy by changing" the soul of all humanity into one mortal man.

"In this way the noble, full, flowing river of old Egypt's wisdom ended in a quagmire of prophecies for the Jews and a dried-up wilderness of desert sands for the Christians. And on these shifting sands the 'historic' Christians reared their temple of the eternal which is giving way at last because it was not founded on the solid rock, and because no amount of blood would ever suffice to solidify the sand or form a concrete foundation or even a buttress for the crumbling building."

The Gospel of the Christians, he expounds, began with a collection of Sayings of Jesus, "fatuously supposed to have been an historic teacher of that name." It originated, he implies, as a set of moral apothegms, but ended as believed history. Even the Jerusalem, which was a name to denote the heavenly Paradise of spiritual bliss, or the Jerusalem above, became in ignorant minds the Jerusalem on the map! And the Exodus of the children of Israel from this mundane sphere in a passage across the Reed Sea of this mortal life to the home of celestial glory, became the screaming farce of 2,125,000 marching men, women, children and camp followers, parading about for forty years over Sinai's and Arabia's desert sands, trailing millions of sheep, oxen, and cattle, subsisting in an arid land with little vegetation and water! Verily "history" must be strained to fairy-tale credulity, when it has to stretch its possibilities to accommodate the free sweep of imaginative typology. Massey concludes one sentence with the clause – "in an Exodus from Egypt which can no longer be considered historical," an Exodus that he says elsewhere "was never more than frankly allegorical." That Massey is not merely indulging in iconoclastic swashbuckling, it is to be noted that whatever pretense the Exodus from Egypt had to being considered as history has been demolished at one blow by Moffatt's proper translation of the Red Sea as the "Reed Sea," a term used by the Egyptians to denote the human body, which is seven-eighths water, and must be crossed by the evolving soul to reach the Promised Land. When it is seen that the Exodus of the Old Testament is finally identical with the Resurrection in the New, it can be granted that the literal rendering of the Israelites' journey from Egypt's bondage to Canaan's milk and honey becomes excellent material for light comedy. But light comedy comes close to turning into heavy tragedy when it is further realized that the soul's dramatized bondage to the flesh in the "Egypt" of the body, has likewise been construed into the "historical captivities" of the Jews in Assyria, Babylon and Nineveh!

Incidentally it may be interjected that according to the evidence so far collected in Massey's day (at least to 1900), there has never been found on the monuments of Egypt any mention or record of the Israelites' sojourn in Egypt, or their having played a part in Egyptian history save in one case. Petrie discovered on a stele erected by King Merenptah II a reference to "the people of Ysiraal." "But," says Massey, "there is nothing whatever in the inscription of King Merenptah corresponding to a corroborative of the Biblical story of the Israelites in the land of Egypt on their exodus into the land of Canaan." The inscription found by Petrie says that the people of Ysiraal in Syria were cut up root and branch by Merenptah. Massey insists that "Israel in Syria was not Israel in Egypt." Israel in Egypt was not an ethnical entity, but the spiritual "children of Ra" in the "lower Egypt of Amenta, which is entirely mythical." Mythical, yes; but typical of the real home of living mortals in this "lower Egypt of Amenta" that is the dramatic ritual name for a planet called Earth, – a fact, it must be confessed which even Massey did not discern. Herodotus, affirms Kenealy, makes no mention of the Israelites – nor of Solomon.

The Book of Revelation, Massey contends, is the drama of the astrological mysteries and has been mistaken for human history; and the mythical aeonial cataclysm at the end of the cycle has been misread into the catastrophic "end of the world." Revelation, he goes on, has been commonly assumed to constitute a historic link between the Old Testament and the New.

"It has been taken as a supplement to the Gospels, as if the history of Jesus had been continued into the wedded life after the marriage of the Bride and the Lamb, and that they dwelt together ever after in that New Jerusalem which 'came down out of heaven' 'as a bride adorned for her husband,' when the tabernacle of God which was to dwell with man took the place of the Old Jerusalem that was destroyed by the Romans. The present contention is that the book is and always has been inexplicable because it was based upon the symbolism of the Egyptian astronomical mythology without the Gnosis or 'the meaning which hath wisdom' that is absolutely necessary for an explanation of the subject-matter; and because the debris of the ancient wisdom has been turned to account as data for pre-Christian prophecy that was supposed to have had its fulfilment in Christian history."

Besides being the parent of a mass of false religious "history," mythicism evidently has been the father of endless ecclesiastical folly. One aspect of this folly has been the misinterpretation of Revelation as aspects of world history, when, as Massey says, "the book as it stands has no intrinsic value and very little meaning until the fragments of ancient lore have been collated, correlated and compared with the original mythos and eschatology of Egypt."

Revelation has been found to be cognate with the Enoch manuscripts and, says Massey,

"Enoch, like John, was in the spirit. His internal sight was opened and he beheld a vision which was in the heavens. But his vision was admittedly astronomical. In it he 'beheld the secrets of the heavens and of paradise according to its divisions' (Ch. 41). The record of his vision is called 'the book of the revolutions of the luminaries of heaven,' and is said to contain 'the entire account of the world forever, until a new work shall have been effected, which will be eternal'" (Ch. 71).

Much more material of the sort shows Enoch to have been the source of Revelation and the contents of both books to be astronomical allegory. Why scholars have been so slow to see the intimate relation between Revelation and its obvious prototype, the Enoch, is another of the riddles of ecclesiastical history which cry aloud for solution.

It was no less a Christian celebrity than Albertus Magnus of the Medieval Church who uttered the following, relative to a connection between Christianity and astrology:

"The Mysteries of the Incarnation, from the Conception on to the Ascension into heaven, are shown us on the face of the sky and are signified by the stars."

The sole fulfillment of prophecy, according to Massey, was astronomical, in the lunar and stellar cycles, marking the stages of cosmic evolution. The basis of Massey's conclusions is well laid if his contention is true – and he presents massive evidence for it – that all that went into the making of the Christian historical set-up was long pre-extant as something quite other than history, was in fact expressly non-historical, in the Egyptian mythology and eschatology. For when the sun at the Easter equinox entered the sign of the Fishes, about 255 B.C., the Jesus who stands as the founder of the so-called Christianity was at least ten thousand years of age, and had been traveling hither as the Ever Coming One through all this preceding time. During that vast period the young Fulfiller had been periodically mothered by the Virgin (of the zodiac!), with Seb (equated by many symbolic indication with Joseph) for his reputed foster-father, and with Anup, the Egyptian baptizer (equated likewise with John) as his herald and precursor in the wilderness. All that time he had fought the battle with Satan in the desert or on the mount during forty days and nights each year. During those ten thousand years that same incarnation of the divine ideal, in the character of Iusa, the Coming Son, had saturated the mind of Egypt with its exalting influence. Little did the men of that epoch dream that their ideal figure of man's divinity would in time be rendered historical as a man of flesh and be hailed as the fulfiller of astronomical prophecy.

If more evidence be needed to show that the origin of the data of the Christ's "life" was in the astronomical mythos, it is at hand in the historical datum that there was in the early Church a diversity of opinion among the Christian Fathers as to whether their Christ was born in the winter solstice or in the vernal equinox. According to Clement of Alexandria the twenty-fifth of March was held by the Christian following to have been the natal day of the Lord from heaven. Others maintained that this was the day of the incarnation. But in Rome the festival of Lady's Day was celebrated on the twenty-fifth of March, in commemoration of the miraculous conception in the womb of the virgin, who gave birth to the divine child at Christmas, nine months afterwards. According to the Gospel of James, or the Protevangelium, the birth was in the equinox and consequently not at Christmas. It is as clear as any fact can be that this uncertainty as to the birth-date of the Christos and the argument as to whether it occurred at the solstice or the equinox imply indubitably that the birth itself was not being considered as transpiring historically, or as an event, but as an item of astronomical symbolism. The very fact that it was placed on such a cardinal point in the year as the solstice, or the equinox, is practically decisive on this point. Indubitably the birthday of the Messiah was hardly ever thought of as a date, but rather always as a point of significance. This was so true in the ancient days that almost it could be said that it was the date that was the significant thing rather than the event allegedly transpiring on it. If the birth of Jesus at Bethlehem had been regarded as purely historical, the only point at issue would have been simply: on what day of the year did it occur? Why was it held that the blessed event necessarily had to occur at the most pivotal point in the solar allegory? Of course the only true answer to all this is that all ancient religion was clothed in the solar myth. No denial of this general fact can stand. On the basis of this datum, so well known to comparative religion students, so little known to the hypnotized occupants of church pews, how can it be denied that in the minds of all people of intelligence in antiquity the fulfillment of sacred "prophecy" was to come in the cloak and guise of astronomical periodicity, and not as once-upon-a-time or once-for-all history? Not only, avers Massey, did the later scribes follow the scheme and ground-plan of Egyptian solar mythicism, but they seem actually to have gone so far as to copy the earlier scriptures.

Khebt, the birthplace of the child in "lower Egypt," and Mitzraim, Egypt, are names of the old Sabaean birthplace in the north belonging to the celestial allegory, and were later applied geographically to Egypt the country. The Egypt of the Hebrew writings is a "country" in the astronomical myth, the "land" of mental bondage, bordered by a "Red Sea" that was never on any map save that ancient uranograph or chart of the heavens picturing the details of the soul or solar myth under astrological signatures. Khebt, Mitzraim, Egypt are names of that lower house of nature where the soul descends to have its incubation and death until the course of growth is finished. At the end of the cycle of mundane experience it hears its Father's voice exclaiming: "Out of Egypt have I called my son." The Exodus out of Egypt, under that or another name, "is the common property of all mythology," says Massey.

Another most important elucidation from his pen is the following (Book of the Beginnings, I, p. 186):

"The earliest nomes of Egypt were astronomes, the divisions of the stars, whence came the name of astronomy; not merely a naming but a noming of the stars into groups, divisions and nomes. . . . Enough at present to affirm that the earliest chart was celestial and that its divisions and names were afterwards geographically adopted in many lands from one common Egyptian original."

Lest this critically vital pronouncement on the science of ancient astrography fail to receive its due consideration in the counsels of modern studentship, it should be added for greater explicitness here that the divisions, localities, features, together with their names, found in all ancient religiography were taken directly in the first instance from the early allegorical charts of the starry heavens and scattered over the maps and insinuated into the histories of all ancient civilized lands. (Perhaps the work most clearly demonstrating this procedure and its startling results is Godfrey Higgins' grand old tome, The Anacalypsis, to which reference should be had for fuller evidence.) He who would interpret the sage scriptures must begin with the uranograph, where consummate wisdom – not childish fancy – first wrote the allegory of man's true history. It is a fact of stupendous significance for those who can see what the ancient books are teaching that in the primitive books of early Egypt Hermes instructs Taht in the nature of the "tabernacle of the zodiacal circle."

Massey can at least cite the Gnostic wing of early Christianity as supporting his conclusions in this field. He writes:

"The Gnostics asserted truly that celestial persons and scenes had been transferred to earth in the gospel and that it is only within the pleroma or the zodiac that we can identify the originals of both." (The Natural Genesis, II, 422.)

This does not need to rest on his bare assertion. Christianity's own historian, Irenaeus, Bishop of Lyons in the second century, corroborates it: "The Gnostics truly declared that all the supernatural transactions asserted in the Gospels 'were counterparts (or representations) of what took place above.'" (Irenaeus, Book I, Ch. VII, p. 2.)

Further Christian testimony along the same line comes from that other early historian of the cult, Eusebius, whose statements are often important, however (as universally recognized and admitted) twisted and unreliable they generally are (Eusebius, b. ii, C. XVII). On this history Massey bases the statement that "it is admitted by Eusebius that the canonical Christian gospels and epistles were the ancient writings of the Essenes or Therapeutae reproduced in the name of Jesus." Eusebius did not admit things he should have admitted, and he certainly was the last historian to admit anything hostile to the Christian movement. If he has admitted this point it was because he could not avoid it. It must therefore be true. And if true, there are no words at immediate command to acclaim the significance of this amazing admission. It concedes the whole truth of Massey's great volumes, and virtually does the same for the contentions of the present work. The Gospels and Epistles of the New Testament were ancient books of the Essenes! Eusebius was merely testifying to what nearly all men of intelligence in his age knew to be the truth, that the Gospels, Epistles and Apocrypha were just portions of the mass of arcane esoteric wisdom transmitted, for centuries orally in the Mysteries, and later in written form, from remote antiquity to their age. One can envision the different, and happier, course that medieval and modern Occidental history might have taken had this admission of the Christian historian not been hidden out of sight for long centuries. The ghost of those dead centuries might justifiably come forth and demand to know why this admission was buried. And the living voice of the present generation, torn with a titanic strife that has grown out of ideologies that were warped by the lack of fundamental truth in traditional religions, might with ample justice rise to demand why the admission is not proclaimed anew at this juncture.

That the Sermon on the Mount is a derivative from ancient arcane religions is seen in the light of the fact that the Seventh Book of Hermes is entitled: "His Secret Sermon in the Mount of Regeneration and the Profession of Silence." The Hermetic books are of great antiquity, perhaps the oldest in the world. Isaac Myer, the Kabalist scholar, so declared them.

Surely the witness of such a high Patristic as Clement of Alexandria is worthy of credence. He says that all who have treated of divine matters have always hid the principle of things and delivered the truth enigmatically by signs and symbols and allegories and metaphors, "yet this foundation of primitive fable has been converted into our basis of fact." We have already noted Diodorus' statement that the Egyptians regarded the Greeks as impostors because they reissued the ancient mythology as their own history.

Justin Martyr, second century Church Father, dashes the foundation stones from under many an arrant Christian claim when he tells the Romans that by "declaring the Logos, the first begotten Lord, our master Jesus Christ, to be born of a virgin mother, without any human mixture, and to be crucified and dead, and to have risen again and ascended into heaven, we say no more than what you say of those whom you style the sons of Jove."

This was written at the early date of the second century, when the new cult found it desirable to emphasize its kinship with paganism, which it did especially through the words of this same Justin Martyr. But only two centuries later the members of this new faith could afford to flout the pagan mythological foundations and brazenly proclaim the uniqueness of their doctrines and rituals.

Zeal to transform allegory into history was not daunted even by the incredible difficulties of changing mythical personages into real human figures. Thus Sut-Typhon, or Sevekh, the crocodile-headed divinity, type of the power of nature buried in the atom, the energies of life submerged in water, the symbol of matter, was converted into Satan, the personal devil. In this line hardly anything could be more revelatory of modern mental ineptitude in the face of the myths than the assertions of such a learned scholar as the Egyptologist, Budge, who after reciting the details of the "life" of the Egyptian Father-God Osiris, that he suffered death and mutilation at the hands of his enemies, that the fourteen cut portions of his body were scattered about and buried over the land of Egypt, that his sister-wife Isis sought him sorrowing and at length found him, that she fanned him with her wings and gave him air, that she raised up his reconstituted body whole and living, united anew with him and brought forth his son Horus, and that Osiris then became God and King of the underworld, – Budge asks us to take this as the literal history of a man on earth! He says that his body was probably buried in the tomb at Abydos. An endless amount of similar fabulous material we have been asked to take as factual history. Is it to be wondered at that the counsels of sanity in a world dominated by such delusions now and again plunge the nations into a vast general wreckage?

Josephus argues that he is under the necessity, when recounting one of the Mosaic "miracles," of "relating this history as it is described in the sacred books," i.e., allegorically, or in the style in which it was given in the writings which were considered divine because they did not relate to human events.

Drews, one of the writers who in the nineteenth century worked at the mythical interpretation of the Gospels, corroborates Massey's identification of Joseph with the Egyptian earth-god Seb, as the foster-father of the divine child:

"Joseph . . . was originally a god, and in reality the whole of the family and home life of the Messiah Jesus took place among the gods. It was only reduced to that of a human being in lowly circumstances by the fact that Paul described the descent of the Messiah upon earth as an assumption of poverty and a relinquishment of his heavenly splendor. Hence when the myth was turned into history, Christ was transformed into a poor man in the economic sense of the word, while Joseph, the divine artificer and father of the sun, became an ordinary carpenter."

In his famous Life of Jesus (1835, Vol. II, Sec. 48) D. F. Strauss states that in the ancient Church the most reflective among the Fathers considered that the celestial Voice of the Old Testament was not like an ordinary voice, produced by vibrations of the air and apparent to the organs of sense, but an internal impression which God produced in those with whom he designed to communicate; and it is in this way that Origen and Theodore of Mopsuete have maintained previously that the apparition at the time of the baptism of Jesus was a vision and not a natural reality. Simple people, says Origen, take lightly the great cosmic processes described in the book; but those who think more profoundly believe that in their dreams they have had evidence by their corporeal senses "when it has simply been a movement of their minds." Had the discriminating practical wisdom evidenced by Origen here been generally exercised throughout the run of the centuries by the simple and the wise alike, the annals of religion would not have contained the record of hallucination and fanatical credulity which they hold.

Drews and Graetz alike regard Josephus' mention of John the Baptist as "a shameless interpolation."

Is it an inconsequential thing that J. M. Robertson (Christianity and Mythology, p. 82 ff.) can write the following?

"That Joshua is a purely mythical personage was long ago decided by the historical criticism of the school of Colenso and Kuenen; that he was originally a solar deity can be established at least as satisfactorily as the solar character of Moses, if not as that of Samson."

He notes that in the Semitic tradition, wherein is preserved a variety of myths, which the Bible-makers, for obvious reasons, suppressed or transformed, Joshua is the son of the mythical Miriam, that is, he was probably an ancient Palestinian Sun-God. Dupuis (L'Origine de Tous les Cultes) places John the Baptist among purely mythical personages and in harmony with many other writers identifies his name with that of Oannes, the Babylonian fish-avatar of Berosus' account, the Ea (Hea) of the more ancient Sumerians.

In his effort to refute the mythical interpretation T. J. Thorburn shows glaringly the bewilderment of scholars anent this theme when he affirms (p. 320) that in the case of the nature-cults the spring revival of the god is simply typical of the annual resurrection of life in nature. This is putting the cart before the horse surely. He goes on to prove the infinite "superiority" and greater "nobility" of Christianity over the pagan mythological idea by saying that in the Christian resurrection (as given by St. Paul in I Corinthians, 15) both Jesus himself and with him all believers rise to a new and more glorious life, in which a "spiritual body" replaces the material or "natural body." The death and revival of the cult-god is an annual matter; Jesus and the Christian die and are raised from the dead "once for all." How great the obtuseness which prevented the scholars from seeing that the pagan typism did not end with the sprouting grain and budding leaf of spring, but from that as type proceeded to the very thing that is claimed to have been the sole possession of Christianity! It is not easy to picture sixteen centuries of the best acumen of the western world floundering over the simple matter of recognizing that the ancient pagans set their cycle of religious expression to the time and tune of nature's solar hymn, as at once the most luminous and moving suggestion of the cyclical advance of man's divinity. Unless we deny to men of the stature of Plato any sagacity beyond childishness, it is naturally assumable that they did not, as Thorburn thinks, lose the spiritual reality in the natural typism. The solar myth was not to celebrate the sprouting of the corn; the sprouting of the grain was called upon to help the mind frame a more realistic conception of the resurrection of the divine seed that had been, like the grain, buried in the earth of flesh and sense. The sages used nature to vivify spiritual processes. As most poets have done, they worshipped spirit through its reflection in nature. They saw that an approach to a lively apprehension of the deeper aspects of truth was vastly facilitated and enhanced by the contemplation of their counterpart in the physical world. How false to charge that the pagan world had only the physical fact and could not go beyond it! The evidence is mountainous in bulk that pagan eyes pierced through the phenomena of nature to the truth of higher levels. Pagan spiritual discernment was all the keener for its close beholding of the natural world. The assumption that in his primitive infantilism the pagan stopped at nature, while the Christian went on to God, is a rank heresy. It is defied by all the fact of antiquity. Rebuttal of this gratuitous depreciation of past civilization is firmly based upon the early production of scriptures of the most exalted wisdom. The authors of these high revelations knew the realm of sublimer truth that lay beyond nature, and they also knew the mighty fact that nature was the outer visible analogue of this other world of truth. Then as now, esoteric genius grasped the distinction between outer and inner, but ancient sapiency recognized better than modern the essential kinship of the two.

An interesting sidelight is cast on our discussion by G. R. S. Mead, already quoted, who in his Fragments of a Faith Forgotten (Gnosticism), says:

"With much sincerity our Gnostics found these numbers and processes in the prologue to Genesis and elsewhere in the Old Covenant Library; . . . But when we find that they treated the Gospel-legends also not as history but as allegory, and not only as allegory but as symbolical of the drama of initiation, the matter becomes of deep interest" to the student of religion.

In his The Story of Chaldea Zenaïde A. Ragozin says that the tenth chapter of Genesis is the oldest and most important document in existence concerning the origins of races and nations, but in order properly to understand it and appreciate its value and bearing, "it must not be forgotten that each name in the list is that of a race, a people or a tribe, not that of a man."

To substantiate his statement on this point Ragozin cites the authority of "many scientists and churchmen" and quotes no less a Church Father than St. Augustine, who pointedly says that the names in the tenth chapter of Genesis represent "nations not men." (De Civitate Dei, XVII, 3.) So again we find racial entities or groups made to masquerade exoterically as "men."

Much data from various sources go to prove that the New Testament – as now known – was compiled from esoteric texts, which were themselves covered by a thick film of allegory and even veiled behind misleading "blinds," the "dark sayings" of fiction and parable. It is unthinkable, impossible that any merely human brain could have concocted the alleged "life" of the Jewish Jesus, culminating in the awful tragedy of Calvary. How, then, came this "life" to be written? Esoteric comprehension answers that it came from the ignorant literalization of the story of the Christ-Aeon of the Gnostic and Essene books, and from the writings of the ancient Tanaim, who connected the kabalistic Jesus or Joshua with the Biblical personifications. The Gnostic records contained the epitome of the chief scenes enacted during the Mysteries of Initiation, from most remote times; although even that was given out invariably under the garb of semi-allegory whenever put on paper. The ancient Tanaim, sage authors of the Kabalah (in its oral tradition) who handed on their wisdom to the later Talmudists, possessed the secrets of the Mystery language; and it is in this language, as has been said earlier, that the Gospels were written. It is possible for us to see, then, what it was that the ignorant literalizers of such material turned into "history."

A fair parallel of the turning of the Christos into "Christ" is seen in the cycle of stories centering about the mythical hero Siegfried. The myths developed as popular tradition, their mythological significance was forgotten and in course of time historical personages were identified with the characters. (See The Perfect Way, Kingsford and Maitland.)

Massey emphasizes the significant fact that there is found no "fall of man" in mythology. The devastating conception, as popularly misunderstood, came in only through the misreading of religious allegory and dramatization. Theologians from the first were bitterly opposed to its antithesis, the ascent of man through evolution. The scientific view of man's ascent clashed with their lugubrious obsession. They clung to the heavy weapon of the "fall" in the sense of sheer "sin" and not understood as the natural, normal, necessary and wholly salutary descent of soul into matter and body, because it gave them a useful psychological cudgel over the laity. From the distorted application of what should have been clear in the myth was hatched that brood of morbid doctrines such as the fall of man into carnal sin, man's whimsical thwarting of God's plan, the depravity of both man and matter, the filthy nature of the flesh, the glorification of asceticism and bodily mortification, original sin, the corruption of natural man, the evil of the world, and others whose only basis of existence at all was the stupid perversion of ancient typology and the literalization of Genesis. And Massey flings the irony of his pen at the fact that "such literalization of mythology is continued to be taught as God's truth to the men and women of the future in their ignorant and confiding childhood." Higgins (Anacalypsis, 514) likewise expostulates against the asinine failure to distinguish between "the real and the fabulous." "It is allowed that Cristna is the sun, and yet they talk of him as a man." He directly charges that "It is evidently almost the only employment of the idle priests to convert their historical account into a riddle and again to give their doctrines and riddles the appearance of history." The temptation to give in full his indignant accusation on this score in his own words is difficult to resist:

"And the reason why all our learned men have totally failed in their endeavors to discover the meaning of the ancient mythologies is to be found in their obstinate perseverance in attempting to construe all the mythoses, meant for enigma, to the very letter. I have no doubt that anciently every kind of ingenuity which can be imagined was exerted from time to time to invent and compose new riddles, till all history became in fact a great enigma. In modern times as much ingenuity has been exercised to conceal the enigma and by explanation to show that it was meant for reality. . . . Before the time of Herodotus every ancient history is a mythical performance, in short, a gospel – a work written to enforce virtue and morality and to conceal the mythos – and every temple had one. The Iliad and Odyssey, the plays of Aeschylus, the Cyropaedia, the Aeneid, the early history of Rome, the Sagas of Scandinavia, the Sophis of Abraham, the secret Book of the Athenians, the Delphic verses of Olen, the 20,000 verses repeated by heart to the Druids, the Vedah or Bedahs."

What has not been understood in the declaration that Cristna is the sun, is that he is not venerated as the sun in the heavens, but as the sun or divine spark in man. It can at last be said positively that the ancients did not worship the sun in itself, but as the analogical cosmic counterpart in the solar system of the central divine fire in the human heart.

In a printed lecture entitled Gnostic and Historic Christianity, Massey makes the positive statement that the early Christians did convert esoteric material into history:

"The claim of Christianity to possess divine authority rests on the ignorant belief that the mystical Christ could and did become a Person, whereas the Gnosis proves the corporeal Christ to be only a counterfeit presentment of the trans-corporeal man; consequently a historical portraiture is and ever must be a fatal mode of falsifying and discrediting the Spiritual Reality."

The last lines of this excerpt carry the burden and gist of the effort here made to assert the psychological and spiritual disservice of the "historical Christ." Massey goes on to enlarge upon the theme and says that Paul chides the "foolish Galatians" for beginning by believing in the spiritual Christos and ending by believing in the Jesus of the flesh; and Massey declares that Paul was himself a Gnostic, the founder of a new sect of Gnosis which recognized only a "Christ-spirit" for the divine Avatar. One must go to the Gnostic writings to discover the pristine teachings of the Jesus in the Mysteries. The literal falsifiers dragged the spiritual divinity of man into matter and the dust. And to cover their fatal work they burned – among other books – the twenty-four volumes of the Gnostic Basilides, by order of the Church. Clement described Basilides as "the philosopher devoted to the contemplation of divine things." The books burned were his works on the

Interpretations of the Gospels, and they would be of priceless value to the world today.

Indications that the scriptures of the Old and New Testament must be something far other than historical record are found in the startling pronouncement made by the Alexandrian Clement (Stromateis, XVII):

"The Scriptures having perished in the captivity of Nabuchodonozar, Esdras the Levite, priest in the times of Artaxerxes, King of the Persians, having become inspired in the exercise of prophecy, restored again the whole of the ancient Scriptures."

As this very claim has been made with Ezra as the inspired prophet instead of Esdras, there is at least the suggested possibility that Ezra and Esdras are two variants of the same name, which could even be the "Isra-" of "Israel" with the divine "el" dropped. In the religious myth it was of course Israel that was to restore the lost substance of the divine revelation! However that may be, if the whole body of scripture that covered the antiquity of the human family and all the particulars of the "race" "chosen" by God to exemplify his dealings with all humanity was lost, and what purports to be that scripture is in fact only the inner vision of a man divinely inspired, the most that can be said for it is that it is a very precarious foundation on which to base the moral and spiritual guidance of the human race.

What meager chance the scriptures ever had of being taken for history must be seen to be reduced to a vanishing minimum when we consider the words of the Egyptian God, Tem or Atum.

"I am Tem," he says, "the dweller in his Disk, or Re in his rising in the eastern horizon of the sky. I am Yesterday; I know Today. I am the Bennu which is in Anu (Heliopolis) and I keep the register of the things which are created and of those which are not yet in existence."

The recording of events that have not yet occurred is a proposal to make the modern scholar run from ghosts. It ought to be a consideration of sufficient force to open the obdurate minds of the deniers of the mythical structure of ancient scriptures to note that in those scriptures much of "history" recorded is still in the womb of time and yet unborn. This portion at any rate is not the record of that which has happened. The answer to this will of course be that it is the record of that which will, objectively happen. As to that, it may be interjected in passing, there is very substantial doubt. One of the largest blind-spots before the eyes of orthodox interpreters of scripture has ever been their fatuous belief in the literalness of so-called Bible prophecy. There is not room for a dissertation upon it here, but only enough space to say bluntly that, in the usual sense of forecast of future objective events, there is not and never was any historical prophecy in the Old Testament or the New. There is some delineation by the seers and sages of the general phases and aspects of later evolution of humanity in the cycle on earth; there is no specific foretelling of coming events on the plane of world history. Evolutionary typism and allegorical scenarios of the shape of things to come can without much difficulty often be made to look like historical description. Events do often match the frame of dramatism in which they are set. Deluded by these appearances, thousands of religious votaries have spilled rivers of printers' ink in the tracing of the configuration of events in their time back to Bible "prophecy." Philological scholarship should have corrected this dupery long ago by announcing the correct meaning of the words "prophecy" and "prophet." From the Greek pro-, "forth" or "out," and phemi, "to speak," the prophet is simply a preacher, one who speaks out the truth, proclaims, gives forth. There is nothing in the word which has any reference to the forecasting of the future. A prophet is simply a preacher, utterer of truth. To this can be added the startling statement that the passages in the Bible which have always been taken for objective prophecies are, like most other material in the scriptures, allegorical visions or poetical depictions of the cyclical processes. This fact should add impressiveness to the strong position here taken that an unbelievable quantity of literal rubbish has to be cleared out of the way before a sane approach to scriptural interpretation can even begin to be made.

There is much support for the fact that the supposed simple origin of the name "Christians," its adoption by a sect that sprang up in the wake of the life of the Galilean preacher called the Christ, is by no means the truth of the matter at all. A passage from Mead's work, Did Jesus Live 100 Years B.C.? (p. 325) tells us a far different story, and indicates we are dealing with something other than history in these things:

"The followers of Jesus had apparently hitherto been 'ashamed' of being called 'Christiani.' . . . It is highly possible that the name Christiani was first used by the Pagans to signify Messianists of all kinds, and was only finally adopted by the followers of Jesus in their public dealings with the Pagans, presumably first in apologetic literature, where we find it is of frequent occurrence from about the second quarter of the second century."

There is scarcely a single common or general belief about the chief items of the Christian faith that may be called orthodox which, on deeper scholastic inquiry, does not turn out to be a popular falsification of something utterly different in its pristine form.

Prof. J. H. Rose is driven to admit (Folk-Lore, Vol. XLVI, 22) that "we have not yet an agreed and perfected technique" for distinguishing history from sagas. No wonder this is so, comments Lord Raglan (The Hero, 61), since there is but one way to mark the difference, and that is by checking alleged history with facts known from other sources. When this is done the sagas break down utterly – as history.

Another scholar, Prof. Nilsson, complains of that utter disregard for history and geography which is peculiar to epic poetry. But, says Raglan, history was not their concern, and geography was an inconsequential side issue. And Prof. Hooke (Myth and Ritual, 6) says that both the Minotaur and Perseus myths pictorialize human sacrifice and are a product of myth and ritual united. Raglan himself states that the true study of Homer has hardly yet begun and will not get us anywhere until students see that the poems have no historical foundation, but are to be taken as documents picturing the evolution of religious ideas, in which sense they become highly important. Again he says that all the difficulties of interpretation disappear when it is realized that these great works are ritual narratives. He asserts that all the main incidents in the Trojan cycle take place in the first and tenth years of the siege and that in the mythological cycles, especially those of Troy and Thebes, all the main events are represented as taking place at intervals of about ten years. There are many resemblances: both cities were built where a cow lay down; both were unsuccessfully attacked, but ten years later stormed and razed to the ground; Hector is a leading hero of both cities. Nearly every state desired to be founded by refugees from Troy or Thebes. There was a Troy in Egypt built by Semiramis (Asiatic Researches, Vol. III, 454), according to Higgins. Trojan refugees are found in Epirus, Threspotia, Cyprus, Crete, Venice, Rome, Daunia, Calabria, Sicily, Lisbon, Asturia, Pamphylia, Arabia, Macedonia, Holland, Auvergne, Paris, Sardinia, Alicia, Scotland, Wales, Cornwall, Libya. The Trojan story was a myth, a sacred history, and became a vast conglomeration of fable and truth.

The origin of the ten-year period so frequently occurring in all these recitals is no doubt the fabulous legend that the Titans fought with the gods for ten years. The Titans represent of course the elementary forces of nature, and the gods stand for the intellectual and spiritual powers. Every traditional myth sought to depict the aspects of this universal conflict.

In Quest magazine of April 1912 a Dr. Anderson writes:

"The critic . . . will proceed to prove that the stories of the trial, arrest and crucifixion are quite understandable as scenes in a mystery play, but are quite inexplicable as facts of history. The trial is represented as lasting through one night when, as Renan points out, an Eastern city is wrapped in silence and darkness, quite natural as scenes in a mystery-play, but not as actual history."

It represents at least some, and possibly great, difficulty to reconcile the fact that Jesus was a Jew with the other fact that the Gospels dealing with him were written in Greek.

"A professional Egyptologist (Dictionary of the Bible, Smith, V. 3, p. 1018) has written respecting the passage of the Red Sea: 'It would be impious to attempt an explanation of what is manifestly miraculous.' To such a depth of degradation can Bibliolatry reduce the human mind! Such is the spirit in which the subject has been crawled over." (Massey: Book of the Beginnings, II, 176).

The reference to the Red Sea brings up one of the most direct and astounding proofs that Old Testament "history" is not history, and can by no possibility be held as such. This has been briefly hinted at, but needs further emphasis. If the partisans of the historical view of archaic literature insist that the Exodus narrative is history, their insistence places them in the most ridiculous of predicaments and in short makes simpletons of them. At the end of the debate they are left holding the bag, the gold brick vanished. For the Red Sea, whether that of the map or that of the myth, is no longer in the Bible! It is clean gone out of the story. The learned scholar, James Moffatt, of Glasgow University, has dropped it out of the correct translation, replacing it with the "Reed Sea," drawn direct from Egypt's mythicism! Assumably his reasons for this rendering, in view of the blasting consequences flowing from it, must have been quite decisive and certain. So if there was no Red Sea in the story, the Israelites could not have crossed it. With this change the whole story falls. Practically, with the deletion from the Old Testament of the historicity of the descent into Egypt and the Exodus from it, the entire structure of "history" in the Bible is shot to pieces. At last the proper mythical translation of one word tears the mask of stupid literalism off the face of ancient esoteric wisdom, and leaves a long deluded and hypnotized world rudely shaken out of intellectual stupor, and with eyes torn suddenly open from its dream, gaping in stunned bewilderment at the wreckage of its illusion. Of all "rude awakenings" this is perhaps the most shocking, but also the most salutary.

Likewise the physical "tabernacle" of the Old Testament, in and at the door of which the Eternal was wont to meet and confabulate with Moses, has vanished along with the Red Sea, and we find the mythical "trysting-tent" in its stead. Male soul and female body in the divine allegory meet and hold their tryst here in the flesh on earth. From it they go on to the marriage, out of which the Christos in man is born.

A word must be interposed here with regard to the bearing of the Jewish rejection of the Messianic Jesus on the debate. Since the wretched persecution of a whole race has gushed from the rejection, there is no lack of warrant for giving the matter full treatment. The work here undertaken is in the large the treatment; but a few conclusions of Massey on the subject can be advanced here with benefit. In his great work, Ancient Egypt, The Light of the World (p. 519) he speaks with great candor. Referring to the Jews who in their popular trends came close to literalizing the scriptural allegories, he says:

"They pursued their messianic phantom to the verge of the quagmire, but drew back in time to escape. They left it for the Christians to take the final fatal plunge into the bog in which they have wallowed, always sinking, ever since; and if the Jews did but know it, the writings called Jewish have wrought an appalling avengement upon their ignorant persecutors, who are still proving themselves to be Christians . . . by igrominiously mutilating and piteously massacring the Jews."

Massey does not mean that the avengement of the Jewish scriptures on Christianity consists of the massacres, of course; he means that the adoption by Christianity of the body of Hebrew scriptures as their Old Testament has been the means of saddling on the back of Christianity the fatal incubus of a vast corpus of myth adopted because it was supposed to be history, and is now seen to be not that at all, but pagan mythology plucked from Egypt! There is no avengement equal to that of the irony of events. The logic of events is inexorable and merciless. Massey speaks in words momentous for the world today and for the time to come, when he writes:

"If the Jews had only held on to the sonship of Iu, the su or sif (the suffix su, sif, sef is Egyptian for son, heir, prince, and the name Jesus came from the combination of the divine Iu(Ju), the Christ, with su or sif, giving us the Egyptian Iusu, or Iusif, Jesus or Joseph) they might have spoiled the market for the spurious wares of the 'historic' Savior, and saved the world from wars innumerable, and from countless broken hearts and immeasurable mental misery. But they let go the sonship of a insert Hebrew (IE or JE) with the growth of their monolatry. They could not substitute the 'historic' sonship; they had lost touch with Egypt, and the wisdom that might have set them right was no longer available against the Christian misconstruction. They failed to fight the battle of the Gnostics and retired from the conflict dour and dumb; strong and firm enough to suffer the blind and brutal Juden-Hetze (baiting of Jews) of all these centuries, but powerless to bring forward their natural allies, the Egyptian reserves, and helpless to conclude a treaty or enforce a truce."

This was the catastrophe entailed for both Judaism and Christianity, as well as for the whole world, in the loss of Egypt's august contribution.

In the finale Massey pays this well-considered tribute to the refusal of Jewry to endorse the historization of mythology:

"And here the present writer would remark that, in his view, the Jewish rejection of Christianity constitutes one of the sanest and the bravest intellectual triumphs of all time. It is worth all that the race has suffered from the persecution of the Christian world."

If there is the providential rulership of the universe that misses not even the fall of a sparrow, it is to be assumed that adjustment of a wrong so flagrant and enormous as the slaughter over sixteen hundred years of a people who merely refused to go along with a doltish substitution of history for allegory, will in due time be made.

Another item of most vivid significance is brought out by Massey (B. O. B. II, 188). He discloses the fact that at a date in the reign of Tahtmes III, some two and a half centuries earlier than the "historical Exodus" – on the scholastic insistence that there was such an event – there were inscribed on a pylon at Thebes in a list of 1200 names of places conquered or garrisoned by the Egyptians, the original names of the towns and districts of Canaan to the number of 115, which, says Massey, is "nothing less than the synoptical table of the Promised Land made 250 years before the Exodus." This comes close to writing the geography and history of a nation before that history has taken place on the actual scene. As we shall find that the "life" of Jesus was in effect written before he "lived," so here we see the geography of a nation charted before the places became the locale of the events which gave their names fame in history. All this points to the whole catalogue of such charts and lists and maps as being allegorical depictions and systematic typographs covering a structure of meaning of the most esoteric and cryptic sort. The Canaanitish names mentioned in the list are Astaroth-Karnaim, Avilah, Berytus, Bashan, Beth-Sappuah or Tebekim, Ephron (Hebron), Hishbon, Hamath, Judah, Kadesh, Kison, Megiddo, Sameshu (Damascus) and others.

Among hundreds of passages to be culled out of early Patristic writing which throw doubt on the veracity of the historical side of Christianity we have a strange statement in Justin Martyr's Dialogue with Trypho: "In the dialogue we find Trypho saying, 'Ye follow an empty rumor and make a Christ for yourselves. . . . If he was born and lived somewhere, he is entirely unknown.'" A more straightforward report on the true situation in the second century, marked by the claims and denials of historians, is hardly to be had. It sounds as if the early Church Father, taking part in the original debate as to the historicity, argues on the side taken by the present work. It was as if he said: "The Christ of the Gospels is the mythical and ritualistic figure; if a historical Christ did live, you have no record of his existence." The entire present debate might be summarized in the same words. His sentences might well be made the concluding ones of our last page. He, too, might have said: "Ye have reduced the cosmic majesty of the Logos to the mean stature of a Galilean peasant."

Clement of Alexandria (Stromata VII, 7, 106) records the astounding fact that the doctrine of the Evangel was delivered to Basilides, the consecrated student of sacred things, by the Apostle Matthew and Glaucus, a disciple of Peter! And there is evidence that the Gospel then delivered must have differed widely from the present New Testament. Tertullian's distorted accounts of this deposit left to posterity are no faithful guide to a true evaluation of it. Yet even the little this partisan fanatic gives shows the chief Gnostic doctrines to be identical with the broader and deeper esoteric wisdom of the East.

And another proof of the claim that the Gospel of Matthew in the usual Greek texts is not the original Gospel written in Hebrew is found with no less an authority than St. Jerome (Hieronymus) for support. The suspicion of a conscious and gradual euhemerization of the Christ principle from the beginning grows into decided conviction as one reads a certain confession contained in Book II of the Comment of Matthew by Hieronymus. For we find in it the proof of a deliberate substitution of the whole Gospel, the one now in the canon having been evidently rewritten by the zealous Jerome. This is well authenticated as genuine history. How far the rewriting and editorial tampering with the primitive gnostic fragments which have now become the New Testament went, may be inferred from reading Supernatural Religion, which ran through some twenty-three editions. The authorities and documentary support cited by its author are overwhelming in quantity and impressiveness. Jerome says that he was sent toward the close of the fourth century by "their Felicities," the Bishops Chromatius and Heliodorus, to Caesarea with the mission to compare the Greek text (the only one they ever had) with the Hebrew original version preserved by the Nazarenes in their library and to translate it. He translated it, but under protest; for, as he says, the Evangel "exhibited matter not for edification, but for destruction." The destruction of what? – must be asked. Doubtless of the doctrine that Jesus the Nazarene and the Christos are one. Hence, for the "destruction" of the newly planned religion which separated the two. In this same letter the Saint – the same that advised his converts to kill their fathers and trample on the bosoms of their mothers if their parents stood between their sons and Christ – admits that Matthew did not wish his Gospel to be openly written, hence that the manuscript was a secret one. Yet while admitting also that this Gospel was "written in Hebrew characters and by the hand of himself (Matthew), in another place he contradicts this and assures posterity that as it was tampered with and rewritten by a disciple of Manichaeus named Seleucus . . . the ears of the Church properly refused to listen to it." (Hieronymus: Commentary to Matthew, Bk. II, Chap. XII, 13).

Gibbon, in a footnote on p. 432 of his great history, gives us material that ought to be granted consideration. He says:

"The modern critics are not disposed to believe what the Fathers almost unanimously assert, that St. Matthew composed a Hebrew Gospel, of which only the Greek translation is extant. It seems, however, dangerous to reject their testimony."

A volume of comment might be made on data of this sort, which could be enlarged to great proportions. There is at any rate enough of it in the Patristic and early sectarian and polemic literature of the Christian movement to provide a sufficient deterrent to the open dissemination of this body of Church history among the general laity. So extensive a policy of concealment, amounting practically to a conspiracy of silence, argues a case difficult to defend.

It may not be inappropriate to conclude this chapter with a reflection forced upon the mind of Gerald Massey toward the later years of a life given to a searching study of the origins of Christianity. It is a tribute of no mean impressiveness to the power of religious influences even when the true inner import of the ritual expressing them is unknown. Dilating upon the Egyptian Mystery ritual, he says:

"In this divine drama the natural realities are represented with no perniciously destructive attempt to conceal the characters under a mask of history. Majestically moving in their own might, of pathetic appeal to human sympathies, they are simply represented for what they may be worth when rightly apprehended. But so tremendous was this tragedy in the Osirian Mysteries, so heart-melting the legend of divinest pity that lived on with its rootage in Amenta and its flowerage in the human mind, that an historic travesty has kept the stage and held the tearful gaze of generation after generation for nineteen hundred years."

If the mere husk of religious truth has exerted so amazing an influence upon mortals, what might have been the transcendent exaltation of the mind and purgation of the life of the race if the golden corn itself had been preserved! But the corn was lost and the husk alone remained when the myths of truth were converted into the falsities of "history."

Chapter VI

CANONIZED ROMANTICISM

Doubtless, despite the evidence assembled, the blunt charge that so apparently impossible a transaction as the conversion of myth into history has really occurred will still remain incredible and unacceptable. The great cry will be raised as to how so amazing and stupendous a blunder could have occurred. With the universal presumption of so much honesty and integrity, and likewise high intelligence in a people divinely inspired as the devout early Christians are believed to have been, it becomes difficult for the general mind to comprehend how such flagrant error could have gained the day and consummated so gross a miscarriage. To what extent was the crime knowingly perpetrated? Was it motivated by sincerity working in ignorance, or by intelligence working in insincerity?

The answer to these queries is by no means simple or easy. It is involved in no end of difficulty arising mainly from the destruction of evidence and the biases and prejudices of the reviewers of what evidence is available. But if all the facts in the situation were truly known, it is pretty certain that the full solution would comprise a vast jumble and admixture of all the varying degrees of intelligence and ignorance, sincerity and insincerity, in one grand plot. Nearly all human and historical transactions are the resultant of a mixed group of forces actuated by every degree of intelligence and sincerity, or the want of them. It may perhaps be questioned whether any act or decision of people anywhere at any time is of downright deliberate insincerity. Some allegedly justifiable "reason" lurks behind or under every deed. People do evil things of deliberate intent, but they hardly do them with insincerity. Justification is found somewhere in the depth of feeling or thought. Generally it will be found that where apparent insincerity is operative, it is unintelligence that warps the action into evil direction. Granting inherent sincerity in human nature, its miscarriage into foul expression must be due to want of keen intelligence. This is indeed the conclusion arrived at in the finale by Plato and Socrates in their dialectical inquiry into the nature of the good. The basic and ultimate evil is nothing but – in one or other of its manifold forms – ignorance. So declared Buddha, Orpheus, Hermes, Solomon and other sage teachers of early man. It is assumed legitimate to accuse a person if he does badly when he should know better. The acme of all evil charge is that a person does wrong knowingly. If in the conversion of myth into history there was this commission of knavery in spite of better knowledge, the verdict must be rendered accordingly. Again, if the wreckage of the myth resulted from ignorance and misguided motives, the judgment must be more lenient, although there is no sentiment in nature and she punishes ignorance as well as knavery.

Our glance at the possibility of insincerity in the motive behind the alteration is actuated by no mere truculent attitude, but is warranted by a more substantial reason. Any history of early Christianity must face and deal with the perpetration of an extensive series of what are known among the historians as "pious frauds" by the Fathers and partisan leaders in the first centuries and the Church's connivance at them then and later. The charge is brought by many chroniclers of the period and confessed by most Christian apologists. The assembling of data substantiating it, while an invidious task, must be made in sufficient force to justify the introduction of it as a count in the case against the historicity of the Son of God. If the charge of fraudulent literary practice in the handling of religious data in the early day can be upheld, it strengthens by so much the likelihood that the transfer of meaning from the impersonal Christos to the man Jesus was made. The proof of fraud and deception greatly heightens the probability that the change occurred. If analysis of the whole situation extant at the time reveals that the transaction was of such a nature that knavery would be suspected of being a highly probable element in it, the discovery of such chicanery in the immediate wake of the suspicion certainly will tend to increase the validity of the non-historical claim. If, in point of fact, it would seem necessary to posit fraud as accessory to the great transformation in the character of the Christos, the disclosure of fraud in the actual situation amounts to strong prima facie evidence that the case was as suspected. It is surely to be agreed that the proven presence and practice of religious fraud in the first centuries of Christian history must be weighed realistically in relation to every development of the ecclesiastical polity then and after. A superficial view would not fail to conclude that there must be a close and perhaps immediate link between such a transaction as the personalizing of the Messiah and the prevalent impostures in the field of religion. If fraud is known to have been a strong feature of the picture, it becomes necessary to determine what part it played in the historization of the Jesus character. To many it is certain that the revelation of such an unknown and unsuspected element in the case will serve as an all-sufficient clue to the solution of the whole complication. It will be seized upon readily as the missing key to the entire mystery. While this may be according too much importance to the item, the presence of fraud is nearly always presumptive testimony to a sinister motive or maneuver.

To begin with, an initial suspicion and distrust is awakened in the mind of the student when he is confronted from the start with the presence and volume of documents, books, gospels and apocrypha bearing the prefix "Pseudo-" to their title. There is the "Pseudo-Mark," the "Pseudo-Acts," the "Pseudo-Dionysus" and others in bewildering profusion. Nothing less than plagiarism and forgery are at once suggested by this phenomenon. Then the field of early Christianity is cluttered up with works controverting alleged "heresies" on all sides. Indeed most of the works that stand as the chief contemporary histories of the first centuries of Christianity bear the title "Against Heresy." This is notably the case with the books of Eusebius, Tertullian, Irenaeus, Hippolytus and Epiphanius, a quintet of historians on whom the Church has relied mainly to buttress its egregious claims to unique authority and its defamations of the "pagan" religions. But it is time to gather the amazing data on this score.

It may be generous to present the most favorable aspect of the evidence first. A passage of this sort is found in Mead's Fragments of a Faith Forgotten (88):

"It must not be supposed, however, that the re-writers and editors of the old traditions were forgers and falsifiers in any ordinary sense of the word. Antiquity in general had no conception of literary morality in its modern meaning, and all writing of a religious character was the outcome of an inner impulse. . . . It should also be remembered that the mythologizing of history and the historizing of mythology were not peculiar to the Jews, but common to the times; what was peculiar to them was their fanatical belief in divine favoritism and their egregious claims to the monopoly of God's providence."

Mead's statement that antiquity did not possess our modern standards of literary morality adds strength to the general claim that the purpose of ancient writing was never strictly to record the facts of history, but rather to depict mystical realities and intellectual concepts. One is obviously privileged to use one's fancy when the truth of objective occurrence is not the theme, and the experience of the inner life is. It may alleviate to a degree the weight of obloquy that may seem to fall upon the perpetrators of so much literary crime to remember Mead's explanation of its religious background.

In The Hero Lord Raglan briefly states that pious frauds of this (and every other conceivable) type were a commonplace of medieval ecclesiasticism. And the medieval was but a prolongation of ancient practice.

In The Anacalypsis (522) Higgins, alleging that it was not uncommon for the priests to charge their opponents with absurd opinions they never held for the purpose of disgracing them, remarks that "this has always been considered by priests a mere allowable ruse in religious controversy. It is yet had recourse to every day."

In Anthon's Classical Dictionary (Fourth Ed. 929, Art. Oraculum) the text stands as follows:

"The only evil spirit which had an agency in the oracular responses of antiquity was that spirit of crafty imposture which finds so congenial a home among an artful and cunning priesthood."

From a source within the fold of orthodoxy itself comes a confession that is singularly and creditably frank. If all Christian authors and apologists had been as candid as von Mosheim, the faith of the Church would have presented a better defense than unfortunately can now be made. Speaking of the Gospel of Hermas in his celebrated history of the early Church (p. 91), he writes:

"At the time when he wrote it was an established maxim with many of the Christians that it was pardonable in an advocate for religion to avail himself of fraud and deception, if it were likely that they might conduce toward the attainment of any considerable good. Of the list of silly books and stories to which this erroneous notion gave rise, from the second to the fifteenth century, no one who is acquainted with Christian history can be ignorant."

He says again (288) that "it is with the greatest grief that we find ourselves compelled to acknowledge" that some of the weaker brethren, in their zeal to assist God with all their might, resorted to such dishonest artifices as could not admit of any just excuse and were utterly unworthy of that sacred cause which they were unquestionably designed to support. One of the illegitimate devices resorted to, he charges, was the measure of composing eight books of Sibylline verses, designed to play upon the general ancient reverence and credulity of the populace respecting the pagan oracles and their pronouncements, in order to win approval of the Christian claims. Some Christian, or perhaps an association of Christians, in the reign of Antoninus Pius, "composed" the books with a view to persuade the ignorant and unsuspecting that even so far back as the time of Noah a Sibyl had foretold the coming of Christ and the rise and progress of his Church. The trick succeeded, says Mosheim, with not a few, nay even some of the principal Christian teachers themselves were imposed upon by it. But it eventually brought great scandal on the Christian cause; since the fraud was "too palpable to escape the searching penetration of those who gloried in displaying their hostility to the Christian name."

Another group of zealots, he goes on, trafficking with the great name and authority of the Egyptian Hermes Trismegistus, concocted a work bearing the title of Poemander, and other books, replete with Christian principles and maxims, and sent them forth into the world. "Many other deceptions of this sort, to which custom has very improperly given the denomination of pious frauds, are known to have been practiced in this and the succeeding centuries." The authors, he claims, were in all probability actuated by no ill intention, "but this is all that can be said in their favor, for their conduct in this respect was certainly most ill-advised and unwarrantable." He shifts the major blame for "these forgeries on the public" to the Gnostics, but admits that he yet can not take upon himself "to acquit even the most strictly orthodox from all participation in this species of criminality: for it appears from evidence superior to all exception that a pernicious maxim, which was current in the schools not only of the Egyptians, the Platonists and the Pythagoreans, but also of the Jews, was very early recognized by the Christians and soon found amongst them numerous patrons, namely, that those who made it their business to deceive with a view of promoting the cause of truth, were deserving rather of commendation than of censure."

Is it possible that we are here standing at the very cradle of what the world has come to call "Jesuitry"? If so it can be seen that this bad excuse for allegedly good action had its remote birth in the methods of ancient sacred writing depicted in our second chapter, used originally with esoteric integrity of purpose, but twisted into fraudulent usage by later piety working with less intelligence and probity. It is another cardinal instance and proof of what is claimed, that all corruption of religion and theology came in through the decay and loss of the principles of genuine esoteric schematism. The case grows more solid with every additional observation that the major cause of all religious decadence and perversion was this early-century transmogrification of allegory into history. This will prove to be the mysterious key to the confusion and chaos in the entire religious domain. Mosheim's honesty in refusing to wash away the knavery here recorded is commendable and will in the end serve the interests of true Christianity.

In Vol. II (p. 5) of his work he again admits he can not deny that pious fraud found a place in the propagation of Christianity in the third century. And again he says it is certain that in the earliest ages of the new faith it was "not uncommon for men to fill up the chasms of genuine history with fictitious conceits, the mere suggestion of their own imagination." And candor could go no further than it does in another passage (Vol. I, 106), in which he admits that when once certain of the Christian writers had been unfortunately tempted to have recourse to fiction, "it was not long before the weakness of some and the arrogant presumption of others carried forgery and imposition to an extent of which it would be difficult to convey to the reader any adequate idea."

The eminent historian Lecky, in his History of Rationalism (I, 164) somewhat ironically records his conclusion:

"Making every allowance for the errors of the most extreme infallibility, the history of Catholicism would on this hypothesis represent an amount of imposture probably unequalled in the annals of the human race."

Bacon, of Yale Divinity School, tells us that an extraordinary license was accorded in John's day to the preacher to employ allegory, myth, symbolism, legend, parable, whatever he would, in the interest of religious edification. He says we know there were others in John's time who used the same liberty of expression.

In a work entitled Discourse of Free Thinking (p. 96) the author, Collins, remarks that "these frauds are very common in all books which are published by priests or priestly men. . . . For it is certain that they may plead the authority of the Fathers for forgery, corruption and mangling of authors with more reason than for any other of their articles of faith."

The Encyclopedia Britannica, dealing with the apocryphal books, says that "since these books were forgeries," the epithet (apocryphal) in common parlance today denotes any story or document which is false or spurious, using the word in the disparaging sense. It adds the significant sentence that each of them at one time or another had been treated as canonical. This lines up a point of considerable importance, testifying to the fact that the books were originally among those esoterically apprehended and hence as genuine as any others, and that when the esoteric sense was lost, their unintelligibility got them rated as false. There is practically convincing evidence to show that the word "apocryphal," like many another, did not have in its original usage any connotation of falsity or baseness. It referred to those books of the ancient wisdom which from the spiritual and mystical profundity of their contents were held as too esoteric for the masses. The etymology of the word apo, "from," and kryptein, "to hide" or "conceal," indicates this fully and categorically. The Apocrypha were the books of the recondite doctrine, hidden from the ignorant populace. This point holds much vital significance for study in this whole field.

Gibbon (Decline and Fall of the Roman Empire, 502) states that "the most extravagant legends, as they conduced to the honor of the Church, were applauded by the credulous multitude, countenanced by the power of the clergy and attested by the suspicious evidence of ecclesiastical history."

Such a Christian authority as The Catholic Encyclopedia (VII, 645) says that "even the genuine Epistles were greatly interpolated to lend weight to the personal views of their author. For this reason they were incapable of bearing witness to the original form."

In an enlightening lecture entitled Paul the Gnostic Opponent of Peter, Massey reveals that "as Irenaeus tells us, the Gnostics, of whom Marcion was one, charged the other apostles with hypocrisy, because they 'framed their doctrine according to the capacity of their hearers, fabling blind things for the blind according to their blindness; for the dull according to their dulness; for those in error according to their errors.'"

A strong statement is made in the History of the Christian Religion to the Year 200, by Charles B. Waite, to the effect that a comprehensive review of the first one hundred and seventy years of Christianity discloses the ignorance and superstition of even the most enlightened and best educated of the Fathers; with rare exceptions they were men who utterly despised learning, especially that of the pagans attempting to study the laws of the material universe. Construing in the narrowest sense the maxim that the wisdom of this world is foolishness with God, they construed the Jewish scriptures and sayings of Christ in the most fanciful and whimsical ways. Their credulity was unbounded and "they had a sublime disregard for truth. . . . Their unscrupulousness when seeking for arguments to enforce their positions is notorious, as well as the prevalence among them of what are known as pious frauds."

Waite says of Eusebius, the Christian historian, that not only the most unblushing falsehoods but literary forgeries of the vilest character darken the pages of his apologetic and historical writings. In speaking of such and other irregularities, Miss Isabel B. Holbrook, a capable student of esoteric religions, writes in one of her brochures:

"Among the most notorious of these forgeries were gross liberties and interpolations concerning Christ into the writings of the historian Josephus, of Porphyry and other heathen and Church writers."

Waite further declares that Eusebius has contributed more to Christian history than any other and "no one is guilty of more mistakes."

"Eusebius has a peculiar faculty for diverging from the truth. He was ready to supply by fabrication what was wanting in historical data."

Niebuhr terms Eusebius "a very dishonest writer."

The thirty-second chapter of the Twelfth Book of Anselm, Evangelical Preparation, bears for its title this scandalous proposition: "How it may be lawful and fitting to use falsehood as a medicine and for the benefit of those who want to be deceived." (From Gibbon, Vindication, 76.)

Chrysostom is quoted (Comm. on I Cor., IX, 19; Diegesis, p. 309) as saying: "Great is the force of deceit, provided it is not excited by a treacherous intention."

Even Cardinal Newman appears to endorse subterfuge for the glory of the faith. In the Apology for His Life (Appendix, 345) he writes: "The Greek Fathers thought that when there was a justa causa an untruth need not be a lie."

What could be more explicit than this entry in the Catholic Encyclopedia (XII, 768)?"

"There was need for a revision, which is not yet complete, ranging over all that has been handed down from the Middle Ages, under the style and title of the Fathers, Councils, Roman and other official archives. In all these departments forgery and interpolation as well as ignorance had wrought mischief on a great scale."

Lecky states that the Fathers laid down as a distinct proposition that pious frauds were justifiable and even laudable. As a consequence of the necessity of enforcing their egregious claims to exclusive salvation, says Lecky, the Fathers immediately filled all ecclesiastical literature with the taint of "the most unblushing mendacity." Heathenism had to be combated, and therefore prophecies of Christ by Orpheus and the Sibyls were forged and lying wonders were multiplied. Heretics were to be convinced, and therefore interpolations and complete forgeries were made. Age after age it continued until it became universally common. "It continued till the very sense of truth and the very love of truth seemed blotted out from the minds of men."

In The Anacalypsis Higgins avers that "every ancient author without exception has come to us through the medium of Christian editors, who have, either from roguery or folly, corrupted them all. We know that in one batch all the Fathers of the Church and all the Gospels were corrected, that is, corrupted by the united exertions of the Roman See, Lanfranc, Archbishop of Canterbury, and the monks of St. Maur."

As to this serious charge he writes (Anac., 697):

"Lanfranc, a Benedictine, was head of the monks of St. Maur about A.D. 1050, and it appears that this Society not only corrected the Gospel histories, but they also corrected the Fathers, in order that their Gospel corrections might not be discovered; and this was probably the reason for the publication by them of their version of the whole of the Fathers."

It is not difficult to see why the labors of Higgins, Massey, Thomas Taylor, the Platonist, and others who were unsparing in their candid handling of obscure facts of history were relegated to oblivion as thoroughly as could be done.

Higgins further says (Anac., 522) that nothing which appears to be told by the orthodox Fathers in a regular and systematic manner against the heretics is credible. He berates Bishop Laurence of the English Church for his destructive translation of the Book of Enoch, and charges the iniquity of his having been made an archbishop, instead of being deservedly disgraced in return for so base an act.

Higgins confesses that his exertions to discover the truth are "in opposition to the frauds of the priests of all religions in their efforts to suppress evidence and to keep mankind in ignorance." He charges that Enoch was quoted by Clement and Irenaeus like any other canonical scripture. The Christians in opposition held it to be spurious, because it so clearly gave the prophecy of the coming of the pagan Avatars.

Lardner is quoted by Higgins as saying that Victor Tununensis, an African Bishop, of about the sixth century, wrote a chronicle ending at the year 566, in which it is recorded that in the year 506 at Constantinople, by order of the Emperor Anastasius, "the holy Gospels, being written by illiterate Evangelists, are censured and corrected."

What must be thought of the declaration of Augustine, founder of Christian theology, when he writes (Civ. Dei, Lib. IV, Cap. XXXI)?:

"There are many things that are true which it is not useful for the vulgar crowd to know; and certain things which although they are false it is expedient for the people to believe otherwise."

In his great work Gibbon asserts that Eusebius, "the gravest of the ecclesiastical historians" "indirectly confesses that he has related whatever might redound to the glory, and that he has suppressed all that could tend to the disgrace, of religion."

Augustine wrote a treatise On Lying, in rebuke to the clergy.

"This work," says Bishop Wadsworth, "is a protest against the 'pious frauds' which have brought discredit and damage to the Gospel, and have created prejudice against it from the days of Augustine to our own times." (A Church History, IV, 93-4.)

Massey says he will speak of certain things "when we begin to explore the monstrous deeds and fraudulent machinations of the evangelists."

From the Editorial Preface to The Lost Books of the Bible the following excerpt is culled. It is in reference to the Gospel of Nicodemus:

"Although this Gospel is by some among the learned supposed to have really been written by Nicodemus, who became a disciple of Jesus Christ and conversed with him, others conjecture that it was a forgery toward the close of the third century by some zealous believer who, observing that there had been appeals made by the Christians of the former age to the Acts of Pilate, but that such Acts could not be produced, imagined it would be of service to Christianity to fabricate and publish this Gospel; as it would both confirm the Christians under persecution and convince the Heathens of the truth of the Christian religion. The Rev. Jeremiah Jones says that such pious frauds were very common among the Christians even in the third century. . . . The same author, in noticing that Eusebius in his Ecclesiastical History charges the Pagans with having forged and published a book called 'The Acts of Pilate,' takes occasion to observe that the internal evidence of this Gospel shows it was not the work of any heathen . . . and Mr. Jones says he thinks so, more particularly as we have innumerable instances of forgeries by the faithful in the primitive days grounded on less plausible reasons."

A note to page 99 of The Lost Books of the Bible states that Tertullian is authority for the allegation that the book called the Acts of Paul and Thecla was forged by a Presbyter of Asia, who, being convicted, "confessed that he did it out of respect of Paul." Pope Gelasius included it in his decree against apocryphal books. Notwithstanding this a large part of the history was credited and looked upon as genuine among primitive Christians.

Another discredited work was named The Death of Pilate, and still another, The Paradise of Pilate, described by Lundy (Monumental Christianity, 243), would regale the reader with some conception of the highly "fanciful" nature of these forgeries, if there was space. We may be pardoned for outlining briefly the first of these two: Tiberius being grievously sick and having heard of the fame of Jesus as a healer of diseases, dispatched a messenger to Pilate to have him send Jesus to Rome to cure him. Pilate replied that he had crucified him as a malefactor. On his way back to Rome with the message, the messenger met Veronica – the woman who touched the hem of Christ's garment – who gave him the cloth handkerchief with which the Lord had wiped his face on the way to crucifixion, and in so doing had impressed his features indelibly upon it. This cloth was brought to the Emperor and he was healed. Pilate was summoned to Rome and thrown into prison, where he killed himself with a knife. His body was thrown into the Tiber and such terrible storms of heat, thunder and lightning followed that the Romans took it up and sent it to Vienne where it was thrown into the Rhone(?). The same storms and tempests recurring, the body was sent again to Lake Lucerne, where it was sunk into the deep waters, said even yet to bubble and boil as if by some diabolical influence.

We might ask in Jerome's words: Would this be matter of edification or of destruction?

Lundy (Monumental Christianity, 245) expostulates against the rejection, as spurious, of two apocryphal Letters of Pilate found in Thilo's and Tischendorf's collections; one addressed to Claudius and the other to Tiberius, in both of which Jesus's miracles, his divine sonship, his crucifixion and resurrection are referred to, and the supernatural signs which attended his coming are read as indicating the end of the world. Lundy then puts forth the question, "Are all these forgeries?" If they are only traditions they are certainly very early ones, and their various statements wonderfully agree, he argues. Taken in connection with early Christian monuments, as to the whole story of our Lord's life, death, resurrection and ascension, they must relate facts of a then recent occurrence, which, he thinks, can not be doubted.

"Were three of four generations of men utterly deceived and mistaken? And is all Christian civilization built upon a lie?" Look at the monuments, he says, and see what pains have been taken to record the verities of early Christianity. "Had the things portrayed not been facts, how could art all at once forsake her fond mythologies and depict such wonderful inventions as these?"

How indeed, millions will ask in concert with Lundy. The answer is – by the most incredible stupefaction of mortal mind that ever befell humanity; through the complete blinding of insight into the original nature of occult portrayals of the verities Lundy refers to, which are spiritual realities and not events of objective history. The monuments portrayed the dramatic enaction as the paintings did, and ignorance mistook them for pictures of factual occurrence. How indeed? By the unbelievable transfer of the hidden purport of scripture from the plane of mind to the plane of "history"; by the whole astonishing series of confusions which this work is written to reveal at last in their glaring falsity and blighting power.

A modern sleuth-hound on the trail of Christian imposture is Joseph Wheless, mainly in his work, Forgery in Christianity, an achievement of great value for its data, but perhaps marred by the Freethinker's irrational hatred of all Biblical religionism. It is a remarkable assemblage of material laying bare the falsity of Christian claims, and all drawn directly from Christian sources. It is a strong case which can be supported entirely upon the admissions of your opponents. On page 43 of the work he affirms that "no one can now doubt that Lecky, after voluminous review of Christian frauds and impostures, spoke the precise historical truth: 'Christianity floated into the Roman Empire on the wave of credulity that brought with it this long train of Oriental superstitions and legends.'"

The Catholic Encyclopedia (IV, 498) admits it was the custom of the scribes to lengthen out here and there, to harmonize passages or to add their own explanatory material. It also maintains that "it is the public character of all divines to mold and bend the sacred oracles till they comply with their own fancy, spreading them . . . like a curtain, closing together or drawing them back as they pleased."

A most curious item that comes to light is a supposed letter prefixed to the Clementine Homilies, an epistle from Peter to James, in which Peter is made to write as follows:

"For some of the converts from the Gentiles have rejected the preaching through me in accordance with the law, having accepted a certain lawless and babbling doctrine of the enemy. And these same people have attempted while I am still alive by various interpolations to transform my words unto the overthrow of the law; as though I also thought thus but did not preach it openly: which be far from me. . . . But they professing somehow to know my mind, attempt to expound the words they heard from me more wisely than I who spoke them, telling those who are instructed by them that this is my meaning, which I never thought of. But if they venture such falsehoods while I am still alive, how much more when I am gone will those who come after me dare to do so!"

The Encyclopedia Britannica presumes that the "enemy" whose lawless and babbling doctrine has exercised Peter is none other than Paul. Massey makes much of the Peter-Paul controversy, declaring that Paul's advocacy of the esoteric spiritual interpretation of all scripture made him the target for the attacks of the Petrine faction that swung over to the exoteric view. The Encyclopedia ventures the theory that the character of Simon Magus mentioned in the Acts and in this letter is a cover for Paul himself, and descants on the identification.

In the article "Midrash" the Encyclopedia testifies that "the tendency to reshape history for the edification of later generations was no novelty" in the fourth century B.C. Pragmatic historiography is exemplified in the earliest continuous sources, viz., the "Deuteronomic" writers, i.e., allied to Deuteronomy, and there are many relatively early narratives in which the details have been modified and the heroes of the past are the mouthpieces for the thought of a later writer or of his age. Numerous instructive examples of the active tendency to develop tradition may be observed in the relationship between Genesis and the Book of Jubilees, or in the embellishment of Old Testament history in the Antiquities of Josephus, or in the widening gaps in the diverse traditions of the famous figures of the Old Testament (Adam, Noah, Enoch, Abraham, Moses, Isaiah, Ezra, etc.) as they appear in non-canonical writings. The Midrash of the Jews and most other ancient sacred literature represented just this tendency to exploit a romantic sense in the old material:

"The rigid line between fact and fiction in religious literature which readers often wish to draw, can not be consistently justified, and in studying old Oriental religious narratives, it is necessary to realize that the teaching was regarded as more essential than the method of presenting it. 'Midrash,' which may be quite useless for historical investigation may be appreciated for the light it throws upon the forms of thought. Historical criticism does not touch the reality of the ideas, and since they may be as worthy of study as the apparent facts they clothe, they thus indirectly contribute to the history of their period."

This nears the statement of truth about the theme, but misses final agreement with it, in the last sentence, which makes the Midrashic style of dealing with truth a mere help in understanding the "history of a period." As so often reiterated already, the ancients were not concerned with the tawdry day-to-day eventualities of history; their aim ever was to dramatize the genius, meaning and spirit of all history in systematic type-forms and personifications of aspects of verity.

It is perhaps impossible that the general public can ever be awakened to the enormity of the corruption of old texts. None but the few scholars who have had time and occasion to go over the immense detail of the inquiry are in position to appreciate the full import and truth of this matter. It is well, then, to ponder deeply the sincere words of a competent and conscientious student, G. R. S. Mead, expressed in his Fragments of a Faith Forgotten (p. 18):

"The Received Text is proved to have suffered in its traditions so many misfortunes at the hands of ignorant scribes and dogmatic editors that the human reason stands amazed at the spectacle."

On page 11 of the same work he says with reference to the Christian religion:

The student of Christianity "is amazed at the general ignorance of everything connected with its history and origins. He gradually works his way to a point whence he can obtain an unimpeded view of the remains of the first two centuries and gaze around on a world that he has never heard of at school and of which no word is ever breathed from the pulpit."

And certainly the truth of his next statement (p. 14) must now be conceded:

"For upwards of one hundred years liberal Christendom has witnessed the most strenuous and courageous efforts to rescue the Bible from the hands of an ignorant obscurantism which had in many ways degraded it to the level of a literary fetish and deprived it of the light of reason."

It is profitable to dwell with Mead on Marcion's view of the Gospels. In that great Gnostic's understanding of theology the Christ had preached a universal doctrine, a new revelation of the Good God, the Father of all. They who tried to graft this on to Judaism, the imperfect creed of one small nation, were in grievous error and had totally misunderstood the teaching of Christ. The Christ was not the Messiah promised to the Jews. That Messiah was to be an earthly king, was intended for the Jews alone and had not yet come. Therefore the pseudo-historical "in order that it might be fulfilled" school had adulterated and garbled the original Sayings of the Lord, the universal glad tidings, by the unintelligent and erroneous glosses they had woven into their collections of teachings. "It was the most terrific indictment of the cycle of New Testament 'history' that has ever been formulated." Men were tired of all the contradictions and obscurities of the innumerable and mutually destructive variants of the traditions concerning the person of Jesus. (This surely points to the certainty that there were no real facts to go upon.) No man could say what was the truth, now that "history" had been so altered to suit the new Messiah-theory of the Jewish converts.

As to actual history, then, Marcion started with Paul; he was the first who had really understood the mission of the Christ, and had rescued the teaching from the obscurantism of Jewish narrow sectarianism. Of the manifold versions of the Gospel he would have the Pauline alone. He rejected every other recension including those now ascribed to Matthew, Mark and John! The Gospel according to Luke, "the follower of Paul," which he might have been expected to embrace, he also rejected, regarding it as a recension to suit the views of the Judaizing party. His Gospel was presumably the collection of Sayings in use among the Pauline Churches of his day.

Mead says Marcion also rejected some of Paul's Epistles because they had been tampered with by the "reconciliators of the Petro-Pauline controversy." Mead calls Tertullian's denunciation of Marcion's party of intelligent people, a work called Against Marcion, "but a sorry piece of angry rhetoric."

In his published lecture on Paul Not an Apostle of Historic Christianity (p. 9) Massey says "it becomes apparent how Paul's writings were made orthodox by the men who preached another gospel than his; with whom he was at war during his lifetime and who took a bitter-sweet revenge on his writings by suppression and addition after he was dead and gone."

Another great Gnostic teacher, Basilides, suffered at the hands of the ignorant party bent on literalizing all the Gospels of a spiritual Christos. Mead says that Basilides' Exegetica were the first commentaries on the Gospel teachings written by a Christian philosopher, and in this, as in all other departments of theology, "the Gnostics led the way." We can only regret, he says, that we have not the original text of the Gnostic doctor himself before us, instead of the very faulty copy of the text of the Church Fathers' Refutation. Hippolytus muddles up his own glosses and criticisms with mutilated quotations, imperfectly summarizes important passages which treat of conceptions requiring the greatest subtlety and nicety of language, and in other respects does scant justice to a thinker whose faith in Christianity was so great that, far from confining it to the narrow limits of a dogmatic theology, he would have it that the Gospel was also a universal philosophy explanatory of the whole world drama. In its proper interpretation such indeed it is.

Heracleon and Bardesanes were other splendid Gnostic Christians whose work was contemned by the bigotry of the ignorant. Bardesanes was the agent directly creditable with establishing the first Christian state, for he induced the Prince Abgar Bar-Manu to make Christianity his state religion. Caracalla dethroned Agbar in 216. In revulsion against this act Bardesanes made an extensive defense of the Christian faith. Even Epiphanius is compelled to call him "almost a confessor." He wrote many Christian treatises in Syriac and Greek. Mead says that the Gnostics were still in the Christian ranks, were members of the general Christian body and desired to remain so; but bigotry finally drove them out "because they dared to say that the teaching of the Christ contained a wisdom which transcended the comprehension of the majority."

Mead cites the great Lepsius as saying (Die Apocryphen Apostelgeschichte, 1883) that "almost every fresh editor of such narratives, using that freedom which all antiquity was wont to allow itself in dealing with literary monuments, would recast the materials which lay before him, excluding whatever might not suit his theological point of view," and substituting "other formulae of his own composition, and further expanding and abridging after his own pleasure."

There was a wide circulation of "religious romances," Mead says, in the second century. Irenaeus himself says there was "a multitude of Gospels extant" in his day.

Considerable authority is back of the broad statement that the Pentateuch contained material other than that now found in it before it was re-composed by Esdras or Ezra. It is pretty certain that even after this re-writing it was still further corrupted by ambitious Rabbis of later times, and otherwise remodeled and tampered with. Sometimes, according to Horne, annals and genealogies were taken from other books and incorporated as additional matter. Such sources were used "with freedom and independence." Indeed this author concludes with the sentence: "They can not be said to have corrupted the text of Scripture. They made the text." This collection made in this free fashion, observes Kenealy, is what the Old Testament is in Horne's view – excerpts from the writings of unknown persons put together by those who, he says, were divinely inspired. "No infidel has ever made so damaging a charge as this against the authenticity of the Old Testament."

As to both the Kabalah of the Jews and the Mosaic Bible, it is just about certain that the Western nations have not the original documents. Both internal and external evidence demonstrates on the testimony of the best Hebraists and the confessions of the learned Jewish Rabbis themselves that an ancient document forms the essential basis of the Bible, and that it received very considerable insertions and supplements in the process of adaptation. The Chaldean Book of Numbers and the Book of the Nabothean Agriculture are mentioned as being very close to the contents of this basic archaic document.

Mead establishes the fact that Celsus categorically accuses the Christians (ii-27) of changing their Gospel story in many ways in order the better to answer the objections of their opponents; his accusation is that "some of them, as it were in a drunken state producing self-induced visions, remodel their Gospel from its first written form and reform it so that they may be able to refute the objections brought against it."

Higgins sums up much data with the conclusion that "there is undoubted evidence that our Gospel histories underwent repeated revisions." He adds that "those who would revise the Gospels would not scruple to revise the Sibyl." This hint is in reference to well-founded charges that the Christians had even reached back into the Sibylline predictions of the pagan oracles and changed them to make them jibe with orthodox preachments.

An evidence of corruption of text is found in an editor's note on page 295 of Josephus' Antiquities, which admits that "Josephus' copy considerably differs from ours."

Joseph Wheless (Forgery in Christianity) is authority for the statement that eight Epistles and the Martyrium are confessed forgeries.

"They are by common consent set aside as forgeries which were at various dates and to serve special purposes put forth under the name of the celebrated Bishop of Antioch."

With reference to the Christian handling of the Sibylline Books and prophecies, one of the strongest indictments of Christian duplicity and insincerity is framed by the facts and the evidence. The Catholic Encyclopedia says that a letter of Polycarp to the Philippians, authenticating the Epistle to them, may itself be a forgery.

Says Higgins (Anac., 565):

"Among all nations of the Western parts of the world the prophetesses called Sibyls were anciently known. There were eight of them who were celebrated in a very peculiar manner, and a work is extant in eight books (published by Gallaeus) which purport to contain their prophecies. This work in several places is supposed to foretell the coming of Jesus Christ. They have been in all times admitted to be genuine by the Roman Church, and I believe also by that of the Greeks; in fact they have been literally a part of the religion; but in consequence of events in very late years not answering to the predictions, the Roman priesthood wishes to get quit of them, if it knew how; several of its learned men (Bellarmine, for instance) having called them forgeries."

"It is the renewed case of the ladder: being no longer useful, it is kicked down. The Protestant Churches deny them altogether, as Romish forgeries. These Sibyls were held in the highest esteem by the ancient Gentiles. And it appears from the unquestionable text of Virgil that they did certainly foretell a future Savior or something very like it. We find, on examination of the present copy of them, that they did actually foretell in an acrostic the person called Jesus Christ by name. The most early Fathers of the Greek and Roman Churches plead them as genuine, authentic and unanswerable proofs of the truth of their religion, against the Gentile philosophers who, in reply, say that they have been interpolated by the Christians. . . . I saw pictures of the supposed authoresses of these prophetic books in several places in Italy. Their figures are beautifully inlaid in the marble floor of the Cathedral Church at Sienna and their statues are placed in a fine church at Venice, formerly belonging to the barefooted Carmelites. They are also found placed round the famous Casa Santa at Loretto."

Higgins says that "Sibyl" means "cycle of the sun." There was supposed to be a prophetess for each Sibyl or Cycle. A new prophetess presided over each Cycle as it passed. There were eight. At the time of Christ another was to come. Elsewhere it is said that the tenth was to mark the consummation of the age.

The Anacalypsis says that The Apostolic Constitutions quote the Sibylline Oracles and say:

"When all things shall be reduced to dust and ashes and the immortal god, who kindles the fire, shall have quenched it, God shall form these bones and ashes into man again, and shall place mortal men as they were before, and then shall be the judgment, wherein God shall do justice."

Justin Martyr, about 160 A.D., says the Cumaean Sibyl prophesied the coming of Christ in express words. Justin tells the Greeks that they may find the true religion in the ancient Babylonian Sibyl, who came to Cuma and there gave her oracles, which Plato admired as divine. Clemens of Rome also quotes the Sibyls in his Epistle to the Corinthians. They are also quoted by Theophilus, Antiochus, Athenagoras, Firmianus, Lactantius, Eusebius, St. Augustine and others.

"Take the Greek books, learn the Sibyl, how she proclaims one God and those things which are to come." Higgins says there are several works extant purporting to be the writings of Peter, Paul and other early Christians, in which the Sibylline oracles are quoted as authorities in support of Christianity.

Dr. Lardner admits (Higgins) that the old Fathers call the Sibyls prophetesses in the strictest sense of the word. They were known as such to Plato, Aristotle, Diodorus, Strabo, Plutarch, Pausanius, Cicero, Varro, Virgil, Ovid, Tacitus, Juvenal and Pliny. What can they have foretold, Higgins asks – and claims he can answer: The same as Isaiah, as Enoch, as Zoroaster, as the Veddas, as the Irish Druid from Bocchara, and as the Sibyl of Virgil: a renewed cycle of the sun and its hero or divine incarnation, its presiding genius. They all admit of ten ages, yet they are not agreed as to the time when the ages commence, some making them begin with creation, some with the flood, but the Erythrean Sibyl is the only one who correctly states them to begin from Adam. He says that ten periods of 600 years each make up the ten ages, or one Great Age.

Some of the testimony regarding the Sibyls is assembled by Wheless in his Forgery in Christianity (p. 142). He says that Justin in many chapters cites these oracles and points for Christian proofs to "the testimony of the Sibyl," of Homer, of Sophocles, of Pythagoras, of Plato. From the Ante-Nicene Fathers he takes this:

"And you may in part learn the right religion from the ancient Sibyl, who by some kind of potent inspiration teaches you, through her oracular predictions, truths which seem to be much akin to the teachings of the prophets. . . . 'Ye men of Greece . . . do ye henceforth give heed to the words of the Sibyl . . . predicting as she does in a clear and patient manner the advent of our Savior Jesus Christ,'" as Wheless adds – "quoting long verses of Christian-forged nonsense." (A.N.F. i, 288-9).

"It is a fact that no critic can deny," says Higgins, "that the Sibylline oracles have been greatly corrupted by the Christians."

Gibbon (D. and F., p. 443) says in re the Sibylline Oracles: "The adoption of fraud and sophistry in the defense of revelation" is apparent in their handling by the Christians.

There must be great significance attaching to Wheless' declaration (Forgery in Christianity, p. 195) that Justin Martyr quotes no Gospels, except loose "Sayings of Jesus," in his writings, but draws profusely from the Sibyls, Oracles, etc. Even Irenaeus makes no mention of the four Gospels (Wheless); and according to Higgins (574) Justin says that "the Sibyl not only expressly and clearly foretells the future coming of our Savior Jesus Christ, but also all things that should be done by him." (Cohort and Gr., p. 36; Lardner: Works, Chap. XXIX.)

The most succinct and telling statement concerning the Sibyls, however, is made by Higgins (576) when he says:

"Almost every particular in the life of Christ as detailed in our Gospels is to be found in the Sibyls, so that it can scarcely be doubted that the Sibyls were copied from the Gospel histories, or Gospel histories from them. It is also very certain that there was an Erythrean Sibyl before the time of Christ, whatever it might contain."

It is hardly probable that any factual evidence can ever be produced at this remote date to substantiate the charges of copying on one side or the other. But it is not reasonable to suppose that a document vastly earlier copied from its successor, although to uphold claims of antecedence for some of their documents, doctrines and ceremonial rites, the Christians did actually resort to the plea of "plagiarism by anticipation" so naïvely put forth by some of the early Fathers. As the oracles of the pagans were adjuncts of all religion for many centuries B.C., the implications of plagiarism fall on the Christians. Whether copied or not, the material fact is that the contents of the oracles and those of the Christian Gospels correspond to such a degree that comparative religion study would rate them both as emanating from a common source and being elements of a common tradition. Practically all the tangled problems of the chronology of documents and priority of texts might be solved on the general terms of this hypothesis.

An early writer bearing testimony to much in Christian history is Papias. He emphatically declares that the Christian Gospels were founded on and originated in the Logia or Sayings. Massey derives "myth" from mutu (Egyptian), "utterance," "saying," and relates it to mati, "utterance of truth," from which he derives, it is believed with good reason, the Gospel of Matthew (Egyptian: maatiu). There is an abundance of evidence to support the contention that the body of the great spiritual tradition handed on from remotest times was incorporated in collections of the most notable and vital utterances taken from the lines assigned to be spoken by the Christos or solar-god figure in the great astronomically-based cryptic ritual of the mighty Mysteries of the past. These collations of sacred utterances of the divine Son to mankind were circulated, but in secret, all over the ancient field under the name, in Greek at any rate, of "the Logia" or "Sayings of the Lord." It is almost beyond question that they were the root documents from which the canonical Gospels were elaborated, or perhaps simply extracted, and to cover deterioration were emended, interpolated, edited by many scribes in turn. In general statement this is as near the true history of the source, origin and nature of the Christian Gospels as can be determined. All the data bearing in any way on the matter can be focused with complete harmony and consistency on this thesis; and there are no data that are hostile to it. The hypothesis precisely fits and elucidates all the data and in turn the data support the thesis. It is the only thesis of which this happy situation can be predicated.

In this connection it seems warrantable that the name Mu, applied (by Churchward particularly) to a "lost continent" and age, is just a form of the word that means "utterance of truth." In the primordial days of cosmic creation, the Lord "uttered his voice" and his utterance was the Logos, which prescribed the form of the universe that his voice called into being. The land of Mu was no more a local region on a globe than "the abyss of the waters" was the Pacific Ocean, or the Garden of the Hesperides was in Spain or that other garden, Eden, was in Mesopotamia, or "the kingdom of heaven" in Germany.

Since the time of the existence of the Gospels some portions of texts have been found in Egypt, Syria and elsewhere called Sayings or Logia, of which whole passages agree almost verbatim with their counterparts in the Gospels. Why such a fact is not accorded its full weight is hard to see. Of course Christian defenders unanimously claim for these documents a date well posterior to the Christian writings and allege they are copies of Gospel material. Yet surely documents containing identical data were extant in very ancient pre-Christian times, and this fact would seem to be in the end conducive for the priority of the Logia to the Gospels.

Shirley Jackson Case, of Chicago University Theological School, in his work to support the historicity thesis, admits broadly that before Paul's time pre-Christian Christianity was in existence not only in Palestine, but also in the Diaspora. A broad admission of this sort could include vast facts and data carrying a very definite refutation of many Christian claims, and in fact does so.

It must have taken much strongly evidential proof to bring Kenealy (The Book of God, p. 408) to say that "assuming that the copies or rather phonographs which had been made by Hulkiah and Esdras and the various anonymous editors were really true and genuine, they must have been wholly exterminated by Antiochus; and the versions of the Old Testament which now subsisted must have been made by Judas or by some unknown compilers, probably from the Greek of the seventy, long after the appearance and death of Jesus."

One of the Church Fathers complains that his writings "had been falsified by the apostles of the devil; no wonder, he adds, 'that the Scriptures were falsified by such persons.'" (Catholic Encyclopedia, V, p. 10.) This complainant was Bishop Dionysius.

According to Wheless, Erasmus and Sir Isaac Newton detected fraud in the translation of passages.

It is probably a record of truth which the Catholic Encyclopedia (VI, pp. 655-6) makes as to the authentic authorship of the four canonical Gospels.

"The first four historical books of the New Testament are supplied with titles (Gospel according to (Greek kata) Matthew, etc.) which, however ancient, do not go back to the respective authors of these sacred writings. . . . That they do not go back to the first century of the Christian era, or at least that they are not original, is a position generally held at the present day. . . . It thus appears that the titles of the Gospels are not traceable to the Evangelists themselves."

While this may not point directly to fraudulent practice, it indicates some manipulation that could possibly hide covert intent.

On the general score of the authenticity of the Gospels Wheless writes as follows:

"The possibility of the pretence that the precious Four Gospels, circulated nondescript and anonymous in the churches for a century and a half, is patently belied by the specific instance of the 'Gospel according to Mark,' of which Gospel we have the precise 'history' recorded three centuries after the alleged notorious event. Bishop Eusebius is our witness in his celebrated Church History. He relates that Peter preached orally in Rome, Mark being his 'disciple' and companion. The people wanted a written record of Peter's preachments, and (probably because Peter could not write) they importuned Mark to write down 'that history which is called the Gospel according to

Mark.' Mark having done so, 'the Apostle (Peter) having ascertained what was done by revelation of the Spirit, was delighted' . . . and that history obtained his authority for the purpose of being read in the churches." (H. E., Bk. II, Ch. 15.)

Wheless gives other data indicating that Peter was dead at the time alleged. But he cites Eusebius from a later passage in his Ecclesiastical History, in which this "historian" gives another version: the people who heard Peter "requested Mark, who remembered well what he (Peter) had said, to reduce these things to writing . . . which when Peter understood, he directly neither hindered nor encouraged it." (H. E., Bk. VI, Ch. 14.) "Peter thus was alive but wholly indifferent about his alleged Gospel" (Wheless). It evidently was not "inspired" if Mark only "remembered well."

It is claimed that Peter was "martyred in Rome" 64-67 A.D. The earliest date claimed for "Mark" is some years after the fall of Jerusalem, 70 A.D. The great Pope Clement I (died 97 A.D.?) first to fourth successor of Pope Peter, knew nothing of his great predecessor's "Gospel according to Mark," for, says the Catholic Encyclopedia (IV, p. 14):

"The New Testament he never quotes verbally. Sayings of Christ are now and then given, but not in the words of the Gospels. It can not be proved, therefore, the he used any one of the Synoptic Gospels."

Wheless comments on this, that of course he did not and could not; they were not yet written. And no other Pope, Bishop or Father (except Papias and until Irenaeus) for nearly a century after "Pope Clement" ever mentions or quotes a Gospel, or names Matthew, Mark, Luke or John.

"So for a century and a half – until the books bobbed up in the hands of Bishop St. Irenaeus and were tagged as 'Gospels according to' this or that Apostle, there exists not a word of them in all the tiresome tomes of the Fathers. It is humanly and divinely impossible that the 'Apostolic authorship' and hence 'canonicity' or divine inspiration of these Sacred Four should have remained for a century and a half unknown and unsuspected by every Church Father, Pope and Bishop of Christendom – if existent. Even had they been somewhat earlier in existence, never an inspired hint or human suspicion was there, that they were 'Divine' or 'Apostolic' or any different from the scores of 'Apocryphal or pseudo-Biblical writings with which the East had been flooded' – that they were indeed 'Holy Scripture.' Hear this notable admission: 'It was not until about the middle of the second century that under the rubric of Scripture the New Testament writings were assimilated to the Old' (C. E., III, 275) – that is, became regarded as Apostolic, sacred, inspired and canonical – or 'Scriptures.'"

Matthew, Mark, Luke and John were all Jews; their Gospels were written in Greek. Also they speak of the Jews in the style and spirit of a non-Jew. Luke adds (I, 1) that there were many other like Gospels afloat. The Cath. Ency. confesses that no one knows why out of many such Gospels the Sacred Four were chosen. Wheless says that Matthew was used by the Ebionites, Mark by "those who separate Jesus from Christ," Luke by the Marcionites, and John by the Valentinians. Wheless will probably be disputed when he says that it is "proven that no written Gospels existed until shortly before 185 A.D., when Irenaeus wrote; they are first mentioned in Chapter XXI of his Book II."

The "heretics" were making use of many Gospels, the orthodox claimed only four for their own. It is claimed and likely with justice that the "gospel" up to the middle of the second century was entirely oral and traditional, or with few written texts, and those held in more or less secrecy by the esotericists of the day. This would quite well accord with the thesis of the existence of Logia or Sayings of divine authorship. The Gnostics or other "heretics" were likely the ones who began to reduce the "gospel" to writing and to bring it out to general use, like the "occultists" of our own age. The orthodox, in self-defense, in all probability did likewise, selecting four and editing them to uphold conceived positions on doctrinal matters. It is confessed in several places that the "heretical spurious gospels" prepared the way and doubtless furnished the incentive for the canonized four. "The Gospels are thus anti-heretical documents of the second century after Gnosticism first appeared." This fact makes them far other in spirit and no doubt in contents than what the Christian populace has always innocently believed them to be – pure historical records of factual occurrence.

Pope Papias – who said that Jesus died at home in bed of old age! – is among the first, about 145 A.D., to name a written Gospel. Quoting the old presbyters (whose memory must have gone pretty far back to the first century), he says that Mark, having become the interpreter of Peter, wrote down accurately whatever he remembered. It is not in exact order that he relates the sayings or deeds of Christ. "For he neither heard the Lord nor accompanied him." Matthew, he says, put the Oracles (of the Lord) in the Hebrew language, "and each one interpreted them as best he could." Papias did not have in his important church any other Gospels and had only heard of such writings from the elders at second hand.

There has been much question of the genuineness of Mark (XVI, pp. 9-20. On this the Encyclopedia Britannica (II, p. 1880) says: "The conclusion of Mark (XVI, 9-20) is admittedly not genuine. Still less can the shorter conclusion lay claim to genuineness." Of the 15th and 16th verses of this chapter the "Go ye into all the world and preach the gospel" and the "saved" and "damned" clauses, etc., are obvious interpolations. Reinach (Orpheus, p. 221) says that it is a "late addition" and "is not found in the best MSS." The New Standard Bible Dictionary (p. 551) states that the longer form has against it the testimony of the two oldest Uncial MSS. (Siniatic and Vatican) and of one of the two earliest of the Syriac versions, all of which close the chapter at verse 8. In addition to this is the very significant silence of Patristic literature as to anything following verse 8. Eusebius says that the portion after verse 8 was not contained in all the MSS. Jerome also says it was wanting in nearly all. But Jerome put it into the Vulgate (Cath. Ency.). The latter authority says:

"Whatever the fact be, it is not at all certain that Mark did not write the disputed verses. It may be that he did not; that they are from the pen of some other inspired writer and were appended to the Gospel in the first century or the beginning of the second."

But the Council of Trent decreed they were part of the inspired gospel "and must be received as such by every Catholic." (C. E., IX, pp. 677-8-9.) The New Commentary on the Holy Scripture (Part III, pp. 122-3) comments:

"It is as certain as anything can be in the domain of criticism that the Longer Ending did not come from the pen of the Evangelist Mark. . . . We conclude that it is certain that the Longer Ending is not part of the Gospel."

Massey says we learn from Origen that during the third century there were various different versions of Matthew's Gospel in circulation. Jerome, at the end of the fourth century, asserts the same thing; and of the Latin version he says that there were as many different texts as there were manuscripts!

Reinach contends that the episode of Jesus and the woman taken in adultery, which was inserted in John's Gospel in the fourth century, was originally in the (apocryphal) Gospel according to the Hebrews. (Orpheus, p. 235.)

As to John XXI the Ency. Brit. has it that, as XX, 30-31 constitute a formal and solemn conclusion, Chap. XXI is beyond question a later appendix. "We may go on to add that it does not come from the same author with the rest of the book." (E. B., ii, p. 2543.)

Even the conclusion of the Lord's Prayer ("For thine is the glory," etc.) is omitted as spurious by the Revised Version. It is not in the Catholic "True" Version. As to that Wheless comments: "It may be remarked that the whole of the so-called Lord's Prayer is not the Lord's at all; it is a late patchwork of pieces out of the Old Testament, as is readily shown by the marginal cross references."

Reinach, citing the Ency. Brit., under various titles, says of the Peter, John, Jude and James Epistles – the "Catholic Epistles" – "not one of them is authentic."

A bit shattering is the word of the same Encyclopedia (I, p. 199):

"John . . . is not the author of the Fourth Gospel; so, in like manner, in the Apocalypse we may have here and there a passage that may be traced to him, but the book as a whole is not from his pen. Gospel, Epistles and Apocalypse all come from the same school."

This was the school of the Mysteries, the Essene Brotherhoods, the Associations of Therapeutae, from which all the oldest documents of a sacred character emanated, and the traditions of which the Gnostics essayed to carry on into the new formulations of Christianity. This is a very important datum. Reinach holds that John – or whoever poses as "John" – is a forger.

Eusebius says that II Peter "was controverted and not admitted into the canon." The Ency. Brit. endorses the view and says its tardy recognition in the early Church supports the judgment of the critical school as to its unapostolic origin.

Tertullian (Cath. Ency., XIV, p. 525) cites the Book of Enoch as inspired, and also recognizes the IV Esdras and the Sibyl, but does not know James and II Peter. He attributes Hebrews to St. Barnabas.

The Apostolic Constitutions, supposed to have been compiled by Clement of Rome and held in high esteem, were until 1563 claimed to be the genuine work of the Apostles. They were composed about 400, and were a collection of ancient ecclesiastical decrees concerning the government and discipline of the Church, in a word, a handy summary of the statutory legislation of the Apostles themselves, promulgated by their own great disciple Clement. Their claim of apostolic origin is manifestly quite false and untenable, Wheless insists. The Catholic Encyclopedia has recognized them as the work of the Apostles and confirmed them as ecclesiastical law.

Likewise the Liber Pontificalis or Book of the Popes, a purported history of the Popes beginning with Peter and continued down to the fifteenth century, Wheless claims is full of spurious correspondence, liturgical and disciplinary regulations, biographies, etc., which certainly must be held under suspicion.

And so the list of tamperings and forgeries runs on down into the Middle Ages, a revelation of duplicity enough to shake the faith of the earnest souls confiding in holy leadership, if it was all known. Lorenzo Valla in 1440 first revealed the forgery of the Donation of Constantine. The Symmachian Forgeries are confessed by the Catholic Encyclopedia. Voltaire pronounced the "False Decretals" of Isidore "the boldest and most magnificent forgery which has deceived the world for centuries." They appeared suddenly in the ninth century, and in them the Popes of the first three centuries are made to quote documents that did not appear until the fourth or fifth century. They are full of anachronisms.

Then comes the sorry recital of lists of deceptions concerning sacred relics, starting with those of the person of Jesus, his bones, his garments, utensils used by him, the cross, nails, bottles of his blood and also of Mary's nursing milk, etc., etc., which are so obviously fraudulent that one would think the ecclesiastical system which either forged them or winked at their exploitation would blush at the record. The Catholic Encyclopedia does confess the policy of tolerance of "the pious beliefs" which have helped to further Christianity and a general indulgence toward all the fatuous superstitions connected with relics, saints, healing and the rest. As no church was to be built without dead men's bones under the altar, so it would seem as if indeed no church system can be historically promulgated without the skeleton of the dead past buried deep in the core of its heart and in its holy of holies.

The Catholic Encyclopedia announces (III, p. 105) that Chosroes (Khosra) II, King of Persia, in 614 took Jerusalem, massacred 90,000 good Christians, captured the cross of Christ and carried it off whole in triumph to Persia. Yet the same authority says that we learn from St. Cyril of Jerusalem (before 350) that the wood of the cross, discovered about 318, was already distributed throughout the world, to show up in enough pieces to have built a colony of summer cottages. This is indeed a miracle of multiplication surpassing Jesus' legerdemain with the five loaves and two fishes. Wheless cites authority for the statement that more than seven hundred relics of the thorns pressed on Jesus' brow have been enumerated. For fuller detail reference should be had to Wheless' book, Forgery in Christianity. Draper in his The Intellectual Development of Europe tells of the shock which the revelation of such unblushing imposture gave to all Europe at different times and which prepared the way for the Reformation.

The vast fraud of his Church is said to have burst upon Luther as he ascended the twenty-eight steps of white marble leading up to the porch of the palace of Pilate allegedly trodden by Christ, which were brought to Rome from Jerusalem by St. Helena. It must be remembered that the great surge of the Reformation came from the natural revolt of the human conscience against dupery and hypocrisy. It will be admitted that the amount of such deception necessary to cause a revulsion sufficiently strong to overthrow a pious system consecrated and venerated by centuries of sacred indoctrination and loyalty must have been of terrific proportions.

Higgins alleges that even the Koran was forged twenty years after Mohammed's death. For priestcraft it may indeed be recognized that necessity is the mother of invention.

Among the writings of St. Anselm, Archbishop of Canterbury in the eleventh century, has been found a verbal description of Jesus in Latin attributed to one Lentulus, a friend of Pontius Pilate and his predecessor in the government of Judea. The letter purports to have been addressed to the Roman Senate by Lentulus. It has been taken to be fictitious. No such person as Lentulus is known of in Judea.

Much of the alleged "historical testimony" supporting Jesus' human existence is material of this sort.

Origen writes that the difference between the copies of the Gospels is considerable, partly from the carelessness of individual scribes, partly from the impious audacity of some in correcting what was written, as well as from "those who added or removed what seemed good to them in the work of correction." (Origen, M. Matt., XV, p. 14.) Wheless asserts that as far as the Gospel of John was concerned, it was not identified with the Christian Church until Irenaeus, Bishop of Lyons, wrote about it A.D. 185, when the Gnostic Gospel was brought forward. This was founded on the Egyptian Mysteries, John being the Egyptian Taht-Aan. Massey endorses this etymology.

Grethenbach (A Secular View of the Bible) refers to the text of Jesus' agonized cry of heroic spirituality from the cross – "Father, forgive them, for they know not what they do" – and says it is omitted from the earlier copies of the Book of Luke, and is probably an interpolation from the similar expression of Stephen (Acts, 7:60), and is missing from the other Gospels. This author likewise points out that all the details of the crucifixion given in the four Gospels are wholly left in silence by the epistolary authors, an extraordinarily singular fact, since, he says, Paul himself must have been in Jerusalem at the time it occurred, and John and Peter are known to have been there likewise.

Mead cites evidence (F. F. F., p. 166) to authenticate his statement that in the "romantic" cycle of "Gospel" writing connected with Simon Magus, the legend of Peter's being in Rome in later versions is belied by data in the earlier ones, in which Peter does not travel beyond the East. We have already noted Jerome's admission that the present Matthew was not the original Gospel of that name, and that the earlier text was "re-written" by a certain Seleucus.

Another work of Mead's – Did Jesus Live 100 Years B.C.? – adduces the datum that the authorized translation of "almost thou persuadest me to be a Christian" is not correct, and that the "imperfect original of it is untranslatable."

This may be the appropriate place to introduce the evidence that is extant as to the mishandling and juggling of the Greek adjective chrestos, meaning "good," "just," "righteous," and the substitution of "Christos," "the anointed one," for it by the Christian writers. It is doubtful, however, if much can be made for or against the historicity from the data available. It is at any rate a matter of considerable importance that the early prevalence of this spelling, or this word, should be known, as such things have apparently been designedly kept from general knowledge.

The etymology of Christos has already been outlined as meaning the "Anointed One," and its evident derivation from the Egyptian KaRaST, the name of the mummy-babe in the coffin, with the significance of divinity buried in flesh, has been indicated. KaRaST has been translated as "fleshed," and it may be of cognate origin with the Greek word for "flesh," kreas. Christos and Messiah are equated in the similar meaning of "Anointed." Oddly enough, the Egyptian mes and the Sanskrit kri both mean "to pour," "to anoint."

It seems that Chrestos is by no means a mere variant of Christos, with the same meaning. The Greek dictionary gives the word as meaning "good-natured," "kind," as applied to men, and "propitious," "favorable," as applied to the gods. The distinguished German savant Lepsius gives the Egyptian nofre (more generally spelled by Egyptologists nefer) as meaning "good," "beautiful," "noble," and says it is equivalent to the Greek Chrestos. He says that one of the titles of Osiris, On-nofre (Un-nefer) must be translated "the goodness of God made manifest," which is probably correct.

Chrestos appears in a number of places throughout the Bible text. In I Peter 2:3 it occurs with the translation of "gracious." In Psalm 34:8 it is rendered "good." W. B. Smith, in Der Vorchristliche Jesus, holds that chrestos as found in the latter passage is equatable with Christos.

Clement of Alexandria in the second century founded a serious argument on his paronomasia (juggling of the spelling, or punning), by which he makes the assertion that all who believed in Chrest (i.e., "a good man") both are and are called Chrestians, that is, "good men." And Lactantius sets forth that it is only through ignorance that people call themselves Christians instead of Chrestians: "who through the mistake of the ignorant (people) are accustomed to say Christ with the letter unchanged." (Lib. IV, Chap. VII.) It is thus apparent that the Greeks were accustomed to call Christ by the name Chrestus, not Christus.

In his The Early Days of Christianity Canon Farrar has a footnote on the word Chrestian occurring in I Peter 4:16, where in the revised later MSS. the word was changed into Christian. The eminent churchman remarks here that "perhaps we should read the ignorant brethren's distortion, Chrestian." Most certainly we should, as the name Christus was not distorted into Chrestus, but it was the adjective and noun Chrestus which became distorted into Christus and applied to Jesus. There is much evidence that the terms Christ and Christians, spelled originally Chrest and Chrestians (Chrestianoi in Greek) by such writers as Justin Martyr, Tertullian, Lactantius, Clement and others, were directly borrowed from the temple terminology of the pagans and meant the same thing, viz., "good," "honest," "gracious," and the noun forms from the adjective.

Philo uses the adjective-combination theochrestos (God declared), which was worked over into theochristos (anointed of God). There may be something in the suggestion that while Christos means "to live" and "to be born into a new life" (the basic meaning of "anointed"), Chrestos signified in the Mystery phraseology the death of the lower or personal nature in man, that part of us which must die daily, as St. Paul sees it. An interesting clue that points in the direction of a cryptic theological meaning of the sort is given by the fact, brought to our notice by chance, that the zodiacal sign of Scorpio was known in esoteric studies as Chrestos-Meshiac, while Leo was called Christos-Messiah, and that this nomenclature antedated by far the Christian era, as a representation or dramatization in the rites of Initiation in the Mysteries. It is clearly evident here that Scorpio stood as symbol of the sinking sun of deity in its autumnal descent into matter, Leo standing for the glorified sun risen to the zenith. This is further attested by a writer of penetrating discernment of ancient structures, Ralston Skinner, who in his profound study, Sources and Measures, brings out a parallel to the Scorpio-Leo, Chrestos-Christos analysis. He writes:

"One (Chrestos), causing himself to go down into the pit (of Scorpio, or incarnation in the womb) for the salvation of the world; this was the sun, shorn of his golden rays and crowned with blackened ones (symbolizing this loss) as of thorns; the other was the triumphant Messiah, mounted up to the summit of the arch of heaven, personated as the Lion of the Tribe of Judah."

It is more than a shrewd guess that we have in this zodiacal characterization, which allocates Chrestos to Scorpio and Christos to Leo symbolism, the true basis of a distinctive use of the two words or spellings. We know well that the vowels in ancient Egyptian, Hebrew and other languages were of quite indifferent rating and value. There seem to have been almost no vowels in the hieroglyphics, and up to the sixth century no vowels were written in the pre-Masoretic texts of the Hebrew scriptures. It is not likely that there was any essentially marked or significant difference between Chrestos and Christos. They may have been used more or less interchangeably. But the insatiable tendency of the ancient mind to devise constructions that would graphically pictorialize basic principles, laws and truths, took form seemingly in this instance in seizing upon the two names, Chrestos and Christos, as descriptive of the two stages of incarnating and resurrected Messianic deity. This is the one inescapable theme of ancient religious writing. It would match the many other twofold designations, such as Sut-Horus, Horus the Elder-Horus the Younger, Osiris-Horus, Cain-Abel, Jacob-Esau, John-Jesus, Judas-Jesus and other pairs that represent the two opposite phases of deity, the God in matter, the Karast, and the God restored to heaven, as the Christ. Much Christian thought even makes the distinction between Jesus the man and Christ the God. It was in all probability the case that the religionists referred to Jesus as the Chrestos, or "good man" who was to be through and after his initiations and transfigurations reborn into the true Christos. The reason, then, for the indicated tendency of the Christians to change the term Chrestos over to Christos is plainly seen. It was their obvious purpose to establish the claim that their divinely prophesied and celestially born Messiah had indeed become the fully deified Savior. This should be a notable clarification and it has the subtle agreement of the zodiacal symbolism to support it.

Incidentally we have in Skinner's data the probably true significance of the symbolic "crown of thorns" so tragically pressed down upon the brow of Jesus in the Gospels.

But it is of no little weight to establish the datum that the term Chrestoi, meaning "good people," full of sweetness and light, was pre-extant to Christianity. This is in part certified by the statement of Canon Farrar in The Early Days of Christianity that "there can be little doubt that the . . . name Christian . . . was a nickname due to the wit of the Antiochians. . . . It is clear that the sacred writers avoided the name (Christians) because it was employed by their enemies (Tacitus: Annals XV:44). It only became familiar when the virtues of Christians had shed lustre upon it. . . ."

It is quite more likely that the Christians chose the name Christian (rather than Chrestian) for the luster that the high name would shed on them than that their virtues shed luster upon the name. The name needed no extraneous illumination; the Christians (as has been seen) doubtless did.

However that may be, the fundamental and crucial fact of the whole matter seems to center in Massey's findings with reference to the derivation of the stem KRST, with whatever voweling, from the mummy KaRaST of Egypt. In the Agnostic Annual he says:

"In a fifth century representation of the Madonna and child from the cemetery of St. Valentinus the new-born babe lying in a box or crib is also the Karest, or mummy-type, further identified as the divine babe of the solar mythos by the disk of the sun and the cross of the equinox at the back of the infant's head. This doubles the proof that the Christ of the Christian catacombs was a survival of the Karest of Egypt."

Justin Martyr uses the word Chrestotatoi, meaning "most excellent." Thirlby alludes to the vulgar custom of the early time of calling the Christians Chrestians. Higgins ventures the supposition that "Christianoi" was likely a corruption of the more common Chrestianoi.

Lucian in a book called Philopatris makes a person named Triephon answer the question whether the affairs of the Christians were recorded in heaven: "All nations are there recorded, since Chrestos exists even among the Gentiles." The Greek is here given as Chresos.

Dr. John Jones (Lex. in voce.) observes that this word is found in Romans 16:18. Higgins comments:

"And in truth the composition of it is Chrestos logia, i.e., Logia peri tou Chrestos, oracles concerning Chrestus, that is, oracles which certain impostors in the Church at Rome propagated concerning Christ, Chrisos being changed by them into Chresos, the usual name given them by the Gnostics and even by unbelievers."

Paul in this Romans passage calls the doctrine Chresologia, and Higgins says Jesus was called Chresos by St. Peter as well as by St. Paul.

Bishop Marsh says of the passage in I Peter 2:3 that some editors give Chrestos, others Christos, "where the preceding verb egeusasthe determines the former (Chrestos) to be the true reading." (Marsh's Various Readings of the New Testament, Vol. I, p. 278.) Higgins asserts that "anointed" covers everything meant to be described by Chrestos.

In Did Jesus Live 100 Years B.C.? Mead states in a footnote that the most ancient dated Christian inscription (October 1, 318, A.D.) runs: "The Lord and Savior, Jesus the Good" – (Chrestos, not Christos). This, he says, was the legend over the door of a Marcionite Church. And the Marcionites were anti-Jewish Gnostics and did not confound their Chrestos with the Jewish Christos (Messiah). Mead says elsewhere that Chrestos was a universal term of the Mysteries for the perfected "saint," and that Christos was more especially limited to the Jewish Messiah idea.

Mackenzie writes that "the worship of Christ was universal at this early date . . . but the worship of Chrestos – the Good Principle – had preceded it by many centuries, and even survived the general adoption of Christianity, as shown on monuments still in existence."

He cites examples of the occurrence of the word Chreste from the catacombs.

It is notable indeed that Justin Martyr, the earliest Christian author, in his first Apology, called his co-religionists Chrestians, not Christians.

In a lecture entitled The Name and Nature of the Christ, Massey writes:

"In Bockh's Christian Inscriptions, numbering 1,287, there is not a single instance of an earlier date than the third century wherein the name is not written Chrest or Chreist."

There is no manifest reason why a fact as significant as this should not be widely recognized and publicized both for the sake of truth and for the sake of the principle now being so strenuously defended, that the citizens of a democracy are entitled to correct information on matters of any importance.

It is also definitely worth noting that in the excerpt from Suetonius' Lives of the Twelve Caesars, one of the four alleged extra-Gospel historical references to Jesus, the name claimed to be an allusion to Jesus is the word Chrestus. Commenting on this, Harry Elmer Barnes, in The Twilight of Christianity, justly ventures the suggestion that the word in this form gives us no assurance that the historical Jesus is the person hinted at, or indeed that it refers to a person at all.

It is frankly in the line of philological speculation, but with the apparent identity of root derivation of two words to suggest its plausibility, to point to a possible relation of the words Chrestos, Christos, with the Greek impersonal verb chrea insert flat line over the e, "it is necessary," "it is fitting," "it is right," "it is good." There is a dialectical or philosophical connection that is by no means far-fetched. All religion is concerned primarily with the relation of the soul to body in its cycles of descent and return. It is to be recalled that these cycles were known in the Greek Orphic and Platonic systems as kuklos (cyclos) anagkes, "the cycle of necessity." Chrea see above) is kindred to the stem of the word "cross," and the Christ on the cross was the Christ-soul undergoing the experience of the cycle of necessity. Also the whole evolution of the Christos is, in a very real philosophical sense, under the impulsion of what may be, and often has been, called divine necessity. The soul advances to divinity, stage by stage and cycle by cycle, under the necessity of its own nature. The fact that chrea means "it is good" as well as "it is necessary" points to the practical certitude that it is cosmically good for the soul to make the pilgrimage round the circle of the cosmos, through the gamut of all values.

The final fact of basic import in the item is that the KRS stem is cognate with the same root that yields the word "cross." The Karest in the mummy-case was a variant figure for the Christ on the cross, the deity in the kreas or flesh. It occurred to some symbologists some time and somewhere to adopt a variant spelling to set over the descending phase of divinity in the cyclical round against the reascending phase, in which the pilgrim soul was called the Christ. The term Chrest was adopted to designate the divine soul going down into the tomb of the mortal body; the Christ was that same soul emerging out of it, "on the eastern side of heaven, like a star." As the Book of Ecclesiastes phrases it, this is almost certainly "the conclusion of the whole matter."

In his History of the Christian Religion to the Year 200, Waite considers certain very old texts to have been basic for the three Synoptic Gospels, and says that these source books contain no evidence as to such matters as the miraculous conception, the physical resurrection, or the miracles. He points out also that the early Apostolic Fathers, Clement of Rome, Ignatius and Polycarp make no mention of the miracles or the material resurrection. Indeed they make no reference to the Gospels or the Acts and produce no quotations from them save such as may have been picked up from extant collections of Logia. He comments on the account of Mary's life given in the Protevangelium, her being given by the priests to the widower Joseph, then about eighty years old, with six children by a former wife.

As to the Vulgate the Catholic Encyclopedia (XII, p. 769) states that under Popes Sixtus V and Clement VIII the Latin Vulgate, after years of revision, attained its present shape. And says Wheless, this translation, which was fiercely denounced as fearfully corrupt, was only given sanction of divine inspiration by the Council of Trent in 1546, under the curse of God against any who questioned it. The tinkering with the text came after the Council, but the latter's decree was not altered to conform to the amended rendering.

Irenaeus either misquotes Mark or the text has been made to differ from his wording in one place, for he says that Mark commences with a reference to the prophetic spirit, and that his is the Gospel of Jesus Christ "as it is written in Esaias the prophet." Eusebius admits "fraud and dissimulation" in the handling of scripts.

Wheless says the proudest boast of the Church today with reference to its ex-Pagan Saint Augustine is that whenever a contradiction between his philosophy and the prescribed orthodox faith arose, "he never hesitates to subordinate his philosophy to religion, reason to faith." (Cath. Ency., II, p. 86.) Augustine himself flaunts his mental servitude when he says: "I would not believe the Gospels to be true unless the authority of the Catholic Church constrained me."

Gibbon adduces much reliable authority to indicate that even in such a matter of historical record as the number of their sectaries martyred in the persecutions under the several Roman Emperors, the Christians have outrageously falsified the figures. Gibbon's pages should be read more generally, so that a saner view might be taken of this item of Christian claims, which have been grossly overstated to win the sympathy which martyrdom arouses.

Miss Holbrook asserts that "Of the 150,000 various readings which Griesbach found in the manuscripts of the New Testament, probably 149,500 were additions and interpolations. One of the Greek manuscripts called 'Codex Bezal' or 'Cambridge Manuscript,' is chiefly remarkable for its bold and extensive interpolations, amounting to some six hundred in the Acts alone."

Gibbon has testified to the "vulgar forgery" of the insertion of the two admittedly spurious passages regarding Christos in the text of Josephus.

Alexander Wilder (Article on Evolution) says that

"such men as Irenaeus, Epiphanius and Eusebius have transmitted to posterity a reputation for such untruth and dishonest practices that the heart sickens at the story of the crimes of that period." A commentator adds: "the more so, since the whole Christian scheme rests upon their sayings."

It is quite possible – and lamentably so – that Massey's bitter words are entirely sane and true, that the "Christian scheme (as it is aptly called) in the New Testament is a fraud, founded on a fable in the Old."

There is a letter written by one of the most respected Fathers of the Church, St. Gregory of Nazianzen to Jerome, which reveals in pretty clear light the early Church's policy of deception. Gregory wrote to his friend and confident, Jerome, as follows:

"Nothing can impose better on the people than verbiage; the less they understand, the more they admire. Our Fathers and Doctors have often said, not what they thought, but what circumstances and necessity forced them to."

Ominous indeed is Massey's serious indictment of Christianity's early duplicity in one of his lectures:

"And when Eusebius recorded his memorable boast that he had virtually made 'all square' for the Christians, it was an ominous announcement of what had been done to keep out of sight the mythical and mystical rootage of historic Christianity. The Gnostics had been muzzled and their extant evidence as far as possible masked. He and his co-conspirators had done their worst in destroying documents and effacing the tell-tale records of the past, to prevent the future from learning what the bygone ages could have said directly for themselves. They made dumb all Pagan voices that would have cried aloud their testimony against the unparalleled imposture then being perfected in Rome. They had almost reduced the first four centuries to silence on all matters of the most vital importance for any proper understanding of the true origins of the Christian superstition. The mythos having been at last published as a human history, everything else was suppressed or forced to support the fraud."

A particularly sharp critic and accuser of Christianity is Alan Upward in The Divine Mystery. He states that in the interests of God and heaven "the theologians have laid their ban on all the sciences in turn, on the lore of the stars, of the rocks, of the atoms, of the frame of man, of his mind, of the Hebrew language and history, of Eastern history, of the history of life." It must be confessed there is much gravamen in this indictment. A religion claiming to be the supremely true one should assuredly have possessed the basic data and correct knowledge which would have enabled it to pronounce unerringly upon every department of truth, in every branch of science. Yet no organic system has ever been found to be so atrociously in error in every arena of knowledge. Outside its own chamber-room of hypnotized faith it has stood for long periods as the enemy of truth in every empirical realm. Truth has had to batter its way through the serried array of ecclesiastical fanaticism, ignorance and stubborn bigotry over long centuries. Truth has never been its chief and primary concern or objective. Instead, it has aimed at psychologization and regimentation of the masses, and to this end it has ruthlessly swept aside all the formulations of intelligence which would have hindered the easy achievement of its goal. Besides fighting every science it has wrecked the splendid temple of ancient mythology and closed the doors of the schools of esoteric truth, and kept them closed to this day. It is with regret that one has to agree with Upward in his stinging accusation against the religion of one's childhood: "Falsehood is found in every religion, but only in the Catholic Christianity is it the foundation of religion." And Upward points to the fact that since with each fresh discovery of truth in scientific fields the cry goes up all over Christendom that science has uprooted the bases of religion, this is sure evidence that a religion resting so far off the center of verihood that every new factual discovery shakes it to its fall, can not be a true or safe religion. A faith that hangs constantly so precariously that the snapping of a single strand in the rope will send it crashing, can not be stabilized in truth.

Chapter VII

THROES OF A BAD CONSCIENCE

It is accounted an evil cause that must support itself by violence and destruction. Unhappily this is the case with Christianity after the third century. Repressed and harassed for about three centuries by popular disapproval and the regnant power, when at last it came into favor and security and a measure of power of its own, the Church of Christ at once let loose the fury of its own virulent passion against every group that would not bend to its narrow and fanatical orthodoxy. It then began its long and almost uninterrupted career of persecution, to its eternal infamy. Because they have been forgotten and largely denied. the interests of truth call for a brief restatement of the facts of ecclesiastical vandalism. It is an integral part of the case here advocated, along with the literary forgeries, tampering with sacred texts and the vitiation of the ancient wisdom on every hand.

Massey well outlines the drift of things from the time that ignorance overwhelmed the Christian movement, cast out the uncomprehended Gnosis, and then resorted to measures of violence to cut all links of connection between their doctrines and antecedent pagan religions. Innocent at first of any knowledge of the derivation of their doctrines from reviled sources in heathenism, great was the surprise and resentment of the Christian devotees when little by little evidence leaked out of the startling and complete identities of their ideas and forms with the material of despised former cults. Hotly indignant, the astonished and desperate votaries of the new faith had to find some way to blot out the tell-tale evidences. So the orgy of destruction set in. There are instances close at hand in our own day to enforce upon our minds the futility and the despicableness of the gesture of burning hated books and exiling their authors. Some of this ignominy can be passed back upon the Christian partisans of the early centuries, when the hot fury of fanatical zeal set fire to libraries of the most precious and irreplaceable books in the world. A fact so well known in history as the burning of the Alexandrian library by Christian mobs need not be dilated upon here. It has not, however, been deeply enough stamped upon general intelligence that this vandal deed was probably the enabling cause of the incidence of fifteen centuries of the Dark Ages, and the postponement of the Renaissance to the latter half of that period. The destruction of a library then meant infinitely more than it would mean today, printing not being extant at the time. It is surely not an unfounded claim to say that the flames of those burning books threw not a light but a murky lurid smoke and smudge over the mind of medieval Europe. The evil consequences are still running their course. The destruction of the Alexandrian library is the main indictment in the bill of vandalism, but there are others not so well known.

The severe charge is made by Higgins (Anac., p. 564) that many of the early Christians of the fourth and fifth centuries in their "fanatical excitement" became Carmelite monks and founded a secret corresponding society, meeting mostly at night. (Night meetings violated Roman law and were in large measure the reason for the persecutions.) The heads of this order, says Higgins, had enough power to correct or destroy at pleasure any Gospel in the world not preserved by the "heretics." This, he avers, is the reason why we have no MSS. older than those of the sixth century. This order's detestation of the "heathen" books was of the deepest virulence, and the fires of their hatred turned into physical flames first at Antioch, as described in Acts, and, says Higgins, were repeatedly rekindled by a succession of councils up to the last canon of the Council of Trent against heathen learning. They sequestered many books for their later destruction. "Here we have the cause, and almost the sole cause, which effected the darkness of the world for many generations."

Higgins relates (p. 565) that St. Gregory is said by John of Salisbury to have burnt the imperial library of the Apollo. (Forsythe's Travels, p. 134.)

The Victor Tunensis, already mentioned, was, according to Higgins and Lardner, the agent of considerable destruction of Gospels about the sixth century, and probably by order of the Emperor Anastasius at Constantinople.

Some twenty-four volumes of the works of the great Gnostic philosopher Basilides, – extolled so highly by Clement of Alexandria – his splendid Interpretations Upon the Gospels, were all burned by order of the Church, Eusebius tells us. These works alone might have changed the course of Western history into pleasanter channels than those of bigotry and slaughter. Several writers affirm that, what with generations of the most active Church Fathers working assiduously at the destruction of old documents and the preparation of new passages to be interpolated in those which happened to survive, there remains of the noble Gnostic literature, the legitimate offspring of the genuine archaic wisdom, nothing but the Pistis Sophia and some few scattered fragments, precious, however, for the hints they give of the mighty treasure lost.

Mead is authority for the reported burning of the manuscripts of French Rabbis by the Inquisition. He says that for one thousand years the Christian authorities hurled all kinds of bulls, anathemas and edicts of confiscation and conflagration against the Talmud. He cites, too, the vandal acts of the fanatical Crusaders, who left smoldering piles of Hebrew scrolls behind them in their path of blood and fire. Official burnings of Hebrew books began at Montpellier in 1233, where a Jew, an Anti-Maimonist, persuaded the Dominicans and Franciscans of the Inquisition, likely unaware of the purely internal conflict between exotericism and esotericism in Jewry, to commit to the flames all the works of Maimonides. In the same year at Paris some twelve thousand volumes of the Talmud were burned, and in 1244 eighteen thousand various works were fed to the flames.

The story of the destruction, not only of books, but of cities, monasteries and temples, of the early pre-Christian Gaelic civilization in Britain, Ireland, Brittany and Gaul, is a sorry narrative of Christian fury. A Christian mob destroyed the city of Bibractis in 389 in Gaul, and Alesia was destroyed before that. Bibractis had a sacred college of the Druids with forty thousand students, giving courses in philosophy, literature, grammar, jurisprudence, medicine, astrology, architecture and esoteric religion. Arles, founded 2000 years before Christ, was sacked in 270 A.D.

A statement in Westrop and Wake's Phallism in Ancient Religions charges Cardinal Ximenes with having burned the old Arabic manuscripts. And Draper shows that the same Ximenes "delivered to the flames in the squares of Granada eighty thousand Arabic manuscripts, among them translations of the classical authors." Wilder states that thirty-six volumes written by Porphyry were destroyed by the Fathers.

A candid and unbiased witness is Edward Carpenter, English philosopher, who, in Pagan and Christian Creeds (p. 204), speaks bluntly of Christian practices:

"The Christian writers, as time went on, not only introduced new doctrines, legends, miracles and so forth – most of which we can trace to antecedent pagan sources – but they took pains to destroy the pagan records and so obliterate the evidence of their own dishonesty."

J.M. Robertson (Pagan Christs, p. 325) writes that of certain books mentioned "every one of these has been destroyed by the care of the Church." The treatise of Firmucus has been mutilated at a passage where he has accused the Christians of following Mithraic usages.

. . . .

The invidious task of mustering a large body of such evidence as this would seem to have been well enough performed with what has been given. But another sizable segment of data remains to be put on record, not at all with the mere aim of heaping disrepute on the dominant religion of the West, but for the purpose of adding convincing reality to the claims here advanced that the Christian system early suffered such deterioration as to make both possible and understandable the catastrophic changes alleged herein. The first reaction on the part of non-studious folks in the Christian faith will undoubtedly be the feeling that a group of people so sanctified by piety and holy faith as the early Christians are commonly reputed to have been, could not have perpetrated the crimes against intelligence and righteousness which this work lays at their door. It remains to be shown, then, that the picture of elevated holiness traditionally painted of the primitive Christians has been colored with unduly bright hues.

On the side of philosophy and religion as an intellectual enterprise Mead has most accurately and faithfully, as well as without undue bias, presented the true picture of the situation in primitive Christianity. In his Fragments of a Faith Forgotten he analyzes the effect of the sudden "throwing open" of the secret esoteric wisdom to the untutored populace, and describes the effect of the blinding new light on the masses. He asserts that the adherents of the new religion professed to "throw open everything" to common view, and the procedure left the unprepared rabble dazed by a sudden flashing of light they could not comprehend. The upshot was that they were thrown into a fever of excitement and emotional frenzy, similar in kind, though greater in degree, to the ferment created by every other marked preachment of new and sensational doctrines in religion. The sage custodians of deep spiritual truth were well instructed and supported by astute knowledge of human nature in their policy of esoteric secrecy. They had been well counseled to this posture by witnessing the inordinate emotional upheaval set in ferment by every untimely release of the dynamic psychological potency of great truths imperfectly comprehended and unsteadied by knowledge. The phenomenon is so glaringly exemplified before our eyes in this day that Mead's words should strike us with singular force:

"The 'many' had begun to play with psychic and spiritual forces let loose from the Mysteries, and the 'many' went mad for a time and have not yet regained their sanity."

The bold affirmation is here made that this comes closer to being the true analysis of the motivation and expression of the forces that made Christianity the religion it was and gave it its distinctive character and direction than any other estimate advanced over the centuries. We have before us at this present so exactly similar a situation in the ferment of extreme and fanatical ideologies exhibited by a host of modern "spiritual" cults of many varieties that there should be little difficulty in our seeing the obvious correctness of Mead's analysis. It is the very charge resounding from hundreds of pulpits today, that thousands of semi-intelligent people are playing with psychic, "spiritual" and "occult" forces which, if coaxed into untimely function without competent philosophical acumen, can prove most perilous to sanity and balance. This can be seen and possibly readily admitted by the clergy. What the clergy will not so readily admit, however, is that its own primitive Christianity (after the fatal third century, at any rate) was as errant, wild and misguided a fanaticism as that of the contemporary cults. It was not so as long as it held on to the philosophy and the esoteric Gnosis of the precedent Mysteries. It became such the moment it destroyed the Mysteries, let down the disciplinary safeguards and "threw open everything" sacred and profound to the impious hands of the gullible masses. The idiotic fervor of piety unbalanced by the intelligence requisite to hold it in line with restraint, swept Christianity out of the channels of sanity into the maelstrom of one of the most rabid of all religious ferments in history, and from that into currents that have borne it forward along courses of violence, bigotry and inhumanity almost beyond belief.

In the same work Mead portrays the situation that ensues when a strong ferment brews among the populace, and a new order is instituted following the sweeping away of old barriers. This, too, can have direct relevance and instruction for the world today. He says the new order gives rise at the same time to a wild intolerance, a glorification of ignorance, a wholesale condemnation of intelligent conservatism, and generally causes a social upheaval which is taken to be the divine expression of a new freedom. Always the peculiar mark of this new freedom is that it shortly becomes as dogmatic as the old oppression. Every one of these stages was manifest in the popular revolt against the conservative aristocracy of intellect in religion which from the third century swept Christianity into the role and spirit of an anti-cultural faith. Such would inevitably be the case when the predominantly mystical and emotional types of religion gain the field against the predominantly intellectual and philosophical strains. Early Gnostic and Pauline Greek Christianity were of the latter strain; orthodox Christianity, mostly Petrine after the third century, was of the former type. This is primarily all that is required as datum to qualify a perfectly clear and correct evaluation of the genius of the movement that founded Christianity. With this view as guide and gauge, there should now be made a thorough re-study of the genesis of Christianity. It would be a most illuminating revelation of what perils are generated the moment reason yields the ground to faith in religion, when piety is not balanced by rational elements, or, in broad sense, when philosophy gives place to religion. Mead ends his treatment of the point with the epigrammatic threnody, "Greek rationalism was lost; symbolism was lost." Indicating the truth of both the fact and its significance may be cited Tertullian's brief announcement that "when one has once believed, search should cease."

On the State of the Church is the title of a treatise written by St. Cyprian just before the Decian persecution. He admits in it that "there was no true devotion in the priests" . . . that the simple were deluded and the brethren circumvented by craft and fraud. Also he declares that great numbers of the Bishops were eager only to heap up money, to seize people's lands by treachery and fraud and to increase their stock by exorbitant usury. (Quoted by Middleton, Free Inquiry.)

The Catholic Encyclopedia (I, p. 555) may be cited to the effect that even in the fourth century St. John Chrysostom testifies to the decline in fervor in the Christian family and contends that it was no longer possible for children to obtain proper religious and moral training in their own homes. The Encyclopedia adds at another place (VIII, p. 426): "The Lateran was spoken of as a brothel and the moral corruption of Rome became the subject of general odium." Practically in every century nearly every large city in Christendom has been charged with harboring vice and moral and political corruption till the odium mounted to scandal. Yet alongside of this record and its own admissions of rottenness in Christian lands and even in the Church itself, this authority (III, p. 34) boasts that "the wonderful efficacy displayed by the religion of Christ in purifying the morals of Europe has no parallel." Vaunting that "the Church was the guide of the western nations from the close of the seventh century to the beginning of the sixteenth," it can be quoted with a string of admissions such as that on VII, p. 387: – "At the beginning of the Reformation the condition of the clergy and consequently of the people was a very sad one . . . the unfortunate state of the clergy . . . their corrupt morals" – that openly belie the validity of the claim. It itself pronounces the Middle Ages, "of all human epochs, an age of terrible corruption and social decadence." "From the fourth century onward . . . the Agapae gave rise to flagrant and intolerable abuses." It describes the

Agapetae as virgins who consecrated themselves to God with a vow of chastity and associated with laymen who like themselves had taken a vow of chastity. "It resulted in abuses and scandals." Jerome arraigns Syrian monks for living in cities with Christian virgins. These Agapetae are sometimes confounded with the Subintroductae or women who lived with clerics without marriage, says the Encyclopedia (I, p. 202).

Even Eusebius refuses to record the dissensions and follies which were rife among the many factions before the Diocletian persecution (Eccl. Hist., Bk. 8, Ch. 2). He delineates the unshepherdly character of the shepherds of flocks, "condemned by divine justice as unworthy of such a charge," their ambitious aspirations for office and the injudicious and unlawful ordinations that take place, the divisions among the confessors themselves, the great schisms industriously fomented by factions, heaping affliction upon affliction, – "all these I have resolved to pass by."

Catholic Encyclopedia says (VI, p. 792) that at the time of Gregory VII's elevation to the papacy "the Christian world was in a deplorable condition." Doctrinal controversy waxed bitter to the point at times of physical combat, especially, says the Encyclopedia (I, p. 191), in North Africa. "One act of violence followed another and begot new conflicts. . . . Crimes of all kinds made Africa one of the most wretched provinces in the world."

Lundy says that the Arian and orthodox factions fought in the streets and in the churches with such fierce animosity that on one occasion one hundred and thirty-seven dead bodies were found in one of the basilicas (Animianus Marcellinus, lib. XXVII, iii, p. 392). Doctrinal controversy waxed so fierce that it gave rise to the phrase "Odium Theologicum" expressed by one writer in the sentence, "Hell hath no fury like an offended saint." This had been previously matched by the Emperor Julian's characterization: "There is no wild beast like an angry theologian."

The Encyclopedia portrays elaborately the "general debasement" which the Church shared with the times. It was worst in the tenth century. Simony and clerical incontinence were the two great evils descanted upon. "Many had lost all sense of Christian ideals." Says the Encyclopedia, with more truth than it suspected, no doubt, "the accumulated wisdom of the past was in danger of perishing." In controversion of the general claim of the Church that in the night of the Dark Ages it was the monasteries and cloisters of Christianity that preserved the ancient classics, we may cite Wheless' sentence: "We shall see that every scrap of Greek and Latin learning which, after twelve centuries, slowly filtered into Christendom, came from the hated Arabs, through the more hated Jews, after Christian contact with civilization through the Crusades." And the Encyclopedia testifies to the fact of sinister force in admitting that even when the development of Scholasticism brought the revival of Greek philosophy, particularly that of Aristotle, "it also meant that philosophy was now to serve the cause of Christian truth." The same force of obscurantism that ten or twelve centuries earlier had blotted out the world's accumulated spiritual light was now upon its return ready to diffract the pure rays of that light into colors of its own composition by passing them through the medium of that dark glass of perpetuated dogmatism and entrenched ignorance that had extinguished it in the first instance. The same obfuscation of intellect that had put out the light a thousand years before was still at hand to distort its pure gleam when it shone again.

The Encyclopedia speaks (XII, p. 765) of "a revival of learning as soon as the West was capable of it" – after being under Christian tutelage for a thousand years.

At a moment when the conscience of cultured people everywhere is horrified at the savage atrocities of a nation diabolically committed to violence, it might be well to remind those on the side of Christian resentment against "pagan" barbarity, that when the Christian Crusaders entered Jerusalem from all sides on July 15, 1099, they slew its inhabitants regardless of age or sex, while Saladin committed no act of outrage.

J. E. Ellam, in his Buddhism and Modern Thought (p. 140), puts in brief compass and strong terms the degradation of Europe under Christianity:

"Yet the moral level of Europe was lower than that of any savages of whom we have record. Its barbarities and cruelties, its vices and brutality, would have scandalized even Dahomey and Benin. Cyril of Alexandria has a lurid description of the vices even of his own followers. Augustine says much the same of 'the faithful' in Roman Africa. Silvianus, a priest of the fifth century, writes: 'Besides a very few who avoid evil, what is almost the whole body of Christians but a sink of iniquity? How many in the Church will you find that are not drunkards, or adulterers, or fornicators, or gamblers, or robbers, or murderers, – or all together?'" (Silvianus: On the Providence of God, III, 9.)

Lundy (Monumental Christianity, p. 353) speaks of the licentiousness in connection with the Agapae or "love-feasts" held in the Christian congregations –

"When in the fourth century . . . the Church, from the necessity of the case, substituted these Agapae for some of the pagan festivities the abuse became so great that the Council of Laodicea forbade their celebration altogether in the churches." Its Canon XXVIII enacts that "it is not permitted to hold love-feats, as they are called, in the Lord's houses, or in church assemblies, nor to eat and to spread couches in the house of the Lord."

Lundy states, however, that they were such a scandal to the Christian name by reason of the drunkenness and licentiousness practiced that entire suppression was the final resort.

"But so popular were these festivals among the poor and ignorant classes of the Christian community, such a strong hold had they obtained in their hearts and lives that it was an exceeding difficult matter to suppress them."

They could still be held in private homes and in cemeteries "and were so held for three centuries longer." They were not suppressed until the seventh century, when the Trullian or Quinisext Council took them in hand.

Paulinus, the good Bishop of Nola, laments that these festivities were carried on during the entire night.

"How I wish," he says in the Ninth Hymn to Felix, "that their joys would assume a more sober character; that they would not mix their cups on holy ground. Yet I think we must not be too severe on the pleasures of their little feasts: for error creeps into unlearned minds; and their simplicity, unconscious of the great fault they commit, verges on piety, supposing that the saints are gratified by the wine poured upon their tombs."

The good Bishop's sad confession that error creeps into unlearned minds is one of the bluntest massive truths confronting humanity. It is also one of the most vital factors involved in the entire history of the Christian religion. Admitted by everybody, it would seem as if, therefore, the very first article in the constitution of a great religion would be to spread honest learning as widely and as deeply as possible.

Lundy sententiously summarizes the situation in the Church, saying (p. 107) that

"Christian doctrine, Christian morals and Christian art degenerated together, and it is called development!" So he can say: "All this is but a repetition of the degeneracy and the debasement of the old Patriarchal faith into Pagan idolatry: of simple truths, as taught by symbols perverted into falsehood by images and idols."

It is hardly necessary to inject the correction of his last statement, that it was not the images and idols that perverted truth, but the failure to go behind those symbols to the sublime meaning now known to be covered by them.

Mead assembles evidence to indicate that the lasciviousness of the Agapae can not be charged against people of such refinement and philosophical acumen as the Gnostics, though

Clement does bring the charge against them; but thinks it probable that some cults calling themselves Christians did confuse the Agapae and love-feasts of the times with the orgies and feasts of the ignorant populace. "The Pagans brought these accusations against the Christians, and the Christian sects against one another."

The volume of accusation and supporting data could be heaped up to hundreds of pages. The modest quantity, gathered in desultory reading, here presented is sufficient to carry home the point that flagrant deterioration had taken hold of the Christian movement on a vast scale, and, since things have their causes, something must have occurred in the movement that for two and a half to three centuries manifested high intelligence and moral purity to reduce it so suddenly to corruption and barbarity. This cause, it is contended, as far as it was an influence detached from exterior economic, political and social conditions, was the loss of the esoteric wisdom, philosophical culture and the whole intellectual side of religion, induced by and further inducing the popular submergence of minority intelligence by majority ignorance. The direct relevance to our theme of this fateful shift from philosophical rationalism to massive irrational pietism is found in the reflection that such a vast transformation in outward life and thought was the evidence of another equally drastic change in basic understanding. The larger and more manifest changes in outward life must spring from significant changes in inner consciousness. That inner change was in major part just that shift from symbolic and allegorical esotericism over to historical literalism, the chief item of which was the mistaking of the Christos for a man of flesh.

As this work is not an attack on Christianity, it must be emphasized that the data here presented reflecting adversely on the name and record of that religion have been given purely for the sake of buttressing the leading argument with the support it gains from its setting in a true, instead of a warped, view of past history. The argument would lose some of its legitimate force if permitted to stand in the poorer light of a history that has been, at any rate to common intelligence, grossly distorted by pious misinterpretation, suppression of honest facts, vandalism and juggling of every sort. The aim has been a purely academic or dialectic one, to show that the loss of high knowledge, the historization of myths and dramas, the literalization of the Gospels, the conversion of the personae of the great universal ritual into living persons, the lethal sweep of ignorance and the ensuing degradation and debasement of the whole movement from the interior heat of theological doctrine clear out to the periphery of moral social conduct, were all wholly necessary and consistent elements of the one completed picture. If history can not be brought into court to support a thesis, point a moral or furnish evidence in straightforward truth-seeking, it is studied to little good purpose. We therefore cite the portions of history that bear with very direct cogency upon the great question under investigation.

Chapter VIII

SUBLIME MYTH MAKES GROTESQUE HISTORY

No single volume could undertake the full task of establishing the fact of the conversion of allegory, myth and drama into "history," but the case has been presented in outline with enough evidence to render it a substantial claim. The stage is now ready for the introduction of the main evidence to validate the further claim that the events taken for the alleged historical narrative of Old and New Testament literature are not and never were occurrences on the plane of objective reality. The case now proceeds directly to the submission of the testimony which proves that the whole web of Gospel history was woven by ignorant assumption out of the traditional material of the rite and the myth.

It is quite possible that with so much of the evidence destroyed, full and final "proof" of the actual change of meaning can never be presented, or that material will never be found that will pin the offense on the actual culprits or show them in the actual work of making the change. There were no lie-detectors, wall-recorders or hidden cameras available to catch the manipulators at work.

The change came first in the minds of the theologians and the people and only later carried out its implications in the alteration of texts and the "correction" of manuscripts. But in the pages ahead so much of the evidence that may be considered as "proof" of the general change on this score will be adduced as the scope of the volume will permit. Again a great quantity is available, and that from rather haphazard reading. A systematic search would uncover whole volumes more. Again much of the data is furnished by Massey and Higgins. It may be claimed that too much reliance is being placed upon the findings of these two delvers into the past, and that their views are prejudiced. We demur to the objection. Both gave their lives to extensive research in the field of ancient religion, both were honest in appraising the value of material and both were to the highest degree sincere in their single aim of finding what was the truth. If they were eventually disposed to a sharply critical view of Christianity, it came directly as the result of what they discovered in the history of that religion. Their hostility was engendered by the force of repellent facts brought to light in their studies, and was not the operation of a merely sectarian prejudice. No more than the present writer did they begin their investigations with a preconceived enmity to Christianity. They probably held no positive enmity against it at any time; they simply wished the world to know the actual truth about it and its history. At any rate they align their judgments and conclusions with the facts and the evidence, and their work must be judged on the basis of its agreement with the data and its competence to meet the demands of exegetical proof, as that of any other scholars. Their testimony is presented here because they saw with clearest vision and described with singular lucidity the pertinent truth in scores of situations in which a clear view has never been had before. A subsidiary aim of this study is to vindicate in the main their important findings in their field. This aim would include also Thomas Taylor in the field of Greek translation and exegesis.

It seems best to begin with what might be generally called circumstantial evidence, and then proceed to more redoubtable testimony. Every item submitted will bear more or less directly upon the case for the non-historicity of the Gospels and their characters.

It is not necessarily true that the workability of a thesis proves its correctness. But if the thesis for the historicity of Jesus piles up great difficulties and obstacles in the way of its acceptance, and that for the non-historicity clears them away, it is a major presumptive evidence that the successful and consistently workable thesis is the correct one. This broad observation will serve to introduce a series of depositions from our scholar Gerald Massey, which, at the risk of some prolixity, it seems eminently desirable to array here. They are of themselves matter of intrinsic value and bear down on our case with most pointed appositeness. Almost alone of Egyptologists this student discerned the chief elements in the great significance of Egypt's lore of wisdom, and therefore had at his service a key by which he could penetrate more deeply into the heart of the Egyptian, Greek and Hebrew systems of religion. His pronouncements and judgments are deemed of especial value because they publish vital truths missed by all the other investigators of the literature of old.

Massey portrays the Egyptian origin and background of the Christian theology and finds it non-historical (The Natural Genesis, I, p. 479):

"Egypt labored at the portrait (of the Christ) for thousands of years before the Greeks added their finishing touches to the type of the ever-youthful solar god. It was Egypt that first made the statue live with her own life and humanized her ideal of the divine. Here was the legend of supreme pity and self-sacrifice so often told of the canonical Christ. She related how the god did leave the courts of heaven and come down as a little child, the infant Horus, born of the Virgin, through whom he took flesh, or descended into matter, 'crossed the earth as a substitute' (Ritual, Ch. xlviii), descended into Hades as vivifier of the dead, their vicarious justifier and redeemer, the first fruits and leader of the resurrection into eternal life. The Christian legends were first related of Horus or Osiris, who was the embodiment of divine goodness, wisdom, truth and purity; who personated ideal perfection in each sphere of manifestation and every phase of power. This was the greatest hero that ever lived in the mind of man – not in the flesh – to influence with transforming force; the only hero to whom the miracles were natural because he was not human.

"The so-called miracles of Jesus were not only impossible on human grounds; they are historically impossible because they were pre-extant as mythical representations which were made on grounds that were entirely non-human, in the drama of the Mysteries that was as non-historical as the Christmas pantomime. The miracles ascribed to Jesus on earth had been pre-Christian religion. Horus, whose other name is Jesus, is the performer of 'miracles' which are repeated in the Gospels, and which were first performed as mysteries in the divine nether world. But if Horus or Iusa be made human on earth, as a Jew in Judea, we are suddenly hemmed in by the miraculous at the center of a maze with nothing antecedent for a clue; no path that leads to the heart of the mystery and no visible means of exit therefrom. With the introduction of the human personage on mundane ground, the mythical inevitably becomes the miraculous; you cannot have history without it; thus the history was founded on the miracles, which were perversions of the mythology that was provably pre-extant."

This is a clear and succinct picture of the truth on the point – except, as has been indicated in our previous work, The Lost Light, that Massey erred in the matter of the mislocation of the nether world, or underworld, of mythology, the Amenta of Egyptian texts. He thought that the Christians erred in mistaking the "earth" of Amenta for this mundane realm and in transplanting the spiritual Christos from this celestial "earth" to the real earth, thereby euhemerizing and falsely historicizing him. In aiming to correct their arrant blunder, he keeps the Christos entirely away from earth, and applies the Christly legend to the "other earth" of Amenta, located somewhere in spiritual spheres. Thus, while Massey retains the Christos as a spiritual entity only, or an element of consciousness, which is assuredly his true character, he in turn errs by keeping him away from earth and the life of man in his supposititious "other earth" of Amenta. The Christos is a real entity and he is spiritual in nature, but he is on earth and in man, yet neither a man on earth (the Christian mistake), nor a spirit in any other earth than this only one we know (Massey's error). The Lost Light has at great length established the truth that Amenta, the underworld of mythology, Hades, is this good earth, where the Christos, a principle and not a man, but at the same time the god in man, performs all the miracles that, as Massey truly represents, were typical allegories in the myth, but were made into miracles in the Gospels when ignorance dragged symbology over into "history." To sum up, the Christians said the Christ was a man on earth in history. Massey says that the Christ was not a man at all, nor was he on earth or in history. He was, instead, the Christ in man, who after death descended into the gloomy Amenta as a shade, and there worked the miracles of healing and implemented the judgment and the resurrection. Massey's mistake was in saying he was not on earth. He was on earth, operating during the life, not after the death, of men, only not as a man, but as a principle of righteousness, in man. The previous work has demonstrated that the ancient theologians called this life "death" (the death of the soul, buried in sense), called mortals "the dead," and by their name Amenta they designated no other region than this nether world which we know as earth. The reorientation of the meanings of these three or four names is pretty nearly the whole clue to the proper interpretation of the scriptures of antiquity. It will be necessary to keep this correction in mind in reading further cullings from Massey's works. It vitiates his main conclusions, but does not destroy the value of his findings with regard to the conversion of myth into history.

A great enlightenment floods the mind from the vast truth couched in the following brief passage from his great work, Ancient Egypt, The Light of the World (p. 77):

"When it is conclusively proved that the Christian miracles are nothing more than the pagan mode of symbolical representation literalized, there is no longer any question of contravening, or breaking, or even challenging any well-known laws of nature. The discussion as to the probability or possibility of miracle on the old grounds of belief and doubt it closed forever."

This indeed is a welcome closure of debate, for few things have so sorely perplexed the reasoning mind and taxed the religious faith of mankind as the alleged "miracles" of Jesus in the Gospels. Whatever militates to break man's utter faith in and reliance upon the invariability of natural law, by so much disintegrates his position of stability in the world, undermines his bases of constancy in conduct and corrodes his entire ground of moral conscience. It tends to reduce his cosmos to a chaos, if the laws of life can be abrogated at any time by a fiat of arbitrary whimsicality, however "good." The philosopher David Hume has written a treatise that lays forever the ghost of "miracles" with impregnable logic: if an event occurs it does so by and through the operation of law and not in contravention of it. There can be no such thing as a "miracle" of the kind believed in by common uncritical religious faith."

The mind of man will be doubly safeguarded against invasion from the side of irrationalism if Massey's golden theological discovery is correct, – that the miracles are only literalized spiritual myths, and never objectively happened. It is the natural law that works no end of miracles, that is, things to make man wonder, such as the rain, the snow, the dew, fire, water, green leaf, bud, flower, seed, death and life from death ever renewed. The Christian introduction of the cult of the "supernatural" into current untutored thought has come closer to unsettling the normal sanity of the world mind and making gullible fools out of millions than any other influence known to history. What the "miracles" – before they were historicized – meant to ancient sapiency was just the truly wonder-working power of the Christ in man to transfigure mortal life and the very bodies of mortals on earth with divine health and beauty. And this knowledge and this conception is worth infinitely more than the physical "healing" by a touch from outside having nothing to do with the beneficiary's own deserts or his own inner divinity, and therefore meaningless. The "healing" of five thousand men and women on any hillside or lakeside in Palestine two thousand years ago is an event of no significance compared with the universal understanding of the immanent Christ's power to heal all men by his divine ferment. Religion badly needs a totally new orientation to this reputed matter of "healing." If people can for long periods violate the laws of life, particularly those connected with food and diet, become gravely ill and then run to a healer or a healing philosophy and be "made whole" by alleged divine power without reference to their demerit or their deserts under the law of life and in contravention of evolutionary justice, chaos will be introduced into the counsels of creation. In fact, the popular religious notions that have made "healing" almost the prime credential of the authenticity of any religious movement, is itself almost wholly grounded on a contempt for natural law. This has gone so far in modern "spiritual" cultism that one strong group has flaunted as one of its banners the outright shibolleth that "the laws of nature are the vaporings of mortal mind." It must basically be assumed that if "spiritual law" in some measure transcends natural law, it does so by fulfilling and consummating it, not by negating it. It is unquestionable that spiritual law bends natural forces to its purposes, as man uses a machine or soul uses body; but it does not disregard the natural energies which it uses any more than the user can disregard the laws of his machine or his body. In this field the vogue of "miracles" has wrought havoc with general sanity. Massey's fine discernment that saw first and clearly in modern times that the "miracles" of "Jesus" were Egyptian mythical rescripts falsely turned into "history," at one stroke robs the Gospel "wonders" of their fictitious value, while restoring to us their real value as dramatic mysteries, and his work in this item puts us under vast obligation to him and to the integrity of his mind and motive. It is this obligation that urges the inclusion of so much of his material in this work.

He writes that no Egyptologist has ever dreamed that the Ritual – the Book of the Dead – still exists in Christian formulations, under the disguise of both the Gnostic and the canonical Gospels, or that it was the fountain-head of all the books of wisdom claimed to be divine. But no initiate in the Osirian Mysteries could possibly have rested his hope of salvation "on the Galilean line of glory," which made individual in one "man" what was spiritually attainable by all. Egypt possessed the knowledge that a kingly power of consciousness had become a voluntary immolation on the altar of sense and fleshly body, in a passion of divinest pity became incarnate, put itself "under the law" of sin and "death" for the salvation of the world; but this knowledge did not run out in futile nonsense in the belief that God had manifested once for all as a historic personality. The same legend of divine sons sacrificing their heavenly birthright for humankind was repeated in many lands with a change of name for the empyreal sufferer, but none of those initiated in the esoteric wisdom ever looked upon Iusa, or Horus, Jesus, Tammuz, Krishna, Buddha, Witoba, Marduk, Mithra, Sabazius, Adonis or any other of the many Saviors as historical in personality, "for the simple reason that they had been more truly taught." (Massey.)

The first "gospel" of the Christians "began with a collection of Sayings of Jesus, fatuously supposed to have been a historical teacher of that name," Massey avers. In some "New Sayings of Jesus" found at Oxyrhynchus, utterances of "Jesus" paralleling those found in the Ritual of remote Egyptian times are to be read.

In a lecture entitled The Logia of the Lord, or Prehistoric Sayings Ascribed to Jesus the Christ, Massey sets forth many vital data. Never, he says, were mortals more perplexed, bewildered and taken aback than were the Christians of the second, third and fourth centuries, who had started their own new beginning, warranted to be solely historic, and then found that an apparition of their faith was following them one way and meeting them in another. This "double" of their faith was obviously not founded on their alleged facts which stood as the base of their original religion, but were ages earlier in the world. It was a shadow that threatened to steal away the body of their substance, mocking them with its factual unreality – a hollow ghost of the same truths they had embraced as a solid possession. It was horrible, devilish. Nothing but the work of the devil could explain the haunting phantom. The Gnostic Ante-Christ had to be made their Anti-Christ. The pre-Christian Gnostics and some of the primitive Christian sects had a Christ who was not based on the person of the living Jesus! One and all had as their divine figure the mystical Christ of the Gnosis and the mythical Messiah, the Ever-Coming One, the type of divine selfhood, manifesting collectively and spiritually in the evolution of the race. Historic Christianity can furnish no explanation why the "biography" of its personal founder should have been held back for several centuries (and strangely the same nearly two centuries elapsed before the books on Buddha's life were circulated); why the facts of its own origin should have been kept (and still are kept) in obscurity; why there should have been no authorized record made known earlier. The conversion of the myths and the Docetic (mystical) doctrines of the Gnosis into human history will alone account for these facts. The singular thing is, points out Massey, that the earliest Gospels are the farthest removed from the supposed human history! That came last and, he affirms, only when the spiritual Christ of the Gnosis had been rendered concrete in the density of Christian miscalculation! Christianity began as Gnosticism, and continued by means of a conversion and perversion that were opposed in vain by Paul. The Mysteries of Gnosticism were perpetuated as Christian, but with a difference, a complete change of character and identity, as interpretation shifted from the mystical to the historical plane. The first Christians based their cult system on secret doctrines whose inner sense was only explained to Initiates during a long course of discipline and study. (Mosheim and other historians testify abundantly to the existence of the Greater and the Lesser Mysteries in the primitive Christian Church.) These secret teachings were never to be divulged or promulgated, and they were not publicized until the ignorant belief in historical Christianity had taken permanent root. We are told how it was held by some that the Apocrypha might only be read by those who were "perfected" in the deeper Mysteries, and that these writings were reserved exclusively for Christian adepts. It must be obvious that the doctrine or knowledge that was forced to be kept so sacredly secret could have had no reference to personal human history that was broadcast to all, or to the teachings of that literal Christianity that boasted so simple an origin. The Greater and even the Lesser Mysteries of Christianity must have dealt with subjects that lay far over in the realm of esoteric truth, having little connection with the outer story in the Gospels. There is bluntly nothing to be esoteric or mysterious about in the direct narrative of Gospel Christianity. If the early Church had its higher Mysteries it is certain that they were of the same general nature as those of pagan Greece and Egypt. Nobody, says Justin Martyr, is permitted to partake of the Eucharist "unless he has accepted as true that which is taught by us," and unless he received the bread and wine as the very flesh and blood of that Jesus who was made flesh. In this we can see the "sarkolatrae" or worshippers of a Christ of the flesh fighting against the spiritual Christ of the Gnostics. There were many sects of so-called Christians and various versions of the nature of the Christ, Kronian or astronomical, mythical and mystical. But the Church of Rome could not escape the evidences that its foundations and ceremonies were drawn from Egypt; the Virgin Mother, the Son, the gods of Egypt were sealed up in the very corner-stone of the Church; the haunting ghost was in the Church itself.

And according to the unquestioned tradition of the Christian Fathers, which has always been accepted by the Church, the primary nucleus of the canonical Gospels was not a life of Jesus at all, but a collection of Logia or Sayings, the Logia Kuriaka, which were written down in Hebrew or Aramaic by one Matthew, as the scribe of the Lord. We have already glanced at the suggested derivation of Matthew from the Egyptian Mattiu, meaning "the word of truth," or "true sayings." Clement of Alexandria, Origen and Irenaeus agree that Matthew's was the primary Gospel, disputing Eusebius' story of Mark's primacy. This tradition rests upon the testimony of Papias, Bishop of Hieropolis and friend of Polycarp. Papias is named with Pantaenus, Clement and Ammonius as one of the ancient interpreters who agreed to accept the Logia as referring to a historical Christ. He was a literalizer of mythology. He believed the Sayings to have been actually spoken by a historical Jesus, written down in Hebrew by a follower named Matthew. He wrote a work entitled Logion Kuriakon, a commentary on the Sayings. Thus the basis of the first Gospel was in no way a biography, record or history of Jesus. It was only the "Sayings of the Lord."

Now there is plenty of evidence to show that these Sayings, the admitted foundations of the canonical Gospels, were not first uttered by a personal founder of Christianity, nor invented afterwards by any of his followers. Many of them were pre-existent, pre-historic and pre-Christian! And if it can be proved that these oracles of God and Logia of the Lord are not original after the year thirty A.D., and that they can be identified as a collection of Egyptian, Hebrew and Gnostic sayings, they would be deprived of any competence to stand as evidence that the Jesus of the Gospels ever lived as a man or teacher. To begin with, says Massey, two of the Sayings assigned by Matthew to Jesus are these: "Lay not up for yourselves treasures upon earth," and "If ye forgive men their trespasses, your heavenly Father will also forgive you." These Sayings had already been uttered by the feminine Logos called Wisdom (Sophia) in the Apocrypha. Wisdom was the Sayer personified long anterior to Christianity. (Let it be noted that the oracular voice in the Biblical Book of Ecclesiastes, or the Preacher, is translated more recently as "the Speaker." This precisely matches the character that is the utterer of truth in the Egyptian Ritual (Book of the Dead), called "the Speaker.") It might indeed with full truth be said, as Massey has just done, that the preacher of the divine words of truth in the world's arcane scripts of old is simply, in Greek terms, Athena, the goddess of wisdom, that is, wisdom personified as feminine. It is sheer imbecility of mind that would attempt to convert the personification into a living man.

More Gospel passages are shown to have been already in the Egyptian Ritual, in Enoch, in 2 Esdras, in the Haggada of the Jews and other pre-Christian documents.

The nature of the Sayings is acknowledged by Irenaeus when he says:

"According to no one Saying of the heretics is the word of God made flesh."

The Christ, the utterer of the Sermons and Sayings, assuredly is not a person preaching on earth.

The "Sayings" were oral teachings in all the Mysteries ages before they were written down. Several of them are so ancient as to be the common property of widely separated nations. Prescott gives a few Mexican Sayings; one of these, also found in the Talmud and the New Testament, is called the "old proverb." "As the old proverb says – 'whoso regards a woman with curiosity commits adultery with his eyes.'" And the third commandment according to Buddha is: "Commit no adultery; the law is broken by even looking at the wife of another man with lust in the mind." Among the sayings assigned to the Buddha is found the one dealing with the wheat and the tares. Another is the parable of the sower. Buddha likewise told of the hidden treasure which may be laid up securely where a thief can not break in and steal. Similarly the story of the rich young man who was commanded to sell all he had and give to the poor is told by Buddha. It is reported that he also said: "You may remove from their base the snowy mountains, you may exhaust the waters of the ocean, the firmament may fall to earth, but my words in the end will be accomplished." These are samples of scores and hundreds of similarities and identities between Christian Biblical material and passages from many pre-Christian books. No one can make the search and discover these numberless resemblances without forming the conviction that the Bible writings are rescripts, garbled and corrupted, of antecedent wisdom literature. To the student who delves into the study and makes the discoveries for himself, the evidence is startling enough to settle the matter beyond all possibility of mistake. For him the argument is closed.

The Buddha, in making his departure, promises to send the Paraclete, even the spirit of truth which shall lead his followers into all truth. The Gnostic Horus says the same thing in the same character. The sayings of Krishna are frequently identical with those of Buddha and of the Gospel Christ. "I am the letter A," cries the one. "I am the Alpha and the Omega," exclaims the other. "I am the beginning and the end," says Krishna. "I am the Light, I am the Life, I am the Sacrifice." Speaking to his disciples, he affirms that they will dwell in him as he dwells in them.

Buddha has his transfiguration when he ascended the mountain in Ceylon called Pandava or Yellow-white. There the heavens opened and a great light came in full flood around him and the glory of his person shone forth with "double power." He "shone as the brightness of the Sun and Moon," identical with that of Christ; and both these are the same as that of Osiris in his ascent of the Mount of the Moon. The same scene was previously portrayed in the Persian account of the devil tempting Zarathustra and inviting him to curse the Good Belief.

But these several forms of the one character did not originate and do not meet in any human history that was lived in Egypt, India, Persia or Judea. They meet only in one place – the mythos, says Massey, with indisputable truth. The mythos arose from Egypt and there alone can we delve down to the root of the origines. The myths of Christianity and Buddhism had a common origin and branched from the same root, whether in Egypt, as Massey claims it did, or elsewhere, as others may insist.

Pronounced in Greek, the Logia or Sayings are the mythoi of Egypt. They are utterances assigned to the personified Sayers in the mythology, which preceded and accounted for our theology and Christology. They existed before writing and were not allowed to be written. They still bear witness, however mangled and mutilated, against historical Christianity. "Myth" and "mouth" are identical at the root.

In the main, the drama of the Lord's death and the scenes of the Christian last judgment are represented in the Egyptian great Hall of Justice, where a person is separated from his sins, and those who have sided with Sut against Horus are transformed into goats. (This doubtless means that they are sent back into incarnation for further experience, and life in the body is typed by the sign of the winter solstice, Capricorn, the Goat, occupying the place of the nadir of descent into matter on the symbolic zodiacal chart. To separate the sheep from the goats is naturally to set off those still needing incarnation in Capricorn position from those who, as sheep in Aries (the Ram, the Lamb) at the spring equinox, are by position and significance out of the area of incarnate life, having made the passover of the line separating physical from spiritual existence when they entered Aries.) Massey points it out as notable that of the four Gospels Matthew alone represents this drama of the Egyptian Ritual. In the Ritual every hair is weighed; in the Gospel every hair is numbered. Many chapter titles of the Ritual are "sayings" of the deceased. Horus is the divine Sayer and the souls repeat his sayings. The original Sayings were declared to have been written by Hermes, or Taht, the scribe of the gods, and they constituted the primordial Hermaean or inspired Scriptures, which the Book of the Dead declares were written in Hieroglyphics by the finger of Hermes himself.

The data of Matthew were put in largely with the motive of fulfilling Old Testament "prophecy." But the compiler was doubtless too uninstructed to know that the "prophecies" belonged to astronomical allegory and that they never could or did refer to human history and were not supposed to be fulfilled on the plane of objective event, except in the minds of the ignorant, who could believe that the zodiacal Virgin Mother would bring forth her aeonial child on earth in a Judean stable or cave. Massey writes an impressive sentence when he pens these momentous words: "Those who did know better, whether Jews, Samaritans, Essenes, or Gnostics, entirely repudiated the historical interpretation and did not become Christians." They were in much the same relative case as those more intelligent persons today who repudiate the bald literal interpretations made by such sects as Jehovah's Witnesses, and just as correct in doing so. "They could no more join the ignorant fanatical Salvation Army in the first century than we can in the nineteenth." The so-called "prophecies" not only supply a raison d'être for the "history" in the Gospels; the events and attendant circumstances themselves are manufactured one after the other from the "prophecies" and sayings, i.e., from the mythos, which was already then of great antiquity. All this was done in the course of the process of literalization of the drama into a human life and its localization in Judea, under the pretext or in the blind belief that the impossible had come to pass. The events of the Gospels were not only thrust forth out of the mythos onto the stage of alleged history, but were mysteriously romanticized with the halo of prophetic fulfillment of Old Testament prediction. Of course the coming Messiah should be foretold to be born in Bethlehem (the house of bread), for the zodiacal allegory had his celestial birthplace long prepared in the sign of Pisces, the house of bread and fishes. He who was to feed the earthly multitude with the miraculously multiplied divinity symboled by bread and fish, would have to be born in the house of the fishes and of the bread which cometh down out of heaven. The Christian scriptures carried forward the salient features of the astronomical allegory, but their ignorant idolaters thought they were purveying sacred history.

Again, the child's being taken to Nazareth was only in order that the sayings might be fulfilled that he should be called a Nazarene. And yet, says Massey, his connection with Nazareth (which, incidentally, has never received any geographical authenticity at any time and perhaps never existed at all) would no more make him a Nazarene than his being born in a stable would make him a horse. Also Jesus came to dwell in Capernaum – "his own city" – on the borders of Zebulon and Naphtali, that a saying of Isaiah might be fulfilled. He cast out devils and healed the sick, for fulfillment of the same prophet's forecast. He taught the multitude in parables, for the same reason. In spite of his miracles and many wonderful works among the populace the people believed not in him, because Isaiah had hinted that the Lord would not be believed. Massey asks why they could be expected to believe when it was prophesied they would not. Jesus sent only two disciples to steal the ass and colt because Zechariah had spoken it so. Judas was on the spot to betray his Lord because the Psalmist had said that the Messiah's trusted and familiar friend "hath lifted up his heel against me." The Speaker in another Psalm had cried, "My God, my God, why hast thou forsaken me?" and the crucified Messiah came in flesh would have to repeat the cry from the cross. "They parted my garments among them and cast lots for my vesture"; "They gave me also gall for meat; and in my thirst they gave me vinegar to drink," had also to be re-enacted to match pre-extant similar passages.

Massey earns our deep gratitude once more for dissipating another of those most fatuous delusions resulting from ignorant misconstruction of ancient mythical material. It is with reference to the so-called "prophecies." It has already been shown that the words "prophet" and "prophecy" by etymology have nothing to do, directly, with forecasting future events in the objective sphere. The prophet meant simply a preacher, or utterer of truth, and his prophecies were simply preachments. The Biblical prophets were not clairvoyant prognosticators, but sages and expounders of lofty wisdom. The prophet was just another variant of the title of "Speaker" given, as just set forth, to the character in the ritual dramas whose part it was, personating divine Wisdom, to utter or preach the sayings of divine knowledge to mankind. The ascription to the word of the meaning attached to it later in common understanding was most unfortunate. It has been responsible for the precipitation into western history of a whole enormous chapter of delusion and lunacy. The amount of insane drivel, excited emotionalism, fear and folly, that the belief in Bible (and more recently "pyramid") "prophecy" has generated in uncritical minds comes to tragic proportions. If the ancient sages, as we now more clearly see, had little concern for factual history of their past or their own present, they must have had even less concern for the equally trivial happenings of the future. What people did at any time was of little value in their eyes, or formed no part of the books of spiritual wisdom. The one thing of prime interest to them was the structure, pattern, form and meaning of all action. Their approach to history was more the Hegelian than the mere chronicler's. And it has to be confessed after mature reflection that in the end that is the only thing about history that matters vitally. No mind can notice or remember a billionth part of the occurrences that constitute history in the factual sense. Therefore its pursuit can have only the final value of instructing the mind on the principles that have determined events, or of admonishing the moral sense or of teaching wisdom. The only worth-while deposit from events acted or studied as history is their "moral lesson." "What does history teach us?" is the only pertinent question to be asked regarding the value of the record of sheer deed. And this consummate recognition will help to dispel at last the perpetual hue and cry of the babbling religionists about Old Testament "prophecy." For it reveals that if events themselves were held of little value, the foreknowledge of them would be even less esteemed. It would assuredly be difficult to locate a single item of practical advantage or service that has ever accrued to the Christians of Europe through many centuries from their having in their possession the sheaf of Old Testament "prophecies." The net effect of their supposed reference was to throw millions of people into wonder, bewilderment and apprehension in every century. Who is ever known to have acted on the warnings and predictions to his clear and obvious profit? And yet the sad story comes to us that the people of Europe in every century since the tenth, at least, have loudly proclaimed that the burden of the "prophecies" fell directly upon their times. The same phenomenon is being repeated in the twentieth as it was previously in the nineteenth, and every one before it. At the best it has always taken a monstrous amount of imagination and stretching to make the prophetic words match the present run of events. But the Procrustean skill of the prophecy-mongers is never less than prodigious, and the gigantic frame of the present history can always be fitted into the small compass of "Bible prophecy." Perhaps this is the place to express the hope that a baleful misconception which has already reduced itself ad nauseam, may now be further reduced ad absurdum ad infinitum.

Massey again adjures us that we have only to turn to the 2 Esdras (written long B.C.) to learn that Jesus the Christ of our canonical books was both pre-historic and pre-Christian. This is one of the books that have been rejected and set apart as Apocrypha, considered to be spurious because they are supposed to contain the secret Gnosis or keys to the true meanings. In this book it is said

"My son Jesus shall be revealed to those that are with him . . . and they that remain shall rejoice within four hundred years; and after these years shall my son Christ die and all men shall have life."

Massey's vigorous comment can be given once more

"The true Christ, whether mythical or mystical, astronomical or spiritual, never could become a historical personage and never did originate in any human history. The types themselves suffice to prove that the Christ was, and could only be, typical and never could have taken form in human personality. For one thing, the mystical Christ of the Gnosis and of the pre-Christian types was a being of both sexes, as was the Egyptian Horus and other of the Messiahs, because the mystical Christ typified the spirit or soul, which belongs to the female as well as to the male, and represents that which could only be a human reality in the spiritual domain or the Pleroma of the Gnostics. This is the Christ who appears as both male and female in the Book of Revelation (a reference to the fact that Jesus in Revelation is described as wearing a golden girdle about the paps). And the same biune type was continued in the Christian portraits of the Christ. In Didron's Iconography, you will see that Jesus Christ is portrayed as a female with the beard of a male, and is called Jesus Christ as St. Sophia – i.e., the wisdom or spirit of both sexes. The early Christians were ignorant of this typology; but the types still remain, to be interpreted by the Gnostics and bear witness against the history. Both the type and doctrine combine to show there could be no one personal Christ in this world or in any other. However the written word may lie, the truth is visibly engraved upon the stones, and still survives in the Icons, symbols and doctrines of the Gnostics, which remain to prove that they preserved the truer tradition of the origines. And so this particular pre-Christian type was continued as a portrait of the historic Christ. It can be proved that the earliest Christians known were Gnostics—the men who knew, and who never did or could accept Historic Christianity. The Essenes were Christians in the Gnostic sense, and according to Pliny the Elder they were a Hermetic Society that had existed for ages on ages of time. Their name is best explained as Egyptian. They were known as Eshai, the healers or Therapeutae, the physicians, in Egypt; and Esha or Usha means to doctor, or heal, in Egyptian. The Sutites, the Mandaites, the Nazarites, as well as the Docetae and Elkesites, were all Gnostic Christians; they all preceded and were all opposed to the cult of the carnalized Christ. The followers of Simon the Samaritan were Gnostic Christians; and they were of the church at Antioch, where it is said the name of Christian was primarily applied. Cerinthus was a Gnostic Christian, who according to Epiphanius, denied that Christ had come in the flesh. The same writer informs us that at the end of the fourth century there were Ebionite Christians, whose Christ was the mythical fulfiller of the time-cycles, not a historic Jesus. Even Clement of Alexandria confesses that his Christ was of a nature that did not require the nourishment of corporeal food."

Mead fortifies Massey's statement regarding the Essenes, saying they "refused to believe in the resurrection of the physical body," either of Christ or of men. The Gnostics, Mead agrees, were the first Christian theologians, and if it is a cause for reprehension that the real historical side of the new movement was obscured in order to suit the necessities of a religion that aspired to universality, then the Gnostics are the chief culprits, he says. To lend some authority to the claim that the Gnostics were not at all rabid "heretics" or fanatical religionists, a Dr. Carl Schmidt may be cited as saying that "we are amazed . . . dazzled by the richness of thought, touched by the depth of soul" of the Gnostic authors, and he speaks of "the period when Gnostic genius like a mighty eagle left the world below it and soared in wide and ever wider circles towards the pure light, the pure knowledge, in which it lost itself in ecstasy."

The alleged heresy of the Gnostics, writes Massey (The Natural Genesis, II, p. 484), which is supposed and assumed to have originated in the second century, the first being carefully avoided, only proves that the A-gnostics, who had literally adopted the pre-Christian types and believed they had been historically fulfilled, were then for the first time becoming conscious of the cult that preceded theirs, and coming face to face with those who held them to be heretics. Gnosticism was not a birth of the second century; it was not a perverter or corrupter of Christian doctrines divinely revealed, but the voice of an older cult growing more audible in its protest against a superstition as degrading now as when it was denounced by men like Tacitus, Pliny, Julian, Marcus Aurelius and Porphyry. For what, asks Massey, could be more shocking to any real religious sense than the belief that the very God himself had descended on earth as an embryo in a virgin's womb, to undergo the precarious ordeal of the pre-natal period, of birth, infancy, the risks of physical embodiment and the suffering of cruelty and persecution, climaxed by an ignominious death on a cross of torture, to save his own created world, or a few in it who might "believe" on him, from eternal perdition? The opponents of the latest superstition were too intelligent to accept so shallow and repulsive a story and a dying deity. Porphyry terms the Christian religion "a blasphemy barbarously bold" (barbaron tolmema). "A monstrous superstition," exclaims Pliny. "A pestilence," cries Suetonius. "Exitiabilis superstitio" (ruinous superstition), says Tacitus. "Certain most impious errors are committed by them," says Celsus, "due to their extreme ignorance, in which they have wandered from the meaning of the divine enigmas." (Origen: Contra Celsum, VI, Ch. XIII.) All of which is as true as it is temperate, avers Massey. The "primitive Christians were men whose ardor was fierce in proportion to their ignorance," as is ever the case. Massey states that when Peter, Philip and John, as preachers of the new creed, were summoned before the Jewish hierarchs to be examined, the Council decided that they were only ignorant men, unlearned in the oral law, unskilled in the tradition of interpretation, believers who did not know the true meaning of that which they taught. They were not punished, but dismissed with warnings, as rude anthropoi agrammatoi kai idiotai (men uneducated and narrow-minded). Idiotai is of course the root of our word "idiots." In the Greek, however, it carries the meaning of being bound up in one's own ideas so closely as not to be able to see beyond one's own small horizon.

Near the end of his greatest work, Ancient Egypt, The Light of the World (p. 905), Massey sums up the data that impelled him toward his momentous conclusions. He says that from the comparative process we learn that the literalizers of the legend and the carnalizers of the Egypto-Gnostic Christ have but gathered up the empty husks of Pagan tradition, minus the kernel of the Gnosis; so that when we have taken away from their collection all that pertains to Horus, the Egypto-Gnostic Jesus, all that remains to base a Judean history upon is nothing more than the accretion of blindly ignorant belief. And therefore of all the Gospels and collections of Sayings derived from the Ritual of the resurrection in the names of Mattiu, or Matthew, Aan or John, Thomas or Tammuz or Tum, Hermes, Iu-em-hetep, Iusa or Jesus, those that were canonized at last as Christian are the most exoteric, and therefore the furthest away from the underlying, hidden and buried, but imperishable truth. With these fateful words he ends his great work.

We have both Philo's and Irenaeus' expressed belief that the Word (Logos) could not become incarnate, Massey testifies. Philo no more knows a Christ that could be made flesh than he knew of a Jesus in human form – and he lived at almost the identical time of the alleged historical Jesus! So it was with the Gnostics. They declared it was not possible that he should suffer who was both incomprehensible and invisible (Irenaeus, b. I, ch. VII, p. 2). According to the Gnostics, says Irenaeus, "neither the Word, nor the Christ, nor the Savior, was made flesh. They maintain that the Word was neither born nor did he become incarnate" (b. 3, XI, p.3). It was impossible that the Gnostics could accept the doctrine of a masculine Logos being made flesh or incarnated in human form. Their Logos was the spiritual antithesis and eternal opposite of matter, not a redeemer of the flesh by wearing it. The advent of the Gnostic Christ could only be in the mind or the spirit. It could only be manifested by an illumination of the mind, a purification of the life, a change of heart in the religious sense. (It is worth pausing to comment that the "true" orthodox Christianity of Irenaeus' day rejected illumination of the mind, purification of the life and change of heart as heresy!) To them the advent was one that could dawn only about a Christ that came from within. The type-form of divine Logos could no more apply to an external history or a personal Savior than the spirit of giving could become Santa Klaus in person. Yet, Massey points out, the Christ of this conception was identical with the Christ of Philo and of Paul. Philo, he says, has defined the incarnation as Archangelos Polyonomos, "the many-named archangel." The power or spirit that incarnated had many names and many forms of manifestation. But this incarnation was not of a nature to be embodied in one man or as one man, either past, present or future. The earliest of the Christian Fathers, Justin Martyr in particular, had given voice to expressions of the multiformity of the Christly manifestation.

The central force of Massey's courageous assault on the ramparts of orthodox Christianity is in his categorical averment that the bulk of the material entering into the formulation of Christian doctrine and practice was long in existence before the Christian era. Let us hear his forthright declaration to this effect in his lecture on The Historical Jesus and the Mythical Christ (p. 22):

"Whether you believe it or not does not matter, the fatal fact remains that every trait and feature which goes to make up the Christ as Divinity, and every event or circumstance taken to establish the human personality, were pre-extant and pre-applied to the Egyptian and Gnostic Christ, who never could become flesh. The Jesus Christ with female paps, who is the Alpha and Omega of Revelation, was the IU of Egypt and the IAO of the Chaldeans. Jesus as the Lamb of God and Ichthys the Fish was Egyptian. Jesus as the Coming One; Jesus born of a Virgin Mother who was overshadowed by the Holy Ghost; Jesus born of two mothers, both of whose names were Mary; Jesus born in the manger at Christmas and again at Easter; Jesus saluted by the three kings or Magi; Jesus of the Transfiguration on the Mount; Jesus whose symbol in the catacombs is the eight-rayed star – the star of the East; Jesus as the eternal child; Jesus as God the Father, reborn as his own Son; Jesus as the child of twelve years; Jesus as the anointed one of thirty years; Jesus in his baptism; Jesus walking on the water or working his miracles; Jesus as the caster-out of demons; Jesus as a Substitute, who suffered in a vicarious atonement for sinful men; Jesus whose followers are the two brethren, the four fishers, the seven fishers, the twelve apostles, the seventy (or seventy-two, as in some texts) whose names were written in heaven; Jesus who was administered to by seven women; Jesus in his bloody sweat; Jesus betrayed by Judas; Jesus as conqueror of the grave; Jesus the resurrection and the life; Jesus before Herod; in the Hades and in his reappearance to the women and the seven fishers; Jesus who was crucified both on the fourteenth and the fifteenth of the month Nisan; Jesus who was also crucified in Egypt, as it is written in Revelation (11:8); Jesus as judge of the dead, with the sheep on the right hand and the goats on the left, is Egyptian from first to last, in every phase, from the beginning to the end."

If the revelation of these identities comes with surprising or shocking force to many readers, the wonder should mount to still greater height when it is stated, as it can be, that Massey has traced out and enumerated some one hundred and eighty of these items of similarity or identity between Horus of Egypt and the Gospel Jesus! And Horus was centuries antecedent to Jesus, and was never pictured as a living person! To the scholarly mind this astonishing fact becomes conclusive of the whole argument. The forced acceptance of the fact that when the only-begotten Son of the Eternal came to earth in all his regal splendor to redeem the fallen race of mortal men, the best he could manage to get in the books that were to establish his mission and perpetuate his influence was a garbled melange of data and symbols already associated with a score or more of previous non-existent typical characters, will bring at last a realistic recognition of the weakness of the case for the historicity. Even were the bald claim for the existence of the man Jesus to be conceded, the victory for orthodoxy and fundamentalism would be almost if not quite as damaging to that side as the refutation. It would indeed be a Pyrrhic triumph, leaving the cause of Christian theology so badly weakened and wounded by obvious inexplicability of many points, as to have forfeited the further support of thinking people everywhere. How could it be explained with rational consistency or with the salvation of respect and prestige, that the historical biography of the one and only Son of God fell into the lines of the merely dramatized "careers" of Horus of Egypt, Krishna of India, Tammuz or Marduk of Assyria, Mithra of Persia, Bacchus of Greece, Zagreus or Sabazius of Phrygia, and a list of others in various lands? The Rosetta Stone has at last brought to an end the centuries-long pretense and hypocrisy of the orthodox Christian party in the study of comparative religion.

One can understand the mental vehemence back of Massey's fling at his critics:

"It is not I that deny the divinity of Jesus the Christ; I assert it! He was and never could be any other than a divinity; that is, a character non-human and entirely mythical, who had been the divinity of various pagan myths that had been pagan during thousands of years before our Era."

He continues with the asseveration that the Christian scheme is founded on a fable misinterpreted, and that the Coming One as the Christ was but a metaphorical figure, a type of immanent spiritual growth consummated in time, who could not take form in human personality any more than Time in person could come out of the clock-case when the hour strikes, like the cuckoo! The "history" in our Gospels is from beginning to end the identifiable story of the Sun-God and the Gnostic Christ who was not "after the flesh." The false belief, he concludes, becomes impossible when we know the true one. But the false one has ever stood in the way of our knowing the true one.

The mythical Messiah was Horus in the Osirian mythos; Har-Khuti in the Sut-Typhonian; Khunsu in that of Amen-Ra; and the Christ of the Gospels is an amalgam of all these characters, and, one may add, of others. Jesus is he that should come; and Iu, the root of the name in Egyptian, means "to come." Iu-em-hetep, the Messianic name in Egypt for thousands of years, signifies "he who comes with peace." And this is the very character in which Jesus is announced by the angels at midnight of December twenty-fourth, a date set by the Egyptian astronomical symbology. A sententious summation of the whole matter is given in Massey's words: "From beginning to end the canonical Gospels contain the Drama of the Mysteries of the Luni-solar God, narrated as human history." The mythos is the magic key that alone will fit the lock of the Bible material and open the door to the explanation of its otherwise unfathomable obscurities. "All that is non-natural and impossible as human history, is possible, natural and explicable as mythos." This is indeed the eventful truth, and the application of it is the only measure that will ever put an end to the farcical irrationality of Christian theology and redeem the body of doctrine from ostensible nonsense to comprehensible sublimity, after centuries of befuddlement.

The catacombs of Rome, says Massey again, "are crowded with the Egypto-Gnostic types which had served the Roman, Persian, Greek and Jew as evidence for the non-historic origins of Christianity." The child-Horus of Egypt reappears in Christian iconography as the mummy-babe in the catacombs, wearing even the tell-tale sign of origin from Egypt, the solar disk! Also the resurrection of Osiris comes into Christian scriptures as the raising of Lazarus, the identification of whom with Osiris makes one of the most thrilling chapters of comparative religion revelation ever to be brought to light. Among the numerous types of Horus repeated in Roman symbols of the alleged historic Jesus are "Horus on his papyrus" as Messianic shoot or natzer (from which root in Hebrew Massey traces the word "Nazarene"); Horus the branch resprouting each cycle for endless ages from the parent vine; Horus as Ichthys the Fish; Horus as bennu or phoenix; Horus as the dove; Horus as the eight-rayed star of the Pleroma; Horus as scarabaeus; Horus as child-mummy with the head of Ra; Horus as the little black child or Bambino; Horus of the reversed triangle.

Massey shows with sufficient clearness the origin of the cross in the Tat-cross of Egypt, or the Ankh-cross, the symbol of Life as resulting from the crossing or union of the two poles of being, spirit and matter. The Tat or cross of stability, symbol of the power that sustains the worlds and all things, was the figure of the pole, thought of as the backbone of the world, the axis of all durability. It united in one the "five supports" or the five-fold tree of the Egypto-Gnostic mystery, the four corner supports and the central axis. This power was personified in Ptah as well as figured in the Tat. The light that the clearer representation of Egypt throws on this symbol is great, for it shows that the cross figure is the insignium of the same power that is personified in the Christ himself and that true depiction should not so much portray the Christ on the cross as that the Christ is the cross. The god in matter and the cross are really one. This personified power in the Egyptian Ritual says, "I am Tat, the Son of Tat" (Rit., Ch. I), or son of the Eternal, who establishes the soul for eternity in the mystery of Tattu (Rit., Ch. 17). Hence we find the figure of the god, as the cross, extended crosswise as sustainer of the universe in Egyptian vignettes. This construction is undoubtedly back of the Gospel legend of Jesus as bearer of his own cross on which he was to "die." In the Christian corruption of the grand conception into impossible "history," the doctrine of the crucifixion, with its human victim raised aloft as a sin-offering for all the world, "is but a ghastly simulacrum of the primitive meaning, or shadowy phantom of the original substance." In what respect are the Flagellantes or Penitentes of New Mexico, lashed on by the fanatic frenzy of Christian doctrine literalized, better than barbarian tribes of the forest or of the South Seas, who are pointed at by the Christians for their inhuman degeneracy in offering living humans in some of the former rites? For they even today come close to actual immolation of a man on the cross on the Good Friday of Passion Week, which Christian miscomprehension and muddled mentality has indeed made into the Black Friday of the year.

The ox and the ass, ever present with Jesus in his stable nativity in the Gospels, were with the Egyptian Coming One, Iusa, ages antecedently. These two animals, which Christians ignorantly assume are pictured in the birth-scenario because they "were there," are evidently typically connected with the birth of divinity because of the exceptional and peculiar type of their breeding. They owe their existence to cross-breeding, and so stood as the type of perfected Christhood, which is raised above sex, or represents sex polarity crossed and unified in one, as before the breaking of cosmic unity apart into biunity. The ox and the ass are present when the Christ comes to indicate to the initiated that the development of the Christ power returns the soul from its state of dual life on the cross to its pristine unity. It is the symbol of the divine androgyneity, or of spirit detached from matter, released from the cross, one again and not two.

A further light is thrown on this by Massey (Book of the Beginnings, I, p. 516), when he speaks of the bifurcation of the child, that is then still without sex (in manifestation), at puberty into the distinctly male or female individual. The calf represented both sexes in the non-pubescent stage, or the mother and the child only, in the phase of nature that did not yet include the father, or the developed creative mind. The bull was the type of the Father or generative force of creative thought. But even the bull, says Massey, was made to conform to the type of spirit-matter in union and neutralizing each other, in the ox. According to Varro, Massey says, there was a vulgar Latin name for ox, viz., Trio. The ox being of a third sex, neither male nor female productively, return was thus made to the primitive Nu-ter or Neuter of the beginning. And as all things are ultimately the A and the O, and begin and end in the same sexless state (in heaven there is neither marriage nor giving in marriage), the ox – and similarly the ass – was the type of fully Christified humanity. Therefore would the Christ be fitly represented as riding into the gates of the Holy City or heavenly Jerusalem on the back of the lowly ass. But why the two beasts, the ass and her foal? The ass was the symbol of the Egyptian God Atum, and ancient typism always depicted the god as creating and procreating, in the two characters of Father and Son. Life was made continuous by the creation in cycles, and the Son typified the new generation as the progeny of the old, ever repeating and recurring. It was the eternal repetition of the projection of new life from old in the time cycles, the previous old cycle being father to the succeeding one, which carried the soul onward in its long journey from the hinterland of matter up to the gates of the Aarru-Hetep of Egypt, which is the Aarru-Salem, or Jerusalem, of the Hebrew version. Iusa is pictured with the ears of an ass, and Iu is both ass and god under one name, Massey states.

A pretty solid support is seen for Massey's general claims as to the association of pagan usages with early Christian worship in that letter of the Emperor Hadrian to Servianus, in which he writes that "those who worship Serapis are likewise Christians; even those who style themselves the Bishops of Christ are devoted to Serapis." The most prominent early Egyptian Christians were at the same time members of the Mysteries of Serapis, as many leading Greek Christians were, like Origen, Clement, Pantaenus and Ammonius, students of the Neo-platonic philosophy.

The Gnostic Jesus in the Pistis Sophia says that he found Mary, who is called his mother after the material body, that he implanted in her the first power which he had received from the hands of his Father, called Barbelo and also the good Sabaoth. Here is the prototype of the great legend in ancient mythical systems of the son impregnating his own mother, as Horus fecundated his mother Isis in Egypt. Christians can spare their spurious indignation at "heathen" sexualism in religious worship, since the meaning carried by the representation is simply that the soul, or son, in man implants in the physical body that gives him his birth the power of spirit that transfigures her also into the likeness of divinity. The soul, as primordial intelligence, is the Father ever; in each new generation it is its own son; and the physical body is the mother. The son, therefore, eternally in each generation impregnates his own mother. Evil minds may see evil in this typing; beautiful minds will see both truth and beauty in it.

Carrying on the train of similarities between Gospel and Egyptian depictions Massey points to the dove symbol. The hawk is a male emblem, the dove the female, he shows. Horus rises again in the form of a hawk in the Egyptian resurrection. As matter is ever feminine, the soul or son descending into physical body would be entering what the ancients called its "feminine phase," its incarnation. Hence at its baptism, or entering the sea of matter, again always typed as water, it would swing to the dove as symbol. The dove made its appearance to attest Jesus' baptism in the Jordan, the Eridanus of the planisphere, the Iaru-:ana of the Egyptian myth, and the "river of life" in any system. Horus rises also in the form of a dove, as well as that of a hawk. He is the dove in his first phase, and the hawk in his second or perfected stage. Elsewhere, swinging the metaphor a grade higher, he says that he came as a hawk and transformed into the phoenix. "I am the Dove; I am the Dove," he exclaims as he rises up from Amenta where the egg of his future being was hatched in the divine incubator, in the An-ar-ef, the hidden land, "the abode of occultation," the house of the blind, – our earth.

Hence in the iconography of early Christianity the child-Jesus is depicted in the Virgin's arms or in her womb, surrounded by seven doves as symbols of the Holy Spirit (Didron: Iconography, fig. 124). For the Holy Spirit, or divine working efficacy of spirit in matter, must fall into the sevenfold segmentation which force ever undergoes when it energizes matter. This had been brought out not only in ancient cosmology and esotericism, but has been in large measure demonstrated by modern physical science, and is corroborated by nature herself in the sevenfold division of light, the octave (septave) of sound, the periodic table of weights in chemistry and the seven-day table of periodicities in the gestation process in all animal life.

A fact that must loom large in the debate as an item of great significance is that mentioned by a number of writers, that neither in the case of Horus nor in those of other "world-saviors," is there any date or history falling in the gap between the ages of twelve and thirty, matching the similar lacuna in the "life" of Jesus! This datum alone points with great cogency to the non-historicity of the Sun-Gods, Christs, Messiahs. Any student of ancient literature knows the esoteric significance of numbers in arcane systematism. The numbers one, two, three, four, seven, ten, twelve, twenty-four, thirty, forty, seventy, three hundred and others are so profusely injected throughout the Bible that it could long ago have been assumed that they carried the deepest recondite meaning. Three, four, seven, twelve and forty are indeed among the most sharply revelatory keys to the entire system of scriptural interpretation. It is ridiculous that Christian exegesis of its own book has for sixteen centuries labored at the interpretation with practically no regard for the meaning of these numbers. It will later be seen as a clear evidence of esoteric incompetence. It has remained for students outside the pale of Christian apologetics to interpret the Bible most capably and profoundly.

The age of twelve in Egyptian myth was one of the indices of transformation from the natural or unregenerate state of humanity into the spiritual kingdom, on the symbolic basis of puberty, change of voice and development of mind. And thirty was the index of completed perfection, type of the spiritual heyday in evolution. The fact that at twelve Jesus left his mother (type of matter and body) to attend to the things of his Father (type of spirit) has never once been discerned as the allegory of the natural man's conversion into the spiritual man, the attainment of his spiritual "thirty years." And a hundred such failures to read their own scriptures aright attest the blindness of exoteric vision on the part of orthodox expounders of scripture.

It is out of the question to transcribe any considerable portion of Massey's (and other) comparative religion data, but some salient items must be introduced. There is a perfect match between the flight of the parents of Jesus into Egypt for the safety of the divine child from the

Herod menace and a similar protection for Horus. The god Taht says to Isis, the mother: "Come, thou goddess Isis, hide thyself with the child," and the place of concealment indicated was in the marshes of Lower Egypt – bringing the Moses analogy to mind at once! This is pure evolutionary symbology and not personal history. That there is any vital significance in the fact that Jesus fled to Egypt to escape the Herod menace, while Horus had to be saved from the Herut menace in Lower Egypt will probably be shouted down by hostile critics. The Herut reptile was another name for the Apap serpent, the water monster that was the Egyptian type of the lower nature in man waiting to devour the child of higher divinity when he incarnated. But the substitution of the tetrarch's name for the reptile's designation is in the highest probability one of the tricks resorted to in the conversion of myth into history. Massey openly charges it.

Then there is the matter of the twelve disciples and their historicity. Massey affirms categorically and likely with full truth, that they "are no more human than was their teacher." But when the Word was made flesh in physical literalism his dramatic supporting cast had to be converted along with him.

What were the twelve disciples, if not men? In the esoteric understanding they were the same in twelve aspects as the three Kings or Wise Men were in a threefold division. Or they were the same three powers of spirit further subdivided into twelve aspects. They were just the spiritual power and intelligence which is the Christ itself, manifesting its wholeness in a twelve-part segmentation. In the same way in which the atomic force of the universe manifests in a seven-part differentiation, so the spiritual nucleus of life manifests in a twelve-part unfoldment. Nature sounds a seven-key octave and Divine Mind sounds a twelve-key diapason. Each in its unfoldment sounds but one key at a time, until the succession covers the gamut. As soul advances through the scale of evolution she passes through twelve grades of being one at a time, adding unto her equipment the quality gained from experience at each level, till her absorption of the essence of all nature is complete finally in a twelvefold unity. These twelve qualities of perfected spiritual cognition are what are represented by the twelve signs of the zodiac, the sun's passing successively through each sign and acquiring the special powers of each, typing the soul's round of the elements and the acquisition of the twelve intelligences. In the Ritual of Egypt the soul had to pass successively through twelve dungeons, each guarded by a god, in each of which it was captive until the door was opened by the god, who held the key and would not use it until the mortal could pronounce his Name. Obviously man is a prisoner to a faculty until he opens up his ability to utilize and command its powers. Ignorance is ever the gaoler and knowledge is the only release. Inasmuch as light produced by suns is the highest aspect of creative energy, the dark dungeon was the appropriate symbol of the benighted condition of the soul when imprisoned in matter. The creative command – Let there be light! – was the divine fiat that ordered the suns to shine and the galaxies to glisten. And light in the physical area was the perfect analogue and symbol of the light of intelligence that was to glow in the domain of ignorance as solar light was to irradiate the universe of space. Twelve lights would therefore be the most apt symbol of the twelve basic powers of divine intelligence, and this brings us back to the primal true designation of the twelve rays of genius in man – the Twelve Saviors of the Treasure of Light! In various other symbolic typings they were also the Twelve Reapers of the Golden Grain, the Twelve Harvesters in the Field of Amenta, the Twelve Builders, Twelve Carpenters, Twelve Masons, Twelve Potters, Twelve Weavers of the Pattern, Twelve Fishermen, Twelve Rowers of the Boat with Horus, Twelve Sailors in the Ship of Ra, the Sun. They are the twelve powers of Sun-God intelligence. And as ancient philosophy brings out the astounding facts that sunlight is the eventual product of divine mentation – "the light of the sun is the pure energy of intellect," says Proclus in one of the most illuminating sentences ever uttered – the twelve "rays" of the solar Logos become at last in men and gods the twelve faculties of spiritual intelligence the evolution of which makes each man in his aeonial career a Christ, instructing and training his "twelve disciples" within the confines of his own individuality. They were the fourfold differentiation, under the symbolism of fire, air, water and earth, of each of the three Kings, or kingly powers of divine intellect into which primordial unity of Mind breaks up in its necessary fragmentation as it descends into matter. As water falling from a height breaks up into fragments owing to the resistance of the air, and the blood-stream divides from the heart, and a tree trunk from its lower stem, so unitary intellect descending from on high breaks up into first a threefold partition and finally into a twelvefold division. In reduction to simplest form, all this means that as in physical matter and its manifestation on earth there are four basic differentiations of expressions as fire, air, water and earth, so in mind there are the four analogous subdifferentiations, again in soul the same four and again in spirit the same four. So the twelve great qualities that are to divinize us are the spirit's fire, air, water and earth, the soul's fire, air, water and earth, and the mind's fire, air, water and earth, all combined in one grand synthesis, the Christ consciousness. All this is represented by the structure of the pyramid, which has the four bases as groundwork, and four three-sided upper faces as the superstructure, with the golden triangle crowning all, and glinting ever with Egyptian sunlight. In the great ancient divine-human drama the twelve facets of solar deity were of course personified in and by twelve characters, and the dark-minded Christian spoliators of sage wisdom had to make twelve uneducated fishermen out of them. There was no escape from their becoming fishermen in the Christian rendition because the Jesus who was the astronomical Avatar coming roughly around 255 B.C., came under the precessional sign of Pisces and so came as Ichthys, the Fish-Avatar. He came as Joshua (Jesus) son of Nun, and Nun is the fish in Hebrew! Can Massey be gainsaid or laughed down, then, when he says the twelve disciples were no more human than their teacher? It is Massey's turn to laugh at the stupidity of his critics.

Jesus himself says in Gnostic literature: "When I first came into the world I brought with me twelve powers. I took them from the hands of the twelve saviors of the treasure of light," that is, from the twelve who are called the aeons in the Gnostic astronomy. And he adds that he took these twelve powers and "cast them into the sphere of the rulers," and "bound them into the bodies of your mothers." By this he means that he has in evolution incorporated them in organic creational systems and finally into the bodies of men, the fleshly body being the mother of the individual soul. Jesus is to reign as king over these twelve powers, the "nine guardians and the three amens," "the five supporters and the seven amens," and all the other characters which were "light emanations," and which would have had no meaning if Jesus had not likewise been an astronomical figure. He unifies them all in himself as he gathers them to himself in passing through the twelve phases of creative manifestation. Beside the twelve "disciples of Jesus" there are found in the Bible the twelve sons of Jacob, the twelve of Judah, the twelve tribes of Israel, the twelve stones Joshua was ordered to set up in the dry bed of the Jordan River, the twelve pieces of the concubine's body cut up (in the nineteenth chapter of Judges), the twelve tables of stone, the twelve commandments, the twelve Urim and Thummim on the breastplate of the High Priest, and others.

Moreover we find striking identity in the Christ's proclamations, the one in the Gospels, the other in the Gnostic texts, of an esoteric doctrine which he will propound openly to his disciples, though he must speak in parable to the multitude. In the Gnostic Gospel Jesus says:

"Rejoice and be glad for this hour. From this day will I speak with you freely, from the beginning of the truth unto the completion thereof; and I will speak to you face to face, without parable. From this hour will I hide nothing from you of the things which pertain to the height."

Matching this with the statement of the Gospel Jesus to his disciples that to them that are without it is given to be taught in parables, but to them in the inner circle it is given to be instructed in the mysteries, there is presented an interesting parallel indeed. More light is thrown on this mystery of esotericism when in the Gnostic scriptures Jesus says, "I will tell unto you the mystery of the one and only ineffable, and all its types, all its configurations, all its regulations . . . for this mystery is the support of them all." Again he says: "I tore myself asunder and brought unto them the mysteries of light to purify them . . . otherwise no soul in the whole of humankind should have been saved." And another excerpt from his Gnostic sayings is of great value, as it clears up a point of meaning which has been sadly misconceived heretofore. When Jesus in the Gospels says that the believer must leave father, mother and kin to follow after him, it has been a "hard saying," too hard to be accepted in literal sense. It therefore should come with great relief to the perplexed faithful to learn at last what the passage actually means in the light of the same unmutilated and unhistoricized text of the Gnostic Gospel:

"For this cause have I said unto you aforetime, 'He who shall not leave father and mother to follow after me is not worthy of me.' What I said then was, ye shall leave your parents the rulers, that ye may all be children of the first, everlasting mystery." (Bk. 2, 341.)

Earlier the parents or "rulers" that were to be left for the Christ ministry were described as the seven elementary or natural powers, the mother powers of nature, giving birth to the first Adam, or natural man, who must be left in the seeking after the higher spiritual genius of divinity! Again it is seen how the literalizing process has reduced high cosmic splendor of meaning to the tawdriness of a family desertion and a flouting of the dearest bonds of mortal kinship.

Jesus gave his disciples power to raise the "dead." In the Pyramid Texts of Teta it is said: "Horus hath given his children power to raise thee up" from the funeral couch.

Massey calls attention to a discrepancy in the version of the miraculous draught of fishes in two Gospels, John and Luke. In John, when Jesus reappears to the seven fishers on board the boat to cause the miraculous haul, it is after his resurrection from the dead. Consequently the transaction, Massey thinks, took place in a region beyond the tomb and not in the life on earth. Whereas in Luke's version his reappearance was in the earth-life and not a reappearance after death. Orthodox idea of course holds that Jesus was resurrected on earth and that Massey's conclusion therefore is not sound. What is true, of course, is that there was no physical or bodily resurrection at all, but only the re-arising out of the grave or tomb of the earthly body of that living nucleus of soul that had descended into the body for incarnation. When the soul from elevated spheres descends and links its refined energies with the coarse life of body, the ancient seers pictured its durance in flesh as its death and burial. Just as naturally, then, its release from body at the end of a life cycle was its resurrection from "the dead." There was no place at all for the historical episode of one man's bursting the bars of a hillside rocky tomb at any time. The resurrection, Paul tells us, was in a spiritual body, dissociating its tenuous substance from the meshes of the fleshly vehicle.

Again that which was a spiritual mystery in Egypt became a "miracle" in Christianity. In the Ritual of Egypt (Ch. 113) Sebek catches the fish in his marvelous net, and it is proclaimed by Ra to be a mystery.

Jesus multiplied the loaves and fishes in the Gospels, and this incident binds wonderfully in with one of the greatest bits of comparative religion data ever to be formulated. When one has grasped from Greek rational theology the significance of the great doctrine of God's deific multiplication of his own life by dividing primeval unity into endless multiplicity, sharing his oneness with the infinity of his creatures, and then applies to it the elucidation of the Christ's multiplying that same divinity under the two zodiacal types of bread and fish (Virgo and Pisces), and then will turn to the Egyptian symbolic writing, he will come upon the amazing discovery that the city of Annu (Anu), (Any in English) – which with the Beth, "house," of the Hebrew gives us Beth-any of the Gospels – was described in the Ritual as "the place of multiplying bread!" From John we learn that "this is that bread which came down from heaven," the divine immortal soul which came here to multiply itself, as an oak multiplies its life in its acorns, in the house of bread, which is the human body. When will the religious mind break through the obfuscations of deadening literalism to see at last that the human body, the soul's tenement on earth, is that Bethlehem, that house of bread, wherein the divine bread comes to be multiplied? Here at last is incontrovertible and irrefutable proof that the Christian has to go back to ancient Egypt's wisdom to discover the keys to the interpretation of his own Bible. If ever the Christian doctrines are to shed any real light on human understanding of the problems of life and immortality, it will be only with the help of Egypt's restored mysteries. As Massey so clearly demonstrated, Christian truth has been sealed up in a fatal obscurantism and Egypt holds the keys to release it.

In the Gospels it is the women who announce the resurrection. "The goddesses and the women proclaim me when they see me," shouts Horus as he rises from the tomb on "the horizon of the resurrection."

Horus was not only the "bread of life" derived from heaven; he also gave his flesh for food and his blood for drink, as did Jesus. He says he has bread in heaven with Ra, and bread on earth with Seb, the earth-god.

Dealing further with the cross as symbol, the arresting fact is brought to light that this emblem in the Egyptian was never the symbol of death – in the sense of the demise of the body – but of life! It was the symbol of "death" only in the transferred sense of the word "death" as the circumscribed life of the soul in the tomb of the body on earth. The cross is the "tree," and the "tree" is the "tree of life which is in the garden" of this world. This chain of identity has not been seen or worked upon. In one form of the symbolism Jesus is nailed on the tree in its form of the cross of wood; but to suit another form of metaphorical approach he IS the tree of life. He is the branch, the shoot (Hebrew natzer, whence probably "Nazarene"), of his Father, the eternal Tree whose branches ramify into all the universe. But for us in turn Christ is the tree, the vine, and we are the branches. A number of allusions in this relation from ancient non-Biblical sources would have kept in better understanding the connection between the tree of Genesis and the cross, or tree, of Calvary. Ancient mythic tradition had it that various typal Christ characters, Noah, Seth, Enoch, Moses, Joshua, plucked a shoot from the tree of life in the garden and planted it on the mount of Golgotha, where it burgeoned anew to become the tree of the crucifixion. And if, in its deepest sense, the cross of crucifixion is only the metaphor for this incarnation in body, which gives ever more abundant life to the soul by multiplying its potentialities through the ordeal of suffering, then the tree of life and knowledge in Genesis remains still the tree or cross of life and salvation, and not the gruesome cross of death. But clearly in the first instance it is the tree of the Father in his original generation of life; in the second it is the tree of the Son, in regeneration, or eternal renewal of life. The legends – some even carried on into Christian exploitation – that the wood of the cross of Jesus became alive and put forth green shoots, solidly substantiate this figurism. It is matched also by the burgeoning of Aaron's rod when cast to earth! Divine life flowers anew from the old stem each time it is planted afresh in the soil of earthly body! The Christmas legend spoke of the rose blooming from the Glastonbury thorn in the winter solstice, and we prate in profound stupidity of the Christ as being a fresh shoot from the rod of Jesse. The mighty truth is in our midst, but goes all unrecognized.

The purely allegorical implications of the cross symbol should have been seen from the Platonic and Gnostic representations of the form of the cross called the Stauros. It was the four-armed structure of the Christ-aeon or emanation extended out over the field of creation, and represented spirit as being "crucified in space," and, Einstein would add, in time. The fourfold division of primary life energy out into space in the creation of universes is, as clearly as could be done, set forth in Genesis, where the river of life split off into four streams, named there Pison, Gihon, Hiddekel and Euphrates. All this is to tell us that life invariably in manifestation "quadrates" itself, or comes to expression in four differentiated aspects, which, be it proclaimed with ultimate clarity at last, are typified in all ancient literature by the four elements of earth, water, air and fire. This partition of primordial life force into the four forms of its manifestation is all that can possibly be meant by the symbol of the four-armed cross in the cosmic range. For the individual its meaning is the quadration of the one energy of consciousness in his life in the four aspects of sense, emotion, thought and soul.

If the Christ was in most real truth crucified in space, the physical timber on Golgotha's ghastly height, hewn and sawed and nailed, might be accepted with enlightenment as pure symbol of cosmic process. But as it stands in common thought among Christian people it is the gruesome sign of the most abject stultification of the godlike principle of intelligence known to history.

Lundy says that Plato must have learned his theology in Egypt and the East, and doubtless knew, from the stories of Krishna, Buddha and Mithra, that other religions had their mythical crucified victims long antecedent to Christianity. Witoba, one of the incarnations of Vishnu, is pictured with holes in his feet.

The nails of the cross have received considerable emphasis in the Gospel story. The nail, Massey shows, was a type of male virility or of the deeper power of nature that binds male (spirit) and female (matter) together for all effective progenation. The nailing of the body of the Christ on the cross would be the dramatization of the incarnational union of the two ends of the life polarity. Spirit must be nailed to matter to give it its quadration, for free from matter it remains in uncreative unity.

Drawing his data largely from Didron's Iconography, Massey brings forth from those recesses of buried ancient secrets which he explored so capably, the fact that must startle all Christian readers with its pertinence to the general theme here elaborated, viz., that with the whole foundation of Christianity resting upon the physical cross and the man nailed on it, the religion that claims to have had its very origin from that cross and man has given no evidence of awareness or commemoration of that pivotal event in all its varied and elaborate iconography for about six hundred years after its founding! Massey records that during the first six or seven centuries no figure of a man appears upon the cross in Christian monumental hierography. There are all forms of the cross except that, the alleged starting point of the new religion! The Christ, and him crucified, says Massey, was not the initial but the final form of the crucifix. Over the first six centuries the representation of the foundation of the Christian faith in a crucified Redeemer is entirely absent from Christian art! Massey writes (Book of the Beginnings, I, 433):

"The earliest known form of the human figure on the cross is the crucifix presented by Pope Gregory the Great to Queen Theodolinde of Lombardy, now in the Church of St. John at Monza, whilst no image of the Crucified is found in the catacombs at Rome earlier than that of San Giulio belonging to the seventh or eighth century. So in the earliest representations of the Trinity made by the 'Christian' artists, the Father and the Holy Ghost (who was feminine as the Dove), are portrayed beside the Cross. There is no Christ and no Crucified; the Cross is the Christ, even as the Stauros was a type and name of Horus, the Gnostic Christ. The Cross, not the Crucified, is the primary symbol of the Christian Church. . . . And that Cross is pre-Christian, is pagan and heathen, in half a dozen different shapes. During centuries the Cross stood for the Christ and was addressed as if it were a living being. It was divinized at first and humanized at last."

The Gospel incident which dramatizes Jesus as running away from his mother at the age of twelve and saying he must henceforth be about the business of his Father, briefly noticed, must be scanned for some further elucidation of hidden purport. (The very first consideration is the thought that if orthodox interpretation insists upon taking "his mother" as his human female parent in the story, by what warrant does it not take "his Father" also as his human male parent? He says in effect that he must leave his mother and go to his father, and if the one parent is taken as human, why not the other?) The esoteric significance of this "incident" has never been divined in theology. It is a grand cosmic dramatization, based on the puberty transformation of the boy into the man. The parallelism is startling and suggestive. With the "mother" typing nature and the "Father" spirit, the transition of the boy over from the care of his mother, in which he had been nurtured up till then, to the interests of his father, along with the first development of sexual creative power and the budding of intellect at the same time, as well as the deepening of the voice, which is a most amazing natural symbol of the power henceforth of the voice to utter the true word instead of the fancies of the child, the physiological climacteric was the most striking possible form of depiction ready at hand of the great central truth of all scriptures – the evolutionary transformation of man the natural, or the first Adam, over into man spiritual, or the second Adam. In Egypt there were two Horuses, or two aspects of Horus, Horus the babe and Horus the man, or Horus the younger and Horus the elder. The younger Horus was the child of the mother – nature-and abode under her tutelage, that is, was ruled by natural instinct and not by reason or mind, until he had risen to the development of the twelve facets of his germina divinity of higher consciousness, whereupon he graduated from the care of mother nature and entered the kingdom of his Father, intellect and spirit. He was then the elder Horus, the grown son of his Father, done with nature and ready to wield the powers of intellect and soul, the business of the Father. With his changed voice allied to developed wisdom he could then utter the "true word" or the echo of the Logos, impossible with his feminine falsetto before! Could anything in nature more completely and admirably typify the profoundest of theological conceptions?

The purpose here, however, is again to indicate that the Gospel mention of the incident, brief as it is, has once more faithfully copied Egyptian prototypes. Every feature of the narrative is found prefigured in the Kamite portrayals. Horus the infant is the child of the Virgin, i.e., matter, or body, produced under natural conditions before the principle of mind (the male element) has unfolded and united with matter to generate the spiritual man. Horus the elder is the child become the man, graduated from the care of mother nature, and having germinated the seed of intellect and spirit into growth and function. Massey is the first to have made this determination clearly, but his work has been left in desuetude. The god Kephr, the world-builder, was symboled by the male beetle or scarabaeus which, the Egyptians alleged, procreated without the aid of the female. This is the type, not of virgin pure matter, but of virgin pure spirit, before union with the female or mother matter in incarnate life.

Astronomically the first Horus or natural man was the child of the Virgin in the sign Virgo; and six months later – which in zodiacal symbology would be at the entire completion of the incarnational cycle – in the sign of Pisces the second Horus, second Adam or the Christ, is reborn of the Fish-mother, or in the house of the Fishes. And in the Gospels Jesus the Christ is born with all the varied forms of the fish-type, as Ichthys the Fish, son of Nun (the Fish in Hebrew), and with twelve "fishermen" as disciples. And Luke's Gospel places the birth of Jesus just six months after that of John the Baptist; who as the forerunner and herald of the Christos is the dramatic character of the first or natural man, preceding him to prepare the way for him and make his paths straight! Will orthodox exegetists tell us how the six months' interval between the births of the natural man and his divine successor, the Spiritual Christ, given by Luke, are to be accounted for on any other basis than that of the zodiacal chart, where in pure typology the two births occur just six months apart on opposite sides of the zodiac? This single datum of comparative religion is enough to put the whole structure of Christian historicity on the defensive. If the unthinkable assumption or claim of historical factuality for the occurrence of Jesus' birth just six months after that of John could be predicated as true, how could the human mind ever contain its wonder at the coincidence of the actual history precisely matching the chart of pagan symbology? This is but one of hundreds of instances in which Christian "history" has had to dance to the tune played by pagan allegorism and typism.

The word "mount" or "mountain" is another link between the Gospels and pre-Christian derivations. The mount is very frequent in Egyptian typology, and the thing it did not mean in esoteric rendering was an earthly hill or elevation. It meant specifically the earth itself. The earth was the mount, raised up in space, where matter and soul, the god and the (animal) man, the one descending "from above," the other ascending from the slime to animal, met for that interrelation that meant evolution. Therefore every great transaction in the evolutionary process "took place" "on the mount." Earth is the only place where spirit and matter ever meet on equal terms or in the balance (symboled of course by the equinoxes), and so it is that God always called man (typed by "Moses") up into Mount Sinai to commune with him. Jesus, the Christ, is drawn up onto the mount to be tempted, he delivers his Sermon or Sayings of wisdom to humanity on the mount (though Luke says it was on a level plain), he was crucified on the hill and was transfigured in the height. Even the ark landed on the "mount of earth," as "Ararat" is a variant of the Hebrew arets (old form areth), "the earth." It is as futile to try to locate "the hill of the Lord," "thy holy hill," "the hills whence cometh my strength," on the map or earth's surface as it is to locate the milk and honey of Jerusalem the Golden in Palestine. Horus was symbolically placed, for all his ordeals and transformations, on the Mount of the Horizon, and this Mount – existing nowhere as a locality on earth, but being the mundane sphere itself – is the Egyptian prototype of all the holy mounts, Gerizim, Horeb, Sinai, Zion, Carmel, Calvary, in the scriptures.

The mount was the "place of emergence" in mythology. This is notable because it aids in the definite localization of its meaning. Life emerges from unmanifestation in the invisible worlds of pure Form (in the Greek sense) to visible manifestation in the physical cosmos, and it can do this only where spirit can achieve its embodiment in matter. A physical planet is the necessary ground for such processing. Spirit emerges from subjective to objective existence on the Mount of Earth. A prominent modern school of philosophy, Bergson's, has dealt so fully with this phase of cosmic procedure that it has taken the name of the "Emergent Philosophy." As life emerged out of darkness into light it gave birth to the suns, the lamps of creation. Hence the mount again was the place of birth for the sun. The solar orb, symbolizing always the divine power of spiritual light, went to its "death" in matter on the Mount of the Horizon on the West, the Western Mount, Mount Manu, and arose in its rebirth on the Mount of the East, or of Dawn, Mount Bakhu. These two names are instructive. Ma-nu is the elementary primordial abyss of the waters, empty space, or inchoate matter, as nu is the hieroglyph for water. Under the symbolism of the sun setting in the western ocean, life goes down from the heights of pure ethereality into the sea of matter. Passing through the round of the material kingdoms it emerges again on the east with a focus of consciousness developed to divine power in a physical organism, and comes forth as a soul or spirit individually conscious. Human-divine consciousness comes from the union in man's body of the two elements of psychic soul and divine spirit, and, oddly enough these two "persons" in man were named by the Egyptians respectively the ba and the khu. The Eastern Mount would then bring divinity to birth as the ba-khu, and so the Mount of Dawn for the divine soul in man was called Mount Bakhu. These two mounts are in Revelation and elsewhere in the Bible.

There is no end of repetition in the Bible of the Egyptian "three days in the tomb." Hosea speaks of the Israelites being held in bondage and being released and raised up "after two days" or "on the third day." The place of captivity for the soul in matter has variable naming, such as Babylon, Egypt, Assyria, Sodom, Arabia, none of which has geographical but only allegorical reference. If final and clinching proof is needed to show that the captivities and bondages in the Old Testament are only mythical representations, we have it in the prophet's assignment to them of a three-days length. The descent of the soul into body to manifest her powers and make her appearance or epiphany (or emergence) is the only substance and reality in any of the "captivities" of scripture. When the soul accomplishes its growth in the dungeons of Amenta, Sheol, Hades, and rises in triumph over the flesh and the grave, she is beautifully said to "lead captivity captive." That the allegories of their Old Testament were known to the Jews as non-historical is shown by the fact that fragments of the original mythos crop up in the Haggadoth, Talmud, Mishna, Kabalah and other Hebrew sacred scripts, Massey points out. This material was known to the Jews, and obviously not as history. Further, most of it had for ages been known to the Egyptians and again not as history. It is fatal to the historical sense of holy writ that we can turn to such old works as the Kabalah and Enoch and the Zohar and find their scenes, names, numbers and personages identical with those supposed to be historical in the Old Testament. An article in the Classical Journal (Vol. 17, p. 264), by T. T. Massey says that "the 600,000 men who came up out of Egypt as Hebrew warriors in the Book of Exodus are 600,000 inhabitants of Israel in the heavens, according to the Jewish Kabalah, and the same scenes, events and personages that appear as mundane in the Pentateuch are celestial in the Book of Enoch." Indeed the first "mapping" and "localizing" of events in the life and evolution of the race were unquestionably first celestial and not mundane. It was never anything but empyreal – until gross ignorance supervened upon intelligence and made the tragic conversion.

Even Swedenborg, a pretty credible testifier albeit he saw only with the eye of inner vision, states that "their historical books were written in the prophetic style and for the most part were made-histories, like those contained in Genesis I to XI." (Arcana Coelesta, 2897.)

In his Jesus and Paul (161) Bacon, who is not specifically aiming at giving the scriptures a mythical rendering, writes that the story of Jesus' walking on the sea in Mark 6:45-52 has a supplement in Matthew 14:28-33, which further draws out the parallel with purely spiritual meaning; saying that in Jewish symbolism power to tread upon the sea or triumph over it signifies victory over the power of Sheol. And in reference to the inner significance of the "captivities" he speaks of victory over the imprisoning powers of darkness. Also he very rightly says (p. 205) that the history of the conception of the Messiah as a great light entering the lower world of darkness and death to effect both judgment and deliverance would carry us far back into pre-Christian interpretative application of the Isaian passage: "The people that sat in darkness have seen a great light; unto them that dwell in the shadow of death hath the light shined." This is just the kind of thing that Massey claims throughout, and supports his claim with mountainous evidence.

But Bacon has a passage which comes dangerously close to repudiating the very fundamental of Christianity in his effort to discredit the Gnosis and early Christian esotericism, or some aspects of them. He says (p. 201) that talk about mystical experiences, gnosis, insight into mysteries, fellowship with God and participation in his eternal life, new birth into eternity and the rest of the current mystical jargon of the day. is all froth and self-deception unless it issues in practical deeds of unselfish service. This pungent asseveration is greeted with the heartiest second from this quarter. Indeed in many respects nothing in religious circles needs to be said so forcefully as just this protest against the extravagances and follies of mystical religion in our day and all days. At the same time it must be recognized that the attainment of these things in a sane and balanced way is certainly the aim and goal of the highest Christian aspiration. If it is not so the whole immense body of saintly mystical rhapsodism in the history of the Church is all froth and self-deception. The point of difference, then, is the degree of sanity and balance with which such experiences are undergone and reacted to. So that once more it is seen that the item in all religion that receives the final and crucial emphasis is philosophical intelligence, as a lever of control over the whimsicalities of mysticism. This point, though touched upon here incidentally, is of absolutely transcendent importance in all estimate of true religiosity.

It is a standing challenge to the proponents of this historical thesis of scripture to explain away the eighth verse of the eleventh chapter of Revelation. If every word, verse, chapter and letter of Holy Writ is – as has been solemnly declared by four or five Church Councils – God's unalterable truth, we then have the Bible itself in the plainest of words declaring the crucifixion of Jesus to be non-literal and non-historical. Speaking of the "two witnesses" (which it explains are the "two olive trees" – therefore certainly not persons or characters) the preceding verse says that "the Dragon shall rise up and slay them." Then follows the eighth verse with its categorical denial of a historical crucifixion in Jerusalem:

"And their dead bodies shall lie in the street of the city which is spiritually called Sodom and Egypt, where also our Lord was crucified."

Jesus crucified not in Jerusalem, but in Sodom and Egypt – two places, geographically, making it necessary to assume two crucifixions or a half crucifixion in each place – and these two "places" expressly described, not as physical localities, but as "spiritually" considered. Here is the Bible's own express declaration that the crucifixion was nothing but a spiritual transaction. Christian exegesis is pretty silent about this verse; it is a question if it has ever been chosen as text for a sabbath sermon. It flies straight in the face of all that ecclesiastical policy stood for from the third century forward to the present. It is the verbatim contradiction of all official Christian theology over sixteen centuries. It is a flat denial of the physical crucifixion and inferentially of the "life" of Jesus, as the Christ. It promises still the final triumph of esotericism. Jerusalem was the "holy city" of the evolved spiritual consciousness, city of "heavenly peace," as its name implies, and never anything else. As a matter of fact, even in its empyreal connotation, Jerusalem was not the locality of consciousness in which the Christ in us is crucified. Jerusalem, on the contrary, is the city of blessedness in which, after the crucifixion, he enters into the peace of his glorious triumph, carried up to the gates of it on the back of the lowly animal, his body. The place of his crucifixion is not in heaven, where peace abides, but down in the depth (Egyptian Tepht, whence Tophet) of matter, the Sodom and Egypt of the fleshly incarnation. There is enough of the primal truth of Christian beginnings left in this one verse to redeem an errant religion from its lost ways and sorry plight.

One of the Sibyl's prophecies was to the effect that the Messiah would come when Rome shall be the ruler of Egypt. "When Rome shall rule Egypt, then shall dawn upon men the supremely great kingdom of the immortal king and a pure sovereign will come to conquer the scepters of the whole earth into all ages." The earliest Church endorsed these Sibylline utterances and cited them to prove the foundation claims of its own religion. Here surely, then, there is a prophecy whose literal fulfillment gave it the lie. Rome did conquer Egypt, and after two thousand years of painful history the world still needs the King of Kings more sorely than ever. Here is an example of fulfilled "prophecy," the folly of which should – but probably will not – carry disillusionment to the rabid mongers of "Bible Prophecy."

But there doubtless was esoteric meaning of intelligent sort back of the Sibyl's utterance. Rome, as the power-center of the world empire, was poetized as the city of epic divine fulfillment, and Egypt, as always in the Bible, was the land of bondage for the soul crucified in body, the "flesh-pots of Egypt." Of course the kingdom of the Lord of spiritual light would come when "Rome," the city of attainment, should conquer and rule over "Egypt," the place of earthly carnal sense. Esotericism redeems another saying of Holy Writ from absurd nonsense and historical contradiction. And it is the only thing that will redeem the whole historical structure of religious meaning from asininity.

Allan Upward writes that in the religion of the inner life "the redemption of the sinner is not so much the historical transaction consummated on the material cross of Calvary as it is the work of the Christ within. . . . Without this feature the history of Christianity can not be understood."

No less a philosopher than Spinoza has this to say relative to the nature of the Christ (Op. I, 510, Epis. To Oldenburg): "that a knowledge of the Christ after the flesh is not necessary to the spiritual life, but the thing that is necessary is a knowledge of that eternal Son of God, the wisdom of God, which has manifested itself in all things and chiefly in the human mind, and most of all in man perfected as Christos."

Paul's verse in I Cor. 15:17 becomes illogical if the historical thesis is held to: "If Christ be not raised, ye are yet in your sins." Every inference of this statement points to a non-historical and purely intimate personal resurrection. If the resurrection was historical and the verse means what it says, then the logic of the situation makes the resurrection dependent upon the state of sinfulness of the people then, or at any time. He did or did not rise, according as the people's general sin is eradicated or is still in force. If people are yet sinful, then Christ can not have risen. The sins or righteousness of people would keep the Christ bobbing up and down between earth and heaven, like a barometer registering the world's batting average in the overcoming of sin. In the esoteric sense the Christ's resurrection is indeed dependent upon the progress of humanity upward to righteousness. We do still bury him deeper with every sin, or raise him up with every sincere act.

He does rise or fall with our advance or backsliding. But if this true theory is applied to the physical resurrection, an ass's bray is not ribald enough to express its ridiculousness. And again despised esotericism alone saves revered scripture from harlequin comics.

Oddly enough the Encyclopedia Britannica (Article: Jews) takes the view that the varied traditions in Jewish religion up to a later stage can not be regarded as objective history. It is naturally impossible, it says, to treat them from any modern standpoint as fiction; "they are honest even when they are most untrustworthy." This peculiar characterization defeats its own intent by obvious self-contradiction. What value honest untrustworthiness has is a bit hard to see. The whole muddle is cleared up if the traditions are regarded as honest and trustworthy allegories. For as honest but untrustworthy history they make no sense whatever, and are valueless if untrustworthy.

Any number of texts throughout the Bible at once lose all comprehensible meaning if taken in the historical sense. For instance, there is the statement in I Cor., 6:1: "Do you not know that the Christians are to be the judges of the world? . . . Do you not know that we are to be the judges of angels, to say nothing of ordinary matters? . . . Do you not know that your bodies are parts of Christ's body?" Taking "Christians" in its historical sense, the picture gives us the ludicrous scenario of good Church folk in the judgment pronouncing sentence upon Mohammedans, Buddhists, Zoroastrians! And taking Christ's body as that of Jesus, the man, we would on Paul's averment be his physical limbs, joints and viscera. Or is it permissible for literalists to take what they like as allegorical and also take what they want as literal? This is their only resort in the end. It makes inconsistency the necessary base of their structure.

Also there is I Cor., 8:6, saying, "yet for us there is . . . just one through whom we live." If the Lord Jesus Christ is Jesus, he is here declared to have made all things, most of which were here and made before he came. As the cosmic Logos, to be sure, he conceivably made the worlds; but as the man Jesus, his hands would have plenty to do with a few mountains and rivers. In the Oxyrhyncus papyri we have the Logos saying, "I am all that was and is and shall be! And my veil it hath never been lifted by mortals" – appropriate for the divine Word, but fatally inapplicable to the man of flesh. Even this lifting of the veil is drawn from the inscription on the base of the statue of Isis at Sais in Egypt.

Also John's passage that "he was in the world, and the world was made by him, and the world knew him not," can have no reference to a personal living Jesus. If this is so it is important to note that even the last clause – that the world knew him not – must have some larger cosmic relevance and can not refer to popular rejection of him and his preachment, according to the accepted interpretation.

A work of great statistical research and vital data is Godbey's The Lost Tribes a Myth. In it he asserts that modern excavations have shown Egyptian dominance in Palestine through the greater part of 3000 years. There were Israelite kings who were political "sons" of Egypt, and Pharaohs warred to establish their authority. (References to the Book of I Kings are given to support this.) "But," says Godbey, "there is no extant effort to append the history of Israel to the antiquity of Egypt." Of course there was not, for the reason that neither Egyptian nor ancient Hebrew literature was dealing with history or antiquity in the historical sense. But if Godbey means that there has been no effort to append Jewish "alleged" history to the religious antiquities of Egypt, Massey's work alone would sufficiently belie his assertion.

A number of utterances of Jesus in his dramatic character of the cosmic Aeon or Logos makes his human personal stature seem futile and puerile beyond measure. His proclamation that he was before Abraham in the loins of the cosmic creation, helping to shape the universe from the foundation of the worlds, sounds senseless when the majestic words are supposed to come from the lips of a mere man on earth. It is the same with his final consummative plea which he makes to his Father in John to restore unto him that glory which he had with him aforetime in cosmic heavens before the worlds were, after he had come into the world whither he had been sent and had done the divine preaching, "healing," "miracle-working," ending with his humiliating crucifixion on a wooden cross, is to reduce cosmic events to the proportion of newspaper chronicles. A great many texts would show the preposterous inapplicability of cosmic characterizations attaching to Jesus as the Logos when referred to Jesus as the man.

The evidence in this chapter is of the kind generally called "textual evidence." It is by no means lacking in either weight or cogency. What is here assembled is a mere tid-bit or filip to what would be a full meal of this significant material. The quantity could be increased to voluminous proportions. Strong as the temptation is to linger in this field, the practical considerations of the task call for a grappling with a series of far more substantial arguments and evidences in the case, which rise in a scale of pertinence and convincing force from chapter to chapter.

Chapter IX

FAITH'S ODD WONDERLAND

An item of sensational testimony bearing upon the pre-Christian origin and character of insignia claimed to be exclusively Christian is the statement of Lundy (Monumental Christianity, p. 125) that the well-known monogram of Christ regarded as an origination of Christianity and a cryptic shorthand signature for the name of their personal Founder, was antecedent to the time of Jesus. Says this author: "Even the XP, which I had thought to be exclusively Christian, are to be found in combination thus: (a insert glyph) on coins of the Ptolemies and on those of Herod the Great, struck forty years before our era, together with this other form so often seen on the early Christian monuments, viz., a insert glyph. And in regard to it, King well remarks, 'although these symbols, as far as regards their material form, were not invented by the Christians, they nevertheless received at this time a new signification and which became their proper one; and everybody agrees in giving them this peculiar signification.'" (King: Early Christian Numismatics, p. 12 ff.). As to this the important thing is that the emblem was not "invented" by the Christians and must have been therefore pre-extant. As to the "new" signification given it, that is another of those rash statements that are based on sheer assumption and the pious necessity of putting a face on the matter reflecting favorably on Christianity and detrimentally upon paganism, as much as to say that the pagans had the emblem, but of course did not know its real and true import and assigned some base meaning to it, and only the Christians elevated it to pure connotations. There has been enough of this brash apologetic for Christian superiority to sicken the conscientious mind. The truth in this instance happens to be precisely the opposite of what is claimed: it was the philosophical pagans who had the insignium and knew what it meant in its profoundest sense; it was the Christians who adopted it in ignorance and reduced it to the empty status of a supposed abbreviation of the name of a man. Lundy himself lets out a hint that confirms this explanation. He says:

"The Greek monogram, therefore, was the prevailing symbol of Christ as the First and the Last during the first three centuries of the Christian era, as more expressive of the faith in His divine character and mission . . . ; while the cross afterwards became the symbol of his human sufferings and death, until it culminated in the ghastly crucifix. Or rather, the primitive Church dwelt more on the divine side of Christ's person and office than upon the human."

This last clause is a hint that entirely falls in consonance with the view that the personal Christ embodied in Jesus was a formulation of later incompetence after nearly two centuries, and not a simple fact stemming from direct original knowledge of such a man's existence. It is perhaps well to add Lundy's supplemental remark, that the sacred monogram, as well as the cross, was used in every act of worship, stamped upon the bread of the Eucharist, marked on the foreheads of the baptized and worn on seal rings, long before the term Pope was ever exclusively applied to the Bishop of Rome, or ever Romanism was dreamed of.

Full value must be given to such a fact as that the early Christian Fathers were insistent on comparing many features of antecedent religion with those of Christianity. For one instance Origen elaborately traces out the agreement of the resurrection of Dionysus in the Greek cult with that of Christ, and does it in such a way as to hint that the resurrection was an allegory of the "Pilgrim Soul" and not historical. Paul carries out this hint in Timothy.

The historicity of the Gospel of Mark is directly challenged by Bacon in his Jesus and Paul (p. 147). He declares that when we look at this Roman Gospel which became so completely standard for this whole class of literature that no other considerable record of Jesus' activity survives, and when we see how the material has been selected and what motive controls the elaboration, it will be perfectly clear that we have in Mark not a biography, not a history, but a collection of anecdotes; and even this collection is made for purposes of edification and not of historical record.

Abraham Geiger, German researcher, agrees with Graetz, one of the most voluminous of German textual critics, in thinking that in Jesus' teaching "there is nothing new, or that what is new is put before us in a somewhat enervated form, just as it originated during an enervated period." (Geiger: Das Judentum und Seine Geschichte, p. 119.)

This allusion to enervation falls in harmoniously with the thesis of deterioration of wisdom in Christian acumen after the second or third century.

No students have surpassed the German investigators in thoroughness of research. Another of this group, G. Friedländer, in his The Jewish Sources of the Sermon on the Mount shows with much learning that not only the Sermon on the Mount, but the entire Christian system (excluding its asceticism) is borrowed from the Old Testament, the Book of Ben Sira, The Testaments of the Twelve Patriarchs, Philo of Alexandria and the earlier portions of the Talmud and Midrash.

Another of the German School, Chwolson, makes a specially noteworthy point that, rightly to understand Pauline and Post-Pauline Christianity, a knowledge of the Sibylline Oracles, Philo and Greek literature generally is most important.

One of the finest Jewish treatises on the subject of Jesus of Nazareth is Joseph Klausner's work under that title. He says definitely that the fourth Gospel is not a "religio-historical, but a religio-philosophical book." It was not composed, he says, until about the middle of the second century, at a time when Christians were already distinct from Jews. The object of John's Gospel is to interpret Jesus as the Logos in the extreme Philonic or cosmic sense, and it therefore passes over such details in the "life" of Jesus as would appear too human! "It may well include a few historical fragments handed down to the author (who was certainly not John the disciple) by tradition; but speaking generally, its value is theological rather than historical or biographical."

Among capable students in the field of this study who entirely disbelieved in Jesus' existence are B. Smith and Arthur Drews. Smith denies the existence of the town of Nazareth, in which determination some others have sided with him. Origen in the latter part of the second century states that he could find no trace of "Bethany beyond Jordan." Smith advances the claim that Jesus was an object of worship to a sect of Nazarites who existed at the time when Christianity came into being, and whom the Christian Father Epiphanius mentions at great length.

It may be noticed in passing that Nietzsche, the philosopher of super-humanity in Germany a half century ago, pronounces the combining of the New Testament artificially with the Old in the Christian system as "perhaps the greatest piece of effrontery and worst kind of 'sin against the Holy Ghost' with which literary Europe has ever burdened its conscience." (Beyond Good and Evil, III, p. 52.)

Nietzsche's view is endorsed by Grethenbach, who feels that "the solemn endorsement of the Jewish Scriptures now embodied in the 'Old Testament' by the Christian Church must stand out forever as one of the most remarkable facts in the history of religion. By this act Christianity made itself liable for and guarantor of a series of writings not a line of which has a known author, and but few incidents of which are corroborated by other testimony; writings which record prodigies and miracles more daring and more frequent than are asserted in the literature of any serious sort promulgated by any other people." (A Secular View of the Bible.)

This virtually amounts, he thinks, to Christianity's chaining itself to a "corpse." However this conclusion must be modified by the knowledge that while the Old Testament literature may be considered a "corpse" if regarded as history – rather a ghost or wraith of history – it must be accepted as a very living thing when taken, as it rightly should be, as vital allegory and drama of verity. Solomon, Grethenbach adds, wise and wealthy as he was, left no inscriptions or other stone witnesses to his name, as did the neighboring monarchs of the Nile and Euphrates.

Meister Eckhardt described the Christ as the collective soul of humanity.

The celebrated Orientalist Rhys Davids in Hibbert Lectures, 1881, (p. 33) declares that historical criticism was quite unknown in the early centuries of Buddhism, "when men were concerned with matters they held to be vastly more important than exact statements of literal history."

And Vittorio D. Macchioro in his fine work, From Orpheus to Paul supplements this with a statement that is of the utmost cogency in its bearing on the general thesis of this work. He says: "In both cases an historical event, which in the opinion of the believers really happened, becomes a spiritual event for every man at all times." This concedes essentially the whole case for our argument. This is the true and graphic description of the position of Christianity at this time and for centuries past. It is doing its best to make inspiring sustenance out of events that it feels must have happened because the belief in them yields spiritual nourishment. The Gospel story must be true history, it asseverates, for witness to which see the good effect it has had on believers. The events of Jesus' life could not have worked so beneficial an effect upon millions and not have happened in reality. There must have been a personal Christ to have made Christianity the religion it has been.

Without the change of a single word this last form of statement may be conceded to be the truth. But if ever truth was a two-edged sword cutting in both directions, it is so in this case, and with damaging consequences for Christianity. True enough (the conception of) a personal Christ was necessary to produce Christianity and make it the religion it has been. The simple contention of this work is that it would have been a far different and far better religion had it been based on the conception of the spiritual Christ instead of the historical Jesus. Would Christian adherents accept their statement in the form which might justly be substituted for the one above? – There must have been a personal Jesus to have made Christianity the witch-baiting, heresy-hunting, doctrine-wrangling, war-waging, bigoted and persecuting religion it has been!

Macchioro testifies to the truth of all that has been claimed here when he goes on to particularize that "in other words, an historical fact, or, if you prefer, a story which Christians regard as an historical fact, I mean the death and resurrection of the Christ, became a mystical fact, the spiritual rebirth of man." The crux of significance in his statements is the point that the spiritual efficacy of the doctrine is in its being believed, not in its factuality. And it can unquestionably be better believed as allegory than as history. Any faith, factually founded or fancifully conceived, can become an effective agent of human psychologization, if only it is believed hard enough. Even what appear to be the splendid fruits of any religion may only be proving the operations of human psychology and not at all the alleged facts on which the religion is based.

"The Baptism and Eucharist," concludes Macchioro, "are in the light of history nothing but acts of initiation."

Bacon admits that Haggadic teaching, whether Jewish or Christian, has no restrictions in the use of fiction save to bring home the religious or moral truth intended. Its one rule is: "Let all things be done unto edification."

Another German critic, Bruno Bauer, thought the Gospels were "abstract conceptions turned into history, probably by one man – the evangelist Mark."

W. B. Smith, Tulane University, in Der Vorchristliche Jesus, derives the "Christ myth" from certain alleged "Jesus cults," dating

from pre-Christian times. Jesus, he thinks, is the name of an ancient Western Semitic cult-god, and he finds a reference to the doctrines held by the devotees of this deity in Acts 18:25, where a Jew, Apollo, coming from Alexandria to Ephesus, already learned in the Way of the Lord, preaches Jesus. He connects the name Jesus with the Nazaraioi, the Nazarenes, a pre-Christian religious society.

Not less summary in his conclusions is Drews, a profound analyst of the Jewish material. He says: "The Gospels do not contain the history of an actual man, but only the myth of the god-man, Jesus, clothed in an historical dress."

Then there is J. M. Robertson, whose labors unearthed much of the buried truth about the Jesus myth. He calls attention to the notable circumstance that the Miriam of Exodus is no more historical than Moses; like him and Joshua she is to be reckoned an ancient deity euhemerized; and the Arab tradition that she was the mother of Joshua (Jesus) raises an irremovable surmise that a Mary, the mother of Jesus, may have been worshipped in Syria long before our era.

According to Preller (Griech. Myth., I, p. 667) the founder of the Samo-Thracian Mysteries is one Jasion, a name cognate with Jesus. No less so is Jason, the recapturer of the "Golden Fleece," – divinity coming under the zodiacal sign of Aries, the Ram.

Robertson is emphatic and decisive in his assertion that "the Christian system is a patchwork of a hundred suggestions drawn from pagan art and ritual usage." No mind open to the relevance of facts and data can study ancient lore extensively without being driven to the same conclusion. Those who deny it simply have not looked at enough of the material.

Even T. J. Thorburn in his work, The Mythical Interpretation of the Gospels (p. 91), says that the cave of Bethlehem had been from time immemorial a place of worship in the cult of Tammuz, as it actually was in the time of Jerome; and, as the "quasi-historic David" bore the name of the sun-god Daoud, or Dodo (Sayce: Hibbert Lectures, pp. 56-7), who was identical with Tammuz, it was not improbable on that account that Bethlehem was traditionally the city of David, and therefore no doubt, was deemed by the New Testament mythmakers the most suitable place for the birth of Jesus, the mythical descendant of that quasi-historical embodiment of the god Tammuz or Adonis.

Among the Gnostics Basilides and Valentinus never did acknowledge any historical founder of Christianity. (Massey: Ancient Egypt, p. 904.) And Clement of Alexandria is authority for the statement that it was after his resurrection that Jesus revealed the true Gnosis to Peter, James and John. (Eusebius: H. E., 2:1.)

Epiphanius, in speaking of the "Sabelian Heretics," says:

"The whole of their errors and the main strength of their heterodoxy they derive from some Apocryphal books, but principally from that which is called The Gospel of the Egyptians . . . for in that many things are proposed in a hidden, mysterious manner as by our Savior." (Ad. Haeres., 26:2.)

Priceless in value would be that same Gospel of the Egyptians if Christian fury had not destroyed it.

Ancient preoccupation with figurism and neglect of history even extended to a denial of the existence of Orpheus, legendary divine instructor of the Hellenic world. Says Lundy (Monumental Christianity, p. 190):

"Both Bryant and Von Doellinger express the opinion that Orpheus was only a name applied to a school of priests who brought the new cult of Dionysus into Greece. Vossius doubts, with good reason, whether any such person as Orpheus ever existed, citing Aristotle and Suidas to this effect. . . . Orpheus was a title under which Deity was worshipped, and he was the same as Horus of Egypt and Apollo of Greece."

In the preface to his work, Prehistoric Religion (p. 18), the author, Philo L. Mills, writes that the written Bible is late in its appearance, but absolutely pure and primitive in its message, while the extrabiblical traditions held a priority of composition, but not of content; "they are valuable only so far as they lend confirmation to the biblical record, which is itself founded on prehistorical records, which have since been lost."

Mosheim (I, p. 482) says of Tatian, one of the later Church Fathers, that he "disclaimed the notion of Christ's having assumed a real body."

And he also says that "Marcion indisputably denied that Christ in reality either suffered or died; but at the same time he affirmed that this imaginary or feigned death was attended with salutary consequences to the human race." By what psychological processes he fancied the Church's perpetuation of a lie could generate salutary consequences for the human race is another of those doctrinal riddles coming down to us from early Christian days which we are supposed to accept without using our reason.

Mosheim adds that the Marcionites were the most fearless in courting martyrdom among the Christian sects, being surpassed by non "either in the number or the courage of their martyrs." If this is so, it only unhappily testifies to the fanatical possibilities even among people of considerable intelligence.

Origen, says Mosheim (II, 160), "thought it utterly impossible that God, a being entirely separate from matter, should ever assume a body, or be willing to associate himself with matter. . . . That is, the divine nature, being generally a different substance from matter, the two substances cannot possibly be commingled."

There is apparent here a singular lack of esoteric systemology on Origen's (or perhaps Mosheim's) part. For that soul everywhere does commingle with matter to effect the work of creation is taught in Platonic-Orphic, Hermetic, and all ancient religious systems. But Origen was astute in recommending to the preachers of Christianity to carry into their practice a set of instructions he prescribed, following the maxim that it is vastly important to the honor and advantage of Christianity that all its doctrines be traced back to the sources of all truth, or to be shown to flow from the principles of philosophy; and consequently that a Christian theologian should exert his ingenuity and industry primarily to demonstrate the harmony between religion and reason, or to show that there is nothing taught in the Scriptures but what is founded in reason. If only sixteen centuries of Christian theologians had followed Origen's prescription!

Mosheim has been quoted as saying that a serious fault of Origen's was that "he lauded immoderately the recondite and mystical sense of scripture and unreasonably deprecated the grammatical and historical sense." If this was or is a fault, how can the existence of a single theological seminary in Christian ecclesiasticism ever be justified? If there is no recondite or mystical meaning underneath the scriptures, why does it need a life training of their expositors, and why are the laity kept in ignorance of their deeper import? The gross absurdity of such whinings against the esoteric side of religion and its sacred books can now be better seen in its bald childishness.

Mosheim has to go to the length of saying the damaging thing that it is not good sense to be enthusiastic over the sublimer interpretations of scripture! And this is precisely the absurd dilemma in which Christian theology has always entangled itself in its efforts to talk down the esoteric element in its own history. It has to repudiate itself at its own best. There is no quibbling over the point: either there is a deeper sense to the scriptures, to all religious exposition, to the profounder experience of religion itself, than the simple-minded can apprehend, or all the labored academic studies in the field have been an extravagance and an impertinence. When they are sincere, all Christian mystics and Christianity's greatest preachers have endlessly emphasized the deeper intuitions of "the life hid with Christ" in the deeper chambers of human consciousness. The ecclesiastical quarrel with and hostility toward esotericism is on the face of it both dialectically irrational, directly treasonable and patently self-contradictory. It is a grave question whether there is not full warrant for characterizing it as a base sell-out of its own true genius for the reward of currying the support of the illiterate masses. It is a betrayal and re-crucifixion of the Christ in man, that has continued from the third century down to this present.

We have also seen, in his strictures upon Origen's addiction to "allegory" how Mosheim reflects the constant theological fear of allegory which is based on the ever-present possibility that if you give free-thinkers and Gnostics an inch of allegory in the scriptures, they may quickly stretch it to a mile and embrace the whole of scripture in your tropes. As between absurd and impossible history and sublime allegorical truth, the truth must be sacrificed for the history.

A light on the date of "Luke's Gospel" is found in the item that Theophilus, the friend to whom Luke addresses himself in the opening chapter, was Bishop of Antioch from about 169 to 177 A.D. (Cath. Ency., XIV, 625). If Luke was written 120 to 130 years after Jesus' death, the chances of its being a legitimate, well-historicized and positive account of events so far past, and entirely quiescent in the interval since their occurrence, are very slim indeed.

To prove Old Testament "history" unauthentic does not directly discredit whatever may be genuine New Testament history. Still it would strengthen the case against the reliability of the latter if the Old can be disproved. So Higgins (Anac., p. 633) remarks how extraordinary a thing it is that the destruction of the hosts of Pharaoh should not have been known to Berosus, Strabo, Diodorus or Herodotus, that they should not have heard of these stupendous events either from the Egyptians or from the Syrians, Arabians or Jews. Yet, he subjoins, the same "events" happened in India. The Afghans or Rajapoutans, shepherd tribes as at this day, invaded south India and conquered Ceylon, then were driven out over Adam's bridge; and the same kind of catastrophe is said to have overtaken their pursuers as that which overwhelmed the Egyptians pursuing the Israelites in the "Red" Sea.

For its circumstantial significance it is well to bring to daylight another feature of historical fact that has received no attention for centuries. This is the matter of the monumental record of Jesus' burial. Says Lundy (Monu. Christ., p. 256):

"The earliest example of our Lord's burial which exists among the monuments of primitive Christianity is, perhaps, that of an ivory in the Vatican, of the sixth century, which represents a square structure surmounted by a dome . . . with a sleeping soldier on one side of it, and two of the holy women who came early in the morning to anoint the dead body of their Lord. No such representations are found in the catacombs or 'early' churches either of the East or West. . . . So careful was early Christian art in abstaining from all painful representation of the Lord. It is a hint to modern idealists in art that they go and do likewise."

Perhaps it is also a hint that the basis of historical factuality behind the story of the Christ's death was too completely wanting.

At the same level of significance is the sister fact that Lundy brings out (Monu. Christ., p. 268). This time it is the resurrection.

"It is a most singular fact that no actual representation of our Lord's resurrection has yet been discovered among the monuments of early Christianity. The earliest that I can find is that published by Mr. Eastlake in Mrs. Jameson's History of Our Lord, representing a temple-like tomb, with a tree growing behind it on which two birds are feeding; the drowsy guards are leaning on the tomb, one asleep, the other awake, and two others are utterly amazed and confounded; an angel sits at the door of the sepulcher speaking to the three holy women; and our Lord is ascending a hill with a roll in one hand, while the other is grasped by the hand of the Eternal Father, as it is seen reaching down out of heaven. It is an ivory carving and said to belong to the fifth or sixth century. It is at Munich."

Lundy adds that as the crucifixion is only indicated by symbol, so doubtless is the resurrection.

Grethenbach reminds us that we must make liberal allowance in our reading of New Testament Scripture for the desire on the part of Jesus' biographers to make the "incidents" of his life conform to the texts of ancient sacred works. Hence, he says, each reader must judge for himself whether he is being treated to fact or to the results of this process of conformity. What a basis for the substantiation of events that have determined the religion of one third of mankind!

In his History of the Christian Religion to the Year 200 Waite affirms there is no evidence that any of those Gospels which were basic documents back of Matthew, Mark, and Luke taught the miraculous conception or the material resurrection of Christ, or contained any account of his miracles, or any references to any book containing such accounts or teachings. Waite says it can not be denied that evidence that the canonical Gospels were unknown to Justin Martyr is very strong, and indeed conclusive, and that his references and quotations were not from them but from other known Gospels, of which Irenaeus says there were many.

A weighty consideration is back of Waite's strong sentence that "no work of art of any kind has been discovered, no painting or engraving, no sculpture or other relic of antiquity, which may be looked upon as furnishing additional evidence of the existence of those Gospels, and which was executed earlier than the latter part of the second century. Even the exploration of the catacombs failed to bring to light any evidence of that character."

It would certainly appear that the event of Jesus' life had no relation to the time of its recording. It has never occurred to partisan zealots that almost indubitably this would be an indication that the "recording" had no relation to the event. An event that begins to be recorded only two hundred years after its occurrence hardly has a legitimate claim to the title of history. It must inevitably be a construction of legend and romanticism, which is exactly what the "life" of Jesus proves to be when examined.

Miss Holbrook says that the four Gospels were written in Greek (by Hebrew fishermen and simple unlearned citizens) and that there was no translation of them into other languages earlier than the third century. No autograph manuscript of any of them has ever been known, nor has any credible witness ever claimed to have seen such a manuscript. Origen says that the four were selected from a very large number, and Irenaeus says that the four were chosen out of many because there were four universal winds and four quarters to the globe. Such a reason for the number selected puts entirely out of court the reason commonly and naïvely believed to have been the guiding one – the selection of four because there were but four in existence. Of the ordinary natural motives that led to the writing and preserving of actual history, not a single one is evident in the production of the Gospels. Neither the time of their composition, nor the character of their material, nor the knowledge of their existence, nor the definiteness of any data concerning them bears evidence of their being veridical history.

Hippolytus claims that the Basilidian Gnostics accepted the Gospel entirely, but Mead asserts that there is evidence to prove they did not. On the contrary they explained such material as the historicized legends of initiation, the process of which is magnificently worked out in the Pistis Sophia treatise. Mead says of the learned Gnostic societies that in their eyes a Gospel was always taken in the sense of an exposition of the things beyond the phenomenal world. As they were the most intelligent of the early Christians, it is warrantable to regard their views as far the most likely version of the truth. The Basilidian view of Jesus was that he was the perfect "man" within the psychic and animal soul of man, or the innermost divine ray of consciousness within the mortal body.

A point of fair cogency is made by Harry Elmer Barnes (The Twilight of Christianity, p. 415) that if Jesus had been the Son of God, neither he nor his Father would have allowed his doctrines to be perverted and later almost wholly supplanted by a jumbled compound of Judaism and paganism.

It counts for much in the argument that Mead (Did Jesus Live 100 Years B.C.?, p. 324) makes it clear that the name "Christian" was not a title given by the early followers of Jesus to themselves. Indeed it is found still unused by a series of Christian writers of the first half of the second century at the time when it was employed by Pliny the Younger in 112 A.D., by Tacitus in 116-117 A.D., and by Suetonius in 120 A.D. These Christian writers were content to designate the early communities of these co-believers by such expressions as "brethren," "saints," "elect," "the called," "they that believed," "faithful," "disciples," "they that are in Christ," "they that are in the Lord," and "those of the way."

A touch of early Christian association of doctrine with Egyptian origins that did not suffer erasure by the vandal hands, is seen in an identification, by Augustine and Ambrose amongst the Christian Fathers, of Jesus with and as the "good scarabaeus," the Egyptian name for the divine Avatar coming under the zodiacal sign of Cancer, the Crab or Beetle. In accordance with the continuation for some time of the Kamite symbolism in Christianity, it was also maintained by some sectaries that Jesus was a potter and not a carpenter. The Egyptian God Ptah was the divine Potter, or shaper of the clay of man's nature into divine form.

Not one person in thousands in the Church today has the faintest idea when the chronology or dating of the Christian era was fixed. Mead states that Dionysius of the sixth century, following Victorious of Aquitaine of the preceding century fixed the date of the nativity of Jesus. Turner of Oxford, in his article on the Chronology of the New Testament in Hasting's Dictionary of the Bible, gives the nativity in B.C. 7-6. In the Ency. Biblica von Soden of Berlin, under "Chronology" gives the Birth "circa 4 B.C." Some encyclopedias give two to three years of the ministry, others but one year.

Likewise Mead cites the judgment of many scholars that the speeches of the persons in the Acts of the Apostles are the most artificial element in a book already vastly discredited as history. Schmiedel pointed out that the author constructed the utterances in each case according to his own conception. Even Headlam, the writer of the conservative article in Hastings' Dictionary, admits that the speeches are "clearly in a sense the author's own compositions."

It is impossible to ignore the force of the rather startling fact baldly stated by Mead (Did Jesus Live 100 Years B.C.?, p. 48) when he writes:

"It has always been an unfailing source of astonishment to the historical investigator of Christian beginnings that there is not one single word from the pen of any pagan writer of the first century of our era which can in any fashion be referred to the marvelous story recounted by the Gospel writers. The very existence of Jesus seems unknown."

Mead goes deeply and carefully into the early use of the term Nazarioi (Nazarenes, Nazarites, Nazarians, etc.) and cites especially Epiphanius' references to it, showing how this careless or over-imaginative "historian" of the "heresies" entangles himself in many flagrant contradictions in his statements. Says Mead:

"The historical fact underlying all this contradiction seems to be simply that 'Nazoraei' was a general name for many schools possessing many views differing from the view which subsequently became orthodox. Their descendants are the Mandaites of southern Babylonia, who have the Codex Nazaraeus."

Epiphanius claims strenuously that the Nazoraeans were the first Christians and that they used both Old and New Testament, – though how they could have used the New Testament when it was not yet in existence, he does not explain! Incidentally the present thesis that there were extant many documents like the Logia or Sayings and various Mystery ritual texts or "Gospels" in all the ancient period, both before, during and after Jesus' "life," is the only one that permits us to solve the difficulty of Epiphanius' claims without charging him with overt lying. The "Gospels" were in existence, yes, but not as the canonical Gospels officially apotheosized at Nicea in 325. But so were they in existence centuries before Christ.

Further with reference to the term Nazar, Mead (Did Jesus Live 100 Years B.C.?, p. 346) has to say that the Old Testament Nazirs were those "consecrated" to Jahweh by a vow, and their origin goes back to very early times in Jewish tradition.

"Now it is to be remembered," he says, "that in Numbers VI the word nezer is applied to the taking of the Nazirite vow of separation and consecration, and the name netzer (branch) is given to one of the disciples of Jesus in the Talmud, and in one of the Toldoth recensions to Jeschu himself, and that the commentators are agreed that this is a play on notzri, the Hebrew for 'Nazarene,'" or Galilean.

In discussing the Ebionites, one of the earliest Christian sects, Mead says that the main charge against them, as related by Hippolytus (Philos., VIII, p. 34) is that they, like all the earliest "heretics" decried the later doctrine of the miraculous physical virgin birth of Jesus. Strange to note again that the closer one gets to the period of Jesus' alleged time, the greater and more general is the denial or ignorance of his existence. The further one draws away from it, the greater and more insistent the "proofs" of it! This again entirely reverses the universal phenomenon of a historical recording. Most living characters are homely and familiar entities during and immediately after their lives, and only wax romantic and haloed after centuries have elapsed. But Jesus was airy and ethereal in the first century, and crystallized into quite concrete personality after several centuries. Every writer about him from the twelfth century on can describe his appearance, his moods, his motives to meticulous particularity far better than anyone writing in the first century.

A curious early Christian document is Justin's Dialogue Cum Trypho, or debate with Trypho, in which (xlix) he puts the following argument into the mouth of his Jewish opponent:

"Those who affirm him to have been a man, and to have been anointed by election, and then to have become a Christ (Anointed), appear to me to speak more plausibly than you," that is, than Justin, who maintained the physical birth of Jesus.

Justin represents his opponent as arguing that Jesus was born naturally like other humans, and not by a miracle of virgin parturition. But this whole debate is wide of the mark, since the question is not whether his birth was natural or supernatural, but whether it was a physical event at all, – not how it occurred, but whether it occurred. The question is not one of quality or manner, but purely one of fact.

A work of Celsus, the pagan debater with Origen, called The True Logos, which certainly would have yielded us much light on all early Gnostic or esoteric interpretation of sacred writings, has been destroyed by the Christians.

It may with many carry weight in the discussion that both Kant and Hegel negate the historical Jesus.

Of the Church Fathers Irenaeus seems never to have subscribed to the legend of Jesus' death on the cross, or his death at all at the early age of thirty-three years. It is a curious thing and hard to explain in the face of the claim that Jesus' life was accepted historically by the universal early Church, that Irenaeus repeats the famous legend which refutes the Gospel "history" flatly. Irenaeus was born in the early part of the second century between 120 and 140 A.D. He was Bishop of Lyons, France; and he repeats a tradition testified to by the elders, which he alleges was derived directly by them from John, the "Disciple of the Lord," to the effect that Jesus was not crucified at the age of thirty-three, but that he had passed through every age and lived on to be an "oldish man." And we are permitted to wonder how such a tradition, attributed to so accredited a source as John, could have lived on for so many years, if the general field was occupied by the factual acceptance of the Gospel narrative, or how it could have been purveyed by a Bishop of such eminence in the Church as Irenaeus.

There are other semi-authenticated tales and legends which keep Jesus alive beyond his early thirties, and afloat in our modern day are works and canards purporting to expose a lost record of the Savior's escape from death in Judea and his travels and teachings in Eastern monasteries, inevitably in Tibet and the Himalayas, that Shamballah of spiritual mystery, where any such fanciful history can safely be localized. The significant thing to note about all this is that the late inventions in the field of etherealized imagination are very likely no more daring and bizarre than those of the earlier centuries.

Candor and honest reflection have both had to be cast aside and a curtain of reticence drawn over the glaring data which operate so directly to contradict the historicity of Jesus, in the material of the famous fifty-third chapter of Isaiah. By theologians it is known as the chapter of the "Suffering Servant." In it are depicted in the most vivid and memorable phraseology the sufferings of the divine agent of human redemption, who sacrifices his heavenly heritage and reduces himself to the form of a lowly servant to bear the sins of wayward men. It is too well known to need quotation. Its impressive recital of the Logos bearing our sins in his body and suffering agony for our transgressions is unforgettable literature. But the point to note is that it is a descriptive summary of exactly what the "historical" Jesus experienced in his earthly career, and it was written centuries before Jesus "lived." Again it appears that Jesus' biography was in considerable part written before he came.

Massey has called attention to the fact, disconcerting to the supporters of the historical thesis, that the Jesus of Revelation is described with female breasts. The conception of supernal deity as androgyne motivated the representation of types of deity as combined male and female. But this was all in the allegorical portrayal and it removes the data from history. In this light Lord Raglan's statement can be well credited, that we can not go far toward the true realization of the meaning of ancient literary formulations without recognizing that the archaic tomes rest on no historical foundations, but that they are documents illustrating the development of religious ideas and systems that are of the highest importance. And when research has fortified itself with this initial instrument of correct comprehension. Raglan avers that all the difficulties will disappear. For that which is difficult and impossible as history, becomes not only possible but sublimely illuminating as mythicism.

This chapter must include an item of the most curious sort, that will doubtless fall with great surprise and some dismay into the minds of many readers. This has to do with the several varying reports or accounts of Jesus' personal appearance and beauty – or ugliness – of physical features. We have here one of the most certain instances of the confusion of allegory with history, for on no other grounds can so eccentric a misconstruction be accounted for. Very understandably all the prevalent notions of the Christ's personality picture him as of the highest order of comeliness. It would not match popular conceptions of his character to think of him otherwise. Surely the Son of God could be nothing less than radiant with charm and beauty. If he had not been comely, he would have had to be made so to give devotees the only picture of him that would have been acceptable to their fancies. Hence every painting and sculpture from the early centuries portrayed him as a man of typical saintliness and beauty. The imaginative genius of artists has extended itself to the utmost to create a form and appearance, mien and expression, that would most fully embody the highest Christian conception of divine character. Jesus was painted to depict what the Christian imagination conceived the perfect man and Son of God in human form to be like. This portrayal represented in the finale a compromise between or composition of the worldly ideal of natural masculine beauty and celestial spirituality, softened by the elements limned in the fifty-third chapter of Isaiah, the man of sorrows who bore our pains in his person. It disturbs many who like to emphasize his humanity, in which he is presented as in all respects like unto us, to read that he never laughed. This tradition precluded his ever being pictured laughing. Laughter, though one of the commonest and most natural of human expressions, does not quite comport with the heavier dignity and gravity of the theological conception of his nature and mission. It is a little too light to harmonize with the more austere solemnity of his earthly errand. Human laughter is not commonly thought of as divine, and if the gods laugh, we are not too certain it befits their empyreal dignity. They might be laughing at us. Laughter is commonly too close to carousal and buffoonery to be seemingly associated with high divinity. Our notion of divinity is inevitably colored with Sabbath sanctity of decorum. Our puritanical bent had pretty effectively debarred laughter from the Sabbath, hence from religion, and hence from the Christ's personality.

The portraiture of Jesus inevitably took the form and character which these considerations dictated, and we have the conventional form, face, bearing and clothing so well known. But it will come with a heavy shock to all who with uncritical minds have accepted this portrayal as at least tentatively a possibility of likeness to the living person of Jesus, to learn for the first time that a number of the earliest Fathers positively stated that Jesus was ugly, ungainly, uncomely and deformed! We can do no better than cite Lundy's findings on this matter (Monu. Christ., p. 232):

"Now it is worthy of special consideration that none of the sculptured or painted representations of Christ in early Christian art exactly agree with the reputed descriptions given of his personal appearance by Agbarus, Lentulus and others. It is not an easy matter to determine when the mere symbols of Christ were developed into pictorial and sculptured representations of his person; but one thing is certain, viz., that the uniform testimony of the earliest writers of the Christian era is to the effect that our Lord's person was insignificant and void of beauty, but that the spirit which shone through his humanity was all beauty and glory."

Again Lundy wrestles (p. 231) with the point:

"The New Testament writings give no account of our Lord's personal appearance. 'Fairer than the children of men' in mind, body and soul was the Hebrew ideal of the Messiah, as the Psalmist expresses it. (XLV:2): and 'He hath no form nor comeliness,' no attractive beauty, is another Hebrew aspect of him, as Isaiah reports it; and with such opposite prophetic anticipations, is it any wonder that the subject of them has actually given rise to two schools of ancient Christian art, or rather two different modes of treating our Lord's personal appearance? One made him the young and blooming and beautiful Divinity, like Krishna, Mithra and Apollo; the other gave him a sad and ugly face, covered by a beard, and made him really and literally 'a man of sorrows, and acquainted with grief.'"

Lundy should have added Isaiah's more specific details of portraiture in the verse which runs: "How was his visage marred, more than any man; and his form, more than the sons of men; disfigured till he seemed a man no more, deformed out of the semblance of a man." The Son of God, deformed more than even humankind! This puts the entire historicity in jeopardy. The structure of Christian theology rests very definitely upon the claim that the babe of Bethlehem was the literal and historical fulfillment of Old Testament "prophecy." It is now caught in the dilemma of having to admit – if Jesus was divinely comely – that the prophecy failed of fulfillment in this important and specific item. To have fulfilled the "prophecy" Jesus must be put down as ugly and deformed! And if Jesus is admitted to have been ill-featured, then millions upon millions of pages of Christian pious effusion about the Galilean's austere beauty must be reduced to what they are at any rate – unctuous froth.

We find Justin Martyr, early second century Father, quoted as follows: "He appeared without comeliness, as the scriptures declared," when he came to the Jordan. Clement of Alexandria deposed to this effect: "the Lord himself was uncomely in aspect . . . his form was mean, inferior to men." Celsus, in his debate with Origen, argues that since the Divine inhabited the body of Jesus, that body must certainly have been different and more beautiful and radiant than common, in grandeur, beauty, strength, voice, impressiveness and influence, "whereas his person did not differ in any respect from another, but was, as they report, little and ill-conditioned and ignoble, i.e., low and mean." Origen in rebuttal protests Celsus' using the prophet's description in literal application to the man Jesus, and argues that any way all human meanness was changed and glorified in his transfiguration, resurrection and ascension. Tertullian decides that no matter how poor and despised that body may be, Jesus is still his Christ, be he inglorious, ignoble and dishonored. David's words that "he is fairer than the children of men" are applicable in that figurative sense of spiritual grace, when he has put on his shining armor of beauty and glory. Tertullian (Flesh of Christ, Ch. 9) says "his body did not reach even to human beauty, to say nothing of heavenly glory." Augustine sidesteps the bald issue by asseverating his beauty in all his functions, offices, acts, miracles, words, character and mission. He summarizes his position in his statement (De Trinitate, VIII, Ch. 4, tom. 8, p. 951, Migne's Ed.): "Whatever the bodily appearance or face of our Lord was, it was but one, yet t was represented and diversified by a variety of numberless ideals." Lundy observes that this passage clearly proves that in Augustine's day the representations of Jesus' features were according to each Christian or Gnostic artist's own conception, and that the theologian-saint would have mentioned any portrait of Jesus if there had been one extant, either of him or of his mother, the virgin Mary. For he adds: "We know not the face or personal appearance of the Virgin Mary." (De Trinitate, VIII, Ch. 5.)

Abarbanel says that the fifty-third chapter of Isaiah can not apply to the personal Messiah, because of the prevailing tradition of the Jewish people that he was a beautiful and blooming youth. This tradition surely had its roots in the imaginative characterizations of the Messiah as the sun-god, which gave to Krishna, Agni, Mithra, Zarathustra, Horus and Apollo the ruddiest bloom of youth and beauty.

It has already been demonstrated that the letter of Lentulus in which Jesus is described ostensibly from first-hand knowledge is a forgery. It goes on to state that Jesus' hair is the color of wine and golden from the root, and from the top of the head to the ears straight and without luster, but descending from the ears in glossy curls to the shoulders, flowing down the back and parted in two portions down the middle after the manner of the Nazarenes; his forehead is smooth, his face without blemish and slightly mantled with a ruddy bloom; his expression is noble and gracious. His nose and mouth are faultless. His beard is full and abundant and of the wine and gold color of his hair, and forked. His eyes are blue and very brilliant. In rebuke and reproof he is awe-inspiring, in exhortation and instruction he is gentle and persuasive. None has seen him laugh, but many have seen him weep. His person is tall and slender his hands long and straight, his arms graceful. In speech he is grave and deliberate, his language and manner quiet and simple. In beauty he surpasses the most of men.

John Damaschius of the eighth century cites an early tradition saying he was like his mother, assuming her features. Lundy, quotes Didron as testifying to the descriptions of him as given by those mystics to whom he appeared in psychic vision. These say that he was tall, clad like a Jew, beautiful of face, the splendor of divinity darting from his eyes, his voice full of sweetness. Lundy notes that these traditions do not agree with the Patristic writings on the subject nor with the portraits copied by Boscio from the frescoes of the catacombs. Lundy concludes by citing the fact that there is nearly a score of examples like the two copied by Boscio, where the ugly and bearded Christ and the beautiful and beardless one occur together on the same monuments!

This whole debate in the early Church forum is a striking instance of the ignorance and confusion concerning their own theological material in which the Christians became entangled by reason of their smothering Egypt's time-honored wisdom. Egypt stood all the while holding in her hands the answer to the riddle of the two contradictory versions of Jesus' personal appearance. Its Messianic Horus was figuratively two characters in one, "the double Horus," "Horus of the two horizons" (west and east). "Horus the Elder and Horus the Younger." As the elder he typified the adult divinity of one cycle; as the younger, he was the new-born son of that aged father. Horus the Elder represented the aged past, Horus the Younger the new-born present and the coming future. As Massey so convincingly shows, the two characterizations passed over into Christianity through Gnostic or other channels, and after some time the inner connections having been lost, both stood facing the ignorant Christians with all explanation gone. Hence the debate in the dark. Again we have a grim demonstration of what a miscarriage of rational sense is produced the moment allegory is converted into history.

There has been grouped in this chapter a long series of data, all of a certain evidential character bearing with accentuated force upon the chief point to be established by the work. It is not the first time that one or more of these points have been raised. But it is the first time that they have been assembled into an organic whole and focused directly upon a single object on the basis of a thesis adequate to give them all a unified coherence and consistency. All acquire a substantial force and pertinence through the application of the keys of the esoteric method and the esoteric wisdom. And while perhaps no one of them may be claimed to exert decisive influence in the final conclusion, the articulated phalanx of them all in linked array does indeed present a massive body of evidence for the case that can not be pushed aside by any critic. If this was the whole evidence the case would still be strong. Limited space has curtailed the expansion of some of the points, as others of far great cogency are awaiting presentation. Many of these are so strong in their testimony that single ones among them might be deemed of sufficient weight and decisiveness to support the main contention. Collectively they must be accounted as constituting final and conclusive proof. The first group of these deals with the incidents and circumstances connected with the Nativity of Jesus. When these incredible circumstances of alleged history are carefully scrutinized and seen at last in their relation to Egyptian elucidative constructions, the weakness of the historical rendition of the Gospels will be apparent with a vividness never before realized. The Gospel narrative has been so romanticized with far-away ideality that the mere act of facing the data in the full realistic sense as history that actually occurred is itself a shocking experience to hypnotized votaries. It is a straight fact that, stripped of their imaginative halo, most of the Gospel events stand forth eerie and grotesque to naked vision. The readiest way to discredit three fourths of the Biblical "history" is to take the narrative strictly at its word – and then reproduce it with literal realism. The general result is slap-stick comedy ready for Hollywood's jaded producers, buffoonery raised to the square or cube.

Chapter X

COSMIC MAJESTY WITH LOCAL ITEMS

The first item to be examined in connection with the Nativity is that which has come to be known as the Slaughter of the Innocents. If any sane and intelligent person will let his reason function for a single minute upon the subject he will be assured that such an episode as the wholesale slaughter of the male babes under two years in Judea by edict of the ruler of the province and for the reason alleged could have held its place in Christian minds as factual history for centuries only through a total paralysis of mentality so great as to surpass all credibility. It would surely seem as if the acceptance of such an incident as part of the history of the Savior of the world could have occurred only among people rated as semi-intelligent or semi-barbaric. The phenomenon of its having gained and long held credible status among people whom history rates as the leaders in world civilization challenges the student with the riddle of such an anomaly. It would almost seem a labor of supererogation to demonstrate its patent non-historicity; but with millions of minds still hallucinated by the spell of the miraculous and the supernatural as being the legitimate essence of "religion," and with the Bible standing in the character of a fetish which must be approached only when the reason has been put in abeyance, the task of disproving what could not by any possibility have occurred must be undertaken.

To begin with, the consideration at once occurs to reflection – when one transfers the episode from romantic subjectivism to concrete realism on the plane of everyday factuality, in the process of which nearly every incident in the Bible at once appears impossible and ridiculous – that to carry out such an edict Herod must have struck at all the infant children of his own political supporters, his friends, his courtiers, the members of the ring that are with him in power. It is incredible that a man in his position, short of being demented, would have risked the infliction of slaughter and grief upon the families of those in his own political "gang." Nor is it conceivable that this powerful coterie of his closest supporters, his cabinet, and the noblemen would have permitted an order that would have involved their own children.

Then the incident is recorded only in the Gospels; and by now it must be clear that the Gospels are spiritual dramas and not histories. There is therefore no historical record of the event. Veridical history knows absolutely nothing about it. It is a total blank as regards this incident in the "life" of Jesus. It is an allegorical formulation and nothing else. It, too, traces its mythological origin to Egypt, where the Innocents – the virgin units of divine mind, our souls-to-be – were attacked, like the infant Hercules in his cradle, by the two reptiles (representing the lower natural forces of the body, in warfare with the newborn Christos taking his initial plunge into carnality), the Apap serpent and the Herut water monster. The soul-units were characterized as "innocent" because they were children of God, newly generated offshoots of his mind, that had not ever previously been wedded to matter in full incarnation. The meaning, as always, is evolutionary, cosmic or spiritual, never objectively historical. On their downward plunge into the world and body they had to withstand the onslaught of the carnal nature with its menace of engulfing, devouring their incipient spiritual nature. This was dramatized as the attack of the serpent upon them in their infancy or childhood. The youthful David overcame the monster Goliath as one version of it, and the fairy legends of the young St. George or petit Jack battling the giant are other forms of it. It is all to typify the danger involving the hosts of young souls from the side of the carnal body on their first venture into incarnation.

Higgins says categorically that the story of Herod and the Innocents is quite unknown to all the Jewish, Roman and Greek historians. Mead states that the Talmud Rabbis know nothing of Herod's wholesale murder of the children as recounted in the introduction of our first canonical Gospel. Josephus knows nothing of it, although he had no reason for whitewashing the character of Herod had such a dastardly outrage been an actual fact. And the Talmud Rabbis so thoroughly hated the memory of Herod that they could not have failed to record such a horror had he been really guilty. Mead adds that we must remember that the Rabbis had no belief whatever in the Gospel tradition as history.

On the subject Lundy has this to say:

"Although persecution began with the very birth and infancy of Christ, when King Herod sent his 'blood-hunting slaughtermen' to Bethlehem to 'spit the naked infants upon pikes and make their mad mothers' howls break the clouds,' yet of this horrible massacre there is no trace at all in the Roman catacombs and none in any Christian art until about the close of the fourth or beginning of the fifth century, when we have an example on a sarcophagus from the crypt of St. Maximin, France. . . . Modern Romish art must needs represent the actual slaughter in all its horrible and sickening details to make it impressive to the vulgar, as Fra Angelico, Raphael and especially Rubens have done. Early Christian art had a more refined delicacy of taste and far better conceptions of the true and only object of art, which is to teach, cheer, comfort and elevate the soul of man, and not fill him with horrors and ideas of cruelty and licentiousness."

(Lundy adduces the valuable testimony also that there is no picturing of the flight into Egypt and return of the holy family to Nazareth in early art, and none of Christ among the doctors in the temple until about the fifth century.)

To accentuate the point that considerations of factual history had little to do with the fixing of a date for Jesus' birth, it is worth inserting a quotation given by Epiphanius (Haer., LI, p. 22) from the Codex Marcianus:

"The Savior was born in the forty-second year of Augustus, king of the Romans, in the consulship of the same Octavi(an)us Augustus, (for the thirteenth time), and of Sil(v)anus according to the consular calendar among the Romans. For it is recorded in it as follows: When these were consuls . . . Christ was born on the sixth day of January, after thirteen days of the winter solstice and of the increase of the light and day. This day (of the solstice) the Greeks, I mean the Idolaters, celebrate on the twenty-fifth day of December a feast called Saturnalia among the Romans, Kronia among the Egyptians, and Kikellia among the Alexandrians. For on the twenty-fifth day of December the division takes place which is the solstice, and the day begins to lengthen its light, receiving an increase, and there are thirteen days of it up to the sixth day of January, until the day of the birth of Christ (a thirtieth of an hour being added each day), as the wise Ephraim among the Syrians bore witness by this inspired passage (logos) in his commentaries, where he says: 'The advent of our Lord Jesus Christ was thus appointed: (First) his birth according to the flesh, then his perfect incarnation among men which is called Epiphany, at a distance of thirteen days from the increase of the light; for it needs must have been that this should be a figure of our Lord Jesus Christ himself and of his twelve disciples, who made up the number of the thirteen days of the increase of the light."

The sixth of January is still traditionally celebrated as the day of the birth of Christ in England and elsewhere. Christian heads are for the most part guiltless of any suspicion of the reason for the date. The quoted passage hints at it, but, without ancient Egyptian backgrounds of data, leaves the matter still obscure. We have already seen that the most primary significance of the number twelve, as pertaining to the disciples, tribes of Israel, months of the year, and other usages, was the Egyptian designation, the Twelve Saviors of the Treasure of Light. The Christ would be fully "born" in humanity when his gradual infiltration into human consciousness had unfolded to perfection the twelve rays of divine mind which man is to express. The inchoate divine light in mankind was to increase by twelve stages of growth to the full shining of Christhood in all hearts. What more natural symbolism then could be adopted than the counting of the first twelve days of increasing light from the solstice of darkness, figured as the twenty-fifth of December? And after twelve days came the thirteenth, on which the whole twelve powers were synthesized in the unified being of the Christos. So that now with the resort again to Egyptian constructions of imagery there can be announced for the first time to the Christian population the correct significance of their celebrating the birth of Jesus both on the twenty-fifth of December and the sixth of January. As the Egyptians would have said, the December solstitial date commemorated the birth of Horus the Younger, the infant Horus, type of the first or natural man Adam; while the January date thirteen days later marked the day of the birth of Horus the Elder, Horus the adult, the homme faît or man made perfect, second Adam. In simpler terms, the December date marked the physical beginning of the birth of the Christ spirit in mankind and the January date marked the concluding stage of its aeonial increase. All of which again throws the meaning of the word "birth," in reference to the

Christos, into its true and proper significance, as a gradual increase of a spiritual quality over a long period, the whole cycle or aeon. Man, who is to be divinized, had first to be physically "born" on a given planet. So the Christ-man as ritualistic type of a divinized humanity, had also to be given his "birth-day" – at the winter solstice, as a babe in the flesh. It will be noticed that the tradition outlined in the Codex Marcianus lays significant stress upon the apparently extraneous fact that the Savior's birth on the sixth of January came in the thirteenth consulship of Octavius Augustus, obviously an obscure hint that Deity fell in with the symbolism to the extent of adding another historical thirteen to the combination. Christians celebrate many a festival day in the year's calendar without the slightest inkling as to the long-lost purport of the ritual commemorations.

Reverting to the Herodian hecatomb of infant death, if the inherent impossibilities of the case do not suffice to determine the matter against the historicity, there is another fact that settles it with finality. This is the date of Herod's death. Christian historians have been relentlessly forced to assent to the year 4 B.C. as the date of the Tetrarch's demise. When verified historical fact is the piper, theological fiction must dance in tune. So back goes the official "date" of Jesus' birth to the year 4 B.C., since Herod must be kept in the story. This throws the whole dating of the Christian era four years out of line with the first guess.

But what will be done now when another authentic date is found and another shift will have to be made on the strength of it? Another ruler is mentioned as on the throne when Jesus was born, and his date is still farther away from the year one. Matthew says that Caesar Augustus levied the great world tax that required Joseph to register at Bethlehem, "now when Cyrenius was Governor in Syria." There has hardly been a period in eastern Mediterranean history when the records of the provincial governments under the Roman Empire were so well kept as just the time referred to. The official annals of the Syrian government are well preserved; and they show no Governor at all by the name of Cyrenius! The closest approximation to the name is Quirinus, and Moffatt's translation of the New Testament inserts Quirinus for Cyrenius in the Nativity narrative. But the authentic date of the governorship of this Quirinus is the two-years period between 13 and 11 B.C.! To accommodate its dating to this item of the "historical" chronicle of Jesus' "life," official ecclesiasticism must now endorse a date eight or nine years farther back than 4 B.C. Two such corrections leave the whole historical structure of Christianity badly shaken, near in fact to the point of tottering. Without a change in the date of the first Christmas the participation of Herod in the infant slaughter becomes impossible. The personal Herod was four years in his grave when the Bethlehem babe arrived.

Comment has already been made on the close similarity of the name of the Egyptian serpent Herut to the Tetrarch's name, and the likelihood of a substitution of the latter for the former when the Egyptian myth was converted into "history." Presumably clinching proof of this jugglery may never be available. It must be left then to rest upon the strong presumptive probabilities inherent in the situation. It must be held deeply suggestive, however, that the name Herod occupies exactly the same place, role and significance in the Gospel "incident" that the Herut reptile fills in the Egyptian allegory! It is the Herut menace to our young divine souls in the one instance, and the Herod menace to the young divinity in the other. This alone is enough to remove it from the realm of coincidence and conjecture and to throw it over into that of identity of character. If it was one isolated single occurrence of such definite correspondence, the case might be classed as accidental. But when it is known to be but one of a long series of such agreements and matchings, sound judgment inclines to call it another historization of Egyptian myth. Such it almost indubitably must be considered.

The fact of Herod's death in the year 4 B.C. alone jars the whole fabric of Christian systematism to its foundations. Christian apologists have belittled in the past, and presumably will again in the future depreciate the importance of the precise date of the birth of their Savior, and will in spite of all facts cling to the historicity of the episode. But we shall see that the structure of the historical claim, severely weakened by the non-authenticity of its very first chapter of events, will be still further assaulted and finally dismantled by a long series of blows from the side of fact, until if it stands at all, it must rest on sheer stolid faith alone. It will be found to be utterly discredited by reason, by data, and by the sheer physical impossibility of the occurrence of Biblical events when they are treated realistically and not romantically. The latter particular will be noted in glaring vividness when the legend of the star of Bethlehem is examined.

From Herod at the birth, it is a short jump to Pilate at the death, of the historical Jesus.

Authoritative data are wanting to present any outright negative evidence as to the participation of the pro-consul in the Gospel events.

But there is a textual detail that looms larger and larger the longer it is considered. It is a phrase in the Apostles' Creed of the Christian Church.

The creed – worthy itself of a whole volume's study – is by no means a mere abbreviated rune or formulary of Christian theological belief. It is that, but it is infinitely more than that. It is a brief of ancient cosmology and creative process, incarnation of spirit in matter, descent of soul into body and return to greater deific state by virtue of the victory won in the lower worlds. An item of the journey of celestial divine spirit through the planes of matter that could not be left out was the "suffering" entailed for it by the necessity of its going "under" the limitations imposed on it by matter's lower range of vibrational sensitivity. Now matter, as has been set forth fully elsewhere, was typified universally and ubiquitously in ancient symbolism by water, so that even the name most generally applied to the mothers of the Christs was in whatever language the word for water, sea, ocean. Mary is incontestably of this origin, being Mare, Maria in Latin, and Thallath, "the sea" (name of a Hellenic "Mother of God"), in Greek. Primeval space, the mother of all things, being matter in inchoate form, was the Great Deep, the waters of the abyss, the firmament of the waters. Now the quality of matter that caused it to be the generator of suffering for the energies of spirit that were "cribbed, cabined and confined" under its sluggish inertness, was its density. It is therefore not a shrewd guess, not a mere chance discernment of a concatenation of phrase and idea that enables us to make a totally new translation of one of the clauses in the Apostles' Creed, by which change the historical Pilate is swept entirely out of the narrative. It is not a sheer stretching of points to make designed ends meet, but must be the result of the rational necessities involved in the only correct and consistent envisagement of the matters discussed in the Creed, when it is asserted that the creedal phrase detailing with the utmost brevity the duress of spirit under the thraldom of matter, must inexpugnably have been in the true original formulation of the ritual statement, "he suffered under the dense sea, was crucified, dead and buried." "Dense sea" would have been merely a euphemism, familiar to all in Mystery Ritual cultism, for "he suffered under the limitation of dense matter," – a shorthand expression in Mystery language. What, then, in the light of this irrefutable statement of the true basic meaning that fits with absolute nicety and exactness into that very place in the Creed, must be our amazement when we turn to the Greek and find a similarity of name even closer to identity than the Herod-Herut one – "dense sea" in the Greek manuscripts is given as a insert Greek equiv. (pontos pilètos)! "He suffered under pontos pilètos: he suffered under the dense sea" (of matter).

It is far from being a merely specious argument, indeed it is a fully warranted contention, that the sudden introduction in this majestic cosmograph in the impressive ritual of the name of a mere man is a misfit and impertinence bordering close on to the sublimest ineptitude. It is exactly like the sudden injection of Bill Brown of 128 North Sixth Street into a line in Paradise Lost. It is too sudden a jerk from the sweep of cosmic drama to page 195 of a school history. A personal reference to our own childhood reaction to this phrase in the Creed may be pardoned. Even from the age of ten or twelve there seemed something wholly incongruous and vaguely disturbing when the Creed jumped without warning from celestial operations on a majestic scale to the judge of a court trial down in Judea. The sudden insertion of one human person's name in the text amid otherwise lofty epic dramatization was jarring and disconcerting. It was an ideological anomaly. It did not ring harmoniously with the context. It stands to reason that the introduction of a local ruler's name into what is provably an august formula of creative cosmology and evolutionary method is obviously an interpolation, and a glaring instance of the wreckage caused by that enormous transposition of allegory and formulae over into supposed history. It will be denied because we can produce no cinema of the scribes caught in the act of changing Herut to Herod and pontos pilètos to Pontius Pilate; but the results of the change glare at us nevertheless.

It must strike anyone who thinks clearly for a moment that the writer of a formulary, as the Creed was intended to be, aiming to express most succinctly the suffering of soul under matter's heavy burden, would have been most unlikely to summarize the long list of dramatic ordeals in mortal career with the phrase "suffered under Pontius Pilate," the proconsul. Even in the "history" of Jesus according to the Gospels, the man Pilate was not at all a central factor in Jesus' sufferings. His part was in fact incidental. Pilate's decree was merely an incident in a chain of events that already had gained such moral momentum that any other decision than condemnation would have been an anticlimax and an artistic faux pas. It would have wrecked the scenario. Pilate's pardon of Jesus would have left Christianity limp and unheroic, much as if in a murder mystery the first-chapter murder victim should recover and defeat the story. Jesus had to be condemned – "it must needs be that Christ should suffer and enter into his glory" – and Pilate's dramatic role was merely mechanical. He has never been taken, even by literalists, for more than a puppet or marionette in the play. And all this inharmony of the elements in the situation is nicely adjusted and resolved if the original reading of "dense sea" is put back in place of the forged proconsul's name.

As to the Apocryphal Gospel of Pilate and the documents entitled Letters of Pilate to Seneca and the philosopher's rejoinders, they are obviously forged Gospels, of which there were scores in existence at the time. A perusal of them suggests forgery in every phase and verse, as is also the case with the so-called Gospels of the Infancy, the Gospel of Mary, the Gospel of Nicodemus, the strange Gospel of Paul and Thecla and others.

Having foisted upon the proconsul's name the ignominy of condemning the Son of God to death, Christian imagination has pursued his shade even beyond the grave, and in various literary concoctions has pictured the anguish of soul which he is undergoing in some darksome Sheol, as post mortem realization of the ghastly crime he had committed upon earth overwhelmed him. Unless sanity returns even these lucubrations may become the canonical Gospels of some later ecclesiasticism.

Chapter XI

STAGGERING TRUTH ON EGYPT'S WALLS

Theologians have written and the clergy have preached in such positive fashion as to the existence of the personal Jesus that the body of the laity has been thrown under the impression that outside the Gospels the historicity of the Master is well attested by the evidence of secular sources. With this prepossession holding the field it becomes necessary to marshal the material bearing on this issue. The average Christian minister who has not read outside the pale of accredited Church authorities will impart to any parishioner making the inquiry the information that no event in history is better attested by witness than the occurrences in the Gospel narrative of Christ's life. He will go over the usual citation of the historians who mention Jesus and the letters claiming to have been written about him. When the credulous questioner, putting trust in the intelligence and good faith of his pastor, gets this answer, he goes away assured on the point of the veracity of the Gospel story. The pastor does not qualify his data with the information that the practice of forgery, fictionizing and fable was rampant in the early Church. In the simple interest of truth, then, it is important to examine the body of alleged testimony from secular history and see what credibility and authority it possesses.

First, as to the historians whose works record the existence of Jesus, the list comprises but four. They are Pliny, Tacitus, Suetonius and Josephus. There are short paragraphs in the works of each of these, two in Josephus. The total quantity of this material is given by Harry Elmer Barnes in The Twilight of Christianity as some twenty-four lines. It may total a little more, perhaps twice that amount. This meager testimony constitutes the body or mass of the evidence of "one of the best attested events in history." Even if it could be accepted as indisputably authentic and reliable, it would be faltering support for an event that has dominated the thought of half the world for eighteen centuries.

But what is the standing of this witness? Not even Catholic scholars of importance have seriously dissented from a general agreement of academic investigators that these passages, one and all, must be put down as forgeries and interpolations by partisan Christian scribes who wished zealously to array the authority of these historians behind the historicity of the Gospel life of Jesus. A sum total of forty or fifty lines from secular history supporting the existence of Jesus of Nazareth, and they completely discredited!

Some of the evidence of spuriousness consists of the differing styles of Greek or Latin in the language used in the interpolations, the place in the context where the passages have been inserted or other indications open to the eye of critical scholars. It is so rare a thing to find unanimous consensus of opinion on such matters among scholars that their practically complete agreement in this case enables the layman to accept the academic verdict with assurance. It will be informative to note some of the commentaries on these passages made by the investigators.

In his work, The Great Galilean (p. 3) Robert Keable writes:

"No man knows sufficient of the early life of Jesus to write a biography of him. For that matter no one knows enough for the normal Times obituary notice of a great man. If regard were had to what we should call in correct speech definitely historical facts, scarcely three lines could be filled."

Had newspapers existed then, no material could have been found for the obituary notice, not even the man's name, asserts Keable. Yet few periods of the ancient world were so well documented as the period of Augustus and Tiberius. But no contemporary writer knew of his existence.

Following his statement as to the complete dearth of reference to Jesus' life by any first and early second century chroniclers and that the very existence of Jesus seems to have been unheard of by them, Mead examines Pliny, Tacitus and Suetonius passages. Pliny was born 61 A.D., Tacitus about the same time and Suetonius some ten years later. All were in position to have gleaned all that was reported of an extraordinary character like Jesus, whose activities and marvels had aroused thousands in the Judean country, if Gospel be history. There are two short statements in Suetonius' Lives of the Twelve Caesars, and they deal chiefly with some disturbances aroused in Rome "impulsore Chresto," "at the instigation of Chrestus." Just what the reference could be to disturbances at Rome, leading to the expulsion of Christians by Claudius, with "Chrestus" as the instigator – when Jesus was never at Rome – is not clear. Doubtless some insurrectionist activities of his followers at the capital, it is presumed. But the Suetonius passage invalidates its reference to Jesus as a man, it would seem. For Mead says that Suetonius' reference to "Christiani" in the second passage might easily apply to Zealots or Messianists of any type. Mead adds that it is a well digested conclusion among schoolmasters and their pupils that, as to Tacitus, we have in him a historical romanticist who has too long fascinated readers by the beauty of his style, and that he is not a sober historian. Tacitus' main statement is that Jesus was put to death under Pontius Pilate in the reign of Tiberius. The famous sentence runs as follows:

"Auctor nominis ejus Christus Tiberio imperitante per procuratorem Pontium supplicio affectus erat."

Mead says this has all the earmarks of being a Christian formula. Tacitus seems to know nothing of the name of Jesus. "Tiberio imperitante" cannot be paralleled anywhere in his vocabulary, and moreover is contrary to regular use, which would be "Principe Tiberio." Hochart (Annales de la Faculté des Lettres de Bordeaux, 1884, No. 2) says:

"This chapter contains almost as many inexplicable difficulties as it does words."

Hochart thinks that a rescript of the Annals and Histories by Poggio Bracciolini and Niccoli is itself a pseudo-Tacitus and that "therefore we are face to face with an elaborate pseudepigraph."

Josephus (Joseph ben Mattatiah) was born 37-38 A.D., and lived to 100 A.D. His spurious passage is in the Antiquities (XVIII, iii, p. 3). Mead says there are a dozen most potent arguments against its authenticity and that it is rejected by all. (He names one scholar, F. Bole, as claiming its genuineness.) We have the explicit statement of Origen in the third century, says Mead, that Josephus had no belief whatever in Jesus being the Christ, whereas the spurious passage states categorically that he was the Christ. The Antiquities (XX, ix, p. 1) has a reference to a certain Jacobus, "the brother of Jesus called Christ." Says Mead: "It follows that Josephus knew nothing of 'the Christ' though he knows much of various 'Christs.'" Josephus, he cites, had been trained in an Essene-like community and seems to have gone to Rome in "Essene" interests. He was at Rome just when the Christiani were singled out for special persecution and cruel martyrdom by imperial tyranny; and yet he knows nothing of all this. He does not know of the gruesome tragedy at Rome or even of the Christ of the Christians. Joseph Klausner in his Jesus of Nazareth (p. 55) reiterates Mead's general observations with reference to the inharmony of the Josephus passages with Origen's statement that Josephus did not admit Jesus as the Messiah. He emphasizes that Jesus' life, if lived, could not have seemed of small and inconsequential moment to Josephus, who wrote in 93, when the Christians were strong and flourishing. Klausner points out the notable fact that Eusebius, of the fourth century, knew the whole of the spurious Josephus passage, whereas Origen of the third century did not. This again points to interpolation between Origen's day and the time of Eusebius. Klausner, on good authority, speaks of "manifest additions by Christian copyists."

But it might be well to note and answer Klausner's concession to general modern opinion in his remark that "it is far more difficult to explain how certain Jewish writers (the Evangelists) invented such a wonderful character than it is to admit that they were describing someone who did really exist." This greater difficulty in the way of seeing the truth of the situation is the tremendous fact of the loss of esotericism in general, the suppression of the knowledge of the Mystery Ritual Drama and its significance and the decay of the original Egyptian crypticism. In the absence of all this guiding intelligence, of course explanation is difficult. Certainly it is difficult to see why the Evangelists should "invent" the Jesus character and personalize him, if one does not know that the Jesus character was already "invented" and had trod the stage boards in the Mystery dramas for centuries B.C. The mere statement of Klausner that the Evangelists "invented" a character that had been the central figure of all ancient Messianic or Sun-God systems for centuries previously, betrays this capable historian's erroneous foundations and approaches to the analysis of the Jesus situation. The Evangelists neither invented nor perhaps even euhemerized the Jesus person. He was already in the documents they rescripted or transcribed. But later ignorance changed him from a typal to a personal entification. The misleading supposition with which these analysts approach the problem is that Matthew, Mark, Luke and John were first century citizens who took pen in hand and wrote the Gospels out of their heads. The final staggering truth about the Bible books is that no "authors" ever sat down and wrote them at all, in the sense in which Sir Walter Scott wrote the Waverley novels. They were never "written" at all in the sense of original creations by given authors. They were in existence long before ink ever met paper to record and preserve them. They were the spoken lines of the great drama, they were the oral tradition, extant thousands of years before they were ever committed to writing. But at some epoch, here, there or elsewhere, the sages or their pupils did at last commit them to writing, lest in some degenerate age they be lost. This is obviously the whole truth as to their origin, and there will be no sanity in the discussion of them until this is known. So let Klausner's remark be thrown into proper form of statement, – that it is not difficult to understand how the Evangelists simply brought out to more popular knowledge the recondite Gospels, with a Jesus long their central figure, which had been theretofore kept more closely concealed within the depths of Mystery cult secrecy. Christianity will not be understood until it is seen as a popularization and consequent fatal vitiation of exclusive secret religious philosophy and ritualism, instead of being considered a new creation and a new advance on previous ignorance.

In his challenging work, The Twilight of Christianity (p. 390), Harry Elmer Barnes reviews the status of the meager amount of extra-Gospel material mentioning Jesus. He ventures the observation that it may greatly surprise some readers to learn that anyone has ever seriously questioned the actual existence of Jesus. As a matter of fact, he asserts, the evidence for the view that Jesus was really a historical character is so slight that a considerable number of the most distinguished students of New Testament times have declared Jesus to be a mythical personage, the product of the myth-making tendencies common to religious peoples of all ages and particularly prevalent at the period of the early Roman Empire. Among the more eminent scholars and critics who have contended that Jesus was not historical, mention might be made of Bruno Bauer, Kalthoff, Drews, Stendel, Felden, Deije, Jensen, Lublinski, Bolland, Van der Berg, Virolleaud, Couchoud, Massey, Bossi, Memojewski, Brandes, Robertson, Mead, Whittaker, Carpenter and W. B. Smith. Of non-Christian evidence, he says, next to nothing exists. Of the twenty-four lines, the total of this sort, not a single line is of admitted authenticity. Barnes quotes the Tacitus passage (from the Annals, XV, p. 44) as follows:

"In order to suppress the rumor, Nero falsely accused and punished with the most acute tortures persons who, already hated for their shameful deeds, were commonly called Christians. The founder of that name, Christus, had been put to death by the procurator, Pontius Pilate, in the reign of Tiberius; but the deadly superstition, though repressed for a time, broke out again, not only through Judea, where this evil had its origin, but also through the city (Rome) whither all things horrible and vile flow from all quarters and are encouraged. Accordingly, first those were arrested who confessed; then on their information a great multitude were convicted, not so much of the crime of incendiarism as of hatred of the human race."

Tacitus wrote the Annals about 117 A.D., by which time the nascent popular notion of the historical Jesus might have gained sufficient vogue to have let the historian assume he was writing definite authentic history. He cites no sources or witness or authorities for his facts.

Barnes points out that the name Chrestus (instead of Christus) used in the Suetonius passage of two or three lines, was a common Greek name, and may not necessarily have referred to the particular man Jesus.

The Josephus excerpt (Antiquities, XVIII, p. 3) is given as follows:

"About this time lived Jesus, a wise man, if indeed he should be called man. He wrought miracles and was a teacher of those who gladly accept the truth, and had a large following among the Jews and pagans. He was the Christ. Although Pilate, at the complaint of the leaders of our people, condemned him to die on the cross, his earlier followers were faithful to him. For he appeared to them alive again on the third day, as God-sent prophets had foretold this and a thousand other wonderful things of him. The people of the Christians, which is called after him, survives until the present day."

Written somewhere between 75 and 100 A.D., Barnes says the passage is admitted even by conservative and pious scholars to be quite obviously spurious. No Jew who rejected Christianity could possibly have written in this vein. It is obviously a late Christian interpolation. It may have replaced an unfavorable reference to Jesus in the original. Philo, Barnes reminds us, the most learned and brilliant Jewish scholar of his day, has nothing whatever to say in regard to Jesus and the Christians. There is therefore in extant Jewish literature of the first century A.D. not a single authentic line making reference to the founder of Christianity.

It is fitting at this place to make answer to the statement of the Freethought proponent Joseph McCabe in his The Story of Religious Controversy (p. 228). He there makes the declaration that is worth our reproducing because it represents the common thought of the average Christian who has not critically looked into the matter. He concludes that it is more reasonable to believe in the historicity of Jesus because there is no parallel in history to the sudden growth of a myth and its conversion into a human personage in one generation. Moreover, he affirms, to those early Christians Jesus was not merely or primarily a teacher. A collection of wise teachings might in time get a mythical name attached to it, and the myth might in time become a real person. But from the earliest moment that we catch sight of Christians in history the essence of their belief is that Jesus was a personal incarnation in Judea of the great God of the universe. The supreme emphasis, asserts McCabe, is on the fact that he assumed a human form and shed human blood on a cross. So it seems far more reasonable, scientific and consonant with the facts of religious history which are known, to conclude that Jesus was a man who was gradually turned into a God.

McCabe's assertion that there is no parallel in history to the sudden growth of a myth and its conversion into history in one generation is a misstatement of the premises, to begin with. It is both a sly subterfuge and an easy way to win a victory in an argument, to twist the premises into shape to support the conclusion. It is simply not true to say that the myth of Jesus was a sudden growth. We have shown that it was a perennial cornerstone of ancient Mystery cultism. Only, it was held in secret and was esoterically apprehended. The only suddenness connected with it came in the way of its rather sudden popularization and exoterization. This indeed was a lone phenomenon without parallel in history – which is the very point our argument advances against the historicity. No doubt there had been previous cases of the exoteric development, but never had this trend swept to such wide-spread and overwhelming volume and power as to smother esotericism completely and to enthrone in its stead the rule of ignorant literalism. The Christian conversion of myth into history, sudden as it appears, was the culminating denouement of a process or trend that was long in fermenting and slow in working to a head. The bloom of a flower is sudden, but it is just the apical point at the summit of a long slow process of growth through many preceding stages. Of course there is no parallel to this phenomenon, for it occurred only after long ages of slow preparation and has kept its direful hold on the religious world ever since. Not perhaps in five thousand years could it occur again on the same colossal scale. It is likely the one titanic calamity in world history. Not the growth of myth, but the historization of myth, is the thing that is, catastrophically enough, without parallel in the world, on the scale and proportions as perpetrated by Christianity in the early centuries.

Then there is the senselessness of McCabe's saying that a collection of myths might get a name attached to it, when there was never a time over centuries previously that the name – Jesus or another of similar purport, always designated the Sun-God in man – had not been attached to such collections. All this shows unconscionable lack of acquaintance with the facts of ancient history that should have been the premises of argument. How can any scholar say it is hard to see why the particular name, Jesus, was attached to the myths when Joshua, Jeshu, Jesse, Joses, Josiah, Joash, Jehoash, Jehoahaz, Jehoshaphat, Joram, Jonah, Jason, Iusa, Hosea and many more variant forms of the very name of Jesus were in archaic literature for hundreds of years B.C.?

Again McCabe both twists facts and draws from them unwarranted conclusions when he says that from the first moment when we catch sight of Christians in history their belief was centered in the personal human Jesus. This assertion has already been controverted by much material gathered in this work, from Clement, Origen, Philo and others of the Christians themselves. Among the unlearned early Christians it may have to some extent been true; but among the intelligent and philosophical ones, the Gnostics, Nazarenes, Essenes, and others, it most certainly was not true. Were these sects not spurned as heretics for the very reason that they repudiated the personal Jesus? The date of a general acceptance of the human Jesus by the parties that had excluded the rest as heretics and established the orthodoxies was not early in Christian history, but on in the third century.

The refutation of these statements in McCabe's short passage goes far to indicate how sorely intelligence and honesty are needed to meet and straighten out many such tangled webs of Christian presumption and falsification of data. Thousands of pages could be given to the labor of correcting misstatements of fact, unwarranted deductions, sly insinuations and other forms of perversion of truth found in hundreds of books dedicated to the defense of the Christian faith.

In a note on page 24 of Josephus' Antiquities there is a statement that Photius says he has seen the chronology of Justus of Tiberias, entitled The Chronology of the Kings of Judah Which Succeeded One Another, and Photius says: "and being under the Jewish prejudices, and indeed he was himself also a Jew by birth, he makes not the least mention of the appearance of Christ or what things happened to him or of the wonderful works that he did." The inference here is obviously that Justus of Tiberius withholds mention of Jesus not because of Jewish prejudices, but in spite of them, the intimation being that had Jesus lived and been known through his wonderful works and Christly status, any Jew would have been prejudiced in the direction of giving the matter all the mention possible. His silence bespeaks his lack of knowledge of the data. He would have been glad to mention such laudable things had he known of them.

Through the creditable scholarship of Klausner, Mead and others we are enabled to approach the next issue that closely and vitally affects the investigation. This is the group of references in the Jewish Talmud to a character whom many have sought to identify with the Gospel Jesus, namely Jehoshua (Jesus) Ben Pandira (Pandera, Pantera, Pantêre). Klausner's treatment of the personage or figure is very full and discerning; Mead has a whole work devoted to him: Did Jesus Live 100 Years B.C.?; and Massey analyzes the situation capably. It is deemed desirable to go into the question of his relation to the Gospel Jesus, not so much because it may contribute any effective data to the main problem under review, as because it may carry to readers the important knowledge that other sacred writings before the Gospels featured a Jesus figure, with much the same narrative material of his "life," as that believed generally to exist only in the Christian canonical writings. The brief outline of the story of this Talmudic Jesus is indeed like a short summary of the Galilean's career: he was born with an accompaniment of certain supernatural manifestations, went to Egypt, became learned in the wisdom of the Egyptians, returned to Palestine, wrought many miracles among the populace through his Egyptian arts or sorcery and magic, incurred the hostility of the orthodox priesthood, was tried and condemned, was given forty days for partisans to come and clear him, and finally stoned to death and his body hanged on a tree. The date of his birth has been placed by the best calculations of scholars at about 115 B.C. It will be seen at once that if this Talmud figure was the Jesus to whom the Gospels could be claimed to refer, or even the prototype of the Gospel Jesus, the dating would throw off base the entire structure of the Nazareth historicity, and would invalidate a thousand "proofs" of the latter based on dates, sequences of events and arguments grounded on and affected by such considerations. The dating of the Christian calendar would be over 100 years off the true.

We may start with the statement made by Massey (The Historical Jesus and the Mythical Christ, p. 2) that in the Book of Acts Jesus is stoned to death and his body hanged on a tree. This establishes a fairly strong point of identity between the two Jesus characters.

Massey declares that this Jewish Pandira was the only Jesus known to Celsus, the author of The True Logos, which was destroyed by the Christians. Celsus says of him that he was not a pure Word, not a true Logos, but a man who had learned the arts of sorcery in Egypt. Massey sums the case when he says that "here is the conclusive fact: the Jews knew nothing of Jesus, the Christ of the Gospels, as a historical character, and when the Christians of the fourth century trace his pedigree by the hand of Epiphanius, they are forced to draw their Jesus from Pandira! Epiphanius gives the genealogy of the canonical Jesus in this wise: – Jacob, called Pandira, Mary – Joseph – Cleopas, Jesus."

The name Pandira is related to the French panthère, "panther," which was credited with being the "nickname" of Jacob, the alleged grandfather of the Talmud Jesus, and this Jacob was said to have been a Greek sailor. "Jehoshua ben Pandira" then means "Jesus, (grand)son of the Panther." That this Talmudic genealogy is found in Epiphanius instead of the long Jesse-David lists appended to the several Gospels is significant of much.

Massey states that Pandira was stoned to death in the city of Lud, or Lydda, and that it must have been around the date of 70 B.C., after the reign of Jannaeus, 106-79 B.C. He says that Queen Alexandra (Salomé) showed favor to him, witnessed his wonderful works and powers of healing and tried to save him from his sacerdotal enemies because he was related to her. The Jews denied the identity of Jehoshua ben Pandira with the Gospel Jesus. Rabbi Jechiels said: "This which has been related of J. ben Perachia and his pupil (J. ben Pandira) contains no reference whatever to him whom the Christians honor as God." Another Rabbi, Salman Zevi, produced ten reasons for concluding that the Jehoshua of the Talmud was not he who was afterwards called Jesus of Nazareth. The matter was unknown to Justus, the Jew of Celsus, and to Josephus, "the supposed reference to him by the latter being an undoubted forgery." Massey asseverates that "the blasphemous writings of the Jews about Jesus," as Justin Martyr calls them, refer always to Jehoshua ben Pandira, and not to the Gospel Jesus.

But Massey is firm and decisive in his conclusion that the Talmud Jehoshua can not be converted into the canonical Jesus as a historical character. The dates can never be reconciled to match contemporary history. Massey repudiates the connection as beyond the remotest possibility. "Make whatever you can of Jehoshua ben Pandira. He is not the Gospel Jesus," he says. From Klausner we learn, however, that the Jehoshua Jewish tradition was entangled at least in Origen's mind with the parentage of the Gospel Jesus. Origen is quoted (Contra Celsum, I, IX, p. 1) as repeating a story that his opponent Celsus related with reference to the current tradition dealing with the family and parentage of Jesus. And this version of the Jehoshua ben Pandira legend is worthy of notice for several reasons. Apart from the question whether it is the truth or a distortion, it is to be considered significant, first because of the sheer fact that such a story was current at the time – the late second century; and secondly because it either carries fact or reflects a perversion of allegorism, and would be notably significant in either case. The character called "the Jew" in Celsus' book (I, p. 28) goes on to say that the dogma of the "virgin birth" was an invention of the Christians; the true facts in the case being: "that Jesus had come from a village in Judea, and was the son of a poor Jewess who gained her living by the work of her own hands; that his mother had been turned out of doors by her husband, who was a carpenter by trade, on being convicted of adultery; that, wandering about in disgrace, she gave birth to Jesus a bastard; that Jesus, on account of his poverty (had to work for his living and) was hired out to go to Egypt; that while there he acquired certain (magical) powers which Egyptians pride themselves on possessing; that he returned home highly elated at possessing these powers, and on the strength of them gave himself out to be a god."

True or false, it is significant that such a story was in vogue in the second century. If one was to employ the usual method of orthodox explanation of such data, which is to assume that the story, however unlikely as truth, took its rise out of some factual foundation, the conclusion would be that it was a garbled version of some more acceptable basis of simple fact. By far the most likely elucidation would seem to be that it was another of hundreds of exotericized myths, being the literalization of a mythical account of the soul's descent into matter in the "Egypt" of the physical body, "the flesh-pots of Egypt." It is worthy of citation just as a sample of how the literalizing tendency could work a spiritual or cosmic myth over into a human story of gross realism! It is more than startling, then, that Mead is found endorsing this explanation of the story (Did Jesus Live 100 Years B.C.?, p. 126). He asks:

"Can this possibly be based on some vulgar version of a well-known Gnostic myth of those days? Jesus went down as a servant or slave into Egypt; that is to say, the Christ or divine soul descends as a servant into the Egypt of the body. It is a common element in the early mystic traditions that the Christ took on the form of a servant in his descent through the spheres, and in many traditions Egypt is the symbol of the body, which is separated by the 'Red Sea' and the 'Desert' from the 'Promised Land.'"

Mead advances this solution of the gossiped illegitimacy of the Christ character because he had studied ancient Oriental religionism closely enough to have found the constant operation of the tendency of the "vulgar mind" to make hash out of sublime allegory. His conclusion is therefore well justified.

But what must be the explanation of another fact which he brings to light in connection with this story, a fact which indeed seems to stand in very sinister shadow? He says that:

"Origen again refers to the quotation from 'the Jew' of Celsus given above, and adds the important detail from Celsus that the paramour of the mother of Jesus was a soldier called Panthera, a name which he also repeats later on (i, 69) in a sentence, by the by, which has in both places been erased from the oldest Vatican MS., and bodily omitted from three codices in this country and from others."

A note by Mead says: "See Notes on both passages by Lommatzsch in his Origenis Contra Celsum (Berlin, 1845)."

According to Epiphanius' original statement (Haereses, p. 78), Origen himself says that James, the father of Jesus' father Joseph, was called by the name "Panther." Origen apparently wished to explain in this way why Jesus, the son of Joseph, was called "Ben Pandera," or "ben Pantere," by the Jews. According to Origen Jesus was so called after the name of his grandfather.

Klausner alludes to the Baraita, a tradition issuing from the Tanaim, quoted in the later Talmud, which says that Jeshu of Nazareth practiced sorcery and beguiled and led astray Israel. And the Talmud speaks of hanging instead of crucifixion, since this horrible form of death was only known to Jewish scholars from Roman trials and not from the Jewish legal system. Klausner cites the Pandira legend "in spite of Mr. Friedländer's various attempts to persuade us that every Talmudist worthy of the name knows that the few Talmudic passages which speak of Jesus are a late addition" and "the Talmudic sources of the first century and the first quarter of the second afford us not the least evidence of the existence of Jesus or Christianity." (Jesus of Nazareth, p. 38.)

The Toldoth Jeshu, says Mead (Did Jesus Live 100 Years B.C.?, p. 303), notes that the Ben Pandera legend had spread so far and wide that we find two Church Fathers compelled to insert the name in the genealogies of Jesus and Mary. The stories say that the trial of Jesus took place before Queen Helene (Helena) and that the sovereignty of all Jewry was in her hands. Her name never appears in the Talmud Jesus stories, nor for a matter of fact, do the names of Herod, or Pilate, or John the Baptist, or any others that confirm the Christian canonical date. The only date indications in the Talmud are, on the one hand, the mention of Joshua ben Perachiah and Jannai in connection with Jesus, and on the other, the Akiba Mary story. Mead says it is true that Helena was the subject of a prolific legend activity in the Middle Ages. Mead (p. 261) does quote the Talmud as saying, "Now the rule of all Israel was in the hands of a woman, who was called Helene"; also he cites the Talmud passage: "And there shall come forth a rod out of the stem of Isai (Jesse), and I am he." And the Toldoth, like the Talmud, he states, also know of a stoning or a stoning and hanging, or of a hanging alone, but never of a crucifixion.

Mead develops a point of some weight when he says that our studies of the works of the philosophers of early times can show us only that all of them regard the wonder-works of Jesus as being due to his magical powers, or rather to the fact of his being a Magus, like many others in antiquity. Such miracles, in the eyes of the philosophers, did not prove the contention of the Christians that Jesus was God, for similar wonders, equally well authenticated, and in a more recent case better authenticated, according to Hierocles, had been done by others. This Hierocles had been successively Governor of Palmyra, Bithynia and Alexandria, and was also a philosopher. In 305 A.D. he wrote a criticism of the claims of the Christians in two books called A Truthful Address to the Christians, or more briefly Truth Lovers. Even Arnobius, in his Against the Nations, sets forth the commonest argument against the Christians concerning Jesus, which was that he was a Magus; he did all these things (sc. Miracles) by secret arts; from the shrines of Egypt he stole the names of the angels of might and hidden disciplines.

Even Jerome was conversant with the legends that floated about as vulgar caricatures of the immaculate conception of the Virgin, and in his letter to Heliodorus, which was written in 374 A.D., the Church Father seems to have in memory the passage of Tertullian (De Spect.) which Mead had already quoted; for he writes: "He is called the son of a workman and of a harlot; He it is . . . who fled into Egypt. He the clothed with a scarlet robe; He the crowned with thorns; He a Magus, demon-possessed and a Samaritan!" Further in his letter to Titus (iii, p. 9) Jerome writes: "I heard formerly concerning the Hebrews . . . at Rome . . . that they bring into question the genealogies of Christ."

Gregontius, Bishop of Tephar in Africa, in the second half of the fifth century says that Jesus had been put to death because he was a sorcerer or magician, so the Jews asserted. John of Damascus in the early eighth century, in the genealogy of Mary tells us that Joachim was the father of Mary, Bar Panther the father of Joachim, and Levi the father of Bar Panther, and therefore presumably Bar Panther himself.

Agobard in the eighth century repeats the Pandera stories.

The Toldoth speak of making a virgin pregnant without contact with a man. In the Talmud Balaam is one of the synonyms of Jesus.

With reference again to the Helene character that figured basically in many of the sacred legends connected with the Christ, there is the detail that the harlot who accompanied Simon Magus was a certain Helen (Greek Helene, Latin Helena). He said his Helen was the Sophia or Wisdom. But the conjecture is that Helene is simply the pseudograph for Selene, the Moon, whereas Simon the magician wielding spiritual powers was a pseudonym of the Sun, the type of all spiritual miracle-working power. (Hebrew for "sun" is Shemesh, whence Shimeon, Shimshon, Samson, Simon.) One of the ancient Biblical typal designations of the women who were lunar goddesses accompanying the sun, as mothers of life, the consorts or concubines of the solar deities, was the "great harlot." This appellation is simply in virtue of Mother Nature's (water's, matter's) prolific fecundity in the production of myriad life, and when held as pure typism has no sensual imputations whatever – as incidentally have none of the phallic representations when apprehended as pure typology.

If the above material seems to be running far afield from base and out into irrelevancy, it is quite worth citation if only to impress the reader, unfamiliar with the quantity of such data encountered in the study of comparative religion, with the feeling that the whole mass of it does indeed run away from solid history and evaporate in sheer myth and allegory. If one will but peruse as little of the Talmud and Toldoth material as is reprinted by Klausner and Mead in their two works from which excerpts have been taken here, one will be convinced that it is not history one is reading, but something less objective, less substantial. It sounds hollow and appears shadowy. And suddenly one finds the supposedly human characters turn to ethereal beings or personifications of the sun and its harlot the moon, in one's hand. To the modern who is unacquainted with ancient method and ancient profundity, this indeed seems to run out into the little end of nothing. To the ancient sage it was the cornucopia of divine wisdom.

Thorburn, in his attempt to refute the mythical interpretation of the Gospels, quotes J. M. Robertson to the effect that "one of the most important details of the confused legend in the Talmud concerning the pre-Christian Jesus Ben Pandira, who is conjoined with Ben Stada, is that the mother is in one place named Miriam Magdala, Mary, the nurse or the hair-dresser." (Jastrow, Dictionary of the Targum and the Midrash, part 2, p. 213, 1888.)

"Isis, too, plays the part of a hair-dresser." (Plutarch, De Iside et Osiride, p. 15) Magdala yields in one ray of its meaning, nursing, rearing, hair-dressing.

Drews adds that Joseph was originally a God. His statement has been already given.

It may be quite fitting to conclude this chapter with a few fragments of positive evidence that true early Christianity, so far from being the outcome of a definite historical event, was instinct with the spirit of ancient pagan symbolic and mythical religion from its very start. These and many more items of similar character intimate indeed that Christianity was close in kinship to the great Sun-God cults of archaic days. The Christs and Messiahs of pre-Christian systems were Sun-Gods, and the great temples of religion were Temples of the Sun, and many hymns were Hymns to the Sun. Rightly apprehended this is not the evidence of heathen "superstition," but the very heart's core of sublimest significance and appropriateness. It may shock orthodox modernism to hear the blunt statement that Christianity will not reach its highest purity and nobility, and hence its highest serviceability until, with realistic grasp of its meaning, it restores the sun-symbol to the central place in its doctrinism. For the divine in man is of the identical essence of the light of the sun.

In Die Christusmythe Drews speaks of the identification of Jesus with an ancient Hebrew cult deity, Joshua, and an old Greek divine healer-hero, Jason, equating Jason with Joshua and Joshua with Jesus, "as all representing the sun." Lundy speaks of the Sun-God of the Persians and Greeks as the true type of Christ, who was himself the sun of righteousness risen with healing in his wings, – the sun with wings being an ancient Egyptian and Chaldean emblem! Lundy says that the Oriental pagan symbols did not indicate a low level of conception, but bespeak the loftiest ideologies, being types of a supreme power and intelligence above matter. Apollo, the Sun-God, he says, must mean far more than merely material light. In the highest philosophical and mystical sense, the pagan types and anticipations of Christ, as Agni, Krishna, Mithra, Horus, Apollo and Orpheus – all Sun-Gods – must be accepted as betokening that the true Sun of Divinity must have been somehow present to give form and character to the ancient shining conceptions of the divine light in man.

"Our Lord the Sun" was used in prayer by Christians up to the fifth and even the sixth century of our era, and embodied in the Liturgy until altered into "Our Lord the God." And the early Christians painted on the walls of the subterranean necropolis the Christ figure as a shepherd under the various emblemisms of the Greek Sun-God Apollo. The very halo that surrounds the head of the Christ and his mother is the suggestion of the solar disk and its radiant light. And of great evidential value is the item adduced by Massey, that as late as the fifth century Leo the Great was compelled to rebuke the "pestiferous persuasion" of those Christians who were found to be celebrating Christmas day, not for the birth of Jesus Christ, but for the resurrection of the spring sun! The power of symbol and of social tradition has proved stronger than indoctrinated dogmatism, as the Nordic Christmas pine tree proves to this day.

Of great suggestive value to Christians would be the item of Philo's having advanced, thirty years before Paul's writing and the Christian presentation of the deific transfiguration, the doctrine of a transfiguration of Moses through his intercourse with God. Describing his ascension to heaven at the summons of the Father, Philo declares that by vision of God Moses' soul and body had been blended into a single new substance, an immortal mind-essence having the appearance of the sun. This is from pagan sources, yet Christian analysts will presume to deny all connection between those wells of early wisdom and the Gospel events on the Mount of Transfiguration, where Jesus' garments became white as the light and his face did shine as the sun; or that other New Testament promise that in the Christian's apotheosis, the righteous shall shine like the sun in the kingdom of their Father.

It would be most interesting to speculate upon the possible psychological reactions of the Christian population if on a given Sunday it was read out from all pulpits in every denomination that in the year 345 A.D., the Pope of Christendom, Julian II, issued a decree fixing December 25 as the day on which all Christians should celebrate the birth of the Christ, instead of March 25, as had been the custom among the Christian people up to that time, in order that their celebration might coincide with that of the followers of Mithra and of Bacchus! And full candor suggests the inquiry why ecclesiastical subterfuge has kept the laity in Christendom in perpetual ignorance of a fact so significant and notable as that Christians for three and a half centuries regarded the annual springtime re-birth of the Sun as the most fitting type of the birth of divinity in the world and celebrated the birth of the Son of God at the vernal equinox instead of the winter solstice. And the Pope's exhortation to his followers that it would be fitting that the Christian celebration matched the time of the Mithraic and Bacchic solstitial festival should not be lost on intelligence. And millions still think that they celebrate the birth of a babe on the calendar day of December 25!

For thousands of years Egypt was dominated by a religion whose gods were typified by the sun symbol. One of the pivotal centers of religious ritualism was Anu (Annu), said to be the On of the Bible, and at any rate the Heliopolis of the Greeks, or "city of the sun." The great pyramid was in reality, as part of its function, a temple of the Sun. Thousands of theological Thorburns have asserted that the birth of the Christian Jesus, the skyey proclamation of the angelic heralds to shepherds, the Gabriel annunciation to the prospective virgin mother, and the adoration of three Oriental Magi before the infant King, were solid events on the plane of occurrence, that their incidence helped to launch the new religion to save humanity from heathen darkness, and that they could have no connection with preceding degenerate pagan idolatry of the physical sun. It is time that this unpardonable obduracy of ignorance be summarily rebuked by the testimony inscribed on the walls of Egypt's mighty structures in stone. Says Massey (Ancient Egypt, p. 757):

"The story of the annunciation, the miraculous conception (or incarnation), the birth and the adoration of the Messianic infant had already been engraved in stone and represented in four consecutive scenes upon the innermost walls of the holy of holies (Meskhen) in the temple of Luxor, which was built by Amen-hetep III, about 1700 B.C., or some seventeen centuries before the events depicted are commonly supposed to have taken place."

Here is witness which outshouts the falsehoods of thousands of pious books, millions of droning sermons and the insincere lucubrations of generations of theologians, with thunder tones of truth that silence forever the claims of Christianity to the historicity of its alleged Founder's Nativity. And how could these four pivotal themes of the incarnation have been thus sculptured upon enduring walls if there had been no Gospels extant at that remote period from which to draw these scenes? If there were no formal Gospels extant so far back, certainly the contents and gist of Gospel material were in some form existent. Evidence of this sort deals sledge-hammer blows at the entire structure of Gospel historicity. The edifice indeed topples under the force of this one telling stroke. Christianity, by subterfuge, vandalism and distortion had buttressed itself against attack on every other side. But it could not fend off the attack of truth from the ancient rear. The Rosetta Stone and the pictured walls of Egypt's tombs and temples have outflanked it and laid its pretensions in the dust. Do what it will, it can not shake off the fact that the annunciation, the incarnation, the nativity and the adoration were already on record, along with the Virgin Mother and her Child, in the Zodiac, in the papyri and on indestructible walls thousands of years before its beginning, and that as religious facts they were old when the Galilean babe was allegedly born in Bethlehem. The Christian organization and system of pious pretension can do nothing in the face of facts such as these. Its arrant claims are silenced once and finally by the deathless voice of ancient Egypt.

Chapter XII

THE SHOUT OF PAUL'S SILENCE

The development of the theme has now brought the discussion face to face with another particular in the volume of testimony that has only been denied its validity as a final crushing blow to the historical view of Jesus by resort to the most specious casuistry and the most dogged denial of reason. It is an item that is so tell-tale in its silent eloquence, so dangerous in its implications, that ecclesiastical policy simply dare not permit its witness to be heard openly in the court. This menacing particular is St. Paul's silence about the personal Jesus. Himself almost contemporary with Jesus, and at any rate on the scene of Christ's life within a few decades after its notable events, and still more, an enthusiastic convert to the new faith following a short period of persecution of its devotees, and fired with an unquenchable zeal for its propagation, he surely must have hounded down all the authentic data regarding the life and acts of the great Divine Founder of his adopted religion with indefatigable eagerness. The likelihood in this direction must have been increased a hundred-fold by the little-mentioned fact that he says in one of his Epistles that he spent two weeks (a fortnight) with Peter (Cephas)! If these things happened on the plane of objective actuality, the most elementary imagination can picture the realistic connotations of it all. Two weeks with Peter! Is it thinkable that the zealous young convert would pass the two weeks of this extraordinary opportunity without plying the impetuous Peter with an endless string of questions as to every detail of all that he had personally witnessed in connection with the series of Gospel events? What did Jesus do here and say there? How did he look, feel, act on this occasion and on that? What were the grand high points in the Savior's career, in the disciple's opinion? What about this, that and the other? The fancy thrills at the electric tension of interest that would have been generated in a meeting between these two! If it also was historical . . . But then, – the scholarly imagination thrills also with just as tense an amazement over the incomprehensible fact that, with all the data of his personal Master's life stored away and glowing in his mind, the dynamic Paul, when he came to sit down and write fifteen Epistles to the young "churches" and congregations of the faith, should never once venture to mention to his brethren the man Jesus! Here is the incontestable, the unanswerable fact. This is the datum that stares the proponents of historicity into silence. Before it sophistry fails and argument goes dumb. There is no answer to this testimony of silence on the side of the orthodox position. If Jesus lived as claimed, and Paul lived and wrote as claimed, it is beyond all cavil unthinkable that the apostle would have left a total blank in his Epistles on the subject of the personal Jesus. Ingenuity can bring up – and has done so – a variety of specious "reasons" to "explain" Paul's silence about his Master. But when they have exhausted their plausibility, they have not laid the ghost of the insistent question nor reduced the pressure of its threat to the orthodox position one whit. It stalks the claim of Jesus' existence like a mocking specter and no legerdemain can exorcise it. The fact stands in all its glaring significance: St. Paul never once mentions the man Jesus! And Paul is the earliest witness among Bible writers, the one nearest to Jesus, says Bacon.

The average man mildly versed in the Bible is amazed when told that Paul does not mention Jesus, for everywhere the assumption prevails that he did. If the matter is broached to a Bible student he will make rebuttal with Paul's own words: "This Jesus whom we have seen," and other passages in the Epistles that sound like testimony to the Galilean's existence, – this Jesus in whom Paul glories and whose witness he bore through pain and travail. How can anyone say that Paul does not mention Jesus?

To be sure, Paul speaks of Jesus. But even the theologians agree that this Jesus of Paul's

Epistles is not a man of flesh. The Jesus Paul dilates upon is the spiritual entity in the core of man's inner being. He is the Christ principle, and not the man.

While this is generally enough conceded by exegetists, the reader may need some assurance on the point. Our first witness is the Yale Divinity School publicist, Benjamin W. Bacon, who in his Jesus and Paul (p. 57) is positive in his position: Paul is the first Bible writer in the first century and he definitely knows no Christ except one not after the flesh. If he had posited a personal Christ, Christianity would not have survived his day

Evidently Bacon does not adhere to the general Christian belief that Jesus became a historical person in Christianity because early Christianity had knowledge of his existence. It is important to notice that he thinks Paul's preachment of a personal Jesus would even have killed Christianity. Here is Bacon declaring that the very element of the new faith which others affirm is the innermost genius of its essence and its very raison d'être is the thing that would have killed it at the start. Others claim it was the tradition of the living Jesus that made it live to become the world power of later years, and that Paul's Hellenism and his spiritual-Christos conception would have killed it. What a confusion we see here in the counsels of Christian theology! One school asserts that the early promulgation of the thesis of a historical man-Christ would have destroyed Christianity in its very birthing, and that Paul's Hellenization of its doctrines saved it. Opposed to this is the general claim that Christianity sprang to life because of its preachment of the personal Christ in the flesh and the asseveration of countless divines that it lived by escaping the esotericism of Hellenic philosophical systems. Compounding these two aspects of Christian thought, we have the net conclusion that the Hellenism that would have destroyed Christianity actually saved it; and the historical thesis that gave it its very being would have killed it. Such illogical entanglements are inevitable so long as the effort is not sincerely to get at the truth, but to make a case for a traditional position on little or no solid foundation of true data.

Bacon adds that it was not the teachings and miracles which we find related in the Gospels that are the bastions and supports of Paul's doctrine, since, he declares, Paul neither possesses these, nor even seems to care for their story. Again the cat escapes the bag, for here is admission of high authority that Paul knew nothing or cared nothing for the Gospel story of Jesus' living career that had allegedly founded the faith he had enthusiastically embraced! It is commonly assumed in Christian circles that of course Paul knew all that the Gospels relate and that this body of history was the basis of his espousal of the faith. But it is clear that the Epistles are in no way related to, or an outgrowth or denouement of, Gospel "history." They would probably be in literature if no personal Jesus had ever lived. They trace to quite another source, which Bacon is frank to tell us of: since Paul is addressing men to whom the conception of the Mystery religions is the commonplace of religious expression, it should occasion no surprise if he uses their phraseology. He employs the familiar esoteric symbols to portray his own exalted experience and thinks his own immortality achieved in terms of Mystery arcana. Paul's language is the vernacular of the Mystery cults. No one familiar with the philosophy of personal redemption through absorption into the nature of dying and risen Christhood can fail to recognize this. The fact can hardly be controverted.

Therefore it will be seen from what a background and in what a philosophical milieu Paul presents his preachment of the attainment of Christhood. It is as detached and remote from Gospel "history" and all its implications as could well be imagined for a body of fifteen Epistles that were to take their place in the same canonical Bible as the complement and companions of those same Gospels! If the general Christian presumption is that Paul's contribution to the scriptures reinforces the Gospel story of Jesus' life, that presupposition has a strong ostensible warrant in the sheer fact that the Epistles are put in on the heels of the Gospels, and certainly not for the purpose of nullifying, but assumedly to reinforce the witness and message of the Gospels. What must be the surprise, then, of the general Christian body to be told that Paul's Christianity is Hellenic theosophy and philosophy, Orphic-Platonic Mystery cultism, almost indeed Hindu Yoga mysticism, with no immediate relation or reference to the Gospel life of Jesus! And this ever bitterly condemned pagan cultism is what saved Christianity beyond Paul's time for later burgeoning into Occidental favor, we are gravely told!

The Yale theologian goes on to identify large and grand aspects of Paul's doctrinism as Hellenic philosophy and Mystery teaching, and even goes so far as to say that Paul's Christianity includes elements that Jesus did not teach! Jesus taught no such doctrine as that of transfiguration by conformation to the likeness of the glorified Lord. According to Paul the adoption of the Christ mind effects a moral new creation here upon the earth, causing the devotee to live no longer unto himself but unto him who died and rose again for man's redemption. It effects also a reclothing with a spiritual body, so that mortality is swallowed up in life. This, says Bacon, is not part of what Jesus taught in Galilee, but it is emphatically Paul's own vision of the risen Christ. Paul is speaking of what he knows because he has seen it, and to express it he is forced to resort to the rich phraseology of the Mystery cults!

This is well conceived by Bacon; but that inevitable narrow contempt for all things pagan and pre-Christian that Christianity has engendered in its adherents asserts itself a little further on in Bacon's work and inspires him to make one of those unfounded assertions which in numberless instances, in sermons and books, indicate nothing more than an inveterate determination on the part of Christian theologians not to admit that any other religion had truth and wisdom equal to that found in their own faith. Bacon admits that Paul borrowed the language that gave majestic expression to the realities of his own (or any man's) divinization from Greek religion. But suddenly realizing that this is impliedly verging on the most egregious praise and glorification of the Mystery religion and imperiling the cherished superiority of Christianity over other systems, the expositor must quickly hedge and retrench. He hastens to assert that Paul's teaching from Hellenistic religion and that the moral ideal presented to the votary of the Mysteries is poor and empty when compared with that of the Sermon on the Mount. Imagine, cries Bacon, the difference between being infused with the mind, or ethical spirit of Jesus, and the mind of an Attis, a Dionysus, or an Asclepios! "Partaking in the nature of" the divinity, "the life in the spirit," "living in Christ," "living the life that is hid with Christ in God," the terms that clothed in words the rapturous experiences of Mystery devotees, – what, Bacon asks, would they all amount to beyond mere magic and superstition, if the convert did not also know the spirit of Jesus? The aspirant must realize a sense of his death to sin and of this union with the Father that can come only through the absolute self-dedication of Jesus. He must be redeemed by adopting the mind of Christ and not that of a pagan god.

It is not often that dignified discussion or scholastic critique calls for or excuses the flat denial of the truth of an argument. But there is little left to do with such a line of sophisticated apologetic save to say it is bluntly not true. More than one item in the statement of Bacon is off the line of truth. To begin with it is disingenuous and logically vapid to speak of the superiority of Paul's teaching to the figures of speech borrowed from Greek theology in which he expresses it. There is no point in contrasting Paul's thought with the forms of speech that utter it. It is well enough known that mind is greater than the capacity of language to express it. Paul chose the best available forms at his command, and those were drawn from his intimate association with the Mystery ritual.

Then follows the inevitable allegation of the poverty of pagan teaching beside the shining splendor of the Sermon on the Mount. This has become decidedly hackneyed in the past fifteen years, or since western universities have instituted courses of real study in Oriental religions and have seen something of the profundity and grandeur of religions which it was until then the old Christian custom to despise. But it is worse than hackneyed; it is not true. Christian prejudice has hitherto prevented that frank, sincere and open-minded examination of pagan systems which would have brought to light the true magnificence of other religions. The proper answer to the smallness and error of the slight that Bacon casts on Greek Mystery morality and spirituality is simply to say that a thousand fair-minded scholars and students have more recently looked at both Christian and ancient pagan systems and have been unable to detect any superiority at all of Christian over pagan faiths. Indeed the consensus of much high opinion is that the palm and laurel would have to be accorded to the pagan.

So when Bacon asks us to imagine the abyss of difference between being filled with the mind of Christ and the mind of Dionysus, the frank reply must be that we see no difference at all. It is only because modern theological professors do not seem to know that in Dionysus, Atys, Bacchus, Adonis, Zagreus, Sabazius and others the Greeks had already expressed everything that a Christian can possibly think of as embodied in his Jesus, that they blunder into instituting comparisons and discovering huge gaps of difference that exist only in their own imaginations. If all the acumen of sixteen centuries of Christian scholasticism has not sufficed to instruct Occidental theologians in the simple fact that the pagan sun-god figures were not historical persons, but were typal characters prefiguring Christly nobility of perfected humanity, and were in fact the very prototypes, pre-extant in literature, of the Jesus personage himself, it would seem as if the credentials of Christian publicists to sit in judgment on pagan representations could be stoutly challenged. So much abject failure and incompetence must go far to disqualify further right to pronounce judgment in this field.

Augustine said that Socrates, antedating Christianity by five hundred years and feeding his mind on the contemplation of the (to Bacon) mean attributes, the poor and empty moral and spiritual natures, of pagan gods, was as grand a Christian as any Churchly saint or martyr. And he said that the pagan brand of Christianity was as lofty and pure a type of it as the kind he knew. He himself received the Christian doctrine of the Trinity from Plotinus, who had fed his mind on the attributes of the pagan divinities and was steeped in Hellenistic rational religion and esotericism. It is because Bacon thinks that Attis and Asclepios were mere tribe-made conceptions of semi-crude humanism that he feels safe in rating them as less authentic and less pure models of divine character than Jesus. It is time that Christian critics who indulge in these gratuitous slurs upon non-Christian systems be told that if they would learn to penetrate through the outward veil of myth and allegory that shrouds these gods from vulgar scrutiny they would find to their astonishment and humiliation that the moral and spiritual grandeur of these typal figures takes no second place in comparison with the nobility of Jesus. How can the mind of one of them be superior to that of the others when they are all, in deepmost essentiality, one and the same? All the solar deities were the embodiments of the same divine majesty. To assert that one of them is superior to another is just to put on display one's ignorance of comparative religion.

But lastly the desperate nature of Bacon's argument is shown by the perilous resort to which he is driven to make a point for his thesis. To prove Greek inferiority he has had to reduce a number of the phrases which express Christian ideality at its loftiest to a low rating because Paul draws them from the discredited poor and empty Hellenistic mystical cult systems. In our turn we ask you to imagine, if you can, the glaring inferiority and baseness of the phrase "partaking of the nature of" the divinity, "the life in the spirit," "the life hid with Christ in God," and such others used by Paul. If these are inferior then Christianity at its highest is inferior, for these Greek pietistic expressions are and have been for centuries current coin to describe the most exalted reaches of the mind of man toward supernal heights in the Church of Christ. But in the twisted logic of a Christian apologist they are classed as base products of a despised Hellenistic pagan culture of the spirit. If Christian mental clarity and moral purity were of so uniquely superior a quality above all paganism, why for some twelve subsequent centuries did the schools of Christian theologians have to go back to two pagan thinkers, Plato and Aristotle, to discover the principles of truth and organic rational structure upon which they could base any dialectical systematization of Christian theology itself? The mind that was in Christ Jesus was apparently not substantial enough or not capably enough known to save Christianity the need of partaking of the mind that was in Plato and Aristotle! Many a claim of cloistered theologians is belied by the record of history.

Bacon quotes Dr. Morgan, who claims that the risen Christ of Paul represents a generalized picture of the historical Jesus. It seems apparent that this word "generalized" is here doing duty as an apology for failure to use the overt words "non-personal" or "non-historical." Dr. Morgan is saying that those features of Jesus which make him so real, and so human – he might have gone on to "so winsome" – pass out of sight in Paul's treatment of the character. Paul's Christ has not the inexhaustible richness or human lovableness of the reputed historical personage. Naturally it would be obvious that if Paul was philosophically, in the spirit of Greek rationalism, delineating the power, functions, grandeur and majesty of the Christly principle in the soul of man, changing man's nature and winning his life to intelligent godliness, he would not be likely to touch the chords of such sympathies and emotions as are awakened by recital of personal human contacts, trials, pains and joys. This is to compare a keen dialectical analysis of a doctor of philosophy with the cooing smile of a babe in the cradle. You obviously can not have the one and the other in the same individual at the same time. Touching human emotion is out of place in a logical or intellectual tournament. And logic has little to do with the baby's fetching charm. One wonders when it will dawn upon the orthodox mind that, to be sure, Paul's Jesus lacks human quality for the very substantial reason that in Paul's understanding he was not a human person at all. Only by elaborate metaphor would Paul's description of a principle of mystic exaltation be clothed in terms of touching human appeal. This is the one substratum fact which explains and resolves all the puzzles and conundrums of the argumentative problem, yet it is the last one the apologists will look at.

And speaking of touching human qualities, it is a grave question whether the unthinkable amount of human sympathy, some of it pleasantly amiable and consolatory, but masses of it gruesome, maudlin and morbid, which the millions of votaries in Christianity expend every year over the babe in the stable at Christmas, and over the horrible scenes when the man of sorrows finally agonizes in physical torture on the Golgotha cross on Good Friday, is psychologically noble and edifying in any way, or whether it is not a futile, moronish and altogether misplaced and degrading wastage of precious psychic force. If Jesus was not personally in history, it is all sheer fatuity and nonsense, a colossal expenditure of costly human emotion over events that never happened. The amount of sentimental gush over the sweetly human side of Jesus, the picture of him saying "Suffer little children to come unto me" while holding one in his arms and two on his knees, – the total amount of hypothetical coddling of Jesus the man as a likeable person of sanctified presence, is enough to deserve the designation "mawkish." The efficacious leaven of the Christ spirit in any man will make him likeably human, of course. And the Jesus character, in this facet, is the type of this humaneness. But to affect surprise because Paul does not introduce a picture of winsome personableness in his dialectical exposition of the nature of Christlikeness is to miss utterly what Paul is dilating upon.

Then Dr. Morgan says that it was to this winsome, touching, appealing human figure of Jesus the man that the churches turned after the death of the Apostle and that the preservation of the Synoptic Gospels meant nothing less than the saving of Christianity. Long search would not have brought to light for the purposes of this work a statement from an argumentative opponent that so fully vindicates and corroborates the general context of this study. But Dr. Morgan sees in a different light and puts a different interpretation upon the great fact he announces. He presents the turn from the mystical Christ to the personal Jesus as a salutary manifestation, wholly beneficial to Christianity, and indeed its savior. The view of this work places an altogether different, a quite unfavorable, construction upon it. Paul had striven to limn and color in the most graphic language available – which evidently he judged to be the phraseology of the Mystery religions! – the Christ he knew, the power and grace of the Christ of the inner chamber of human consciousness. To do so he pictured the Christ of the Greek Mystery dramatization. While Pauline Christology, Gnostic esotericism and Mystery initiation doctrine held the Christian movement for two and a half centuries up to a high intellectual and philosophical level, it was Paul's type of Christos that inspired this lofty achievement. Intelligence restrained the uprush of the ignorant masses' literalized and carnalized conception of the Christ that was so soon to swamp all cultured spiritual ideology in the movement. But with the Apostle gone and the uncultured masses streaming into the Church, with the Gnostics ousted as heretics and the voices of intelligence repressed into silence, the sad and fatal turn of Christianity from the loftiness of spiritual realizations to the basest degradation perhaps known in all religious history marched on to consummation of its tragedy. How fatally right Dr. Morgan is, neither he nor his Church has ever known. To its own catastrophic desolation the Christian movement did surely enough turn from the higher and fuller conception of the Christ as the ever-coming world Messiah of a divine spirit transfiguring humanity, to the winsome-gruesome personal Jesus. This happened when its personnel had fallen to so low an intellectual ebb – amply testified to by leading writers of the time – that compromise had to be made with its incapacity to rise to a more spiritual conception of an Avatar, and the calamitous substitution of the euhemerized Christ that would have shocked Clement, Origen, Philo, Ammonias and Paul had to be pronounced blessed, if the thousands who could reach no higher were to be held in the fold. Only too true is it that when Paul was gone the Church took that fatal plunge into a vitiated and utterly false exotericism that perpetrated the unbelievable debacle resulting from the personalizing of a purely dramatic figure. This step was indeed the "salvation" – rather the initial establishment – of historical Christianity; that Christianity that reduced purely spiritual doctrines to as low a level of mental skullduggery as not even the naked sons of the forest and the sea isles had ever been guilty of doing; that Christianity which closed the academies of the most illumined wisdom the race has known, burned libraries with fiendish fury, pronounced its own most philosophical students heretics, perpetrated centuries of the most barbarous cruelty in religious persecution ever known in the world, and founded a civilization that at last has consummated its perversion of guiding wisdom by plunging all the world into the climactic holocaust of slaughter in human history. The turning of the Christian masses from the spiritual Christ to the man Jesus indeed "saved" Christianity, which is no more than to say that it perpetuated that kind of Christianity, certainly one that was both derationalized and despiritualized. It utterly wrecked the true Christianity of the ancient Sages, who have given to the world the priceless legacy of lofty truth and tested wisdom. Christian proponents will continue to read victory and blessedness into this saddest of all debacles in the cultural life of the world, for the legend of Christian superiority must be maintained at all costs.

The implications of this confusion in the thinking of Bacon and Dr. Morgan should not escape observation. Bacon has been quoted as saying it was Paul's Greek Mystery systematism that saved Christianity; Dr. Morgan avers that salvation came through the preservation of the Synoptic Gospels with their personalized Master. As the Synoptics rest on a thesis that is in the main diametrically opposite to that of the Johannine and Pauline writings, we have here two eminent Christian exegetists arguing that Christianity was saved by two forces as nearly opposed to each other as could well be. These two views are seen to clash today; how bitterly they clashed in the earliest days of Christian history, and with what lamentable consequences the one prevailed over the other must be later included in our study.

Notice has already been taken of Bacon's declaration that we have in Mark not a biography, not a history, but a selection of anecdotes, and those not for the purposes of history, but for spiritual edification. If Paul's Jesus is not a man, and Mark not Jesus's biographer, pretty nearly one third to one half of New Testament support of the historical Jesus is gone already! More of Bacon's fine material must be scrutinized in this chapter, as it expresses with great aptness just those points in the case that badly need review. For the moment other data bearing on Paul's silence must be presented.

There is Klausner, who remarks the significance of Paul's giving testimony to the existence of Jesus (he evidently assumes that Paul is referring to Jesus as a person) and scans Jesus' influence on Paul, but admits that Paul shows no interest in the events of the Savior's career. He quotes a writer (name not given) who says:

"To Paul's mind the center of interest was not the teacher, the worker of miracles, the companion of publicans and sinners, the opponent of the Pharisees; it was the crucified Son of God raised from the dead, and none other."

A phrase picked from many similar ones in Massey's work reads: "the Jesus of Paul, who was not the carnalized Christ."

Drews briefly in one place refers to Paul, "who," he says, "knew no historical Jesus."

"Instead of preaching the Jesus of the historicalized Gospels, Paul preaches the doctrine of the mystic Christ," writes Mead.

Grethenbach (Secular View of the Gospels, p. 243) remarks on the tell-tale fact that in its very earliest stage of propagation the legend of the miracles performed by Jesus is absent from the writings which came from or are accredited to those who were closest to him, and are found only in later accounts by Gospel authors whose names are wholly suppositious.

"As for Paul it might appear from his own ardent avowal that had he ever heard of these prodigies done for Jesus and by him, he (Paul) would not have hesitated to use them for the great glory of God (Romans 3:7-8); and his silence about them comes with the force of absolute denial."

In Paul's own account of his conversion he writes in this remarkable fashion:

"Immediately I conferred not with flesh and blood; neither went I up to Jerusalem to them who were apostles before me; but I went away into Arabia."

"Flesh and blood" is a strange expression by which Paul indicates that he did not confer with the Christian folks at Jerusalem or elsewhere. It indeed sounds very much like a garbled mistranslation of a Mystery or ritual phrase referring to the soul's no longer having consort with the flesh of incarnation after its conversion from carnal appetencies. And if Jerusalem is taken in its Mystery signification of the city of heavenly peace, the whole passage can not illegitimately be regarded as an epitome of the soul's transformation, its choice of a middle path, going neither to flesh and blood, nor retreating to heavenly Nirvana, but going away into the intermediate region between Egypt, signifying the flesh, and Jerusalem, the spirit, or into Arabia. It should be remembered, if scholastics begin to snicker at such a suggested rendition, that Mount Sinai, the middle point of meeting between man and God, is placed by Paul himself in Arabia, as seen in the fourth chapter of Galatians. If this reconstruction of the lostoriginal esoteric meaning is correct – and it is more likely than many will think, for ancient method handled allegorism in just such fashion – it is good case and example of how the historicizers of the spiritual myth turned allegory into history. By turning it back again one can begin to see what the original formulation may have been.

Again Paul almost categorically denies that he is preaching a Gospel of a living Jesus when he says:

"I made known to you, brethren, as touching the Gospel which was preached by me, that it is not after man. For neither did I receive it from man (or from a man), nor was I taught it, save through revelation of the Christ revealed within."

Massey comments that in short, Paul's "Christ was not at all that Jesus of Nazareth whom he never mentions, and whom the others preached, and who may have been, and in all likelihood was, Jehoshua ben Pandira, the Nazarene."

As to the Christ in the Epistle to the Hebrews, a document claimed to have been written by Paul, Massey says:

"Now in this Epistle the Christ is non-historical, he is the Kronian Christ, the Aeonian manifestor, of mythical, that is, astronomical prophecy; he is after the order of Melchizedek, who was 'without father, without mother, without genealogy, having neither beginning of days nor end of life.'"

It would seem that we have in this characterization of Melchizedek, after whose "order" the Christ was, enough to convince any but mystically derationalized "believers" that there could be nothing humanly personal and individual about Melchizedek, and inferentially about the Christ, as of his kind and nature. There are those who think and assert that Melchizedek was a man. He could no more be a man than righteousness could be a man, or liberty or virtue be a lady. By name he is the "King of Righteousness," as in Hebrew melchi is "king" and zedek is "righteousness." "He" is that "spirit of truth" which, when it has fully swept into all hearts and minds, will lead us all into truth and establish the kingdom of righteousness upon earth. The description of him as without father and mother and genealogy, certainly does not refer to human father and mother and ancestry. It means that "he" is "born" or generated from that highest form and level of spiritual being which is yet undifferentiated into spirit (father) and matter (mother), and is called in the arcane nomenclature "parentless." In the highest worlds there is neither marriage nor sex to induce it. Out of this pure essence comes the unit of soul and consciousness that is to descend into matter, marry it and through union with it generate the cosmos. This is why it can be further described as being "before the worlds," "before the foundation of the earth," "before Abraham," "in the bosom of the Father," "in the womb of creation." "A" (Greek alpha privative) means "not." Brahm is the Eternal and Absolute. A-Brahm (Abraham) is therefore "not the Absolute," but of course the first emanation from the Absolute, the first form of manifestation that is not the Absolute and Infinite, but the manifestation of the relative – and to us the real. Melchizedek, the power of the spirit of rightness and the great aeonial Messiah, ever-coming from the beginning of man, that could by no possibility "come" at any one moment, since it must come to all men as they slowly grow in grace, or in any one personality, since it must dwell in all alike, is that genius to which all Christified men will give body and instrumentality as humanity is redeemed and glorified.

It is in the sense and reference just elucidated that Paul therefore admonishes Titus and Timothy to give no heed to "fables and endless genealogies," and to "shun foolish questionings and genealogies." Of course Paul would warn them away from "genealogies," since it was not likely that one in a thousand of the laity would grasp the impersonal significance of the word, and since Paul knew that the popularization of what would be misconceived as lineal ancestry instead of spiritual descent would certainly lead to the disastrous outcome of the personalizing of the Christos. Paul's warning was against an aspect of esotericism that he saw clearly enough would act as a trap. He was merely guarding the esoteric purity of the loftier conception, and advising Titus and Timothy to do the same. As Paul was (Bacon and others admitting it) fully steeped in Mystery cultism, he was simply acting as any Mason would do today, cautioning his confreres against using the secret vocabulary indiscreetly. It is notable that genealogies are absent from John, the one Gospel that preached the Christos as the ray of the cosmic Logos, and not the man. This is quite consonant with what would be expected. Presenting Christ as non-human and impersonal, it would omit the externally hazardous"genealogies." Marcus the Gnostic eliminated the genealogies from Luke! The Docetae, a sect preaching the purely spiritual Christ, "cut away the genealogies in the Gospel after Matthew." (Epiphanius.) Tatian also struck them out. He had first accepted them, but when he learned better, rejected the gospel of the Christ made flesh. "Barnabas, who denied the human nature of Christ, assures us that it was according to the error of the wicked that Christ was called the Son of David" – in the literal exoteric sense, doubtless. Paul also tells us that no "man can say that Jesus is the Lord, but by the Holy Spirit" (I Cor. 12:3). Marcion does not connect Jesus with Nazareth. Paul's Christ is nowhere called Jesus of Nazareth, nor is he born at Bethlehem, – the town, but in Bethlehem, the "house of bread," the sign of Pisces, in the astrological symbolism.

There is a ludicrous mixture – as was to be expected and inevitable – of the historical Jesus and the spiritual Christ in the first Epistle of Paul to Timothy, where Jesus Christ is spoken of as he "who, before Pontius Pilate, witnessed the good confession"; and half a dozen lines later, Paul's Jesus is the "Lord of Lords dwelling in the light unapproachable, whom no man hath seen nor can see." Massey comments that this is the Christ of the Gnosis who could not be made flesh to stand in the presence of Pontius Pilate. Let the reader note, from the analysis of the name "Pontius Pilate" made earlier in the work, how difficulty such as this vanishes the moment the esoteric non-historical rendition is adopted in place of the historical. Slight and inconsequential as this matter may seem in an instance of the kind, it is the key to the redemption of the Christian religion from its theological irrationality. It may be indeed the key to the salvation of all religion, now threatened as never before with total obscuration.

It is time to meet and answer a typical orthodox retort to the implications of Paul's silence about Jesus. We find such a rebuttal in Shirley Jackson Case's The Historicity of Jesus. This is a representative work, written by an outstanding modern theologian, of the University of Chicago Divinity School. Case speaks first of Paul's having acquaintance with relatives and friends of this Jesus. A little later he discusses the claims of scholars and Paul's own (apparent) statement that he had "seen Jesus our Lord" (I Cor. 9:1). He cites Paul's incidental remark to the Corinthians that "we have known Jesus after the flesh" as proof that he had actually seen the earthly Jesus. Then he affirms that Paul had come into intimate contact with individuals of note, and a host of others unknown to us by name, who had contacted Jesus. There is of course no evidence anywhere for the claim that Paul had met many persons who had seen or heard Jesus. It is just the assumption – and no more – that if Jesus lived and did what the Gospels report, Paul, living immediately after the events, must naturally have heard, known or contacted the historical aftermath of occurrences that had made such a stir in Palestine at the time. This gratuitous presupposition Case uses as the warrant for his further presumptive statement that this knowledge and first-hand acquaintance would have made it impossible for Paul to mistake a primitive doctrine about an anthropomorphized god for belief in the actual existence of a historical individual. We have to admit, is Case's argument, that Paul stood too close to the age which professed to know Jesus to be successfully hoodwinked on the historical question. If Jesus never lived, it is not at all probable that even the most enterprising propagandists could have succeeded in persuading Paul of the reality of this mythical person in the generation to which Paul himself belonged. Paul everywhere takes for granted the existence of Jesus, whose memory was fresh in men's minds; and also a good part of his attention is given to resisting opponents who claim superiority over him because they have been, or have received their commission from men who have been, personal companions of Jesus – a fact, says Case, which Paul never denies, though he disputes the legitimacy of the inference regarding superiority which they deduce from the fact.

It is certainly permissible to state that Case's conclusions from the premises in this facet of the argument are not dialectically supportable. We have ourselves mentioned Paul's statement that he spent a fortnight with Peter. Even without that it would be reasonable to think that he may have known and associated with others who had been close to Jesus – assuming that he lived. For argument's sake, we may concede the major premise of Case's reasoning: that Paul could have known many who had met Jesus. But the deductions Case draws from the premises seem wholly unwarrantable. Paul need not mention Jesus because everybody already knew of his existence, is the tacit claim. Such knowledge was a commonplace and there was no occasion to refer to it. Because Jesus was a definite historical character, his life and personal doings need never be spoken of. Paul could dilate at greatlength upon the fundamentals of the religion Jesus assumedly founded and had no need to speak of the founder! Jesus was the inspiration of the greatest religion on earth, a man whose life was so epochal that history was redated from his birth, a man whose preachment of the first divine wisdom vouchsafed to men was to free the human race from the bondage of sin and evil, a man whose mission was so mighty that stars beckoned and angels choired, and heavenly halleluiahs mingled with earthly songs to celebrate the descent of deity to the planet, – and when Paul descants with holy enthusiasm upon the marvels of this world-changing message, he found no occasion to speak of the man who was the genius of it all! For Paul to write fifteen Epistles, basic treatises on the religion that this man founded, and find no reason to refer even once to anything he said or did, would be on the order of one's writing a thorough treatise on the American Revolution and never once mentioning George Washington, – forsooth because everybody knows that Washington had something to do with it! This is the sort of reasoning that Case is treating us to. Of course everybody knows that Jesus, like Washington, was there; so there was no need to mention him. The fact that Paul wrote profound discourses on the religion established by Jesus and does not mention him, proves that Jesus lived! This is a new way for a historian to put a man in history – to remain silent about him. Herodotus or Gibbon or Macaulay does not mention Proxon; therefore Proxon must have lived. The best way to promulgate the religion Jesus founded is not to mention the founder! But, says Bacon, Paul's writings do not even dissertate on the teachings of Jesus primarily. Therefore, on Case's line of reasoning, it must have been in Paul's mind that the best way to advance the new Jesus-inspired faith was to write letters on it that leave out both the founder and his teachings! Scholars admit that it was Mystery cult teaching that Paul expatiates upon, and not specifically "Christian" cultism at all, in the ecclesiastical sense. All this, Case would argue, proves the existence of Jesus. All this is logical ribaldry, but it becomes tragic when it is realized that the whole of post-third-century Christianity rests upon the silly foundation of that sort of "logic."

From the standpoint of human sentiment alone, it surely would seem as if such high motivations as gratitude, reverence, honor, and the like, by which it can be assumed with perfect logic that Paul would have been actuated toward the man who was the author and finisher of his ecstatic faith, would have prompted him to express at least an occasional outburst of praise and thanksgiving toward the man himself, instead of confining all his tribute of high feeling toward the purely abstract principle of Christhood. But again the apologists may allege that Paul's reverence for the man was so supreme that it awed him into silence. It is in congruity with every high human presumption in the case to assume that had Paul known of a surety about Jesus' existence, no amount of pressure of any kind could have deterred this impetuous apostle from pouring out his lavish meed of adoration upon the life that had transfigured his own being. He would have been ashamed not to do so. If Paul knew Jesus had been there, how do we account for this unchristian churlishness and repression of such a man's natural gratitude?

Every implication of the situation would argue that if Jesus lived and Paul had known Peter and others closely allied to Jesus, nothing could have prevented him from extolling the wise words and miraculous achievements of his idol to the highest point his pen could exalt them. That is the only reasonable presumption permissible in the case; to keep silent would be the extraordinary, the bizarre and illogical thing. There is no dodging the fatally damaging involvements of Paul's silence about Jesus. Even if Case's contention were true that Paul keeps silent because he and the people he was writing to took Jesus' life for granted, that still would not explain Paul's characterization of the Jesus he does speak about as a spiritual principle, and not a personality. If Paul knew of Jesus' existence so well that he need not prove it by any reference to it at all, there would be all the more and not less reason for his describing him as a man. Why would Paul descant only upon the impersonal Christos, if he knew all the while that the personal Christ had just been present in his own land! Why write of him only as a psychological entity, when Paul knew him as a man?

Thus it is glaringly preposterous for Case (and others) to construe Paul's silence as evidence for the historicity, or to excuse Paul's failure to mention the Galilean on unwarranted deductions from premises that are themselves only daring conjectures. But there is one other premise that Case posits that proves to be quite untrue. He asserts that Paul stood close to the age that professed to know Jesus. It is true that Paul stood close to the age in question, but it is not true that this age "professed to know Jesus." Data already adduced have established the strange fact that the age of Paul was as silent as was Paul himself about Jesus the man. It was a later age that proclaimed the historical Jesus, later by at least three or four generations. Over a century had to elapse before the legend of the human babe and miracle-worker found voice. Paul and his and Jesus' own age were alike silent. Philo and Josephus were close at hand in the same age, and writing volubly of just such things as were vitally concerned with what Jesus represented, and they are silent, save for the tiny squeak of some daring interpolator in Josephus' book.

As to the argument that no one could have persuaded Paul about the reality of this mythical person Jesus, it again is the weirdest pass at logic, for no intelligent person ever needs to be "persuaded" about the reality of a mythical figure. No person conversant with the Mystery teachings, as was Paul, could fail to know the difference between a mythical hero and a living mortal. Millions of the intelligentsia of many ages of ancient times were acquainted with the mythical personages without once falling into the stupid error of taking them for living persons, as the Christians did, or charged the pagans with doing. The Christians of Paul's type most certainly did not. Case's point is just another instance of the groundless fatuity that features the debate on that side, based on abject failure to apprehend the genius of ancient allegorism.

It is worth the time to examine several bits of Paul's writing that point with great decisiveness to the apostle's spiritual Christ conception. In I Cor. 7:29 he speaks of "waiting for the revelation of our Lord Jesus Christ." What is the point of their waiting any longer for a revelation that every Christian preacher and writer shouts to the world had come with the historical appearance of Jesus of Nazareth? What an anomalous situation – the long-expected Avatar of the ages had at last come in the person of this Jesus! He was here, he had wrought his marvels, proclaimed his message, the odor of his sacred presence was still in the air, when Paul wrote! Yet Paul says they are still waiting for the revelation, the Epiphany, the showing forth in Israel! He had come, and apparently his own had not recognized him. What a miscarriage, what blindness, for Paul and his age to miss him, and to keep pathetically looking ahead in expectation when he had been just now behind them, at their very elbow!

Again in I Cor. 7:4-5 ff. Paul writes of "judging nothing before the time, until the Lord come." A row of exclamation points would hardly mark the significance of this verse. Case himself cites Paul's writing to the Philippians his confidence that God, who had begun a good work in them "will perfect it until the day of Jesus Christ." Further he counts on them to remain "void of offence unto the day of Christ," and encourages them to stand fast. How could the apostle write such things pointing to the future for fulfillment if he knew that the Messiah had just been among them?

Massey points out that according to James (5:7, 8) the coming or presence of the Lord was still being awaited. He pleads: "Be ye patient" until "the coming of the Lord," for "the coming of the Lord is at hand" – when it had just taken place! From Peter (3:10) Massey quotes:

"The day of the Lord will come like a thief, when the heavens will vanish with crackling roar, the stars will be set ablaze and melt, the earth and its works will disappear."

The Lord had come, and in spite of an earthquake and a darkened sun and other convulsions of nature, the good old earth had kept on in its course. It is important to note in passing that secular history records none of these supremely extraordinary natural phenomena, which we must assume would have been the case had they occurred. It is quite worth noting what Gibbon has to say on this score in his great history of the Roman Empire:

"But how shall we excuse the supine inattention of the Pagan philosophical world to these evidences which were presented by the hand of Omnipotence, not to their reason, but to their senses? During the age of Christ and his apostles and of their disciples, the doctrine which they preached was confirmed by innumerable prodigies. The lame walked, the blind saw, the sick were healed, the dead were raised, demons were expelled, and the laws of Nature were frequently suspended for the benefit of the Church. But the sages of Greece and Rome turned aside from the awful spectacle, and pursuing their ordinary occupations of life and study, appeared unconscious of any alterations in the moral or physical government of the world. Under the reign of Tiberius the whole earth, or at least a celebrated province of the Empire, was involved in a preternatural darkness of three hours. Even this miraculous event, which ought to have excited the wonder, the curiosity and the devotion of mankind, passed without notice in an age of science and history. It happened during the lifetime of Seneca and the elder Pliny, who must have experienced the immediate effects or received the earliest intelligence of the prodigy. Each of these philosophers in a laborious work has recorded all the great phenomena of Nature, earthquakes, meteors, comets and eclipses which his indefatigable curiosity could collect. Both the one and the other have omitted to mention the greatest phenomenon to which the mortal eye has been witness since the creation of the globe." Etc. (D. and F., p. 443.)

Again Paul's characterization of Jesus as "the first-born," "the first-born of all creation," "the first-born from the dead," "the first-born among many brethren," would not fit a personal Galilean. "Now hath Christ risen from the dead and become the first fruits of them that slept." But, Massey asks, in what sense? It is impossible, he avers, to apply such descriptions to any historical person. No historical Jesus could be the first-born from the dead. In the gross exoteric sense this would mean that no man in all preceding centuries had risen out of his physical grave in a body of any kind, physical or spiritual. In a somewhat more exalted esoteric sense it would mean that Jesus was the first in all the history of humanity ever to rise as a spiritually glorified being from his body of clay in his final transfiguration into immortality. It would mean that no one before Jesus had ever accomplished the resurrection of his spiritual body out of the earthly body of this death, which is the true meaning of the resurrection. But in any of the possible eventualities that fulfilled resurrection doctrine, taken historically, it is unthinkable and presupposes vast injustice on the part of God to the millions antedating 33 A.D., that no mortal had ever achieved spiritual victory up to that time. One has to go over to the deeper esoteric sense to catch the rational significance of the statement that Jesus was the first fruits of them that slept. For obviously the Christ-type of consciousness is the first power of divine rank that is awakened to full and immortal function out of the deep sleep of age-long incubation in matter into which the living energies of spirit are plunged at the beginning of each cycle. The Christ-mind is the first perfected fruitage on the tree of life and nature. This is precisely what is embodied in many cryptic constructions in sacred lore, representing the tree in Adam's garden as bearing the Christ as its topmost and richest fruit. The golden bough on the tree or the bright star on the highest tip of the Christmas pine carries the meaning still. After long ages of gestation in her womb, Mother Nature in her old age (Sarah, Hannah, Elizabeth!) brings forth the Christ consciousness, as the first divine fruitage of the natural order. With this knowledge and conception sane comprehension can at last replace prevalent logical dementia.

Paul also speaks of "building up the body of Christ, until we all attain unto the unity of Faith and to the knowledge of the Son of God, unto a full-grown man; unto the measure of the stature of the fulness of Christ." How could each of us build up the body of Christ, if he be a physical man? If we take such a saying of Paul as that he "knew a man in Christ," we at once run into ludicrous impertinence if we think of Christ as a man. What it would be to be "in" a Christ who is physical, would be difficult to say. Does the orthodox protagonist pronounce this a silly and preposterous argument? But he could call it silly only on the presupposition that of course the phrase means to be "in" Christ in the purely spiritual sense of being in the vibration of the same mind and soul that Christ manifested. But that is to admit nearly all that this work stands for: that the Christ is a spiritual nature in us, and not a man in history. Orthodox strategy falls back on the definition of Christ as spiritual principle whenever the argument would take a disadvantageous turn on the personal rendering, but jumps back to the latter when it seems safe to do so. But the Christ is either one or the other. The one excludes the other and the vacillation back and forth between the two prevents the fixing of one clear and determinate meaning to the term. It is beyond question that the word "Christ" means the flower of divine consciousness in man and nothing else whatever. All ancient sacred books presented a type of this beauteous development in man's organism at the summit of his growth, and – ignorance later mistook the figure for a man. This is the whole – tragic – story.

That the life, crucifixion, death and resurrection of the Son of God were distinctly not behind Paul, but still to come as a consummation for all humanity is indubitably indicated by Paul himself in II Timothy (2:16-18) where he says:

"But shun profane and vain babblings; for they will increase unto more ungodliness. And their word will eat as doth a canker; of whom is Hymenaeus and Philetus; who concerning the truth have erred, saying that the resurrection is past already; and overthrow the faith of some.""

What testimony from the scriptures themselves could be more cogent than this? Paul is warning his Christian brethren to quit the silly talk about the resurrection being accomplished once and for all for humanity, through the exoterically misapprehended physical resurrection of the man-Christ. It was as if Paul cautioned them to be on their guard against countenancing and enhancing the disastrous vogue of the exoteric exploitation and garbling of deeply esoteric material. There is every reason to think that this is the true picture of the import behind Paul's words here, a picture which we owe chiefly to Massey's clear vision.

Then we come to the matter of Paul's vision on the road to Damascus, which is the chief reliance of the flesh-worshipping party in the debate. This incident is supposed to clinch the verdict for the historicity. What doubt can there be when Paul saw Jesus in his vision, and the appearance of the Master to him was so overwhelmingly genuine that it led to Paul's conversion? How can Jesus' existence be doubted when he actually appeared to Paul (and others)?

But the matter is not so simple. It involves much that needs understanding. Was the apparition to Paul the wraith of the dead Jesus or the spirit-body of Jesus still living? Massey cites data of much cogency to intimate that the vision came to Paul while Jesus was still living, if facts of Gospel "history" be considered. He shows by data from the Acts that Paul's conversion, supposed to have occurred after the year 30 A.D. at the earliest, must have occurred as early as 27 A.D. He reasons as follows: Paul stated that after his conversion he did not go up to Jerusalem for three years. Then after fourteen years more he went again up to Jerusalem with Barnabas. This second visit can be dated by means of the famine, which is historic, and known to have occurred in the year 44, at which time relief was conveyed to the brethren in Judea by Barnabas and Paul. If we take seventeen years from the 44, the different statements go to show that Paul had been converted as early as 27 A.D. The conversion then could not have been by a spiritual manifestation of the supposed personal Jesus, who was not then dead, and further had not at that time been regarded as, or converted into, a living person of the later canonical Gospels.

But that point can be let go, as a bit indecisive. Modern Spiritualists and Theosophists can supply plentiful data as well as a full-fledged rationale of spiritual science to make it possible for Jesus, living in 27, or dead in 33, to "appear" to Paul in vision. Whether spirit or wraith, little is the difference. But a far more vital point is one which, of course, the pro-flesh debaters have never commented upon. Quite – and refreshingly – unlike medieval and modern visionaries who see the radiant figure of "Jesus" in their inner world, Paul distinctly does not make the unconscionable mistake of the latter by asserting the identity of the figure or personage of his vision with an allegedly former living character whom he had never seen. We have covered this point in the first chapters. He simply designates the figure appearing to him as the Lord Jesus Christ, which can be seen to stand here for a generic name of such a type of radiant manifestation, apart from any necessary connection with any former or present living personality. Ancient Egyptian necrological science predicated that the gods and the elect of perfected humanity could appear to men in whatsoever garments of solid or etheric matter they chose. They could appear in many different forms, clothed in flesh or clothed in light. Paul, with his Mystery cult associations, must have been familiar with these possibilities in a commonplace way. It was enough for him to know that he had experienced a spiritual vision, that an apparition of a celestial-appearing figure, an angel of light, had flashed across his inner eye. He did not presume to tie the vision back to any earthly personage, particularly to an individual he had never seen. He only says that the radiant light of the Christos enfolded and blinded him.

Strange as this may sound to theological ears, there is much solid reason to suspect that the whole episode of Paul's great vision was the rescript almost verbatim of a portion of Mystery dramatism. For Paul says that the stunning, blinding radiance of Christly glory threw him with his face to the ground, after which a voice out of the light spoke to him and said, "Stand on your feet, Paul." This hardly seems like personal history, for in the Mystery philosophy the descent of the divine soul into incarnation in the early human beginning stage sent it into the bodies of animals who yet walked on all fours, with face to the ground. And as the Christ consciousness gradually asserted its rulership, the humanized animal forms slowly rose to their feet, upright! For the god-soul to incarnate at the beginning of the cycle was for it to fall to earth with its face to the ground, and then the divine voice within spoke and bade it stand up on its feet as the upright human-divine! It is not hard to presume that an age saturated with the effort to dramatize mythical typology would have introduced into the Mystery ceremonial just such a typical representation of the soul's descent into lowly animal body and its resurrection to the upright human status.

Furthermore the transformation was accompanied by a change of name – Saul to Paul, as Abram to Abraham, Jacob to Israel. "A new name shall be given unto" the Christified human, carved on a white stone, says Revelation. The whole recital may not unwarrantably be construed as a bit of the initiatory ritualism of the Mystery societies, which was itself just a dramatic typing of the transformation of man, starting with his face to earth in brute body, and rising from his animal nature to spiritual stature, when he received his new baptism. In all probability it stood at first as pure typism in Paul's writings, and may have been made over into an alleged personal experience of his by the hands and fancies of those redactors who transmogrified sublime mythicism into startling history.

In Myth, Magic and Morals (pp. 6-9 ff.) F. W. Conybeare says that Paul's Christ is an a priori construction of his own, owing little or nothing to the historical man of Nazareth, and to those who knew that man and cherished his memory. The most that Paul owed to him was the name Jesus. Paul's Jesus is an ideal superhuman Savior, destined from the beginning of the world to play an ecumenic role. Paul, he says, shows no acquaintance with the Sermon on the Mount or with the parables.

Paul could not remember in another instance of mystic vision of his (I Cor. 12:1 ff.) whether certain experiences occurred to him "in the body or out of it, I know not; God knoweth," – twice repeated. This can serve as the legitimate foundation for the suggestion that Paul's ecstatic vision may have been one of those super-conscious experiences which many people have had, so detached from objective reality that they can by no possibility be related to actual events in the world at all.

Chapter XIII

ROBBING PAUL TO PAY PETER

The study now touches upon a phase of Paul's relation to Christianity that involves a portion of early Christian history which is generally unknown to the laity or the people at large. It is the Peter-Paul controversy, so-called. It was a factional dispute in the early Church between two sides representing respectively the spiritual and the literal construction of Scripture. There appears to be evidence that there was a Petrine party upholding the historical interpretation of the Messiahship and the Gospel narrative, opposed to a Pauline faction that stood for the esoteric mystical meaning of all Scripture.

Massey is speaking of the great gulf that separated these two views and their factional advocates in early Christianity when he makes this drastic declaration:

"The bodies of two million martyrs of free thought, put to death as heretics in Europe alone, and all the blood that has ever been shed in Christian wars, have failed to fill that gulf which waits as ever wide-jawed for its prey."

There is first the matter found in the Clementine Homilies, which is ostensibly inspired by the Petrine faction. The author, assumed to be Clement of Rome, designates Paul as "the Hostile Man." Peter is made to say to Paul, "Thou hast opposed thyself as an Adversary against me, the firm rock, the foundation of the Church." Paul's conversion by means of abnormal visions is attributed to the false Christ, the Gnostic and Spiritualist Christ opposed to a historic Christ. Peter is hitting obviously at Paul in Homily 17, when he says, "Can anyone be instituted to the office of a teacher through visions?" Paul is treated as the arch-enemy of the Christ crucified – he is declared the very Anti-Christ! He is predicted to be the author of some great heresy expected to break out in the future. Peter is said to have declared that Christ instructed the disciples not to publish the one true and genuine Gospel for the present, because false teachers must arise, who would publicly proclaim the false Gospel of the Anti-Christ, that was the Christ of the Gnostics. "As the true Prophet has told us, the false Gospel must come from a certain misleader." The true Gospel was confessedly "held in reserve, to be secretly transmitted for rectification of future heresies." The Petrine party knew well enough what had to come out if Paul's preaching, proclaimed in his original Epistles, got vent in wide broadcast. Hence those who were the followers of Peter and James anathematized him as the great apostate and rejected his Epistles. Justin Martyr never once mentions this founder of Christianity, never once refers to the writings of Paul. Strangest thing of all is that the Book of Acts, which is mainly the history of Paul, should contain no account of his martyrdom or death at Rome. Paul's writings seem to have been withheld for a full century after his death.

According to Massey, "The Praedicatio Petri declared that Peter and Paul remained unreconciled until death." Klausner (85) refers to the dispute between Peter and Paul over the observance of the ceremonial laws, circumcision and forbidden foods.

Clement of Alexandria states that Paul, before going to Rome, said that he would bring to the brethren the Gnosis, or tradition of the hidden mysteries, as the fulfillment of the blessings of Christ, who, Clement says, reveals the secret knowledge and trains the Gnostic by Mysteries, i.e., revelations made in the state of trance. Thus Paul was going as a Gnostic and therefore as the natural opponent of historic Christianity, the promulgation of which was the aim of the Petrine party. Massey declares it was the work of Peter to make the Mysteries exoteric in a human history. It was the work of Paul to prevent this by explaining the Gnosis. Paul warns against the preaching of that "other Gospel" and that "other Jesus."

The data on the subject are none too full or explicit. Controversy could easily rage over it. The gist of the matter is, however, apparent. Christianity started as Gnosticism, became vitiated by the introduction of exoteric elements and proceeded along the track of that course of literalization and historization which made it acceptable to all the ignorant and repellent to all the intelligent. Endless controversy arose between the leaders of the two trends and it appears that Paul was arrayed against Peter. If it was not Paul, the subjective esotericist, against Peter, the objective exotericist, it was at least Pauline spirituality against Petrine literalism. As has so often been admitted by scholars, Paul preached the gospel of the immanent Christ; Peter stood for the fact and the message of a personal Jesus. The resolution of the controversy in favor of the Petrine party was fateful for the whole future of Christianity and the Occident. It committed the Catholic Church to an effort to organize the whole world under its aegis in an earthly body, in which effort it has achieved so large a success, but also in which, by the very fact of its adapting its message to a form of attraction for the less intelligent masses, it has lost its own interior meaning, its profoundest spiritual genius. No one can predict history unless he is blessed with some power of vaticination, but it is reasonable to assume that had the Pauline wing of the early movement prevailed, the service of Christianity to the Western peoples over sixteen centuries would have brought more of benison than it has done.

But the matter of this controversy is not ready to be dismissed with the treatment given. The obligation to deal fully with its historical implications rests heavily on anyone treating the development of early Christianity. The early Petrine victory has fixed the character and set the course of all following Christian influence, and as this course and character have been defended, ecclesiastical polity has ever since stood stoutly behind the historical interpretation of scripture. Scholars and theologians in every camp have inveterately lauded the Church's third-century choice of Petrine as against Pauline theology and they have without limit hailed that choice as Christianity's escape and salvation from the evils of Gnostic doctrinism and Pauline mystical spirituality. It is the purpose of this study to challenge the dominance and the tenability of this posture and to refute its basic contentions. It is the thesis that the Church, Christianity and religion itself lost immeasurably by following after Peter instead of Paul. Our contentions on this score will fly directly into the face of all orthodox scholastic opinion and will doubtless invite bitter scorn and condemnation. But truth is important and worth the cost one often has to pay for it.

Bacon has so well stated the conventional and established view on the matter that it will serve the purpose handidly to let him present it. In his Jesus and Paul (p. 138) he is speaking of Mark's Gospel and says that, try as he would, Mark finds it impossible to make his recital the story of a real man under actual historical conditions, and at the same time the story of the superhuman being who steps down into incarnation from "heaven" and who is treated in the Christology of the Gnostics as a "principle" and not as a man. The combination is attempted, however, says Bacon, and Paul's influence is seen pressing on the side of the subjective Christhood. John carried the subjectivization of the Christ even further, but, says Bacon, it is fortunate indeed for us that the move in the direction taken by Paul and John could not be carried through to triumph. John came close to making the "life" of Jesus one long ode of spiritual transfiguration, ignoring the mundane Jesus on his personal side. John was more a history of abstract Christhood than of the Christ himself. Then, asserts Bacon, we all know how fatal would have been the result for real religious values if the later Gospel – John – had completely superseded all its predecessors. Mark superseded all earlier Gospels (this is a bit strange, since many scholars have made Mark the earliest Gospel). Then John had carried the apotheosis still beyond Mark. Had the transference of human to purely spiritual character in the Christos been carried through to final victory, the real and historical Jesus would have been completely eclipsed behind the raptures of spiritual exaltation and mystic rapports. The solid ground of plain, hard fact underneath the Christian structure would have disappeared. Our science of religion would have been reduced, alleges Bacon, to the tiny dimensions of a figure scarcely more substantial than the mythical heroes of the Mysteries. We can be thankful that the whole Gospel was not written in the mystic style, as displayed in the stories of the baptism and the transfiguration, that there was so much rugged fact, defying all imaginative effort to romanticize it into sheer ideality, so much narrative established in the mouths of many witnesses, that those who aimed to idealize the man clear over into pure spirit could not have their victory. Well is it that the Church did not follow the lead of that ultra-Pauline element which for so long in the movement sought to exalt the impersonal Christos and to ignore the Galilean mechanic whom Paul had not known in the flesh. Sober moral common sense led the body of the movement to fall back rather on the Petrine reminiscences of the sayings and doings of Jesus the man.

One has to wonder whether the eminent and learned writers of this and similar material – to be found in endless profusion in Christian apologetic literature – have ever paused long enough in their laudable zeal to vindicate the Christian record to reflect upon the implications and commitments of their position thus stated. As a matter of simple fact these grandiose assertions to the effect that Christianity was fortunate to escape the Pauline influence come close to being a blank confession that Christianity has never been a wholly spiritual religion, and from the third century was not capable of absorbing and assimilating the completely spiritual message and import of the true Gospel! The realization has never seemed to dawn upon orthodox defenders of the faith once delivered to the saints that to proclaim its good fortune in escaping Paul's thoroughgoing preachment of the indwelling spirit of God is practically the equivalent of proclaiming Christianity to be a system that refuses to go the whole way in the direction of inner spiritual illumination. The inference of good fortune in escaping a certain element implies the presence of evil in that element. If the Church is proclaimed fortunate in having escaped Paul's spiritual systematism, the plain deduction from the syllogism is that Paul's high spirituality was and is a dangerous and evil thing. Yet a million sermons have taken Paul's beautiful runes and rhapsodies of the spiritual life and gone on to magnify and extol their sanctifying power in the Christian experience. If this is the benign thing that Christianity escaped (and it is our assertion that this beauteous influence is just the thing it did lose), how in the name of all that is reasonable can a religion be declared fortunate in escaping the highest blessedness of spiritual exaltation? If Paul's ethereal afflatus, his lofty flights on the wings of beatific realization of the presence of God in the soul, are things of danger to be sedulously escaped, it is imperative, then, that the Christian system turn to repudiate Augustine, Thomas à Kempis, Bonaventura, St. Francis and its thousands of idolized saints and enchanted mystics, whom it has persisted in holding up as heroes of the sacred life. In striking, however glancingly, at Paul and his contribution to their movement, the exegetists are shouting aloud the ultimate spiritual deficiency of their own cult. Their attitude represents mental insincerity, if not open duplicity, inasmuch as the condemnation of Paul's exalted communion with inner deity clashes diametrically with a stupendous volume of experience on the part of Christian devotees from Augustine to Rufus Jones as to the supreme excellence of the Gnostic pathway to the vision of divine light. In the face of this enormous volume of most highly acclaimed and venerated mysticism of Christian votaries, which, if anything, outdoes even Paul in pure rapture – since Paul never relaxes his hold on rational elements, and the Christian mystics often do – it is surely disingenuous for theologians to decry the Pauline influence or hold it up as a potential peril happily escaped.

And if the Church was fortunate to escape the fate of being ridden with the highest and sanest type of rational mysticism perhaps ever to be introduced into religion, its good fortune did not continue longer than the fourth century. For Augustine straightway fell into exalted ecstasies more unrestrained than any Paul expressed. And a whole catalogue of saints and ascetics since then have followed the same path to what they reported to be the acme of inner blessedness. Not even the Hindu Yogi has surpassed the line of Christian revelers in transcendental enchantments. When the holy saints and nuns of medieval and modern Christianity have fallen into such white-hot rapture of identity with the suffering Jesus of Passion Week that the replicas of his wounds opened and bled on their very bodies, and all this (and much else) has been held in awesome regard by the Christian body in general, it comes close to downright insincerity for scholars to denounce Paul's lofty rational spirituality as not genuine Christianity.

It is time that someone called attention to the glaring inconsistency of this position. That which has been exalted as the noblest and highest strain in Christianity over the centuries is precisely the attainment of inner rapport between the individual soul and the God consciousness, and this is the Pauline influence that we have seen denounced as a peril. If Paul's emphasis on this experience was a life-and-death danger to Christianity, then it was not fortunate to escape it, for it never did escape it! Not only did it adopt it – on one side of its life at least – but it became the religion's brightest crown! If that influence spelled catastrophe, then the religion has suffered vast catastrophe, for that influence is exactly what it exalted to the highest. It is surely strange that the very element which these critics pronounce the gravest danger that Christianity escaped has never been seen as calamity, but is on all sides held to be Christianity's truest expression. And again can be seen how decisively historic fact gives the lie to an ingrained facet of stereotyped ecclesiastical pietism.

Bacon confesses that it would have been fatal if Christianity had gone the whole way with

Paul into the inner realization of divine presence and communion. This is to say by inference that it was all right to go a little way into realization of inner divine values, but not to go into it with whole-hearted intensity. It must be granted that moderation in all things is commendable, indeed is the sum of most virtue. And no one goes beyond us in decrying the dangerous tendencies and extravagances that so often engulf the unwise or unbalanced dabbler in the mystic ocean. There is here full and even hearty accord with those who press that side of the case. But still it is the height of anomaly to assume that any true goal of human aspiration is to be striven for only half way. No goal of real worth will be reached without consummate care and balance at every stage of approach. That is understood in any effort at perfection.

Bacon holds that it would have been a calamity if the real historical Jesus had been eclipsed behind the glories of apocalyptic vision. Then Christianity is headed for calamity, for its confessed and approved aim is eventually to eclipse any outward value or nucleus of value behind supreme inner realizations. If this is not so, a thousand Christian books and ten million Christian sermons have been a resounding lie. The pro-Jesus argument is a bubble that bursts and vanishes under the touch of the final consideration in all religious experience, that no Savior external to man's own mind and heart can avail to help any mortal win his immortal crown unless and until that mortal has incorporated into his own nature the mind and self of the Christ spirit. No Christ outside can transfigure a mortal until the mortal feeds on that body of divine essence, transubstantiates his own being with it, becomes transfigured by the ineffable infusion of a higher consciousness and ends by being changed in a moment into the likeness of a divine soul. Be there a thousand holy Messiahs in body on earth, they would not alter the conditions of the individual's apotheosis one whit. The eclipse of an alleged personal Jesus behind individual spiritual attainment and a true estimate of the relatively minor importance of a personal Avatar, could not be fatal to Christianity or any religion, because in the end, with evolution the judge and jury, any historical "Jesus" must be eclipsed behind a real divine achievement in consciousness. If this is not true, all religious or ethical exhortation for the spiritual purification of the life is waste and impertinence. On the other hand, the eclipse of the Pauline emphasis on the life of spiritual realization, irrespective or regardless of the solid fact of Jesus' personal career, could and did become a terrible handicap to the promulgation of the only true Christianity worthy of the name – that Christianity which builds the Christ mind and heart into the ranks of humanity.

By what species of clairvoyance Bacon and his fellow apologists profess to see more terrible consequences flow from centuries of Christian effort to incorporate divine graciousness into the European and American consciousness than have accrued to history from that same amount of effort to commemorate a solidly real Jesus, we do not pretend to know. A myriad of the grossest forms of man's inhumanity to man, fifty millions of people, historians estimate, murdered by Christian bigotry and hatred, religious wars of frightful proportions, persecutions, intercreedal antagonisms, hopeless division and hostility, the total suppression of free thought and free inquiry, of scientific investigation and search for truth for ten to twelve centuries – all this is but a suggestion of the record of that same Christianity which drew its motivations from the (alleged) solid fact of Jesus' existence. Surely the challenge can be flung down to the theologians to tell us on what sound knowledge they dare to assert that the record of their religion would have been still far more terrible if the millions of devoted followers had been actuated by the esoteric motive of trying to incorporate as much of the Christ mind within the area of their own lives as Paul would have taught them to do. If the Church's dodge from Paul's rational mysticism back to the exoteric factuality of Petrine doctrine saved it, it saved it for a record of brutal and conscienceless inhumanity that would utterly discredit any other organization on earth. Every rational assumption in the situation gives us the right to assert that had it held to Paul instead of turning to Peter, it might have been saved from the horrible record it has made in being saved from the still more horrible record it would have made – as claimed – if it had not been saved to make the horrible record it did make! Crazy as this sounds, it is exactly where the logic of this conventional line of theological reasoning leads us. It robbed Paul to pay Peter; far better had it been to rob Peter to pay

Paul. And the Peter's pence it has paid have not bought it remission of any of its sins against the glimmering of the esoteric light of spiritual truth in many corners here and there in Europe in the intervening centuries, light which it has with fell fury rushed to black out as soon and often as it appeared. For from the days its ignorant masses elevated the Petrine doctrine in triumph over the Pauline esotericism to this present, it has been crucifying not only the spirit of Paul but the heart and soul of the true Christ in humanity. And this is the institution and the creed that Bacon defends. The real historical verdict after sixteen centuries is that it was a calamity that the solid ground of plain hard fact of Jesus' personal existence did not disappear behind the living reality of inner grace.

Had the personal Jesus disappeared, as Bacon laments the possibility of its having done, we would have had left nothing more substantial than the mythical heroes of the Mysteries and a vague general idea of a god somehow dwelling within us, is the claim. But our early chapters have dealt with this point. Since the work of saving grace must be consummated eventually by each individual for himself, and a model or paragon was provided by ancient sage wisdom in the form of the Messianic Sun-God figures in the Mystery dramatic rituals, man's only inspiration toward the task of his salvation is the knowledge that the excellence of the model can be achieved by him in time. A living exemplar can do no more. And since he can not, all the claims that a historical Jesus is the only solid basis for the one true dynamic religion fall out as untrue.

All the writers in the strain that Bacon labors to express lay great stress on the fact that the hard plain data of Jesus' actual career are the only solid or substantial elements to which a religious faith can attach itself and feel under its feet the firm ground of certitude from which dynamic fortitude can be drawn. But we have particularized the item that if this is the one rock to which we can safely moor our bark, it is by the very fact of its "onliness" most unsafe and insecure after all. If Jesus alone attained, our victory is far off. As a matter of truth, there is no safe ground for humanity to stand upon in religion save the rock of divine instinct in the inner self. If, as said, this is insecure, no historical man is of avail to save the individual. The sad effect of teaching the masses to look outward for their salvation to a historical person is seen in the helpless bewilderment and resourcelessness of people today when they are suddenly told for the first time that their only God is the Christ within their own souls. They are filled with dismay, they are overwhelmed with desolation, and they turn and cry: "They have taken away my Savior – on whom shall I lean now?" They have so little cultivated the acquaintance of their inner divine guest that they have certitude neither of his presence nor of his competence to save them. Through dearth or desuetude of the doctrine and practice of the immanence of God, millions today stand trembling in helpless terror when this challenge leads to the sudden revelation of their own inner poverty. When they are told they have nothing more substantial to count upon than their feebly-glowing spark of divinity – all drowned in the welter of human loves and hates, greeds and cruelties – their situation appears to them hopeless indeed. No wonder they find consolation and safety when the sanctified priest assures them that the personal Jesus will look benignly upon them and be their vicarious benefactor.

Paul, Bacon agrees, had not known the Galilean mechanic in the flesh. He had apparently never heard of him and writes nothing of him. Yet this bereavement and deprivation did not prevent him from being the actual founder of the true Christianity and possibly its foremost expounder and teacher. The spiritual model of the Mystery drama was quite as dynamic an inspiration as ever was needed to lift a man to near-divine intelligence and holiness. Paul's own life and writing put out of court the arguments of his unworthy successors in the great religion he promulgated. Paul himself disproves that the existence of a living Jesus is a necessary element in the psychology of Christly attainment. He attained without knowledge of a personal Savior, as did, shall we say, Plato and Socrates long before him.

There is nothing in the whole of the illogical position upheld by Bacon in this passage that would not be readily corrected by a proper study of comparative religion, with especial reference to the Egyptian sources of all Bible material. But the idiosyncrasies of the argument can not be seen until such study has been made in considerable volume and with proper insights, as well as freedom from established biases. The entire body of supposititious data on which criticism and judgments have so far been based must be drastically altered, and a new foundation for both criticism and interpretation formulated, on the basis of the inclusion of later and sounder Egyptian studies in comparative religion. The perennial weakness of the Christian essay to evaluate its own scriptures has been the delimitation of the scope of its survey to the too narrow bounds of the Christian movement alone. Contempt of "pagan" influences has kept Christian perspective focused on the narrow study of a body of literature that has been believed capable of standing alone and revealing its meaning without reference to its relation to antecedent and environing connections. The truth is that the total of its form, nature and meaning is so closely intertwined with these antecedent elements that without them the study can proceed only in dense darkness. The sun of truth that is needed to throw light into the dark recesses of the mystery, confusion and unintelligibility of the Christian exegetical problem is that luminary of wisdom that shone of old in Egypt, but that was eclipsed by the uprush of popularized Christianity and buried until the Rosetta Stone opened the long-sealed door to let the light shine forth once again. Only with that torch in hand will the scholars have the light to see both their former erroneous methods and the true nature of the problem.

Chapter XIV

A QUEEN DETHRONED

Nor immediately apropos to the theme of Paul's silence, but closely cognate to the broad implications of Bacon's position as above set forth, and of great general interest in relation to the vital changes in early Christianity which affect the study, is a statement from the Yale theologian on page 230 of Jesus and Paul, to the effect that it has been credibly estimated that Christianity lost one half of its following to Marcion and other Gnostic "heretics" bent on divorcing it from its Jewish affiliations and making it over in the true likeness of a Hellenic Mystery cult of personal redemption. Mead asserts, too, that the great Marcionite movement had cut Christianity entirely apart from Judaism. Valentinus tried with some modest success to harmonize the two elements. This datum as to the Marcionite invasion into the ranks of Christianity must be considered a fairly true estimate. Mosheim also says that Origen "had introduced the Academy" – Orphic-Platonic esotericism – entire into the fabric of Christian theology. Augustine a little later came from sitting at the feet of Plotinus, and, previously tinged with Manichaeism, introduced the Plotinic-Platonic doctrine of the "three fundamental hypostases" into Christianity from early Jewish popular exoteric tendencies over to an alignment of doctrine with the most enlightened philosophic wisdom of ancient days. It represented an effort on the part of the more illumined elements, the real intellectual leaders, who had affiliated with the movement perhaps from the motive of saving the strong popular surge of religious ferment from swinging completely out of hand and degenerating into exoteric rubbish. The danger of the deterioration of high spiritual religion into vulgar misrepresentation of truth, which only the most clear-sighted sagacity can envision and guard against, is always great. But it was never so acutely crucial as in the very epoch under review. It seems likely that there was a lessened tone of spiritual character and perhaps some moral laxity in the personnel of the Mysteries, provoking some wide-spread disgust. Likely also was it that resentment and impatience prevailed among the masses over the exclusiveness of the Mystery cults, and there probably was a growing desire on the part of the people to break down the barriers of secrecy and spread the teachings abroad to the world. Discerning that it was both impossible and undesirable to resist this sweep, which represented grave danger to the inner teachings, but also perhaps feeling some sympathy with it, the philosophical element allied itself with the movement, seeking to direct its currents into safe channels. Almost every great popular movement – like the French Revolution – engages at its inception the interest and support of idealists. Later on, when more grossly human interests surge to the surface and find expression, the idealists are disappointed and disillusioned and drop out. A typical example of this in an individual case is the poet Wordsworth in connection with the French Revolution. The philosophic thinkers who joined the early Christian movement later either dropped out or were forced out by the overwhelming surge of crude exotericism that made hash of the doctrines after two and a half or three centuries. Origen was in particular posthumously excommunicated and anathematized three hundred years after his death for having introduced into the theology the great Oriental doctrine of rebirth or reincarnation.

The high-minded endeavor of the philosophic Christian leaders to hold Christianity up to the superior levels of sage wisdom and interior insight, could it have held its own, is the thing that would in truth have saved the religion of Christos. Yet this most salutary and enlightened trend in leadership and following, Pauline and not Petrine, is the influence that the theologians say Christianity was lucky to escape. In the ironical long and short of the matter, the claim is that Christianity was saved from a worse fate than its now known despicable record of centuries, by following a trend that left every one of its doctrines void of true or intelligible meaning and introduced chaos into every interpretation. We are asked to believe that another trend that would have retained the true inner essence of vital significance, to the eternal enlightenment of mankind, would have represented a great and catastrophic danger to the faith. If this does not reveal the poverty of exegetical and interpretative insight on the part of Christian theologians, we would not know how otherwise to read it.

Brief notice must be taken and rebuttal made of an excerpt from Dr. Morgan quoted by Bacon. He says that the Hellenistic conception of fellowship with God is intellectual and mystical rather than moral, a participation in divine omniscience and immortality by enlightenment or ritual. The Church, on the moral side, insists on conduct. This is one of those fine-spun differentiations that, to have the force intended, must slur the highest tenets and accredited principles of Christianity itself. To hit at Hellenistic philosophy, elements of its doctrine or practice must be belittled. But the odd thing is that these same elements condemned in Hellenism turn out to be influences that have been lauded and glorified in Christianity itself. What Christian Church would not feel itself highly blessed to know that its ministry brought to its people the most intimate mystical fellowship with God? The sad thing to note is that if it does not attain that much of victory, it also does not attain the straight moral purity advertised as more distinctly a normal Christian performance. Forsooth the attainment of communion with God in the inner sanctum of conscience and character must be decried as second rate performance because it is Greek and not distinctively Christian. It is a weird logic that has to defend the probity of moral conduct by slandering the sanctity or sincerity of mystical and intellectual fellowship with God. Their efforts to translate history into the meaning they wish to give it force them into the necessity of condemning fellowship with God as evil. All this bespeaks the reduction of Christian dialectic to a one-sided belittlement of everything non-Christian. Even the highest elevations of the human soul in aspiration for union with God must be written down as dangerous, because Greek rational religion inculcated them first.

One other venting of Christian antipathy to the lofty systems of pagan religion is worth closer scanning, as it is found expressed in another passage from Bacon (247). After saying that he had made special effort in his survey of the fourth Gospel to show its completely Pauline character, he declares that Gentile Christianity faced its critical hour forty years after Paul's death when the churches of Asia lay between the Scylla of reaction toward Jewish legalism and the Charybdis of Gnostic theosophy. That the stream of Christian development was able to take a clear and open course by preaching to the world the spiritual Christ of St. Paul and interfusing also into the teaching of Jesus the Pauline doctrine of grace, is owing to the Ephesian evangelist. If this so great boon came to Christianity through Paul's influence, again it must be asked: why the universal orthodox judgment that the adherence to Paul's type of religion would have wrecked Christianity? Again it is difficult for the laymen to understand how Paul's contribution both saved Christianity and threatened it with obliteration.

The later years of development in the early Church, says Bacon, were marked by the incoming of grievous wolves not sparing the flock, by a teaching of Anti-Christ, threatening to sweep away the whole Church from its relation to the historical Jesus. The Asiatic wing of the Church was in danger of forsaking the way of approach to God by moral self-dedication in the spirit of love and taking its course along the dangerous path of Gnosis. By what license or chicanery of logic a Christian theologian can stigmatize the inner realizations of divine grace and divine presence aspired to (and often, apparently, attained) in the practice of Gnostic Christianity as Anti-Christ, is not clear either on the surface or in the depths of the situation. The realization of inner sanctification is apparently to be belittled or stigmatized because it was not attained with the help of the doctrine of a personal Jesus. And how it can be contended that a Gnostic's achievement of divine grace is Anti-Christ and spurious, while the same realization by a Christian saint is the legitimate divine unction, can not readily be apprehended. What can all this narrow logic-chopping mean but that Christian jealousy of its own asserted virtues has reduced its apologists to the childish maneuver of declaring the Christ it proclaims as the only true one, and the Christ non-Christians cultivate as a false one? The presence of such a motive is at hand in the egregiously overweening presumptions on which the whole Christian missionary movement was based. "We have the only true religion, because we alone have the true Christ," was the cry that accompanied the attempt to force Christianity willy-nilly upon all the rest of mankind. It took a hundred years of pretty nearly flat failure to open the zeal-blinded eyes of vaunting Christians to the fact that other religions had found ways to reach the true Christ within the heart.

If it is true that Christianity would have been ruined by following "the delusive path of Gnosis," it should be expected that those who for centuries did follow that path would show in their lives and fate the awful consequences of having lived this baneful doctrine. The Gnostics themselves, it is to be presumed, must have presented in their history the evil results of the system. What did the acceptance of Anti-Christ do to them, as a horrible example of false teaching? Surely those who devoted their lives to following such a pestiferous perversion of true doctrine must have given evidence of the disastrous effects of such a plague in their own lives. If it would have ruined Christians, surely it must be clear that it ruined its own devotees. Bacon and his fellow slanderers of Gnosticism have surely put themselves "out on a limb," which can be sawed off in quick order. For what do we find when we turn back to look at the Gnostics and their careers? Let the great and competent Gibbon answer for us (Decline and Fall of the Roman Empire, Vol. I, p. 393): "The Gnostics were distinguished as the most polite. the most learned and the most wealthy of the Christian name." Mead and other scholars testify to the high character of the Gnostics.

And the modern Harnack is fair enough to say, in comment on Irenaeus' strictures against the Gnostics, that these fine Christians have been severely misjudged. He writes:

"Owing to omissions and because no effort was made to understand his opponents, the sense of the by-no-means absurd speculations of the Gnostics has been ruined by the Church Father."

The great German exegetist adds this:

"According to Hippolytus (Philos., VI, 42), the followers of the Gnostic Marcus complained of the misrepresentations of their teaching by Irenaeus; the followers of our newly discovered book (the Akhmim Codex) could also have complained of the incomprehensible fashion in which Irenaeus had represented their teachings "

The time is ripe at last, after eighteen hundred years, to scotch this unfounded and unjust canard that Christian bigotry has kept alive against these highly intelligent and philosophic early Christians whom ignorance designated as heretics. There is nothing but an arrant Christian prejudice to support the Christian claim that the embracing of Gnostic religion by the early Church would have been calamitous. On the other side we have the clear verdict of that court of last appeal

– history – that Gnosticism, if it did not itself produce the most excellent type of Christians, was produced and held by them. Its unimpeachable testimony gives the lie direct to this habitual slander of the splendid protagonists of one of the world's noblest religious enterprises. Christians themselves would have their eyes opened upon a new perspective of historical values in the appraisal of their own faith if they would scan the verifiable item of history that has perpetually been held from their knowledge, the fact that in the early proscription of "heretics" by the orthodox party in the Church, it was a case of the worst elements pronouncing judgment against the best, exoteric blindness striking as esoteric insight, a fury of zealotry tramping down calm balance of philosophy. It was Christianity at its worst smothering Christianity at its best. To say this today is open lèse majesté against official attitude, but it happens to be on the line of truth. We are asked to believe that Christianity found a salvation, still apostrophized in spite of a record of historic failure, by rejecting the well-grounded religious systematism of the most cultured, intelligent and philosophical class of the third century, who at least had inward discernment adequate to the comprehension of a purely spiritual Christos, and adopting in place of it the crass literalized theological melange of a rabble of the lowest grades of intelligence who were so completely incapable of grasping the spiritual conception of immanent divinity in man that the Church was compelled to feed them on the fiction of the Christ as a living man. Celsus and others have testified that the orthodoxy of the time made its appeal only to the most abject in mind and social station in the Roman Empire. Indeed Celsus tells us that it would tolerate no persons of learning and intelligence in its fold. He says it reached out after only the most wretched and "god-forsaken." It spurned the counsels of philosophy and erudition. Libraries and learning were anathema in its eyes, that in rejecting the Gnosis as heresy, the ignorant leadership of the early institution condemned Christianity to ages of error, blindness and fateful miscarriage of true religion, with a record of inhumanity that crushes the human spirit merely to read it. If this was the salvation from the dreadful menace of Gnosticism, Christianity had better not been saved.

And how is all this impeachment of Gnostic Christianity to be held consistent with a summary statement made by Bacon – one with which there can be ready accord – that Jesus and Paul were the champions of the only gospel that has real promise for our struggling world? How can it be both safe and salutary for the world to pin its faith to a Pauline preachment now, if the cause of the true religion saved itself by turning its back to Paul and its face to Peter long ago? This makes Paul both a menace and the bearer of salvation at the same time. The purpose in laying stress on such a point as this is to show up the precarious and unsound nature of whole volumes of the sort of critical Christian apologetic, Bible analysis and academic investigation in this field that has been under discussion here. One must ask what becomes of the tedious hair-weighing lucubrations of eminent theologians speculating on the Pauline authorship of certain New Testament books, when other schools of thought just as plausibly demonstrate that Paul did not even write the Epistles attributed to him. It all points to one thing clearly, – the uncertain authorship of all the material of the scriptures and the shaky status of all determinations arrived at concerning it. Inasmuch as the whole case for the historicity of Jesus rests upon just such insecure bases, occasion is taken here to introduce some of the available testimony of scholars on the question of the Pauline authorship of the books assigned to him in the canon.

In his Did Jesus Live 100 Years B.C.? (p. 38) Mead cites the authority of a distinguished Dutch scholar, Van Manen, to whom had been assigned the writing of the article on Paul in Hastings' Dictionary. What so eminent a specialist has to say on the subject of Paul's literary work must weigh with considerable force on opinion. Says Mead:

"Van Manen emphatically repudiates the genuineness not only of the Pastoral, but of the whole of the rest of the Letters traditionally ascribed to Paul."

And Mead says this is of great moment, since it is not the opinion of an isolated scholar, but the outcome of the studies of a school. Van Manen himself is definite in his statements:

"With respect to the canonical Pauline Epistles, the later criticism here under consideration has learned to recognize that they are none of them by Paul; neither fourteen, nor thirteen, nor nine or ten, nor seven or eight, nor yet even the four so long 'universally' regarded as unassailable."

Mead follows with this comment:

"Van Manen is unable any longer in all simplicity to hold by the canonical Acts and Epistles, or even to the Epistles solely, or yet to a selection of them. The conclusion it has to reckon with is this: (a) that we possess no Epistles of Paul; that the writings which bear his name are pseudepigrapha containing seemingly historical data from the life and labors of the Apostle, which nevertheless must not be accepted as correct without clear examination and are probably, at least for the most part, borrowed from the 'Acts of Paul,' which also underlie our canonical book of Acts. (b) Still less does the Acts of the Apostles give us, however incompletely, an absolutely historical narrative of Paul's career; what it gives is a variety of narratives concerning him differing in their dates and also in respect to the influences under which they were written."

Important is Van Manen's statement that the Paulinism of the lost Acts of Paul and of the canonical Epistles of Paul, is not the "theology" or the "system" of the historical Paul, although it ultimately came to be, and in most quarters still is, identified with it. "It is the later development of a school, or, if the expression is preferred, of a circle, of progressive believers who named themselves after Paul and placed themselves as it were under his aegis." This would not be an inordinate supposition, by any means. Much of "Aristotle" is believed to have been written down by the students in the Academy. But it is of greater importance for us to be told that this group that "edited" the Pauline Epistles was, according to Van Manen, "among the Gnostic-heretics." If this be true – and its probability is very great – the tangle, confusion and logical rout of Bacon's thesis are overwhelming. The whole structure of his argument falls down in a debacle of ruin. For having said that it was Paul (now declared by such an eminent scholar as Van Manen to be a group of Gnostics) who saved Christianity from popular superstition and Jewish legalism to flower out beyond his generation, and having denounced the Gnostics at the same time, he is by his own opinions thrust into the logically senseless and untenable position of denouncing the school and the influence that he has said saved the faith.

Mead quotes McClymont of Aberdeen, the conservative writer of the article The New Testament in Hastings' Dictionary, who frankly states that the so-called Pastoral Lectures (I and II Timothy and Titus) "are distinguished from all others by their want of historical agreement with any period in St. Paul's life as recorded in the book of Acts, and also by their strongly marked individuality alike in style and substance."

That there must be great strength in Van Manen's view is attested by the data which show that the oldest witnesses to the existence of the Epistles are Basilides, Valentinus and Heracleon. Marcion is the first in time. And these men were all Gnostics. As we learn from Tertullian, traces are to be found of an authoritative group of Epistles of Paul. It is notable that Tertullian still calls Paul "the Apostle of heretics," and, addressing Marcion, speaks of Paul as "Your Apostle"! What do these little items intimate but that "Paul," whether as man or group, school or circle, was of the Gnostic persuasion if not indeed of the Gnostic party?

Van Manen dates his "Paul circle" about 120 A.D. and assigns 130-150 to the Acts. Justin Martyr, in the second century, knows nothing of the Acts, even when referring to Simon Magus, a reference which he could not have omitted had he known of Simon's mention in that treatise, and one which all subsequent heresiologists triumphantly set in the foreground of their "refutations" of that famous "heretic" and impostor. Also there is no clear quotation from the Acts known till 177 A.D.

A matter that is full of meaning from every point of view and is especially corroborative of our position, is the postulation by Van Manen and indeed many others of the existence of a "common document" under or behind the Gospels. This represents the sanest approach or tentative in all textual Biblical investigation to what must be the genuine nub of explanation of sources, origins, context and authorship. The close similarity of three Gospels, or four, has never been interpreted in its clear implications. The explanatory theory was that one of the Evangelists wrote his document first and three others copied it – with variations. Weight of opinion settled upon Mark as the first-written text. Much more likely would it seem to be that all four were variant renderings of a hoary oral tradition, the first setting down of which on paper became the "common document" behind the four and all others – as there were many. Irenaeus told us a valuable thing – though it is known from other evidence – when he said that there was "a multitude of Gospels extant" in his day. Were facts exactly known, it is quite likely that some of the "other Gospels" considerably antedate the canonical four. There is no datum which proves that these four were the earliest. The air of the day was filled with Gospels, and common sense closes the door on every other thesis than the only one naturally assumable, – that they were all essays on the part of many writers to render the truest version of the great oral tradition. On every hand there were members of the several Mystery Brotherhoods, and one after another writer would be inspired to try his hand at transcribing portions of the memorized Mystery ritual, adding his own glosses and elucidations, omitting some sections of the great mystic drama, or some of the allegories and sayings, inserting others. Many scholars predicate the existence of the collections of the Sayings of the Lord, the origin of which it seems easy to attribute to the program of the Mystery ceremonial, where in each performance a large part of the typical drama of the descent and career of the Soul in incarnation, its "death," "burial," "crucifixion" and "resurrection" in and from the "tomb" of the fleshly body, consisted of an elaborate set of discourses which constituted the message, given orally, by the Messianic spiritual principle to mortals on earth. Since, as seen, the earth itself was the "Mount" both of crucifixion and of transfiguration, the discourse of the Christ character in the ritual came to be known as the Sermon on the Mount. Burton Scott Easton, in his book Christ in the Gospels, a quite erudite treatise, says it is silly to speculate on the geographical location of the "Mount" on which Jesus preached his discourse, as it is likely not to be taken in its physical or material sense at all. This is a welcome ray of light penetrating the gloom of theological obtuseness. The "Sayings" were the body of the verbal or declamatory interludes in the acted drama. The parables were other spoken specialties. From century to century at least a few innovations or novel features might be introduced in this or that country. Though all depicted the same mystery of the Incarnation, or the oblation of the Son (Sons) of God on the altar of fleshly humanity, the various national Mysteries such as those of Samothrace, of Phrygia, of Eleusis, of Bacchus, of Atys, of Osiris, Serapis, Isis, Aten and others were modifications in one of another pronounced direction. The Mysteries solve the great mystery of the Gospels. In whole or in part, the Gospels were just the written transcript of the great religious ritual-drama that had been almost the ancient world's sole theme of sacred literature. The assumption on the part of Christian leaders at the start, and of Christian apologists ever since, that the great body of "Gospel" literature afloat in the middle East in the early centuries of our era – and quite obviously also before it – bore no relation to the total organic religious effort of the world before the time specifically marked "Christian," is on the face of it manifestly a stultification of both scholastic judgment and common sense. To attempt to place a specific date of the first origin, which date must at all costs be kept after the year 35 or 40 or 50 A.D. – of a body of literature that in either oral or written form must have had an immemorial antiquity behind it even then, must be seen at last as the prize folly of the ages. Unquestionably there was a "common document" behind the Gospels; and some of the hoary books of wisdom that survived the besom sweep of Christian destruction, give us inklings of its contents.

    The endless aspersions cast on the Gnostics and their philosophy come with bad grace from the Christian side in view of the manifest advantage in standing, repute and character which accrued to the early Church from the adherence to it of various philosophical groups, however much some of them might still be adjudged "heretical" from the dogmatic point of view. It might profit the Gnostic traducers to turn back and read again what Mosheim has to say on the close intimacy between early Christianity and Greek philosophy. It must be noted in glancing at this material that the word "philosophy" had come to connote in the minds of third-century Christians a thing of reproach. It was to them the genius and embodiment of heresy. A faint idea of what inspired this antipathy to philosophy may be gained by putting it side by side with the recent American popular animus against the incursion of the "brain-trust" into the political arena, and the vulgar distrust of the cap and gown or the university degree. There is inevitable, no doubt, a submerged subtle resentment against the cult of intellectualism or pretensions thereto from the masses who lack it. When Christianity gathered in the lowest elements of the Roman population and propagated itself by catering to their level of hysterical religionism, the resentment against learning, genuine or superficial, was widespread and deep-seated. There are ever two vastly divergent planes on which the thing known as religion can deploy its psychologizations in human life, that of the intellect and that of the emotions. Like other religions, Christianity has swung its emphasis back and forth at different epochs between these two modes of the force. In the third century it was in the throes of a movement sweeping it from the intellectual aspect to the emotional. It brought, as we have seen, a hatred of books, learning, philosophy. But before the debacle became overwhelming and catastrophic philosophy had rendered the Church great service, which it is quite worth our while to recall and cogitate.

Mosheim (Vol. I, p. 341) analyzes the contribution and influence of Clement of Alexandria. Clement tells us, he writes, that he would not hand down Christian truth – that is, the truth about the Christos in its purely spiritual form – bare and unmixed, but associated with or rather veiled by and shrouded under the precepts of philosophy. For, according to Clement, the seeds of celestial wisdom communicated by Christos to the world lay hid in the philosophy of the Greeks, after the same manner as the succulent part of a nut lies concealed within the shell. For he appears to have been firmly persuaded that the essence of Greek philosophy was sound, wholesome and salutary, in fact that it was consonant with the spirit of Christian wisdom, but that it was reconditely veiled by a cloud of superficial images and fictions (which we know were the mythical and allegorical dramatizations) just as the kernel is hidden by the shell.

It should be the business of Christians then to endeavor industriously to penetrate this exoteric covering in order to discover the true relation between human and divine wisdom. The origin of Greek philosophy he attributes to Deity himself – would that such liberality had prevailed in the Christian hierarchy ever since! – but its transmission to humanity had to be through inferior agents. Philosophy was the way to eternal life before Christ himself came, and therefore he allows that the Grecian sages were saved. He reiterates that philosophy was divinely communicated to the Greeks. (Deity must have chosen Chaldea and Egypt as his agents of this communication, since Greek philosophy emanated from those lands.) It was given to Greece as a special testament or covenant, and it in fact constitutes the basis of that doctrine which the world has since received from Christos. Mere inner persuasion of the spirit must always be strengthened by that more accurate knowledge of religion which was to be acquired through the aid of philosophy.

This sagacious counsel of Clement the Church would have been wise to follow. But Mosheim goes on. With a view to accomplishing this desirable end, the Christians not only adopted the study of philosophy themselves, but became loud in their recommendation of it to others, declaring that the difference between Christianity and philosophy was but trifling. And it is most certain that this kind of conduct was so far productive of the desired effect as to cause not a few of the philosophers to enroll themselves under the Christian banner! Those who have perused the various works written by such of the ancient philosophers as had been induced to embrace Christianity, can not have failed to remark that the Christian discipline was regarded by all of them in no other light than as a certain mode of philosophizing. (Sad the day when this liberal spirit was replaced by that of dogmatic bigotry!)

Much light peeps out through obscuring veils in the next observation of Mosheim: the opinion was held by many that philosophy had been surreptitiously brought down from heaven and communicated to mankind by those angels whom, according to the ancients, a love of pleasure had induced to rebel against God and who descended to earth to unite their divine intellection with material bodies for the sake of the opportunity thus afforded pure spirits to enjoy the sense of life. (The real motive of "rebellion" was not hostility to God, but revolt against the inane passivity of the purely ideal world – vide Plato.) Clement himself seems to have adopted this opinion; and he is at pains to refute those who maintained that philosophy was a device of the evil one to deceive the human race. (This tell-tale hint gives positive evidence of the virulence of the proletarian revulsion against the rational wing of Christianity, which this work claims has never been given its due place in historical analysis.) Mosheim adds that from this position of Clement we may assume that the alleged origin of philosophy in diabolism had taken deep root among the multitude. Clement explains that Paul, in warning Christians to beware being spoiled by philosophy, obviously was speaking to the more perfect Christians, those "who had attained to the very heights of Gnostic intelligence," cautioning them that the philosophies were but an elementary discipline and should not be permitted to obscure the fuller realities of the Christian experience. It will readily be apparent how widely the views of modern commentators like Bacon, who indulge in the conventional derogation of the Gnostic Christians, diverge from the attitude of Clement, who had first-hand acquaintance with Gnostic philosophy. It is Clement, not Mosheim, who here equates "more perfect Christians" with "the very heights of Gnostic intelligence." Not only Gibbon, but Clement, makes the Gnostics the elite of the Christian personnel.

Mosheim adds that through Origen and Heraclas, pupils of Clement, and through pupils of Ammonias Saccas, who mostly entered the ministry, the love of philosophy became pretty generally diffused throughout a considerable portion of the Church. Porphyry says that Ammonias, a father of Neo-Platonism, had taken up Christianity and later renounced it. Eusebius says that he held to it to the end.

We can see in Clement's – and no less in Origen's – high regard for Greek philosophy, as being indeed the innermost kernel of rational Christianity, the sufficient answer to the indignant howl let out nearly two hundred years before Augustine's day by that loud and blatant protagonist for doctrinal Christianity, Tertullian. That fierce zealot had written:

"What indeed has Athens to do with Jerusalem? What concord is there between the Academy and the Church? . . . Away with all attempts to produce a mottled Christianity of Stoic, Platonic and dialectic composition!"

True enough, by the time Christianity had been adulterated and transformed to the thing of literal gibberish and pious emotionalism to which it had degenerated in Tertullian's day, little enough of its pristine kinship with the lofty Platonism and the splendid eclecticism out of which it originally flowed was discernible. Also, hidden under esoteric veils as its highest teachings and revelations had been, of course the crassness of blunt exoteric vision could detect no connection with the primal system of arcane philosophy in which the deeper Christianity of Gnosticism had had its roots. But the sad mistake of the Church had been manifest in its propensity and its final historic choice to follow its blind and fanatic Tertullians instead of its clear-seeing philosophical Clements and Origens – and Dean Inges.

The supreme lesson that the whole historical episode should teach is that, in the words of Mosheim (I, 346) upon Clement's attitude on the relation of basic philosophy to religion, ". . . our conviction of mind must necessarily be strengthened and confirmed by our acquiring that more accurate knowledge which was to be obtained through the assistance of philosophy."

Whenever the principles of this maxim are transgressed religion swings into channels of irrational behavior. In short religion is never safe until it is well grounded upon and stabilized in the rudiments of truth discovered by a profound study of philosophy. Christianity despised, then threw out its early sage philosophy, and a hideous historical sequel trailed its long shadow over the ensuing centuries.

It is too much to expect that attack and denunciation will not fall heavily upon the thesis here advanced that Christianity was a movement of ignorance against mental culture and rational philosophy. It is found, however, that Mosheim directly confirms this position. He goes on to describe the growth of a party in the Church which violently resented the encroachments of philosophical interests on the religion of "simple piety," and which feared that the spread of earthly philosophy (they must have forgotten that Clement said it came down from heaven) would injure the cause of celestial truth. The two parties, then, of the philosophical enthusiasts and the dour pietists, "opposed each other with the utmost warmth," the one contending for the utility and excellence of philosophical discussion and urging the teachers of the Church to demonstrate the harmony between religion and reason; the other regarding every species of human learning, and more particularly philosophy, with detestation and contempt, and urging the brethren to maintain the faith in all its genuine simplicity. And the theologians of the modern Church still exhort us to regard as our true Christianity the bewildering irrational literalisms of the Christian party – which is what Christian doctrine became in its "simplicity" – that held instruction, learning, reason and philosophy in utter detestation and contempt!

In the finale of his discussion of this point Bacon ends by asking the very pertinent question whether we may hold that there is still need of the Gospel as theology. He notes that in our time few pay homage any more to the fallen "queen of the sciences," as it was denominated in ancient days. The cry today is for religion without theology.

There is not room here to debate this question. It is of the utmost importance, however, that the sheer fact of theology's having fallen into desuetude in Christianity should be fully analyzed and comprehended in its true significance. That the one religion vaunting itself to be the truest, highest, purest in world history should have shifted so far from its pristine constitutional character as to find itself in these latter times of world stress entirely out of unison with its original intellectual foundation, is attestation enough that great and vital divergence from basic principles must have occurred at some epoch. A long chapter would not suffice to detail the nature and immense import of the divergence that did assuredly occur. But however searchingly we may probe, it will come back in the end to the one fact that the far distant root-cause of Christianity's defection from its own theology was generated back in that fatal third century, when the Gnostic and philosophic wing of the movement was amputated by the rising power of the tide of ignorant exotericism that flooded in upon the new religion at that time. It would be easy enough to trace the effects right up to the present aggravated scorn and neglect of theology. When the shift from allegory, myth and drama to history was made, the cryptic esoteric keys to the lofty and sublime inner meaning of theological formulations were lost. The doctrines of the faith were thus left standing as little more than empty shells, devoid of intelligibility and hence bereft of dynamic power and so, finally, powerless to engage interest. They became relegated to the cloister, the library shelves and the theological seminaries. They sank into the background and were covered by the dust of oblivion from the sheer fact that the cord of relevance and meaning by which they would have been tied to living human interests and problems had been cut, and they became a thing apart and out of meaningful relation to life itself. The Bible also, of which theology is the intellectual exposition of its meaning, shared largely the same neglect and ostracism out of living experience. No voice raised today would be a more desolate bleat in the wilderness of uncomprehending stolidity than one which proclaimed anew the need of theology as the solvent of the world's gripping problems of this age. It would go utterly unheard, shouted down by the raucous chorus chanting the total inadequacy of theological doctrine to meet even the mental needs of our time. Yet the early Church proclaimed those doctrines as the saving truth of God for the guidance of men through this life. And the profound wisdom of the purest philosophy in history, the Greek, blessed these teachings with its sanction.

Perhaps nothing, then, will surpass the surprise of the Church itself when it hears the plaintive bleat for theology rise from this end of the field. For there is ample ground to support the forthright declaration that every single dogma, creed article and ceremonial item in the original Christianity was, and still is, the very truth, and likewise is knowledge critical for the practical needs of the world today! It is an unbelievable anomaly that while Christian theology is the saving truth of life, the religion that promulgated it has so weirdly perverted it into unintelligible gibberish that it no longer bears the stamp of either truth or utility, and the Church is itself forced to disown its own primal genius as unrelated to the problem of practical good. So recreant has the institution been to the teaching of truth it itself proclaimed in creed and scripture and theology that it must now turn and disavow its own organic constitution. The enormity of this dereliction must be seen as proportionate to the vastness of the change and degradation necessary to have brought it to pass. The prodigious extent of the transformation from sublime meaning to unconscionable jargon in Christian theology can be seen in all its appalling significance only by those who will make the comparison and see the shocking contrast between the present corruption of the doctrines and their transcendent majesty of import in the minds of the ancient sages who clothed the body of truth in the romantic garb of allegory.

In rounding out this long chapter it is supremely desirable that the full import of Paul's silence that so damages the case for the historical Christ be summarized and crystallized. On the basis of the premises established it is simply inconceivable that the ardent Apostle – the actual founder of Christianity! – could have left in his writings a total blank about the man Jesus. No amount of sophistry or mental chicanery can set aside the verdict of common sense. Any argument advanced to "explain" it rings from the start with the hollowness of sounding brass and the feebleness of a tinkling cymbal. Paul was in essential leanings a Gnostic, one of the Hellenic philosophers so despised by the anti-philosophical wing of fanatical Christianity in the third and fourth centuries. The ineluctable reason why Paul does not mention a historical Jesus is that he had obviously never heard of one, and further could not have conceived of one. No more could he have believed in a personal Logos than could Philo, who was about contemporary with him. Paul and John, says Bacon, saved Christianity from vitiation for the generations beyond their own. Yet Paul and John had no theology of a personal Jesus, obviously and admittedly. So logic concludes that it was a theology that had no room for the personal Christ that saved Christianity.

The final word here should be a dissertation on the true inward meaning of the phrase – the Word made flesh. The easy step from the esoteric collective sense over to the exoteric personal caricature of the idea spelled a swift and facile "descent to Avernus" for Christian theology. With the total loss of the formulae and keys of the antique arcana, the fateful transmogrification of true meanings into nonsense fell speedily upon ecclesiastical doctrinism through many avenues. But one of the chief and most immediately damaging misconstructions was that which inhered in the misreading of single names of type characters in a singular instead of a multiple or distributive sense. Just as it would be a misconstruction to read Santa Claus as one character giving gifts to all children, instead of the spirit of giving distributed among all parents, so it was a mistake to predicate the flesh which the Logos was to assume as the mortal flesh of one man. Naïve thinking, if the more discerning truth is withheld, jumps to the conclusion that if the Word is to become flesh, it must be encased in the body of one man. But the thinking and the knowledge behind Biblical esotericism is by no means naïve. It is inexpressibly recondite, unbelievably cryptic. It takes at least as much acumen to decipher the occult sense thus embalmed in allegory as it required constructive genius and inventive deftness to embody it there. What the vital phrase then signifies in its original cryptic intimation is that the Logos, the ideal archetypal structure-form of God's thought, which was to be borne out to utterance by the resonant thunder of his Voice or spoken Word – precisely as our voices carry out in their tones the ideas of our minds and stamp them upon the living world – was to go vibrating down to the lowest levels of the reach of the creative emanation and finally stamp its image and form upon the highest creature of flesh. The pulsing electronic energy of divine Mind was in the end to become the presiding genius in bodies of flesh. Not in the flesh of a man, but in the flesh of humanity was the light of the Word to be born, glimmer and shine. It was to enter and become flesh collectively, with its rays distributed among all men, and not confined in one single body alone. The Egyptians have the term from which indeed, in utmost likelihood, the very name "Christ" has come, to designate the "soul made flesh." It is their Karast, the name of the deceased in the mummy-coffin, and it means "fleshed." Modern theology will never recover the genuinely correct sense of much of the ancient sacred writ until it restores to a central place in its structure of exegesis the forgotten doctrine of "Dismemberment," the idea of the fragmentation or cutting of deity to pieces, or as the Greeks put it, "the distribution of whole natures" of the gods into infinite partition, so that a seed fragment of divine Mind may be planted in the life of every creature. This principle is indeed clearly embodied in Christian theology and ritual in the Christ's breaking of the loaf – after declaring that it typified or "was" his own body – and distributing a portion of it to each participant in the divine transubstantiation. Each fragment of his deific nature thus transplanted in the body, heart and mind of the communicants became "fleshed" or Karast; and this became the Christ on the cross of flesh. The Christ in each of us is the Word made flesh, which after the analogy of the broken pieces of the loaf, came and dwelt among us, telling us that indeed unless we take and "eat" of this divine essence, our aeonial salvation will not be accomplished. The mind can see at this juncture that the moment one leaps from the meaning of the incarnation of the Christos "in all men" to the other sense of "in one man, Jesus," the groundwork for a rational and intelligible comprehension of the fleshing of the Logos, and with it the whole basic sense of ancient religion, flies away, and confusion stalks the effort to grasp the purport of all theology. The entire edifice of theology is built upon and around the central fact of the descent of the Logos into flesh and matter. It is the nub of the entire system. It is the key to the scriptures. The planting of the seed fragment of divine nature distributively in humanity was and is the advent of Christos, the great aeonial divine coming. That the Son of God was collectively the Sons of God, or the principle of Sonship distributed like bread to the "multitude," has never been decisively grasped as the prime key to the theological systemology. "The gods distribute divinity" is one of the most sententious and revealing items in the profound Platonic philosophy belittled by Christian dogmatists. "Each superior deity," explains Proclus, "receiving from on high the excellent nature of those gods who are above it, imparts it in divided measure to those natures immediately secondary to themselves." The gods in the rank above us offer us their very bodies, i.e., the essence of their divine natures, the substance of intellect and will, for us to feed upon by appropriation, or "eating." If the bread is the body of the Christ's nature, how can it be implanted germinally in the flesh of billions unless it be broken into as many fragments as there are to be communicants?

This is the meaning – all lost in the historicizing process – of the multiplication of the loaves (and fishes) to feed the multitude.

The Logos was made flesh, but not in one man only. Paul thrilled to this knowledge, and the Bible hardly anywhere rises to such majesty and loftiness as in those passages in his Epistles wherein he dissertates on the forming of the Christ in us through the growth of charity in our hearts. There is no confusion there. That comes in only when the man-Christ is thrust into the picture.

Chapter XV

A STAR—AND LUNA

The resources of the dictionary are hardly adequate to pictorialize what has to be styled the doltish fatuity of popular conception in Christian countries of such an accouterment or embellishment of the Oriental dramatization of spiritual history as the heralding of the birth of Christos by the appearance of a star and its guidance of three Magi of Persia to the stable in Bethlehem. When this incredible instance and example of the devastation of sane reason by the psychological seductions of miracle and divine fiat has been looked into closely, some realization must begin to take form in the minds of many that Clement's injunction to balance faith with critical thought is a quite indispensable counsel of wisdom. The power of blind faith to stultify the reason is brought out in glaring flagrancy in the instances to be cited. The point is accentuated here in all its ribald ridiculousness for the twofold purpose of awakening the narcotized intellects of thousands to a realization of the amount of inherent absurdity that must be swallowed if the narrative of Jesus' historical "life" is to be accredited, and of adding another stone of solid strength to the building of the case for the non-historical interpretation of scripture. The climactic reflection from the critique should be that if the acceptance of the Jesus story as history rests upon a series of such mental infatuations as this, it can be received only by minds that have undergone nearly complete paralysis, and that the whole basic structure of Christianity thus stands upon perilously weak foundations indeed.

In a lifetime of reading there have been encountered only two slight or glancing allusions to the illogicality and inherent impossibility of the story of the guiding star of Bethlehem. There may be others that have not been seen. It is to illustrate or exemplify the shallowness of general orthodox thinking on matters of scripture and theology that an attempt is made to present this matter in realistic baldness. When the ordinary person at Christmas time purchases one of the greeting cards picturing the five-pointed star in a dark blue heaven of night; with a streak of rays streaming down as distinct as the beams of searchlights upon a humble structure on the edge of Bethlehem, directing the three camel-mounted Magi to the spot of the Savior's nativity, the aura of interest and devotion in the scene is probably not dimmed or diminished by any roguish consideration that there may be a single irrational item in the representation. If the current query of American cleverness – "What is wrong with this picture?" – were put to the card purchaser, he or she would doubtless be shocked and taken aback to be apprised that there was anything amiss with it. It must be true as pictured, for it is so described in the Bible. And of course to those who have been educated to think of the Bible as a book wherein is inscribed the record of how God turned nature and its laws upside-down to impress his creature man with his almighty power, the physical impossibilities in the picture present no mental difficulties. God simply caused it to happen that way.

But it is a different story when looked at from the standpoint of reason and natural law. As intimated before, all that needs to be done to prove that the Bible is not a historical record of actualities, is to take it at its word and see what you have. It involves the process of de-romanticizing the narrative and transposing its detail over into the realm of factual realism. The result is sometimes just inane, but more frequently is deliciously ludicrous. A rare treat of the latter variety awaits a realistic probing of the Bethlehem starry portent.

The non-reflective Biblical idealist might be persuaded under pressure to admit, in the first place, that stars have been universally known to shine only at night, not very brightly if it is in moonlight season, and not at all (visibly) if it is cloudy. This detail would have necessitated traveling only by night for the three Magi. This would put the star under the awkward necessity of hiding somewhere in the intervening daylight periods, and holding up its speed of motion or resting, or somehow "killing the time" until dusk came on, when it would appear again and announce that it was ready to continue the journey. Otherwise it would get too far ahead of the camel train to serve as reliable guide. To cover the eight-hundred miles across the Arabian desert from Persia to Judea it would have to repeat this daily routine for a month or more, neglecting its ordinary celestial functions until the miracle of founding Christianity was attended to. Having landed the three men at the feet of the aureoled babe, it would bid them a grateful adieu and dash off into stellar normalcy again.

It may be a somewhat more difficult operation, however, to convince the hypnotized devotee of the miraculous and the supernatural, that no star – assuming now that it is a real star and not some hypothecated ignis fatuus of Christian fancy – could by any possibility become or act as a local guide to a given spot on earth. If there is any lingering remnant of protest that perhaps it could be done, let anyone go out under the open sky at night and try to determine at what moment he is exactly under a particular star, or exactly what spot that star is pointing to. With this corrective of his idle fancy, let him recall that the earth is constantly turning under the stars at the rate of over a thousand miles an hour, or about eighteen miles, roughly, a minute. Any locality thus would be rushing under the star at about four times the speed of the swiftest airplanes, and to keep over the desired spot the star itself would have to sweep around on its orbit at an unthinkable rate of speed. Even if it could shoot downward one distinct ray to point to the stable in Bethlehem, the latter would in a few hours turn around from under its finger and disappear on the underside of the planet. A star can give compass direction and nothing more. It can not be a local guide.

There has been no end of the weirdest and most fantastic speculation, much of it given out seriously by astronomers who should be ashamed, and by religious heads who think such things are permissible and indeed laudable because piously motivated, as to the possible actual astronomical nature of the Bethlehem phenomenon. One theory is that at about that period, or within a hundred years of the date, there was a conjunction of four, five or six of the planets, making such a bright cluster that the childish ancient world straightway fell into hysteria and paroxysms of superstitious fear, standing in awe of some great portent, the Bethlehem babe being somehow or other announced by the planets in one voice. Another typical version is that there flared up a mighty comet which aimed straight toward, or trailed its wispy tail right over, the Judean stable. It is distasteful to be called upon to emphasize the degree of mental folly necessary to hypostatize such stupidities, yet the consequences have been so fatal that a final satirical treatment seems called for. The astronomers and divines who are heedless enough to permit their names to go under these wild conjectures to keep the credulous in line with "the sacred story," seem to imagine that if they succeed in putting some unusual luminary in the sky about the year one, they have adequately explained the legend of the star, and thus substantiated Biblical prestige. It is not enough merely to have accounted for a star in the heavens; it must be brought down to earth and made to hover motionless over the cave in Bethlehem! For Matthew says that "it came and stood over where the young child was." Imagine a cluster of five or six of our planets, including Jupiter, which is many times the size of our earth, hanging on the outskirts of Bethlehem villages and pointing to the stable! No astronomer that ever lived knows anything about a star that came within a hundred feet of the earth and stood still there. No star ever known has "stood" anywhere, since all are rushing at invariable speed along an orbit. Again, the diameter of a star that could point to a single building of tiny dimensions in a village could not be twenty to thirty feet at most. The tiniest of the asteroids has a diameter of some five miles. The only sizable star left that might fulfill the conditions is a meteor, but no meteor ever led travelers patiently across a desert and then stood still over a village. As an actual phenomenon, the "star of Bethlehem" is the most childish absurdity ever perpetrated by unscrupulous priestcraft upon religiously derationalized humans.

But the story is not only inherently preposterous; it holds a self-contradiction as well. An amazing and, to the orthodox view, most disconcerting fact comes to light in an observation that reveals absolute contradiction between the conventional legend and the Gospel text. The legend universally has it that Balthasar, Gaspar and Melchior, the "three Kings of Orient," were Magian astrologers from Persia or Chaldea, who by stellar or other forecast divined the date of the Messianic birth. Under the spur of news of such aeonial magnitude, they made the camel journey across the Arabian desert to greet the divine Messenger in Judea. According to the best geographies it is safe to say that this is going west on the map. So the Magi traveled west. But the Gospel story does not agree. It says they traveled east! For when they came to Herod and informed him of the purpose of their visit, and frightened him with their oracular prophecy that the new-born king would unseat him from his throne, they said: "We have seen his star in the east, and are come to worship him." The star that appeared and led them till it stood over the birthplace was seen "in the east." The "dodge" out of this predicament will probably be the reminder that all stars rise in the east and then "travel" west. The text says nothing to this effect. The plain implications of the language of the Gospel is that the wise men saw the star in the east and therefore went there, i.e., to the east, where it indicated the locality of the Savior's birth. But popular legend takes them westward. Something is indeed wrong with this picture.

Mention of these tangled absurdities was made a few years ago to the leading Episcopalian clergyman in Boston. With Christmas approaching he introduced matter from the discussion into his next two Sunday sermons, saying it was obvious that Christians would have to give up the assumed historicity of this aspect of the Nativity story, and regard it all as a beautiful allegory. The moral of the incident – and it is a weightier moral than appears on the surface – lies in the fact that this splendid and liberal divine had never before sensed the realistic impossibilities of the star's role in the Gospel "history." The moral grew still heavier when it appeared likely that neither had any other minister thought it through. That so superficially glaring a knot of inconsistencies and physical absurdities should never have been noticed and commonly taken into account speaks loudly as to the mental narcotization of the votaries of a religion of blind faith. And the matter takes on still a graver import when it is considered that a hundred other constructions in both Old and New Testaments can similarly be reduced to nonsensical rubbish by the simple process of imaginatively actualizing what is described as taking place. The story of the Exodus of the Israelites from Egypt makes particularly diverting "comic strip" when the details as narrated in holy writ are realistically reconstructed. Joseph Wheless has obligingly done this for us in his Is It God's Word?

The purpose here is not primarily interpretative, but the challenge will come to us to produce a rational meaning for the star allegory if it was not a factual verity. It will carry some credence for the denial if it can be shown that it has another meaning on the esoteric side that is both clear and acceptable to reason. The explanation is not difficult. It is simple enough to anyone who has become familiar with ancient Egyptian symbology. One of the most patent emblems by which the Egyptians typified the soul as a nucleus of intellectual "fire" was the star, and the evolutionary descent of the soul into matter, typified as earth and water, was allegorized as the sinking of a star into the earth or ocean with the rotation of the globe. Soul and star unite in meaning in the Egyptian word Seb, says Massey. And souls, like the stars, sank periodically into the domain of matter. A star falling or sinking below the horizon was the typograph of a soul going down into incarnation in the earth, or into the earthy and watery elements of the body. The "west" was therefore the typical "region" where souls went to their "death," or semi-dead condition of existence under the limitations of matter, in which state they gained a new life, were reborn at Christmas and finally resurrected at Easter. The soul that, as a star, had sunk into flesh "on the western horizon of the sky," rose in its new birth or liberation "on the eastern side of heaven." Or, putting it a bit differently, the soul that as the aged one of a previous incarnational cycle, descended anew into matter and body to be regenerated after "death" and to be reborn as its own son, would show the light of its star rising in the east. The birth of the Christos then was the emergence above the eastern horizon of the new Adam resurrected out of the dying embers of the old. The advent of the Christ principle in man was therefore mythically embellished by the legend of the star of soul rising in the east. It was an integral part of the Egyptian and other dramatizations of the divine Nativity.

The three Wise Men, rather the three Kings of Wisdom, who attend the appearance of the star are none other than the three differentiations of the "star" or soul itself, the three aspects or rays into which it breaks its primal unity when it comes to organic manifestation in and through a body or instrument. Naturally they would appear when the "star" of soul has its birth in the east, as they are its own three aspects raying forth, and they must come with the star. This illumination of the mind with the true sense of a beautiful allegory is worth more than a hundred volumes of silly speculation in the effort to make the "history" of the Jesus life stand up in the face of obvious irrationality. It is a wholesome relief to know that it is allegory, and to know also that one's faith and religion do not have to be supported any longer on the unstable foundation of the star's claimed factuality. The star must be believed if the personal Jesus is to be accepted. Rejected as preposterous on factual ground, the star can still become a virile aid to spiritual realization if the

Jesus story also is taken as the dramatization of wondrous truth. The drama, more potently than the "history," was to impress this indefeasible veritude upon the early life of humanity. It represents the genius of the whole ancient literature, which has been woefully misread because this fundamentum was ignored.

Less allegorical but equally fictitious must have been that other item of Nativity accompaniment which is introduced in order to account for the parents' visit to the village of Bethlehem, through which new scriptures were to be made to fulfill "prophecies" in old ones. This was the alleged decree of Caesar Augustus "that all the world should be taxed." The first thought that occurs – to a politician, at least – is that the Romans must have been slow to rise to their lush opportunities for income if the idea of a tax had not occurred to them before this! The student of Roman history is pretty well assured that the Imperial government had not been unduly neglected of the taxing prerogative of a conquering nation at any time in the Republic's or the Empire's period. But the sum and substance of the story of the Augustus tax is that there is no official Roman government record of this world-wide levy anywhere extant or ever known. And the records were well kept at this epoch. The declaration has been thundered forth from a million pulpits that the Gospel story of the Christ stands accredited by facts of authentic history. Here is one of the most salient of such facts, and it is found to be no fact of history at all. It is more fictitious than any myth. It is untrue, whereas a myth is brimming with (hidden) truth.

It would not be difficult to amass a great amount of authors' data to support the claim as to the fictional nature of this tax and the Cyrenian (Quirinian) census preparatory to it. But an authority lies at hand that will be used extensively in this section of the study, and it is desirable to summon the witness of a defender of the historical point of view to our side of the discussion. This particular authority can well be used as representative and typical of hundreds of others, which can not all be brought forward in evidence. It has been selected out of scores of "Lives of Jesus" because its handling of many items in the "life" of the subject is fairer than usual to the realistic or concrete view, and less haloed with mystic romanticism. The work is The Historical Life of Christ, by Joseph Warschauer, an eminent European scholar. In the Preface the author aims to embody in his work the method and theories of another leading European student, Albert Schweitzer, who in turn has stated that the ideal "Life" of Christ would be one that H. J. Holtzmann did not write, but should have written. The Warschauer book, therefore, may be taken as the mouthpiece of a "school" of orthodox thought in Christianity, confessedly modernistic and liberal, and certainly highly influential in shaping and formulating present Christian attitudes. It must be kept in mind throughout that his book is building the case for the historicity of Jesus.

This writer, then, is quite frank in admitting that the total silence of history concerning the tax and census in the reign of Augustus makes such an event highly improbable. He admits the 4 B.C. date of Herod's death and rightly says that the census would not likely have been taken in his reign by any Roman authority, since Herod was an independent ruler and an ally of Rome. A "first census" was apparently taken about A.D. 6, after the deposition of Herod's successor Archelaus, when Judea became part of the Roman province of Syria, under Cyrenius (Quirinus). This "governor in Syria" mentioned in the Gospel as in office when the Bethlehem birth occurred, is placed as early as 13-11 B.C. This dating would change and disarrange whole blocks and chains of evidence laboriously assembled. Warschauer concedes that if the date of Quirinus was earlier (than 4 B.C.), the census could not have been conducted under his supervision. For the census over which Quirinus did preside was carried out in A.D. 7 and caused the popular revolt alluded to in Acts 5:37, for the reason that it was the first time that the Jews had been thus levied upon. And, Warschauer adds, Joseph was a subject of the tetrarch Antipas and not liable to Roman taxation! Not only that, but the issuance of such an order would have entailed almost a miniature migration of inhabitants, an unlikely act of the Roman power. And finally, he adds, even if Joseph's journey to his ancestral city can be explained over these difficulties, no unprejudiced mind would believe that he would have taken with him his wife in her then physical condition. There is no real or plausible reason for the trip, he asserts, beyond the literary or legendary necessity of having the Messiah born in Bethlehem. He even most truly concludes that Luke's attempt to link the birth of Jesus with Bethlehem must be regarded as unsuccessful. Yet what must be considered most remarkable in this connection is that Warschauer's own correct vision of the non-historicity of this (and scores of other) events in the detail of Jesus' "life" builds no grave doubt in his mind as to the historicity of the whole structure. Childhood indoctrination and traditional prepossession will not yield even to the forthright evidence of massed opposing data. Jesus must be kept alive in spite of mountainous evidence.

He is entirely convinced, however, of the preposterousness of the star's going ahead of a group of travelers and resting over a house in a village, saying it belongs to poetry and not to history. Yet again he gathers no hint from all this that the entire story of the Gospels might with as sound reason be consigned to the domain of (spiritual) poetry, and dropped as history. The ingenious explanation of the presence of an enormous percentage of poetry masquerading as history in the Gospel narrative is the time-worn claim that in lack of more than the most meager substratum of real data about the real Jesus, the poetry crept in and was incorporated through the, as he avers, particular proclivity of the first and second centuries toward indulging "popular legend." Just as the Norse elements of the pine tree, mistletoe, Yule log, holly, and other symbolisms crept into later Christianity, so elements of Greek and other mythologies became interwoven into the actual background of Jesus-fact. One wonders how long it will be ere the minds that go so far toward the truth, will not go the few additional steps to the goal of the full truth – that, far more than were the first and second centuries, the entire ancient period was transfused with the spirit of poetic and mythic representation of wisdom, and that the entire Gospel content was a formulation of this nature, and of immemorial antiquity. And it must be asked, since the apologists cling to the legend of much poetry clustering around some solid data, what and where and how many are those data, that stand as the rock of fact to which the barnacles of popular fancy have clung. Let Warschauer himself supply this interesting answer on almost his first page: he says that of this historical personage, to whom oceans of pious devotion have been poured out and to whom men of every age have turned as the revelation of God, we must say that we know next to nothing! A work to prove the historical life of Jesus begins with this admission. But, this is no deterrent to zeal; in fact, it serves the immediate purpose of enabling him to say in the same breath that since we know next to nothing about this extraordinary personage, we therefore know everything! This well matches its companion gem of Christian logic, the averment of Tertullian that the bases of Christianity were credible because they were impossible. This proves something else not so creditable to Christianity – that when once the mind is committed to fanatical obsession, an element contrary to reason becomes the gauge and standard of proof.

And what is the logic that builds up the astonishing conclusion that we know everything about Jesus because we know nothing? The piously sophistical answer is that Jesus' mind and character have stamped themselves ineffaceably upon the consciousness of the race. We know him to have been the kind of man he was because of the kind of impression he has made upon us. We know him, as it were, by his psychological fruits in our lives. Again, this is an argument for the psychological efficacy of some exalted paragon, some hypostatized ideal, and as Warschauer admits, the ideal was presented to Christian adoration on little or no basis of actual knowledge whatever. This whole situation is covered by the statement that an ideal stereotype, the alleged historical Jesus, was held before the Christian imagination for centuries and naturally produced a psychological reaction consonant with the character of the figure presented. The psychological effect says nothing whatever either as to the historicity of the ideal personage or as to our definite knowledge about him. Once the paragon was dangled before the devotees, the psychological effect would be registered whether he lived to our definite knowledge or not. Beyond all refutation Mithra, Bacchus, Sabazius, Hercules, Izdubar, Marduk and Horus, as types and ideals of divine qualities, had also stamped the mind and character of ancient civilizations with their excellence. Yet they were not living persons; no one has even a little knowledge of their life histories. Portia,

Hamlet, Othello, Tiny Tim and Cinderella have stamped much noble imagery into the life, mind and character of millions, and are not historical. Writers like Warschauer pooh-pooh the claims of a mythical foundation for Gospel writing. Yet, when their own admissions of the elements of impossibility, improbability, poetry and legend that were interpolated into the meager quantity of material that alone stands as the history of divinity on earth are added up, there is so little left of credible solid fact that it is indeed they who are basing a Gospel upon purely mythical grounds! What is the "historical life of Christ" but a myth if its historian is compelled to start out with the concession that almost nothing is known about his subject? It is far better to work with a myth that is true in the mythical manner, than to deal with a myth that pretends to be history, but is not. The first will at least not deceive you; the second will both deceive and delude. Advocates of the historicity found their structure of religion squarely on myth, and the deadly, not the sustaining, kind. The edifice of historical Christianity is founded on a reputed base of fact which can be made to stand up only by the endless resort to guess, conjecture, surmise, supposition, strained probability, the unbelievable proportion of which in the works of the apologists can only be hinted at here, and the total weakness of which can be realized only by the reading of scores of volumes that labor at the task of upholding the historical thesis. Indeed the surest way to enhance a doubt as to the existence of the living Jesus is to read enough books that essay to prove it. The instability of the groundwork on which it rests will be more sharply accentuated with each new reading.

Other features of the Nativity story engage attention. Warschauer almost puts the case irrevocably in our hands when he says that there is indeed hardly a single statement among those in which Luke tells us of the Bethlehem birth that can survive dispassionate scrutiny. He deals frankly with the Matthew-Luke flat contradictions as to the Bethlehem-Nazareth birth and residence problem. Matthew represents Bethlehem as the birthplace of Jesus, and Nazareth as the adopted home of Mary and Joseph. But Luke has them residing in Nazareth before the birth of Jesus. Matthew brings the holy family from Bethlehem to Nazareth, while Luke moves the parents from Nazareth to Bethlehem. Matthew says nothing of the journey and enrollment. Luke is silent about the Herod plot and the flight into Egypt, and has nothing concerning the three Magi, or their star, or the massacre of the babes. Warschauer resolves the contradictions and discrepancies on the theory that we are dealing with two traditions which can not be harmonized. He does not know that the solution of the numerous Gospel contradictions must be sought further back than two opposing traditions. Nor does he explain how two irreconcilable traditions arose out of one original tradition. He does not know that there were more than two divergent versions of most legendary material and that the mythical representations of many aspects of the human-divine allegory branched off from one original formulation into many variations and recensions, in the same way as, supposedly, did language from one primal stock. Some of the variants can be attributed to copyists' errors; others no doubt to scribal corrections, emendations, interpolations and forgery.

He notices the Slaughter of the Innocents and very justly equates it with a great diversity of Greek, Persian and Syrian "popular legend," in which kings were divinely warned of danger from their own infant sons. Yet it is to be assumed that Warschauer would protest the conclusion which a student of comparative religion would feel legitimately qualified to establish from these premises, that the Herod slaughter was itself derived from this common stock of pervading myth. It is time to remark here that the great – the inestimably great – service which Lord Raglan's work, The Hero, has performed in clearing up the status of all this type of speculation is in the fact that it establishes, for the edification of these Bible analyzers and for all understanding, the truth that what they term "popular" legend and thus by a mere name brush aside as of no intrinsic import, was not the upgrowth of popular fancy and therefore mere superstition of the folk sort, but is all traceable to the one primal religious ritual-drama, to which must be assigned an authorship of truly Olympian sapiency. If it can ever be driven home to the seat of theological intelligence that the whole Christian Bible is just a somewhat specialized collection of the same stories, myths and allegories as constituted the mythical aggregations of Greece and other countries, it will mark the day-break of the new and true light on Biblical exegesis.

The role of the shepherds in the fields by night, the blinding flood of light, the celestial heralding of the advent, the proclamation of the glad tidings of great joy, are all likewise found by Warschauer to parallel similar features of the Mithra, the Dionysus, even the Augustus cycles of legends. The flight into Egypt is seen to be matched by a similar episode in several mythological quarters. The "stable" is admitted to be a "cave" in second century stories. The great Christian doctrine of the virgin birth is treated with sanity, as being akin to a series of divine progenations of both Greek and Old Testament heroes. In the Hebrew scriptures we have stories of the "wondrous births" in connection with Isaac, Samson and Samuel. The Talmudic Moses has a virgin mother; Samuel's mother became pregnant after receiving divine seed; Zipporah was found by Moses pregnant, but by no mortal man. Tamar became pregnant by an infusion of divine seed and Isaac was not the result of generation, but of the shaping of the unbegotten. On the Greek side not only were the heroes of legend, Herakles, Theseus, Perseus, Jason and others believed to be the sons of divine fathers and human mothers, but the same legend reached down even to historical figures like Pythagoras and Plato, both of whom were "Sons of Apollo," the first by Parthenis – which Warschauer remarks sounds most intriguingly suggestive of parthenogenesis, or "virgin birth," – the second by Periktione. It ought to be observed that the clue here noticed by Warschauer is fundamentally of far more significance in pointing the way to the truth than volumes of the blind speculation indulged in by students who flout the claims for the mythical origin of Bible material.

One encounters the frequent assertion that the Christians adopted many pagan myths and brought them from meaningless superstition to relevant intelligibility by weaving into them a new and worthy meaning. With an appearance of plausibility in a few cases, this ruse has been employed in many books as one of the numberless big and little sophistries that have served to maintain the legend of Christian superiority and pagan depravity. Needless to say, this is not true. Indeed the true lies the other way around. It was the exoteric folly of Christians that took the many high typifications of spiritual and cosmic knowledge and warped them out of all semblance of any truth, either esoteric or exoteric. Warschauer indulges in this unworthy subterfuge in several instances.

Short shrift is made of the genealogies by this author. First the difference between the two lists as given by Matthew and Luke is noted. They are hopelessly irreconcilable, he agrees. Then the inevitable necessity of the Messiah's being proclaimed as of King David's line, in order that "prophecy" might again be fulfilled, is set forth. He must be of Davidic descent and of Bethlehem birth. But the notable feature of the genealogies, in Warschauer's estimation, is the fact that both lists trace the Davidic descent through the mother's husband, who was not Jesus' father, but was only his foster-father. (Massey shows the identity of Joseph's role in the Gospels with that of the Egyptian Seb (Keb, Geb), the god of earth, who, though not the planter of the divine seed from which the Son of God sprang, yet nourished and nurtured him from birth onward.) The genealogies are included, he assumes, for the express purpose of establishing that Joseph was of David's house and lineage. But the whole force of the set-up evaporates the moment the Holy Spirit steps in to usurp the function of human fatherhood. Christian poverty and pagan sufficiency are here seen in glaring contrast, for resort must be had to pre-Christian systems to catch the splendid hidden meaning of this cryptic situation – which was adopted by Christianity from pagan usage, but with interior meaning lost. To be sure, no power can implant the seed of divine sonship save the Holy Spirit, which is the Mind or Logos of God injected into the womb of matter, the Mother. Nothing but spirit can fecundate matter, to make it reproductive of new birth. No mere earthly parent could stand in the allegory as the divine father of the Christ. But once the seed is implanted and the matter-mother impregnated with the divine spark, then the earthly father can assume his role of rearer and protector of the divine-human child. After centuries of abuse of paganism, Christianity must now in humility turn to that despised source to learn for the first time the true meaning of its own elements. But Warschauer is quite fair and concise on this point. He says the genealogies are worthless, and ends by saying that had either Evangelist wished to prove the view of the Lord's birth that afterwards became dominant, he would have given Mary's and not Joseph's line of ancestry. For if the genealogies prove anything, it is that Jesus was not of David's line, as the Davidic descendant, Joseph, was not his father.

Yet again the obduracy of orthodox obsessions shows its hand in Warschauer's assertion that the genealogies do not disprove the Lord's Davidic descent. This once more is a sample of the inveterate arguing backwards, or sheer turning of "no" into "yes," to which resort such apologists have been so often forced that it has become an addiction.

The "flight into Egypt" is a vivid example of how a feature of ancient Egyptian representation of lofty cosmic and creative procedure came into Christianity in the merest fragmentary form. The full elucidation of the grand sweep of the meaning back of this allegorism has been made in the companion work to this, The Lost Light. But in the mighty Kamite system the flight into Egypt is the glyph for the descent of the hosts of embryo souls from celestial spheres into incarnation on earth. There is no disputing this rendering; "Egypt" clearly is the type-name for earth and body, or matter. It is a main item in Egyptian systematism, whereas in the Christian scheme it becomes a mere incident along the way, and is no essential part of the story.

It would be delightful to consider a paragraph on page 19 of Warschauer's work. It details the pageantry attendant upon the Savior's birth, – the Holy Child laid in the manger, the shepherds with their flocks by night, the angel's appearance to announce the birth, the heavenly choir chanting their carol of glory to God and peace on earth, and the halo of holy thrill around the entire event. And he rightly says that in the whole of literature there is no more exquisite idyll than this. Even with the limitation of its meaning to the sheer event of one babe's birth, it is so vibrant with imaginative glamor that its inherent beauty touches the aesthetic susceptibilities of all. But perhaps the world is not yet ready to agree with a lone voice, when it asserts that even this impressiveness is raised to a pitch of psychological intensity that is quite ineffable and cathartic beyond anything ever dreamed of, when a mind at last knows that the paean and halo are types and touches of a veritable rapture of adoration paid to the birth of Christ-love in all men.

What seems difficult to tell an age that has never learned to go beneath or behind the symbol to verity is that exotericism ends with the beauty of the symbol, whilst esotericism only begins with the symbol and goes on from it to the undreamed-of wealth of a whole new world of revelation. The symbol serves but to touch off the release of a flood of luminous conceptions, which would never leap into organic and meaningful array until marshaled into relationship by the magic of the symbol's suggestiveness. Thousands of pulpits yearly resound with the sentiment that the vital significance of the Christmas festival lies in the stimulus it furnishes all celebrants to press on to bring to birth the Christ within themselves. This is commendable and good; but with the alleged historic reality of the Bethlehem scene engrossing so much of interest and attention, the detached aim has little chance to swing clear and sweep to more than touching sentimentalism. The vigorous force of a symbol or drama is caught in full when the meanings and intimations adumbrated by it can be carried away from the starting point and applied in the deep regions of personal consciousness. This transfer can be effected all the more smoothly for the very fact that the symbol or drama is itself known to be pure fiction. When, however, that which should be mere meaning-vane is alleged to be itself the event about which meaning is to center, itself the thing to which the meaning points, instead of being merely the pointer to a meaning higher and deeper, the native strong force of symbol and drama is choked in its cradle, so to speak. The alleged historicity of the cycle of Christmas pageantry ties the significance of the festival too close to itself. The meaning can not escape its own symbols and fly with main force into the hearts and minds it should be elevating. So long as the historicity clings and the Christmas festival purports to be the anniversary celebration of the physical birth of a human babe, the wings of the spiritual effort to transfer the meaning from the alleged event over to personal beatification of character are clipped, and the designed cathartic purification and exaltation of the human spirit is thwarted. Instead of sweeping into the mind and heart, the cleansing fire of the great Yule ceremony flows back into the symbol and ends there. As the result of the third-century debacle of esoteric wisdom, therefore, the millions in Christendom continue to celebrate their great solstitial festival without any competent realization of its full import and without ever experiencing anything of the divinely potent theurgy which the symbolical dramatization of the Christ-birth in all men was anciently designed to effectuate.

To stay with the symbol and pageantry and not go beyond them was the crime of Christianity. To stay with the symbol was to cut off the soul and mind from the possibility of their soaring aloft into the highest of their capabilities of rapport and rapture. With symbolism a dead language and a lost art for many centuries, culture in Christendom has been forced to limp on as best it could without the uplifting and sustaining power generated by a true science of symbolic drama. What is here discussed is something that was known to the ancient theurgists, lost in all the intervening time, and not safely recovered as yet. To see truth through the lens of a natural symbol was a consummate attainment of the ancient Egyptians, and is hardly even surmised today. To begin to apprehend something of its potency one must have lived and dreamed with symbols for some years. It is an experience that wholly transcends the power of language to depict its gripping efficacy and beauty. From this point of view it can be said that the full release of the hidden majesty and grandeur of the Nativity pageantry – that aspect of Yuletide festivity that Warschauer termed a "poetic idyll" – is only possible when at last the mind knows of a certainty that the idyll is purely poetry and not history. The tragedy is that so few can go beyond the symbol to the deeper plummeting. Erroneous tradition presses so heavily in upon them that they are afraid to let go of the symbol as fact itself and reach for the wondrous grace of the miracle of meaning beyond it. The legend of the historicity has atrophied the cultural capacity to catch what the event meant as symbol. There must first, of course, be some clear intellectual perception of what the pageantry and symbolical embellishment stood for, which is mostly as yet a secret of the ancient Egyptians. This itself constitutes a revelation beyond the belief of anyone who has not had the good fortune to discover it. The poverty of intellectual illumination and psychological afflatus to which the Christian literalization of arcane science has reduced us will be known only when the transcendent sublimity of the Christmas pageantry as an exquisite dramatic idyll is brought to realization again through the recovery of symbolic genius. That genius has mastered the art of employing an appropriate symbol as a lens to magnify the truth seen through it. The highest adroitness and skill in the usage consisted in keeping the symbol diaphanous, the lens transparent, so that it never distorted, obscured or shut out the object from view. This is just what Christianity did not do with ancient symbols. Its sin was to render them all concrete and opaque! Looking at the symbol, it sees that, but nothing beyond. The ancient world used symbols, allegories, dramas, because it knew how to keep them clear and translucent. No thought of history obtruded to congeal the translucency of pure emblemism into opaqueness. The symbol was an unobstructed pathway for the passage of the light.

It must be reiterated, then, as the summit truth in all this, that the Nativity idyll is, as idyll, as poetry, as luminous, gripping myth of truth in all its purifying power, far more potent for the beautification of the mind and the life than ever it can be as event. This is not treason to Christianity, but the uttermost loyalty to the more enlightened Christianity, it is so only to that hybrid pseudo-Christianity which exoteric blindness brought into existence after the third century. It never can be treason to the Christianity of the Christos.

The dynamic power of symbol and typology apostrophized in the foregoing elucidation finds powerful reinforcement in the inceptive revival of a science that is only now beginning to be formulated by modern insight, but which must have been well understood and exercised by the more learned and intelligent ancient esotericists, – the science of symbolism. It is finding its modern reincarnation in the new science of semantics, the meanings of signs. It is a really momentous denouement for the modern world and promises to put the mind of the race back in more harmonious rapport with the enlightened mentality of the early sages, whose view swept over the field of truth in comprehensive scope and crystal perspicacity. Likewise it will go far to restore to thought the great fundamental principle of knowledge which was particularly central in the philosophy of Spinoza, – that the order and structure of man's mind is harmonious with the order and structure of nature. Symbolism alone reveals this harmony. As yet, however, the modern approach along this avenue of illumination is hesitant and tentative. The ancients clearly had a deeper grasp on what might be called a psychic luminosity of apperception, which was generated by and supervened upon the constant habit of reflecting upon natural symbols until hidden harmonies of meaning and the identity of structure between thought-form and nature-form burst upon inner vision. High thought in both the Pythagorean and the Platonic schools asserted that the contemplation of mathematical truth was the mind's path of closest approach to deity. It seems likely that for the sapient Egyptians the highest path was considered to be the contemplation of natural symbols. It is evident that they regarded the forms and phenomena of nature as the living shapes of truth, structuralizing in material concreteness the unseen but concordant structure of archetypal forms in the noumenal world. With sonorous voice Emerson proclaims that the world of nature is the mirror of God's thought and the visible things are his ideas crystallized in matter. He, then, who can discern the Logos of divine mind shining through the concrete forms of nature, becomes the priest of God, says Emerson. He interprets God's language and reads the Word printed on the pages of the open book of nature. The Egyptians used the phenomena of nature as the glass by which the meanings of the creation were made clear and large. No one will have a basic understanding of the relation of soul to body until he grasps the essential facets of the relation between seed and soil, for the two are homologous. A hundred aspects of spiritual verity likewise come into lucid comprehension when viewed through the lens of natural analogy. Perhaps a much further recovery of this lost science of seeing through nature's eyes is necessary before the fullest implications of the chief theses of this work can be grasped.

Some further comment is needed on Warschauer's statement that the Christmas scenario is poetry of the deepest charm and that only a pedant would try either to prove or disprove what is so plainly the work of devout and tender imagination. But it is certainly legitimate to ask such a writer by what right he can pick and choose, out of a given body of what he himself designates as idyllic poetry, certain portions to be labeled poetry, while reserving other portions to be regarded as actual event. He merely assumes that a central event – the birth – occurred in fact, and then proceeds to classify almost the whole of the accompanying detail as poetic embellishment, clearly not history. On what ground does he dodge the inherent presumption that if the large body of concomitant detail is idyllic fiction and adornment, the central event, or the whole of the construction, may be equally embellishment? It has not seemed to occur to expounders in this field that if so large a series of alleged episodes in the "life" of their subject is proven to be work of the decorative imagination, there might be at least a presumptive possibility that the whole construction may be accounted for on the same basis. And one may legitimately ask also why so much respectful indulgence can be conceded to the play of devout and tender imagination in the formulation of Christian presentations, while the meed of respect for the same imagination when used by the ancient sages to portray the spiritual truths of religion is so churlishly denied. It is the contention here that the entire body of archaic sacred literature, the whole construct of mythology and the great universal ritual-drama that so definitely set the form of religious ceremonial the world over, were all the work not only of devout and tender imagination, but also of a consummate artistry and a genius for the pictorialization of supernal truth and wisdom unparalleled elsewhere in human history. That not only the fringe and the hem of the garment of ancient biblical literature, but the entire garment was a work of this consecrated embroidery, is the thing that seems so difficult for modern scholastic insight to recognize. Warschauer has gone a little way toward recognition of the pivotal truth when he removes a considerable segment of alleged Gospel history from the pale of heretofore claimed factuality, and he ennobles this portion with the dignity of sanctified mythicism. But when will insight go the whole way and see at last that the entirety of the ancient religious literary product is of the same stamp and mold?

Next to be noticed is Warschauer's mention of the circumstance that Luke has no reference to the flight into Egypt. Instead, the parents go openly to Jerusalem, without fear of the threat from Herod, to present the child in the temple and offer sacrifice. Warschauer thinks it doubtful that every infant born in a Jewish household had to be presented in Jerusalem. It could not be carried out in all cases at any rate. But the presentation in this case is made the peg on which to hang the episode of Simeon and Anna in the narrative, which attests the Lord's mission as Savior of Israel. But even these incidents in the temple, Warschauer admits, are not records of fact, but are introduced to emphasize the element of Messianic expectancy then so widely extant. He even notes that the "marvel" of Joseph and Mary at Simeon's rapturous declarations is hardly natural after Mary had herself heard the annunciation of her divine motherhood from Gabriel.

It is a mite disconcerting to find Luke, after all, accrediting the babe's natural paternity to Joseph. The Gospels thus contrive in the end to give Jesus two fathers, if not three, God, the Holy Ghost and Joseph. On the historical thesis this reduces to absurdity. It can be resolved into comprehensible meaning only by resort to ancient subtlety and deeper understanding. Warschauer's version of explanation is that while Jesus was the natural child of Mary and Joseph, his divine paternity as the only begotten Son of God was insinuated into the narrative to meet and fulfill the age's current prepossession with the earthly advent of a divine Avatar. He even asserts that the element of the virgin birth is a foreign importation. But in this sense it can be asked what element in Christianity is not of "foreign" origination. There is not a single doctrine or ceremonial of Christian theology and worship that has not been drawn from antecedent pagan religions.

Warschauer is driven to the extremity of falling back upon a claim of textual tampering to account for the injecting of the supernatural fatherhood into the story, when both Matthew's and Luke's intent was so obviously to regard Joseph as the begetter of Jesus. Incidentally he alludes to the undeniable fact that the text of the Gospel underwent some manipulation in the interest of dogma. A fact which is so generally hushed up, is thus made use of when it can prove a very present help in exegesis.

One paragraph on page 26 of Warschauer's book is worthy of being transcribed verbatim. It is again a glowing instance of an argument that can be turned against the very point it is aimed to establish. It practically concedes the case for the opposition. Having yielded so much of the history to legend and poetry, he is forced to uphold the importance of these in the Nativity story. So he says that even if so much of the detail is only legendary embellishment, by which admission he robs the birth of all its supernatural staging, we must not therefore conclude, he insists, that the legends are worthless. The discovery of the non-historical character of a narrative does not require us to throw the whole thing on the rubbish heap, or to conclude that we have exposed the whole account as another literary hoax. We have to see what the legend means in connection with the story. And tracing its origin as far as we can into hidden springs, we may have to assign to it a very high significance and treat it as authentic contribution to the final message which it adorns. The legends are not history, but they are added to the modicum of history as a natural effort to testify to the divinely transcendent and really superhuman quality of the main event. To portray in some manner adequately the ineffable splendor of the Messianic advent the writers had to fall back on legends of supernal suggestiveness.

It is assuredly a strange circumstance that puts into the mouth of a writer who is conducting the case for the historicity the identical estimate of the value of myth that has here been used to dispute the historicity. It was hardly to be expected that our dissertation on the exalted function and value of the myth would have received so unequivocal a seconding from an opponent of our position. It really concedes everything to this side, if only its just implications are followed out. But who is it that has decried mythology and thrown on the ash-pile the whole marvelous structure of ancient mythicism? It is the Christian party. It is bad grace and an unfair fight to emphasize the value of myth in a carefully circumscribed sphere, where its usual condemnation would have endangered a large segment of the purported history of the Christ, and at the same time applaud its derogation in the large and everywhere else. That the value of the myth is supreme in the whole ancient field, and that the Christian habit of belittling it is a heinous error of vast proportions, is close to the nub of the entire debate. It is we who are arguing that the Gospel story is not to be cast out as rubbish just because it is myth. Warschauer will applaud legend in a minor province and as far as it can be useful to his purposes, but he is not sure enough of the universal value of myth to commit the entire Gospel story to that category and expect it to retain supreme value. The history or a modicum of it must be held on to as the irreducible solid rock of fact to rest the foundation of Christianity upon. A little fringe of the story – and it becomes a dangerously large one in the total – can be yielded over to myth; and while myth is thus sheltering a segment of the sacred canonical literature, it must be hoisted in importance, to uphold and not disqualify the history. That the ancients knew the ultimate value of the myth and were willing to let go all history for it, basing their solid foundations on the truth behind the myth, which was in the finale the gist of all history, the Christian scholar has never yet seen. All final true grounding of his studies yet awaits his coming to this perception.

The legend which reported that the name "Jesus" had been chosen for the new Messiah before he was conceived is granted Warschauer's half-cynical indulgence as a concession to the poetizing instinct. He gives the name "Joshua," the equivalent of Jesus, as meaning "God's help." It is not the place to enter into philological controversy; but that the root of the many variants of the name "Jesus" traces back to Egyptian origin and has a far profounder etymological significance than "God's help" is known to many.

Warschauer represents Jesus as a Jew from the start, well versed in Hebrew scriptures, brilliant and skilled in exposition, defense and attack. Just how a still-young carpenter could have gained this literary and intellectual training, reached generally only by long schooling crowned with university courses – and years of teaching – without any known education, deponent sayeth not. The synagogue is one source suggested, and it could be assumed that he had some schooling or special rabbinical instruction.

Of his growth and development nothing is known, Warschauer admits. Yet that nothing is better than the grotesque tales of his childhood found in some spurious gospels, which are plainly clumsy inventions. The one item recorded – the Passover visit to Jerusalem at the age of twelve, and his tilt with the temple doctors – may be fact, thinks Warschauer; but he regards it as highly unlikely that his parents would have gone three days on the homeward journey before they missed him! That Jesus lost himself (for three days?) in his absorption in the debate and forgot to join the caravan is accepted by Warschauer as credible enough to permit the incident to stand on historical footing! On such feeble bases rests much of the main temple of Christianity.

Our authority is frank in adducing data that militate against the thesis he aims to uphold. He reveals that Luke's narrative of the nativity of John the Baptist is modeled on Old Testament prototypes of famous and wondrous births. This story includes the central mythological element of a conception and birth from the womb of a mother past nature bearing age. This is of course pure allegory and only to be understood with reference to ancient theogonies. Sarah and Hannah are earlier prototypes of the same imagery. The mother is nature, and the natural order only in its great age – after millions of years of evolutionary development – produced man and his brain in which to bring the Christ child to functioning. Other identities with previous births are cited. So Warschauer admits that such a striking literary copying would of itself justify full doubt as to the historical character of any account so evidently constructed upon former models. But why will he not see that this frank admission and discerning observation holds with exactly the same force and relevance when extended to embrace the whole and not merely minor features of the Jesus birth and the Gospel set-up? Not only the birth of John the Baptist, but the entire body of Gospel occurrence can be just as completely matched by earlier figurations of sage dramatic genius, – and all of it mythological! What would amaze Warschauer, surely, is the extent to which correspondence, similarity, identity, between Christian material and pre-Christian mythology runs. Had he devoted the same zeal to the pursuit of such a comparison as he has done to sifting Gospel data, he would have realized that he is not warranted in clipping off merely a thin fringe of detail from the Gospel body, surrendering it to myth, while retaining the main bulk as history, but that he would have to resign it all to be catalogued as pagan dramatism. To his surprise and perhaps dismay he would have found with sufficient study that such parallels as he has detected in one case run consistently throughout the entire structure. If he can concede truly that identity with antecedent non-Christian mythical material invalidates the historicity of some portions of Gospel matter, then the invalidation extends over the whole of the ground and not only claims a margin. Conceivably he would dispute this as an arrant claim that could not be substantiated. The answer is that the all-sufficient evidence exists, and many who have examined it attest its adequacy. Its potent relevance, however, can not be seen until it is examined. At any rate it is a pleasure to cite Warschauer's open admission that Luke's wonder-tale of angelic apparitions, child-birth in the mother's old age, lyrical rhapsodies, quite certainly belong to the domain of religious poetry and can not stand as fact. What he seemingly has not threshed out and can not see, is that poetry is itself one language of fact, and that the ancients in their wisdom delineated the entire range of cosmology, creative process, evolutionary pattern and lofty subjective experience by the method of myth and drama. Calamity ensued when later stupidity mistook the objective portrayals of subjective reality for the subjective portrayals of objective reality. Truth demands that Christianity recognize this and go the whole way to correct its mistake. To go part of the way is not enough. The whole truth is demanded.

The Zacharias hymn is a Messianic psalm, he rightly states. But difficulty is encountered when it is noted that the cousin relationship between Mary and Elizabeth, stated by Luke, is directly repudiated by John's Gospel. The remainder of the story, he somewhat sadly confesses, is an instance of haggada, or fanciful religious narrative that later Judaism so delighted in. The fact that Judaism was prepossessed with a flair and fancy for poetic figurism is lightly touched by Warschauer, as just an incidental circumstance that accounts for an annoying feature of the Gospel historicity that must be explained. Had he the perspicacity to concede to the fact itself – that an age of a nation's religious life was dominated by such an (to him) eccentric and irregular tendency – that poetic allegorism prevailed and predominated in Judaism at the time. And it is rather gratuitous that he limits it to this particular period. What he fails to recognize is that this tendency was part of the universal literary spirit of the whole ancient world over many centuries, and is in itself a powerful adjunct to the present contention that the whole of ancient scripture was allegorical, both in spirit and in method. His slighting treatment of this very central datum indicates a lack of perspective and understanding of the elements of his problem.

We step out of the flowery field of romantic legend over to firm ground of history in Warschauer's elucidation, only when we reach the fifteenth year of the reign of Tiberius, when John, the forerunner of the Messiah, issued the call to the age to repent in view of the imminent coming of the "Kingdom." But what evidence of factual objectivity is there in the narrative to differentiate what goes on thereafter from what had gone before? Obviously nothing more than the type of material encountered there, which is only a shade or two less romantic on the side of imagination than the more frankly mythic trimmings sewed on to the Nativity. Yet even here the expositor admits, item by item, that many occurrences connected with the story from that point onward are as obviously non-historical as the birth anecdotes. Some of these must be set down.

As early in fact as Mark's citation of Isaiah's announcement of the messengership of John, Warschauer says we are not dealing with history, but an Evangelistic attempt to match John's herald role with popular expectation. The scholar even points out to us that Mark's description of John's voice as that of one crying in the wilderness is from Isaiah (40:3) where it is not even a reference to Messiah, but to Yahweh restoring his exile-ridden people to their homeland. And he is frank to tell us that while John proclaims the nearness of the Kingdom, he does not prophesy the Messiah either in person or in spirit.

Attention needs to be called here to the misapplied usage of the word "eschatological." Warschauer uses it here in relevance to the coming of the Kingdom, which Christian theology has erroneously connected, through the misinterpretation of several scriptural passages, with the "end of the world" (itself a fatal mistranslation of the Greek for "the end of the cycle"), and the pronouncing of judgment upon all humanity in a final scene. It can be said at last that the imagery of John's language carried no such eschatological implications whatever. The coming of the Kingdom has no more extended reference than that which goes with the "Christification" of collective humanity. When the common variety of mortal men has accomplished the transfiguration of its life from animal or "Gentile" rating into the likeness of the shining radiance of spiritualized being, or the "Israelite" status, then the kingdom of heaven has materialized or "come" to earth. It is not likely that geological convulsions will have anything to do with it. Nor is it likely that the dawn of spiritual consciousness in the race as a whole will be delayed for the many millions of years the good earth has yet to run on in its course around the sun. Many righteous individuals have already brought their contribution to the kingdom of peace and good will here now. The matter makes clear how immediately dangerous the reading of the sage books of antiquity becomes the moment an objective rendering is introduced into what must be kept purely subjective to guard its sane reference. There is no history in antique books of wisdom. But the ideal patterns of all history are there. The eschatological suggestion, if it is such, embodied in John's cry for repentance goes no farther than the reference to the general cry drawn from the Mystery stage character's lines, when in the great drama the Messianic actor cries to mortals or "Gentile" man to awake to the realization that he must prepare his mind and heart for a great and always in some degree imminent transformation into the higher nature of the Christ whom "John," the natural man, precedes. The event impending is not one that is to supervene historically, that is, objectively, at any given moment, as a thing of outward observation. The "Kingdom," Jesus himself specifies, cometh neither here nor there, and not with observation. It comes silently in the hearts of men and women. The amazing ado about the age's expectation of a personal Messiah, to be injected into the milieu of the world's political, economic and social life, is a vast misreading of arcane meaning. Nothing in religion has ever driven sensible humans to such folly as the objective expectation of the coming of Messiah. Warschauer says that John's prefatory preachment of the coming day of judgment created a stir and commotion in all Judea, so that the multitude flocked out to be ready to witness the expected prodigy. So did Miller's deluded preachment of the same thing in all New England and west to Ohio in 1836 to 1843, when the whole bubble of delusion burst in ridiculous and shameful disillusionment. The "Millerite Delusion" should be read up by all who need to be impressed with the lesson of religious gullibility and the utter folly of taking scriptures as literal history.

Our scholar suggests that the multitudes who flocked out at the clarion call of the Messiah's herald for repentance were not necessarily corrupt or sunk in iniquity. They were ill-used, oppressed and mistaught people, feverishly longing for release from hard conditions. Their greatest defect, Warschauer hints, was due to a mechanical conception of religion! They were taking the herald's words too literally! They understood John to be predicting the coming of a great man, a king, who would redeem their lowly status, instead of a Christly or kingly instinct in the heart: this was their fault! There is entire agreement here with Warschauer on this point. But to our vision there is no reason perceptible on the horizon anywhere that makes clear why the fault of the populace of the first century in mistaking Messianic prophecy by translating it too literally and mechanically, and thereby turning the Christos, the Prince of Peace, into a human figure, is any more reprehensible then than now. The ironic possibilities and eventualities of the argument are left to the reader's predilections.

The next bit of presumptive "history" that the scholar throws out the window is the romantic story of the circumstances precipitating the Baptist's death: the "Salome" dance before

Herod, his impetuous promise to give the damsel whatever she might ask, her intrigued demand for John's head on a charger, and the rest. He says the entire episode is open to the gravest doubts, and again is admittedly molded over the pattern of Old Testament stories, especially that of Jephthah in Judges. John's head is represented as being brought in and presented to the dancing daughter of Herodias then and there, whereas, says Warschauer, John was in prison at Machaerus, distant by four days' journey from Tiberias, where such a banquet would have been held. Lastly Herodias was not a wanton character, but a loyal and steadfast queen.

Warschauer betrays his lack of acquaintance with deep and recondite ancient esoteric symbology when he says that John's description of the one greater than he, who, though coming after him, is preferred before him, wielding a winnowing fan and bringing fire from heaven to burn the chaff, does not fit Jesus. One, however, must study the great system of Egyptian portrayal under glyph and symbol to see how perfectly it does fit the Jesus or Christ character.

It is desirable to call attention to this investigator's tribute paid in his book (p. 46) to religious genius as a thing of subjective depth beyond all fathoming of ordinary mentality. It is the very thing that has been predicated of it in our work as the basis of the necessity for portraying its deeper intimations by the singular method and appliances of allegory and myth or drama. The religious intuition plumbs the wells of mystic realization to such depths that it is past depiction by any other typism. This is adduced here by way of showing that a Christian apologist can himself strengthen the case for esoteric methodology at moments when bias is not immediately concerned.

The next Biblical event of reputed historicity to be shunted aside by Warschauer is the opening of the heavens at the end of the baptism, the proclamation of the celestial voice that this was God's beloved Son sent for the world's acceptance, and the descent of the dove upon Jesus' head. The disqualification of this as history is accomplished by the averment that it was a purely subjective intuition of Jesus himself and not an outward event witnessed by the assemblage on the river bank! The account given of the event by Matthew and Luke carries its own refutation, he acknowledges. For had Jesus' mission thus been authenticated by such a marvel wrought openly in the sight of a concourse of people to bear it witness, neither Jesus nor the populace could have hesitated, they to acclaim and he to accept, the Messianic character of his person and his status. That no such sweeping demonstration followed, is regarded by this critic as conclusive proof that the divine approbation expressed out of heaven at the baptism could not have been objectively perceived.

Then he testifies to a realistic envisagement of the improbability that a man who a week or two previously had been a humble mechanic could suddenly register a serious realization of his being, in his own slender person, the embodied divinity of cosmic majesty and proportions, prefigured in and by the universal conception of Messiah. This is surely a sensible discernment on Warschauer's part, knowing, as he must, the jibing rain of skeptical abuse and derision that any common man today, or any day, would call down upon his devoted head if he openly and seriously proclaimed himself the cosmic Christ and the Logos of God! No amount of the most genuine saintliness, or worthy character, of nobility of life, could support in any person today the self-announcement of his divine Messiahship, and save him from universal presumption of insanity. Hardly less suspect would be the claim for such a status advanced by others on behalf of any mere mortal, however saintly. Humanity will never be able to rationalize or render acceptable on any sane basis the claim of or on behalf of any one member chosen out of its own group to the unique status of "the elect of all the nations" or the only Son of Deity. It is psychologically impossible. So that it is a disappointment when Warschauer, with all his circumspection and realistic caution, in the end goes with Jesus in the latter's eventual realization, stunning and awesome as it must have been to him, that he is personally the cosmic Messiah! All of which attests again how wretchedly the historical acceptance of scripture can twist human mentality. For it entails the acceptance of situations and events that the intellect can swallow only with repressed qualms and with rational nausea.

Another acknowledgment weakening to the historical claim is Warschauer's reminder that every one of Jesus' answers to Satan in the wilderness temptation is taken from Deuteronomy VI to VIII, and that such an encounter between the Savior and the personified evil principle is paralleled in Zoroastrian and Buddhistic and other religious literature. Warschauer unctuously attests that the piety of the age loves these parallels, but he still does not see that ancient love of analogues by which to typify eternal spiritual truth is a more smashing witness against the Gospel historicity which he defends than he possibly realizes. So general and constant was the pressure of this tendency to exploit the parallelism of events that, he says, we may expect to find the disposition manifest itself in attempts to relate nearly all the events in the "life of Christ" in the outward form of an analogue with some event in the Old Testament. He admits that this procedure involves some sacrifice of historical accuracy, and he grants that indeed in regard to the Lord's temptation of forty days at Satan's hands we are not dealing with history at all, declaring that this should need no confirmation. He is thus driven by his own intellectual probity to ask if there is any nucleus of veridical fact left in the incident for faith to feed upon. His answer is – as always – that the episode could not have become current and got into the record if it had not some basis of factuality beneath it. This has become a stock argument on the side of the historicity. It is used mechanically, without regard to the fact that in hosts of instances legendary figures, such as Lord Raglan shows Robin Hood and King Arthur to be, have acquired as much historic reality in the general mind as many a historical character. On this argument it is to be presumed that we would have to agree that doubtless there was some basis of truth back of Little Jack Horner, Little Bo-Peep, Tom the piper's son, Jack Spratt and his wife, Old King Cole, Jack the giant-killer, Cinderella and Moby Dick. A thousand years from now some historical literalist will be saying that we must assume there was some personal ground for the characters of Portia and Shylock. It should be remarked, then, that the New Testament story of the temptation must be put down as resting on nothing stronger than conjecture. Warschauer himself disqualifies it as history.

The next item to be likewise disqualified is Jesus' commissioning his twelve disciples upon a mountain. This, as given in Mark, Warschauer dismisses with the statement that it bears the stamp of legend and not that of history. Also is noted the fact that while there are four lists of these chosen "fishermen," not two of them quite agree.

With regard to the cleansing of the leper cited by the three Synoptists, he says that if it belongs to history, it could not well have happened when it is reported to have occurred. And the scholar reverts to sane criticism when he declares that for anyone who knows the deep-rooted nature of leprosy, it is difficult to believe that Jesus healed the disease with a mere word. He sees the account as just an attempt to analogize Jesus' power with that of Moses and Elijah, who were said to have cured lepers. As to the account of Jesus healing the paralytic let down through a hole in the roof, he speaks of the glaring improbability of this detail. He calls in the modern psychological discovery of the power of auto-suggestion to account for the possible cure as narrated. He takes a wavering stand on the accredited miraculous power of the divine healer.

He comments again on the improbability that Jesus would have met the challenge as to his keeping company with publicans and sinners with the remark that he comes to call not the righteous but sinners to repentance, unless indeed it was uttered in irony. In regard to another cure, he says its credibility need not concern us, – its historicity being questionable. In another case he says Mark reports an incident with what we would judge to be a touch of exaggeration. He cites a remarkable instance of textual manipulation in Mark 3:21 after Jerome's revision. Utter want of both historical and evolutionary perspective is exhibited by the exegetist – and thousands of others similarly conditioned by orthodox persuasions – in his viewing the Kingdom's incidence upon earth as a thing that might be consummated by Jesus' preaching of its imminence and his soulful exhortation to the masses, within the matter of a few years' lapse. It can be safely predicated as to this that any mind which can seriously envisage the complete perfection of all humanity from present low stage to the lofty purity needed to bring in the Kingdom of Righteousness within the space of two years, as Warschauer postulates (p. 85), has had its capacity for sound judgment warped sadly out of focus. It can be asked what more is needed as evidence of the correctness of this statement and the folly of any immediate or early expectation of the arrival of the Kingdom of Christliness on earth than the fact that two thousand years have passed, with the western world in possession of the inestimable and unfailingly efficacious help of the Christ's own (alleged) teachings, and we are sure at this moment that the Kingdom is if possible farther away than ever before. Humanity must indeed be slow to learn if the pointed moral of two thousand years fails to teach it so simple a determination as that. One of the stock delusions of religious folly to which the "common people" are always pitiably susceptible by reason of want of training in critical reflection, and which is therefor used by designing modern "evangelists" to prey upon their gullibility, is the notion that a heavy surge of feverish emotionalism can induce God quickly to wind up the affairs of the planet in deference to our regard for the inviolability of Old Testament "prophecy"! God is alleged to have written the Book; it seems to say clearly that the time is at hand; the Kingdom is imminent; the promised signs can be discerned (with a slight stretch of the imagination); therefore the cataclysmic holocaust must be only a matter of days or weeks away. Not even a thousand rebuffs to the fell presumption of this overweening expectation in the centuries of theological befuddlement have availed to dampen the ardor of unintelligent Christian sectaries for what these writers call "eschatological" and "apocalyptic" consummation. If it is a credit to have afflicted millions of ordinarily good humans with a series of pitiable delusions of this sort, Christianity has that credit. Repentance and the worthy fruits of repentance were to compel the Kingdom to appear, and that speedily, avers Warschauer, saying that Jesus sympathized warmly with the eager, zealous, activist mood of the times.

It is impossible to forego the opportunity to hold this idea up to realistic view. The author under discussion goes on to say seriously that the professedly religious in Jesus' day believed that the coming of the Kingdom was merely delayed by the sins of the people. The rigorously ritualistic Pharisees felt that the general failure to conform to ceremonial observance with sufficient strictness was holding back the great Day of the Lord. Had not the Talmud said that Israel would be redeemed if the nation would keep only two sabbaths with the proper solemn decorum? Warschauer does see that this approaches caricature of the Messianic concept, but he still insists that Jesus himself fell in with popular belief that Jahweh would return to his people when they returned with pious devotion to him. Jesus instinctively adopted this prophetic persuasion, he states. He adds, of course, that Jesus interpreted it in terms of a more gradual moral regeneration; yet he does not let this in any way upset the schedule of a few years' time for the striking of the clock of apocalyptic doom. If the present generation would but sow the seeds of righteousness, the same generation, or surely the next, would reap the harvest of the Kingdom's descent from heaven. So even the omniscient Son of God is committed by his own followers to this moronic conception of infantile-minded religionists. For it was not only the sentiment of the unlettered rabble that did flock into the Christian communion a little later; it was, says Warschauer, the grandiose conception of the Savior, his own plan to call the Kingdom into existence quickly, immediately, with the challenge of power and the compelling unction of zealous faith. The Golden Age was to be dragged in by the violence of heroic ethic in obedience to God's will; the Kingdom of Heaven was to be assaulted and captured by storm. And Warschauer subjoins that it is open to us to see the essential truth of this conception. He does indeed turn the sense into the more reasonable channel of a gradual transformation of the inner consciousness of individuals, instead of a sudden cataclysmic denouement. Yet he permits even Jesus to be fooled by its failure to appear at the beck of the pious zealotry of the age at the time expected. This presumes that Jesus himself had so lost the sense of evolutionary proportion as to believe a general stiffening of piety and good behavior would roll up the scroll of the heavens and melt down this planet as predicted with the fervent heat of Messianic zealotry. Surely his devotees could honor him with the imputation of a little more intelligence than that.

Wrestling with the problem of Jesus' own recognition of his cosmically unique divine Sonship, Warschauer avers that this supervened upon his consciousness in full and mystically irresistible force at the baptism. He had there been seized with the intuition of his unique supernal cosmic status; in spite of all his sense of his humanity he was forced to realize that he was the Messiah! And that realization came to him with such strength, intimates Warschauer, that it even brought with it the temptation to regard himself as the earthly King, destined, according to exoteric popularization of the idea, to rule the nations politically. But Jesus put this glittering lure resolutely behind him, as the real Satanic temptation, says the commentator. He permits us to hazard the guess as to why Jesus dismissed the outward rulership idea and confined himself to the role of a spiritual messenger. This guessing is the thing of considerable significance both here and elsewhere along the way. If a chain is no stronger than its weakest link, the chain that holds up the whole structure of Gospel Christology is pitiably weak, for it is composed of an unbelievable number of linked guesses, conjectures, surmises, suppositions, inferences, some of which break under a laugh.

The paragraph raises the grave question anyhow as to the psychological sanity of the view that any mortal creature born of woman, with normal brain and strictly human powers of consciousness, could in any way, shape or manner possibly arrive at the conviction that he, in his own human nature and constitution, was THE cosmic Christ that the Bible and Christian theology have delineated. It is flatly and blankly impossible for any normal human being to gather from any source and entertain the conviction that he is standing outside the pale of humanity and that he belongs to a cosmic divine order instead of the human genus. He could not do this within the bounds of sanity. The possibility of his doing it would come only with the breakdown of his mentality. It is absolutely impossible for any mortal man to conceive of himself as holding some status or being commissioned with some grandiose errand which is not equally within the capability of other humans in the course of growth. For Warschauer and others to foist on Jesus the recognition of this utterly unconscionable and preternatural character for himself in all history is for them to place him in the class of a derationalized human. He deserves better treatment at the hands of his votaries. It is conceivable that a man may come to think of himself as a Christ, a mortal who has immortalized himself by having adopted the mind of true Christliness. But it is unthinkable that in sane, sober and serious consciousness any man of our race could come to think of himself as being THE Christ, that Christ of the Gospels and Christian doctrine in whose person were centered divine cosmic attributes and functions inconceivably remote from human category or accomplishment. If any individual reached and announced such a conviction now, his action would stand out as an ugly affront to general intelligence and be heartily resented by all ranks of people, the more vehemently in the ratio of their culture. If any segment of the population received such a Messiah seriously, we know what type it would be, – the most ignorant, uncritical and psychologically gullible element. This was indeed largely the kind that did receive and accredit the Gospel Christ in the form of a human person in that fatal third century. It can be maintained on grounds of sheer logic and common sense realism that Jesus, if a man, could not possibly have arrived at any such inner persuasion about himself and his mission consistently with the consummate sanity attributed to him generally. Any man can gain a conviction that his life is set apart for a unique work of first importance in world history. But this is a normal reaction and is a thousand miles away from that conception of cosmic uniqueness and hierarchical grandeur which the idea of Messiahship involved in its Biblical characterization. It is indeed the very thought – which Christian devotion had to strain at and swallow – that the cosmic aeonial Avatar, a figure of astronomical proportions, of solar and celestial grandeur, the co-creator of the worlds with the Father, could be compressed without garish ridiculousness within the compass of the personal stature of a man on earth, that has engendered even subconsciously a natural incredulity about the tenability of Christian theology, and brought the latter at last to the position of an outcast even from its own courts and temples. It is almost certain, indeed, that the simple explanation of that theology's repudiation even in its own house, is nothing more involved than the revulsion of common human good sense and instinctive logic against an idea so grotesquely unnatural as that the cosmic Logos should come walking down the street or drop in for lunch! It comes close to being fairly well analogized by the idea of going in and purchasing the whole of Virtue or Integrity physically compressed in a drug-store capsule! But is it far from this to the assertion, which on the basis of all Christian dogmatism can be squarely made, that at the crucifixion the Logos was wounded in the side, hands and feet? A Roman soldier raised his spear and struck the cosmic universe below the heart! For the Logos is the manifest universe, and Christ was declared the Logos and Jesus was the Christ! The saddening reflection from all this is that such obfuscation should have been produced by a distorted theology upon the intellects of Biblical exegetists with the result that they could soberly write of a man in any age conceiving himself to be the Logos of God, with all the superhuman involvements going with the character. No amount of ascription to such a one of the most touching modesty and sanctification of motive could save him from the imputation of egotism beyond the reach of human thought. The conclusion of the whole matter is reached in the lamentable consideration that the mentality of a whole civilization had to be twisted askew to make such a conception tenable, and that the age-long prevalence of such a conception twisted that mentality still further askew. And with such premises to build upon, who can say that this distorted mentality has not been the breeding ground of the outward follies and mistakes that have cast this civilization into the most awful inferno of calamity in world history? It could well be so.

In passing Warschauer remarks that a meticulous regard for chronological accuracy is not a strong point with any of the Synoptists, – which is cited as just another weak link in a long chain of weak links.

It is his own argument that the term "bar nasha," translated "the Son of Man" in the Gospels, does not refer to Jesus as the Christ in person, but generically to "man" or humanity. What is this but a subsidiary and indirect, but still implied, corroboration of our contention here that the other terms alluding to the divinized man as the Christos, the Anointed, etc., escape the same particularized limitation and point to the larger and more general connotation?

The author confesses on page 103 that he is moving, however reverently and haltingly, in the direction of surmise, when he fixes the time of Jesus' final realization of his Messianic role. On page 107 we encounter such admissions as that Mark's statement is open to serious doubt, and that the graphic touches in the description of one of the miracles may possibly be attributable to the Evangelist's own imagination. The amount of credit given to the story of the storm on Lake Gennesaret is not great. It, too, seems to have been modeled over the lines of the story of the Jonah storm. The parallelism extends far. He questions how far the prototypal story rests on a basis of fact, and he says that in such a problem surmises are cheap and knowledge is dear. His way out is to say that what may have happened is that Jesus fell asleep in the boat in the storm, and that all the rest was supplied from that ever-handy well of popular legend that slaked the thirst of the age for romantic afflatus. Mark is charged with great indifference to geography. He even locates the Gardarene miracle in the wrong place, according to Warschauer.

Coming to the great climactic miracle of the whole Gospel collection, the raising of Lazarus, the scholar quotes Prof. E. F. Scott (The Fourth Gospel, p. 45) as saying that it can not with real probability be given a place in any intelligible scheme of the life of Christ; that it is inconceivable that a miracle of such omen for all mankind, performed in the one week of the Savior's career of which there is a full chronicle, and in the presence of multitudes just outside Jerusalem, with the miracle itself forming the direct occasion of the crucifixion, should have been left totally out of the narratives of the three other Evangelists and be given only by John, – the one, we may remark incidentally, who, like Paul, presents a Jesus who is scarcely personally human at all! And Scott ends by making the very sensible suggestion we are almost pushed to the conclusion that the raising of Lazarus is, in the main, symbolical! When will scholars receive that extra little push that will thrust them at last into the circle where alone the full truth as to the nature of all this material and its interpretative problem can be seen? When will they take that one further step beyond Prof. Scott's suggestion that will enable them to see that not only the Lazarus story but the entire literature is symbolical?

Indeed the next author quoted by Warschauer practically does take that step. It is Prof. Burkitt, who (in The Gospel History and Its Transmission, p. 223) says that for all its dramatic setting we can not regard the Lazarus miracle as the account of a historical event! Warschauer agrees that the other (Lukan) mention of Lazarus in the story of the rich man and the beggar is pure moral apologue and suggests a very plausible connection between the two episodes. By we know not how many intervening stages, he writes, the moral fable grew through the haggadic tendency into the historic legend. It is our reflection prompted by this explanation that if he admits that the Bible material was a final outgrowth of a number of successive stages of transformation of original moral apologue into history, he has gone far in the very direction of granting the major premises on which our work stands. It is precisely our position that all ancient Biblical content began as apologue and became, in Christianity, transmuted into history. To refute that position in the large, this scholar supplies us with much data in the small, that support our contention. And after all, it is no small thing in this debate to concede the non-historicity of this particular Lazarus miracle. In fact the edifice of Christianity rests, as Paul loudly proclaims, on one single fact, the resurrection of Jesus. But this pivotal item has been considered to have been stoutly buttressed by the auxiliary death-to-life miracle of similar significance and portent at Bethany. To wipe away the latter as history is seriously to weaken the main girder in the temple of Christianity.

Then comes Warschauer's analysis of the incident noted only by Luke (VII:36-50) when at a supper in the house of a Pharisee a woman who had been a sinner came in from the dark streets to pour out her gratitude to Jesus as the agent of her moral regeneration. It is introduced here to form the background of the scholar's comment that the verses 44 to 46 read like a later elaboration, being too didactic and out of all relation to the human side of the situation as narrated. He even deletes the words "but to whom little is forgiven, the same loveth little" from the Savior's speech, claiming they are a singularly uninspired gloss. So one more item of "history" goes by the board, – when it serves a particular scheme of interpretative motive to oust it from the narrative.

Additional strength is given by Warschauer to his contention that Bethlehem could not have been the actual birthplace of Jesus by his treatment of material detailing the Savior's later visit to Nazareth, "his own country," where he found himself strangely without honor. Also the disqualification of another item of the "history" is made by Warschauer's statement that the clause – "save that he laid his hands upon a few sick folk and healed them"-sounds decidedly like interpolation, either by the Evangelist of some later editor.

Mark, he says, knows nothing of the attack of the crowd on Jesus that nearly led to his murder, from which danger he escaped by "passing through the midst of them"; and this incident, too, is dismissed as likely not historical. Also the Lord's sayings about Elijah and Elisha manifesting their powers only for the heathen and not for the Israelites, seem to our critic as of doubtful authenticity. They belong, he significantly states, to the realm of primitive Christian apologetics!

He questions, too, the credibility of Jesus' commissioning two groups, one of twelve, the other of seventy-two, disciples to go forth and preach the Gospel unto all the world. He thinks they are two variants of the one event, and comments quite adversely as to the anti-climactic upshot of the whole grandiose missionary program, which, had it been historically true, would have shown some concrete results, either in failure or success, worthy of recording. Neither profane nor sacred history carries a single item of report on the outcome of the great strategy of the Son of God to publish the glad tidings of salvation to the nations.

Comment on Herod's later suspicions of Jesus and fear of his power to stir up undesirable political ferment includes Warschauer's statement that study of the incident is calculated to raise doubts as to the historical character of what is there said of Jesus' identity. Admission is made in another connection that the true order of events can only be conjectured, with probability as our sole guide, – again a feeble basis for history to rest upon. Matthew made a most happy conjecture of his own, he ventures. Thus even the authors of Gospel "history" were not sure of what they recorded.

Mark is again accused of guessing, – as to why Jesus went into a period of retirement.

That Jesus should have twice withdrawn from the Galilean country following the two feedings of the multitude is put down as unbelievable and reduces the course of events to chaos. Resort is even had to the fictional reconstruction of occurrences to account for certain things mentioned in the history. If this liberty is permissible now, there should have been no condemnation of similar practice in the early centuries. Our safety is in being told that it is invention and not something else. A lengthy hypothetical construction is made by Warschauer on page 149 to serve as at least a not impossible explanation of the origin of the legend of the master's walking on the waves.

The cure of the blind man at Bethsaida is allocated to the category of symbolic legend and is not to be taken as a historical reminiscence. It may stand as a symbolic representation of the gradual enlightenment of the disciples, who were initially dull. Some history then admittedly could have been made out of pristine spiritual allegory. It is stated that Mark's setting of the cure of the epileptic boy is quite inappropriate for it, and his allocation of the incident is declared to be quite impossible. Of very doubtful historicity, too, is the disciple's question as to why they could not exorcise the demon, and Jesus' reply that this kind can only be dispossessed by prayer. The cure may have occurred before the commissioning of the twelve instead of after the transfiguration, is the surmise. On page 167 Warschauer speaks of the truly desperate task of reconciling the Synoptists with the Johannine version. Desperate indeed, if taken as history; infinitely less difficult if taken as spiritual drama. On page 168 he is confronted with, as he avows, the even more formidable task of fitting into the framework of events the recorded sayings of the Lord. This task frankly denies accomplishment, and the guesses of the Synoptists are often conflicting, it is admitted. Confusion, faulty memory, conflict of already corrupted manuscripts, all complicated the Evangelic labors. Mark follows one plan, Matthew and Luke others. Which saying followed what event was, as a rule, not so much matter for surmise as indeed past all accurate surmising, is the candid and damaging admission.

We may conclude this résumé of testimony from this typical author with his own climactic statement, confirming finally the chief theses of our own position, that the Gospels were written in the first place not as works of history, but of edification, and that purely historical considerations were at most of only secondary interest to the sacred writers! The purpose envisaged in our amassing so much material from a single work of this kind is exactly to demonstrate to readers that any rational attempt to build the case for the Gospel historicity, if it is honest enough to look closely at the factual content of that history, can save itself from entanglement in contradiction, absurd predicament and bizarre situation only by denying an enormous percentage of the history itself. It must indeed be accounted an odd situation when the claim for an important conclusion can be supposed to be strengthened or validated by the disqualification of by far the major evidence for it! At such a desperate pass stands the defense of the Gospels as history. It will have been noted that scarcely an event in the narrative touched upon by Warschauer (and he covers the main events of the Gospel "life" of Jesus) has not been undermined and severely weakened, if not put entirely out of court as history. Since the Gospels are, to begin with, the only source of supposed historical knowledge of the Savior's life, even if they could be accredited as history, something like nine-tenths of their testimony is invalidated by Christian writers like Warschauer. These special pleaders rest their case for the historicity upon the extant history, and then turn to and make poetic or legendary or symbolical moonshine of that same history. If the Gospels are not histories, but mythical dramas – as obviously they are – there is no extant credible evidence to rest historical claims upon. Even in the hands of its own defenders the body of the history melts down until there is left nothing but a substanceless shadowy mirage of historical foundation, a veritable wraith of reality. Warschauer has been called in as witness to impress upon unstudied folk the astonishing extent to which the body of historical evidence, vaunted as of such solid substantiality and redoubtable proportions, does thus melt down under the rays of the sun of common sense and sane judgment. Warschauer might himself be dumbfounded to realize how little material he has left intact as veridical historical data upon which to support the thesis of Jesus' life. He himself has stripped the already slim body of claimed factual history to skeletal tenuity.

The data supplied by such a work positively establish the fact that a very large segment of the Gospel material must be relinquished as history. What has been gullibly assumed to be history is now discovered to be – exactly what this work claims – poetic legend and typism.

Chapter XVI

AN EPOCHAL DISCOVERY

The general proposition herein advanced that the Bible is a literary work executed in accordance with ancient patterns of design and method which are scarcely as yet envisaged in relation to their significance receives an astonishing confirmation and reinforcement from a source that came to hand only recently and as it were by accident. It has to do with the literary form-structure of the Bible books and not with their contents. But so startling is this revelation of a definite arrangement of material according to one or more peculiar form-patterns that the conviction of a hidden purpose and cryptic significance far beyond the recording of mere history in the Bible is overwhelmingly stamped on the mind. The form of this peculiar structure is so organically articulated that its claims on the attention reduce the content almost to secondary significance. This discovery has been released to the world by N. W. Lund in a book bearing the non-revealing and uninspired title of Chiasmus in the New Testament. With great detail and system and no little ingenuity the author has segregated portions of material in both Old and New Testaments into unit or constituent groups and then systematized the phrase and sentence elements of each group into the scheme of a surprisingly methodological arrangement, which roughly forms when diagramatically represented the Greek letter "Chi," whence the word Chiasmus, the name of the scheme. (For practical purposes the letter "Chi" is our "X.")

There is a progressing succession of elements (words, phrases, constructions, whole sentences) more commonly numbering three (A, B, C or 1, 2, 3) reaching a climactic culmination in the fourth member, D, from which there is an anti-climactic recession through the same or repetition of the same or similar elements in the reverse order, D, C, B, A, or 4, 3, 2, 1. The author has succeeded in making an unbelievably large amount of Bible material fit this model structure without the usual necessity of stretching it to make his thesis hold good. Perusal of his work fixes the inexpugnable conclusion that this strange arrangement is not fortuitous and that a very large portion of the whole of the Bible was cast in the mold of this diagram or variants of it! Indeed as one finishes his work one stands pretty close to the persuasion that form was almost the primary consideration of the Bible writers and content secondary. There seems to have been a greater concern with the poetic mechanics of the writing than with the message or meaning. There is indeed something bordering on a suggestion of an eerie element in all this, as if the purpose of scriptural writing was to impart a conception of structure as an integral element in the total message, or as a cryptic haunting of a cosmogonic design behind the flowing content. Students have labored and claimed to uncover such woven-in patterns in the plays of Shakespeare.

We are challenged to adduce some theory as to the significance of this remarkable formation. It seems obvious that it is an attempt to introduce what the Hindus call "mantric force," a power of suggestion much like, but greater than, that of rhyme and meter in poetry, into the recital of verses chanting the import of cosmic creation and the life movement. If it was possible to sing of creation in the identical analogue and symbolic lines of that creation, a magically powerful psychological efficacy might be superinduced upon the mind.

Now the ancients conceived of divine spirit as descending into matter through three and one half kingdoms (see the number three and a half in the exact middle chapters, 11 and 12, in the Book of Revelation), reaching its nadir of full manifest expression in the middle of the fourth (the Gospels' "fourth watch in the night"), and then returning with its fruits of experience to its celestial home through the same three kingdoms, in reverse order. From top down these three and one half kingdoms might be denominated the Nirvanic, Atmic, Buddhic and Intellectual (in Hindu nomenclature), or perhaps Super-Spiritual, Spiritual, Intuitional and Mental. The outward or downward progress of spirit through these three and a half states of consciousness was the emanation of soul into matter or embodiment of which all the ancient scriptures speak. It was the Greek "descent of the soul." At the same time the life in the still inchoate atom began an evolution from below upward, and it, too, progressed onward through three and one half kingdoms of nature, the mineral, vegetable, animal, and the animal-human, landing in the middle of the fourth or human, where it met and conjoined its physical energies with the unit of divine potency that had come down from above. Here at a common meeting place the two forces, spirit and matter, pressing ahead in opposite directions but toward each other, combine in what the old scriptures universally denominate a marriage, from which is to come the progenation of the next surge or cycle of ongoing life. It is at this meeting point of spirit and matter, soul and its body, that all meaning and all experience-value are localized. Soul descends half way from the summit of being and matter and rises half way from the bottom, and the two meet at the only place their energies can be synchronized and eventually harmonized, which is just exactly at the middle point in the seven levels of the gamut of being. For man the meeting point is right in his body and brain.

Again this is diversion into exegesis, which is not the quest in this work; but it may be of great value if it reveals to the detractors of the esoteric and symbolic systems of Biblical construction how far they are off track and how far they must penetrate into the scorned intricacies and subtleties of the obvious esoteric methodology of the ancients who wrote the scriptures if they would unlock the doors leading to the buried treasures of a manifestly cryptic bibliology. To chant the verses in measured cadence and lift, or in successive crescendo and diminuendo, with the movement of the creative life waves expressed and felt through the miniature imitation of that cosmic rhythm would be to sway mind and soul in rapport with the cosmic pulse. It would be to join in living grasp of their fundamental meaning the two mightiest symbols of all religion, the cross and the number seven, in one dramatic and tonic linking, that would powerfully stir the ritualistic instinct in human nature. Nothing less than this is indeed the genius of ritualism: a small measured action of body and voice while symbolic emblemism tugs at the mind, copying in miniature the basic structural movement of the universe of life. When the little action of man falls into exact rapport with the beat and rhythm of the pulse of life and the movement of the cosmic creation, something in the creature's natures rises in strong joy to acknowledge the harmony. It is a synchronization of beat and wave-length that provides a wireless channel for the free discharge of a higher force. This is the ground of the mantric efficacy of all music and poetry. Then when to this perfect accord of the swing there is joined the intellectual perception that goes with full appreciation of the meaning of the accompanying symbols, the combined mental-emotional effect is something of grandeur in man's inner life that has been lost out of religious experience since ancient days. The loss came through the vitiation of the esoteric significance of rite and symbol; so that one half the elevating power of its own ritual and emblemism has been lost to Christianity as the result of the debacle in esotericism in the third century.

In connection with Lund's important disclosure may be noted his own statement that the study of folk-lore is especially valuable from the consideration that it presents a similar development to that of the Gospel tradition. This is a discernment almost if not quite equal in significance to his discovery of the chiasmus Lord Raglan's The Hero had hinted at this same perception and Massey had been working in the spirit of it for forty years. The incredulous reader may well demand to be shown the nexus of relationship between folk-lore and the Gospel tradition, for it is superficially not apparent. However, things not connected by visible links may be united subterraneously. It is so here. The cord of linkage lies deep and runs far back in time, in fact to the very origins of human culture. In reality folk-lore and the religious deposit emanated from the same source. They represent but two divergent streams from the same fountain. The one took the path of intellectual studiousness and remained couched in philosophic, symbolic and dramatic esotericism; the other advanced outward toward popular expression and took the form of legend, hero-tale and nature-cultism, frequently becoming entwined with local reference. The first maintained itself on the mysticism of the intellect, the other on the mysticism of nature, and hence the latter included the activity of nature spirits, elementals, sprites of forest, hill and vale. One needs but to go back far enough in the analysis of the folk-tale to find that it runs at last into the same sub-vein of meaning as that from which the Bibles sprang. New and again most significant testimony to this same effect is advanced by the eminent psychologist, C. G. Jung, who says that he finds the same alphabet of symbolic characters appearing in the type-dreams of his clinical patients as appears in the folk-lore and religions of the nations. Some of the characters in this symbolic alphabet are the cross, the tree, numbers, the serpent, the star, the bee, fish, water, fire and the rest.

Of great pertinence, then, is Lund's statement (p. 17) that what he calls form-history is a preliminary study to the history of literature. The critical interest of form-study is not the Gospel content, or the Gospels as they now stand, but it lies in the small component units of Gospel formation. These portions – which can be strangely cut off from the context and stand unsupported – Lund says have had a long history before they entered the written Gospels! As astonishing corroboration of earlier statements to the same effect made in this work, this pronouncement of Lund merits all possible emphasis. Our declaration that the Gospels were re-editions of material of venerable antiquity in the first and second centuries may have sounded like the veriest raving of insanity and heresy. But here is an orthodox spokesman who, in the wake of one of the most sensational discoveries in all Bible study, asserts that whole sections of what now purports to be Gospel writing of the first century had a long history before they became a part of canonical scriptures! And that which was proclaimed herein in the very teeth of all Christian opinion to the contrary is additionally confirmed when Lund goes on to assert that the writer of the Gospel does not create these sections; they were, he avers, the product of the folk-spirit operating unconsciously in the shaping of the material. The Gospel writer acted merely as an editor, the material handled lying already at his hand in the popular tradition. And still further strength is lent to previous assertions of this work when he says that the parts revamped by the Gospel "editors" are not now in their original pure form, having been surrounded with introductory and supplementary comment in the editing.

There is one point, however, in which Lund's analysis does not coincide with the view here taken. This is his assignment of the origin of the Gospel sections spoken of to the folk-spirit operating unconsciously. Lord Raglan has so capably shown that the intricate, well-articulated and artfully dramatized constructions that made up the general body of national folk-lore could not have been produced in the first place by countryside illiteracy and cultural inadequacy. They must have been the products of advanced intellectual and dramatic sagacity. This conclusion of Raglan's is one of the greatest determinations in the field of world literature in modern times and it vastly alters the aspect of all such study.

It is clear now that Gospels, Revelation, the Epistles and the folk-tales must now be approached from the same point and with the same dramatic motivation and all carrying the same basic purport. Likewise they must at last be recognized as the work, not of merely general grades of human intelligence, but of that intelligence exalted to the point of knowing and dramatically portraying the experience and the deepmost significance of the world of life.

But Lund's study in chiasmus will definitely add new strength to the perception that the element of form in ancient literary construction held an importance in the eyes of scripture compilers which has never hitherto been recognized. To us all now comes the sobering reflection that it took us two thousand years to make even this discovery, which, once seen as Lund illustrates it by diagram and graph, is so manifest before our eyes that the possibility of our having missed it for centuries heavily underscores our stupidity. Yet right now it is fitting to ask how many more centuries it may take before we will awake to the true recondite significance of the ancient's employment of such a signal and unique formalism.

Out of these considerations there takes shape the concluding realization, itself of weighty import, that it is now beyond the scope of reason longer to hold the claim of the Gospel's authorship by any writer as a first-hand literary creation of his brain and pen. Authorship of course they had, but in no sense authorship as we understand it today. It was more nearly in the sense in which we would understand the authorship of a new geometry text, or a geography or even a work on the history of philosophy. The "author" of such a work does not produce the content, but takes old established content and simply readapts it to some new scheme of presentation or elucidation. In this prescribed editorial sense only were the Gospels ever "written." They were just fresh editions of the sublime "old, old story," republished and, falling into the hands of the populace with their mysteries cryptically concealed, turned eventually into literal nonsense.

The sudden discovery that the divine or divine-human authorship of the ancient scriptures laid an emphasis heretofore never dreamed of upon literary form-structure must cause a drastic revision in the standards of appraisal, evaluation, appreciation and interpretation. The Old and New Testaments alike will stand in a totally new character, aureoled in a brilliant and beautiful glow of something that is more than mere meaning, something that is indeed the apotheosization of meaning. It is something that transcends sheer intellectuality and rises to a realm of appreciations that belong to a higher order of consciousness. In transcending the intellect, however, it does not become the negation of the intellect but its complete vindication and consummation. It is as if the intellect, struggling through mists and tangled labyrinths of darkened paths, came out on a height from which all locations and directions could be clearly viewed. The ancient sages, it now seems clear, worked in the glow of a great inner light. They were indeed called "Illuminati." It required no small genius to create voluminous scriptures and great dramatic recitals in which the scheme of cosmic truth was inwoven into constructions which themselves were molded in the form of creational procedure. This attempt to synchronize the consciousness of man, the microcosm, with the lilt and tempo of the macrocosmic movement, has dropped totally out of human ken for two thousand years. It has never had the remotest touch of recognition or apprehension in Christian intelligence. The custodians of Christian scriptures have never had the least inkling that their own sacred texts harbored this new-found evidence of so majestic a lost art as the chiasmus indicates. Words are of course a feeble instrumentality by which to convey the sweep and swell of such conscious afflatus as was experienced by those whose mind and sensibilities were attuned to the register of those loftier and subtler emotions produced by participation in the mighty ritual-drama of the Mysteries. Yet this inadequacy of words alone to convey high values is undoubtedly one phase of the reason why ancient esotericism resorted to the complementary agencies of dance, ritual, rhythm and chiasmic structure in the effort to solemnize both the spoken and the written representation of evolutionary truth. The Greek envisagement of catharsis holds deeper intimations of prime value for the modern world than anyone has yet seen. The drama was designed to throw the individual man's mind into the sweep, the swing, the stride and the roll – the feel of the movement – of cosmos, and thus induce repercussions that would sift out the dross of unworthiness and accentuate the elements of rich veritude in the personal life. Beneath the superficial consciousness wrapt up with the concerns of ordinary existence in each mortal there slumbers the unawakened energy of a divine nature. To cause this dormant virgin energy to awake and exert its powers there is needed the impact or incidence of a vibration that for it is analogous to the vibration of the rising warmth and sun of spring to the latent energies in seed, plant or tree. And this magical efficacy was known and operated by the ancients. It was produced and effectuated by the combined elements of movement, music and meaning in a masterly blending. It was in brief the rational meaning of the universe set to the movement of the universe. It reached inner depths of mind and psyche and there bestirred into conscious activity the slumbering powers of man's latent divinity. The dance in the Mysteries repeated the rhythmic pulse of creation and the chorus accompanying it duplicated the "music of the spheres." And this composed the mighty choral dance, the bewitching song of the divine enchanter, designed by adept wisdom from the foundation of humanity to keep the race in memory of its lost divine birthright. It is the kiss of Eros that awakens the sleeping Psyche to her new life. The continual reproduction of this sanctifying and purifying influence for the cultural refinement of humanity throughout its history was the pristine motive and function of all religion. In most religions it has been obscured, lost, corrupted, smothered. The cultural salvation of the race may depend upon the quick recovery of this essential instrumentality for revivifying the "dead" divine spirit in the whole world.

After a disquisition of this sort a great deal more significance than would otherwise have been sensed can be discerned in a sentence glimpsed in A History of Jewish Literature, by Meyer Waxman (p. 2). He observes that in the so-called prophetic books symbols are only occasionally used as a means of enforcing the message; whilst in the apocalyptic books allegory occupies the most important place, and a regular symbolic mechanism, in which annual sober symbols predominate, is built up. Here is a hint that meaning was aimed at through a fixed system of symbols and allegories, and that the purpose back of the writing was not directly to communicate a simple message, but to intrigue the mind by imagery and dramatism into subtler realizations.

We have noted Burton Scott Easton's rejection of "the mount" as a geographical localization. He displays forthright sense and courage in going further and declaring that as an actual discourse the Sermon on the Mount was never delivered at all, and that "the mount" is mere rhetorical or theological decoration; even in the Sayings it may have been – as in Matthew it certainly is – a Christian counterpart of Sinai. Such an utterance is indeed a notable step in the direction of sane exegesis. But the plaudits that spring forth to greet it are somewhat tempered by the thought that it is still a long way from this recognition to the understanding that both Mount Sinai and the Mounts of the Temptation, of the Sermon, of Transfiguration and of Crucifixion are all in the ultimate rendering just this good earth no less.

Further refreshing candor as to the obvious non-historicity of much in the Gospels is displayed by Easton. The final verdict as to the authenticity of the miracles, he writes, must on the whole be a non liquet. We do not know that special miraculous forces were at work or that they were not. We can hardly think that Jesus would have expected to find figs on a tree in March, nor that he would think it sane to curse the poor plant because it did not violate the due order of nature. We must doubt the story of the fish that despite the stater in its mouth could still take a hook. We can not be expected to take literally the tale of a star standing over a house. In all such cases we would be recreant to our duty as rational beings if we did not look beneath the surface of the narratives to the underlying motive. The same principle must be carried into the analysis of the miracle stories, to an extent to be determined by the special circumstances in each case. But this author does not seem to think that this version of the miracles makes further damaging inroads into what little strength remains to the historical foundations of the Christ life.

A realistic view is taken by him in regard to the maps of Jesus' journeys constructed by following mechanically the topography described in the Gospels. He says they represent quite literally nothing whatever. Nor, he adds, are we better off in the chronology, except in the broadest outlines.

Again, he declares himself in agreement with what has been demonstrated earlier in this treatise, that Jewish and Christian literature from, roughly, B.C. 250 to A.D. 250, teems with pseudepigraphs of all sorts.

And he asks if we are to class the writers of Daniel, Enoch and II Peter as outright dishonest men. Oddly enough the answer to such a query can not be given until our whole view of ancient writing has been reoriented in the direction of understanding the methods of esoteric motive. When that orientation has been made it will be found that the question need not be answered, because the question itself will not need to be asked. The "pseud-" in the pseudepigraphs can be dropped when it is esoterically understood. From the exoteric or historical standpoint nearly all cryptographic writing is "pseudo." But this is only because it is supposed to be something – history – that it was never intended to be. The only false thing in the situation is the judgment that mistakes it for history.

In discussing Mark Easton comments that of course this Gospel is not held up as a model of historical precision; his story already contains palpable allegorical elements. He adds that the naïve character of John's historical writing is still more clearly seen in the account given in John 6:22-26. Again he says that the paragraph detailing the ferrying of so many thousands of people across the lake from Tiberias to Capernaum can surely be taken as a mere literary device, without historical foundation. In another place he protests that in any case we should certainly understand that, whatever may have been John's purpose, it was surely not to write history, as we understand that term. Later he says that if the Gospel is really by an eye-witness, he has written with but little regard for what he actually saw and heard. This general observation would seem thoroughly warranted with regard to the whole of the four Gospels. It would be hard to conceive of any writing purporting to be history that sounds less like it than the Gospels.

Another rather remarkable confession is made by Easton when he says that as a matter of fact many of the second and third century Christian rites have long defied explanation. No one knows, he avers, why oil was poured into the baptismal water, or why a candle or a staff of olive wood was dipped into it. It can be said, however, that these two ceremonial transactions are not only known, but are among the easiest and clearest of symbolic riddles. Water was the universal type of the lower natural man or animal, carnal nature; fire was the equally general emblem of the higher or spiritual nature; the introduction of fire into a moist material, to dry it and set it on fire, was the broad symbolic dramatization of the transforming power of spirit upon the carnal nature of the first Adam, man unregenerate. As the natural man, he is baptized with water; as the spiritual man he undergoes the higher baptism of fire (intellect or spirit) precisely as John declares. Oil, as the fuel for fire, carries the connotation that went with it. So the pouring of oil into baptismal water typified the injection of fire of mind and spirit into the baser, "moister" part of man's nature, to transform and light it up. It certainly does not detract from the force of the symbology that when oil is introduced into water it floats on the surface. To dip a candle – the agent of fire again – or a staff of olive wood (either itself inflammable or the tree from which oil – olive – is produced) into the water would indicate in slightly variant form the same basic process. Our modern orthodox theologians, with minds bound down to the "history" theory of scripture, cry out in irritation and impatience over such alleged flimsy fol-de-rol of the ancient mythical construction and the modern interpretation. They will not brook it for a moment that the men inspired of God to write Holy Scripture would descend to such indirection and mental frivolousness. As to this, what must be observed is that if this emblemism is fol-de-rol, then the bulk of Holy Writ is fol-de-rol. And this does not necessarily convict the "inspired" amanuenses of Deity of writing a lot of ridiculous drivel. For symbolism, when apprehended by minds not bound to gross realism, can impress deeper meanings and awaken more powerful intimations than can words. If theology will return to its pristine origins in symbolism, it may lay hold again of the dynamic force of human worship and regain its forfeited influence in human life. Easton's final comment in this connection is to the effect that we have not only to explain the appearance of certain ceremonies in Christianity; we have also to explain their almost universal acceptance there. Massey located the identic sources of explanation in the books of ancient Egypt; later study has authenticated that explanation. But unyielding habits of mental obduracy prevent recognition of the true elucidation even when it is presented. This is a world tragedy. Our titanic holocaust of mechanical fury may be one of its repercussions.

On the question of chronology he advises it is needless for us to waste time; whether Jesus was executed on the Passover or the eve of the Passover we shall never know. One account gives the date as the 14th of the Hebrew month Nisan, the other account puts it on then 15th. Here again it is symbolism that holds the key to the answer, since the 14 was determined by lunar typology and the 15 by solar. The full moon of a symbolical lunar month falls on the fourteenth day, and of a solar month on the fifteenth. History has nothing to do with it.

Taking Jesus' statement that if they destroyed this temple he would raise it up again in three days, John, says Easton, explains it as pure allegory.

There are several expressions and statements in the New Testament that have always baffled comprehension or at best offered only a semi-rational meaning, because they were taken literally. One such is the designation "the poor," as used in the two passages: "The poor ye have always with you," and "the poor have the Gospel preached unto them." Literal rendering of the word "poor" (in the economic sense) makes the received meaning of these two passages ridiculous. Especially is this the case in the one which rates the preaching of the Gospel as a compensatory balance against the misfortune of being (economically) poor! In the opinion of many, if the "poor" had to listen to the Sabbath droning from the average pulpit, they might be understood if they regarded it as an added hardship and no blessing or comfort. Obviously the term here refers to the spiritually as yet unregenerate, the undivinized mortal, the first or natural man. They doubtless shall be with us to the end of the aeon; and they in time shall have the consolation of having the Gospel (not the sheer material of the Bible books, but the essence of the divine tidings from deity to man on earth) preached unto them, until they pass from the poverty of ignorance to the richness of the kingdom's spiritual treasures.

Then there is the matter of Jesus' proclaiming himself as Messiah and as King. There are many angles to this line and it is difficult to handle as an argument. But again it is as clear as a case as many another in revealing that what is silly if taken literally and historically resolves back into the highest rationality when taken in deeper meaning. Indeed it does this in unusually striking fashion.

Easton and other writers are at pains to show that Jesus was crucified on the charge of claiming to be king and Messiah. The Sanhedrin judged the declaration by Jesus as to his kingship strictly according to Jewish law. A claim to be a prophet was, if proven false, a capital offense; a claim to be Messiah was a crime of blacker stain; but a claim to be the celestial Messiah, to sit on God's right hand, was a blasphemy beyond pardon. That Jesus made claims to be both king and Messiah is supported by appropriate texts cited and by inferences from his acts and statements. Easton says that this brings us face to face with the basic question of all: Jesus' claim to be not only Messiah, but celestial Messiah, Messiah in the most exalted sense, the heavenly and cosmic Son of Man. And he thinks that Jesus used the term "Son of Man" in its fullest apocalyptic force. As far as such claims constituted criminality, Jesus was guilty of both violating religious law and, in the eyes of his fellows, blaspheming God.

It requires but a moment's clear thinking and a realistic visioning of the case to enable us to see at once that the assumed unconscionable arrogance and personal self-exaltation implied by these claims made for himself by himself inheres in Jesus' position only when he is taken in his historical personality. It drops away the moment he is taken in his true original character as the Christ spirit in man. Of course the Christ consciousness is Messiah, long awaited by the teeming sons of men, who by his visitation in their hearts will be changed into the Sons of God and released from earth to eternal liberty. The dramatic figure of the Christos in the Mystery ritual could appropriately utter these declarations as to his status and role in the human drama, for it would be his part to announce his nature and mission. But if he is conceived as a man in the flesh such claims as to himself are too preposterous and unnatural; and besides are psychologically unthinkable as emanating from any sane human. No soul under the limitation of tiny human body could possibly so think of himself, much less proclaim it.

Warschauer represents Jesus as wrestling with his own spirit and intelligence to determine whether he should be a political king of the nations or exercise his kingship only in the silent motivations of the human heart. He represents this as the deeper inner meaning of "the temptation." Blind credulity prompts unthinkable devotees to assume that in actual history the carpenter had but to forget his divine mission and say "yes" to an actual Satan's proposition and the throne of the Caesars would have been his. Whether as God or man, the imputation to him (as an actual person) of such a chimerical thought as a serious consideration makes of him a hallucinated dolt. The whole situation can be seen in its flaming preposterousness only when the true sense of the "temptation" is brought to light. Of course when the soul migrates to earth from celestial mansions, there is before it the choice of throwing all its interests and energies into the delights of sense, the acquisition of riches and the things of this world, or of rising above these to the rulership of the things of the heart, mind and spirit, in remembrance of the covenant and its divine mission. Satan is man's lower animal sense nature, and of course this Satan offers the higher Ego the riches of the world and its kingdom of enjoyment. But see what egregious travesty this all becomes when the soul is historicized and carnalized!

He was charged with proclaiming himself king and the title "King of the Jews" was on the cross above his martyred head. This title or phrase has been the culprit in misleading all theology along a false trail into the wilderness of error. The phrase never had a historical reference, to begin with. The "Jews" in it were in no sense the historical racial group. In the Mystery ritual the Christos personage was announced and designated as the king, in the spiritual sense, of course, of those mortals who had adopted the nature and mind of the Christ and had become the divinized and the elect. To denominate this grade of perfected men a term derived from Egypt and its Mysteries was employed. It is the same term that the Hebrews early in their history adopted and appropriated to themselves, as Gesenius tells us in his Hebrew Grammar, "in token of their descent from an illustrious ancestry." The "illustrious ancestry" were none other than the graduates or adepts of the highest rank in the Mystery discipline, or in fact the divinized humans. The Hebrews at an early date simply took to themselves the exalted and illustrious title of the class of men who had risen to shining divinity. The Egyptians called them the short name that was the first element in the name of their Christ Messiah character for thousands of years. This great name was Iu-em-hetep. Iu in Egyptian is 'the Coming One," or "He who comes," meaning the power that comes as our divinity. The highest adepts in the Mystery ranks then were called the "Iu's." They were those in whom the Christ had come. In Latin the "Iu" form shifted to "Ju," as seen in the name of the Romans' King of the Gods, Ju-piter. The Hebrews took to themselves this exalted name and called themselves the Jus, which became in English spelling later, Jews. The Jesus character in the various Mysteries had for centuries borne the title of King of the Ius, or Jus, with never the most remote historical reference attaching to its meaning. But when the historization of the drama took place, the Messiah figure had to be saddled with the claim that he was King of the Jewish nation.

In this light it is of interest to note Easton's observation that what the twentieth century Occidental deems mental sanity is not a fair criterion to apply to first century Galileans. He says that many now expect a proximate millennium without losing their mental balance; and in first century Palestine every sign of the times pointed irresistibly to the fulfillment of God's promises to interpose in the course of this earth's normal progress. As to this, if good folk in the first century were any more gullible or hallucinated about the coming (first or second) of a personal Messiah than large numbers of folks are at this present epoch, it speaks ill for the level of intelligence at that time. If many among us expect the millennium, as, sad to say, they do, without losing their mental balance, the unfortunate implication must be that mental balance has already been pitiably disturbed. For none but religiously hypnotized minds can think seriously of a millennium in realistic historical terms occurring in any near future on this earth. The sects and cults holding millennial views are almost universally regarded with indulgent contempt by intelligent people. According to nearly all Christian writers, the people of Jesus' day were all a-tremble with expectation, being assured of the immediate coming of Messiah and his millennial kingdom. Modern equally certain tremblers are just as certainly deluded. The spirit of charity and wisdom that is Christos is no doubt slowly spreading his gracious rulership over the lives of men on the planet; and the gradual increase of that spirit until it divinizes all the race is the only millennium anywhere visioned in ancient scripture. That it will ever be marked off historically with definite beginning and precise date of end, and only for one thousand short years, is a crazy idea for people to hold in first, tenth or twentieth century.

As has been noted earlier, the odd thing about millennial advent theory is that its visionary and enraptured anticipators have declared in every century since at least the tenth that the particular century then in course exhibited those precise signs of the times, mentioned in the Bible, that indicated the approach of the crack of doom. This indeed shows the whole concept to be emotional fol-de-rol, with cap and bells. Yet Jesus himself is written down as having announced it would come before his generation had passed away! And so it turns out that the only-begotten Son of Omniscient Deity committed a blunder in historical judgment that no ordinarily intelligent person would make at any time. For nineteen hundred years have elapsed and the Savior's prediction is still unfulfilled. His miscalculation has put his apologetic followers who write books about him to no end of exertion in casuistry to "explain" his error. There is sorely needed a comprehensive survey of the entire theme of Messiahship in religion. It will be undertaken in the last chapters.

The discussion of Gospel historicity could not well skip the item of the casting out of demons, evil spirits, demoniacal obsessions. It may not be feasible to wash the whole subject away as impossible history, though in the end it must come close to that. The practice and the very fact of it are thrown out of court in sane psychological quarters today. Christians would not themselves be found committed to a credence in such things, nor would they be caught indulging in any countenance of them or traffic in them. The matter is held to be outside the pale of normal Christian activity, and is left to the unorthodox cults of Spiritualism to deal with. But in books on Jesus it would not do to charge the Master with being involved in unorthodox and spurious religionism of any sort. So the writers report the exorcisms as legitimately within the province of Christian healing. To be sure, modern psychology studies the phenomena of dual or multiple personality, schizophrenic possession and other varieties. But this is still a great deal softer than blunt assertion of obsession by the power of Satan. This is diabolism pure and unrelieved. The question raised was by what authority and in whose name did he cast out the devils. His Messianic credentials were indeed supposed to be established or refuted by the answer he could give to the question put to him by his enemies. The argumentative strategists accused him of casting out devils by Beelzebub, the Prince of Demons. If he said he did it by God's authority, they would have him on the claim of being God's Son. The Christians have been in much the same dialectical predicament as was their Master. If they credit the miracles of exorcism, they authenticate a disclaimed superstition; if they refuse standing or reality to the phenomenon of obsession, they discredit their Founder-Teacher. To uphold the paragon, they must accept an unpleasant rider on the bill.

Chapter XVII

TRUTH EXORCISES DEMONIAC OBSESSIONS

The debate on diabolic obsession and the predicament in which the history thesis plunges it are both beautifully resolved and reason is restored to the throne in the kingdom of Biblical exegesis once more by the simple device of understanding that the entry of Christly love-wisdom into the life and consciousness of the race and the individual drives out those irrationalities, fixations, obsessions of error, those almost literally demoniac possessions, which the rampant elemental forces, centered in the lower carnal mind, stamp upon the psychic nature. This is all that could ever have been sanely meant by the myth of the Christ casting out evil spirits. The Bible stories are but the scripts of the dramatizations of the inner change.

Likewise, it can be said summarily, the diseases, leprosies, palsies, "deaths," infirmities, cripplings, which are the subject of Jesus' whole run of miraculous cures, belong to the same general category of typology. The touch of Jesus' physical hand, or his magic words, upon the human sufferer is beyond any doubt or controversy the type, and type only, of the general healing and integrating power of the impact of true Christliness in the subjective life. The miracles, as Massey so clearly noted, can not be taken as objective historical occurrences. It has been seen how even a writer like Warschauer has thrown grave doubt over the most of them. Again it is seen that as history a large section of the Gospels is unacceptable and stirs incredulity; as allegory it takes its high place in both understanding and cultural stimulus. In every case gain is won by discarding the history and accepting the allegorism.

Then there is the matter of the several numbers used over and over again in Gospel narrative. Nothing has so glaringly revealed the pitiable meagerness of the orthodox scholar's equipment for archaic interpretation and the innocence of his mind as regards knowledge of ancient systems of numerology in scriptural writings as does his blindness or opacity of mind as to the meaning of these numbers. This want of insight into a profoundly technical subject and the inveterate refusal to credit the matter with any definite significance whatever, have become a trifle pathetic in these late days, when competent research has well established the bases of intelligible comprehension of a profoundly abstruse science. Even chiasmus would have been howled down before this epoch; now it is accredited. Number symbolism must now also be legitimatized. The recurrence of such numbers as 2, 3, 4, 7, 10, 12, 30, 40 and 300, more especially 3, 7, 12 and 40, should have spoken to the dullest of imaginations as to the lurking presence of great significance in their ubiquitous appearance in scripture. It would take pages of elaborate exposition to set forth here the meaning of the three days in the tomb, the walking on the water at the fourth watch of the night, the five wise and five foolish virgins, the servant's setting out six pots of water to be turned into wine and this happening "after three days," Jesus' going up into the Mount of Transfiguration "after six days," his tarrying at certain places seven days, and the 40 days' duration of the temptation. The number forty occurs sixty-three times in the Old Testament. It is surely a bit naïve to ask coincidence to explain why so many events in the natural course of actual history should run just forty days or forty years. The very unlikelihood of so much coincidence should have taught students that they were dealing with symbolism and not factuality. Forty was a universal number used to typify the period that the seed of divine consciousness must lie dormant in incubation in matter before germinating in a new birth. The human foetus is forty weeks in the maternal womb. In Egypt the grain was said to lie in the ground forty days before sprouting.

There is the item of Jesus' unknown years. Can it be imagined that if the Gospels were in any real sense intended to be biographies, or even merely works designed to link the principles of the new religion with the ostensible life and acts of the divine Messenger who allegedly brought it into being, they would leave a nearly total blank in his history from the birth events up until the last few months of his abbreviated life? The very doubtful incident of his temple argument with the doctors at twelve is the only item that breaks the long hiatus. This plan of the presentation of the material does not suggest history. The claim is that the data were – by the time Mark came to think of writing his recollections – meager and scant enough. In the first place, the Gospel that is alleged to have been written first does not read in any respect like the work of a man who is really trying to piece together what he recalls of events that he had once had actual knowledge of. No man in any age would produce a work that reads as those Gospels do, if he were aiming to restore a series of veridical historical events in a historical narrative. He would not inweave and embellish it with so large a proportion of admittedly legendary garnish. Reading it, one gathers the feeling that one is reading a work of allegorism. If it is history it is surely the most lyric type of history ever written. Practically there is little to its very substance save a cluster of prodigies at the birth and a larger cluster of prodigies and miracles, interspersed with discourses and moral philosophy, and a dramatic denouement at the end. Anyone with a cultivated sense for ancient dramatism can feel that it is allegory he is reading, and not history. The three years of his "ministry" – all there is of his life – have even been reduced by some scholars to one and a half, or even to one. The ancients did indeed represent the cycle of spiritual initiation, or symbolic history of the Christian life, under the typism and within the frame of the solar year, with its twelve solar months and its thirteen lunar ones. The festivals around the year were all set to match the symbolism of the dying sun of autumn, the resurrected one of spring, the balance (of spirit and matter) at the two equinoxes, and the alternate victory of light (spirit) and darkness (matter) at the two opposite solstices. Samuel, a type of the Christos, is said to have made an annual circuit of Ramah, Bethel, Gilgal and Mizpah, which can be equated with the four "corners" of the annual zodiac, or the two solstices and the two equinoxes. The Biblical "year of the Lord" was a phrase that had this typological reference. The sun being always masculine and the moon feminine, several of the patriarchs were given a progeny of twelve sons and one daughter! It is of no avail for the modern theologian to snort in annoyance at such renditions of meaning, or such a method of exegesis. The snort is silenced by the fact that the ancient sages did resort to such devices to embalm the precious core of meaning in structures of subtle indirection. If we would interpret what they wrote, we must at least follow their method and cease grumbling at its peculiarities. We shall no longer be annoyed if we yield our recalcitrancy, follow their scheme and find at last that apparent nonsense is replaced with the most luminous intelligence. We are annoyed at their method because our own presuppositions defeat our efforts to comprehend. Our key won't fit their construction and we blame them for stupidity. When we have sense enough to use the key they used, or the key that alone fits their lock, the obstructing door can be opened and the light let in. The events between birth and final climactic end of the Christ story are missing, not because Mark forgot anything in that interval, but because those given were the episodes featured in the allegorical depiction. It must be put down as a very unlikely circumstance that if Mark could remember even the words spoken by many characters throughout, and short speeches of long discourses in places, and the minutiae of the miracles and journeys, he could not recall a single item between the birth and year twelve, and between twelve and thirty! Massey is authority for the observation that the same two lacunae occur in the "lives" of other legendary Messiahs; so that again every rational implication points to its being allegory and not objective fact.

The triumphal entry into Jerusalem: not only is this as unlikely a historical event as could be imagined, but it is definitely an episode in the dramatic ritual of initiation. It did not need to happen on the streets of Jerusalem to get into Gospels; it was already in the scripts of the ritual drama. Like many another incident and miracle of the narrative, it would have been in the "record" if no Jesus had ever lived – for it was already there centuries before Christ. Every religious dramatization or initiatory ritual had as part of its climactic denouement the entry of the candidate into a room, palace or "city" emblematic of the "city of heavenly peace" – St. Augustine's "City of God," Bunyan's "Celestial City" – as the place to which the exiled pilgrim soul returns to its empyrean "homeland." This feature of dramatic topography originated – as did nearly all others – in Egypt, where the prototype of the Greek Elysian Fields was found in the form of the Aarru-Hetep. "Hetep" is the Egyptian for "peace" and so is the equivalent of the Hebrew Sholom or Salem. Aarru is the origin of the "hiero" – meaning "sacred," which became the "Jeru" of Jerusalem, the city of "sacred peace," or finally the celestial paradise. Jerusalem is spelled in old manuscripts "Hierosolyma." The entry of Jesus into the Holy City is but the historicized drama of the soul making its regal entry into the "city" of blessed peace and rest after its triumphant battle with the lower forces on earth. Each nation of antiquity used its capital city, named often to fulfill this function, as the earthly counterpart of the heavenly city of the allegory. That he entered it riding on an ass and her colt is the cryptic fashion of representing the soul's being carried from the outlying regions of the material experience up to and through the gates of the Holy City by the agency of the animal portion of its own dual nature. And the presence of two generations of the faithful animal is to typify the fact that the soul's journey from animalism up to divinity can not be consummated in one cycle of experience in the flesh, but must proceed through a succession of lives, passing continuously from the older phase of one generation to the succeeding younger phase. If this seems far-fetched and strained, it will be seen in its proper relevance if one studies the functionism of the Egyptian pair Osiris-Horus, Father-Son, Horus the Elder-Horus the Younger, and Kheper, the beetle-god, and the ideologies connected with them. Each younger generation of animal bodily life took up the labor of carrying the soul ahead through its progression and the ideograph of this had to represent the older and the younger stages in the line of procreation to convey the full meaning. If literalism pictures Jesus as entering astride both animals at once, it faithfully preserves the idea that he has won his victory by virtue of what both generations of the animal embodiment have done for him.

On its realistic side the incident seems logically impossible. How Jesus – if he had stirred up the popular hostility that was to hound him to his death within a week – could have found the populace at Jerusalem in mood to welcome him with hosannas and strewn palms, and how he got the crowd out for the reception, is a little more than credulity can swallow. And to crown the whole procedure with anomaly, the episode, taken from the drama, got into the Gospel scenario at the wrong place. It was put in too soon. The Gospels being a dramatization of the unfolding history of the soul in its struggle through the elements, it is an anachronism to put the final episode of his return from earthly exile to his celestial home ahead of the crucifixion and death. It would logically even follow the ascension, and should be the final and climactic act of the entire drama. Life proceeds outward from the silence of the inner chambers of creation at the beginning of a cycle of new growth, fights its battle on the plain or on the "mount" of open visible manifestation then retires again within the inner sanctum of the temple of the universe, its last tones ringing like an echo over the scene of its late activity. The church recessional symbolizes the return of the evolutionary pilgrim to his Father's house, chanting its song of triumph as it enters the gates of the "Holy City," "Jerusalem, the Blest." If one will in imagination rise to some degree of appreciation of the grandeur of this evolutionary drama, and then displace it suddenly with the imagined realism of Jesus' riding the lowly animal into the Judean capital, one will gain a realizing sense of the tragedy which befell human culture when allegory was turned into history. By feeding our minds on the grossness of historical realism instead of the dynamic psychic power of allegorism and typology, we have lost touch with the bases of cathartic purification.

The crucifixion! The longer and more closely one ponders it – realistically – the less it seems possible as an actual occurrence. It, too, had its dramatic prototype in the Mystery ritual where the candidate for initiation was tied or bound or symbolically nailed to the cross and even put into a hypnotic coma to be awakened from "death" after three days on Easter morning. Thus the non-historical source of the feature is clearly evident. There is much doubt as to the Roman practice of physical crucifixion, and particularly on a Tau cross. It was not a Hebrew custom, or sanctioned by Hebrew law. It was resorted to, as far as known, only in exceptional and rare occasions. It seems on the surface more like a ritual procedure than a physical event. Again, like the temptation, the Sermon, the transfiguration and ascension, it was consummated "on the Mount," which is the hieroglyph for the earth. And it is surely not without occult significance that "Calvary" is from the Latin calvus, meaning "the head," and "Golgotha" is Hebrew for "the place of the skull." It is of course clear that the inner significance of all that goes into the interior experience of the crucifixion of the Son of God as immortal soul on the cross of matter, is "localized" within the head or brain, or mind, of man. This datum is enough to enable anyone familiar with ancient habits of typology and dramatization of truth to penetrate to the heart of the mystery behind the names of the Mount of Crucifixion. Prometheus, whose name signifies the archetypal creative Fore-Thought, was chained to a rock on a Mount and tortured there. The allegorical background and archetypes of the Gospel crucifixion are complete and perfect; the historical evidences and possibilities are far from similarly strong. It makes much greater sense as drama than it possibly can do as history.

The picture of the Son of God coming to earth to show mankind how to be victorious over the conditions of mortality, and then demonstrating his victory by the method of physical helplessness and an ignominious death of his body on the cross, has never seemed anything but unnatural to the naïve mind. The mind even of piety and devotion has to be "conditioned" by subtle sophistries before it can accept the postulations of Christianity. Not until one studies the Egyptian and Greek philosophies and views the resultant findings through the eyes of symbolic depiction can the feature of sacrifice and immolation in the mission of the divine Son to earth be aligned with the reasonable background of our position. Long lost to ecclesiastical philosophy is the ancients' characterization of matter as the cross on which the Christ-soul is crucified, and this physical life itself as the "death" of the divine Ego. These two concepts were the ribs or spine, so to say, of the archaic wisdom. For the Christ to die on the cross was simply a dramatic glyph for its incarnation. Incarnation was the ground and primary base of all meaning in religion. Therefore to represent the incarnating divinity as being immolated on a cross was to dramatize the basic experience from which all religion flows. Any soul is being crucified on the cross whenever it is alive in a physical body. This life is its (comparative) "death," for in all ancient systems the body, living, was the tomb of the soul's "death." Witness the Greek sema, tomb, and soma, body. Even sarcophagus is from the Greek for the physical body, – sarx. Here, then, is the full meaning of the crucifixion: – the soul's life in body in its incarnational experience, with the infinitude of varied signification attaching to or flowing from that ground. Drama portrayed it by the binding or nailing of a man on a cross of wood. That is drama; the thing dramatized is the god's life under the limitations of mortal flesh. But the drama was not history. It merely depicted the meaning of history. But who can calculate the tragedy of the annual wastage of emotional stress and strain in the pouring out of oceans of maudlin sympathy and vicarious grief over the Passion Week sufferings of a man who never lived? The numberless crucifixes seen on every side stand as a most gruesome and lugubrious sight, filling the beholder not only with morbid revulsion at its positive ugliness, but with a sense of the lamentable breakdown of reason under the force of indoctrinated ignorance. For it stands not as luminous symbol of high meaning, but as the graven image of alleged but impossible historical fact. It stands as the sickening seal of the enslavement of the human mind under the force of a gross delusion and a lie. As the picture of alleged fact it is ugly; for the fact itself – if true – is ugly, because it is incompatible with reason and intellectual integrity. Anything which mocks the reason and strikes at the probity of the mind is ugly. The crucifix, as monument of historic event, is the darkest, most dispiriting object in any landscape, for it speaks of the darkness of the human intellect under the pall of religious superstition.

And the resurrection? So majestic, so powerful in the reach of its grandeur is this doctrine that even though the deeper meaning may not be apprehended, it is deeply affecting. It is so sublime that no inadequacy of conception or representation can quite mar its beautiful suggestiveness. Yet again, it must be said that if it is still full of majesty even in its misconception, how infinitely more moving must it be when rightly comprehended! As the supposed miraculous bursting of the bars of a rocky hillside tomb by a man in human form, risen from bodily death, it leaves us in wonder, awe and – incomprehension. As the dramatization of our own eventual bursting of the bars of "death" and the physical limitations of the mortal body, and our ecstatic stepping out of this prison-tomb through the rent in the veil of this bodily temple into the glorious resurrection-body of light, it leaves us truly lost in wonder, reverence and – comprehension. Surely a more salutary repercussion for the whole of the Ego's mind, soul, body flows from the adequate grasp of a great metaphysical reality than could possibly accrue from the same representation completely misapprehended. If this is not granted, then the argument is that incomprehension is more beneficial than understanding. This is indeed a frequent resort of ecclesiastical helplessness in face of questions that children can – and do – ask. As a glyphic representation of the climactic rapture of our final apotheosization the resurrection is transcendently meaningful and exalting; as the claimed exhibition of one exceptional man's miraculous power, it arouses speculative wonder.

Paul says that if Christ has risen, the bases of Christianity are sound. For if he rose, we, too, shall rise. Yet nineteen hundred years have passed and not one believing in him has ever risen in the same (alleged physical) manner. If more were needed to prove that the Gospel resurrection could never have been meant to be taken in the objective historical sense, it is found in Paul's statement – which indicates that Christianity has put a wrong interpretation on the incident – that the divine Ego is sown, i.e., incarnated, in a natural body, but is resurrected from that physical tomb in a shining spiritual body. Equally, then, with the crucifixion, the resurrection is dissipated out of its historic character and becomes resolved into its infinitely more marvelous transcendental significance. And as in every other case, for it to die as history and be reborn as dynamic enlightenment, is gain.

The ascension, in any physical sense, is similarly a degradation and caricature of its lofty transcendency. At a high rate of speed, a physical body rising off the earth nineteen hundred years ago would not yet have reached the nearest star. The perfervid but not very realistic imagination of piety assumes that Jesus arose in the sight of his disciples in his body (that Thomas touched) and when he got up a fair distance, his physical substance somehow changed over into what angels are thought to be composed of. And that is enough for faith and credulity. Does "heaven" begin at forty thousand feet above the earth?

There is left one situation that comes under critical view in the Gospels, which certainly bears weighty testimony to the disqualification of another large group of events recorded as history in the Jesus "biography." This relates to the long list of "events" that allegedly transpired on the night before the crucifixion on Good Friday morning, of Passion Week. When zeal for history outran intelligence it did not seem to occur to the ignorant transformers of the myth into that category, that in a case where Egyptian wisdom had concentrated many aspects of meaning into a single symbolic point of time, the transferal of allegorical representation over into factual occurrence might meet unexpected difficulties in the crowding of a long series of symbolic "happenings" into a limited period of actual time. Mythical depiction requires only hypothetical time; history demands actual time or measured duration. This very predicament developed in connection with the incidents recounted in the Gospels as taking place on this last night of Jesus' life. It was the night of the Passover, placed by one account on the 14th of Nisan, by another on the 15th, and both dates symbolical of the first full moon after the vernal equinox, a fact which at once gives it the simple significance of Easter. It was the night in the religious (solar) year on which all the significance of the entire course of incarnate experience came to a head in its last (symbolic) climactic moments. On this "night," under solar symbolism, the soul in the flesh on earth came to the end and consummation of all its labors in the body, finished its assigned task, accomplished the final stages of its perfection and stood on the door-sill of its liberation forever into celestial freedom out of earthly bondage. On that night all things heaped up in consummation and in victory. It was the night of triumph. All phases and lines of development reached their apical convergence in the glorious unfoldment into light, as the Greeks call it, of all the latent potentialities of the spiritual Ego in that final consummatum est. In the nineteenth chapter of the Egyptian Ritual (Book of the Dead) the symbolic narrative recounts a long list of allegorical processes which depict the concluding stages and steps of the many varied forms of portrayal under which the soul's experience had been typed. It was all one experience, but it comprised the blending in one grand climactic moment or realization of many strands and facets of growth in man's composite nature, and each phase had been allegorized under its appropriate typism. It was the final merging of all the varied rays into the ultimate white light. So in this nineteenth chapter there is a description of the climactic stage of each aspect. So to say, each stream of the living force had to be brought up to empty its final product and consummation into the crystal sea of complete divinization. The chapter therefore speaks of this last "night" of the soul on earth as "the night of" some fifteen or more apparently different transactions, when in fact it is descriptive of but the one grand collective denouement of salvation. And this "night" in the Ritual is none other than the night of the full moon of the vernal equinox! Symbolically the soul then crosses the line (of the equinox) which in the diagram of meanings marks the boundary between earth and heaven; and thus at its climactic moment in all its earthly experience it "passes over" from earth to heaven, to become "a pillar in the house" of its God, to "go no more out."

Frankness calls for the admission that the Egyptian list of "events" occurring on that meaningful "night" has apparently not been reproduced or copied in the Gospel story. Several of them correspond and might point to transmission from Egyptian into Palestinian literature. However, the difference in most of them can readily be accounted for on the ground of the great diversity of symbolic representation and the constant attempt throughout the ancient day to vary the systems of typing. Hebrew symbology did assume a quite different face from the Egyptian in many respects. But it still remains highly significant that in both the Egyptian and the Hebrew (or Greek) scriptures the narrative crowds a long list of "events," factual or ritualistic, into the few hours of this night of the Passover. The meaning of both groups of occurrences is, if the symbolism be penetrated, one at base. But the Egyptian was frankly allegorical; the Hebrew, under Christian handling, purports to be history. This difference becomes exceedingly, overwhelmingly embarrassing to the claims of the historical rendition. For it turns out that there could not possibly have been time enough – on the historical presupposition – in that night to enable the events narrated to have occurred in reality. On the symbolic basis one can crowd any number of developments into a single "night," for meaning expands into a fourth dimension and occupies no space or fills no time. But when one converts these imponderables over into history, they require time to occur. It makes a vast and in this case catastrophic difference. It all conspired to give the personal Christ a very full program and a busy time on his last night on earth! It is interesting to list the card for the hours from sunset until the next morning's gruesome finale. This schedule began with the "Last Supper" with the twelve, which, if held at "supper-time" would have started off the night's activities. This would have taken several hours, perhaps, if the animated discourse pictured so vividly by Leonardo in the famous painting be accepted as possible reality. After that came the walk out to the Mount of Olives and return. As there would have been no point in turning back the moment of arrival there, this item would have consumed time running on toward midnight. Then came the switch of scene to Gethsemane and the detailed series of incidents there, including time for Jesus' long agony and sweat; his chiding of the disciples for falling asleep and not being able to watch with him "one little hour"; his arrest by the special guard sent out to take him; the cutting off and healing of the ear of the centurion's servant; then – wonder of wonders! – three separate and distinct court trials, involving the presence of officials, the procurator, the Sanhedrin, and the masses, all in the late hours of the stillness of an Oriental night; then the mockery of the soldiers, the casting lots for his garments, the pressing of the crown of thorns on his brow; – then at last the toilsome journey up the hill, with cross on bleeding shoulder, to Golgotha; the erection of the cross, with those of the two thieves; and the final agony. It may be argued that this program could have been run through in the ten or twelve hours that have been assigned to it. But the three court trials seem to throw the decision against the possibility. To accept this all as history is indeed asking us to swallow a camel. It seems clear that in this instance history overreached itself and betrayed its own incompetency as an interpretative key. History here at last breaks down under its own impossible weight. It reads itself out of court. It fails when tested empirically. As fact it goes down; only as allegory can its material retain plausibility and sane meaning.

Writers spin fine theories to render it all acceptable as occurrence, but in the end it comes back to the point of obvious impossibility in any common sense view of it. The legerdemain of miracle must be called upon to rescue it. There is really no likelihood that it could all have taken place as narrated. And once more all unseemliness and difficulty vanish through the simple expedient of viewing it for what it obviously is, – a dramatic play, garbled and altered to make it fit the dimensions of history.

Although it is by no means the whole of the available material, this much of the refutation of the Gospel narrative as history must suffice. Here, then, we have the record of events making up the biography of the man Jesus of Nazareth, a biography acclaimed by hundreds of learned scholars as one of the best authenticated of historical lives. The entire story is found only in one book, in four varied "editions." We take this book's elaborated detail and, instead of finding it to be admittedly genuine history, we are amazed to discover that, even on the admission or by the declaration of the supporters of the historic interpretation, event after event, whole series of events, whole sections of the text, evaporate into the thin mist of legend and poetry, leaving next to nothing of solid substance to ground the historic position upon. The very material that has been advanced as proof of the historicity is admitted to be not history at all! Orthodoxy is found to have for centuries maintained the claim of the historicity of a character whose available life record turns out to be myth and fable. And the egregiously vaunted unimpeachable history of the man of Galilee rests only upon allegory at last. In the plainest of words Paul says that the Abraham-Sarah-Isaac-Hagar-Ishmael story in the Old Testament "is an allegory." His own silence as to Jesus and a hundred other silent but logical voices seem to proclaim that the whole Gospel story is likewise allegory. The whole of its "history" fades at the touch of realism into the unsubstantial hues of dramatic romance. And this verdict comes as forcefully out of the mouths of its confessors as from its opponents. And the final devastating blow to the historical thesis falls with the recognition that not only does the supposed historic framework prove to be in the end mythic invention, but it turns out to be in the main a mere copy of mythic material from originals drawn from earlier pagan systems. The grand upshot of the whole investigation is that the life of Jesus reduces to nothing but the re-edited body of ancient Egyptian mythology.

Chapter XVIII

THE ANOINTING OF MAN

No critical survey of the question of the Biblical Christ could be considered thorough unless it covered the entire theme of ancient Messianism, since the Gospel Jesus came in the aura and setting of this concept and his alleged mission and the movement founded on it derive most of their essential meaning from it. It will be found as the result of such a survey that a clear grasp on the features of this great ancient persuasion yields for us finally the substantial bases for determination of the main question of the historicity. In curt statement, when it is known fully and correctly what the conception of Messiahship really was, it will be seen that it never looked to its fulfillment through the birth or advent of a historical person, no matter how divine. If Jesus came as the fulfillment of all ancient Messianic expectation, and came as a human babe, his coming was not after all the true fulfillment, and the proclamation and belief of his Messiahship was a miscarriage of the true import of the tradition. No intelligent adherent of ancient religious systems ever dreamed of the Messiah's coming as a man. It was clearly understood that that which was to come was a principle, or spirit, or rule of righteousness in all humanity. The Nativity, to be sure, under the sway of symbolic method, took on the aspect of the birth of a babe in the zodiacal house of bread, or Bethlehem, and of course from the kingly line of divine Davidic intellection. But esoteric intelligence knew where symbolism began and also where it ended. Symbolism can sweep in strong force over the human spirit, carrying it straight into the core of vital meaning as it presents to the mind the reality of that which it adumbrates. But it can not thus enlighten and empower the mind if it holds it down to its own level and insists on its own factuality. A symbol is not to engage the thought longer than to give it a vigorous push and send it away from itself as from a springboard into a realm of apprehension never glimpsed before. A symbol is only the initial energization of a thought, which is to proceed from it to more distant flight. With the literalist or exotericist thought ends with and at the symbol. The tragedy of this is that while the symbol is powerful enough to suggest the vital import of meaning symbolized, it can never contain that meaning within itself. But a strange phenomenon occurs in the psychological field if one dwells with symbols attentively for a long time. At the same time that the meaning passes beyond the symbol to the inner regions of mind and thought, it tends in the end to reflect back upon the symbol and transfuse it with the glow of the greater light which through it as lens has been thrown upon the screen of a subjective world lying beyond. So that while the symbol is overpassed, it is not discarded, but itself becomes more vividly irradiated with sublime pertinence. He who celebrates Christmas knowing that the Bethlehem babe is only a symbolic type of something remote from the physical and not an event at all, still will find the stable, the manger, the babe, ox, ass, and star all in themselves radiantly alight with transferred meaning poured down upon them from above. Though they are not the containers of the meaning, they will be freshly lighted up with meaning reflected from on high. Being the adjuncts and indicators of that high meaning, they will by repercussion come to share the meaning itself. The whole pageantry and accouterment of meaning can be heartily entertained and in no sense (save the historical) rejected, when a reference to reality beyond it is accepted and one that it can not carry is rejected. It becomes translucent with beauty through simply being the agency of the mind's grasp of supernal beauty beyond it. The greater light that it helped the mind to discover flows back to bathe it in the hues of a mystical iridescence. It may be a paradox, yet it is thoroughly true that religious imagery and pageantry exercise a far stronger dynamism when they are known to be allegorical than if they are believed to be memorials of fact. The symbol helps the mind to grasp greater reality over in the subjective world; from that clearer vision the mind can swing back and embrace the symbol as an integral part of the great treasure of light caught by its aid. It will not be cast aside as worthless when the full gods of glorious meaning arrive. It can be carried along as the outer coin and mnemonic seal of the golden revelation. This is to refute the charge that if the events of religious ceremonial and festivity are thrown out as non-historical, the whole celebration of such festivals as Christmas and Easter will lose all their gripping impressiveness. On the contrary the symbols will exert a ten-fold weightier significance when they are envisioned truly as symbols and not falsely as events.

The theme of the ancient Messianic conception is a majestic one. It seems clear that no true knowledge of it has been extant since remote antiquity. Every rendition of it, every view or exposition of it in the centuries down to the present has been a gross material caricature of it. The best effort to reinvest it with its pristine magnificence may not be adequate to the task. But the fuller glory of the mighty cosmic event it illustrates can not be sensed until at least the mental statement of its profound significance is attempted.

The name – Messiah – calls for examination, to begin with. It is of combined Egyptian and Hebrew etymology. The mess is from the Egyptian mes, meaning to give birth to, to be born. The -iah is the well-known Hebrew terminal, meaning in its broadest sense "God" or "divinity." In deeper connotation it is a hieroglyph for deity that has descended into matter to be born anew. (As such it is an abbreviated form of the seven-lettered Jehovah, denoting male-female deity in union.) The word Messiah then means "the born God," or "the born deity," in the fuller sense of the "reborn deity."

Another meaning of mess in Egyptian is "to sprinkle" or "anoint." Through this etymology the word comes to have the secondary meaning of "the anointed God." Anointing with oil was throughout ancient days a ritualistic typing of the more abstruse meaning of a baptism of the lower nature by the higher divine influence. It carried the idea of pouring on the head of a man a substance that could be set on fire. The key is to be found in John Baptist's statement that while he, the preparer of the way for a higher influx, baptizes us with "water" – type of the life of the natural order – the more exalted one coming after him is to baptize us with "air" (Latin: spiritus) "and with fire." Oil symbolically is higher than water, for the reason that it always rises to the top of water and besides is the fuel for fire, which water is not. It is a substitute symbol for "fire" itself, being its fuel and giving a bright and shining appearance. So then the Messiah, as the "anointed God," was the Christos, come or coming to earth to be gradually reborn into his next stage of expanded life and consciousness through a baptism or anointing with the "oil of" divine "gladness."

The "anointing" facet of the meaning allies the term "Messiah" with the Greek name of "Christos." We have already traced this as a likely derivative from the Egyptian KaRaST, the name of the mummy, or the god "fleshed" (Greek: kreas, "flesh.") It is probable that all these are kindred to the Sanskrit kri, "to pour out," "to rub over," i.e., "to anoint." Messiah and Christos are therefore identical in meaning. The kri derivation of the word at once establishes Krishna as a Messiah of the first order.

The intellectual roots of the Messianic tradition lie away down in the ancient cosmogonic formula that the Logos was to become fleshed and dwell among the inhabitants of earth. The fleshing of the Logos, which was the condition and concomitant phenomenon of his earthly advent, was the coming of Messiah. Begotten before all the worlds in the bosom of the Father, dwelling in the inchoate depths of the "abyss" of matter before the creation swept into organic form, he was destined to come to the fullness of his manifestation in the flowering of the genius of his divinity in a race of human but potentially divine men on this planet. As much of his cosmic power as could function through the mechanism of fleshly body on such a planet was to be brought forth in full epiphany, or to full appearance in human fleshly embodiment. This segment or ray of its power was the Christos. The Logos is the unbounded Power that informs and ensouls the whole manifest creation. In no way could the totality of its energy be circumscribed and contained in a single solar system, a single planet, or a single race of beings on a given planet. How much less, then, could it be embodied in the tiny confines of the body of a single man? But that degree, measure and aspect of its universal vibration – that one note of its infinite gamut of tones and chords – which the brain and nervous system of a race of conscious beings on a globe could embody and express, or in the etymological sense of the word, per-sonal-ize (i.e., sound through, from sonum, "sound," and per, "through,") that form of the universal expression was the Christos. It would come to birth in the milieu of mortal strife, in the body of a biologically developed animal race wherein animal carnality would contend furiously with its incipient new order of gentleness until subdued by the all-conquering power of a higher order of intelligence. It would gradually grow into the fullness of its stature of conscious power and at last take over the rulership of all the motivations of action and end by seating himself on the throne in the kingdom of the world. The Christos was one ray of the energy of the Logos, that ray which could rule in the kingdom of man's mind, heart, soul. Its gradual growth in the spirit and consciousness of the human race was the coming of Messiah.

Playing the role of the central event, and embracing indeed the entire inner significance of the whole process of human racial evolution, it was at once the dominant theme, the nub and focus, of all the schematism in religion and philosophy. The gist of all the meaning in scriptures and theology falls within its pale. The coming, that is, the birth, of the Son of God, his chain of experiences dramatized as his circumcision, baptism, temptation, trial, condemnation, crucifixion, death and resurrection, formed the ritualistic outline of his life on earth, his sojourn in the flesh.

But the first onset of the rush of perception that springs from this basic statement brings with it the vitally significant realization that the "coming" of Christos to humanity would be a process covering the whole life span of humanity itself. It would be a coming of such gradual movement that it would far better be described as a growth carried forward over the entire history of man. It would be a coming only in the sense in which we say that a child comes to be a man. There is seen to be no possible place in the conception for a "coming" in the sense of an arrival in objective manifestation at a given moment or year. It is to be seen as a coming that is always being forwarded, ever taking place from one end of the cycle to the other, from the beginning of a period of creation to the end of the aeon. The basic conception of Messiah thus rules out from the start the idea of its fulfillment in and through the birth of a man at any "date" in history, and reduces any such statement of it at once to the category of symbol.

The correctness of this view is found immediately at hand in the several titles prefixed to the Messianic figure in ancient Egypt. He is "the Ever-Coming One," "He Who Ever Comes Periodically." The idea is emphasized also in one of the many addresses uttered by Horus, who is the Messiah, when he announces himself in the words "I am Horus, who steppeth onward through eternity." Again it is the background of his declaration: "Eternity and everlastingness is my name."

He says he is Yesterday, Today and Tomorrow, and the name of his boat is Millions of Years." "I am the persistent traveler on the ways of heaven." A score of other appellations and descriptions would fortify the diuturnity of the conception. The "regular" and "periodical" nature of the coming will be dealt with more at large when the astronomical aspect of the typism is reviewed. Nothing is clearer than that the ancient tradition of Messiah connoted nothing whatever in the form of an event that could be dated in history. It definitely reads as the unfoldment of a power through a process that runs on continuously through the cycle of the race. It is a growth that takes place in the life and consciousness. It has its beginnings, its mid-course and its climactic denouement. But while all these stages are accomplished through an instrument that binds the operation to a scene in time and place, still no stage, aspect or crisis in the process is a local temporal event. The birth can be said to take place in "Bethlehem" or in "Abydos" or in "Annu." But these were names of subjective realities long before they were assigned to cities when the allegory was foisted on local geography. The birth would have taken place in "Bethlehem" and "Annu," and the crucifixion on "Golgotha," no matter what particular localities later received these names. The baptism took place in the Jordan, yes, if the Jordan is the river of life that runs on the borderline between the kingdom of the flesh and the Holy Land of spirit, and must be crossed by the peregrinating souls to reach the Promised Land of blessedness. The temptation took place on the Mount, if the "Mount" is the planet earth. And the resurrection took place in and from the tomb, if that "tomb" is the mortal body. The death took place on the cross, if that "cross" is the deadening inhibition of the sluggish vibration or inertia of the material corpus in which soul comes to be housed for a season. Yet in no soul's experience can these "events" be organized into a series of historical occurrences as for an individual human being. Although they are in themselves the essence and meaning-gist of all historical event, they do not transpire in the realm of three-dimensional space, nor are they commensurable with the human sense of temporal happening. They do not occur "once upon a time." They are rather the final deposit of the whole historical stream upon the ocean bed of basic consciousness undergoing its initiation into reality. If, as Tennyson avers, life is ever going from more to more, the birth and transformation of the Christ nature is the cycle of cosmic event that gives a particular mode of life or type of consciousness its baptism into a larger sweep of sentient being. It was and is the event of human history; but still not an event in human history. It was the one event and not one of the events. None of the typologies by which ancient genius dramatized this chapter of evolutionary history could be detached and called an event in that history. The whole straggling line of linked events in world history make up this one cosmic event. We are all living now, individually and collectively, the baptism, the temptation and the transfiguration of the Christos, yet no single event of our lives is any of these transactions. The gradual upsurge of the spirit of charity and good-will in human hearts was the birth of the Christ on earth, and the continuous expansion and growing sway of that spirit among men was his ever-coming.

Massey's unequivocal declaration is that the advent of Messiah was periodic, not once for all. His words are stirring:

"Once-for-all could have no meaning in relation to that which was ever-coming from age to age, from generation to generation, or for ever and ever. Eternity itself to the Egyptians of the Ritual was aeonian, or synonymous with millions of repetitions, therefore ever-coming in the likeness of perennial renewal, whether in the water-springs of earth or the day-spring from on high, the papyrus-shoot, the green branch, or as Horus the child, in whom a Savior was at length embodied as a figure of eternal source. At the foundation of all sacrifice we find the great Earth-Mother, following the human mother, giving herself for food and drink. Next the type of sacrifice is that of the ever-coming child. . . . Thenceforth the papyrus-plant was represented by the shoot; the tree by the branch; the sheep by the lamb; the Savior by the infant as an image of perpetual renewal in life by means of his own death and transformation in furnishing the elements of life."

The phrase of central importance in this passage is that which describes the life as unfolding its germinal potentiality into product through millions of repetitions. The first of all principia in the knowledge of life is that it eternally renews itself in periodic cycles of birth, growth, decay and death (of its forms), building its constructions each time anew out of the debris of the old, and unfolding a segment of its predetermined pattern in each renewal. That which becomes ever increasingly apparent to the student of Egyptian wisdom is the great fact of the eternal renewal. It is the hub of the universe and the nub of all discourse about it. The understanding that life endlessly renews itself, dying to be born again, turning the very wrack of death into the sustenance of new life, and so advancing to its purpose through the series, is the first fundament of knowledge, the ground of all wisdom.

And that which "comes," which manifests itself in increasing revelation at each successive wave of ongoing, is just the archetypal design, the ultimate as it was the primary goal, of the whole movement. This structural and organic whole is Logos, the "logical" form that the creation is to take. Obviously that which conforms to and harmonizes with the primordial cosmic mental design is "logical"; that which does not is "illogical."

We can not doubt that through the ages one increasing purpose runs, and that life is making its epiphany through the circling of the suns. In its minor cycle, too, the Christos, arm of the power of the Logos, ray from its larger cosmic fiery heart, manifests its developing beauty through its successive reincarnational expressions in material body on earth. Each descent to earth, where it dies as seed of former growth to be renewed as new shoot, brings to view a larger graciousness, a more resplendent loveliness of its nature. It makes many "comings" in order finally to be here in full. The endless repetition of cycle in the life movement makes the coming of deific power both periodic and regular, as the Egyptians have it.

If the fundamental truth about life is that it eternally renews itself, the human mind has not far to go to find the natural analogue of the principium. Two types of endless renewal confront the eye of man at all times. The one is the seasonal death and rebirth of nature; the other is the periodical cycles of the stars. The seasonal renewal of nature has an astronomical basis and background. It will readily be seen, then, how this determination operated to throw the whole delineation of Messianic advent into the forms of astronomical cycles. It was but a matter of looking at nature, which herself set the norms and figures of cyclical periodicity, to discern the types that would exemplify the ceaseless adventing of the Christos into the mundane sphere. Utilizing primarily the two most patent cycles of the day and the year, as well as the annual cycle of growth and death in the vegetable world, the fashion under the typism of the zodiacal precession and the great mythical and stellar-cycles. These will be elaborated presently.

In the Rubric directions to Chapter 149 of the Ritual (Birch) there are given the secret instructions "by which the soul of Osiris is perfected in the bosom of Ra." This perfecting of the soul of deity is the equivalent of the "coming" of the Christ on earth to establish the reign of good-will among men.

"By this book the soul of the deceased shall make its exodus with the living and prevail amongst, or as, the gods. By this book he shall know the secrets of that which happened in the beginning. No one else has ever known this mystical book or any part of it. It has not been spoken by men. . . . Carry it out in the judgment hall. This is a true Mystery, unknown anywhere to those who are uninitiated."

It is ever to be remembered that the "deceased" in the Egyptian Ritual is the living mortal, not the earthly defunct; and therefore its making its exodus among the living is a reference to its coming to full development in the life on earth. The great Mystery is of course the whole import and the reality of life in the cycles, the secret wisdom that the soul picks up throughout its whole peregrination through the kingdoms of organic existence. It unfolds in course as the cycling spiral of experience extends.

Massey's further delineation of the Christos principle is enlightening:

"The Messu, or the Messianic prince of peace, was born into the world at Memphis in the cult of Ptah as the Egyptian Jesus, with the title of Iu-em-hetep, he who comes with peace or plenty and good fortune as the type of eternal youth. Here we may note in passing that this divine child, Iu-em-hetep, as the image of immortal youth, the little Hero of all later legend, the Kamite Heracles, had been one of the eight great gods of Egypt, who were in existence 20,000 years ago; (Herodotus, 2:43) known as Khepr, Horus, Aten, Tum or Nefer-Atum according to the cult. . . . His mother's name at On was Iusaas, she who was great (as) with Iusa or Iusu, the ever-coming child, the Messiah of the inundation." (For even the periodicity of the Nile overflow was used to portray the rhythm of the coming.)

One of the most revealing of all ancient scriptural indices is this great Egyptian name of the Messianic Christ-figure that held in Egypt for some thousands of years B.C. – Iu-em-hetep. It is nearly the whole story in itself. Iu is the verb "to come" ; em is "with" or "in"; and hetep is, most significantly, both the noun "peace" and the number "seven." As all cycles are encompassed in seven stages or sub-cycles, the "peace" that is to be consummated in this seven-part cycle of human development is thus the equivalent or counterpart of the seventh and climactic tonal vibration which synthesizes the whole expression. When humanity shall have reached the apex of its seven-toned perfection, its "peace" will be the harmony of seven keynotes synchronized in one grand master-tone. Therefore "peace" and "seven" are identical, and the Egyptian expressed this profound knowledge in the one word "hetep." (It is our "seven" even now, as the hetep form shortened to "hept," the "h" roughened, as it has often done, into "s," and so the Latin has its "sept-em" and the English its "septenary" and "September.") Iu-em-hetep then reads: "(He who) comes with or in peace as number seven," or as the seventh or climactic stage of the cycle. This name is alone enough to negate all historical assumptions connected with the coming of Messiah. It declares that Messiah comes in his last and consummative stage only in the last round of the cycle. If Messiah came in person two thousand years ago, it was an untimely and futile advent. He came too soon and wholly out of relation to cyclical denouement. The Bible itself is loud in its proclamation of the aeonially cataclysmic accompaniments of the last days of the cycle, when the Son of Man (the product of the "man" cycle and therefore its Son) shall come in the clouds of heavenly consciousness to pronounce the final judgments on the results of the cycle's effort. The "coming" in Judea in the year one A.D. is therefore like the entry of an actor into the play long before his cue and out of all pertinence to his part in the drama. In the premature appearance of the Christ in embodied form at a given date in world time the whole framework of the ancient theological structure would have been disorganized. In brief, a personal Messiah at any time is not necessary to the meaning or fulfillment of ancient theology. In fact the latter can not in any way accommodate in its essential structure a historical Messiah. The introduction of such an element into the system deranges the logic and upsets the meaning of the whole. Ancient theology had no place for a man-Savior.

The Jesus-legend, says Massey, was Egyptian, but, he adds, it was at first without the dogma of historic personality. The latter was a spurious addition made to it by misguided Christians.

In the Ritual Horus, the Egyptian Christ, says:

"I am Horus, the prince of eternity. Witness of eternity is my name." (Ch. 42.)

He steps onward through eternity without ever stopping or standing still. Or he sails in "the boat of Horus," the name of which is "Millions of Years."

It is significant that, according to Higgins in the Anacalypsis (p. 591), seven Zoroasters are recorded by different historians. The Avatars of Persia bore the name of Zoroaster, and thus it is to be inferred the Chaldean priests of Babylon and Persia simply designated one Messiah to each of the seven stages of the cycle. Again one reads that there were fourteen Zoroasters. As nearly every aspect of life force or intelligence was susceptible of a double or two-fold representation, or was the result of the interplay of two opposing energies, the twice-seven enumeration is understandable without change of essential connotation. But we have a very direct and likely correct hint as to the inner purport of the name Zoroaster in Higgins' conjecture that, as he suspects, "he was merely the supposed genius of a cycle." It is hardly possible for us to light upon a more sententious true definition of a Messiah or Avatar than this phrase of Higgins: the genius of a cycle. Life runs its course through the kingdoms and the cycles, and it is more than poetry to say that it sounds out a given note in a scale of tones in the cosmic tone-poem in each cycle. The dominant note produced by the energic vibration in each cycle, understood in terms of conscious expression as sense, emotion, thought and intuition, would be the divine Messenger, the Messiah or Avatar of that cycle. As Heraclitus so well says, "man's genius is a deity." In the light of this truth we have the links that form at last a chain to bind our thought fast to a stratum of all theology, namely, the enlightened meaning of Messianism. Higgins says (Anac., p. 616) that every cycle has its muse, its song and its Savior. Doubtless, too, if we were conversant with cosmic schematism, we should find it has its dominant vibration, its key rate or frequency, its color, its number, its proper name. We are yet, perhaps, too ignorant of cosmic graphology to evaluate the import of the fact that the color of earthly vegetation is green.

We find Democritus saying that "Deity is but a soul in an orbicular fire." There is in a pronouncement of this kind a fathomless well of profundity, which our minds must struggle to comprehend. The soul is a fragment – and a seed fragment, capable of reproducing its parent – of God, an embryonic child of his Mind; and the fragment is set whirling through the cycles under the force of a fiery creative energization. This energization sets up, as it were, a draught or a friction by the power of which the divine potencies slumbering in the seed are awakened to budding, growth and fruition. The universal direction of the movement engendered by the energy of creation produced by God's thought is "orbicular." The helix or spiral is the ancient Greek symbol of all creative motion.

It may be noted in passing that, as Higgins narrates, Zoroaster was born in innocence and of an immaculate conception, of a ray of the Divine Reason. When he was born the glory arising from his body lighted up the room, and he laughed at his mother. He was called a splendid light from the tree of knowledge, and in the finale he or his soul was suspended a ligno (from the wood), or from the tree, the tree of knowledge. Here again we find the cross or tree of Calvary, the tree of the Christ, identified with the tree of knowledge of Genesis. It is in the imputations of such data as this, strewn prolifically over the field of comparative religion study, that the true significance of the literature of which the Gospels are but a fragment is found.

Iamblichus, the "divine doctor" of the Neo-Platonic school, writes that the sun was "the image of divine intelligence," and Plato speaks of the sun as "an immortal living Being." But no statement surpasses the mighty pronouncement of Proclus, as he discourses on Plato's theology, that "the light of the sun is the pure energy of Intellect." The energy of thought in man's tiny brain is found to be able to engender a glow of light, heat and power, electric in nature. Thought, divine from the start, was the first General Light and Power plant. The ineffable universal power that lights the suns is the energy generated by God's Mind in process of thinking and willing! As man's puny thought organizes his life and his world in his fragmentary sphere, so God's thought organizes and controls the universe. Souls are seed-sparks of the mighty fiery glow and gleam that flash out in the darkness of the void to become the centers of light. Little wonder the Egyptians equated the two words "star" and "soul" in the same word, Seb, as they equated "peace" and "seven" in the word hetep. And even Seb likewise means "seven," since each soul is in reality the potentiality of seven souls, or a soul building itself up to perfection in seven cycles, unfolding a segment of itself in each. Most instructive is the promise found in the Sibylline books: "He will send his Son from the Sun."

The first seven emanations from the heart of Deity were called the "Sons of Fire" in the sacred scriptures of all great nations. They were the seven lights on the Tree, the seven archangelic "candles." The Jewish book of esoteric truth, the Kabalah, denominates them the seven Sephiroth upon the Sephirothal Tree. They are the seven Powers before the Throne. A word of seven letters in each different tongue is found carved in the architectural remains of every grand religious structure in the world, from the Cyclopean remains on Easter Island to the earliest Egyptian pyramids. The seven candles of the churches still mutely flaunt their ineffable cosmic meaning before the blind eyes of the flocks of modern worshippers, who are sublimely innocent of comprehension.

Quoting Clement of Alexandria, Thomas Aquinas says the candle "is a sign of the Christ, not only in shape, but because he sheds his light through the ministry of the seven spirits primarily created and who are the seven eyes of the Lord." Therefore the principal planets are to the seven primeval spirits, according to St. Clement, that which the candle-sun is to Christ himself, namely – their vessels, their phulachai, or guardians.

It has been proven more difficult to find the clear and explicit significance of the number fourteen, or twice seven, already glanced at, than that of most other forms of symbolism or numerology in the ancient formulations. That the number has real relation to cosmic or evolutionary fact, however, must be presumed on the strength of numerous occurrences of it in ancient lore. There is a possible base of meaning in the fact that, since life is the result of an interplay between spirit and matter, and each stage of growth is consummated in a cycle embracing seven steps, there would be a seven on the physical side and a corresponding seven on the spiritual. Every sign of the zodiac is dually aspected, presumably to indicate that the particular ray of potency expressed through it is the resultant of opposed spirit-matter energies. (Likely these are the four-and-twenty elders of Revelation.) Possibly the seven planes or stages of the physical creation are taken dually in the same way. At any rate we find Damascius saying:

"There are seven series of cosmocrators or cosmic forces, which are double; the higher ones commissioned to support and guide the superior world, the lower ones the inferior world (our own)."

We have significant allegorical treatment of the twice-seven in the Old Testament, when Jacob has to serve seven years for Leah and an additional seven for Rachel. But there is other use of it in Genesis, where it is said that from Adam to the Flood is fourteen generations, from the Flood to the going down into Egypt is fourteen generations, and from the going down into Egypt to the Exodus is fourteen generations. Every intimation seems to point to the genealogical lists of Patriarchs in the Old Testament as being type-names of the cycles, as one generates, or "begets" its successor. This is indeed the verdict of the best students in the field of esoteric and comparative religion. It turns out, on the basis of much clear evidence, that the "Patriarchs" of Jewish "history" are the names of what the Hindus have called "Manus." Capt. Wilford in Asiatic Researches (Vol. V, p. 243) says: "The Egyptians had fourteen dynasties, and the Hindus had fourteen dynasties, the rulers of which were called Menus." These "dynasties" are obviously not the dynasties of lines of historical monarchs. They are clearly evolutionary epochs, distinguished, at least in schematic diagram, by the predominant key-note of expression of the life or consciousness in each epoch. As "man" is the Sanskrit verb "to think," this term "Manu" seems to say with the utmost definiteness that these fourteen Manus or "genii of cycles" were actually the designations for fourteen (or seven taken doubly) types of progressive manifestations of the thinking principle in evolution. This clarification of otherwise meaningless and baffling Old Testament recondite narrative is an important gain in understanding.

The "rulers" of the dynasties just as clearly would not be men, certainly not men of the strictly human category, but rather the dominant key-type of mentality of the different stages.

Still another signification of the fourteen is advanced by Massey, who takes from the

Egyptian phrase, "house of a thousand years," – "house" being used in the sense of a zodiacal sign – the meaning that makes it equivalent to another phrase, "fourteen life-times," rated at seventy-one years each, or nine hundred and ninety four. Horus or Iusa, in the "house of a thousand years," was the bringer of the millennium. Sut, or Satan, released for "seven days" – the period of matter's dominance over spirit, buried in its inertia – was then bound for a thousand years – the period when in turn spirit gains ascendancy over matter and turns it to its service – and religious typology worked this out as roughly fourteen life-times. What more typical example or instance of a true cycle than a human life-time?

If the title of address to deity by early Christians was "Our Lord, the Sun!" up to the fifth or sixth century (when it was altered into "Our Lord, the God!"), it is not difficult to see the profound and fundamentally true meaning of the most general statement that can be found in ancient literature to describe the nature of the Messiah or the Avatar, which was, "the Messiahs were all incarnations of the Sun." This is indeed a sentence which holds the pith and marrow of all theology. Yet it falls meaningless upon the mind of this age because the great Sun-myth in religion has been misconstrued by ignorance into rankly materialistic conception. Through this miscarriage spiritual ideology has been warped into physical sense. The mighty truth hidden behind all sun-symbolism in ancient thought escaped recognition when that great item of knowledge had been lost which revealed that the sun is the blazing effulgence of divine intellect. It is the ineffable light of Mind. If the light of this truth could be made once again to enter the mind of man, all the alleged material degradation of the conception of the Sun as God – the charge brought by shallow and uncomprehending Christianity against the wiser ancients – would be swallowed up in the magnificence of the truer conception. When will it be seen – as the ancients knew it – that the Christos, the deity in man, is a seed fragment of the deity that glows in insupportable grandeur in the sun, is in fact a little sun of divine intellect embodied in each man? Only when again that luminous truth is regained, will the full grand import of ancient "sun-worship" dawn to cognition in the modern brain, and the slur of arrogant modernity against pagan worshipers of the heavenly luminary be ended by reverent understanding.

We can now take a passage such as the following from Higgins (Anac., p. 588) and see its essential truth. Referring to the many Messianic figures as repeated incarnations of the solar deity, he says:

"Here we see the renewal of the incarnation just spoken of in the fact of identity in the history of most of the ancient hero-Gods, which has been fully demonstrated by Creuzer in his second volume. The case was that all the hero-Gods were incarnations – Genii of cycles, either several of the same cycle in different countries at the same time, or successive cycles – for the same series of adventures was supposed to occur again and again. This accounts for the striking similitudes in all their histories. Some persons will not easily believe that the ancients could be so weak as to suppose that the same things were renewed ever 600 years. Superstition never reasons."

If comment on Higgins' concluding fling was seemly, perhaps it would be enough to observe that modern Christians may gather some stimulating reflections from the thought of their having for sixteen centuries accepted as literal history a long and involved series of such dramatic "adventures" of their own purported hero-God, which had been the twentieth or the fiftieth or the one-hundredth recorded repetition of the same adventures of solar deity in the flesh.

The truer view of the import of the saga, says Lord Raglan, was not confined to the Norse, but was, according to Prof. Hooke, general in the ancient world. That the ritual-drama and the hero-legend that grew out of it were dealing with elements of knowledge far higher and more meaningful than mere adventures of an ancestral hero in the flesh, is evidenced by what was behind the representation. Some of these features were: the cyclic movement of the seasons and of the heavenly bodies, together with the ritual system associated with them, which "inevitably tended to produce a view of Time as a vast circle in which the pattern of the individual life and the course of history was a recurring cyclic process." (The Labyrinth, p. 215.) Raglan comments that this view of time as a ritual circle seems to have been carried over into Christianity, since, according to Prof. James (Christian Myth and Ritual, p. 268) in the Eucharistic sacrament the redemptive work of Christ was celebrated not as a mere commemoration of an historic event; for in the liturgy the past becomes present, and the birth at Bethlehem and the death on Calvary were apprehended as ever-present realities independent of time and space. This is welcome light amid modern darkness.

A remark of Higgins may fall in appropriately here. He contends that it is philosophical to hold in suspicion all such histories (as the legendary recitals concerning Roger Bacon), but unphilosophical to receive them without suspicion. The mythos, he says, has corrupted all history. Who can doubt, he asks, that the Argonautic expedition is a recurring mythos? As Virgil has told us, new Argonauts would arise from time to time. But while one can sense the legitimate connotation of Higgins' observation that the mythos has intruded on the ground of actual history and "corrupted" it, this is a great deal like saying that music and poetry have come in to corrupt real life. The mythos was designed to irradiate history with meaning, as music and poetry are adapted to halo life with deeper significance. The only mistake – and it is the invariable and unfailing one – was in reading the mythos for history, and not seeing it as the light of history. And if new Argonauts would arise from age to age, so new Christs would arise in future times and countries, – but in the recurring mythos, not in human embodiment. As a thousand adaptations of the love-lyric have arisen in every age to celebrate the great passion, so the equally vital theme of the soul's incarnation in flesh was reissued in ever new mythical and allegorical dress.

Higgins adds:

"I suspect that new Troys were expected every six hundred years. In the case of the Romans this was a superstition, which could not be corrected by that kind of experience which we acquire from history. What we call their history, Mr. Niebuhr has shown, was mere mythos. This will account for a degree of superstition which would be otherwise scarcely credible among the higher ranks of the Romans. . . . An Englishman called Lumsden has asserted that many of the incidents in Roman history were identical with those in the heroical history of the Greeks, and therefore must have been copied from them. . . . They were not copies of one another, but were drawn from a common source; were in fact an example of remaining fragments of the almost lost, but constantly renewed, mythos which we have seen everywhere in the East and West – new Argonauts, new Trojan Wars" – and new Messiahs under changing names, though always a name indicating solar deific character.

This is well and truly discerned; and in connection with it Higgins sets forth his consistent thesis that all early histories were originally composed and written in verse for the sake of correct retention in memory, and further set to music for the same reason. The most ancient of the ancients had nothing of the nature of our real history. Real history was not the object or aim of their writing, any more than it was Virgil's or Milton's or Dante's.

Cristna (Krishna), Moses, Cyrus, Romulus and others were all exposed, Higgins reminds us, but all were saved from the tyrant's power. And, like Alfred the Great (whom Raglan shows to have been also a semi-mythical character), they were all preserved by a cowherd. The cowherd would have relevance under Taurian zodiacal symbolism, and the figure would have been changed to a shepherd at the incidence of the next sign in the precessional order, Aries, the Ram.

And very enlightening is Higgins' comment on the deification of the Caesars:

"Much nonsense has been written concerning the heroes of antiquity being converted into Gods, but now in the Caesars I think we may see the real nature of the apotheosis. They were not supposed to be men converted into Gods, but were incarnations of a portion of Divine Spirit; at least this was the real and secret meaning of the apotheosis. They were men endowed with the Holy Ghost. They were nothing but men supposed to be filled with more than a usual portion of that

Spirit.

"Like Christian saints they were not generally declared till after their deaths. . . . I am surprised that we have not a life of Octavius by a Latin Xenophon to match the heathen gospel called the Cyropaedia."

Higgins cites the ancient mythical figure known as "Nimrod" as interpreting "the Beast" of Revelation, which had seven heads and ten horns, as a glyph for the Great Cycle of Life in animal (beast) embodiment, during which the ten later spiritual powers were developed in the seven sub-cycles; or in Kabalistic language, the perfection of the ten (twelve) higher spiritual faculties or Sephirothal powers through the seven elementary cycles.

Chapter XIX

LOST CYCLES OF THE SUN

It is of immense significance that the name "Sibyl," which has earlier been discussed, is given by Higgins as probably meaning "cycle of the sun." Ancient wisdom, or ancient mythologies proclivity, or both in co-operation, conspired to allot to each cycle its presiding genius, its Christos, conceived as a ray of the solar divine fire of intelligence. But it assigned also to each cycle its female guardian, its prophetess or "Sibyl." Higgins states that we have the prophecies of eight of these Sibyls, which indicates that eight of the cycles had passed. In the first century one was still awaited. This would seem to harmonize fully with the tradition extant in Roman history as to the visit of the aged Sibyl to King Tarquin with nine of her books containing the forecast of future Roman history; going off and burning three upon his refusal to buy them; coming back and offering the remaining six for the same price asked for the nine; burning three more; and finally receiving her original price for the remaining three. The prophecies of the Cumaean Sibyl were quoted by many of the earliest Christian Fathers from Justin and Clemens to Augustine, as credible authority for the belief in the coming of the Christ on whom the Christian faith was based. Clemens of Alexandria quotes these words from St. Paul in Latin: "Take the Greek books, learn as to the Sibyl, how she foretells one God and those things which are future." St. Austin says that the Sibyl, Orpheus and Homer all spoke truly of God and of his Son. (Sir John Floyer, On the Sibyls, p. IX.)

Dr. Lardner admits that the old Fathers call the Sibyls prophetesses in the strictest sense of the word. The Sibyls were known as such to Plato, Aristotle, Diodorus Siculus, Strabo, Plutarch, Pausanius, Cicero, Varro, Virgil, Ovid, Tacitus, Juvenal and Pliny. But what can they have foretold? – Higgins asks. And he answers: the same as Isaiah, as Enoch, as Zoroaster, as the Vedas, as the Irish Druid from Bocchara and as the Sibyl of Virgil, – "a renewed cycle of its hero or divine incarnation, its presiding genius."

We can perhaps locate the aeonial construction of the Sibylline theory in the fact stated by Higgins that all the purveyors of the tradition admit of ten ages, which, each six hundred years long, constitute the "great Age" of six thousand years. Yet, he says, they do not agree as to the time when the ages commence; some making them begin with the creation, some with the flood; but the Erythraean Sibyl is the only one who correctly states them to begin from Adam.

The most important part of these Sibylline oracles, says Higgins, is a very celebrated collection of verses in the eighth book of the prophecy of the Erythraean Sibyl, which in its first words forms the acrostic in the Greek language: Iesous Chreistos Theou Uios Soter Stauros; or, Jesus Christ, Son of God, Savior, Cross, the initial letters of which (in Greek) without the last "S" spell the Greek word Ichthys, or "Fish," the zodiacal designation of the Christian Jesus in the Hellenic world all through the first centuries. The Christians in Italy and elsewhere in the early centuries were called by the pagans Pisciculi, or "Little Fishes," and both Tertullian and Augustine refer to Christ in the world as the Great Fish in the sea.

Tertullian carries out this symbolism in a notable sentence (De Bapt., c. 1):

"We little fishes, according to our ICHTHUS, Jesus Christ, are born in water, nor have we safety in any other way. . . ."

Cicero, speaking of the prediction of the Savior's advent in the Sibyls, says: "But that they proceeded not from fury and prophetic rage, but rather from art and contrivance, doth no less appear otherwise than from the acrostic in them." Eusebius (vide Floyer's Sibyl, Pref. xx) says the acrostic was in the Sibylline books at the time of Cicero. And we have given Justin's statement that the Sibyl had foretold the coming of Christ.

It is certainly indicated from positive utterances that a comparative study of the Sibylline remains and the Gospels should be made with the greatest despatch and care.

A succinct statement of the general belief in the cyclical order of Messianic return is made by Higgins (Anac., p. 200):

"It was the belief that some great personage would appear in every cycle, as the Sibylline verses prove; but it was evidently impossible to make the birth of great men coincide with the birth of the cycle. But when it was desirable to found power upon the belief that a living person was the hero of the cycle, it was natural to expect that the attempt should have been made, as was the case with the verses of Virgil and others. This great personage is, according to Mr. Parkhurst, the type of a future savior."

Nothing accentuates better than this passage the advantageous manipulation of a universal sacred tradition by the human side of priestly zeal for very human ends. Supplementing this is Higgins' revealing conjecture, which is almost certainly a bull's-eye hit at the truth:

"I suspect that the vulgar were taught to expect a new divine person every six hundred years, and a millennium every six thousand; but that the higher classes were taught to look to the year of Brahm, 432,000 years, or perhaps to 4,320,000 years."

The latter number was the Hindu reckoning of the length of the Great Year of Brahm, or a Day of Manifestation. The statement brings out the difference between esoteric and exoteric teaching. And it conveys a most direct hint to guide us in the effort to locate the full truth about the Messianic announcements in days of old. It tears away the whole mask of furtive practice on the part of the ancient priesthood, and discloses the policy that is more than anything else responsible for the world's uncertainty and confusion over the great doctrine of the Messiah. It tells us clearly that while among the initiated and the intelligent the purely spiritual nature of the Avatar was known and treasured in secret, the masses of uninstructed people were kept hugging the delusion that the cycle was to be heralded and fulfilled by the birth of a great Hero and Savior. "They can not grasp the meaning of a spiritual coming – they must be told it is a man" – might be put as the gist and genius of the exoteric delusion.

Mention has been made of the ancient Avataric theory as embracing ten cycles of six hundred years each, making a "great cycle" of six thousand years, presumably heralding the millennium in the seventh thousand. This – if such was the scheme – would simply represent the six Genesis "Days" (cycles) of active physical world-building, followed by the Sabbath (seventh) Day, consummating the work of creation with the flowering out of divine genius in the highest creature, man, in the seventh aeon. Each period was roughly equated with the "house of a thousand years" already mentioned. The "ten horns" of the Beast would be the ten sub-periods of six hundred years each. About the time of Jesus it was believed that nine of the ten sub-cycles had passed, and world-wide expectation was set to await the coming of the tenth and climactic aeon of the great cycle. We may have here one of the answers to the oft-propounded questions: Why, if there was no historical Jesus, did the whole great movement of Christianity start at that time? There must have been a living personage at that time to give the initial impetus to so great a sweep toward a new religious formulation as took shape in Christianity. Christian writers on Jesus all emphasize the universal deep-seated expectation of Messiah prevalent then. The religious atmosphere was electrically charged with this fervent looking and longing for the aeonial consummation, with its proclaimed advent of the Savior, exoterically believed to be about to descend into the flesh. It will surely come as a shock to many Christians, with minds fed on the all-convincing claims of the Church, to learn that the expectation of Messiah's arrival was so deep and general that various groups of sectarians in and out of the Christian circle, looking around to locate the true Avatar in the person of some great one, actually picked on more than one prospective candidate. Among those thus marked for Messianic characterization were Apollonius of Tyana, Marcion, Montanus, Simon Magus and Arion, much as Plato and Pythagoras had been considered divine births five and six hundred years before. This probably by no means exhausts the list. And that Marcion and Montanus were chosen for the honor several hundred years after the life of the Jesus figure indicates beyond cavil that there had been no consensus of certitude as to the birth and Messiahship of the man of Galilee. Those who picked later candidates assuredly could not have been convinced that the Christ had come definitely and surely in the man Jesus in the first century.

Higgins cites old works, among them one entitled Tavanibr's and Bermei's Travels (Vol. II, p. 106) as speaking of the ancient belief that the second Person of the Trinity had incarnated nine times.

"The Gentiles do hold that the second Person of the Trinity was incarnated nine times, and that because of divers necessities of the world, from which he hath delivered it; but the eighth incarnation is the most notable; for they hold that the world, being enslaved under the power of the giants, it was redeemed by the second Person, incarnated and born of a Virgin at midnight, the angels singing in the air and the heavens pouring down a shower of flowers all that night."

He then goes on to say that incarnated God was wounded in the side by a giant, in consequence of which he was called "the wounded in the side," and that a tenth incarnation is yet to come. He then relates a story that the third Person of the Trinity appeared in the form of fire.

"It is allowed in the Dialogues on Prophecy (Part 4, p. 338) that we are now in the seventh Millenary of the world. This is exactly my theory," writes Higgins. "When Daniel prophesied to Nebuchadnezzar of the Golden Head about the year 603 B.C., he clearly spoke of four kingdoms, including that then going, for he calls Nebuchadnezzar the golden head. . . . These kingdoms are cycles of six hundred years and bring the commencement of the millennium to about the year twelve hundred, according to what I have proved, that the era of the birth of Christ was the beginning of the ninth age of the Romans and Sibyls and the ninth Avatar of India."

It is more than likely that the allegory of the great image in Daniel, whose head was of gold, breast and arms of silver, belly and thighs of brass, legs of iron, and his feet partly of iron and partly of clay, refers to the four elements or planes in the constitution of man and not at all to measurable cycles of years. It is stretching the word "kingdom" pretty far to make it refer to a mere lapse of a few hundred years of historical time. "Kingdom" as used by ancient allegorists denotes a realm, type or stage of consciousness, and nothing temporal or historical in a political sense. Its meaning in the phrases "kingdom of heaven" and "kingdom of God," as well as "kingdom of this world," decry such a rendering. Yet as each kingdom of evolving consciousness was established during a given cycle, there is after all a correlation of the meaning with the time or period sense. But the allegory is clearly referring to evolutionary cycles and not to groups of a few hundred years along the historical time-lapse. Obviously the millennium did not begin at the year 1200, and the time-table of this interpretation sadly miscarried.

But it is not risking much likelihood of error to assert that there is a startling clue to a very definite delineation of the cycle-graph in this image construction that has never hitherto been analyzed or interpreted with the true key. The image of a man from head to foot, composed of a series of elements running in order of fineness and preciousness from gold at the summit to iron and clay at the feet, is conclusively a typing of the composite nature of man, who from his head of gold (spirit) to his feet of miry clay (matter) is a four-ply creature, constituted of spirit (gold), mind (silver), emotion (brass) and sense-body (iron and clay combined), in the allegorical depiction. Higgins is indeed partly vindicated in his judgment of these four element-divisions as time cycles, by a mass of legendary data to be found in the opening chapters of all ancient histories or world cosmographs. It is there said that ancient "poetic" tradition spoke of the reign in the earliest racial dawn of an Age of Innocence when mankind was childlike and knew no evil; and this is called the Golden Age. It was followed by the age of Silver, when life grew a little less halcyon. As man came to adulthood his childlike simplicity and naïveté was replaced by sterner qualities in the Age of Brass. And when finally consciousness had descended fully into the hard realism of earthly embodiment, came the Age of Iron, when the feet of the former angel race were enmired in the heavy clay of sense and body. All the books of the ancient wisdom say that this full course of the descent of the soul into earthly body was consummated in three and a half cycles from angel to man, while also the evolution of the body itself from mineral to human fineness requisite to house the descending spirit was achieved in a similar three and a half cycles or kingdoms. Downward as soul, or upward from the clod as body, man stands exactly where his two constituent elements of god and animal have met and conjoined their powers in the middle of the fourth kingdom counted either way. And this being the background of the imagery in Daniel's mind, what could be more true and astonishing than that the fourth kingdom should be represented by the half-and-half valence of two symbols, iron and clay? For it is precisely at the point of three and a half stages, kingdoms or cycles from start that life, measured either as soul from above or as body from below, breaks into a twofold balance or fission into two countervailing elements, each of which is the summation of three and a half cycles. Conceived diagrammatically, this would again yield the chiastic structure outlined in an earlier place. Daniel's grand metal image is therefore a quite true symbolical graph of man's evolutionary development to his status as a being of three and a half kingdoms or modes of conscious life on both the spiritual and the animal sides of his nature.

On the side of the natural or animal man we have here the basis of a correct interpretation for the first time of one of the pivotal numerical symbolisms in scripture, – the three days in the tomb. "Days" here indubitably refers to cycles, as in Genesis. The text of key significance in the Bible is the verse which reads: "As Jonas was three days in the belly of the whale, so must the Son of Man be three days and nights in the bowels of the earth." The plain meaning is that the unevolved germ of spiritual consciousness must, like a seed, be implanted in matter and evolve through the three lower physical kingdoms, the mineral, vegetable and animal, until in the middle of the fourth or human kingdom it blossoms out to full function and fruition in the organic brain of man.

This clarification also prepares the way at last for the epochal pronouncement that three is not after all the correct number! Three is a blind or cover for the true number, which is or should be three and a half! Evidence for this will be found in the eleventh and twelfth chapters of Revelation, where the number three and a half occurs three times, though it is presented in such cryptic fashion that its true import has been missed. Animal man evolving from sea water rises to full development at the end of three and one half cycles, where it meets soul descending through a corresponding series of three and a half kingdoms of ethereal essence. The body evolving from below thus gives soul its incarnation and divides the area of consciousness with it, sharing its own sense and emotion life with the other's mental and spiritual powers. Material is not at hand to verify the estimate, but it must be found a curious circumstance, hardly pure coincidence, that Higgins, who gave all such matters life-long consideration, and who did not know of the diagrammatic significance of the three and a half as it has just been analyzed, sets the length of the ministry of the Gospel Jesus at precisely three and a half years. As the estimates of the thousands of scholars who have studied the Bible through the centuries vary from one to three years or more, Higgins' guess is as good as any.

The important outcome, however, of all this is that the weight of such considerations presses heavily toward the conclusion that the length of the "ministry" of the Jesus figure is wholly numerological allegorism, and has nothing to do with the facts of an alleged biography. Many assign to it one year. This is "the acceptable year of the Lord," or the cycle of astronomical events in the annual round of the solar year, which become the apt symbols of the events in the whole circuit of human evolution. Then there is the three-year assignment, which is the looser use of three instead of three and a half. The true symbolic period of the interrelated and reciprocal ministry of soul to flesh and flesh to soul (as Browning so well notes) is three and a half "years" or "days." As the two chapters in Revelation also so clearly bring out, the meaning behind the number 1260, given there twice, is that it is the number of days in forty-two months (also mentioned twice), or three and one half years. Daniel gives the same number, but for some reason as yet unfathomed he gives also the numbers 1290 and 1335 in the last verses of his book. Whether some zealous scribe deliberately altered the number 1260 to the other figures to throw the exoteric mind off the scent is only to be guessed. The full number of days in three and a half years would be 1278. The computation in Revelation that yields 1260 counts thirty days to the month. Just as is the case with the dates of Easter and Christmas, the fact that definite numerical (or historically factual) figures are not given indicates mathematical or astronomical symbolism. The "history" is discredited at every turn.

Higgins calls attention to the noticeable item that comes to light in the study of ancient cycles, that there were always two classes of Avatars running at the same time. Yet, he explains, though there are two, they are after all but one. This was because the Avatars were identical with the cycles, and the two cycles, united, formed a third. He does not clarify this last, but possibly means that the cycle gains a wholly new understanding when it is seen that the Avatar (as a divine "messenger") is the gist, as it were, of the time cycle. The time period is the Avatar in one sense; the Messenger (or more properly the Message) is the Avatar in another sense; and the two combined yield the complete meaning of the term. If he means that two cycles of six hundred years each unite in length and form a third cycle of twelve hundred years, the meaning may be thus simplified. Naturally the multiples of smaller cycles would form greater cycles. He does not seem to imply that the "third" cycle is composed of the ten presiding geniuses or Neroses, and the ten presiding geniuses of the signs of the zodiac. The Neroses and signs revolve over and over and cross each other, so that finally at the end of the ten signs they conclude at the same time after a period of 21,600 years; thus founding the great cycle. Or if the period be doubled, we have a larger cycle of 43,200 years, which, taken ten times, gives the still greater cycle of Brahm, of 432,000 years.

The word "mundus" (Lat. "the world") itself was used to refer to a cycle, Higgins claims. He traces the name of Cyrus' mother, Mundane, to the combination of "Mundus" and "Anna" (a year), meaning "the year's cycle" or circle of the year, "Cyrus" means the sun!

But the central word in this connection is the Greek aion, "aeon" or "age." The mistranslation of this word in the phrase teleuten aion in the Bible as "the end of this world," instead of "the end of the cycle" has been productive of more mental havoc and psychological suffering on the part of millions of misguided dupes than perhaps any other crude bungling of rendition in all the scriptures. To be sure, the final conclusion of great cycles that run over millions of years may fall synchronously with the extinction of life on our planet. But this falls quite outside the pale of any meanings commonly given to religious interpretation. Many cults have used the phrase – "end of the world" – to justify their wild millennial and eschatological expectations. They took it literally to mean the incidence of the great final cataclysm. But any interpretation which envisages the possibility of a planetary crisis within less than several millions of years must be regarded a farrago of childish nonsense.

A remark dropped by Higgins may be very helpful in solving one of the everlasting perplexities of Old Testament meaning: the great ages of the Biblical "patriarchs." Says Higgins: "The age and its hero personage have been confounded"! Here is the most likely solution of the great conundrum of Methuselah's nine hundred and sixty-nine years. Not the man, but the age which bore his name, reached the extended limit.

The ninth age was to bring a blessed infant whose coming would restore the beatific Age of God that went out when Paradise was lost. The age, not the child, was to live six hundred years. The coming of this infant was the nub of the expectant faith of the Oriental world for many centuries. Moreover he was to be the ninth (or tenth) great Avatar and close out one of the greater cycles of six thousand years. Nations vied with one another in claiming him as the product of their religion and their national life. He was to be of the lineage of their exalted royal house. Every sect of religionists following the millenary system believed itself to be the favorite of God. Therefore of course its people believed that the Avatar would appear among them. They were therefore ready to catch at any extraordinary person as the great one sent to be the desire of all nations. Thus, says Higgins, we have several ninth and several tenth Avatars running at the same time in different places. Bishop Horsley, he says, could not help seeing the truth that the Fourth Eclogue of Virgil referred to the child to whom the kings of the Magi came to offer presents. He adds the detail that Scipio Africanus, Buddha, Arion, Hercules, were pointed to in many places as the child of Virgil's prophecy. He adduces the fact – if it is such – that Augustus, Solomon and others who bore Messianic reputations were strangely enough all of a ten-months pregnancy, – to fulfill, one assumes, the tenth Messianic numerical status. Also Alexander, as well as several Hindu Sages, as Salivahana and Gautama, bore the mantle of divine birthhood, being said to have been produced by a serpent entwining around their mothers. As a symbol of divine wisdom, the immaculate conception through a serpent's impregnation of the mother could well have been one of the forms of allegorical depiction in archaic usage. The Naga or Serpent was a universal symbol of all evolution, and the cycles of seven-period evolution did make the Universal Mother – Nature – pregnant and fruitful.

That there was much credence in the Avataric cycles in the early Church itself is evident from many things. For instance Theodoret is confused about the Christos, stating that sometimes he is regarded as a spirit, and sometimes that he had a virgin for a mother, while again it is written that he was born as other men. And others claim, he says, that the Christ in Jesus reincarnates again and again and goes into other bodies, and at each birth appears differently. Hippolytus, writing of "heretical" beliefs, says Christ is held to be the son of Sophia (Wisdom) above, that he was the male potency of God when the Heavenly Man descending, separated into the two poles of being, spirit and body, and that the Holy Ghost is the female power.

Mead includes the "Holy Spirit" as one of the names of the Mother Sophia. Also "She of the Left Hand" as opposed to the Christos, "Him of the Right Hand." The Christian creed, which speaks of the Son, who sitteth on the right hand of God, is thus using Gnostic terminology and imagery. And both Gnostics and orthodox Christians were using imagery drawn from long anterior systems. It would be interesting to enlarge upon the Gnostic schematism or systemology which outlined the creations in the microcosmic and macrocosmic phases, and set the elements of the universe in proper relation in the great plan. The purpose of the whole of Life's creational energization of the universe was to evolve mind to perfection. The emanation and evolution of the World-Mind in cosmogenesis, and of the human mind in anthropogenesis, is the main interest of the secret and sacred science of old. Midway between the upper worlds of spirit and the lower worlds of material constitution, Sophia, Wisdom, has been dwelling. There between the Ogdoad, or Eight Great Powers of Light above, and the Hebdomad, or Seven Spheres of psychic and material substance below, she fashioned her house, and there she mediates between the two worlds of being. In Proverbs (9:1) we have the statement of this in remarkably direct form: "Wisdom hath builded her house; she hath hewn out her seven pillars." For she projects from above the Types or Ideas of the Divine Mind into the cosmos, stamping them by her power upon the plastic substance of the matter below. But a long disquisition sets forth how she attempted of herself, without the informing power of the First God, to give form to the creation, and failed. This is called the Great Abortion, the effort, so to say, of matter, without the aid of formative Mind, to stamp logical form upon the material universe. Lost and wandering in chaos, then, she is represented as being rescued by Divine Love, or the Christ Aeon, which, like the Christ of the Gospels who healed the abortion of the woman with the issue of blood through the power flowing into her from her touch with his garments, stopped her fruitless wastage of life-blood and made her fruitful for the production of the Sons of Mind. Thus was her abortion stopped and she became the fecund mother of the Mind-born creation. So productive indeed did she become that she was named by a name opprobrious among men, but descriptive purely of her endless and teeming fecundity – the Great Harlot. Mead lists other of her names: Man-Woman, Prouneikos or the Lustful One, the Matrix, the Genetrix, Paradise, Eden, Achamoth, the Virgin, Barbelo, the Daughter of Light, Ennoea, the Lost or Wandering Sheep, Helena and many more.

The "abortion" spoken of by the Gnostics is in many respects just another representative version of the virgin birth. It depicts the effort of pure matter to produce the creation, as it was expressed, "without a syzygy" or pair of opposites. Nature, the eternal Mother, had to be fecundated by the germ of Mind, projected from the male aeon. The Holy Ghost, the power of the highest, had to come upon her, to end her abortive virginity and make her the Mother of the Worlds.

A variant of the virgin birth typology that emphasizes the abortive aspect by means of the additional feature of life-long barrenness, is found in the stories of at least four women in the Bible, Sarah, Hannah, Machir and Elizabeth, who in their old age are made to bring forth the divine child. The import of this allegorism is of course that Mother Nature only succeeds in finally producing her child-product, the Christ consciousness, far along in her creational effort, near the end of her cycle, or in her "old age." She could not give birth to the Christ-child until six long aeons of physical effort had at last brought the creation of the brain of man, in which such a specialized ray of Mind could function. The birth of the Savior-consciousness in any cycle would come in the seventh or last round of the period, therefore in the old age of the mother-nature forces.

Massey has well analyzed the virgin motherhood and what lay behind it. Of Isis he says she was the virgin mother who produced a purely natural and hence spiritually abortive or inferior type of creation, "without the fatherhood," but who regenerates or gives new birth to the "dead" Osirian powers of Mind, buried hopelessly in her material womb, until she is fructified by the later copulation with the Christ aeon, or Holy Ghost.

There is the story of Salivahana, a divine child, born of a virgin in Ceylon, which shows such close affinity to that of Jesus that it would be hard to deny a common source for both. He was the son of Tarshaca, a carpenter. His life was attempted in infancy by a tyrant who afterwards was killed by him. Most of the other circumstances, with slight variations, are the same as those told of Krishna. Western scholars have been too blind to the obvious inferences from such identities in comparative religion. Bali, Semiramis, or Eros, Buddha and Cristna had long before the "time" of Jesus suffered crucifixion in like fashion as narrated of him. Moreover Salivahana was again a ninth Avatar. The affirmation was made that the tenth Avatar would come in the form of a white horse. The Hindu Bala Rama, says Higgins, is another cycle of Neros, or Cristna of the Ram sign. Rama was to Cristna what John was to Christ. Rama, he asserts, was known by the names of Menu and Noah. He also points to the striking similarity between Noah and Janus, the Roman god of opening doors, and says their virtual identity has been admitted by every writer upon these subjects. In the Tibetan language, he says, John is called Argiun (Ar-John), and was the coadjutor of Christna. It seems evident that these two are the Tibetan counterparts of the great epic characters in the Mahabarata, Arjuna and Krishna, whose names are not very far in sound and spelling from John and Christ! And the related characters occupy exactly the same or corresponding positions, forerunner or lower way-opener, and following Lord. Even the so-named Fish-Avatar of Vishnu in

Berosus' account of the Chaldean Genesis, Ioannes (Joannes), avers Higgins, was blended with the ninth Avatar. Jesus is called a Fish by Augustine, who says he found the purity of Jesus Christ in the word "fish," "for he is a fish that lives in the midst of the waters." Both Jonah and Hercules were swallowed up by the sign of the Fishes, at the very same place, Joppa, and for the same period of three days. (Dupuis, Histoire de Tous Les Cultes, pp. 335, 541.) The sun was called Jona, as appears from Gruter's inscriptions, says Higgins. Augustine also writes that "Ichthys" (Greek: "Fish") "is a mystical name of Christ, because he descended alive into the depths of this mortal life, as unto the abyss of waters." Lundy (Monumental Christianity) says the early Christians drew a fish on the sand as a Lodge sign.

Enoch refers to the shed blood of the crucified elect long before the time of Jesus.

All these identities, correlations, equivalences, can't be sheer coincidence. When coincidence is a constant element in a hypothetical situation, it is considered proof.

Chapter XX

TWELVE LAMPS OF DEITY

It is time now to note the play in ancient days of this Avataric formula and tradition in secular history outside the Bible purview. There is not space to touch upon its incidence in the field of epic poetry, save to hint at its evident usages by Virgil in his great Aeneid. It is obvious that he wrote this epic of Roman "history" as a complimentary tribute to the Roman nation generally and the Emperor Augustus in particular. In doing this he did nothing that was in the least degree unique or exceptional in the ancient domain. It was the custom in all countries of the Orient to attempt to graft the divine epic of the soul onto both the geography and the history of each particular land, representing its named places as the scenes of the epical incidents, and identifying its leading king with the divine hero. This practice was no doubt at the start pure and legitimate allegorism, with no attempt to falsify or deceive. But when allegorical intent and purport were forgotten, the results proved a deception to all later dullness.

It is worth the space to quote the great Virgilian aeonial prophecy in Eclogue IV, as it is the chief prototype doubtless of all the Sibylline and other pagan predictions of Messiah.

"The last era of Cumaean song is now arrived, and the grand series of ages begins afresh. Now the Virgin Astraea returns and the reign of Saturn recommences. Now a new progeny descends from the celestial realms. Do thou, chaste Lucina, smile propitious to the infant Boy, who will bring to a close the present Age of Iron and introduce throughout the whole world the Age of Gold. . . . He shall share the life of Gods and shall see heroes mingled in society with Gods, himself be seen by them and all the peaceful world. . . . Then shall the herds no longer dread the huge lion, the serpent also shall die; and the poison's deceptive plant shall perish. Come, O dear child of the Gods, great descendant of Jupiter! . . . the time is near. See, the world is shaken with its globe saluting thee! The earth, the regions of the sea, and the heavens sublime."

This was called the Sibylline prophecy about the coming of Christ, lauded and extolled by the Christians until it became safe and polite to denounce everything pagan. In the aura of Virgilian heroics, however, the prophecy was dressed up to indicate Augustus as the scion of the Gods and to hint at the divine origin of the Roman nation. The legend would probably be in the background of Italian world politics today.

Irenaeus and the first Christian Fathers said that during this new Age of Gold the lion should lie down with the lamb, and the grapes were to cry out to the faithful to come and eat them!

Beside the Caesars, Cyrus the Great of Persia was one of those monarchs who was heralded as the aeonial child and the tenth Avatar. But nothing in all Biblical interpretation is more doltishly fatuous than the reading of the name of this earthly sovereign into the Greek word Kurios (Eng.

Cyrius), meaning "Lord." It is generally equivalent to Christos itself, and is often used with it, as in "Lord Christ" or "Christ the Lord." It is often a generic term for God himself. To take it anywhere as referring to Cyrus of Persia in the historic sense is obviously an unwarranted translation. It often renders the meaning of its passage nonsensical.

So thoroughly did the Avataric theorization permeate the ancient world, both religious and secular, that it became impossible for the Christian movement, no matter with what vehemence it later wished to repudiate pagan influences and usages, to escape the general power of the conception. Not only at the earlier stage of its inception, but far on into the later centuries it continued to exert its strategic determination upon Christian theory and polity. Indeed, if Higgins' data are to be accepted (and he was a scholar of intellectual probity and sincerity), the tradition exercised such persuasions upon the Christian masses up to the opening of the thirteenth century that the Church powers have found it politic to hide in oblivion a most remarkable chapter of events which Higgins has chronicled. They are brought to light here out of their obscurity, not for the purpose of sensational disclosure, but to support the correctness and cogency of the general argument of the work.

At the time of Richard the First, Higgins sets forth, about 1189 – the end of a cycle of twelve hundred years, or two Neroses, approaching – a general belief prevailed that the end of the world drew near, a belief which, in a great measure, caused the Crusades to Palestine, where the devotees expected the Savior to appear. This is attested by St. Bernard of Clairvaux and was forecast by Joachim, abbot of Curacio in Calabria, a most renowned interpreter of prophecy in those days. Antichrist was to appear at Antioch, and the Crusade was the gathering together of the kings of the earth to the battle of the great day of God Almighty. (Rev. 16:12, 14; Nimrod, III, p. 393.) It appears from the accounts that the possession of Antioch was made a great point, almost as much as that of Jerusalem. It was among the first cities taken by the Crusaders.

It is surprising enough to most Christians to be informed that the ancient theory of Messianic cycles had anything to do with the timing of the Crusades and indeed their motivating purpose. It will doubtless come as an even greater surprise to be informed that those within and outside the Church who held to the cyclical program of Messiahs regarded Mohammed as the Avatar of the six-hundred-year-cycle running from six hundred to twelve hundred A.D., and the tenth Avatar of the ancient Great Cycle. Higgins says that Mohammed was accredited as the Avatar succeeding Jesus, and that he was expressly foretold by Haggai, the Prophet, under the Hebrew name of H M D. Of this prophecy, says Higgins, Parkhurst (Christian apologist) was an unwilling witness. The Crusaders flocked into Jerusalem in twelve hundred, the end of the Mohammed cycle, which, he affirms, began in the year six hundred and eight, and cites Faber as authority for this date. According to Higgins Mohammedans have made the claim that a passage has been expunged from the Romish Gospels which ran as follows:

"And when Jesus, the Son of Mary, said, O children of Israel, verily I am the apostle of God sent unto you, confirming the law which was delivered before me, and bringing good tidings of an apostle who shall come after me, and whose name shall be AHMED."

This is cited as the burden of the Haggaian prophecy.

But the crowning act in this run of serio-comics – which must ever ensue when the outer framework of spiritual allegory is taken for objective history – is yet to be recorded.

The Crusades expended their fanatical zeal and filled nearly two centuries with the history of one of the most shocking exhibitions of religious infatuation of all time (involving even the children in its frenzied insanity). But as the year twelve hundred drew nearer, the Messianic expectancy increased in fervor. In the great ferment of half-demented pietism, the year twelve came and went, with no miraculous appearance of the Messiah of the Age. Then – so relates Higgins – after the devotees and followers of the new Gospel, or Gospel of the new Avatar, had in vain looked for the holy one who was to come, they at last pitched upon St. Francis of Assisi as having been the divine Messenger; and of course the most surprising and absurd miracles were conjured up to match the character. (It could be asked if this was the basis of the cycle of miracle-sagas that came down with his name to later days.) Some of the fanatics, having an indistinct idea of the secret doctrine of renewed incarnations, or letting their knowledge of the principle of recurrent incarnations escape in the heat of controversy, maintained that St. Francis was "wholly and entirely transformed or transfigured into the person of Christ – totum Christo configuratum." (Vide Litera Magistrorum de Postilla Fratris, P. Joh. Olivi in Baluzii Miscellan. Tom., I, p. 213; Waddingi Annal, Minor Tom., V, p. 51; Mosheim, Hist. Cent., XIII, Pt. ii, Sect. XXXVI). Mosheim says (Higgins) that by some of them the Gospel of Joachim was expressly preferred to the Gospel of Christ.

It appears that this Joachim, abbot of Curacio and renowned interpreter of prophecy, had published a book called Evangelium Eternum (The Everlasting Gospel), in which, presumptively, he had set forth the theory of Avataric cyclical reincarnation, and declared another Messiah due in the year twelve hundred, end of another Neros cycle. This work, which circulated throughout the European Church and stirred a great ferment, was never censured or suppressed by any act of the Pope, but only the introduction to it was placed under the ban. John of Parma preferred the Gospel of Joachim above the canonical Gospels.

Higgins tells us that a Rev. Dr. Maclaine said the the Evangelium Eternum consisted, as productions of that nature generally do, of ambiguous predictions and intricate riddles. This, says Higgins, is what we might expect. After it had been published some time and had received the greatest support possible from the Popes and all the orders of monks, the Franciscan fanatic Gerhard published a work called an Introduction to this Gospel, in which he censured the vices of the Church of Rome and in set terms prophesied, or deduced from the Evangelium Eternum, the destruction of the Roman See. This appeared in the year twelve hundred and fifty, close upon the last period to which the millennium could be delayed, viz., twelve hundred and sixty A.D. (Here obviously the numerology of another than the Neros cycle came into play. This was the cycle of twelve hundred and sixty years, based on the three and a half years, or twelve hundred and sixty "days," taken from the eleventh and twelfth chapters of Revelation, as before noted. The days were now figured as years, following the method as prescribed in Exodus, where the forty years in the wilderness were expressed in the formula "forty days, for every day a year.") As the fateful and climactic moment of the end of the year twelve hundred and sixty approached, the passions of the different orders of monks were excited to the greatest pitch and tension. Gerhard's book was burned and its author persecuted, though his followers among the Franciscans claim for him the gift of prophecy and place him among the saints. The followers of St. Francis generally – the strong supporters of the new Gospel – and Gerhard maintained that he, St. Francis, who was the angel mentioned in Revelation XIV:6, had promulgated to the world the true and everlasting Gospel of God: that the Gospel of Christ was to be abrogated in the year twelve hundred and sixty, and was to give place to this new and everlasting Gospel, which was to be substituted in its room: and that the ministers of this great reformation were to be humble and barefoot friars, destitute of all worldly emoluments. This was stripping off the veil and showing the meaning of the eternal Gospel without disguise. It excited the most lively feelings of surprise, of hope, or of indignation, according as it met favor or disfavor from the opinions of the different fanatical partisans. The Pope did not, according to the usual plan, burn the author; the book only was burned, and its author mildly censured and banished to his house in the country. This took place in the year twelve hundred fifty-five when the parties, expectant of the millennium, must have been in the highest state of fear and anxiety, suggests Higgins.

The year twelve hundred and sixty arrived and passed away; but, mirable dictu, the sun did not cease to give its light, the moon and the stars did not fall from heaven; nothing in particular happened; the pious fools stared at one another and impious rogues chuckled. The Popes and Cardinals at Rome, half fools (Higgins), and the dupes everywhere else, finding themselves all in the wrong, soon began to charge folly upon one another; and as they had quarreled before as to who should display the most zeal for the new glad tidings, they now began to quarrel about who should bear the blame, each shuffling the odium on to some other. Dr. Maclaine and Mosheim have clearly established the great – and Higgins ventures to add, almost universal – reception of the Evangelium Eternum. After some time, the fanatics having by degrees ceased to preach, and the Pope to support, the new Gospel, the old Gospels recovered their credit and vogue, and the friends and promulgators of the new Gospel died away, or were burned as they came to be considered heretics. The court of Rome endeavored to guard against whatever might arise.

Lest the reader may conceive from this recital the feeling that so preposterous a miscarriage of sane balance could not occur in modern days, let the reminder come that the mistranslated Bible phrase, "end of the world," has worked an almost equally flagrant debacle of reason in a very similar ferment as late as the year 1843, in the Millerite delusion that swept over New England and all northeastern United States. And but a few years back of the present writing (1943) the world was taken aback by the proclamation of the aeonial Messiahship of the great Lord of the spiritual worlds, Maitreya, who was to come in the body of the Hindu youth, Jiddu Krishnamurti. A number of sects still preach the imminent coming of Christ and the dissolution of the world.

It seems certain that the increase in the monastic orders about the fifth and sixth centuries and again in the late eleventh and twelfth, arose from the expectation of the millennial denouement.

The aftermath of the twelfth century hallucination is interesting. After the expectation of the extraordinary manifestations had died away and the power of the Saracens seemed to increase, the Popes, says Higgins, became more than ever embittered against the Mohammedans and equally furious against all who supported anything relating to the now obsolescent Gnostic or cyclic doctrines of millennial expectation. This accounts, says Higgins, in a very satisfactory manner for the zeal of the Popes up to a certain time for the new Gospel, and their bitterness afterwards towards the Templars and Albigenses, among whom some remnants of these superstitions remained. The ecclesiastical hierarchy in the Church had had a severe lesson in the resurgent sweep of erratic esotericism, projected or prolonged from ancient pagan sources into its own history, and became cool to all things savoring of the Messianic idea ever since. And again it is the prerogative of this study to announce that the egregious predicament of error came simply because an ancient allegorical structure clothed in astronomical typology was misread in a literal and objective sense instead of a spiritual one. It would certainly seem within our warrant to say that a hypothesis which can be supported and illustrated by such positive evidences direct from world history must be regarded as solidly established.

There is now to be considered, following a look at the cycle of Neros, that other still greater period known as the Phoenix cycle. This possesses elements very germane to the entire theory of Messiah, and yields most interesting data and correlations. Lundy (Mon. Chris., p. 422) says that when Herodotus was in Egypt he was told that the Phoenix was a bird of great rarity, only coming there once in five hundred years, when it dies and another arises from its ashes. It is reported to be like the eagle and of a red and golden plumage. But Herodotus never saw one, except in pictures. Then there is Pliny, who says:

"It surpasses all other birds; but I do not know if it be fable that there is only one in the whole world and that seldom seen. . . . It is sacred to the sun; lives six hundred and sixty years; when old it dies in its aromatic nest (frankincense and myrrh) and produces a worm out of which the young phoenix arises; and it carries its nest to the altar of the temple at Heliopolis in Egypt. The revolution of the year corresponds to the life of this bird, in which the seasons and stars return to their first places." (Bk. X; 2.)

And Tacitus says "that the opinions vary as to the number of the years, the most common one being this, that it is five hundred years, though some make it 1461 years." (Annals, VI:28.)

Lundy directly asserts that no such bird as the Phoenix ever existed; that it was only one of the constellations in the old Egyptian zodiac. It had been identified by the laborious researches of Mr. R. S. Poole, as the bird of Osiris, or Osir, so often invoked by the souls in Hades for their deliverance, as the Book of the Dead shows us. The Phoenix is elsewhere the Bennu (Benno), the Swan of the Greeks, the Eagle of the Romans, and, he adds, the Peacock of the Hindus, as the symbol of ever-renewing immortality in the heavens. In the Egyptian constellation of the Phoenix or Bennu, the dog-star Sothis (Sirius) was the most conspicuous, the brightest star in the whole heaven, even brighter than the sun by three hundred times, and greater in bulk by two thousand times, according to Proctor, though from its great distance it does not appear so. When this Dog-Star marked the summer solstice, it was the period of the new year, i.e., the great year or cycle of 1461 years, when the stars and planets return to the same position. Also it was then, or about the time of the summer solstice, that the Nile began to rise, which is the very life of Egypt. This Phoenix cycle of 1461 years was discovered not long since on the ceiling of the Memnonium at Thebes, and was identified there as the Bennu or Osir of Osiris. It signified, like the great Sothiac and other lesser periods and cycles, the beginning and the ending of all things, or the end of one cycle to be followed by the birth of another. Mr. Poole says (Horae Aegyptiacae, p. 35):

"Sothis, the Dog-star, was considered as sacred to both powers of nature, Osiris with Isis as the Good Power, and Typhon as the Evil Power; since at the time of its rising they were considered as conflicting; for the Nile then begins to show the first symptoms of rising, and at the same time the great heat was parching up the cultivated soil."

The Bennu, Nycticorax or Phoenix, was then the sign of the constellation in which the Dog-star rose to mark a new era and a new year together; just as when the star or conjunction of Jupiter and Saturn in the constellation of the Fishes marked the advent of Christ. "There can be no doubt," continues Mr. Poole, "that the Bennu is the Phoenix, or the constellation partly or wholly corresponding with the Cygnus, and perhaps also with the Aquila." (Horae Aegyp., p. 42.) "And the period of its appearance was ascertained and its manifestation was celebrated on the first day of Thoth, the beginning of the Egyptian year." (Ibid., p. 46-7.) "This constellation was one of the principal festivals of the Egyptians. It took place at the summer solstice when the Nile began to rise."

Nearly a century before either Mr. Wilkinson or Mr. Poole wrote of the Phoenix and its cycle, concludes Lundy, the great French astronomer Mr. Bailly thus spoke of it:

"It is impossible to doubt that the Phoenix is the emblem of a solar revolution, which revives in the moment it expires. If any one question the truth of this, he will find the proof of it in those authors who assign to the Phoenix a life of 1461 years, i.e., the time of the Sothis period, or of a revolution of a great solar year of the Egyptians." (Hist. of Astr., 214.)

Fourteen hundred and sixty and a fraction years is the period of time in which the calendar would correct itself if leap year's extra day each four years was omitted, or, as it was put, the stars would return to their first places according to months.

Higgins states that the six hundred or six hundred and eight years is the period between two conjunctions of the sun and moon. He does not indicate how this is to be understood, as there are solar eclipses by the moon oftener than six hundred years and at irregular intervals. He says that the Phoenix was a portion of the universal principle of Divine Love, or Eros, which eternally moved over the waters (the inchoate matter of space) and which in the form of a dove was incarnated every six hundred or six hundred and eight years. Eros was the Greek Phanes, one of the deific hierarchy, so luminously analyzed in Proclus' great dissertation on the theology of Plato. The similarity between Phanes and Phoenix must be an evidence of common origin of both names. Bennu is likewise of cognate derivation. Higgins gives us more of the hypothetical description of the bird. It was the bird of the morning, he says, and also the bird of Paradise; its dwelling was in the East at the gate of heaven, in the land of spring and in the forest of the sun, in a plain of unalloyed delights lying twelve cubits higher than the highest mountains. Phoenix was also a tree; and upon the highest convexity or umbo of Achilles' shield stood a palm or Phoenix tree. (Nimrod, III, p. 395.) Another name for palm tree is Tamar, which is the name of one of the Old Testament mothers of divine sons. Then there was the tamarand, tamarack or tamarisk, one of the sacred trees of Egypt. Grethenbach tells us that one equivalent of tamarisk is Asar in the Egyptian. The cycle is complete when we reflect that Asar is the original name of Osiris.

Naturally the great astronomical cycle of 1461 years would not be overlooked by symbologists seeking cyclical periodicities in the stellar revolutions. It was therefore made the date of the end and new beginning of the Avataric cycle. The fact that it was set at five hundred years, at six hundred and sixty and finally at fourteen hundred and sixty-one makes its reference to the lifetime of a "bird" – of which there was but one in existence at a time! – quite fabulous. Massey, with considerable chance of being correct, traces the word "Phoenix" to p-h-ankh, the Egyptian combination meaning "the joining for life," or in a living relation (of male and female life-powers, or spirit and matter), which took place at the end or beginning of such a cycle, symbolically. Nature achieved each new cycle of on-going life through the union of her two polarized opposite energies, so that the union of male and female potencies periodically would typify the beginning of a new birth or a new era. Ankh means "life-tie" in Egyptian. The word Sphinx Massey derives from this p-h-ankh with the "s" of causative or initiative action prefixed, – s-p-h-ank. The Sphinx would be the universal power of nature which causes male and female forces to unite for the reproduction of a new generation of life. It is the human in front and female animal behind.

Further mention must be made of the Nile inundation, which the Egyptians wove into the annual succession of stellar phases. One must read Massey's Ancient Egypt, the Light of the World, to gain any adequate conception of the remarkable harmony and coincidence of the water stages of the great river with the star movements and positions throughout the year. It is a source of never-ending wonder that earthly phenomena and heavenly economy work together with such articulation and appropriateness. Or it is a testimony to the shrewd mythicizing instinct of ancient sages that they named a star in Virgo constellation, for instance, Vindemeatrix, the grape-gatherer, a star which rose when the grapes were ripened. And this is made to stand for the Virgin who rises on the world, as matter in evolution, to bring forth in the mature season the fruit of the vine, from which the wine of divine spiritual intoxication will be available to raise men, symbolically, in ecstasy to the gods! Thus did the Christs and the Horuses and the Krishnas and Bacchuses come as winebibbers, or to turn "water" of the natural life into "wine" of spiritual consciousness. Only through this transformation of lower element into the symbol of the higher mind could man's ability to partake freely of his divine fruitage be aptly portrayed.

Egyptian analogical – and anagogical – genius traced the correspondence in physical nature between the cosmological data on which the structure of their heaven-taught theology was based and the yearly phenomena of the overflow of their mighty river. It may seem to us a mere poetization to assume that the rising of the fresh waters of the river in the growing heat of summer could be an interpretation by nature, or her fulfillment, of the great religious conception of the coming of the divine life to mankind. Yet the rising waters, bringing coolness and renewed fertility to the land, were the coming of the "savior" in every practical sense. The waters began to rise in the lowlands of northern Egypt in June. The Egyptian name of the June month was Mesore. Massey traces this name to Mes-Hor. Mes is the root of the word Messiah, as we have seen, and means "to be born." Hor is "Horus," free of its Latin "us" masculine termination. So Mesore is "the re-born Horus." June was the month Dazu in the Assyrian calendar, and it was the month of Tammuz in the Aramaic calendar. Horus, says Massey, was the great Father deity Tum, reborn, like the beetle, as his own renewal, or his own son. So the name of the month was Tum-mes, which worked over into Tammuz, and which became the later Thomas of the Bible! The spiritual water of life was reborn under the symbolism of the physical waters that came to revive a land parched to death with solar heat. All through the period of July and August the waters swelled to bless and fructify the land; and they stood at their highest even level at the very time of the autumn equinox. Then they began to fall and went to their lowest at the time of the death of the solar deity in the winter solstice.

As the moon was the type of the material mother bringing the solar god to his birth once a month symbolically in the new moon and to his perfection in the full moon glory, the full moon typified the coming of divinity in its fullness in humanity. The full moon must be seen to yield the full glory of the Father's light on the body of the mother-matter. Translated, this stands as type of the mightiest of all truths for man, – that the light of the Father or spiritual Mind, long buried in the bosom of mother matter, at last comes to its birth with the full release of its shining power, in the body composed of the elements of the natural world, its mother. This revelation of divinity in the world of nature is the birth of God as his own Son, or himself in a new birth. If it had ever been once known that the lunar phenomena carried to the ancient mind all this splendid typology, the ancient scriptures could have been read with fine appreciation of their luminous meaning. So both Horus and Khunsu, a cognate deity in the same character, were placed in the disk of the full moon in the zodiac at Denderah, when the moon was at its full in the sign of Pisces, the house of bread, or, in Hebrew, Bethlehem! As the night symbolized incarnation, when the light of spirit was submerged in the darkness of matter, the child in the full moon was the type of the divine solar light, hidden and buried, yet shining in and through matter, as the light of the world by night, or the light of the spirit shining even in the darkness of fleshly embodiment. Now, when the Nile deluge began with the sun in the sign of the beetle or crab, and in the month of Tammuz or Mesore, the moon rose at full in the sign of the Sea-Goat (Capricorn), and the divine child was therefore born of the full moon at the winter solstice.

An interesting sidelight is thrown on all this when it is known that the Akkadian name of the June month is Su-Kul-Na, "seizer of seed," to explain which we must go back to the sign of the beetle set above by the Egyptians, and consider the fact that the beetle (symbol of the God Kheper, the Creator) began to roll up his seed in a ball of earth at that time to preserve it from the rising flood. This is only a portion of the story, and the list of correspondences between the astrological data and the river's stations is quite astonishing. Modern scholastic religion professes vast contempt, impatience and irritation over this business of ancient fancy-work, and protests that if religion has to rest upon such idle speculation and "superstition," it must remain childishly inconsequential. Not so with the ancients, and not so with any modern that will live with these symbols long enough to catch the terrific power of their suggestiveness and their educational lucidity. The endless correspondences between cosmic truth and the very nature of the living world were of old, and can be today, the positive demonstrations of the ubiquitous presence of deific principle in every natural phenomenon. Surely the high truths of a divine wisdom would stand doubly accredited in the human mind if their principles were found to be matched and corroborated in the actual world outside man. The ancient thinkers lived close to nature and watched her processes; the moderns have cut the link between man and nature.

Most definite, perhaps, of all the cycles was that of the precession of the equinoxes, the period of 2160 years during which the sun at the vernal equinox continues to fall in one of the twelve zodiacal signs, or passes through one-twelfth of its entire circuit that is completed in about 25,900 years. It will be found that the symbolic implications of this cycle, with the sun's successive occupancy of each of the twelve signs, constitute nothing less than the most recondite of keys to a large segment of all scriptural exegesis. It can be unfolded here in the merest outline.

With the Neros, the Phoenix, the 1260 and the 1461 cycles denoted, the road is open to pursue the astronomical basis of the Messianic theory to still farther reaches. These will be discerned through the instrumentality of the intimations of the features of the grand cycle of equinoctial precession. It is here that will be found the full and final purport of the great tradition, or more at any rate of its particular detail. That it was wholly an astronomically based periodicity, to serve, however, as the analogue for the greatest of all meanings in spiritual evolution, there can be little doubt when the evidence has been examined.

It seems incomprehensible that a thing as large and significant as that which is now to be disclosed could have been lost out of general knowledge and so far consigned to oblivion that its restoration will be greeted with opposition and scorn in those quarters where its loss has wrought the direst mischief. Sixteen centuries of mental beguilement of the most atrocious character is a pretty dear price to pay for the suppression of the school of astronomical allegorism in the make-up of the scriptures which still hold sway over communal acceptances. The item thus heralded with so much unction is the method employed by the sagacious formulators of the religious typologies in representing the successive cyclical incarnations or "comings" of the Messiah under the name and character of the twelve signs of the zodiac in turn.

So evidently did astronomical and astrological presuppositions underlie theological doctrinism that the very name and function of the Avatar "coming" in each precessional period of 2160 years was assigned to him in reference to the zodiacal sign. He bore the designation and was vested with the characteristic qualities of the sign. As the Messiahs were incarnations "of the sun," the "personality" of the incarnated power was assumed to embody and manifest during the cycle those special differentiations of universal deity which were severally the distinguishing characteristics of the signs themselves, or that one of the twelve aspects of completed deific nature which each sign was figured to express. Ancient astrology assigned to each of the twelve signs, and indeed to each decanate of a sign, a particular ray of influence, as one might say, each one had its proper color, tone, virtue, radiation or vibration. Hence, being the presiding genius of the sign, its expressive revelator, it must needs bear its name and number and manifest under every phase of its typical character. Hence the Messianic personage changed his name and the whole scheme of portraiture under which he was represented at the beginning of each new period of precessional advance. And not only were the distinctive sign characteristics attributed to him, but the seasonal types and the monthly traits in the annual solar round were wrought into his "life and history." With nature, he died in the autumn, was quickened at the winter solstice, and rose again "from the dead" at the vernal passing over the boundary line between heaven and earth. At one season he was the ingloriously defeated victim of his "enemies" and persecutors; at another he strode forth in triumph over all his foes. A hundred minor characterizations are germane to his office and mission, as well as to his essential nature, at the different stations in the yearly cycle. Only in the large is it possible to trace these many aspects of his astrological representation.

A large portion of the confusion that has crept into the exegetical problem has arisen from the fact that a number of designations and picturizations of Messiah in the many past cycles have survived and overlapped, and so have introduced complexity through the very abundance and variety of descriptive data of the Savior. It proved hard to absorb and assort twelve whole sets of divine characterizations in the person of deity in manifestation, when it was long forgotten that deity was given a twelvefold catalogue of changing attributes, in accordance with the phenomena of precession. We have here, then, a new-old formula which should enable us to introduce great clarification into a situation wherein miscomprehension has so long prevailed.

It must further be prefaced that every one of the twelve signs is a dual or double representation of its particular facet of divinity. Every sign is said to be "double." This is accounted for by the consideration that the sages endeavored to portray the divine nature as expressing itself in both its positive and negative phases in conflict or interplay in each day of manifestation. Indeed it is so in actuality. Manifestation can come only through the tension of forces set in between the positive and the negative ends of life's polarity. Also it was the intent to present each aspect of deity indicated by the sign in its two opposite phases of dying and being reborn which each annual circulation of the sun was made to portray. Such phases of opposition or reversal always fell just six months apart at stations directly opposite each other on the zodiacal chart.

When the two forces of life are not polarized in relation to each other, life is not in manifestation. We shall see, then, how each sign presents the Messianic character and epic in the dual aspects suggested by its name and distinctive features.

Following Massey, a beginning can be made – for no particular reason – at the station of Leo in the zodiac. Under this sign, in which the vernal equinox fell some fourteen thousand years ago, the Savior manifested in his twin aspects in the character of what the Egyptians called "the Lion of the Double Force," or the twin lions, the old and dying lion, adult of the previous generation or cycle, and the reborn young lion, the "lion's whelp" of the Old Testament. They were also called the two Cherubim, and the word "cherubim" derives from the Egyptian name of the two lion figures, which was Kherufu. These two lions were represented as guarding, the one the western and the other the eastern gates of life at the two equinoctial points of September and March. On its visit to earth the soul, in the Egyptian Ritual, cries, "I come that I may see the processes of Maat (the Goddess of Truth) and the lion-forms." The Hebrew so far carried original Egyptian typism over into their own constructions as to denominate the divine Avatar as "the lion of Judah," or "the lion of the house of Judah," – the title still retained by the monarchs of Ethiopia. The Old Testament references to the lion and the lion's whelp attest the continued use of the symbol over a long period. What the soul means by saying it comes to earth to see the "processes of Maat" is that its life in the flesh will bring under its conscious experience and scrutiny the concrete manifestations of Truth in living situations. Here it will see Truth in actual operation, coming to light in the acts and fates of men. Also in seeing the two "lion-forms" it will gain cognizance of the reality of its own selfhood under the two aspects or phases through which its experience in every cycle of descent and return, its death and resurrection, takes it. It will come to know itself as in the one phase, represented by its image standing at the gate of the western equinox of September, the dying old one of the past generation; and in the other phase, represented by the image or Kherub standing at the eastern gate of March, as itself reborn out of its own "death" into its youth of the new generation. It is the fruit of one cycle of growth going to its death in the autumn, and the germ springing forth out of that fruit to inaugurate the new cycle in the following spring. Maat is commonly known to Egyptologists merely as the Goddess of Truth or Justice. She is that, but in a very comprehensive sense. She is really the Goddess of the balanced relation between the cosmic forces of spirit and matter, wheresoever manifested, and her prerogative is to mete out the justice that is invoked by the disturbance of the just balance between the two eternal forces. All the issues of life are determined by the soul's adeptness in maintaining that due balance, which alone is the condition of life's orderly evolution. Maat is "Lord of the Balance," and each soul, as it rises to mastery of the elements of life, becomes its own "Goddess Maat" and must maintain its control of the even balance. It comes to earth time and again to become ever more expert in the science of maintaining the balance, or manifesting truth and righteousness. As the soul is the embryonic Christ, the Messiah coming in its Leonine phase was dramatized as the Lion of the Double Force, or as the lions of the two horizons, east and west.

As the precession moves apparently backwards, the next sign is Cancer. This is the sign of the Crab, but more anciently of the Beetle. Under its nomenclature the Coming One was designated as the Good Scarabaeus. He was dual in the two aspects of the old beetle dying as he went into the ground along the Nile's edge, and the young beetle reborn, like the Phoenix, out of its parent's death. It would be difficult to find a symbol or phenomenon in nature more faithfully matching the ideology of the incarnational "death" and the following resurrection of the soul in its periodical shuttling between heaven and earth, than the living economy of the beetle. It makes a perfect analogue with the experience of the Ego, which "dies" and is reborn with each embodiment in matter on earth. The crab offers a cognate symbolism, as it spends its life alternating constantly between the elements of water – companion symbol with earth for matter – and air. Its frequent climbing up out of the water onto the land is a type of the soul's rising out of the lower material realm into the light and air of intellectual and spiritual being.

The beetle was the emblematic key to one of the greatest of all theological conceptions of ancient cosmology or creation, and the lost answer to the greatest of all religious controversies that ensued in the early Christian Church, one which eventually divided the Church into Roman and Greek Catholic factions. This was the Arian-Athanasian controversy and the so-called "filioque dispute." This was over the question whether the third person of the Trinity was produced from the Father alone or from the Father "and from the Son," – "filioque" in Latin. Had not Egyptian allegorism been held in scorn and contempt and already forgotten, the beetle symbolism held the answer for the disputants all the time. For the Egyptians declared that the beetle or scarabaeus produced its young through the Father alone, without union with the female. This was simply a nature-type of the great cosmic fact of the Divine Mind, or the Father, projecting from his own intellectual being those children of his thought creation which became the mind-born Sons of God. They are born of mind alone, not of mind and matter in conjunction. The beetle presented a type of this unilinear begetting in its life habit.

The ass, another Biblical zootype closely associated with the Christ, is found in this house.

Next comes Gemini and its dual aspecting is readily seen in the Twins. Here the name is simply the Two Brothers or the Twin Brothers. These figure in many Biblical and ancient scriptural allegories, such as the Tale of Kamuas, the stories of Cain and Abel, Jacob and Esau, and Pharez and Zarah, Tamar's twins; but more definitely in the Egyptian Sut-Horus and the Persian Ormazd-Ahriman pairs. The Romulus-Remus legend of Rome's founding is a variant of it. The two brothers are pictured as in direct opposition to each other, as they battle for alternate victory and suffer alternate defeat in their successive and never-ending conflict in the sphere of manifestation. As spirit descends under the power of sluggish matter the material brother, or power of darkness, is hailed as victor; when spirit overcomes the flesh to put all things under its feet, hell is vanquished and the Christ is triumphant. The one brother can be taken as the spiritual aspect of life, the other as the material, and the two are ever in combat during a cycle of manifestation. As the one increases the other must decrease, and most remarkably this is precisely what John the Baptist declares to be the case as touching him and the Christ. The names of two mythical brothers in a Roman classic fable, Castor and Pollux, have been given to the two twin-stars in the constellation of Gemini. Astronomically it is said that one of them is decreasing in magnitude, the other increasing.

Passing to Taurus, we have the Egyptian typing of the Messiah, Iusa, the second Atum, as born of Hathor, the "cow-goddess" in the sign of the Bull. According to Massey this period ran from 6465 B.C. to 4310 B.C. Under bovine typology the Messiah was born in the stable, and the Greek Hercules, also a Christos figure, had to clean the filth of the animal nature out of the Augean stables. Duality is shown by his turning the streams of two rivers into the stables, meaning of course the streams of spirit on the one side and matter on the other, carrying for us the instructive moral that the lower nature is purified by the admixture of soul and sense in our lives. Again in dual character the Christos under Taurian symbolism was the adult bull of the past generation, dying to be reborn as his own son, the golden calf of Old Testament figurism. In the Assyrian version he became the winged bull so commonly found in the temples and architecture of that land. Candidates for initiation in the cult of Mithraism were baptized in the dripping blood of a slain bull. It was called the taurobolium or bull-bath. The initiated man was thus "washed in the blood of the Bull." The much-condemned worship of the Golden Calf in the alleged backslidings of the children of Israel into idolatry was no more reprehensible or an offense against the God of Abraham, Isaac and Jacob than the later adoration of Christos under the signature of the Lamb of God. So far as can be seen the only sin in the matter was their holding on to the emblem of the previous cycle after a new cycle with its changed figure had dawned. It was in no sense, even if historically true, a bald worship of the physical image of a Golden Calf, instead of the spiritual being of Deity. Any nation that had been esteemed worthy to be chosen by Almighty God as his favorite human group, yet proved to be so weak as to turn from the worship of the spiritual Lord of the worlds and bow down to a metal calf as the embodiment of an actual divine power preferable to God, must be thought a freakish genus of humanity indeed. It would have been as unaccountable and bizarre an occurrence as, for instance, it would be for a modern nation of high intelligence to give up suddenly its trust in moral and natural law and turn to expect better providence from ivory elephants or bronze dachshunds. And the children of Israel, overwhelmed time and again with the signal evidences of their God's miraculous preservation of them, yet turned from his worship to bow down to the Golden Calf of Baal not only once, but as often as one turns the pages in Exodus and following books. And yet learned theological pundits descant on this assumed historical occurrence with undisguised gravity.

Following Taurus comes Aries. As Taurus had extended from 4310 B.C. to 2155 B.C., Aries began at the latter date and ran to about 155 B.C., close to the time of the Christian Messiah. This is indeed a notable datum, as it alone would account for the almost equal use of Arian and Piscean symbology in connection with Jesus in the Gospels. The old forms and symbols of Aries had not had time to be discarded and replaced by those of Pisces, the next sign, and were kept along with the new ones adopted from Pisces just coming in. For Jesus was introduced as Aries was going out and the sun entering Pisces.

As Aries was the sign of the Ram, the adult dying phase was balanced by the renewed youthful phase in the Lamb of God. Here is found the warrant for the angelic announcement of the Avatar's advent to a company of "shepherds" in the fields; the parables of the Good Shepherd and the sheepfold; Jesus' figurative title of the Shepherd of Souls (and the Church "pastor"); the shepherd's crook as an ecclesiastical symbol; and the congregational "flock." The sacrificial lamb on the altar was again an emblem of the immolation or oblation of God-life for man. "Other sheep I have" would be a sentence put into the mouth of the Messiah figure in a Mystery-drama when the typing was molded on Arian lines. Likewise such an utterance as "I am the door of the sheepfold" and "The sheep know me when they hear my voice" would have this astrological origin.

Pisces follows Aries and blends its sign-types with those of Aries in Christian allegorism. It is the true sign of the Galilean Savior, and this dramatic character lived up to its proper emblemism with full fidelity. Tertullian and Augustine and other early Fathers exalted Jesus as the Great Fish in the mortal sea and designated his followers as "little fishes." The Christians dubbed themselves Pisciculi, the Latin for "little fishes." The Greeks named the Piscean Avatar Ichthys, the Greek for "fish"! We have noticed the famous sentence whose initial letters spelled Ichthus. The twelve "disciples" were "fishermen." The gold for the taxes was found in the fish's mouth and the last miracle was the overwhelming draught of fish. The Roman catacombs were replete with images of the two fishes everywhere with the Christ figure One of the two typical articles of divine food with which the Messiah fed the multitude was fish, and fish was also constellated in the heavens as a type of divine sustenance. Jesus offered himself as sacrifice for humanity not only as the lamb led to the slaughter, but also as fish to be eaten along with bread for mortal salvation. Duality is seen in the two fishes of the sign. Pisces is the plural form, as Piscis would be the singular.

The roll of the cycle brings us now to Aquarius, into which sign the new age or dispensation is entering about the present time. But where are the hierophants of old who watched the time-table of the cycles and were alert to introduce the new typology and hail the new-born Avatar and adorn him with his new panoply of characterization? Alas! for the first time in world history there are no Magi, no Council of Sages, no Demi-gods to change the nomenclature and salute the incoming Genius of the Cycle with his proper figuration. Nor is there a populace reverent or intelligent enough to do aught save jeer at it if it were announced.

Pisces was the "house of bread" as well as of fish, and this in Hebrew reads "Bethlehem." As being just six signs distant from and therefore directly opposite Virgo, in which the first or natural man was born, Pisces was the inevitable symbolic birth-place of the Christ or divine man.

Aquarius is the Waterman, pouring out the ichor of divinity from his urn in two streams, again representing the division of the life-stream into spirit and matter, both equally beneficent. Nu is the watery fount of primordial origins, elemental source, and holds the waters of the abyss. From it emanates that water which is to generate life for all the universes, as the sea water generates life on our planet. Aquarius is the only man in the zodiac of animal signs; so in man the two streams of living water flow together to purify the nature for the generation of the Christ consciousness. Jesus proclaimed himself as the bringer of that water of life which all men must drink to be immortalized.

Capricorn, beginning at the winter solstice, is the Sea-goat. Matter's most consistent symbol in the ancient type-language is water. Spiritual consciousness is most deeply buried in matter at the point in evolution symbolized by the winter solstice. But as the Sea-goat is an animal mythically combining the forefront of a land animal with the body and tail of a sea creature, the representation is that of man, who is a god immersed in a body composed of combined earthly and watery elements, though seven-eighths water. "Capricorn" means "goat-horn," and the horn was an emblem of intellect and spirit, probably as growing from the head. Christ is described as "the horn of our salvation." But also he is, as sacrifice for mortals, the "Scape-Goat" of ancient dramatism. His death for man spells tragedy, which, oddly enough, in Greek means "goat song."

Sagittarius yields duality in the half-man, half-horse constitution of the Archer. Man is a god in the body of an animal, according to the pronouncement of ancient philosophy which must be seen to be the key to the meaning of this Centaur figure of Sagittarius. He is the Bowman drawing his bow. What is he aiming at? The answer to this has been found in only one place in archaic literature. A verse from the Book of the Dead in the mouth of Shu, a high spiritual God, says: "I am the lion-god, who cometh forth with a bow; what I have shot at is the Eye of Horus." Coming in the late autumn with shortening days and waning sun-power, the shooting out of the Eye of Horus, great Egyptian symbol of divine sight, was a typing of spirit's loss of intellectual and intuitive spiritual vision as it descended into the darkness of material embodiment. So here the God Shu is figured as the mighty hunter, a title carried by Orion, Nimrod, Hercules, and other deific characters in the mythic annals.

The same autumnal loss of divine genius, but under a quite different allegorical guise, is portrayed in Scorpio. Instead of the loss of his spiritual eye, the deity, plunging into matter and coming under its spell of inertia, here is typed as suffering the scorpion sting of matter's inhibitions, represented as poisoning the divine soul and throwing it into a lethal sleep or "death." It is not the god himself who is personated by the scorpion, but the power which the god must overcome and transmute into the agent of his own resurrection on the other side of the zodiac. Or it may be thought of as the beneficent influence that inducts spirit from above into the lower realms where its victory over material opposition will exalt it to higher status through the regeneration of powers sown in weakness and raised in strength. An intimation of this is shown in a singular statement in the Egyptian texts otherwise incomprehensible, that Serkh, the Scorpion goddess "stings on behalf of gods and men." This is a clear assertion, badly needed in general understanding, that the "sting" of incarnation, the temporary submersion of spiritual powers "under the law" of flesh and sense, is wholly salutary and beneficent for the purposes of evolution. For eventually the risen Christ in the heart imparts to all his followers as they grow to spiritual adulthood the power "to tread on serpents and scorpions." Students of astrology are well aware that the sign was represented by the eagle in very remote times. As the eagle above and the stinging poisonous insect below, it is again dual. Indeed it is possible to see in this double aspecting the basis of the Phoenix myth, the bird as the one phase and the worm which is to renew its dying life as the other. Job says that he shall die in his nest and renew his life like the eagle. Christ is the swift eagle, renewing himself periodically from the worm.

Standing on the great "horizon" line that divides spirit from matter, and so indicating the point of equilibration between the two evolutionary forces is Libra, the Scales of the Balance. Duality is seen here in the two, positive and negative, scales of the balance. This is one of the most philosophically instructive of all the signs, as it connotes one of the greatest of all principles of human understanding of the basic meaning of all life in the flesh. The great truth carried by the sign is that while in the body man is standing directly on a horizon line separating the two kingdoms of life, spirit and matter; that he lives in both regions, heaven and earth, at the same time; and that consequently his whole experience is an ordeal of "being weighed in the Balance." The mighty significance of this fact is that it is the substance of the doctrine of the Judgment, which is thus incontrovertibly demonstrated to take place or earth during the life in body, and not in heaven after death! One of the greatest of theological discernments is thus brought to light after centuries of groping error in the misconception of a great cardinal doctrine. The Messiah's title under this symbolism was "Lord of the Balance" in Egypt. He was addressed as "thou who weighest all souls in the Balance." Human history might well be made to run in happier courses if it was general knowledge that souls are being weighed in the Balance of the Judgment here on earth.

It was practically inevitable that a sign denoting matter should stand in immediate juxtaposition to Libra, and facing it across the boundary line. This is Virgo, Mother Nature, matter in its primordial "virgin" state. It is an "earth sign"! This "virginity" of primal matter is shown by the position of the sign in the (symbolic) zodiac, which is just above the border line between spirit and matter, still, so to say, in the heavenly or spiritual world and not yet substantialized or concretized into physical substance, but preparing to become the mother of the forms of creation that would eventually bring the body of man as the birth-house of the Christos. The Christ of this sign is of course not the Virgin, but her Son. He is in the sign in his Mother's arms. Just under her feet is the head of the great serpent, Hydra, whose elongated body stretches across seven signs of the zodiac below the horizon line, with open jaws ready to devour the Christ-child if she should let him fall. Two great truths are adumbrated by this relationship. The first is that the Christ principle in its incarnational experience must pass through a cycle of seven stages in the realms of matter, figured as the devouring serpent which swallows the eggs of the bird of spirit. The second is meaningful in reference to the Genesis promise that the heel of the woman and her seed (the Christ) should bruise the head of the serpent. The Christly power to tread on serpents and scorpions is immediately cognate also. The ancient zodiacs and planispheres placed the universal Mother, Eve, where she could crush the serpent with her heel.

In Virgo is the constellation cluster called the Grapes. Rising in the autumn as the sign emerges above the horizon, this signalizes the coming of the Christos into the flesh and suggests the potent meaning that he will give mankind the higher "intoxication" of the Wine of Life, an uplift of consciousness which Plato calls "a divine mania." It is something more than a chance play on words, really full of the sublimest sense, when one says that the Christ comes to intoxicate man with divine "spirituous liquors." We have here the ground of all the wine symbolism in ancient Bibles, and the origin of such an ancient festival as the Hakera of old Egypt, at which Har-Tema (Horus) came "full of wine," and was styled "the Jocund." This is matched, somewhat at a distance, in the Gospels in the person of Jesus, who came "eating and drinking," the copying of an Egyptian allegorism, which represents him as making merry with the lowly of earth. This is the closest the Gospels come to representing the man of sorrows as "jocund." The scene is the counterpart of a similar dramatization found in the Noah allegory, where Noah, the "no-etic" or divine intellectual principle, on his return to earth after the flood that washes away all forms, plants a vineyard and shortly becomes intoxicated, so that his sons have to go in backward to cover his nakedness. The Father principle of spirit, descending to earth loses its divine vesture, becomes "naked" and must be reclothed by the renewal of its heavenly garments by its own sons. All this is pure Egyptian typism, matched in every feature in the Kamite texts. The elevation of mortal mind by the buoyant afflatus of divine thought quality, which, to speak in the figure, goes to the head and induces ecstasies and raptures, is what the ancients symbolized by the ideogram of intoxication resulting from man's imbibing the Wine of Immortality poured out for him by the gods. As all such symbolizations are dual, there is also an intoxication of another sort, that undergone by the god himself when he, like Noah, lands again on earth and becomes intoxicated with the wine of sense, reveling in it like a drunkard, forgetting his divine nature. The carousal and buffoonery of the Hallowe'en festival are survivals of the original representation of this typology. The god-man and the animal-man in us mutually intoxicate each other, until in the end the higher intoxication neutralizes the lower and man becomes soberly wise.

As each one of the twelve months in the annual round brings its distinctive characteristics and types of weather, so the zodiac was designed in ancient sagacity to intimate that in the whole round of the aeonial cycle the passage of the sun through each of twelve signs, symbolizing the peregrination of the soul through twelve stages of expanding growth, brought out in manifestation the final twelvefold perfection of its power. As the Christ unfolds successively each new aspect of his developing faculty, he "comes" to that further extent. So he "comes" in every new and full moon; in every morning sunrise; in every springtime; in every month of the year; in every precessional thousand years; and in every Great Year of twenty five thousand years. He "comes" in every cycle large or small. Each age and aeon brings a particular segment of his nature to manifestation. He "comes" regularly and periodically because each throb of life's pulse pushes the living stream of divine energization farther out to the remotest periphery of being. Nothing less can accrue to knowledge from the perusal of our brief sketch of zodiacal typology than the summary realization that the various scriptural accounts of Messiah's coming were all grounded on astrological figurism, and had nothing whatever to do with history. All people have been mildly aware of the use of a few touches of Arian, Piscean and perhaps Taurian symbolism in connection with Christly religionism. The Lamb, the Bull and the Fish seem to be interwoven for some reason into the story. The Virgin is there, too; but as long as she is assumed to be a mortal young woman in history, her astrological connotations have not been evident. Perhaps this work announces for the first time since ancient days that the Christ was figured as coming in each sign and under each sign's particular symbolic characterization and significance. It is therefore an epochal revelation for all religion.

Chapter XXI

ORION AND HIS DOG

One must ask, in the wake of this disclosure of the astronomical and astrological character of ancient Messianism, how it is that the birth of the Christian Messiah, claimed to be a purely historical event at a given hour about the year 4 B.C., still carries with it so many of the marks and vestiges of the non-historical astrological depiction. The fixing of the Christmas date on December 25, three days after the winter solstice, was done confessedly to match Bacchic and Mithraic cult practice; and the dating of Easter on the first Sun-day following the first full moon on or after the vernal equinox equally has not a single shred of linkage with history. Both these great festival dates speak purely of solar mythicism. Likewise, if scrutinized closely, nearly every major and minor incident in the career of the Gospel Jesus is interlaced with one or more features of cyclical or constellational typism. It would take another book to present this body of correlative material. One instance may serve to give substance to the claim.

Take the lowly figure of the animal type (zoötype Massey calls it) so definitely interwoven with the Gospel Messiah, – the ass. It was present, along with the ox, at his birth; along with its foal it bore him in triumph into the celestial city at the end; again with its foal it was brought in to help him toward his crucifixion. The Christ as the Good Samaritan was mounted on it. Out of his life-long study of astrological types, what has Massey to give us about this animal symbol?

"The ass has been obscured by the lion and other sacred animals, but it was at one time great in glory, particularly in the cult of Atum-Iu, the ass-headed or ass-eared divinity. The ass has been badly abused and evily treated as a type of Sut-Typhon, whereas it was expressly a figure of the solar god, the swift goer, who was Iu the Sa (Iusa) or Atum; and Iu-sa is the coming son, or the Egyptian Jesus on the ass." (Sa is the Egyptian suffix meaning "Son," "Heir," "Prince,"

"Successor.")

"The Ass in ancient mythology was a symbol of great importance," says E. Valentia Straiton, in The Celestial Ship of the North (p. 47). The ass originally typified the deity of the Dog-Star, then known as Sut, son of the Typhonian Mother, who had the honor of rearing the first child in the heavens. The Book of the Dead says: "The Great Words are spoken by the Ass." (Baalam's ass speaks in the Old Testament.) In original Egyptian the Hebrew Jah, Iah, Iao or Ieu (Iu) mean an ass, the type of the Sabaean Sut, who was the earliest El, the Son or Sun. An ideograph of an ass's head was the equivalent of a period of time and a cycle. Oddly enough, says Miss Straiton, the ass was an ideographical hieroglyph of the number 30, symbol of a luni-solar month, which was divided into three weeks of ten days each in the twelve-month year. The twenty-eight days of a lunar month belonged to Sut-Typhon. What is called Sut's resurrection – perhaps better his transformation into spiritual being – was symboled by the shift from the lunar cycle of twenty-eight days to the solar thirty-days cycle, and from Sut's day, Saturday, to the solar Sun-day. A three-legged ass found in Persian scriptures, says Miss Straiton, typified a month of three ten-day weeks.

Even the Christian St. Ambrose, Bishop of Milan, calls Jesus "the Good Scarabaeus, who rolled up before him the hitherto unshaken mud of our bodies." (Egyptian Mythology and Egyptian Christianity, Samuel Sharpe, London, 1863, p. 3.) And St. Epiphanius has been quoted as saying of Christ, "He is the Scarabaeus of God." Christian forms of the scarab yet exist, used as an emblem of the Savior.

In his introduction to the Nubian Grammar, the noted German savant Lepsius says: "At every step we meet in Babylonia with the traces of the Egyptian models." And it is surely unlikely that if Babylonia absorbed Egyptian prototypes, it could have done so without transfusion through Hebrew, Syrian and Greek channels.

Bailly is quoted by Miss Straiton as saying, "All the classics support Herodotus in the knowledge of the three Divine Dynasties preceding the coming of the human race." It is also noted by De Rouge in The Turin Papyrus: "Most remarkable of all, Champollion, struck with amazement, found that he had under his eyes the whole truth. . . . It was the remains of a list of Dynasties embracing the furthest mythoic times, or the reign of the gods and heroes." Citing Pandoros he continues: "It was during this period that those benefactors of humanity descended on earth and taught men to calculate the course of the Sun, Moon and Stars by the twelve signs of the Ecliptic." Creuzer writes that it is "from the spheres of the stars wherein dwell the Gods of Light that Wisdom descends to the inferior spheres. . . . In the system of the ancient Priests, all things without exception – the gods, the genii, manes (souls), the whole world, are conjointly developed in Space and Duration. . . . The Pyramid may be considered as a symbol of the magnificent hierarchy of Spirits."

Miss Straiton (p. 36, op. cit.) verifies what has here been affirmed as to Egyptian city-naming and typing:

"The Egyptians expressed the place of birth and rebirth of the Sun and its burial below by saying, 'The tomb of one life was ever the womb of another.' They built their cities accordingly, as places of Resurrection."

Abydos, Annu (On, Heliopolis), Thebes, Sais, Luxor, Memphis and others were particular examples of this usage.

"When the vernal equinox receded from the sign Aries, the Lamb, into Pisces, the Fishes, and the Sun-gods were born under this sign, the Gnostics or early Christians, who were versed in ancient wisdom, typified the Sun-gods as Fishes."

Venus, who was the same as the Norse Freia, and whose day is Friday, is exalted in Pisces;

so fish is eaten on Friday. Well does Miss Straiton observe that "all the falsities found in the interpretation of the myths are due to their having become literalized."

Each movement of the sun into a new sign in the precession brought about the fixing of a new birth-place in the heavens. A significant basis of meaning is attached to the rising of one sign as its opposite sign went to its death. The Bull, Taurus, dies with Scorpio opposite rising. "Scorpio is the sign of night, darkness, death, while Taurus is the sign of life, physical generation." In the eternal conflict between spirit and matter, the one waxes as the other wanes. The "death" of the one is the increased "life" of the other.

Our attention is called to the fact that one of the calendars in use among the Hebrews shows all the remarkable events of the Old Testament occurring on the days of the equinoxes and the solstices. Likewise on the same calendar days the most outstanding events of the New Testament happened, as for instance the Annunciation, the Birth, the resurrection, the birth of John the Baptist. Such a fact goes far to prove that the founders of the Christian religion, so far from being under the driving persuasion that they were giving to the world the first light of a true revelation, quite obviously were trying to adjust whatever they felt was unique in their message to the time-honored forms and programs of ancient pagan usage.

The Dog-Star, Sirius, rising in the south to announce the beginning of the year, on the imagery of the farmer's dog barking to announce the dawn of day, may be a poetization that has nothing to commend it but its prettiness. Yet when it is taken along with a hundred other such constructions in a system of uranographic depiction, all of which go to make the most lucid portrayal of the entire meaning of the basic religion and philosophy of the world, it becomes far more than merely playful fancy. In limning the history of man's soul in relation to its body in the imagery of the celestial movements and cycles, the sages of antiquity took the most eligible method open to man to perpetuate in one great universal language of nature-myth the sublime meaning of this cosmos and man's life in it. They wrote their unforgettable advertisement on the one signboard that would forever command man's view, – the open face of the sky. God obliged by writing the exact counterpart of it on the surface of Mother Earth. So that whether man looked below or looked above, he found the heavens telling and the earth making reply. The one shouted God's eternal message and meaning, and the other echoed it. With its daily voice in his ears, how could man ever lose or forget it? The allegedly silly childish myths of the stars were intended to be the most vivid mnemonics to all the human race of its own cosmic being and destiny.

Another lucid sketch of constructive fancy is seen in the myth that is linked with the origin of the "dog days" that fall in August. Astrological theory places the beginning of the "dog days" at the time when the sun rises simultaneously with the Dog-Star. The common tradition that a mad dog shuns water or will die if he drinks water, almost certainly had its origin in remote astrological symbolism. For the constellation of the Dog, Canis Major, has his back turned toward Cancer, a water sign. The great Dog-Star, Sirius (the name based on the root of the word "Osiris"), typified the divine nature, as Anup, the Dog, Jackal, Fox in the Egyptian mythology, represented the keen-scented Deity that could guide man through the darkness of incarnational night. The great Sirius, that blazed brilliantly in the dark night of winter, fitted and filled this conception. Water, as always, represented the body of man in whose humid confines the soul descended for its incarnation. The body is seven-eighths water. Along with and exactly akin to the representation of the soul's falling into an intoxication by the strong wine of sense in its fleshly experience, was the analogue of its going mad when it bathed in or imbibed of the waters of incarnation. The great Dog of soul went "mad" when it dipped into the waters of the bodily life. It therefore turned away from the water, and no doubt is turned toward an air or fire sign. The twelve zodiacal and the thirty-six other constellations have been designed to depict the several aspects of general truth under a varied but always deeply enlightening allegorical modus.

Then there is the legend of the "three Kings of Orient" who came on Christmas to adore the new-born God. Who shall say that the term or title, Three Kings of Orient, as the Christmas hymn phrases it, is not some early zealous and jealous scribe's work of shunting out of sight a bit of too evident and open pagan astrological symbolism from the Christian material? For from of old the Three Kings were the three conspicuous stars in the belt of Orion, the mighty Hunter, that so easily distinguish this notable constellation, making it next in prominence in all the heavens to the Great Bear itself. And their title was for long centuries the Three Kings of Orion. The three King-Stars in Orion, himself the personification of the Horus or Christos power, rise in the east on Christmas Eve and ascend to the mid-heavens on the celestial equator. Sirius, the Dog of Divinity, rises right after Orion, being the Hunter's dog, lesser deity following in the wake of higher deity everywhere in nature. And man in evolution, the thinker, is followed on the upward path by the animal, who will at a later day stand where he now does. Some thousands of years ago, when on Christmas Eve the Dog-Star stood at the height of the sky, on the horizon of the east rose in its turn the constellation of the Virgin, bearing in her one arm the Christ-child himself, and in the other hand gripping the great star Spica, the head of wheat, for that divine bread which cometh down from heaven, the eating of which will sate man's everlasting hunger for God.

The births of Abraham, Moses, Caesar and many other great figures were all foretold by the appearance of a star, according to Higgins.

"I flatter myself," he says, "that I shall convince my reader that this story of a star was no fiction, but only a mythological or allegorical method of representing the conjunction of the sun and moon, and the conclusion of the cycle at the end of every six hundred years, and the periodical restoration of some star or planet to its old place, or to its periodical rising in a place relative to the sun and moon at the end of the time. Thus whenever the star arrived at its proper place they knew that a new cycle commenced, a new savior would be born; and for every Avatar a star was said to have appeared."

How a conjunction of the sun and moon, or of some six of the planets, as some modern guessers have predicated, could guide three Magi slowly across the Arabian desert and stand still a few feet above a stable in Bethlehem, deponent sayeth not. Otherwise Higgins' delineation of the cyclical basis of the Avatar tradition is both clear and sound.

It is worth noting the concession to ancient allegorical custom made by Bishop Laurence in the preface to his translation of the Enoch:

"That singular and to those, perhaps, who penetrate its exterior surface, fascinating system of allegorical subtleties, has no doubt a brighter as well as its darker parts; its true as well as its false allusions; but instead of reducing its wild combinations of opinion to the standard of Scripture, we shall, I am persuaded, be less likely to err if we refer them to the ancient and predominant philosophy of the East; from which they seem to have originally sprung, and from which they are inseparable as the shadow is from its substance."

Obviously we are likely to catch the hidden meaning of the allegorical subtlety only if we refer the constructions embodying it to the philosophy of the ancient East, since they are the positive expressions of that philosophy. Once their true significance is seen, they prove to be not only fascinating but illuminative of all our darkness.

Higgins asks how the French and Italians came to dye their own god Cristna black before they sent icons of him to India. And how came his mother to be black? – the black Venus, or Isis the Mother of Divine Love, the Aur or Horus, the Lux of St. John, the Regina Coeli (Queen of Heaven), treading in the sphere on the head of the serpent – all marks of Jesus of Bethlehem, of the temple of the sun, or Cris, but not marks of Jesus of Nazareth? Summing up much of the material Higgins declares that there can be no dispute about the prevalence of a common doctrine both east and west of the Indies, purveying the same elements; and the only question will be whether the East copied from the West before the birth of Christ, since the same doctrines were there before his birth, or the West copied from the East at a later time.

In Egypt, Massey tells us, the ordinary year was timed largely by the inundation of the river and the heliacal rising of Sirius. In the cycle of the Great Year of precession, the time was marked by the retrogression of the equinoxes and the changing position of the pole. This time was kept by double entry. And when the birthplace of the Messianic child was made zodiacal it traveled around the backward circuit of precession. The birthplace of Horus, the divine babe, born of the Virgin of the zodiac, was made coincident with the vernal equinox, and the "date" thus became subject to the change of precession. It parted company with the lesser year and the inundation to travel from sign to sign round the circuit, staying in each sign 2160 years. Fourteen thousand years ago, the calculations reveal, the vernal equinox coincided with the sign of Virgo, and the autumn equinox with the sign of Pisces. So Eratosthenes (276 B.C.) testifies to the fact that the festival of Isis, which was celebrated in his time at the autumn equinox, had been celebrated when the Easter equinox was in Virgo. Higgins claims that a great part of Moses' object was to make the shift of the festival of the equinox from Taurus to Aries, thus throwing the onus of sin upon the worship of the Golden Calf (Taurus) when the proper emblem should have been the Lamb of God (Aries).

Modern religious ritualism has only the fragments and tatters, so to say, of the majestic fabric of the ancient Sun-worship. And in the main even those remnants stand without any competent appreciation of their original moving significance. In the distant past every festival of the religious year was replete with a meaning of great moment, since every phase and position of the sun in the annual zodiac carried a corresponding meaning with reference to the pilgrimage of the soul round the cycle of outgoing into matter and return to spirit. The (apparent) progress of the sun through the four seasons, the two equinoxes and solstices, and the twelve solar and thirteen lunar months, as well as the sun's position at critical or meaningful points in the circuit, were made the basis of a correspondent movement, progress and position of the divine Ego or Self in man in its aeonial round. How perfect this correspondence is and how graphically the meaning of the soul's experience in its cyclical evolution could be represented or dramatized by these features of the solar year, can not be realized until one scrutinizes this material with a bit more than lackadaisical interest. One must take the time and pains to see the remarkable exactness with which the transactions of the solar, lunar and stellar movements re-enact the eternal drama of the soul and the body, in their alternate phases of union and dissolution. The great commemorative or ritualistic festivals were of course those dated at the two solstitial and the two equinoctial points, fixing the Christmas festival in December, Easter in March (or April), the ancient Fire-festival in June and the Michaelmas or Hallowe'en festival in September (or October). But astronomical configurations and conjunctions brought significance to other periods in the year. There is, for instance, the beautiful but little-known festival of the Assumption of the Virgin. Some pretense is made at keeping it by ritual observance in a few churches, but it is doubtful if any unction can go with its perfunctory celebration, since the depth of its real meaning is no longer plumbed by the celebrants. Dupuis gives us the background for understanding:

"About the eighth month, when the sun is in his greatest strength and enters into the eighth sign, the celestial virgin appears to be absorbed in his fires, and she disappears in the midst of the rays and glory of her son."

This, comments Higgins, represents the death or disappearance of the virgin. The sun passes into the Virgin the thirteenth before the Kalends of September. The Christians consider this as the reunion of the Virgin and her Son. The feast commemorates the passage of the virgin. At the end of three weeks the birth of the Virgin Mary is fixed. In the ancient Roman calendar the assumption of the virgin Astrea, or her reunion with her son, took place at the same time as the assumption of the Virgin Mary; and her re-birth, or her disengagement from the solar rays, occurred at the same time with the birth of Mary. This was the eighth of September in our calendar.

One has to go back to the most recondite view of cosmic operations to divine the hidden meaning of this Assumption of the Virgin in the rays of the Solar Lord. With the Virgin and the Sun personalized in the characters of Mary and her son Jesus, in the Gospel legendary form, it is not easy to work out the reference. An alleged historical man and his mother are hardly dimensional enough to carry the burden of the vast cosmic representation in their tiny personalities. Resort must be had to the language of symbolism, which was the current coin for the transmission of such profound meanings in the olden time.

Now, to begin with, the Virgin represents matter in its pure primordial form. It is engendered in the bosom of Absolute Being by the first fiat of Divine Creative Will. The first act of this Creative Will is the division of itself into the two elements of the eternal bipolarity, the interaction of which two forces is the condition necessary for its own manifestation or creation. The separation thus entails the detachment of matter and of spirit severally out of each other's arms, the abstraction of the one soul of life from the polar opposite and the setting of the two in mutual tension with each other.

The next point to be noted, with symbolic language as our guide, is that matter was invariably personalized by the great Mother or Mother-Goddess character, and represented by the symbol of water. Water was the element out of whose womb all life was to come to birth, and, with the magical consistency with which this symbolic language spells a thrilling meaning, it is water that is the first mother of all life! All first life on the planet emanated from sea water. The human birth issues out of a sack of water. This water, or matter, was the "water of the firmament," which Genesis notes as the very first creation, divided into its two segments or forms of the upper and the lower firmament. The upper firmament of water is matter in its super-atomic, ethereal or invisible state, that is "above" the substantial creation; the lower firmament is matter in its visible, concrete, substantial or atomic construction.

So Being detaches its watery (material) part from its fiery (spiritual, solar) part and sends both forth upon the creative business of the Divine Mind. On the material side the work begins with the formation of the atom and proceeds to the evolution of all the forms which it is designed to provide for the organic expression of life in all its creative fancy. It builds up the visible universe which gives Life its manifold play throughout the cycle. But when the cycle has run its long course and the day of dissolution arrives, matter, the Virgin of the world, is drawn back into union with the fiery principle from which it was separated in the beginning, and is once more absorbed into the enveloping rays of Infinite Being.

Each new expression of life in and through matter – each new birth from the Virgin Mother – generates a new type of advanced realization of its fiery spiritual principle. Yet this is always achieved through a course of experience of the germ of mind in a body of matter, and is therefore the Virgin's own Son. Matter is the mother of the Suns, which are her Sons. Hence the fiery power of life on its spiritual side reabsorbs into its bosom at the end of each cycle the masses of matter which entered into the form-structure of spirit's ideation. And see how astonishingly earthly Nature carries out the symbolism! In the period of the summer's greatest solar power the fiery energies have barometric capacity to absorb more water than at any other time of the year! It is commonly the period of drought; the air moisture is absorbed and not precipitated. It is the season when the watery element is absorbed by the fiery. Ancient philosophical poetic fancy must needs seize upon the natural fact and use it to give body to cosmic truth.

Each new generation of life produced by a cycle of manifestation and growth is the Son of Virgin matter. But the material creations inevitably must dissolve away and be reabsorbed back into the bosom of the primordial and eternal Infinite. In each cycle of manifestation, which by definition in the symbolic language is Matter's or the Virgin's Son, it is this newest release or formulation of spirit's fiery energy that absorbs matter's potencies at the period of dissolution. Hence it is said that the Virgin is taken up or assumed by her own Son and lost in his fiery rays. So the Assumption of the Virgin is the climactic act in the aeonial round. And after three weeks in the tomb of non-being, the new year begins with the rebirth, i.e., the reappearance of the Virgin as the drought ends with the equinoctial rains! Matter's reappearance on the creative scene is intimated by the reappearance of the water, its symbol, on the earthly scene. The Virgin is absorbed in the glowing bosom of her own Son, the Sun, but emerges again to become mother of the next generation of being. The New Year's festival that is dated in mid-September is indeed well placed.

Another interesting item of ancient symbolical and astrological reference is the legend of the "Halcyon Days." Ordinary dictionary or encyclopedia sources explain the name as referring to a period of about fourteen days during the winter solstice, when the kingfisher, otherwise called the halcyon bird, nests on the waters, supposedly bringing them to a tranquil smoothness. Halcyon has therefore come to mean tranquil and peaceful. The supposed origin of the legend is the Greek myth of Halcyone, daughter of Aeolus, God of the winds, who in grief over the loss of her husband Ceyx, cast herself into the sea, which became calm.

It would seem, however, that the etymology of the word – halcyon – points to some more recondite reference in relation to the Dog-Star, Sirius. The "hal" is obviously the Hebrew form of the Egyptian "har," – Hebrew "l" and Egyptian "r" being equivalent, as the Egyptian has no "l" – and "har" is the equivalent of the "Hor" of "Horus." It therefore means "God" or "deity." The cyon is unmistakably the Greek Kuon, meaning "dog." "Halcyon" thus comes to mean "the divine Dog," or "God (as) the Dog(star)." As the coming of the Day-Star from on high was to bring "peace" to earth, the birth of the God at the winter solstice would fittingly be thought of as the basis of a legend that placed the "Halcyon" days at the winter solstice.

Another solar date in the year, of early significance now forgotten, is the second of February, Candlemas Day, or the holy day of the Purification of the Virgin. It marks the termination of another period of forty days length, of which there are at least five in the year's course. The Christ was born symbolically on the night of December twenty-fourth, and February second ends a stretch of forty days from that date. As forty days was the ancient cryptogram in number for the period of the seed's incubation in the ground or matter before germinating, therefore a glyph for the general fact of incarnation, the end of all the forty-day periods would signalize the perfection of the product of the incarnational experience. Hallowe'en ends the forty days from the autumn equinox, and May-Day ends forty days from the vernal equinox, as Easter ends the forty days of Lent. So Candlemas ends forty days from Christmas. The conclusion of the period of soul's tenancy of the body is presumed to have raised the constituent matter of the body in which it was housed to final purification. The candle flame, drawing up and transmuting into its own glorious essence of fire the lowly elements of the animal body of the candle (animal tallow), is the grand symbol of this transfiguration of essence which soul works upon lower body. And this is the Purification of the Virgin.

Albert the Great (Lib. de Univers.) says that the sign of the celestial Virgin rises above the horizon at the moment in which we fix the birth of Christ, that is, at midnight of December twenty-fourth. He adds that all the mysteries of his divine incarnation and all the secrets of his miraculous life, from his conception even to his ascension, are traced in the constellations and figured in the stars which announced them. (See Dupuis: Histoire de Tous Les Cultes, Vol. 3, pp. 47, 318). This symbolic allegorism was the true and high employment of ancient astrology. Higgins (Anac., p. 314) strengthens this assertion in remarking that "the trifling but still striking coincidences between the worship of the god Sol and the stories of Jesus are innumerable." It should be noted that if the resemblances are sometimes apparently "trifling," this is the fault of the ignorant copying of earlier definite constructions, due to the loss of esoteric insight, and is not attributable to any want of exact correspondence or identity in the material originally.

Chapter XXII

OUR DAY-STAR RISES

In Lundy's Monumental Christianity (p. 120) there is a paragraph of some length which it would be a crime of the deepest dye not to mention here. It stands as such a choice morsel of that combined arrogance and sad ignorance and misjudgment which the host of Christian writers has exhibited for centuries in their treatment of the religions of "paganism," that not to serve it up to the reader in this feast of clarification would be gross niggardliness. Comment must be restrained until the end. (The most egregious statements are emphasized by (our) italics.)

"It is a marvelous thing that Paganism has these Avatars or appearances of God on earth, whether as copies or as independent types or prophecies of Christ's manifestation of God to men it matters not; and so we have the Bel of the Assyrians and Babylonians; the Mithra of the Persians; the Agni of the Hindus; the Horus of the Egyptians; and the Apollo of the Greeks and Romans, all bearing a striking analogy to the Real Son of God, being all of them sun gods themselves. Because the sun was the great creator and restorer in nature, he was adored or made the medium of the adoration paid to the Creative, Preserving and Restoring Power of the universe by all these ancient peoples. They were seeking after God; for to the greater part of the Pagan world God was unknown. Their mistake was in identifying nature and God, and not retaining nature as a mere symbol. Their religion as a consequence became unreal; and their gods mere fictions – mere forces of nature deified – mere creatures of the imagination. If nature be God and made itself, then there is an end to all argument about religion. In that case religion becomes natural science or natural history. God as a Supreme Being or Person above and beyond and independent of nature there is none; and religion is an impossibility. But religion is a fact; and has been a fact ever since the existence of the human race. It stands, therefore, as a witness to the universal belief in Something or Some Being behind nature and beyond it; and when the sun was at first chosen as the most conspicuous symbol and the most fitting type of God's unknown being and attributes, they were feeling their way after him and making their images of the material sun like the grace and beauty and fresh bloom of nature acted upon by his warmth and light. If Christianity and this Sun of Righteousness are but copies or adaptations of this old Paganism, then how did it take the place of Paganism? It would be a house divided against itself. Some real and not merely ideal Divine Personage had appeared among men, or Christianity is but a fiction like the rest. It was not afraid of the Pagan Apollo, when it adopted the beautiful ideal of this youthful sun-god to express the divinity of Jesus Christ as a fact."

The passage deserves by way of comment and critique a whole extended essay instead of a few sentences. It is indeed an inviting pièce de résistance. The main puzzle, however, is to tell duck from turkey. Indeed it is a fact that the more of such underhand blows of Christian writers at paganism one reads, the more impressed one becomes with the realization that most of the presumed stones of slander and reproach they hurl at paganism turn out to be bouquets of the highest praise. The diatribes of intended abuse more often than not resolve themselves through an unguarded utterance into the highest encomiums.

Lundy begins by admitting that it is marvelous that the pagans had Avatars and Messiahs in their religions. But when he says it matters not whether they had them as copies, or as independent types and prophecies of the Gospel's Christ's manifestation, and that either way it proves the superior truth of Christian teachings, he gaily plunges right through a wall of impossible logic and contrary facts stout enough to stop any force but religious zealotry. It is the same fatal predicament that caught one Christian reviler of paganism after another in the net of its illogical absurdity. It being too confessedly humiliating to admit that the early Christians copied their unexampled true religion from the pagans, forsooth the copying had to be laid at the door of the pagans! But, horrors! The pagans were first, centuries ahead of them! A thing is not copied before it is in existence, but after. Later copies earlier, not vice versa. There was but one dodge to escape the dreadful onus of the logic of the situation, and peerless Christianity saw it and resorted to it. This was to charge that the pagans, instigated by the devil, copied the matchless Christian doctrines that were still to come with the birth of the true Messiah in the year one (or four, or twelve) A.D. Paganism was of the devil and the scheming serpent that whispered blandishing words in Eve's ear came on the scene again to dictate artfully to the many pagan seers the "plagiarism by anticipation" of the faith to be. The pagans craftily copied the Christian religion centuries in advance.

Alternative to copying the items of Christian dogma ahead of their pronouncement, Lundy admits that the pagans may have preconceived the realities of Christ's manifestation as "independent types and prophecies," with or without Satan's whispering aid. If so, all that any sane mind could think of their accomplishment is that it was a feat of wondrous genius. If Christianity be the transcendently lofty pure revelation it is claimed to be, the pagans soared high to match its conceptions in advance. Yet a Christian writer musts needs treat it with a slur.

Then Lundy calmly admits that Bel, Mithra, Agni, Horus and Apollo all "bear a striking analogy to the Real Son of God," without the remotest suspicion that such an admission points with practical conclusiveness to the fact that Jesus was just another Sun-god figure with the others.

But the apex of both poor reasoning and bald untruth is reached in his statement that the mistake of the pagans was in identifying nature with God and not retaining nature as a mere symbol. He here charges pagan philosophy with making the enormous mistake that it took endless care never to make. The whole base of pagan religious systems is the explicit differentiation between nature and God, since nothing is more emphasized everywhere than the more exalted status of the Christ, second Adam or child of the spirit, over the first or natural man, of the earth, earthy, who comes first to prepare the way for the later and higher guest. The Christ comes in the fullness of time, in mother nature's old age, to elevate and transform the child of nature. Paul states that the whole (natural) creation groaneth and travaileth in pain, waiting for its transformation by the power of manifested spirit. The great Egyptian religion is built on the conflict between Sut and Horus, who typify the natural forces and the spiritual. Horus' victory over Sut is the symbolization of the highest aim and goal of all religious aspiration. The ancients expressly did not intrude the area of nature into the kingdom of spirit. To retain nature as mere symbol of higher values is precisely the thing they did do. And they did it so grandly that if Christianity does not turn back and adopt the same method of natural analogical representation and depiction of spiritual laws, it will continue to hobble along groping in semi-darkness, ignoring the natural correspondences that alone could eliminate its labyrinthine difficulties.

To assert that pagan religion was unreal, that its gods were mere fictions of the imagination, is simply to state what is not true and never was. Their gods were the real forces of both nature and mind, but personalized for the simple purposes of dramatism. To declare that Isis was a fiction, that Thoth was pure imagination, is to declare that Mother Nature is unreal, that Intelligence is not a true element.

God is a Supreme Being behind and beyond nature, though unquestionably in nature as well; but there is no body of evidence that the pagans ignored this knowledge. Any student who does not find that ancient religion is infinitely more than natural science or natural history has not read his books with eye to see what is there. Lundy simply reveals his total failure to grasp the profundities of archaic wisdom if he contends there is in it no Supreme Being above, beyond and independent of nature. This is sheer unwillingness or inability to see what is there for any mind to perceive. What Lundy has not seen, nor those who belong still to his party, is that the ancients discerned a relation subsisting between nature and nature's God which they worked upon to achieve a greater lucidity in the formulation and exposition of the most recondite and cryptic truths of life. Though at a lower level than mind and soul, nature was known to be the analogue of cosmic truth, and as such provided the visible living types of that truth. It was the physical counterpart of all spiritual law, and its processes and phenomena were an unerring key to the mysteries of all subjective revelation. And the ancients never spurned nature or vilified it with the philosophical contempt which the Christians heaped upon it in virtue of its supposed inferior status. God was far more than it, to be sure; but it was a segment of his being, as much as a man's body is a portion of his selfhood, and as such it had its own proper place in the sacredness of the whole.

The amount of charitable condescension Christian writers have lavished upon the poor pagans for their laudable seeking after God amid their prevailing spiritual darkness should certainly induce God to indulge them in his tender mercy They were cut off from all true light, yet by some blind instinct they groped for what was vouchsafed in full panoply of glory a little later to the Christians. Heroically they struggled toward the light. So they chose the sun as the most conspicuous manifestation of the powers of light, life and creation, because, of course, they could go no higher toward a metaphysical idea. In dull blundering hazy fashion they could think far enough to see that the sun was the author of the beneficent provision that surrounded them on earth. With no power to see a Divine Mind working at a far higher level than that evidenced through the power in the physical sun, they were limited to their conception of the Creator in the garb and role of a sun-god. And if Christianity broke away from paganism and spurned it as a bundle of crude childish misconceptions, how, asks Lundy, can it be said that it was not infinitely higher than the system it so far transcended? How, he asks, as if it was a clinching argument of unanswerable force, how did Christianity take the place of paganism? How, indeed, we ask in turn. This volume contains the gist of the answer, and it is not the answer that Lundy assumed to be the only and the true one. Contrary to every element of his implied answer, Christianity is not only a copy or adaptation "of this old paganism," with every single one of its doctrines rooted in an ancient item of symbolic portrayal of truth, but, sad to say, it is a vitiated and degraded copy of the shining original. This answer has never been given before Christianity, grievously enough, took the place of paganism because it swept an overpowering wave of fanatical resentment against the aristocracy of the esoteric intellectual mysteries and drowned it out. This is the simple truth of the matter, so long submerged. The episode contends for the honor of being perhaps the direst tragedy of world history. The recrudescence of the esoteric movement widespread in the world today is the most general effort in sixteen centuries to regain what was then lost. And all the forces of the intervening centuries of obscurantism, reaching right up to the present and opposing the light now as then, are set to block the recovery.

The most fatal legend that clutches at the general mind today and stultifies all right exertion to regain what ancient pagan wisdom once held for humanity, is the legend that the Dark Ages are long past. On the intellectual side of religion and spirituality we are still dwelling in the lingering shadows of medieval night, hypnotized and victimized by superstition of the weirdest types flaunted from pulpit and seminary. This beclouded day of gloom must continue as long as we have not the acumen to dissociate sublime myth, allegory, drama and symbol from the dregs of history. For philosophical science has at last, in recent development, gone far enough toward the light that it now announces that the core and gist of all philosophy is summed up in the one word, meaning. And the transcendent meaning of the richest legacy of religious wisdom imparted to the race in all time has been lost for two millennia because it was preserved in an amber of allegory, which, mistaken for history, has yielded a farrago of clownish nonsense in place of the gold of truth. This is the biggest chapter in the cultural history of mankind.

Yet Lundy hits close indeed to the real truth of the matter in many other passages. He says, for instance, that Plato learned his theology in Egypt and the East and must have known of the crucifixion of the Buddha, Krishna, Mithra and others occurring long before the day of Christianity. He even argues that if the mythos has no spiritual meaning, all religion becomes mere idolatry. And he admits that the symbols of Oriental pagan religions do indicate a Supreme Power and Intelligence above matter. He says that the Greek and Persian Sun-gods were true types of the Sun of Righteousness. He even reaches the point of magnanimity at which he can say that surely the God and Father of all has not withheld a knowledge of the way of life and salvation from his pagan children and revealed it only to Israel, before the advent of his Son. Yet it is the Christian system which has not been at too strenuous pains to discourage a general belief that such had been the case. Indeed that very conclusion is practically enforced upon the mind as a necessary implication of all the Christian claims put forth as to the benightedness of the pre-Christian world. Lundy comes to the advanced point of admitting that the true Sun must have been somewhere close in the background to produce such shining types and anticipations of Christ as Agni, Krishna, Mithra, Horus, Apollo and Orpheus on the pagan horizon. But he, like all others standing in the same orthodox tradition, winks his mental eye at the obvious true implication of this admitted datum, which is that they and Jesus were alike representations of the one Christos who was never a person.

Lundy cites the "eagerness with which the pagans embraced Christianity" as evidence that it gave them in more comprehensible form what they had been imperfectly taught in their own systems. It explained the mystery of their own creeds. The entire religious world had long been looking for the birth of a "man-God," he says. The Redeemer promised to fallen man had been announced uninterruptedly from age to age. He had been eagerly looked for at Rome, among the Goths and Scandinavians, in China, India, in High Asia especially, where all the religious systems were founded on the dogma of a Divine Incarnation. Zoroaster had foretold it, and Zoroaster's disciples, the Magi of Persia, had followed the star to the birth-chamber. Pagan oracles and the Sibyls had foretold it. So, concludes Lundy, when at last the news broke upon the pagan world that Messiah had indeed come in Judea, the nations eagerly flocked to hail the babe who brought the consummation of their hopes.

To summarize a long argument in brief, not only is Lundy's picture of the "eagerness" much overdrawn, if not an actual fiction, but, as has been shown herein at an earlier place, the mass support that accrued to Christianity in the early centuries was the result of far other causes than the belief that the Avatar of the new astronomical aeon had appeared in personal form on a given day in Bethlehem. Lundy's brief can best be answered by noting that there is no evidence whatever of a general widespread flocking of the nations to the banner of the new cult. So far from this being the case, there was for nearly two centuries almost no notice taken of the event at all. And the rabble of the Roman Empire that did after two and a half centuries flock into the fold, did so through default and decay of esoteric understanding rather than from any true recognitions.

The eminent psychologist, C. G. Jung, says that the mind of man, before it is inundated and indoctrinated or conditioned with fictions and falsities, is a clean tablet, a virgin womb, and that if it is properly nourished with truth it can give birth to the Christos. This is a pretty tropism and true enough; but it is not quite the meaning of the virgin birth of the Christos in the ancient glyphs. The Virgin Mother is matter, not mind. Matter is to evolve an organism in which Mind and a Spiritual Soul would grow, bloom and bear fruit of the highest divine consciousness. The planting of this soul in matter's garden, its germination, growth, cultivation, blooming and fruiting were the birth and the "coming" of that Messiah to which the sages of antiquity taught the human family to look with eager expectation. Any preachment which distracts the concentration of the entire world's aspiration and striving away from this goal of our racial evolution and dissipates it in sentimental release upon an isolated historical event (that proves in the finale to be no event at all, but only garbled allegorism), by so much defeats the vital message of ancient truth and thwarts the direct purpose of the early divine guardianship of the race. The true and only true expectation of Messiah's birth in the world must be watched for in the mantling spread of Christly graciousness among all peoples. When the watchman, peering from the mountain top through the night and fog of low human selfishness and animal brutishness at last proclaims the signs of the appearance of the Sun-god in the rising tide of good-fellowship among the nations and the brotherly congress of all peoples in mutual amity, then and in no other way will the world be able to join with the angels above in filling heaven and earth with choric halleluiahs. Till then all Yuletide gladsomeness is but token of that which is still to come. The mythic birth of a babe amid all the pageantry of beautiful emblemism is a moving drama of the grand reality. But, alas! If the mind have nothing to carry it beyond the pageant to the transcendent actuality, or, worse, if the mind has been taught to take the pageant for the whole body of the actuality, it becomes travesty and tragic abortion.

Lundy is long departed, but it is for his followers and successors to contemplate the implications of his and their own historic claims. We have noted the odd fact that whenever the

Bible narrative is accepted as historic truth and its accounts of factual occurrence are transposed into realism, monstrosities of unnaturalness are the result. Even more prodigiously fatal is the consequence of accepting in full realism the great Christian claim that Messiah has come and gone and left the world wholly unredeemed. No more tragic reflection could afflict the mind of sincere humans than the assurance – if the Christian claim be true – that the world's great Messianic hope has been fulfilled – and that it has meant so little! If the nineteen hundred years of historic record that have followed this supposedly crowning event of the human aeon are to be taken as the actual fulfillment of Messianic promise, then we have witnessed the supreme anticlimax and disillusionment of the ages. So crushing would this realization be to the natural sanguine spiritual instinct and the hope of the race that in the face of it the human heart would cry out to Deity for the assurance that it may indeed not have been so It is little to be wondered at now why Paul urged the brethren to shun profane and vain babblings of such as Hymenaeus and Philetus, who, he says, concerning the truth have erred, saying that the resurrection is past already. Of similar urgency today is the message that we should shun the vain babblings which err in saying that the Messiah has come already. Human courage and constancy would fail if the world was assured that the great aeonial denouement of all fervent aspiration and age-long faith had actually taken place, and meant nothing more than the record since then. The mind refuses to accept the centuries of medieval darkness and the nearly equally futile centuries of modern confusion of tongues as the laurel crown of historic consummation, the golden fruits of the mundane effort. From present view it would be almost to suffocate the heart with the chill of terror to admit the thought that the great culminating event of human life has already taken place – and proved so futile. Mortal spirit must sink in despair if the history since Bethlehem and Golgotha is the upshot of Messiah's coming. The only salvation of that spirit is the assurance that Messiah has not come, but is yet to come. For discomfiture and dismay seize the mind at the thought of the pitiable historical denouement of the alleged Messianic fulfillment. If what the world has seen in the actual since the angels chorused to the shepherds is the reign of Messiah, then the dream of faith must die in the morn of hard disillusionment. As far as anyone can see, the world could have been no worse off if it had not happened at all. Indeed it proves to have been largely the cause and beginning of an initial period of sixteen hundred years of such spiritual benightedness as the world had not known before. It inaugurated the Dark Ages and in just those lands over which its blessings of "light" were distributed. And now, after nineteen hundred years of the supposed benignant effects of the reign of the planetary Messiah, the most blatant denials of his influence and blastings of his teachings are rampant in the world, and in that portion of it predominantly to which he delivered his message. Blessed with the unction of his wondrous message for nineteen centuries, the nations today are plunged in the depths of horrid chaos and direst tribulation. If Messiah has come and world history is the upshot of it, the mountain of ancient hope and prophecy has indeed labored and brought forth a mouse of human defeat and disappointment.

The only escape from the fatality of this dismay is to know thankfully that Messiah did not come in personal embodiment in the year one, four or twelve, or in any year on the calendar, but that he has come in part in the spirit of good-will among men as far as it prevails, and is still to come in the fullness of his birthing in all human breasts. Thus only can faith, hope and sanity be saved, and the dignity and meaning of sage ancient scriptures be maintained.

The actual sequel over so many centuries if proof final and positive that the alleged and never authenticated birth of Jesus the man was not the fulfillment of ancient Messianic prophecy. It is proof unanswerable that this prophecy was never intended or expected to be fulfilled in and by the birth of any historical personage. Until the ignorant debacle of wisdom in the third century the Christos to come was a spiritual principle and never a man, though dramatized in human form, as it was to manifest in man. The Christ was to come in man. The ignorant were told that it was to come in a man, and the Dark Ages were born. Ignorance is told now that it has come, and the subconscious thought of its proven historical futility grips the world mind with chaos and despair. What is there to buoy the religious hope of mankind if Messiah has already come and all in vain?

Having corrupted every high doctrine of archaic wisdom into rank nonsense, it has remained for Christianity in the end to wreck also the great Messianic tradition. Christianity has dashed the high hope of the world into the dust of two thousand years of ignominious history. By fixing a specific date for the Messiah's coming in a single man, Christianity has made the following two thousand years of appalling record of brutal inhumanity stand as the crushing sequel of that advent. And the inglorious character of that sequel drags the spirit of man down into hopeless defeat.

There is but one way by which that pall of perpetual hopelessness can be lifted and the psychological boon of perpetual high expectation given back to man again, and that is by mental rejection of the entire Christian thesis of the Messianic coming in the year one. Chaos and despair can be escaped only by the denial of the basic claim of Christianity, through the assured knowledge that Christ did not come in the form of Jesus of Nazareth on any given day. The only way to gild the skies of the future with the roseate hues of high expectation and ever kindling rational hope is to dash to pieces the whole structure of historical Christianity and clear the mental ground of its littered rubbish. Only then can the true form of the Messianic doctrine grip mind and heart with perennial buoyancy and anoint mankind with the oil of gladness.

Nowhere in either general study or in so-styled "occult" investigation has the real reason for the cyclical representation of the Messianic coming ever appeared to have been perceived and stated. That cryptic reason not only gives a light by which to solve the riddle, but at the same time adds perhaps the final crowning argument for the untenability of the man-Messiah theory. It has been seen that by ancient sagacity the coming of Messiah was pictured as taking place regularly, cyclically and periodically, under the figure of a star rounding its orbit to reappear again and again. This portrayal brought the representation as close to an analogue with the actual method of the coming as it was possible for the human mind to bring it. The Avatar was depicted as coming to earth under the symbolism of a long sweep of lunar, solar and stellar cycles, for the reason that, precisely like these revolutions, his coming was not a single historical occurrence, falling in a line of other single events, but was the one grand event that summed the whole series, and progressed to its consummation through the endless repetition, like the stellar revolutions, of smaller cycles of advance. It took the multiple repetition of minor cycles to round out the major grand cycle, which was in itself and in its product the coming, though each minor cycle within it was not only the prefigured type of the whole movement, but an actual integral portion of the coming itself. Not being a person, but a quality or degree of consciousness, and coming not in one man but in the character of all men, it could come in no other way than by a graduated approach, advancing a little further toward full arrival at each step and in each cycle. In all the life of nature, progress or evolution invariably makes headway by an endless series of forward steps, each one bearing the development ahead a certain distance, and generally receding somewhat to be picked up and carried forward by the next surge a little farther than before. This is unquestionably the logic back of the ancient thesis of reincarnation for the soul of man. It is unthinkable that the soul, starting its human experience from just above the level of the brute, can crash the gates of heaven in one short life. From animal selfishness up to godlike graciousness there is a gap that evolution can bridge only in a long course of the slow development of conscious powers through mingled sorrow, joy and discipline. The soul being an entity that can hold its gains in its interior ark of the sanctuary of life, it circles down to earth again and again, adding an increment of experience and its fruitage of wisdom, as well as developed faculties, at each round of the wheel of birth and death. The ever accumulating capital of enhanced godliness in the whole body of individuals thus brings the Christly soul of the world periodically nearer its full epiphany. This envisagement of the fixed rationale of the evolutionary movement sets the determinative seal on the logic of the argument. To predicate the coming of the Christ consciousness in one man only, would be to deny it to the race in which it has its real coming. To predicate it as coming all at once at a given historical epoch would be to interdict nature and annul the rhythmic movement and the cyclical advance. The true image of the coming was the sun, or the star, or the season, that came in endless repetition. There is but one story that nature has to tell, and that is the story of the endless coming of ever new life, the eternal renewal through endless time. The claim of the historical coming of Messiah in the first century A.D. would be as anachronistic as it would be for a playwright to throw the climactic denouement of his drama into the middle of the second act. From the strategic view of evolution's long course the incidence of the climactic event anywhere in mid-stream is premature and abortive. It has not been prepared for, the forces at work have not had time to flow into position for the consummative effect. It is untimely and out of setting. It would break in upon the organic growth of the movement, would destroy the rhythm of nature, disrupt sequences and wreck the plan. The birth of the aeonial Christ, as a man, in the year four or twelve B.C. would precipitate a miscarriage of all ancient scriptural meaning and structure and would engender, as it has done, a hybrid prodigy of mocking irrelevance. Instead of being the fulfillment of all sacred prophecy, it has proven to be the untimely abortion of that prophecy. There is no logical place for it in the scheme of ancient religion, and its injection into the scheme disconcerts and nullifies the whole splendid order. If the sublime portent of ancient Messianism is allowed to discharge its whole body of meaning upon one historic person at a given year in the course, the great ancient drama of majestic purposiveness in the whole run of history crashes into wreckage by the roadside two thousand years back. If the coming of Christos is already past, the rest of history will represent man's blind staggering forward with no goal of grand allurement ahead. For that kingly attainment which was designed to be the aeonial loadstone to draw mankind on to the end of the human epoch will have been drained out into one single (alleged) historical event, leaving the race still unenlightened and without its guiding star of knowledge, and further demoralized by a stupendous hallucination from the fulfillment of a great prophecy without visible result. Paul warns that the words of those vain babblers who say that the resurrection is already past "eat as doth a canker." The echoes and reverberations of those brave words of the Apostle have been rolling from age to age, as the centuries have brought the evidence of the canker corrosion of the Western mind by the vain babblings that Messiah has come already.

Sublimely sacred is the Nativity drama of the Yule. Let no heart reject its gripping import, let no mind disdain its reference. But it is the tragedy of twenty centuries that any soul should rejoice in it as the mere commemoration of an event that has happened and is not still to happen. If this tawdry notion can be lifted and expanded to the immensity of the conception that the drama prefigures the mighty reality of a cosmic event that is even now running its thrilling course in ever increasing grandeur of meaning, there is no power that will stop the voices of millions caroling joyous Noels unto the coming of the King of Love. Not until the Bethlehem stable scene is removed from mass consciousness as past history, and reintegrated in a wondrous new concept of heightened majesty and power on the understanding that it is sublime allegory of a racial denouement still in process and still awaiting consummation, will the song which set heaven's arches ringing and filled earth's temples with the echo at the solstice of winter sweep the human heart into abiding joy.

As it is no derogation of the greatness and dignity of the One God to cease to think of his power and intelligence and love as being confined within the personality of one grandiose Being isolated and detached from the universe, and instead to conceive of him as the life and mind manifesting in all creations, neither is it a derogation of the Christos to cease to think of him as one person and to pay homage to him as the irradiating charity transforming all human hearts. Surely to contract the religious idea of the Christ into the meager confines of one personality in history is to belittle that which we would magnify. To adore him as the King of Love ruling the immeasurable hosts of earth's mortals and distributing his benignant influence out in million-fold streams to irrigate all lives, must be the conception that will mightily glorify itself through the infinite multiplication of its nature distributed out into countless creatures. Life never contracts into one except when it dissolves away all the forms of its multiple expression at the end of a cycle and retires back into unity. It is then retreating into dormancy in its condition of absoluteness – which to us is the negation of all our values, – nothing. Whenever its energies are pushing outward into manifestation in creation, its oneness is divided, then multiplied, into infinite diversification and modification. The creation would itself be both impossible and meaningless if it were not so.

Oneness precludes all possibility of structure, or organism. It abolishes relationship among diverse elements, and with that goes meaning.

In the reflection of this great truth the coming of Christhood in one only character in history is meaningless. It lays no foundation for organic unity in humanity. Indeed by its unrelatedness to living mortals, by its isolation and exceptionality, it itself destroys the one link of unity that should bind the members of the race together in structural wholeness. No fitting place can be found or made for it in the beautiful system of ancient theology. And if it is forcibly thrust into it, the gleaming significance of the whole structure is blasted. The Christos in the heart of the race is adequate to carry with comeliness and consistency the magnificent meaning of the ancient scriptures. But no man-Christ in Judea or elsewhere is able to encompass in his tiny personality that range and sweep of significance. It is an anomaly, a lamentable malformation of ignorance dealing unwittingly and ruinously with the elements of cryptic beauty.

A priceless item of ancient knowledge was the recognition that each small cycle in nature is the type and analogue of the whole movement and design of life. The sages therefore read into certain of the most familiar cycles those epochs, stages, turning points which prefigured the momentous significance of ultimate reality, which itself comes to light little by little in an endless round of renewed cycles. Nature repeats endlessly in the small the analogue of that which is the reality of the large and the whole. Both the small and the large are the reality which alone is. That which in the day, month, year and precession appears over and over again and passes – and so has got the name of mere appearance as over against abiding reality – yet bears the stamp and image of that one omnipresent reality which does not pass. The returning star was the sign and harbinger of the Christos because it was the image and portent of that coming. The advent of Messiah was exactly prefigured by the features of every rolling cycle. The star in the east is that bright and morning star whose rising on the field of general human consciousness will deify humanity. It is the day-star from on high, but having plunged into earth and ocean "on the western side of heaven" in its descent into matter, it must rise again after its night of incarnation "in the east," as token that deity that goes periodically to its "death" in body will just as often have its joyous resurrection.

A Christmas carol has the following lines:
And the sky was bright
With a holy light –
'Twas the birthday of a King!

Christmas celebration extols the wondrous significance of the birth of humanity's King. A fine Christian hymn begins with the line – The King of Love my shepherd is.

A common religious phrase is "Christ the King." A Christmas hymn exhorts:

Let earth receive her King!

In a world in which the ideal of democracy is rampant the rule of a King has lost some of its idyllic glamor. This is in the political field of human interest. Children need kingly rule and naturally pay homage to kingship. So the race in its childhood honored regal position and power. But neither the adult individual nor the race in its maturity cherish kingship so unreservedly. The reason for the change is that as the individual and the world grow to their adulthood, they feel the divine instinct to discard outward rulership and set up the function of divine kingship within themselves. The ideal of kingship is not lost; it is simply shifted from outside to the inner courts of the Self. In the spiritual world, then, the divine right of the King to rule his domain of consciousness and conduct is still inalienable and inviolable. A sad day for humanity when the ideal of the spiritual rule of a principle of love and righteousness in the inner life of mortals falls into disrepute. Hail then with renewed acclaim the solstitial birth of the King of Love!

This King of Glory was named by the ancient Egyptians I U. This became later J U and Y

U. As he was also God, the Hebrews added their word for Deity – E L. This gave Y U-E L, eventually YULE. The French form used the short root of the divine principle of intelligence, N O (cognate with our English know), the No-etic faculty, with the Hebrew E L and derived NOEL.

As fortune would have it, the study is completed in December, on the very fringe of the winter solstice. In ancient typism the period of the god's incarnation in flesh and matter was dramatized as the midnight and the midwinter of its cycle. At midnight in midwinter the mighty constellation of Orion, followed by the great Dog-Star Sirius, takes its position in the central heavens south of the zenith. Orion prefigures the greater divinity; and as divinity endlessly seeks the thrill of life that accrues to it from becoming periodically incarnated in matter in its seven-period cycles, so the mighty hunter, Orion, with his Dog, is dramatized as pursuing the Seven Sisters, the Pleiades, ahead of him, – matter being eternally feminine.

But in the belt of Orion, the part of his dress that gives organic stability to his whole body, are the three stars known as the Three Kings. They point almost in a direct line to the following Dog.

Man is most philosophically described as "a God in the body of an animal." The God is leading in evolution, but it is bringing the animal behind it along toward the same high goal. Within the animal is the God that, like the dog, can dower the mortal animal-man with the divine instinct to guide himself unerringly through the darkness of incarnational night. So Sirius was made the type of the Christ-soul in mankind. He is preceded by the Three Kings who anticipate his coming and hail and adore him on his arrival. The Three Kings of evolving consciousness are Mind-Soul-Spirit, the ineffable trinity of divine life. In man's ordinary consciousness they manifest as Goodness, Truth and Beauty. When brought to glowing intensity in the field of conscious being in man, the three fuse into one grand power of divine Love. This is the three-starred, three-rayed King whose birth is hailed at midnight of December twenty-fourth.

When Yuletide carolers raise paeans of joyous song to greet the birth of humanity's King at midnight of the winter solstice, it is all in token of the birth of the three kingly elements of consciousness that are destined to rule in the life of man on earth, – Goodness, Truth and Beauty. Fused in the white heat of Love, they become that Prince of Peace who can touch the animal in man with his wand of magic and transform him into the fairy spirit. And only then will begin that reign of Saturn, that Golden Age, when the "halcyon days" set in, and the King-fisher of the souls of men can build its nest in safety on the tranquil waters of the erstwhile stormy sea of mortal life, in the winter solstice of evolution.

We three kings of Orion are;
Bearing gifts we traverse afar;
Field and fountain,
Moor and mountain,
Following yonder star.
Oh! Star of wonder, Star of might,
Star with royal beauty bright!
Westward leading,
Still proceeding,
Guide us to thy perfect Light!

HE IS THE KING OF GLORY

www.ingramcontent.com/pod-product-compliance
Lightning Source LLC
Chambersburg PA
CBHW022354040426
42450CB00005B/179